The New Commodity Trading Systems and Methods

The New Commodity Trading Systems and Methods

PERRY J. KAUFMAN

JOHN WILEY & SONS

New York • Chichester • Brisbane • Toronto • Singapore

Library of Congress Cataloging in Publication Data:

Kaufman, Perry J.
  The new commodity trading systems and methods.

  Bibliography: p.
  1. Commodity exchanges—Statistical methods.

I. Title.
HG6036.K38   1987   332.64′4   87-6073
ISBN 0-471-87879-0

Printed in the United States of America

10 9 8 7 6 5

TO MY PARENTS

Preface

The equipment and techniques for trading futures markets have expanded at a remarkable rate since the writing of the first edition 10 years ago. At that time, it was difficult to find enough systems to use as examples; the chapters on regression analysis and cycles had no applications, only the idea that these tools would become useful. The solutions to the more complex mathematics were given as programs for the TI-59, a handheld programmable calculator just released.

The chapters in this edition have been completely rewritten to include advancements in research, many more systems, and the use of a computer. Regression analysis is developed into ARIMA modeling, and cycles have become Fourier spectral analysis; both techniques are now available on a home computer. The most important concept in computerization has become Chapter 15, Optimization. Although essential to system development, computerized testing may lead to the wrong solution as well as the correct one; in Chapter 15, both sides are explored. The computer studies that appeared in "Pattern Recognition" have been retested and analyzed. Those programs previously given for the TI-59 are now in FORTRAN.

Although this book is longer than the first edition, it is more concise. Repetitious examples have been eliminated, along with sections that have not proved useful. Chapters on charting have not drastically changed but are reorganized and include new available systems.

Most of all, I have 10 more years of experience in researching and trading. All the analyses, summaries, observations, and comments are my own. Although I have tried to be objective, strong opinions have occasionally filtered through. I hope they will be viewed as useful.

PERRY J. KAUFMAN

Casa de Mar, Bermuda
May 1987

Acknowledgment

My thanks to John Deuss for providing the environment and guidance necessary to produce the best possible results.

Contents

If you have a minute, I'll tell you how to make money in stocks. Buy low and sell high. Now if you have five or ten years, I'll tell you how to tell when stocks are low and high.

JRL June, 1966

The New Commodity Trading Systems and Methods

1
Introduction

Quantitative methods for evaluating price movement and making trading decisions have become a dominant part of market analysis. At one time, the only
acceptable manner of trading was by understanding the factors that make prices
move, and determining the extent or potential of future movement. The market
now supports dozens of major funds and managed programs, which account for a
sizable part of commodity open interest and operate primarily by decisions based
on "technical analysis." Many commercial participants in the markets, who once
restricted research to supply, demand, and related factors, now include various
technical methods for the purpose of "timing" or confirming price direction.

In many ways, there is no conflict between fundamental and technical analysis.
The decisions that result from economic or policy changes are far-reaching; these
actions may cause a long-term change in the direction of prices, and may not
necessarily be reflected immediately. Actions based on long-term forecasts may
involve considerable risk and often can be an ineffective way to manage a position. Integrated with a technical method of known risk, which determines price
trends over shorter intervals, many commercial firms have gained practical solutions to their trading problems.

Leverage in the commodities markets has a strong influence on the methods of
trading. With margin deposits ranging from 5 to 10% of the contract value (the
balance does not have to be borrowed as in stocks), a small movement in the
underlying price can result in large profits and losses based on the invested margin. Because high leverage is available, it is nearly always used. Methods of
analysis will therefore concentrate on short-term price fluctuations and trends, in
which the profit potential is reduced, so that the risk is often smaller than the
required margin. Commodities systems can be characterized as emphasizing price
moves of less than 20% of the contract value. Trading requires conservation of
capital, and the management of investment risk becomes essential.

Even with the distinction forced by high leverage, many of the basic systems
covered in this book were first used in the stock market. Compared to securities,
the futures markets offer great diversification and liquidity. The relative lack of
liquidity in a single stock lends itself to index analysis, whereas the "commodity"
index has never become popular.

1

TECHNICAL VERSUS FUNDAMENTAL

Two basic approaches to trading commodities are fundamental and technical analysis. A fundamental study may be a composite of supply-and-demand elements: statistical reports on production, expected use, political ramifications, labor influences, price support programs, industrial development—everything that makes prices what they are. The result of a fundamental analysis is a price forecast, a prediction of where prices will be at some time in the future.

Technical analysis is a study of patterns and movement. Its elements are normally limited to price, volume, and open interest. It is considered to be the study of the market itself. The results of technical analysis may be a short- or long-term forecast based on recurring patterns; however, technical methods often limit their goals to the statement that today's prices are moving up or down. Some systems will go as far as saying the direction is indeterminate.

Recently, technical systems have used tools previously reserved for fundamental analysis. The popularization of the computer now allows the more complex studies required of fundamentals to be performed on the same home computer once housing only technical systems. There will always be purists on either side, rigid fundamentalists and technicians, but a great number of professionals combine the two techniques. This book draws on some of the more popular, automated fundamental trading systems.

One advantage of technical analysis is that it is completely self-contained. The accuracy of the data is certain. One of the first great advocates of price analysis, Charles Dow, said:

The market reflects all the jobber knows about the condition of the textile trade; all the banker knows about the money market; all that the best-informed president knows of his own business, together with his knowledge of all other businesses; it sees the general condition of transportation in a way that the president of no single railroad can ever see; it is better informed on crops than the farmer or even the Department of Agriculture. In fact, the market reduces to a bloodless verdict all knowledge bearing on finance, both domestic and foreign.

Much of the price movement reflected in commodity cash and futures markets is anticipatory; the expectations of the effects of economic developments. It is subject to change without notice. For example, a hurricane bound for the Philippines will send sugar prices higher, but if the storm turns off course, prices will drop back to prior levels. Major scheduled crop reports cause a multitude of professional guessing, which may correctly or incorrectly move prices just before the actual report is released. By the time the public is ready to act, the news is already reflected in the price.

PROFESSIONAL AND AMATEUR

Beginning traders often find a system or technique that seems extremely simple and convenient to follow, one that they think has been overlooked by the professionals. Sometimes they are right, but most often that method has been rejected. Reasons for not using a technique could be the inability to get a good execution, the risk/reward ratio, or the number of consecutive losses that occur. Speculation is a sophisticated business. As Wyckoff said, "Most men make money in their own business and lose it in some other fellow's."

To compete with a professional speculator you must be more accurate in anticipating the next move or in predicting prices from current news—not the article printed in today's newspaper ("Government Buys Beef for School Lunch Program"), which was discounted weeks ago, and not the one on the wire service ("15% Fewer Soybeans and 10% More Fishmeal"), which went into the market two days ago. You must act on news that has not yet been printed. In order to anticipate changes, you must draw a single conclusion for the many contingencies possible from fundamental data, or

1. Recognize recurring patterns in price movement and determine the most likely results of such patterns.
2. Determine the "trend" of the market by isolating the basic direction of prices over a selected time interval.

The bar chart, discussed in Chapter 8, is the simplest representation of the market. These patterns are the same as those recognized by Livermore on the ticker tape. Because they are interpretive, more precise methods such as point-and-figure charting are also used, which add a level of exactness to charting. Point-and-figure charts are popular because they offer specific trading rules and show formations similar to both bar charting and ticker-tape trading.

Mathematical modeling, using traditional regression or discrete analysis, has become a popular technique for anticipating price direction. Most modeling methods are modifications of developments in econometrics and basic probability and statistical theory. They are precise because they are based entirely on numerical data.

The proper assessment of the price trend is critical to most commodity trading systems. Countertrend trading is just as dependent on knowing the trend as a trend-following technique. Large sections of this book are devoted to the various ways to isolate the trend, although it would be an injustice to leave the reader with the idea that a "price trend" is a universally accepted concept. There have been many studies published contending that trends, with respect to price movement, do not exist. The most authoritative papers on this topic are collected in Cootner, *The Random Character of Stock Market Prices* (MIT Press).

RANDOM WALK

It has been the position of many fundamental and economic analysis advocates that there is no sequential correlation between the direction of price movement from one day to the next. Their position is that prices will seek a level that will balance the supply–demand factors, but that this level will be reached in an unpredictable manner as prices move in an irregular response to the latest available information or news release.

If the random walk theory is correct, the many well-defined trading methods based on mathematics and pattern recognition will fail. The problem is not a simple one, and is dependent on both the time interval and the frequency of data used. When a long time span is used, such as 20 years, and the data to be analyzed are averaged quarterly, an apparent inflationary trend will appear with seasonal and cyclic variations. Technical methods, such as moving averages, are often used to isolate these price characteristics. The averaging of data into quarterly prices smooths out the irregular daily movements and results in noticeable correlations between successive prices. The use of daily data over a long time interval introduces noise and obscures uniform patterns.

In the long run, commodity prices may return to initial levels; however, short-term price movement is very different from a random series of numbers. It contains two unique properties: exceptionally long "runs" of price in a single direction, and "asymmetry," the unequal size of moves in different directions. Although the long-term trends identified by quarterly data are not of great interest to the commodity trader, short-term trends that focus on these characteristics are successful.

Further study of this area is possible using references found in Teweles, Harlow, and Stone, *The Commodity Futures Game, Who Wins? Who Loses? Why?* (McGraw-Hill). The most well-known studies are by Holbrook Working, Paul Cootner, Hendrik Houthaker, and A. B. Larson.

BACKGROUND MATERIAL

The contents of this book assume an understanding of speculative markets, particularly the commodities futures markets. Ideally the reader should have read one or more of the available "trading guides," and understand the workings of a buy or sell order and the specifications of contracts. Experience in actual trading would be helpful. A professional trader, a broker, or a purchasing agent will already possess all the qualifications necessary. A farmer or rancher with some hedging experience will be well-qualified to understand the risks involved.

The basic reference book for general contract information is the *Commodity Trading Manual* (Chicago Board of Trade). For beginning or reviewing the basics there is Powers, *Getting Started in Commodity Futures Trading* (Investors Publications). Other comprehensive books are Schwager, *A Complete Guide to the Futures Markets* (Wiley) and Kaufman, *Handbook of Futures Markets* and *The Concise Handbook of Futures Markets* (Wiley). The introductory material is not repeated here.

A good understanding of the two most popular charting methods can be developed by reading the classic by Edwards and Magee, *Technical Analysis of Stock Trends* (John Magee), a comprehensive study of bar charting, and Zeig and Kaufman, *Point and Figure Commodity Trading Techniques* (Investors Intelligence). This book briefly reviews the elements of each before going on to develop the techniques further. Writings on other technical methods are more difficult to find. The magazine *Technical Analysis of Stocks & Commodities* stands out as the best source of regular information; *Futures* magazine has a limited number of technical articles, and most other commodity books express only a specific technical approach. Excellent coverage is given in Seidel and Ginsberg, *Commodities Trading* (Prentice-Hall). A few comprehensive studies, such as Maxwell, *Commodity Fu-*

tures Trading with Moving Averages (Speer) would be worth studying. On general market lore, the one book that stands out is Lefevre, *Reminiscences of a Stock Operator* (Doran). Wyckoff mixes humor and philosophy in most of his books, but *Wall Street Ventures and Adventures Through Forty Years* (Harper & Brothers) may be of general interest.

A reader with a good background in high school mathematics can follow most of this book except in its more complex parts. An elementary course in statistics is ideal, but a knowledge of the type of probability found in Thorp, *Beat the Dealer* (Vintage) is adequate. A good calculator, one with mathematical functions, will be of great help. A home computer is better.

RESEARCH SKILLS

Before starting, a few guidelines may help make the task easier. They have been set down to help those who will use this book to develop a trading system.

1. **Know what you want to do.** Base your trading on a solid theory or observation and keep it in focus throughout development and testing.
2. **State your hypothesis or question in its simplest form.** The more complex it is, the more difficult it will be to evaluate the answer.
3. **Do not assume anything.** Many projects fail on basic assumptions that were incorrect.
4. **Do the simplest things first.** Do not combine systems before each element of each system is proven to work independently.
5. **Build one step at a time.** Go on to the next step only after the previous ones have been tested successfully. If you start with too many complex steps and fail, you will have to simplify to find out what went wrong.
6. **Be careful of errors of omission.** The most difficult part of research is identifying the components to be selected and tested. Simply because all the questions asked were satisfactorily answered does not mean that all the right questions were asked. The most important may be missing.
7. **Do not take shortcuts.** It is sometimes convenient to use the work of others to speed up the research. Check their work carefully; do not use it if it cannot be verified. Remember that your answer is only as good as its weakest point.
8. **Start at the end.** Define your goal and work backwards to find the required input. In this manner, you only work with information relevant to the results; otherwise, you might be proving the existence of the universe before long.

2

Basic Concepts

. . . economics is not an exact science: it consists merely of Laws of
Probability. The most prudent investor, therefore, is one who
pursues only a general course of action which is "normally" right
and who avoids acts and policies which are "normally" wrong.

L. L. B. Angas

ON THE AVERAGE

In discussing numbers, it is often necessary to use representative values. The
range of values or the *average* is substituted for the purpose of specifying a
general characteristic and solving a problem. The average (*arithmetic mean*) of
many values can be a preferable substitute for any one value. For example, the
average retail price of 1 pound of coffee in the northeast is more meaningful to a
cost-of-living calculation than the price at any one store. However, not all data
can be combined or averaged and still have meaning. The average of all commodity prices taken on the same day would not say anything about an individual
commodity that was part of the average. The price changes in copper and corn, for
example, would have little to do with one another. The average of a group of
values must meaningfully represent the individual items.

The average can be misleading in other ways. Consider coffee, which rose from
40¢ to $2.00 per pound in a year. The average price of this product may appear to
be $1.40; however, this would not account for the time that the product spent at
various price levels. Table 2-1 shows that the time intervals needed to achieve
these price levels varied, with the longer intervals at lower prices.

When the time spent at each price level is included, it can be seen that the
average price should be lower than $1.40. One way to calculate this, knowing the
specific number of days in each interval, is by using a weighted average of the
price and its respective interval

$$W = \frac{a_1 d_1 + a_2 d_2 + a_3 d_3 + a_4 d_4}{d_1 + d_2 + d_3 + d_4}$$

$$= \frac{6000 + 8000 + 8400 + 7200}{280}$$

$$= 105$$

Table 2-1   Weighting an Average

Prices Go		Average	Total Days		
From	To	During Interval	For Interval	Weighted	$1/a$
40	80	$a_1 = 60$	$d_1 = 100$	6000	.01666
80	120	$a_2 = 100$	$d_2 = 80$	8000	.01000
120	160	$a_3 = 140$	$d_3 = 60$	8400	.00714
160	200	$a_4 = 180$	$d_4 = 40$	7200	.00555

Although this is not exact because of the use of average prices for intervals, it does closely represent the *average price relative to time*. There are two other averages for which time is an important element—the *geometric* and *harmonic means*.

Geometric Mean

The geometric mean represents a growth function in which a price change from 50 to 100 is as important as a change from 100 to 200.

$$G = \sqrt[n]{a_1 \times a_2 \times a_3 \times \cdots \times a_n}$$

The solution to the geometric mean can be either of two forms:

$$\ln G = \frac{\ln a_1 + \ln a_2 + \cdots + \ln a_n}{n}$$

or

$$\ln G = \frac{\ln(a_1 \times a_2 \times a_3 \times \cdots a_n)}{n}$$

The two solutions are equivalent. Using the price levels in Table 2-1, disregarding the time intervals, and substituting into the first equation:

$$\ln G = \frac{\ln 40 + \ln 80 + \ln 120 + \ln 160 + \ln 200}{5}$$

$$\ln G = \frac{3.689 + 4.382 + 4.787 + 5.075 + 5.298}{5}$$

$$\ln G = 4.6462$$

$$G = 104.19$$

The geometric mean has advantages in application to economics and prices. A classic example is to compare a rise in price of tenfold from 100 to 1000 to a fall of $\frac{1}{10}$ from 100 to 10. An arithmetic mean of 10 and 1000 is 505, while the geometric mean gives

$$G = \sqrt{10 \times 1000} = 100$$

which shows the relative distribution as a function of comparable growth. Due to this property, the geometric mean is the best choice when averaging ratios that can be either fractions or percentages.

Quadratic Mean

The quadratic mean is as calculated:

$$Q = \sqrt{\frac{\Sigma(a^2)}{N}}$$

The square root of the mean of the square of the items (root-mean-square) is most well-known as the basis for the *standard deviation*. This will be discussed later, in the section "Dispersion and Skewness."

Harmonic Mean

The harmonic mean is more of a time-weighted average, not biased towards higher or lower values as in the geometric mean. A simple example is to consider the average rate of speed of a car that travels 4 miles at 20 mph, then 4 miles at 30 mph. An arithmetic mean would result in 25 mph, without considering that 12 minutes were spent at 20 mph and 8 minutes at 30 mph. The weighted average would give

$$W = \frac{12 \times 20 + 8 \times 30}{(12 + 8)} = 24$$

The harmonic mean is

$$\frac{1}{H} = \frac{\dfrac{1}{a_1} + \dfrac{1}{a_2} + \cdots + \dfrac{1}{a_n}}{n}$$

which can also be expressed as

$$H = n \left/ \sum_{}^{n} \left(\frac{1}{a_i}\right)\right.$$

For two or three elements, the simpler forms can be used:

$$H_2 = \frac{2ab}{a + b} \qquad H_3 = \frac{3abc}{ab + ac + bc}$$

This allows the solution pattern to be seen. For the 20 and 30 mph rates of speed, the solution is

$$H_2 = \frac{2(20)(30)}{20 + 30} = 24$$

which is the same answer as the weighted average. Considering the original set of numbers again, the basic form of harmonic mean can be applied:

$$\frac{1}{H} = \frac{\dfrac{1}{40} + \dfrac{1}{80} + \dfrac{1}{120} + \dfrac{1}{160} + \dfrac{1}{200}}{5}$$

$$= \frac{.05708}{5} = .01142$$

$$H = 87.59$$

DISTRIBUTION

The *frequency distribution* can give a good picture of the characteristics of the data. To know how often sugar prices were at different price levels, divide prices into 1¢ increments (e.g., 5.01 to 6.00, 6.01 to 7.00, etc.) and count the number of times that prices fall into each interval. The result will be a distribution of prices as shown in Figure 2-1. It should be expected that the distribution of prices for a commodity will be *skewed* towards the left-hand side (lower prices) and have a long *tail* towards higher prices on the right-hand side. This is because prices remain at higher levels for only a short time relative to their long-term characteristics. Commodity prices tend to be bounded on the lower end, limited in their downside movement, by production costs and resistance of the suppliers to sell at prices that represent a loss. On the higher end, there is not such a clear point of limitation; therefore, prices move much further up during periods of extreme shortage relative to demand.

The measures of *central tendency* discussed in the previous section are used to qualify the shape and extremes of price movement shown in the frequency distribution. The general relationship between the results when using the three principal means is

arithmetic mean > geometric mean > harmonic mean

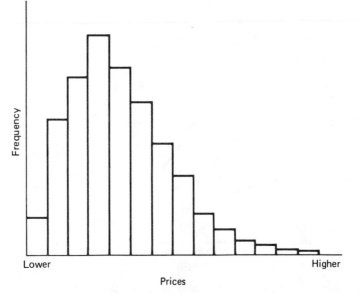

Figure 2-1 Hypothetical price-frequency distribution.

Median and Mode

Two other measurements, the *median* and the *mode,* are often used to define distribution. The median, or "middle item," is helpful for establishing the "center" of the data; it halves the number of data items. The median has the advantage of discounting extreme values, which might distort the arithmetic mean. The mode is the *most commonly occurring value.* In Figure 2-2, the mode is the highest point.

In a normally distributed price series, the mean, median, and mode will all occur at the same value; however, as the data becomes "skewed," these values will move farther apart. The general relationship is:

$$\text{mean} > \text{median} > \text{mode}$$

Characteristics of the Principal Averages

Each averaging method has its unique meaning and usefulness. The following summary points out their principal characteristics:

The *arithmetic mean* is affected by each data element equally, but it has a tendency to emphasize extreme values more than other methods. It is easily calculated and is subject to algebraic manipulation.

The *geometric mean* gives less weight to extreme variations than the arithmetic mean and is most important when using data representing ratios or rates of change. It cannot always be used for a combination of positive and negative numbers and is also subject to algebraic manipulation.

The *harmonic mean* is most applicable to time changes and, along with the geometric mean, has been used in economics for price analysis. The added

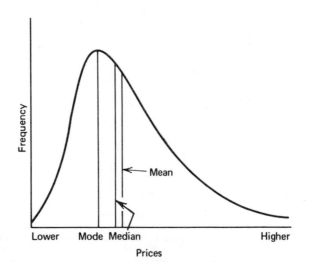

Figure 2-2   Hypothetical price distribution skewed to the right, showing the relationship of the mode, median, and mean.

complications of computation has caused this to be less popular than either of the other averages, although it is also capable of algebraic manipulation.

The *mode* is not affected by the size of the variations from the average, only the distribution. It is the location of greatest concentration and indicates a typical value for a reasonably large sample. With an unordered set of data, the mode is time consuming to locate and is not capable of algebraic manipulation.

The *median* is most useful when the center of an incomplete set is needed. It is not affected by extreme variations and is simple to find if the number of data points are known. Although it has some arithmetic properties, it is not readily adaptable to computational methods.

DISPERSION AND SKEWNESS

The center or central tendency of a data series is not a sufficient description for price analysis. The manner in which it is scattered about a given point, its *dispersion* and *skewness,* are necessary to describe the data. The *mean deviation* is a basic method for measuring distribution and may be calculated about any measure of central location, for example, the arithmetic mean. It is found by computing

$$MD = \frac{\Sigma \, | \, x \, |}{N}$$

where MD is the mean deviation and $\Sigma \, | \, x \, |$ is a sum of deviations of each value from the arithmetic mean or other measure of central location with *signs ignored*.

The *standard deviation* is a special form of measuring average deviation from the mean, which uses the root-mean-square

$$\sigma = \sqrt{\frac{\Sigma \, (x^2)}{N}}$$

where σ is the standard deviation, x is the deviation from the mean $(x_i - \bar{x})$, and N is the number of items in the data series.

The standard deviation is the most popular way of measuring the degree of dispersion of the data. The value of one standard deviation about the mean represents a clustering of about 68% of the data, two standard deviations from the mean include 95.5% of all data, and three standard deviations encompass 99.7%—nearly all the data. These values represent the groupings of a perfectly *normal* set of data, shown in Figure 2-3.

Most commodity data, however, is not normally distributed and must be measured and corrected for *skewness*—the degree of distortion from the normal symmetry. In a perfectly normal distribution, the median and mode coincide. As the data becomes more extreme, which could be at very high commodity prices, the *mean* will show the greatest change and the *mode* will show the least. The difference between the mean and the mode, adjusted for dispersion, gives a good measure of skewness

$$K = \frac{\text{mean} - \text{mode}}{\sigma}$$

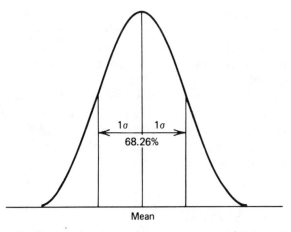

Figure 2-3 Normal distribution showing the percentage area included within one standard deviation about the arithmetic mean.

This can also be expressed using the median as

$$K = \frac{3(\text{mean} - \text{median})}{\sigma}$$

Transformations. The skewness of a data series can sometimes be corrected using a *transformation* on the data. Price data may be skewed in a specific pattern. For example, if there are $\frac{1}{4}$ of the occurrences at twice the price, and $\frac{1}{9}$ of the occurrences at three times the price, the original data can be transformed into a normal distribution by taking the square root of each data item. The characteristics of price data often show a logarithmic, power, or square-root relationship.

Skewness in Price Distributions

Because the lower price levels of most commodities are determined by production costs, price distributions show a clear boundary of resistance in that direction. At the high levels, prices can have a very long "tail" of low frequency. Figure 2-4

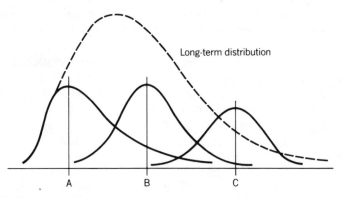

Figure 2-4 Changing distribution at different price levels. A, B, and C are increasing mean values of three shorter-term distributions.

shows the change in the distribution of prices as the mean price (over shorter intervals) changes. This pattern indicates that a "normal" distribution is not appropriate for commodity prices, and that a "log" distribution would only apply to overall long-term distributions.

THE INDEX

The purpose of an average is to transform individuality into classification. When done properly, there is useful information to be gained. Indices have gained popularity in the futures markets recently; the stock market indices are now second to the financial markets in trading volume. These contracts allow both individual and institutional participants to invest in the overall market movement rather than take the higher risk of selecting individual securities. Furthermore, investors can hedge their current market position by taking a short position in the futures market against a long position in the stock market.

A less general index, the Dow Jones Industrials, or a grain or livestock index can help the trader take advantage of a more specific price without having to decide which products are more likely to do best. An index simplifies the decision-making process for trading. If an index does not exist, it can be constructed to satisfy most purposes.

Constructing an Index

An index is traditionally used to determine relative value; the increase or decrease in value over time as seen in the Consumer Price Index (CPI). Most indices have a starting value of 1 or 100 on a specific year. The index itself is a ratio of the current or composite values to those values during the base year. The selection of the base year is often "convenient" but should represent a stable price period. For commodities, most years prior to 1973 would be adequate with certain key years as exceptions. If a set of commodities is selected for the index and combined using a weighting method, the index for a specific year is the ratio

$$\text{Index (year } t) = \frac{\text{commodity values (year } t)}{\text{commodity values (base year)}} \times 100$$

If the value of the index is less than 100, the composite values are lower in year t than they were in the base year. The actual index value represents the percentage change.

A *simple aggregate index* is the ratio of unweighted sums of commodity prices in a specific year to the same commodities in the base year. Most of the popular indices fall into this class. A *weighted aggregate index* biases certain commodities by weighting them to increase or decrease their effect on the composite value. The index is then calculated as in the simple aggregate index.

PRACTICAL USE OF DATA

Most applications of statistics are not based on a set of perfect data, as is technical analysis. Even econometrics, which uses the best data available, introduces error when its data are *representative*. The average price received by all farmers for corn on the fifteenth of the month cannot be the exact number. For both economic and practical considerations, most statistics are accumulated by *sampling*.

When using incomplete or representative sets of data, the approximate error in the sample should be known. This can be found by using the standard deviation as discussed in the previous section. A large standard deviation means a large error or an extremely scattered set of points. This process is called the *testing of significance*. Sample data usually becomes more significant as the number of items becomes larger, and the measurement of deviation or error will become proportionately smaller.

$$\text{Error} = \frac{1}{\sqrt{\text{number of items sampled}}} = \frac{1}{\sqrt{N}}$$

Therefore, if only one item is sampled, the error is considered 100%; for four items, the error is 50%. The size of the error is important to the reliability of a commodity trading system. If a system has had four trades, whether profits or losses, there is a 50% possibility of error in the conclusions. There must be sufficient trades to assure a comfortably small error factor. In order to reduce the error to 5%, there must be 400 trades. Forecasting errors can be grouped together and measured collectively. By keeping the sample error small, the risk of trading can be better understood.

The Law of Averages

The *law of averages* is a greatly misunderstood and misquoted principle. Its most common use in commodity trading is in referring to the expectation of an abnormally long series of profits or losses being offset by an equal and opposite run. That is not what is meant by the law of averages. Over a large sample, the bulk of events will be scattered close to the average in such a way as to overwhelm an abnormal set of events and cause them to be insignificant.

This principle is illustrated in Figure 2-5, where the addition of a small abnormal grouping to one side of a balanced group of near-normal data does not affect the balance. A long run of profits, losses, or price movement is simply abnormal and will be offset over time by the large number of normal events. Further discussion can be found in "The Theory of Runs," Chapter 16.

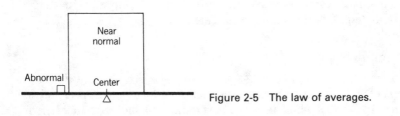

Figure 2-5 The law of averages.

Bias in Data

When sampling is used to obtain data, it is common to divide the entire subsets of data into discrete parts and attempt a representative sampling of each portion. These samples are then weighted to reflect the perceived impact of each part on the whole. Such a weighting will magnify or reduce the errors in each of the discrete sections. The result of such weighting may cause an *error in bias*. Even large numbers within a sample cannot overcome intentional bias introduced by weighting one or more parts.

Commodity price analysis and trading techniques often introduce bias in both implicit and explicit ways. A *weighted average* is an overt way of adding a positive bias (''positive'' because it is intentional). On the other hand, the use of two analytic methods acting together may unknowingly rely doubly on one statistical aspect of the data; at the same time, other data may be used only once or may be eliminated by offsetting use. The daily high and low used in one part of a program and the daily range (high to low) in another section would be considered bias.

PROBABILITY

Calculation must measure the incalculable.

Dixon G. Watts

Change is a term that causes great anxiety. However, the effects and likelihood of a chance occurrence can be measured, although not predicted. The area of study that deals with uncertainty is *probability*. Everyone uses probability in daily thinking and actions. When you tell someone that you will be there in 30 minutes, you are assuming:

Your car will start
You will not have a breakdown
There will be no unnecessary delays
You will drive at a predictable speed
You will have the normal number of green lights

All these circumstances are extremely probabilistic, and yet everyone makes the same assumptions. Actually, the 30-minute arrival is intended only as an estimate of the average time it should take for the trip. If the arrival time were critical, you would extend your estimate to 40 or 45 minutes, to account for unexpected events. In statistics, this is called *increasing the confidence interval*. You would not raise the time to 2 hours because the likelihood of such a delay would be too remote. Estimates imply an allowable variation, all of which is considered normal.

Probability is the measuring of the uncertainty surrounding an average value. Probabilities are measured in percent of likelihood. For example, if M numbers from a total of N are expected to fall within a specific range, the probability P of any one number satisfying the criteria is

$$P = \frac{M}{N} \qquad 0 < P < 1$$

Laws of Probability

Two basic principles in probability are easily explained by using examples with playing cards. In a deck of 52 cards, there are 4 suits of 13 cards each. The probability of drawing a specific card on any one turn is $\frac{1}{52}$. Similarly, the chances of drawing a particular suit or card number are $\frac{1}{4}$ and $\frac{1}{13}$, respectively. *The probability of any one of these three possibilities occurring is the sum of their individual probabilities.* This is known as the *law of addition.* The probability of success in choosing a numbered card, suit, or specific card is

$$P = \frac{1}{13} + \frac{1}{4} + \frac{1}{52} = \frac{18}{52} = 35\%$$

The other basic principle, the *law of multiplication,* states that the *probability of two occurrences happening simultaneously or in succession is equal to the product of their separate probabilities.* The likelihood of drawing a three and a club from the same deck in two consecutive turns (replacing the card after each draw) or of drawing the same cards from two decks simultaneously is

$$P = \frac{1}{13} \times \frac{1}{4} = \frac{1}{52} = 2\%$$

Joint and Marginal Probability

Price movement is not as clearly defined as a deck of cards. There is often a relationship between successive events. For example, over two consecutive days, prices must have one of the following sequences or "joint events": (up, up), (down, down), (up, down), (down, up), with the *joint probabilities* of .40, .10, .35, and .15, respectively. In this example, there is the greatest expectation that prices will rise. The *marginal probability* of a price rise on the first day is shown in Table 2-2. Thus there is a 75% chance of higher prices on the first day and a 55% chance of higher prices on the second day.

Table 2-2   Marginal Probability

		Day 2				
		Up	Down			
	Up	.40	.35	.75	Up	Marginal Probability on Day 1
Day 1						
	Down	.15	.10	.25	Down	
		.55	.45			
		Up	Down			

Marginal Probability
on Day 2

Contingent Probability

What is the probability of an outcome "conditioned" on the result of a prior event? In the example of joint probability, this might be the chance of a price increase on the second day when prices declined on the first day. The notation for this situation (the probability of A conditioned on B) is

$$P(A|B) = \frac{P(A \text{ and } B)}{P(B)} = \frac{\text{joint probability of } A \text{ and } B}{\text{marginal probability of } B}$$

then

$$P(\text{up Day 2}|\text{down Day 1}) = \frac{\text{joint probability of (down, up)}}{\text{marginal probability of (down Day 1)}}$$

$$= \frac{.15}{.25} = .60$$

The probability of *either* a price increase on Day 1 or a price increase on Day 2 is

$$P(\text{either}) = P(\text{up Day 1}) + P(\text{up Day 2}) - P(\text{up Day 1 and up Day 2})$$
$$= .75 + .55 - .40$$
$$= .90$$

Markov Chains

A method of solving a more complex situation of conditional probability is the *Markov process* (*Markov chain*). For example, the possibility of a clear, cloudy, or rainy day tomorrow might be related to today's weather.

The different combinations of dependent possibilities are given by a *switching matrix*. In our weather prediction example, a clear day has a 70% chance of being followed by another clear day, a 25% chance of a cloudy day, and only a 5% chance of rain. In Table 2-3, each possibility today is shown on the left, and its probability of changing tomorrow is indicated across the top. Each row totals 100%, accounting for all weather combinations. The relationship between these events can be shown as a continuous network (see Figure 2-6).

The Markov process can reduce intricate relationships to a simpler form. First, consider a two-state process. Using the commodities markets as an example, what is the probability of an up or down day following an up day, or following a down

Table 2-3   Switching Matrix

		Tomorrow		
		Clear	Cloudy	Rainy
	Clear	.70	.25	.05
Today	Cloudy	.20	.60	.20
	Rainy	.20	.40	.40

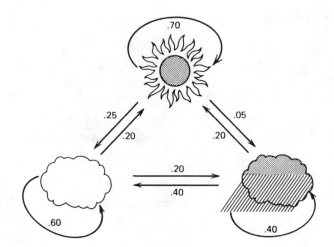

Figure 2-6   Probability network.

day in a market with an upwards trend? If there is a 70% chance of a higher day following a higher day and a 55% chance of a higher day following a lower day, what is the probability of any day within an uptrend being up?

Start with either an up or down day, and then calculate the probability of the next day being up or down. Because the first day may be designated as up or down, it is an exception to the general rule and therefore is given the weight of 50%. The probability of the second day being up or down is the sum of the joint probabilities

$$P(\text{up})_2 = (.50 \times .70) + (.50 \times .55)$$
$$= .625$$

The probability of the second day being up is 62.5%. Continuing in the same manner, use the probability of an up day as .625, the down as .375, and calculate the third day,

$$P(\text{up})_3 = (.625 \times .70) + (.375 \times .55)$$
$$= .64375$$

and the fourth day,

$$P(\text{up})_4 = (.64375 \times .70) + (.35625 \times .55)$$
$$= .64656$$

which can now be seen to be converging. To generalize the probability of an up day, look at what happens on the ith day:

$$P(\text{up})_{i+1} = [P(\text{up})_i \times .70] + [(1 - P(\text{up})_i) \times .55]$$

Because the probability is converging, the relationship

$$P(\text{up})_{i+1} = P(\text{up})_i$$

can be substituted and used to solve the equation

$$P(\text{up})_i = [P(\text{up})_i \times .70] + [.55 - P(\text{up})_i \times .55]$$

giving the probability of any day being up within an uptrend as

$$P(\text{up})_i = .64705$$

Predicting the weather is a more involved case of multiple situations converging. By approaching the problem in the same manner as the two-state process, a $\frac{1}{3}$ probability is assigned to each situation for the first day; the second day's probability is

$$P(\text{clear})_2 = (.333 \times .70) + (.333 \times .20) + (.333 \times .20)$$
$$= .3663$$

$$P(\text{cloudy})_2 = (.333 \times .25) + (.333 \times .60) + (.333 \times .40)$$
$$= .41625$$

$$P(\text{rainy})_2 = (.333 \times .05) + (.333 \times .20) + (.333 \times .40)$$
$$= .21645$$

Then using the second day results, the third day is

$$P(\text{clear})_3 = (.3663 \times .70) + (.41625 \times .20) + (.21645 \times .20)$$
$$= .38295$$

$$P(\text{cloudy})_3 = (.3663 \times .25) + (.41625 \times .60) + (.21645 \times .40)$$
$$= .42791$$

$$P(\text{rainy})_3 = (.3663 \times .05) + (.41625 \times .20) + (.21645 \times .40)$$
$$= .18815$$

The general form for solving these three equations is

$$P(\text{clear})_{i+1} = [P(\text{clear})_i \times .70] + [P(\text{cloudy})_i \times .20]$$
$$+ [P(\text{rainy})_i \times .20]$$

$$P(\text{cloudy})_{i+1} = [P(\text{clear})_i \times .25] + [P(\text{cloudy})_i \times .60]$$
$$+ [P(\text{rainy})_i \times .40]$$

$$P(\text{rainy})_{i+1} = [P(\text{clear})_i \times .05] + [P(\text{cloudy})_i \times .20]$$
$$+ [P(\text{rainy})_i \times .40]$$

where each $i + 1$ element can be set equal to the corresponding ith values; there are then three equations in three unknowns, which can be solved directly or by the matrix method as shown in Appendix 3, "Solution to Weather Probabilities Expressed as a Markov Chain."[1] Otherwise, it will be necessary to use the additional relationship

$$P(\text{clear})_i + P(\text{cloudy})_i + P(\text{rainy})_i = 1.00$$

The results are

$$P(\text{clear}) = .400$$

$$P(\text{cloudy}) = .425$$

$$P(\text{rainy}) = .175$$

---

[1] A full mathematical treatment of Markov chains can be found in John G. Kemeny, and J. Laurie Snell. *Finite Markov Chains*, Springer-Verlag, New York, 1976.

Bayes Theorem

Although historic generalization exists concerning the outcome of an event, a specific current market situation may alter the probabilities. *Bayes theorem* combines the *original probability* estimates with the *added-event probability* (the reliability of the new information) to get a *posterior* or *revised probability*,

$$\frac{P(\text{original and added-event})}{P(\text{added-event})}$$

Assume that the price changes $P(\text{up})$ and $P(\text{down})$ are both original probabilities, and an "added-event," such as a crop report, inventory stocks, or money supply announcement is expected to have an overriding effect on tomorrow's movement. Then

New probability $P(\text{up}|\text{added-event}) =$

$$\frac{P(\text{up and added-event})}{P(\text{up and added-event}) + P(\text{down and added-event})}$$

where *up* and *down* refer to the original historic probabilities, and $P(A \text{ and } B)$ is a joint probability.

Bayes theorem finds the conditional probability even if the joint and marginal probabilities are not known.

New probability $P(\text{up}|\text{added-event}) =$

$$\frac{P(\text{up}) \times P(\text{added-event}|\text{up})}{P(\text{up}) \times P(\text{added-event}|\text{up}) + P(\text{down}) \times P(\text{added-event}|\text{down})}$$

where $P(\text{added-event}|\text{up})$ is the reliability of the new event being a correct predictor of an upwards move, and $P(\text{added-event}|\text{down})$ is the probability of prices going down when the added news indicates up. For example, if a decline in soybean plantings by more than 10% has a 90% chance of causing prices to move higher, then

$$P(\text{added-event}|\text{up}) = .90$$

and

$$P(\text{added-event}|\text{down}) = .10$$

would be used in Bayes theorem.

SUPPLY AND DEMAND

Price is the balancing point of supply and demand. In order to estimate the future price of any product or explain its historic patterns, it will be necessary to relate the factors of supply and demand and then adjust for inflation, technological improvement, and other indicators common to econometric analysis. The following sections briefly describe these factors.

Demand

The demand for a product declines as price increases. The rate of decline is always dependent on the need for the product and its available substitutes at different price levels. In Figure 2-7a, D represents normal demand for a product over some fixed period. As prices rise, demand declines fairly rapidly. D' represents increased demand, resulting in higher prices at all levels.

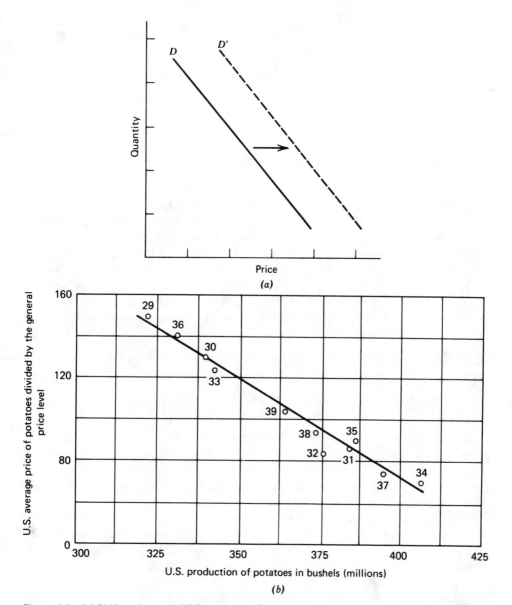

Figure 2-7   (a) Shift in demand. (b) Potatoes: U.S. average farm price on December 15th versus total production: 1929–1939. (*Source:* Shepherd, Geoffrey S. and G. A. Futrell. *Agricultural Price Analysis,* Iowa State University, Ames, IA, 1969, p. 53.) (c) Demand curve, including extremes.

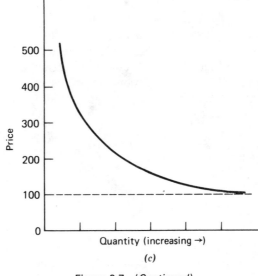

Figure 2-7   (*Continued*)

Figure 2-7*b* represents the demand relationship for potatoes for the years 1929–1939. In most cases, the demand relationship is not a straight line; production costs and minimum demand prevent the curve from going to zero. On the higher end of the scale, there is a lag in responding to increased prices and a consumer reluctance to reduce purchasing even at higher prices (called "inelastic demand"). Figure 2-7*c* shows a more representative demand curve, including extremes, where 100 represents the minimum acceptable income for a producer. The demand curve, therefore, shows the rate at which a change in quantity demanded brings about a change in price.

Elasticity of Demand. Elasticity is the key factor in expressing the relationship between price and demand. It is the relative change in demand as price increases,

$$E_D = \frac{\text{relative change (\%) in demand}}{\text{relative change (\%) in price}}$$

A market that always consumes the same amount of a product, regardless of price, is called *inelastic;* as price rises, the demand remains the same and E_D is negatively very small. An *elastic* market is just the opposite. As demand increases, price remains the same and E_D is negatively very large. Figure 2-8 shows the demand curve for various demand elasticities.

If supply increases for a product that has existed in short supply for many years, consumer purchasing habits will require time to adjust. The demand elasticity will gradually shift from relatively inelastic (Figure 2-8*b*) to relatively elastic (Figure 2-8*a*).

Supply

The supply side of the economic equation is the normal counterpart of demand. Figure 2-9*a* shows that, as price increases, the supplier will respond by offering

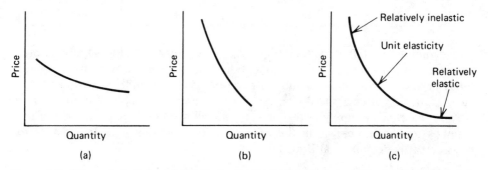

Figure 2-8 Demand elasticity. (a) Relatively elastic; (b) Relatively inelastic; (c) Normal market.

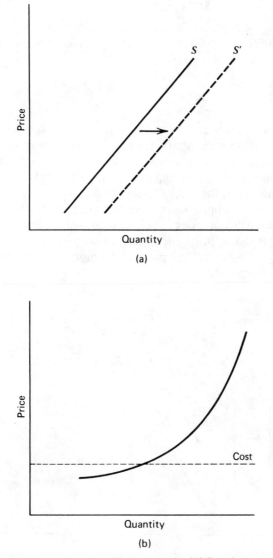

Figure 2-9 Supply-price relationship. (a) Shift in supply. (b) Supply curve, including extremes.

greater amounts of the product. Figure 2-9*b* demonstrates the supply at price extremes. At low levels, below production costs, there is a nominal supply by those producers who must maintain operations due to high fixed costs and difficulty restarting after a shutdown. At high-price levels, supply is erratic. There may be insufficient supply in the short term, followed by the appearance of new supplies or substitutes, as in the case of a location shortage. In most cases, however, it is demand that brings price down.

Elasticity of Supply. The elasticity of supply E_S is the relationship between the change in supply and the change in price,

$$E_S = \frac{\text{relative change (\%) in supply}}{\text{relative change (\%) in price}}$$

The elasticity of supply, the counterpart of *demand elasticity,* is a positive number because price and quantity move in the same direction at the same time.

Equilibrium

The demand for a product and the supply of that product meet at a point of *equilibrium*. The current price of any commodity represents the point of equilibrium for that product at that moment in time. Figure 2-10 shows a constant demand line *D* and a shifting supply, increasing to the right from *S* to *S'*.

The demand line *D* and the original supply line *S* meet at the equilibrium price *P*; after the increase in supply, the supply line shifts to *S'*. The point of equilibrium *P'* represents a lower price, the consequence of larger supply with unchanged demand. Because supply and demand each have varying elasticities and are best represented by curves, the point of equilibrium can shift in any direction in a market with changing factors.

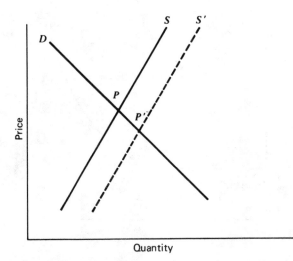

Figure 2-10   Equilibrium with shifting supply.

Building a Model

A model can be created to *explain* or *forecast* price changes. Most models *explain* rather than forecast. Explanatory models analyze sets of data at concurrent times, that is, they look for relationships between multiple factors and their effect on price at the same moment in time. They can also look for *causal,* or "lagged" relationships, where prices *respond* to other factors after one or more days. It is possible to use the explanatory model to determine the normal price at a particular moment. Although not considered forecasting, any variation in the actual market price from the normal or expected price could present trading opportunities.

Methods of selecting the best forecasting model can affect its credibility. An *analytic* approach selects the factors and specifies the relationships in advance. Tests are then performed on the data to verify the premise. Many models, though, are refined by "fitting" the data, using regression analysis or "shotgun" testing, which applies a broad selection of variables and weighting to find the best fit. These models do not necessarily forecast but are definitely optimized hindsight. Even an analytic approach that is subsequently "fine-tuned" could be in danger of losing its forecasting qualities.

The factors that comprise a model can be both numerous and difficult to obtain. Figure 2-11 shows the interrelationship between factors in the cocoa industry. Although this chart is comprehensive in its intramarket relationships, it does not emphasize the global influences that have become a major part of price movement since the mid-1970s. The change in value of the U.S. dollar and the volatility of interest rates have had far greater influence on price than normal fundamental factors for many commodities.

Models that explain price movements must be constructed from the primary factors of supply and demand. A simple example for estimating the price of fall potatoes[2] is

$$P/PPI = a + bS + cD$$

where P is the average price of fall potatoes received by farmers; PPI is the Producer Price Index; S is the apparent domestic free supply (production less exports and diversions); D is the estimated deliverable supply; and a, b, and c are constants determined by regression analysis.

This model implies that consumption must be constant (i.e., inelastic demand); demand factors are only implicitly included in the estimated deliverable supply. Exports and diversion represent a small part of the total production. The use of the *PPI* gives the results in *relative* terms based on whether the index was used as an *inflator* or *deflator* of price.

A general model, presented by Weymar,[3] may be written as three behavior-based equations and one identity:

(a) *Consumption*

$$C_t = f_C(P_t, P_t^L) + e_{C_t}$$

[2] J. D. Schwager, "A Trader's Guide to Analyzing the Potato Futures Market," *1981 Commodity Yearbook,* Commodity Research Bureau, New York.
[3] F. H. Weymar, *The Dynamics of the World Cocoa Market,* MIT Press, Cambridge, MA, 1968.

(b) *Production*

$$H_t = f_H(P_t, P_t^L) + e_{H_t}$$

(c) *Inventory*

$$I_t = I_{t-1} + H_t - C_t$$

(d) *"Supply of storage"*

$$P_t' - P_t = f_P(I_t) + e_P$$

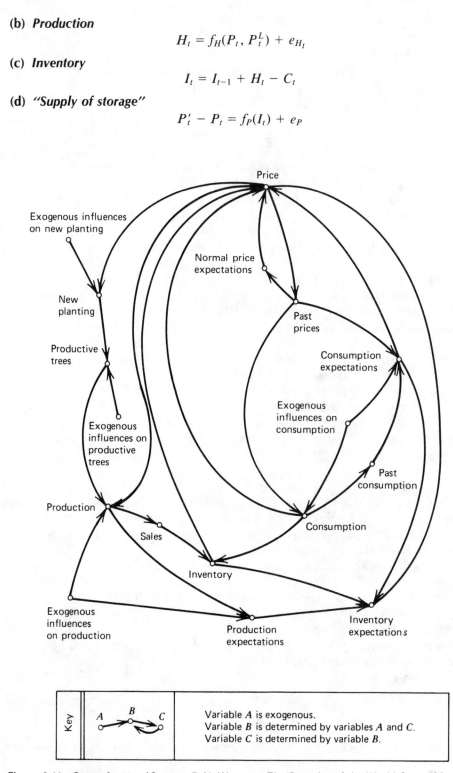

Figure 2-11   Cocoa factors. (*Source:* F. N. Weymar. *The Dyamics of the World Cocoa Market,* MIT Press, Cambridge, MA, 1968, p. 2.)

where C is the consumption, P is the price, P^L is the lagged price, H is the production (harvest), I is the inventory, P' is the expected price at some point in the future, and e is the corresponding error factor.

The first two equations show that both demand and supply depend on current and/or lagged price, the traditional microeconomic theory; production and consumption are thus dependent on past prices. The third equation, inventory level, is simply the total of previous inventories, plus new production, less current consumption. The last equation, "supply of storage," demonstrates that people are willing to carry larger inventories if they expect prices to increase substantially. The inventory function itself, equation (c), is composed of two separate relationships—manufacturers' inventories and speculators' inventories. Each reacts differently to expected price change.

RATE OF RETURN

The calculation of *rate of return* is essential for assessing performance as well as for many arbitrage situations. In its simplest form, the *one-period rate of return R*, or the *holding period rate of return* is

$$R = \frac{P_1 - P_0}{P_1} = \frac{P_1}{P_0} - 1$$

where P_0 is the initial investment, and P_1 is the value of the investment after one period. In most cases, it is desirable to standardize the returns by *annualizing*. Although calculations on government instruments use a 360-day rate (based on 90-day quarters), a 365-day rate is common for most other purposes. The following formulas show 365 days; however, 360 may be substituted.

The *annualized rate of return on a simple-interest basis* for an investment over n days is

$$R_{\text{simple}} = \frac{P_n - P_0}{P_0} \times \frac{365}{n}$$

The *annualized compounded rate of return* is

$$R_{\text{compounded}} = \left(1 + \frac{P_n - P_0}{P_0}\right)^{365/n}$$

The geometric mean is the basis for the *compounded growth* associated with interest rates. If the initial investment is \$1000 (P_0) and the result is \$1600 (P_n) in 12 years ($n = 12$), there has been an increase of 60%. The simple rate of return is 5%, but the compounded growth shows

$$P_n = P_0 \times (1 + R)^n$$

or

$$R = \sqrt[n]{\frac{P_n}{P_0}} - 1$$

$$= \sqrt[12]{\frac{1600}{1000}} - 1$$

$$= .04 \text{ or } 4\%$$

3

Regression Analysis

Regression analysis is a way of measuring the relationship between two or more sets of data. An economist might want to know how the supply of wheat affects wheat prices, or the relationship among gold, inflation, and the value of the U.S. dollar. A hedger or arbitrageur could use the relationship between two related products, such as palm oil and soybean oil, to select the cheaper product or to profit from the difference. Regression analysis involves statistical measurements which determine the type of relationship that exists between the data studied. Many of the concepts are important in technical analysis and should be understood by all "technicians," even if they are not used frequently. The techniques may also be directly used to trade, as will be shown later in this chapter.

Regression analysis is often applied separately to the basic components of a *time series*, that is, the *trend*, *seasonal* (or secular trend), and *cyclic* elements. These three factors are present in all commodity price data. The part of the data that cannot be explained by these three elements is considered *random*, or unaccountable.

Trends are the basis of many commodity trading systems. Long-term trends can be related to economic factors, such as inflation or shifts in the value of the U.S. dollar due to the balance of trade and/or changing interest rates. The reasons for the existence of short-term trends are not always clear. A sharp decline in oil supply would quickly send prices soaring, and a Soviet wheat embargo would force grain prices into a decline; however, "trends" that exist over periods of a few days cannot always be related to economic factors but may be strictly behavioral.

Major fluctuations about the trend are attributed to *cycles*. Both business and industrial cycles respond slowly to changes in supply and demand. The decision to close a factory or shift to a new crop cannot be made immediately, nor can the decision be easily changed once it is made. Opening a new mine, finding crude oil deposits, or building an additional soybean processing plant makes the response to increased demand slower than the act of cutting back on production. Moreover, once the investment has been made, business is not inclined to stop production, even at returns below production costs.

The *random* element of price movement is a composite of everything unexplainable. In later sections ARIMA, or "Box-Jenkins" methods, will be used to find shorter trends and cycles that may exist in these left-over data. This chapter will concentrate on trend identification, using the methods of regression analysis. Cycles and seasonality will be discussed in Chapter 7. Because the basis of a strong trading strategy is its foundation in "real" phenomena, serious students of price movement and traders should understand the tools of regression analysis to avoid incorporating erroneous relationships into their strategies.

CHARACTERISTICS OF THE PRICE DATA

A time series is not just a series of numbers, but *ordered pairs* of price and time. Most trading strategies use one price per day, usually the closing price, although some methods will average the high, low, and closing prices. Economic analysis operates on weekly or monthly average data, but might also select a single price (week on Friday) as representative. Two reasons for the infrequent data are the availability of most major statistics on supply and demand, and the intrinsic long-term perspective of the analysis. The use of less frequent data will cause a *smoothing* effect. The highest and lowest prices will no longer appear, and the data will seem more stable. Even when using daily data, the intraday highs and lows have been eliminated, and the closing prices show less erratic movement.

A regression analysis, which identifies the trend over a specific time period, will not be influenced by cyclic patterns or short-term trends that are the same length as the time interval used in the analysis. For example, if wide seasonal swings occurred during the year but prices were about the same each year at the same time (shifted only by inflation), a 1-year trendline would be a straight line, splitting the fluctuations in half (see Figure 3-1).

The time interval used in regression analysis is selected to be long (or multiples of other cycles) if the impact of short-term patterns is to be reduced. To emphasize the movement caused by other phenomena, the time interval should be one-half of that period (e.g., a 3- or 6-month trend will exaggerate the seasonal factors). In this way, a "trend" technique may be used to identify a "seasonal" or "cyclic" element.

Figure 3-1   A basic regression analysis results in a trendline through the center of prices.

LINEAR REGRESSION

A *linear regression* is the straight-line relationship of two sets of data. It is most often found using a technique called a "best fit," which selects the straight line that comes closest to most of the data points. Using the prices of corn and soybeans as an example, their linear relationship is the straight line (or "first order") equation (see Table 3-1).

$$Y = a + bX$$

where Y is the price of corn ("dependent" variable)
$\quad\quad X$ is the price of soybeans ("independent" variable)
$\quad\quad a$ is the "Y-intercept" (where the line crosses the Y-axis)
$\quad\quad b$ is the slope (angle of the line)

METHOD OF LEAST SQUARES

The most popular technique in statistics for finding the best fit is the *method of least squares*. This approach produces the straight line from which the actual data points vary the least. To do this, calculate the *sum of the squares* of all the deviations from the line value and choose the line that has the smallest total deviation. The mathematical expression for this is

$$S = \Sigma(y_i - \hat{y}_i)^2, \text{ where all uses of } \Sigma \text{ implies } \sum_{i=1}^{N}$$

S is the sum of the squares of the error of each of the data sets, and the value $y_i - \hat{y}_i$ is the difference between the actual value of y_i at x_i and the predicted line value $\hat{y}_i$. Graphically, the individual deviations, or errors, for four points may look like those in Figure 3-2.

Each actual data point is (x_1, y_1), (x_2, y_2), (x_3, y_3) and (x_4, y_4), and the approximated position on the line is $(x_1, \hat{y}_1)$, $(x_2, \hat{y}_2)$, $(x_3, \hat{y}_3)$, and $(x_4, \hat{y}_4)$. The sum of the

Table 3-1   Annual Average Corn and Soybean Prices

	1956	1957	1958	1959	1960	1961	1962	1963	1964	1965
Corn	1.27	1.19	1.10	1.10	1.05	1.00	.98	1.09	1.12	1.18
Soybeans	2.43	2.26	2.15	2.07	2.03	2.45	2.36	2.44	2.52	2.74

	1966	1967	1968	1969	1970	1971	1972	1973	1974	1975
Corn	1.16	1.24	1.03	1.08	1.15	1.33	1.08	1.57	2.55	3.02
Soybeans	2.98	2.93	2.69	2.63	2.63	3.08	3.24	6.22	6.12	6.33

	1976	1977	1978	1979	1980	1981	1982
Corn	2.54	2.15	2.02	2.25	2.52	3.11	2.50
Soybeans	4.92	6.81	5.88	6.61	6.28	7.61	6.05

Source: 1956–1965—Illinois Statistical Service; 1966–1982—Commodity Research Bureau *Commodity Yearbook.*

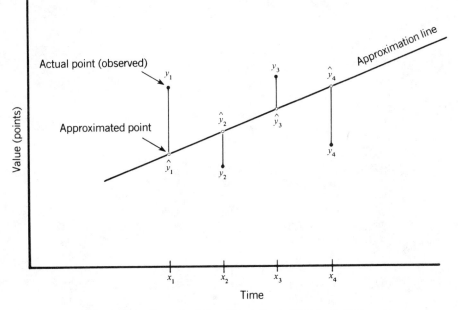

Figure 3-2   Error deviation for method of least squares.

squares of the errors is

$$S = \Sigma(y_i - \hat{y}_i)^2$$
$$= (y_1 - \hat{y}_1)^2 + (y_2 - \hat{y}_2)^2 + (y_3 - \hat{y}_3)^2 + (y_4 - \hat{y}_4)^2$$

The line that causes S to be the smallest possible will be the best choice for these data points. The square of $y_i - \hat{y}_i$ is always positive, thereby magnifying the importance of those data points that are far from the approximated line on either side and reducing the significance of those points for which the approximation is good.

To use the least-squares method for solving the corn–soybean price relationship, look for the solution to the straight line, $y = a + bx$, expressed as

$$b = \frac{N\Sigma xy - \Sigma x\Sigma y}{N\Sigma x^2 - (\Sigma x)^2}$$

$$a = \frac{1}{N}(\Sigma y - b\Sigma x)$$

Here, N is the number of data points and Σ represents the sum over N points. In order to solve these equations, construct a table of corn and soybean values and calculate all the unique sums in the preceding formulas individually[1] (Table 3-2).

---

[1] Appendix 2 offers a computer program to solve the straight-line equation using the method of least squares, as well as the other nonlinear examples.

Table 3-2 Totals for Least-Squares Solution

	i	Corn y_i	Soybeans x_i	x_i^2	x_iy_i	y_i^2
1956	1	1.27	2.43	5.90	3.09	1.61
1957	2	1.19	2.26	5.11	2.69	1.42
1958	3	1.10	2.15	4.62	2.36	1.21
1959	4	1.10	2.07	4.28	2.28	1.21
1960	5	1.05	2.03	4.12	2.13	1.10
1961	6	1.00	2.45	6.00	2.45	1.00
1962	7	.98	2.36	5.57	2.31	.96
1963	8	1.09	2.44	5.95	2.66	1.19
1964	9	1.12	2.52	6.35	2.82	1.25
1965	10	1.18	2.74	7.51	3.23	1.39
1966	11	1.16	2.98	8.88	3.46	1.34
1967	12	1.24	2.93	8.58	3.63	1.54
1968	13	1.03	2.69	7.24	2.77	1.06
1969	14	1.08	2.63	6.92	2.84	1.17
1970	15	1.15	2.63	6.92	3.02	1.32
1971	16	1.33	3.08	9.49	4.10	1.77
1972	17	1.08	3.24	10.50	3.50	1.17
1973	18	1.57	6.22	38.69	9.76	2.46
1974	19	2.55	6.12	37.45	15.61	6.50
1975	20	3.02	6.33	40.07	19.12	9.12
1976	21	2.54	4.92	24.21	12.50	6.45
1977	22	2.15	6.81	46.38	14.64	4.62
1978	23	2.02	5.88	34.57	11.88	4.08
1979	24	2.25	6.61	43.69	14.87	5.06
1980	25	2.52	6.28	39.44	15.83	6.35
1981	26	3.11	7.61	57.91	23.67	9.67
1982	27	2.50	6.05	36.60	15.13	6.25
Σ sums		Σy 43.38	Σx 106.46	Σx^2 512.95	Σxy 202.35	Σy^2 82.27

Substitute these values into the formulas and solve for a and b.

$$b = \frac{27(202.35) - (106.46)(43.38)}{27(512.95) - (106.46)(106.46)}$$

$$= \frac{5463.45 - 4618.23}{13849.65 - 11333.73}$$

$$= .336$$

$$a = \frac{1}{27}(43.38 - .336 \times 106.46)$$

$$= \frac{7.61}{27}$$

$$= .282$$

The equation for the least-squares approximation is

$$y = .282 + .336x$$

Selecting values of x and solving for y gives the results shown in Table 3-3.

Table 3-3   Least-Squares Relationship for Corn and
Soybeans: 1956–1982

Soybeans	x	1.00	2.00	3.00	4.00	5.00	6.00	7.00
Corn	y	.61	.95	1.29	1.63	1.97	2.31	2.65

The results of the linear approximation are shown in Figure 3-3. The slope of .336 indicates that for every $1 increase in the price of soybeans, there is a corresponding increase of 33.6¢ in corn. This is not far from what would be expected for farm income. Because the corn yield per acre is 2.5 times greater than the soybean yield in most parts of the United States, the slope is expected to be about .4. Considering areas where soybeans are alternatives to cotton and other crops, and the tendency for midwest farmers to plant mostly corn, a relatively higher price for soybeans is not surprising.

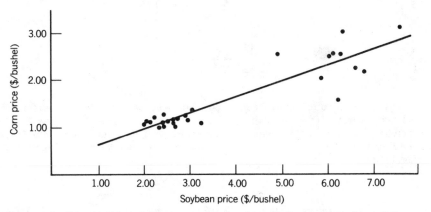

Figure 3-3   Scatter diagram of corn, soybean pairs with linear regression solution.

LINEAR CORRELATION

Solving the least-squares equation for the best fit does not mean that the answer is usable. There will always be a solution, but there might not be a valid linear relationship between the two sets of data. The *linear correlation* refers to a value called the *coefficient of determination* r^2, or the *correlation coefficient*, which expresses the relationship of the data on a scale from +1 (perfect positive correlation), to 0 (no relationship between the data), to −1 (perfect negative correlation), as shown in Figure 3-4.

The correlation coefficient is derived from the deviation, or variation in the data. It is based on the relationship

Total deviation = explained deviation + unexplained deviation

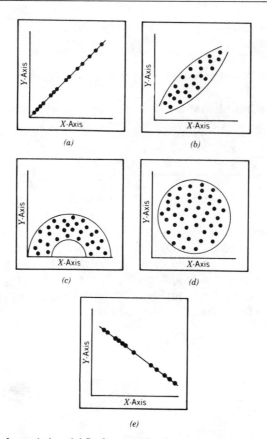

Figure 3-4   Degrees of correlation. (*a*) Perfect positive linear correlation ($r^2 = 1$). (*b*) Somewhat positive linear correlation ($r^2 = .5$). (*c*) and (*d*) No correlation ($r^2 = 0$). (*e*) Perfect negative linear correlation ($r^2 = -1$). (*Source:* Mendenhall, William and James Reinmuth. *Statistics for Management and Economics,* 2nd ed., Wadsworth, Belmont, CA, 1974. Reprinted by permission of the publisher, Duxbury Press.)

where   *total deviation* is $\Sigma(y_i - \bar{y})$, the sum of the individual differences
                      from the average;
       explained deviation is $\Sigma(\hat{y}_i - \bar{y})$, the sum of the differences between the
                      points on the fitted line and the average;
  unexplained deviation is $\Sigma(y_i - \hat{y}_i)$, the sum of the remaining forecast error
                      terms.

Changing this into a ratio gives

$$r^2 = 1 - \frac{\text{unexplained deviation}}{\text{total deviation}} = 1 - \frac{\Sigma(y_i - \hat{y}_i)^2}{\Sigma(y_i - \bar{y})^2}$$

The value r^2 can also be determined using sums already calculated in Table 3-2, by applying the following formula:

$$r^2 = \frac{(N\Sigma xy - \Sigma x \Sigma y)^2}{[N\Sigma x^2 - (\Sigma x)^2][N\Sigma y^2 - (\Sigma y)^2]}$$

This is easy to calculate; it requires only one sum in addition to the solution of the least-squares problem. The results r^2 are interpreted as follows:

$r^2 = +1$ A perfect positive linear correlation. The data points are along a straight line going upward to the right (Figure 3-4a).

$+1 > r^2 > 0$ The scattered points become more uniformly distributed about a positive approximation line as the value of r^2 becomes closer to +1 (Figure 3-4b).

$r^2 = 0$ No linear correlation exists (Figures 3-4c, 3-4d).

$-1 < r^2 < 0$ The scattered points become more uniformly distributed about a negative approximation line as the value of r^2 becomes closer to −1.

$r^2 = -1$ A perfect negative linear correlation, the line going downward to the right (Figure 3-4e).

Applying the formula to the corn–soybean data and using the sums from Table 3-2 gives

$$r^2 = \frac{[27(202.35) - (106.46)(43.38)]^2}{[27(512.95) - (106.46)^2][27(82.27) - (43.38)^2]}$$

$$= \frac{(5463.45 - 4618.23)^2}{(13849.65 - 11333.73)(2221.29 - 1881.82)}$$

$$= \frac{714396.84}{(2515.92)(339.47)}$$

$$= 83.6$$

The results show a strong relationship between the prices of soybeans and corn. The value of r^2 may also be considered as having accounted for 83.6% of the price relationship between the two products.

Correlation Adjustments When Using a Time Series

Because most price analyses involve the use of two time series, precautions should be taken. A long-term upward or downward trend will overshadow the smaller movements around the trend and exaggerate the correlation. The following methods may be used to correct the problem:

1. The deviations from the trend $(\hat{y}_i - y_i)$ may be correlated
2. The first differences $[(\hat{y}_i - \hat{y}_{i-1}), (y_i - y_{i-1})]$ may be correlated
3. The two series may be adjusted for trend

Forecasting Using Regression

A distinct advantage of regression analysis is that it allows the analyst to forecast price movement. In the case of the linear regression, the forecast will simply be an extension of the line. Later in this book, there will be other *nonlinear* solutions that are used to predict more complex patterns.

The regression forecast is the basis for the *probabilistic model*. Instead of the corn–soybean relationship, regress the price of soybeans against time using the linear least-squares method on the data in Table 3-2. The result is

$$y = .987 + .221x$$

where y is the price of soybeans for the year x. Because the solution used 1 for 1956 and 27 for 1982, the average farm income per bushel of soybeans is forecast as 7.32 in 1985 ($x = 30$) and 8.38 in 1990 ($x = 35$).

Confidence Bands. Regression analysis includes its own measure of accuracy called *confidence bands*. It is based on a probability distribution of the errors in the fitted equation and the size of the data sample. Looking at Figure 3-3, the straight line cannot touch all the points, but its "goodness of fit" may be measured by using the *standard deviation of the errors* to determine the variance over the

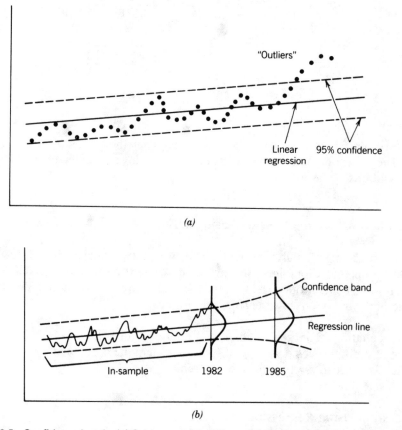

(a)

(b)

Figure 3-5   Confidence bands. (a) Soybeans with 95% confidence band. (b) Out-of-sample forecasts lose confidence.

total number of data points N. If the actual data points are y_i and their corresponding value on the fitted line $\hat{y}_i$, then

$$\sigma = \sqrt{\frac{\Sigma e^2}{N}}$$

where

$$e_i = y_i - \hat{y}_i$$

Referring to the table of normal distribution (Appendix 1), the 95% level is equivalent to 1.96 standard deviations. Then, a confidence band of 95%, placed around the forecast line, is written

$$95\% \text{ upper band} = y_i + 1.96\sigma$$

$$95\% \text{ lower band} = y_i - 1.96\sigma$$

Figure 3-5a shows the soybean forecast with a 95% confidence band. The points that are outside the band are of particular interest and can be interpreted in either of two ways.

1. They are not representative of normal price behavior and are expected to correct the levels within the bands.
2. The model was not performed on representative or adequate data and should be reestimated.

Figure 3-5b also indicates that the forecast loses accuracy as it is further projected; the forecast is based on the size of the sample used to find the regression coefficients. The more data included in the original solution, the longer the forecast will maintain its accuracy.

NONLINEAR APPROXIMATIONS FOR TWO VARIABLES

Data points that cannot be related linearly may be approximated using a curve. The general polynomial form that approximates any curve is

$$y = a_0 + a_1x + a_2x^2 + \ldots + a_nx^n$$

The first two terms on the right side form the first-order equation for a straight line. By adding the next term a_2x^2, the shape of the resulting line changes to a *parabolic* curve, one with a single, smooth change of direction. The third term a_3x^3 adds an *inflection* to the pattern. For most price forecasting, the *second-order* equation, also called *curvilinear*, is sufficient (Figure 3-6). The corn and soybean prices from Table 3-1 will be used to give examples of this and other nonlinear approximations.

The curvilinear form

$$y = a + bx + cx^2$$

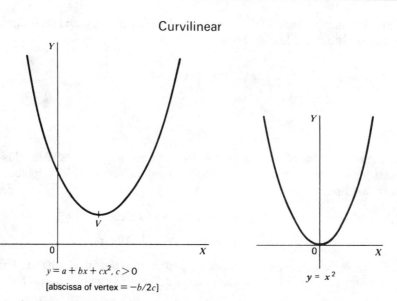

Curvilinear

$y = a + bx + cx^2, c > 0$

[abscissa of vertex $= -b/2c$]

$y = x^2$

Figure 3-6   Curvilinear (parabolas). (*Source:* Reprinted with permission from *Standard Mathematical Tables,* 24th ed. CRC Press, Inc., 1976 pp. 321, 322.)

must be solved for the coefficients a, b and c using the simultaneous equations

$$Na + b\Sigma x + c\Sigma x^2 = \Sigma y$$
$$a\Sigma x + b\Sigma x^2 + c\Sigma x^3 = \Sigma xy$$
$$a\Sigma x^2 + b\Sigma x^3 + c\Sigma x^4 = \Sigma x^2 y$$

The calculations from Table 3-2, including the additional sums for x^3, x^4, and $x^2 y$, can be substituted into the preceding equations. The system of simultaneous linear equations can be solved by the process of matrix elimination[2], a technique that should not be performed without the help of a computer. An alternate solution can be obtained by continuing with the already familiar least-squares method.

SECOND-ORDER LEAST SQUARES

The concepts of least squares can be extended to the curvilinear (second-order) equation by minimizing the sum of the errors[3]

$$S = \sum_{i=1}^{N} (y_i - a - bx_i - cx_i^2)^2$$

[2] See Appendix 3 for examples of matrix solutions.
[3] F. R. Ruckdeschel, *BASIC Scientific Subroutines*. Vol. I, Byte/McGraw-Hill, Peterborough, NH, 1981.

First, it is necessary to separate the various intermediate sums before expressing the solution for a, b, and c.

$$S_{xx} = \frac{1}{N} \sum_{i=1}^{N} (x_i - \bar{x})^2$$

$$S_{xy} = \frac{1}{N} \sum_{i=1}^{N} (x_i - \bar{x})(y_i - \bar{y})$$

$$S_{yy} = \frac{1}{N} \sum_{i=1}^{N} (y_i - \bar{y})^2$$

$$S_{xx2} = \frac{1}{N} \sum_{i=1}^{N} (x_i - \bar{x})(x_i^2 - \bar{x}^2)$$

$$S_{x2x2} = \frac{1}{N} \sum_{i=1}^{N} (x_i^2 - \bar{x}^2)^2$$

$$S_{yx2} = \frac{1}{N} \sum_{i=1}^{N} (y_i - \bar{y})(x_i^2 - \bar{x}^2)$$

The constant values can then be found by substitution into the following equations

$$b = \frac{S_{xy}S_{x2x2} - S_{yx2}S_{xx2}}{S_{xx}S_{x2x2} - (S_{xx2})^2}$$

$$c = \frac{S_{xx}S_{yx2} - S_{xx2}S_{xy}}{S_{xx}S_{x2x2} - (S_{xx2})^2}$$

$$a = \bar{y} - b\bar{x} - c\bar{x}^2$$

The procedure is identical to the solution of the linear least squares. Fortunately, there are simple computer programs that have already been written to solve these problems. Using the program found in Appendix 2, the result is

$$y = .310 + .323x + .002x^2$$

Table 3-4 shows the relationship using selected values of x. Notice that this relationship is essentially linear due to the small second-order coefficient. It is not necessary to solve both the linear and curvilinear models because the second-order equation can be used in the linear form when this situation occurs.

Table 3-4   Curvilinear Values for Corn and Soybeans

Soybeans	x	1.00	2.00	3.00	4.00	5.00	6.00	7.00
Corn	y	.63	.96	1.29	1.63	1.97	2.31	2.66

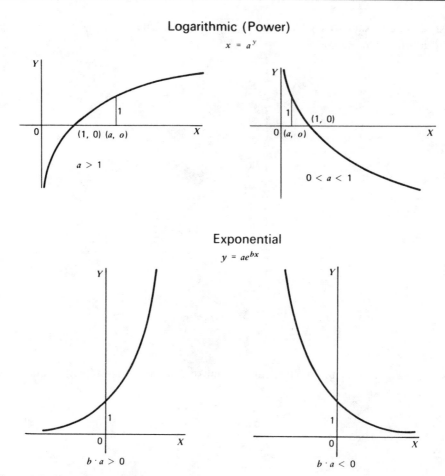

Figure 3-7 Logarithmic and exponential. (*Source:* Reprinted with permission from *Standard Mathematical Tables,* 24th ed., CRC Press, Inc., 1976 pp. 316, 320.)

Transforming Nonlinear to Linear

Two curves that are often used to forecast prices are *logarithmic* (*power*) and *exponential* relationships (see Figure 3-7). The exponential, curving up, is used to scale price data that become more volatile at higher levels. Each of these forms can be solved with unique equations; however, both can be easily transformed into linear relationships and solved using the method of least squares.

	Logarithmic	Exponential
General form	$y = ax^b$	$y = ae^{bx}$
Transformed	$\ln y = \ln a + b \ln x$	$\ln y = \ln a + bx$
Linear form	$y = a + bx$	$y = a + bx$
	where $y = \ln y$	where $y = \ln y$
	$a = \ln a$	$a = \ln a$
	$x = \ln x$	

Table 3-5   Log and Exponential Values for Corn
and Soybeans

Soybeans	x	1.00	2.00	3.00	4.00	5.00	6.00	7.00
Corn (log)	y	.54	.94	1.30	1.64	1.96	2.26	2.56
(exp)	y	.84	1.02	1.24	1.50	1.83	2.22	2.70

The significant difference in the transformations is that the value of x is not scaled for the exponential. Taking the original data and performing the appropriate natural log functions *ln* results in the linear form that can be solved using least squares. Selected results from the computer program in Appendix 2 are shown in Table 3-5.

EVALUATION OF TWO-VARIABLE TECHNIQUES

Of the three curve-fitting techniques, the curvilinear and exponential results are very similar, both curving upward and passing through the main cluster of data points at about the same incline. The log approximation curves downward after passing through the main group of data points at about the same place as the other approximations. To evaluate objectively whether any of the nonlinear methods are a better fit than the linear approximation, find the standard deviation of the errors, which gives a statistical measurement of how close the fitted line comes to the original data points. The results show that the curvilinear is best; the logarithmic, which curves downward, is noticeably the worst (see Figure 3-8).

In the case of the corn–soybean relationship, the model with the smallest variance makes the most sense. Prices will usually remain within the range tested, and the realities of production-price relationship support the selection of the linear (or curvilinear) values.

The use of regression analysis for forecasting the price of soybeans alone has a different conclusion. Although 27 years were used, the last 10 showed a noticeable increase in soybean prices. This rising pattern is best fit by the curvilinear and exponential models. However, forecasts using these formulas show prices continuing to rise at an increasing rate. Had inflation maintained its double-digit rate, these forecasts would still lead to unrealistically high prices. The logarithmic model, which leveled off after the rise, turned out to be the best for the actual situation. This shows that the problem of forecasting is more complex than this naive solution. The logarithmic model, which showed the worst statistical results, provided the best forecast. Major factors that cause significant price shifts, such as interest rates, inflation, and the value of the U.S. dollar must be monitored carefully. The model must be reestimated whenever these factors change. The section on "Multivariate Approximations" will discuss this in more detail.

Direct Relationships

Many products are dependent on the prices of other commodities in both the cost of production and product substitution. Arbitrage is often based on these relation-

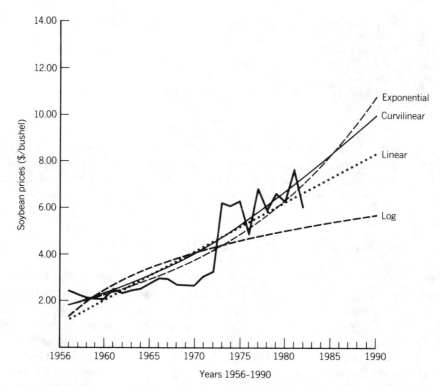

Figure 3-8 Least-squares approximation for soybeans using linear, curvilinear, logarithmic, and exponential models.

ships, which are carefully monitored and quickly corrected by traders; interest rate vehicles of the same maturity, "strips" of interest rates, interbank rates for the same currencies at different locations, the soybean "crush," and other processing margins do not stay out of line for long. The following nonfinancial markets have close relationships that can be found using regression analysis.

Products Related	Reason
All crops	Relative income for farmers
Grains	Protein substitution for feed
Livestock to feedgrains	Feed, cost of production
Livestock	Food substitution
Sugar and corn	Sweetener substitution
Hogs and pork bellies	Product dependency
Silver, gold, and platinum	Investor's inflation hedge

MULTIVARIATE APPROXIMATIONS

Regression analysis is most often used in complex economic models to find the combination of two or more independent variables which best explain or forecast prices. A simple application of annual production and distribution of soybeans will determine whether these factors are significant in determination of soybean prices. Because the demand for soybeans and products is complex, a high correlation should not be expected between the data. However, there is no way of knowing how much impact other factors have on the prices over a long term.

Using the method of least squares which was employed for a simple linear regression, the new equation is

$$y = a + bx_1 + cx_2$$

where y is the resulting price

x_1 is the total production (supply)

x_2 is the total distribution (demand)

a, b, c are constants to be calculated

As in the linear approximation, the solution to this problem will be chosen by minimizing the sum of the squares of the errors at each point

$$S = \sum_{i=1}^{n} (y_i - \hat{y}_i)^2$$

Substituting $\hat{y}$ from the previous equation,

$$S = \sum_{i=1}^{n} (y_i - (a + bx_1 + cx_2))^2$$

The solution to the multivariate problem of two independent variables x_1 and x_2 requires the following three least-squares equations:

$$an \quad + b \sum x_1 \quad + c \sum x_2 \quad = \sum y$$
$$a \sum x_1 + b \sum x_1^2 \quad + c \sum x_1 x_2 = \sum x_1 y$$
$$a \sum x_2 + b \sum x_1 x_2 + c \sum x_2^2 \quad = \sum x_2 y$$

The procedure for solving the three simultaneous equations is the same as the curvilinear method of coefficient elimination. The sums are calculated in Table 3-6, then substituted into the last three equations:

$$12.00a + 13.546b + 12.582c = 44.4$$

$$13.55a + 15.980b + 14.75c = 53.28$$

$$12.58a + 14.75b + 13.86c = 49.264$$

The coefficient matrix solution is[4]

$$\begin{pmatrix} 12.00 & 13.55 & 12.58 & 44.40 \\ 13.55 & 15.98 & 14.74 & 53.28 \\ 12.58 & 14.74 & 13.86 & 49.26 \end{pmatrix}$$

$$\begin{pmatrix} 1 & 1.239 & 1.048 & 3.700 \\ 0 & .6798 & .5451 & 3.145 \\ 0 & .5451 & .6720 & 2.714 \end{pmatrix}$$

---

[4] Matrix elimination is the necessary solution to the multivariate problem. Appendix 3 contains the computer programs necessary to perform this operation.

$$\begin{pmatrix} 1 & 0 & .1429 & -1.5240 \\ 0 & 1 & .8018 & 4.6264 \\ 0 & 0 & .2349 & .1922 \end{pmatrix}$$

$$\begin{pmatrix} 1 & 0 & 0 & -1.641 \\ 0 & 1 & 0 & 3.9703 \\ 0 & 0 & 1 & .8183 \end{pmatrix}$$

The results show $a = -1.641$, $b = 3.9703$, and $c = .8183$, so that the multiple linear approximation of the price is

$$\hat{y} = -1.641 + 3.9703x_1 + .8183x_2$$

where x_1 is the production in billions of bushels and x_2 demand in billions of bushels. The coefficient of supply is the principal factor in the determination of price. Had either coefficient of x_1 or x_2 been small, it would have indicated a lack of significance. The selection of which data to try when determining price components is not obvious and may result in a useless answer. In the example, supply-and-demand figures were chosen to determine price, but perhaps supply and inflation or demand and inflation would have been better. To find out which sets of data are best, each combination would have to be tested and the results compared.

Generalized Multivariate

In general, the relationship between n independent variables is expressed as

$$y = a_0 + a_1x_1 + a_2x_2 + \cdots + a_nx_n$$

Table 3-6   Totals for Multivariate Solution

			Supply	Demand					
			x_1	x_2	x_1^2	x_2^2	x_1x_2	x_1y	x_2y
		y	(Billions)		(Billions)			(Millions)	
1964	1	2.67	.700	.677	.490	.458	.474	1.869	1.808
1965	2	2.88	.845	.738	.714	.545	.624	2.434	2.125
1966	3	2.98	.928	.839	.861	.704	.779	2.765	2.500
1967	4	2.93	.976	.874	.953	.764	.853	2.860	2.561
1968	5	2.69	1.107	.900	1.225	.810	.996	2.978	2.421
1969	6	2.63	1.133	.946	1.284	.895	1.072	2.980	2.488
1970	7	2.63	1.127	1.230	1.270	1.513	1.386	2.964	3.235
1971	8	3.08	1.176	1.258	1.383	1.583	1.479	3.622	3.875
1972	9	3.24	1.271	1.202	1.615	1.445	1.528	4.118	3.894
1973	10	6.22	1.547	1.283	2.393	1.646	1.985	9.622	7.980
1974	11	6.12	1.215	1.435	1.476	2.059	1.744	7.436	8.782
1975	12	6.33	1.521	1.200	2.313	1.440	1.825	9.628	7.596
Σ		44.40	13.546	12.582	15.977	13.862	14.745	53.276	49.265

The solution to this equation is an extension of the problems in two variables. The $n + 1$ equations in $n + 1$ variables are created by summing the $n + 1$ equations developed from the general equation by multiplying the second by x_1, the third by x_2, and so on:

$$a_0 n \quad + a_1 \sum x_1 \quad + a_2 \sum x_2 \quad + \cdots + a_n \sum x_n \quad = \sum y$$

$$a_0 \sum x_1 + a_1 \sum x_1^2 \quad + a_2 \sum x_1 x_2 + \cdots + a_n \sum x_1 x_n = \sum x_1 y$$

$$a_0 \sum x_2 + a_1 \sum x_1 x_2 + a_2 \sum x_2^2 \quad + \cdots + a_n \sum x_2 x_n = \sum x_2 y$$

$$\vdots$$

$$a_0 \sum x_n + a_1 \sum x_1 x_n + a_2 \sum x_2 x_n + \cdots + a_n \sum x_n^2 \quad = \sum x_n y$$

The solution to this system of equations can be calculated on most computers using a standard program available for this purpose (see Appendix 2). Those with only a little experience in regression analysis should remember that the model is most accurate within the range of the data points; when projecting outside the bounds of the sample data, the predictive qualities of the regression formula decrease with time.

Many dependent variables (x_i) may be used to increase the possibility of finding a good correlation. The predictive quality of this solution will depend on the relevance of the independent variables. It is best to start with the obvious components of a time series: inflation, using the Wholesale Price Index or Consumer Price Index; the industrial cycle, often represented by the accumulation of stocks or overall production; and a seasonal variation, in terms of an index of adjustment. Measuring the error of the estimates will help determine whether additional factors are necessary.

Least-Squares Sinusoidal

A special case of the multiple linear predictor occurs when periodic peaks can be observed in the sample time-series data. These peaks and valleys suggest that the time series may have a cyclic pattern. One of the more well-known uses of cyclic analysis was performed by Hurst in *The Profit Magic of Stock Transaction Timing* (Prentice-Hall), in which there is an interesting example of Fourier analysis applied to the Dow Jones Industrial Averages.

The equation for the approximation of a periodic movement is

$$y_t = a_0 + a_1 t + a_2 \cos \frac{2\pi t}{P} + a_3 \sin \frac{2\pi t}{P} + a_4 t \cos \frac{2\pi t}{P} + a_5 t \sin \frac{2\pi t}{P}$$

which is a special case of the generalized multivariate approximation

$$y = a_0 + a_1 x_1 + a_2 x_2 + a_3 x_3 + a_4 x_4 + a_5 x_5$$

where P is the number of data points in each cycle and

$x_1 = t$, the incremental time element
$x_2 = \cos(2\pi t/P)$, a cyclic element
$x_3 = \sin(2\pi t/P)$, a cyclic element

$x_4 = t \cos(2\pi t/P)$, an amplitude-variation element

$x_5 = t \sin(2\pi t/P)$, an amplitude-variation element

The term $a_1 t$ will allow for the linear tendencies of the sequence. The term 2π refers to an entire cycle and $2\pi t/P$ designates a section $(1/P)$ of a specific cycle t; this in turn adds weight to either the sin or cos functions at different points within a cycle.

The solution is calculated in the tabular manner of the other methods, using simultaneous linear equations derived in the same way as the generalized multivariate equation, substituting from the table of sums and solving the coefficient matrix for $a_0, \ldots, a_5$. A complete discussion of curve fitting using trigonometric functions appears in Chapter 7.

ARIMA

An Autoregressive Integrated Moving Average (ARIMA) model is created by a process of repeated regression analysis, resulting in a forecast value. An ARIMA process automatically applies the most important features of regression analysis in a preset order and continues to reanalyze results until an "optimum" set of parameters or coefficients is found. In Chapter 15, the selection and testing of individual parameters within a trading strategy are discussed. This involves approximating their initial value and identifying a testing range. An ARIMA model does all of this as part of its special "process."

G. E. P. Box and G. M. Jenkins refined ARIMA at the University of Wisconsin[5] and their procedures for solution have become the industry standard. This technique is often referred to as the *Box-Jenkins* forecast. The two important terms in ARIMA are "autoregression" and "moving average." *Autoregression* refers to the use of the same data to self-predict, for example, using only gold prices in the analysis to arrive at a gold price forecast. *Moving average* refers to the normal concept of smoothing price fluctuations, using an average of the past n days. The moving average and popular variations are discussed thoroughly in Chapters 4 and 5. This process uses an "exponential smoothing" technique, which is among the most popular methods.

In the ARIMA process, the autocorrelation is used to determine to what extent past prices will forecast future prices. In a "first-order" autocorrelation, only the prices on the previous day are used to determine the forecast. This would be expressed as

$$P_t = a \times P_{t-1} + e$$

where P_t is the price being forecast (dependent variable)

P_{t-1} is the price being used to forecast (independent variable)

a is the coefficient (constant percentage)

e is the forecast error

[5] G. E. P. Box and G. M. Jenkins. *Time Series Analysis: Forecasting and Control*, 2nd ed., Holden-Day, San Francisco, 1976.

In a "second-order" autoregression, the previous two prices are used as follows:

$$P_t = a_1 \times P_{t-1} + a_2 \times P_{t-2} + e$$

where the current forecast P_t is based on the two previous prices P_{t-1} and P_{t-2}; there are two unique coefficients and a forecast error. The moving average is used to correct for the forecast error, e. There is also the choice of a first- or second-order moving average process,

$$First\text{-}order: E_t = e_t - b \times e_{t-1}$$

$$Second\text{-}order: E_t = e_t - b_1 \times e_{t-1} - b_2 \times e_{t-2}$$

where E_t is the approximated error term
e_t is today's forecast error
e_{t-1} and e_{t-2} are the two previous forecast errors
b_1 and b_2 are the two regression coefficients

Because the two constant coefficients, b_1 and b_2, can be considered percentages, the moving average process is similar to exponential smoothing.

The success of the ARIMA model is determined by two factors: high correlation in the autoregression and low variance in the final forecast errors. The determination of whether to use a first- or second-order autoregression is based on a comparison of the *correlation coefficients* of the two regressions. If there is little improvement using the second-order process, it is not used due to its time-consuming calculations. The final forecast is constructed by adding the moving average term, which approximates the errors, back into the autoregressive process

$$P_t' = P_t + E_t + e'$$

where P_t' is the new forecast, and e_t' is the new forecast error. The moving average process is again repeated for the new errors e', added back into the forecast to get a new value P'' and another error e''. When the variance of the errors becomes sufficiently small, the ARIMA process is complete.

The contribution of Box and Jenkins was to stress the simplicity of the solution. They determined that the autoregression and moving average steps could be limited to first- or second-order processes. To do this, it was first necessary to detrend the data, thereby making it *stationary*. Detrending can be accomplished most easily by *differencing* the data, that is, creating a new series by subtracting each previous term P_{t-1} from the next P_t. Of course, the ARIMA program must remember all of these changes, or *transformations*, in order to restore the final forecast to the proper price notation by applying these operations in reverse. If a satisfactory solution is not found in the Box-Jenkins process, it is because the data are still not stationary and further differencing is necessary.

Because of the three features just discussed, the Box-Jenkins forecast is usually shown as *ARIMA* (p, d, g), where p is the number of autoregressive terms, d is the number of differences, and g is the number of moving average terms. In its normal form, the Box-Jenkins ARIMA process performs the following steps:

1. **Specification.** Preliminary steps for determining the order of the autoregression and moving average to be used.

a. *The variance must be stabilized.* In many price series, increased volatility is directly related to increased price. In stocks, the common assumption is that this relationship is "log-normal." A simple test for variance stability, using the log function, is checked before more complex transformations are used.

b. *Prices are detrended.* This uses the technique of first differences; however, a second difference (or more) will be performed if it helps to remove further trending properties in the series (this is determined by later steps).

c. *Specify the order of the autoregressive and moving average components.* This fixes the number of prior terms to be used in these approximations (not necessarily the same number). In the Box-Jenkins approach, these numbers are usually small, often one for both. Large numbers require a rapidly expanding amount of calculation, even for a computer.

How many terms are necessary? This is a critical part of the ARIMA solution and often requires manual intervention in the computer program. The object of this step is to find the fewest terms necessary to solve the problem. All ARIMA programs will print a *correlogram*, a display of the autocorrelation coefficients. The correlogram is used to find whether all the trends and well-defined periodic movements have been removed from the series by differencing. Figure 3-9 shows three patterns of correlograms printed by *EASI/ARIMA* on a microcomputer. The top scale shows the

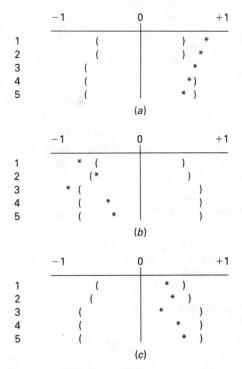

Figure 3-9   ARIMA correlograms. (*a*) Ideal correlogram results, showing significance in the first and second lags only. (*b*) Significance in the first and third lags, indicating that further trend elimination is necessary. (*c*) No significant correlations at any lag values.

importance of the coefficients. If they fall within the brackets, they have no importance, and if they fall outside the brackets, they are highly significant (greater than two standard deviations, or 95%). The left scale gives the *lag* relationship, that is, the relationship of the current price to the price *n* days ago. An asterisk will appear on line 3 outside the bracket (see Figure 3-9*b*) if a strong pattern in the lag 3 relationship to current prices has not yet been removed. To remove this, additional differencing of the data must be performed. If successful, the resulting correlogram will appear as in Figure 3-9*a*, where only the lag 1 and 2 values are outside the bracket. If further differencing results in a pattern shown in Figure 3-9*c*, all correlation of any importance in the data have been lost. If the pattern in Figure 3-9*c* were to occur in the first step, it would mean that there is no relationship to be found by autoregression. If it occurs after some differencing has been performed, the data have been differenced too many times.[6]

2. **Estimation: determining the coefficients.** The previous step was used to reduce the number of autoregressive and moving average terms necessary to the estimation process. The ARIMA method of solution is one of minimizing the errors in the forecast. In minimization, it will perform a linear or nonlinear regression on price (depending on the number of coefficients selected), determine the errors in the estimation, and then approximate those errors using a moving average. It will next look at the resulting new error series, attempt to estimate and correct the errors in that one, and repeat the process until it accounts for all price movement.

To determine when an ARIMA process is completed, three tests are performed at the end of each estimation pass:

a. *Compare the change in the coefficient value.* If the last estimation has caused little or no change in the value of the coefficient(s), the model has successfully converged to a solution.

b. *Compare the sum of the squares of the error.* If the error value is small or if it stays relatively unchanged, the model is completed.

c. *Perform a set number of estimations.* Unless a maximum number of estimations is set, an ARIMA process might continue indefinitely. This safety check is necessary in the event the model is not converging to a solution.

Once completed, the errors can be examined using an *O*-statistic to check for any trend. If so, an additional moving average term may be used to eliminate it.

Forecast Results

Once the coefficients have been determined, they are used to calculate the forecast value. These forecasts are most accurate for the next day and should be used with less confidence for subsequent days (see Figure 3-10).

What if the forecast does not work? First, the process should be checked to be certain that it was performed properly. Pay particular attention to the removal of

---

[6] Examples of the correlogram come from Eric Weiss, "Applying ARIMA Forecasts," *Technical Analysis of Stocks & Commodities*, May 1983. Refer to Weiss's two other articles on ARIMA in earlier volumes of the same magazine, especially "ARIMA Forecasting," January 1983.

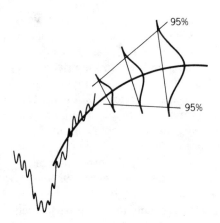

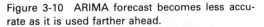

Figure 3-10   ARIMA forecast becomes less accurate as it is used farther ahead.

trends using the correlogram. Next, check the data used in the process. If the data
sample is changing (which can be observed on a price chart) select either a
shorter or longer period that contains more homogeneous data.

Trading Strategies

In the article that originally piqued the interest of commodities traders,[7] Anon
uses a 5-day-ahead forecast. If the ARIMA process forecasts an uptrend and if
prices fall below the forecast value, the commodity can be bought with added
confidence (lower risk and more profit). This technique of selecting "better" entry
points may compensate for some of the inaccuracies latent in any forecasting
method. The danger of this approach is that prices may continue to move counter
to the forecast, so that caution and a stop-loss are necessary.

Following the Trend. Use the 1-day-ahead forecast to determine the trend position. If the forecast is for higher prices, a long position should be held; if it is
predicting lower prices, shorts are necessary.

Countertrend Indicator. Use the ARIMA confidence bands to determine over-
bought/oversold levels. Not only can a long position be entered when prices
penetrate the lowest 95% confidence band, but they can be closed out when they
return to the normal 50% level. A conservative trader will enter the market only in
the direction of the ARIMA trend forecast. As shown in Figure 3-10, if the trend is
up, only the penetrations of the lower band will be used to enter new long positions.

Use of Highs and Lows. Both the implied highs and lows as well as the independently forecasted highs and lows can be the basis for other interesting strategies.[8]
The following two are used with intraday prices.

[7] Louis J. Anon, "Catch Short-Term Profits with ARIMA," *Commodities Magazine*, Dec. 1981.
[8] John F. Kepka, "Trading With ARIMA Forecasts," *Technical Analysis of Stocks & Commodities*,
Aug. 1985.

1. Using confidence bands based on the closing prices, buy an intraday penetration of the expected high or sell a penetration of the expected low, and liquidate the position on the close. Use a stop-loss. Consider taking positions only in the direction of the ARIMA trend.

2. Using the separate ARIMA models based on the daily high and low prices, buy a penetration of the 50% level of the high and sell a penetration of the 50% level of the lows. Liquidate positions on the close. Use a stop-loss.

Kalman Filters

Kalman offers an alternative approach to ARIMA, allowing an underlying forecasting model (*message model*) to be combined with other timely information (*observation model*). The message model may be any trading strategy, moving average, or regression approach. The observation model may be the floor broker's opening calls, market liquidity, or, in the case of existing foreign markets, earlier trading activity—all of which have been determined to have some overriding reliability in forecasting.

Assume that the original forecast (message) model can be described as

$$M(P_t) = c_f P_{t-1} + \text{me}_t$$

and the observation model as

$$O(P_t) = c_o P_t + \text{oe}_t$$

where *me* and *oe* are the message and observation model errors, respectively. The combined forecast would then use the observation model error to modify the result

$$P'_{t+1} = c_f P'_t + K_{t+1} \text{oe}_t$$

where K is the Kalman gain coefficient.[9]

LINEAR REGRESSION MODEL

A linear regression, or straight-line fit, could be the basis for a simple trading strategy similar to a moving average. For example, an *n*-day linear regression, applied to the closing prices, could be used with the following rules:

1. *Buy* when the closing price moves above the forecasted value of today's close.
2. *Sell* when the closing price moves below the forecasted value of today's close.[10]

---

[9] For a more complete discussion, see Andrew D. Seidel and Philip D. Ginsberg. *Commodities Trading,* Prentice-Hall, Englewood Cliffs, NJ, 1983 or R. E. Kalman, "A New Approach to Linear Filtering and Prediction Problems," *Journal of Basic Engineering*, Mar. 1960.
[10] These rules were used by Frank Hochheimer in *Computerized Trading Techniques 1982*, Merrill Lynch Commodities, New York, 1982.

There is an important difference between a model based on linear regression and one founded on a moving average. There is no "lag" in a regression strategy. If prices continue higher at the same rate, a moving average system will initially lag behind, then increase at the same rate. The lag creates a safety zone to absorb some changes in the direction of prices, without getting stopped out. (See Chapter 4 for a complete discussion of moving averages.)

A regression model, on the other hand, identifies a change of direction sooner by using a linear regression. A steady price move, however, will place the fitted line right in the center of market movement, subject to frequent whipsaws. A uniform trend is the worst case for such a system (see Figure 3-11). It would be necessary to place a band around the regression line and only accept signals caused by price moves of extreme directional change.

In Figure 3-11a, the three positions of the regression line all show numerous penetrations of the price, resulting in many losing trades. To avoid this, the

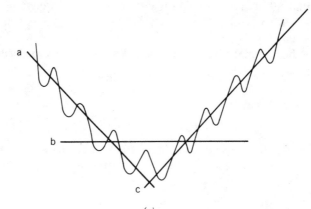

(a)

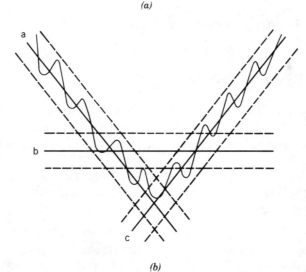

(b)

Figure 3-11   Linear regression model. (a) Simple penetration of the regression lines. (b) Penetration of the channel formed by confidence bands.

market must have no price declines within an uptrend and no rallies within a downtrend, or the regression line calculation must use only a few days. However, the use of only a few days is inconsistent with the nature of such a statistical measurement, which gains significance with more days. Figure 3-11*b* shows the use of a *confidence band* spaced equally around the regression line. Using a *high-confidence* band (e.g., 95%), it is possible to turn the erratic performance in Figure 3-11*a* into two clearly identifiable trends. Interestingly, the use of a confidence band with the regression analysis looks remarkably similar to a channel on a standard bar chart.

Hochheimer's 1982 study, performed without a channel or confidence band, shows the best selection of the regression interval at 60 to 70 days (the maximum tested was 70 days). Silver had a remarkable 1615 trades—one each day. Only two commodities showed average trade duration greater than 2 days.

4

Moving Averages

The linear and nonlinear techniques used in Chapter 3 produced forecasts that used the properties of dependence and correlation. The predictive qualities of these methods are best within the area bounded by existing data and decrease sharply when values are based on extrapolation outside the previous occurrences. The techniques most commonly used for evaluating the direction or tendency of commodity prices both within prior ranges or at new levels are classified as *autoregressive* functions. Unlike the forecasting models, they are only concerned with evaluating the current price direction. This analysis will result in one of three conclusions: Prices are moving in an upward, downward, or sideways direction. From this single building block, it will be possible to form rules of action and develop complex strategies of anticipation.

In an autoregressive model, one or more of the previous day's prices determine the next sequential price. If t represents today's price, $t - 1$ yesterday's, and so on, tomorrow's price will be

$$P_{t+1} = a_0 + a_1 P_t + a_2 P_{t-1} + \cdots + a_t P_1 + e$$

where each price is given a corresponding weighting a_i and combined to give the resultant price for tomorrow $P_{t+1} \pm e$ (e represents an error factor). The simplest example is the use of yesterday's price alone to generate tomorrow's price:

$$P_{t+1} = a_0 + a_1 P_t + e$$

The autoregressive model does not have to be linear; each prior day can have a nonlinear predictive quality. Thus P_t could be represented by a curvilinear expression, P_{t-1} by an exponential or logarithmic formula and so on. All of these expressions would then be combined to form an autoregressive forecasting model for P_{t+1}. In going from the simple to the complex, it is natural to want to know which of these choices will perform best. The answer can only be found by experimentation and application to a specific problem. Various methods must be attempted and applied to actual data in a real-time or extrapolated situation to determine the predictive quality of any model. Chapters 5 and 15 will discuss which choices have been most popular.

LEAST-SQUARES MODEL

The least-squares regression model can be applied in an autoregressive way by recalculating the model daily and using the slope of the resulting line or curve to determine the direction of the trend. A simple error analysis evaluates its predictive qualities. Assume that there is a lengthy price series for a commodity and that we would like to know how many prior days is optimum for predicting the next day's price. The answer is found by looking at the average error in the predictions. If the number of days in the calculation is increased and if the predictive error decreases, the answer is improving; if the error stops decreasing, the accuracy limit has been reached. As an example, start by using only one prior day to find the price forecast

$$P_{t+1} = a_0 + a_1 P_t$$

$$P_t = a_0 + a_1 P_{t-1}$$

$$P_{t-1} = a_0 + a_1 P_{t-2}$$

$$\vdots$$

$$P_2 = a_0 + a_1 P_1$$

and work up to a large number of days:

$$P_{t+1} = a_0 + a_1 P_t + a_2 P_{t-1} + \cdots + a_n P_{t-n+1}$$

$$P_t = a_0 + a_1 P_{t-1} + a_2 P_{t-2} + \cdots + a_n P_{t-n}$$

$$P_{t-1} = a_0 + a_1 P_{t-2} + a_2 P_{t-3} + \cdots + a_n P_{t-n-1}$$

In the last case, it takes n days of prior prices to generate each new prediction. In all cases, $n + 2$ equations can be written to solve the $n + 1$ coefficients a_0, a_1, . . . , a_n using matrix elimination (see Appendix 3). The result is a predicted price $\hat{P}_t$ for each actual price P_t. The notation $\hat{P}(n)_t$ means the predicted price for day t using an n-day linear regression; therefore, $\hat{P}(3)_{25} = 58.00$ means that the predicted value of P on day 25 was 58.00 using a 3-day linear regression analysis (a straight-line fit of the 3 prior days). The error occurring in each prediction is defined as

$$\hat{E}(n)_t = P_t - \hat{P}(n)_t$$

the difference between the actual and predicted values for that day using the n-day linear regression. As an example of error analysis, May 77 Copper was selected for a period of 20 trading days showing a slight upward and a slight downward move, with some intermediate changes of direction. Table 4-1 shows the actual predictions using linear regressions with from two through seven prior prices and prediction of one day forward. Table 4-2 shows the relative error in these predictions and an analysis of the errors. The *mean* is a simple average of all the points and determines the net trend bias during the sample period; the *standard deviation* measures the accuracy of the forecast.

The standard deviation and coefficient of variance are both measurements of the distribution of points about the approximation line. As discussed in Chapter 2, the standard deviation measures the occurrence of points near the predictions; the

Table 4-1   Analysis of Predictive Error, May 77 Copper, November 1, 1976
through November 30, 1976

Date	Sequence t	Price P_t	Price Predictions for $P(n)$-Day Linear Regression					
			$\hat{P}(2)_t$	$\hat{P}(3)_t$	$\hat{P}(4)_t$	$\hat{P}(5)_t$	$\hat{P}(6)_t$	$\hat{P}(7)_t$
10-21	1	60.30						
10-22	2	59.30						
10-25	3	58.70						
10-26	4	57.80						
10-27	5	59.80						
10-28	6	58.20						
10-29	7	58.40						
11-01	8	58.90	58.60	57.40	58.60	58.52	58.30	57.95
11-03	9	59.10	59.40	59.20	58.20	58.86	58.75	58.53
11-04	10	61.00	59.30	59.50	59.45	58.67	59.10	58.98
11-05	11	62.10	61.90	61.77	61.35	60.15	60.15	60.30
11-08	12	62.00	63.20	63.73	63.15	62.75	62.37	61.53
11-09	13	62.50	61.90	62.70	63.50	63.38	63.20	62.94
11-10	14	63.50	63.00	62.60	63.00	63.68	63.71	63.64
11-11	15	61.30	64.50	64.16	63.70	63.84	64.34	64.38
11-12	16	61.70	60.10	61.23	62.05	62.25	62.69	63.36
11-15	17	62.00	62.10	60.36	61.10	61.66	61.87	62.30
11-16	18	62.20	62.30	62.37	61.10	61.36	61.71	61.86
11-17	19	61.70	62.40	62.47	62.55	61.57	61.64	61.85
11-18	20	61.50	61.20	61.67	61.95	62.17	61.47	61.51
11-19	21	62.40	61.30	61.10	61.35	61.61	61.85	61.31
11-22	22	61.40	63.30	62.57	62.05	61.99	62.07	62.20
11-23	23	59.90	60.40	61.67	61.75	61.57	61.61	61.73
11-24	24	59.80	58.40	58.73	59.85	60.29	60.37	60.58
11-26	25	59.10	59.70	58.76	58.85	59.22	59.59	59.71
11-29	26	59.50	58.40	58.85	58.30	58.06	58.55	58.87
11-30	27	59.10	59.90	59.17	59.10	58.56	58.20	58.48

smaller the value, the closer the grouping. The variance is another way of looking at the deviations; the smaller the variance, the better the forecast. The copper error analysis shows the smallest values for $\hat{E}(4)_t$, the 4-day linear regression. Because of the simple, uniform pattern in the short test period, a fast model worked best. Regressions using more days were less sensitive to price change, resulting in larger errors.

Determination of the best predictive model using error analysis can be applied to any forecasting technique. It may be practical to carry the error analysis one step further and include the results of the prediction error on day $t + 1$, $t + 2$, and so on. Knowing that the forecast has maintained accuracy for 2 or 3 days would ensure more latitude in executing the resulting buy or sell order and help to determine the rules of a trading program.

Having selected the most accurate forecast model, the size of the prior day prediction error can be used to resolve trading decisions. Consider the following situations:

1. The prediction and the actual price are very close (high confidence level)
2. The prediction is within one standard deviation of the actual price (65% confidence)
3. The prediction is greater than one standard deviation from the actual price but less than two standard deviations (65% to 95% confidence)
4. The prediction is greater than two standard deviations from the actual price (95% confidence)

In the first case, the current trend is continuing in a highly uniform manner. The second case indicates that, although not uniform, the price move is within the normal predictive bounds. In cases 3 and 4, prices are outside the normal forecast range. If greater than one but less than two standard deviations, as in case 3,

Table 4-2   Analysis of Predictive Error, May 77 Copper, November 1, 1976 through November 30, 1976

Date	Sequence t	Price P_t	Predictive Error for $E(n)_t$-Point Linear Regression					
			$\hat{E}(2)_t$	$\hat{E}(3)_t$	$\hat{E}(4)_t$	$\hat{E}(5)_t$	$\hat{E}(6)_t$	$\hat{E}(7)_t$
10-21	1	60.30						
10-22	2	59.30						
10-25	3	58.70						
10-26	4	57.80						
10-27	5	59.80						
10-28	6	58.20						
10-29	7	58.40						
11-01	8	58.90	−.30	−1.50	−.30	−.38	−.60	−.95
11-03	9	59.10	.30	.10	−.90	−.24	−.35	−.57
11-04	10	61.00	−1.70	−1.50	−1.55	−2.33	−1.90	−2.02
11-05	11	62.10	−.20	−.33	−.75	−1.95	−1.95	−1.80
11-08	12	62.00	1.20	1.73	1.15	.75	.37	−.47
11-09	13	62.50	−.60	.20	1.00	.88	.70	.44
11-10	14	63.50	−.50	−.90	−.50	.18	.21	.14
11-11	15	61.30	3.20	2.86	2.40	2.54	3.04	3.08
11-12	16	61.70	−1.60	−.47	.35	.55	.99	1.66
11-15	17	62.00	.10	−1.64	−.90	−.34	−.13	.30
11-16	18	62.20	.10	.17	−1.10	−.84	−.49	−.34
11-17	19	61.70	.70	.77	.85	−.13	−.06	.15
11-18	20	61.50	−.30	.17	.45	.67	−.03	.01
11-19	21	62.40	−1.10	−1.30	−1.05	−.79	−.65	−1.09
11-22	22	61.40	1.90	1.17	.65	.59	.67	.80
11-23	23	59.90	.50	1.77	1.85	1.67	1.71	1.83
11-24	24	59.80	−1.40	−1.07	.05	.49	.57	.78
11-26	25	59.10	.60	−.34	−.25	.12	.49	.61
11-29	26	59.50	−1.10	−.70	−1.20	−1.44	−.95	−.63
11-30	27	59.10	.80	.07	.00	−.54	−.90	−.62
σ (Standard deviation)			1.209	1.217	1.069	1.151	1.149	1.220
M (Mean)			.030	−.037	.012	−.027	.037	.065
V (Variance)			1.389	1.406	1.086	1.260	1.255	1.415

prices may have reversed from their prior direction but not enough to ensure a permanent change. The last case gives a high confidence level of a sustained change.

THE MOVING AVERAGE

The simplest and most well-known of all smoothing techniques is called the *moving average*. Using this method, the number of elements to be averaged remains the same, but the time interval advances. Using a generalized time series as an example, $P_1, P_2, \ldots, P_t$ is a set of time-sequential elements. A moving average measured over n of these points at time t would be

$$M_t = \frac{P_t + P_{t-1} + \cdots + P_{t-n+1}}{n} = \frac{\sum_{i=1}^{n} P_{t-i+1}}{n}, \qquad n \le t$$

In other words, the most recent moving-average calculation is the average (arithmetic mean) of the prior n data points. Consider the use of three points ($n = 3$) to generate a moving average:

$$M_3 = \frac{P_1 + P_2 + P_3}{3}$$

$$M_4 = \frac{P_2 + P_3 + P_4}{3}$$

$$\vdots$$

$$M_t = \frac{P_{t-2} + P_{t-1} + P_t}{3}$$

If P_t represented a commodity price at a specific time, the moving average would smooth the price movement. The more prices that are used, the less effect a new price will have. Five successive prices form a *5-day moving average*. When the next sequential price is added and the oldest is dropped off the prior average is changed by $\frac{1}{5}$ of the difference between the old and the new values. If

$$M_5 = \frac{P_1 + P_2 + P_3 + P_4 + P_5}{5}$$

and

$$M_6 = \frac{P_2 + P_3 + P_4 + P_5 + P_6}{5}$$

then $C = P_2 + P_3 + P_4 + P_5$ can be substituted for the common part of the moving average, solved for C, and substituted to get

$$M_6 = M_5 + \tfrac{1}{5}(P_t - P_{t-n})$$

This also gives a faster way to calculate a moving average. It can be seen that the more terms in the moving average, the less effect the addition of a new term is likely to have:

$$M_t = M_{t-1} + \frac{1}{n}(P_t - P_{t-n})$$

The selection of the proper number of terms is based on both the technical consideration of the predictive quality of the choice (measured by the error) and the need to determine price trends over specific time periods for commercial use. The more days or data points used in the moving average, the more *smoothing* will occur; variation lasting only a short while will have less effect. There is also a danger of losing cyclic or seasonal variations in prices by the choice of the wrong value of *n*. For example, a repeating cycle of four data points 5, 8, 3, 6, 9, 4, 7, . . . , which advances by one each complete cycle, will appear as a straight line if a moving average of 4 days is used. If there is a possibility of a cyclic or seasonal pattern within the data, care should be taken to select a moving average that is out of phase with the possible pattern.

The length of the moving average must also correspond to its use. A purchaser of silver for jewelry may need to buy each week. The purchaser will wait as long as possible while prices continue to trend downward during that week but will buy immediately when an upward turn is identified. A 6-month trend cannot help his problem, but a 5-day moving average may.

What Do You Average?

The closing or daily settlement is the most obvious price to apply to a moving average. It is generally accepted as the "true" price of the day and is used by many analysts for calculation of trends. But other alternatives exist. The average of the high and low price of the day will smooth the results by preventing the maximum difference from occurring when the close is also the high or low. Similarly, the closing price may be added to the high and low and an average of the three used as the basis for the moving average.

Another valid component of a moving average can be other averages. For example, if P_1 through P_n are prices, and M_n is a 3-day moving average, then

$$M_3 = \frac{P_1 + P_2 + P_3}{3}, \qquad M_4 = \frac{P_2 + P_3 + P_4}{3}, \qquad M_5 = \frac{P_3 + P_4 + P_5}{3}$$

$$M_5' = \frac{M_3 + M_4 + M_5}{3}$$

where M_5' is a "twice smoothed" moving average, which gives added weight to the center points. Chapter 5 gives an example of a system based on triple smoothing.

Another popular use of the moving average is to smooth the highs and lows independently. The result is a band representing the daily trading range, or volatility. This can be important for the development of a trading system.

Types of Moving Averages

Besides varying the length of the moving average and the elements that are to be averaged, there are a great number of other modifications of the moving average.

An *accumulative average* may be used for a long-term trend. It does not satisfy our strict definition of a moving average because it adds data but does not discard any, therefore, is cumulative. It is traditionally started at the beginning of a contract and continued until the contract expires. Due to the constant accumulation of prices and the increase in the length of the average, the effect of the additional price at day t on the old moving average will be $(P_t - \bar{P}_t)/t$, where $\bar{P}_t$ is the average of all prices through t. This becomes very small towards the end of a 1-year contract, which has approximately 250 trading days. A *reset accumulative average* is a modification of the standard accumulative average and attempts to correct for the loss of sensitivity as the number of trading days becomes large. This alternative allows you to reset or restart the moving average whenever a new trend has started or at some specified time. The use of this technique has been combined with trendlines to develop a trading system.

Truncated moving averages are the most common; they are simply called *moving averages*. The most basic has already been discussed in detail. The simplest way of continuing a daily moving average calculation is to keep the total of the past n days. Each new day then only requires the addition of the new value and subtraction of the oldest one. That total is both saved for the next day and divided by n to find the new moving average value. An interesting twist to this technique is the *average-modified method,* in which the new day is added and the last moving average value is subtracted. Returning to the example of a 5-day moving average, day 6 was

$$M_6 = M_5 + \tfrac{1}{5}(P_6 - P_1)$$

This becomes

$$M_6 = M_5 + \tfrac{1}{5}(P_6 - M_5)$$

The average-modified version is convenient because past components of the average may be discarded; only the prior moving average value and the new price are necessary. The substitution of the moving average value tends to smooth the results even further. Its use prevents the difference $(P_6 - P_1)$ from becoming too extreme; it effectively cuts the possible range in half and dampens the end-off impact.

The *weighted moving average* opens many possibilities. It allows the significance of individual or groups of data to be changed. It may restore proper value to parts of a data sample, or it may incorrectly bias the data. A weighted moving average is expressed in its general form as

$$W_t = \frac{w_1 P_t + w_2 P_{t-1} + \cdots + w_n P_{t-n+1}}{w_1 + w_2 + \cdots + w_n} = \frac{\displaystyle\sum_{i=1}^{n} w_i P_{t-i+1}}{\displaystyle\sum_{i=1}^{n} w_i}$$

This gives the weighted moving average at time t as the average of the previous n prices, each with its own weighting factor w_i. The most popular form of this technique is called "front-loaded" because it gives more weight to the most recent data and reduces the significance of the older elements. Therefore, for the front-loaded weighted moving average (see Figure 4-1)

$$w_1 \geq w_2 \geq \cdots \geq w_n$$

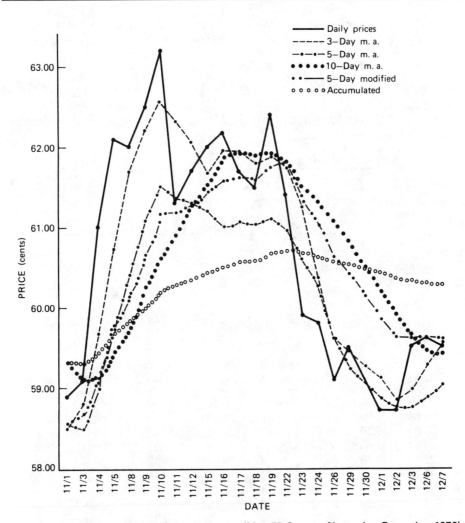

Figure 4-1 A comparison of moving averages (May 77 Copper, November-December 1976).

The weighting factors w_i may also be determined by regression analysis, but then they may not necessarily be front-loaded. A common modification to front-loading is called *step-weighting* in which each successive w_i differs from the previous weighting factor w_{i-1} by a fixed increment

$$C = w_i - w_{i-1}$$

The simplest case takes integer values for an *n*-day step-weighted moving average:

$$w_1 = n$$
$$w_2 = n - 1$$
$$\vdots$$
$$w_n = 1$$

This gives the weighting factors the values of 5, 4, 3, 2, and 1 for a 5-day average. Another approach would be a percentage relationship between w_i elements,

$$w_{i-1} = a \times w_i$$

where $a = .9$; then, $w_5 = 5$, $w_4 = 4.5$, $w_3 = 4.05$, $w_2 = 3.645$, and $w_1 = 3.2805$ (see Table 4-3).

Prices may also be weighted in groups. If every two consecutive data elements have the same weighting factor,

$$W_t = \frac{w_1 P_t + w_1 P_{t-1} + w_2 P_{t-2} + w_2 P_{t-3} + \cdots + w_{n/2} P_{t-n+1}}{2 \times (w_1 + w_2 + \cdots + w_{n/2})}$$

or, grouped with n even,

$$W_t = \frac{w_1(P_t + P_{t-1}) + w_2(P_{t-2} + P_{t-3}) + \cdots + w_{n/2}(P_{t-n+2} + P_{t-n+1})}{2 \times (w_1 + w_2 + \cdots + w_{n/2})}$$

Any number of consecutive data elements can be grouped for a step-weighted moving average.

Table 4-3　Sample Moving Averages Using May 77 Copper (NY)

	Date	Price	3-Day	5-Day	10-Day	5-Day Average Modified	Accumulative	10-Day Step-Weighted
				60.60	61.40	60.30	59.30	58.70
1	11-01	58.90	58.50	58.56	59.31	58.56	59.31	58.90
2	11-03	59.10	58.80	58.48	59.08	58.67	59.29	58.84
3	11-04	61.00	59.67	59.04	59.15	59.13	59.43	59.18
4	11-05	62.10	60.73	59.78	59.43	59.73	59.64	59.72
5	11-08	62.00	61.70	60.40	59.76	60.18	59.81	60.21
6	11-09	62.50	62.20	61.08	60.23	60.65	59.99	60.74
7	11-10	63.20	62.57	61.52	60.60	61.16	60.19	61.33
8	11-11	61.30	62.33	61.36	60.91	61.18	60.26	61.48
9	11-12	61.70	62.07	61.30	61.24	61.29	61.34	61.67
10	11-15	62.00	61.67	61.20	61.55	61.43	60.42	61.85
11	11-16	62.20	61.97	61.00	61.86	61.58	60.49	62.00
12	11-17	61.70	61.97	61.08	61.93	61.61	60.55	62.00
13	11-18	61.50	61.80	61.04	61.87	61.59	60.59	61.91
14	11-19	62.40	61.87	61.12	61.91	61.75	60.67	61.98
15	11-22	61.40	61.77	60.96	61.80	61.68	60.70	61.86
16	11-23	59.90	61.23	60.60	61.47	61.32	60.67	61.48
17	11-20	59.80	60.37	60.26	61.32	61.02	60.64	61.13
18	11-26	59.10	59.60	59.60	61.06	60.63	60.58	60.71
19	11-29	59.50	59.47	59.22	60.81	60.41	60.54	60.41
20	11-30	59.10	59.23	59.06	60.50	60.15	60.49	60.07
21	12-01	58.70	59.10	58.84	60.20	59.86	61.43	59.72
22	12-02	58.70	58.83	58.76	59.92	59.62	60.37	59.42
23	12-03	59.50	58.97	58.76	59.63	59.60	60.35	59.33
24	12-06	59.60	59.27	58.86	59.45	59.60	60.32	59.29
25	12-07	59.50	59.53	59.02	59.41	59.58	60.30	59.30

These moving averages can also be plotted in different ways, each way having a major impact on their interpretation. The conventional plot places the moving average value M_t on the same vertical line as the last entry P_t of the moving average. When prices have been trending higher over the period of calculation, this will cause the value M_t to lag behind (or below) the actual prices; when prices are declining, the moving average will be above the prices (see Figure 4-2).

The plotted moving average can either *lead* or *lag* the last price recorded. If it is to lead by 3 days, the value M_t is plotted on the vertical line $t + 3$; if it is to lag by 2 days, it is plotted at $t - 2$. In the case of leading moving averages, the analysis attempts to compensate for the time delay by judging price direction using a forecast based on current rate of change and direction. A penetration of the forecasted line by the price may be used to signal a change of direction. The lag technique may also serve the more sophisticated purpose of *phasing* the moving

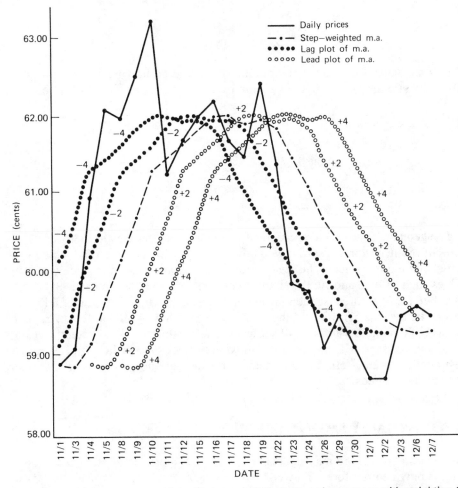

Figure 4-2 Plotting lag and lead for a 10-day step-weighted moving average with weighting 10, 9, 8 . . . (May 77 Copper, November-December 1976).

average. A 10-day moving average, when lagged by 5 days, will be placed in the midst of the actual price data. This technique will be covered later.

GEOMETRIC MOVING AVERAGES

The previous discussion could equally apply to a geometric average, in which case the basic equation for the last n points at time t would be

$$G_t = (P_t \times P_{t-1} \times \cdots \times P_{t-n+1})^{1/n} = \left(\prod_{i=1}^{n} P_{t-i+1} \right)^{1/n}$$

The daily calculation is more complicated but, as shown in the discussion of averages, could be rewritten as

$$\ln G_t = \frac{\ln P_t + \ln P_{t-1} + \cdots + \ln P_{t-n+1}}{n}$$

$$= \frac{1}{n} \left(\sum_{i=1}^{n} \ln P_{t-i+1} \right)$$

This is similar in form to the summation of a standard moving average based on the arithmetic mean. A weighted geometric moving average would have the form

$$\ln G_t = \frac{w_1 \ln P_t + w_2 \ln P_{t-1} + \cdots + w_n \ln P_{t-n+1}}{w_1 + w_2 + \cdots + w_n}$$

$$= \frac{\sum_{i=1}^{n} w_i \ln P_{t-i+1}}{\sum_{i=1}^{n} w_i}$$

The geometric moving average itself would give greater weight to lower values without the need for a discrete weighting function. In applying the technique to actual commodity prices, this distinction is not as apparent. For widely ranging values such as 1000 and 10, the simple average is 505 and the geometric average is 100, but for the three sequential cocoa prices—56.20, 58.30, and 57.15—the arithmetic mean is 57.2166 and the geometric is 57.1871. A similar test of 5, 10, or 20 days of commodity prices will show a negligible difference between the results of the two averages. If the geometric moving average is to be helpful, it would be best applied to long-term historic data with wide variance, using yearly or quarterly average prices.

EXPONENTIALLY SMOOTHED MOVING AVERAGES

Exponential smoothing may appear to be more complex than other techniques, but it is only another form of a weighted moving average. It has the added advantage of being simpler to calculate than any other method discussed; only the last *exponentially smoothed value E_{t-1}* and the *smoothing constant a* are necessary to compute the new value. The technique of exponential smoothing was developed during World War II for tracking aircraft and projecting their position—the immediate past is used to predict the immediate future.

The geometric progression

$$1, a, a^2, a^3, \ldots, a^{n-1}$$

applied to the terms of a weighted moving average

$$W_t = \frac{w_1 P_t + w_2 P_{t-1} + \cdots + w_n P_{t-n+1}}{w_1 + w_2 + \cdots + w_n}$$

gives $w_1 = 1$, $w_2 = a$, $w_3 = a^2, \ldots, w_n = a^{n-1}$. If $a = \frac{1}{2}$, also said to be 50% *smoothed*, the resulting sequence is

$$1, \tfrac{1}{2}, \tfrac{1}{4}, \tfrac{1}{8}, \ldots, (\tfrac{1}{2})^{n-1}$$

This shows the rapidly decreasing importance of each older price. Substituting the geometric progression into the equation for the weighted moving average, gives

$$E_t = \frac{1 P_t + a P_{t-1} + a^2 P_{t-2} + \cdots + a^{n-1} P_{t-n+1}}{1 + a + a^2 + \cdots + a^{n-1}}$$

By a lengthy arithmetic process using the formula for the sum of a geometric progression the same equation can be stated as

$$E_t = (1 - a)P_t + a E_{t-1}$$

where P_t is the most recent price and $0 \le a \le 1$. It can be seen that 100% of the combined value of past prices are distributed such that $a \times 100$ goes to the previous exponential moving average and the balance to the most recent price. If $a = .70$, the current price P_t will receive a weighting of 30% of the total moving average. A more popular form, and one which reverses the weighting notations is:

$$E_t = E_{t-1} + a(P_t - E_{t-1})$$

Start the smoothing process at P_2 by letting $E_1 = P_1$ and calculate the next value:

$$E_2 = E_1 + a(P_2 - E_1)$$

The interpretation of this last equation can be seen in Figure 4-3 as

New exponential value = prior exponential value + some % of (today's price
— prior exponential value)

An important feature of the exponentially smoothed moving average is that all data previously used is always part of the new result although with diminishing significance. In general:

$$E_t = a(P_t + (1 - a)P_{t-1} + (1 - a)^2 P_{t-2} + \cdots + (1 - a)^n P_{t-n} + \cdots)$$

For example, if the smoothing constant $a = .10$, add 10% of the new difference to the old average:

$$E_t = E_{t-1} + .10(P_t - E_{t-1})$$

That in effect will reduce all data from points 1 through $t - 1$ by 10%; the next calculation for $t + 1$ will cause the data from t back to be reduced again by 10%.

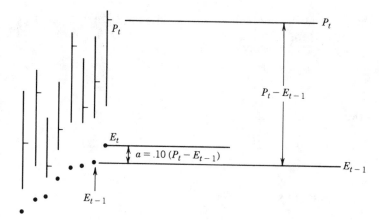

Figure 4-3   Exponential smoothing.

Therefore, at any time t the impact of data used at time k is based on the number of days elapsed, $t - k$, and the smoothing constant a. Let the significance of $P_k - E_{k-1} = k = D_k$. Then on day k we have

$$k = a \cdot D_k$$

$$k + 1 = a \cdot D_k - a \cdot a \cdot D_k$$

$$\vdots$$

$$k + n = a \cdot D_k - (a^2 \cdot D_k + a^3 \cdot D_k + \cdots + a^{n+1}D_k)$$

$$= a \cdot D_k - \sum_{i=2}^{n+1} a^i D_k \quad \text{(written in summation form)}$$

$$= D_k \left(a - \sum_{i=2}^{n+1} a^i \right) \to 0 \quad \text{as } n \to \infty$$

This shows that the significance of the data on day k goes to zero as n gets infinitely large. Consider the following example. An investor has 10% of the shares of stock in a corporation where there are t investors. The corporation decides to take in another investor and gives that investor 10% of the total outstanding shares. There are now $t + 1$ investors, and the original are diluted to 9% of the total. Another investor buys in at 10% of the total; there are now $t + 2$ investors, and the original investor has 8.1% of the stock (10% less). As more investors are added, the stock holding dwindles to 7.29%, 6.561%, and 5.9049%. Even though the number of shares that are held remain the same, their significance to the whole has been reduced. No matter how many investors are added at 10%, the original shares will always have some minor percent of the whole. In exactly the same way, the original price used in an exponentially smoothed moving average always retains some relevance; with a standard moving average of n days, the $(n + 1)$th day is dropped off and ceases to have any impact.

Double Exponential Smoothing

As a trend continues in its direction, the exponentially smoothed moving average will lag farther behind. By selecting a smoothing constant nearer to 1, the magnitude of this lag will be lessened but it will still increase. If the lag is considered the predictive error in the calculation, then

$$e_t = P_t - E_t \qquad \text{(error)}$$

where E_t is the exponential smoothing approximation of the price P_t. The same exponential smoothing technique can be applied to the pattern of increasing or decreasing error to get

$$F_t = F_{t-1} + a(e_t - F_{t-1})$$

and then add the difference between the original smoothing value and the double (second-order) smoothing back into the approximation:

$$EE_t = E_t + F_t$$

The effect of error due to lag will be corrected so that instead of the lag increasing it will decrease. This method can be extended to "third-order" smoothing.

RELATING EXPONENTIAL AND STANDARD MOVING AVERAGES

Most people grasp the time relationship of a standard moving average much more rapidly than an exponential. Because of the diluting effect of the exponential smoothing, a comparison with respect to days is based on both the smoothing constant and the elapsed time. Intuitively, a 50% smoothing is somewhat slower than a 2-day moving average, a 10% smoothing is slower than a 10-day moving average, and a 5% smoothing is slower than a 20-day moving average. The important factor is that for any specified smoothing constant, the exponential moving average includes all prior data. If a 5-day moving average was compared to an exponential with only 5 total days included, the relationship would be closer to a straight moving average than if the exponential had 10 or 20 days of elapsed calculations.

Look at the situation of continuously increasing numbers from 1 through 15 and back to 1. Comparing a 5-day moving average with an exponential moving average will show the relationship. The exponential is calculated two ways: once using only the last five prices (a modified approach for our example); the other using all prices from the beginning (the standard method).

Figures 4-4 and 4-5 and Table 4-4 show the relationship between the standard exponential and the modified exponential using five points. During the period of constant increase and decrease of at least 5 consecutive days, both the 5-day standard and exponential with five points stabilize; those 5 days represent their entire set of calculation values. At the peak, the standard moving average reacts faster than the other methods in staying closer to the current price; the 5-point exponential gives 20% of its weight to the most recent price, and less to prior prices, causing it to react slower than the standard moving average.

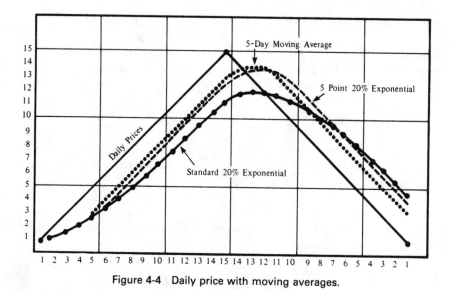

Figure 4-4   Daily price with moving averages.

The standard exponential smoothing is different, lagging farther behind each day but increasingly *approaching* the value of one, as the data increase by one, for long time periods. The weighting of the near values is offset by the retained significance of the oldest data, which is never fully lost, causing the exponentially smoothed moving average to lag the farthest behind the current prices. Although there are 14 days of constant decline, the standard exponential has not yet stabilized, still reflecting the turning of prices from up to down at 15.

To form the specific relationship between exponential smoothing and standard moving averages, create a table showing the significance of each oldest day in the exponential calculation. In Table 4-5, the .50 smoothing constant gives 50% of the total value to the current price, 25% to the prior day, 12½% to the next oldest, until the 7th oldest day adds only .8% to the total value of the exponential moving average. Table 4-6 accumulates these weights to show how much of the calculation has been completed by the elapsed days printed across the top. Table 4-6 is plotted in Figure 4-6. The most recent days (on the left) receive the bulk of the

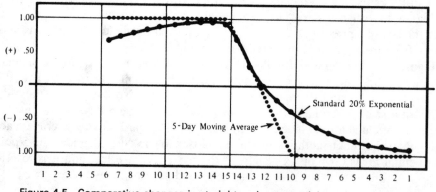

Figure 4-5   Comparative changes in straight and exponential moving averages.

Table 4-4   Comparison of Lag Between Standard and Exponentially Smoothed Moving Averages

Price	Standard 5-Day	5-Point 20% Exp	Standard 20% Exp	Change		
				5-Day	5–20% Exp	20% Exp
1	—	1.00	1.00	—	—	—
2	—	1.20	1.20	—	—	—
3	—	1.56	1.56	—	Not enough	—
4	—	2.05	2.05	—	data	—
5	3	2.64	2.64	—	—	—
6	4	3.64	3.31	1.00	1.00	.67
7	5	4.64	4.05	1.00	1.00	.74
8	6	5.64	4.84	1.00	1.00	.79
9	7	6.64	5.67	1.00	1.00	.83
10	8	7.64	6.54	1.00	1.00	.87
11	9	8.64	7.43	1.00	1.00	.89
12	10	9.64	8.34	1.00	1.00	.91
13	11	10.64	9.27	1.00	1.00	.93
14	12	11.64	10.22	1.00	1.00	.95
15	13	12.64	11.17	1.00	1.00	.95
14	13.6	13.24	11.74	.60	.60	.57
13	13.8	13.52	11.99	.20	.28	.25
12	13.6	13.54	11.99	−.20	.02	.00
11	13	13.36	11.79	−.60	−.18	−.20
10	12	12.36	11.43	−1.00	−1.00	−.36
9	11	11.36	10.95	−1.00	−1.00	−.48
8	10	10.36	10.36	−1.00	−1.00	−.59
7	9	9.36	9.69	−1.00	−1.00	−.67
6	8	8.36	8.95	−1.00	−1.00	−.74
5	7	7.36	8.16	−1.00	−1.00	−.79
4	6	6.36	7.33	−1.00	−1.00	−.83
3	5	5.36	6.46	−1.00	−1.00	−.87
2	4	4.36	5.57	−1.00	−1.00	−.89
1	3	3.36	4.65	−1.00	−1.00	−.92

significance; the oldest prices are of little impact. The .10 smoothing calculation is 90.1% complete by day 22; the total remaining days added together only account for 9.9% of the value.

Figure 4-6 relates the fully calculated exponential smoothing (to within 1%) to the standard moving average. Find the smoothing constant on the left, and the number of days in a standard moving average along the bottom. Observe that testing various equally distant smoothing constants may give an unexpected distribution relative to past days.

Equating standard moving averages to exponential smoothing								
Smoothing constant (%)	.10	.20	.30	.40	.50	.60	.70	.80	.90
Standard (*n*-day average)	20	10	6	4	3	2.25	1.75	1.40	1.15

Table 4-5 Evaluation of Exponential Smoothing—Significance of Prior Data

	Past Number of Days																						
Weighting (%)	1	2	3	4	5	6	7	8	9	10	11	12	13	14	15	16	17	18	19	20	21	22	23
1.00	100.0	—	—	—	—	—	—	—	—	—	—	—	—	—	—	—	—	—	—	—	—	—	—
.90	90.0	9.0	.9	—	—	—	—	—	—	—	—	—	—	—	—	—	—	—	—	—	—	—	—
.80	80.0	16.0	3.2	.6	—	—	—	—	—	—	—	—	—	—	—	—	—	—	—	—	—	—	—
.70	70.0	21.0	6.3	1.9	.6	—	—	—	—	—	—	—	—	—	—	—	—	—	—	—	—	—	—
.60	60.0	24.0	9.6	3.8	1.5	.6	—	—	—	—	—	—	—	—	—	—	—	—	—	—	—	—	—
.50	50.0	25.0	12.5	6.3	3.1	1.6	.8	—	—	—	—	—	—	—	—	—	—	—	—	—	—	—	—
.40	40.0	24.0	14.4	8.6	5.2	3.1	1.9	1.1	.7	—	—	—	—	—	—	—	—	—	—	—	—	—	—
.30	30.0	21.0	14.7	10.3	7.2	5.0	3.5	2.5	1.7	1.2	.8	—	—	—	—	—	—	—	—	—	—	—	—
.20	20.0	16.0	12.8	10.2	8.2	6.5	5.2	4.2	3.3	2.7	2.1	1.7	1.4	1.1	.9	—	—	—	—	—	—	—	—
.10	10.0	9.0	8.1	7.3	6.6	5.9	5.3	4.8	4.3	3.9	3.5	3.1	2.8	2.5	2.3	2.1	1.8	1.7	1.5	1.3	1.2	1.1	1.0

Table 4-6 Evaluation of Exponential Smoothing—Significance of Prior Data

	Total Inclusion Through Nth Day																						
Weighting (%)	1	2	3	4	5	6	7	8	9	10	11	12	13	14	15	16	17	18	19	20	21	22	23
1.00	100.0	—	—	—	—	—	—	—	—	—	—	—	—	—	—	—	—	—	—	—	—	—	—
.90	90.0	99.0	99.9	—	—	—	—	—	—	—	—	—	—	—	—	—	—	—	—	—	—	—	—
.80	80.0	96.0	99.2	99.8	—	—	—	—	—	—	—	—	—	—	—	—	—	—	—	—	—	—	—
.70	70.0	91.0	97.3	99.2	99.8	—	—	—	—	—	—	—	—	—	—	—	—	—	—	—	—	—	—
.60	60.0	84.0	93.6	97.4	99.0	99.6	—	—	—	—	—	—	—	—	—	—	—	—	—	—	—	—	—
.50	50.0	75.0	87.5	93.8	96.9	98.5	99.3	—	—	—	—	—	—	—	—	—	—	—	—	—	—	—	—
.40	40.0	64.0	78.4	87.0	92.2	95.3	97.2	98.3	99.0	—	—	—	—	—	—	—	—	—	—	—	—	—	—
.30	30.0	51.0	65.7	76.0	83.2	88.2	91.8	94.2	96.0	97.2	98.0	—	—	—	—	—	—	—	—	—	—	—	—
.20	20.0	36.0	48.8	59.0	67.2	73.8	79.0	83.2	86.6	89.3	91.4	93.1	94.5	95.6	96.5	—	—	—	—	—	—	—	—
.10	10.0	19.0	27.1	34.4	41.0	46.8	52.2	57.0	61.3	65.1	68.6	71.8	74.6	77.1	79.4	81.5	83.3	85.0	86.5	87.8	89.1	90.1	91.1

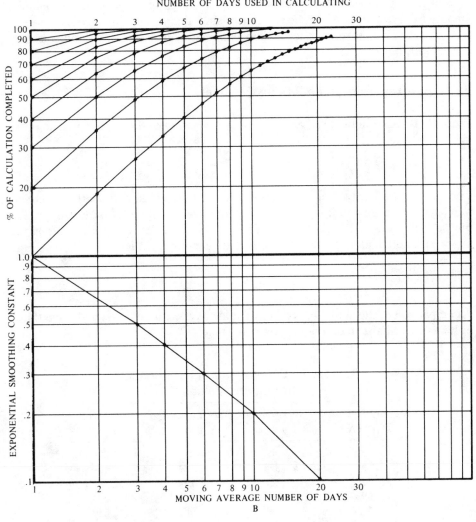

Figure 4-6 Evaluation of exponential smoothing.

If the smoothing constants shown above are tested, half of the tests will analyze moving averages of 3 days or less. If the testing program is to relate to the standard moving average, reverse the process, finding the smoothing constant for a known number of days.

Equating exponential smoothing to standard moving averages									
Standard (*n*-day average)	2	4	6	8	10	12	14	16	18	20
Smoothing constant (%)	.65	.40	.30	.235	.20	.165	.14	.125	.11	.10

The distribution of smoothing constants is very close to logarithmic and is plotted on log paper for emphasis. To test a range of days using exponential smoothing, use a logarithmic distribution of smoothing constants across the range, with closer values taken at the smaller numbers. This may seem an unnecessary precaution, but it is not.

Best Approximation of Smoothing Constants

Work by Hutson[1] indicates that a close approximation of the exponential smoothing factor c is

$$c = \frac{2}{N + 1}$$

where N is the equivalent number of days in the standard (linearly weighted) moving average. In addition, *second- or third-order exponential smoothing*, based on the weighting of the past 2 or 3 days' prices, may be desirable. This is the exponential equivalent to step-weighting. Its general form is

$$c_p = 1 - \left(1 - \frac{2}{N + 1}\right)^{1/p}$$

A comparison of the standard moving average days with first-, second-, and third-order exponential smoothing is shown in Table 4-7.

Table 4-7   Comparison of Exponential
Smoothing Values

Moving Average Days (N)	First-Order $p = 1$	Second-Order $p = 2$	Third-Order $p = 3$
3	.500	.293	.206
5	.333	.184	.126
7	.250	.134	.091
9	.200	.106	.072
11	.167	.087	.059
13	.143	.074	.050
15	.125	.065	.044
17	.111	.057	.039
19	.100	.051	.035
21	.091	.047	.031

Estimating Residual Impact

The primary difference between the standard moving average and exponential smoothing is that prices impact the exponentially smoothed value indefinitely. For

[1] Jack K. Hutson, "Filter Price Data: Moving Averages vs. Exponential Moving Averages," *Technical Analysis of Stocks & Commodities*, May/June 1984.

Table 4-8   Comparison of Exponential
Residual Impact

N	$2/(N + 1)$	RI (%)	10% RI	5% RI
5	.333	13.17	.369	.451
10	.182	13.44	.206	.259
15	.125	13.49	.142	.181
20	.095	13.51	.109	.139

practical purposes, the effect of the oldest data may be limited. A general method of approximating the smoothing constant c for a given level of residual impact is given by

$$c = 1 - RI^{1/N}$$

where RI is the level of residual impact (e.g., .05, .10, .20), a lower percent level implies more residual impact, and N is the equivalent moving average days.[2]

The approximation for the smoothing constant, given in the previous section as $2/(N + 1)$, can be shown to have a consistent residual impact of between 13 and 14%. The use of the preceding formula, as shown in Table 4-8, would allow the specific adjustment of residual impact.

[2] Donald R. Lambert, "Exponentially Smoothed Moving Averages," *Technical Analysis of Stocks & Commodities*, Sept./Oct. 1984.

5

Moving Average Systems

Chapter 4 developed the tools for calculating moving averages—standard, weighted, exponentially smoothed, and regression-based. To profit from identifying the trend requires the establishment of trading rules and the selection of specific parameters which define the trend speed and trade risk, among other factors. Often, the selection of rules is seen to be dependent on additional parameters. This chapter will first discuss those rules that are necessary to all trading strategies, then give examples of actual systems. The selection of trend speed is handled only briefly here but is continued with a detailed analysis of these and other systems in Chapter 15.

BASIC BUY AND SELL SIGNALS

Regardless of the selection of moving averages, the smoothed trend calculation will lag behind the actual current market price. In bull markets, this lag will cause the moving average to be below the price; in bear markets, it will be above. When prices change direction, the moving average and the actual commodity prices cross because the moving average still reflects the previous trend. These crossings provide the opportunity for the basic trading signals

Buy when rising prices cross the moving average.
Sell when declining prices cross the moving average.

It is also necessary to decide what "prices" are to be used. The answer depends on the construction of the average and the testing of the system. If the average is composed only of closing prices, it is reasonable to start testing with the modified signals

Buy when rising prices close above the moving average.
Sell when declining prices close below the moving average.

If an average of high and low prices were used, a buy or sell would be signaled when the new average (*high* + *low*)/2 was above or below the corresponding moving average value. In all cases, consistency is important. The system that is tested and the one that is traded should be the same. In the following discussion, the term "close" will be used. To find out if a trading signal occurred each day, wait until the close of trading, calculate the new moving average value, and then see whether a crossing occurred according to the basic buy and sell rules.

In order to speed up the response to price change, the value of the closing price that would cause a new signal can be calculated in advance. This would allow execution on or near the close of the current day. The rules of the system can also be changed to buy or sell on today's close if that price is above or below yesterday's moving average value. A small amount of testing by longhand calculation will determine which approach works best. Still another modification would be to test today's close against yesterday's projected moving average, so that if the moving average values for the past 2 days were

$$M_{t-1} = 432$$

$$M_{t-2} = 429$$

the difference $M_{t-1} - M_{t-2} = 3$ would be added to M_{t-1} to get the turning criterion of $\hat{M}_t = 435$ for today. That means that the *rate of change* must differ for a signal to occur. More sophisticated approaches to projecting the moving average will be covered later.

Variations in Timing

Lead and *lag* are features common to moving average systems discussed in Chapter 4. The opposite in purpose, a lead of n days advances the plotted value of the moving average M_t from beneath the current price P_t to the position n columns ahead. In actual trading, this gives an advance criterion for a trading signal; prices must remain above this level to maintain the current position. A lag time of n days plots the current moving average value in the same column as P_{t-n}, n days sooner. This indicates that a signal has already occurred, but no action may be taken for n days. The lead plot tries to anticipate a trend change whereas a lag is a commitment to holding a position. Both lead and lag techniques may use the same basic buy and sell signals as standard moving averages.

Entry and exit timing may be improved by a *delay* in taking action on a signal, usually from 1 to 3 days. This technique allows a number of days for the newly developed trend to reverse and show a "false signal" at the cost of missing the beginning of the trend. Systems that have a large number of short losing trades and a high profit/loss ratio can benefit from a delay of 1, 2, or 3 days.

Reversing a position on each trade signal results in a constant commitment to being in the market. This philosophy will show greater profits when the trade is successful, but more frequent losses because of the constant commitment to trend changes during whipsaw periods. An entry delay may also improve a reversal system.

BANDS

Thus far, modifications have been based on a simple moving average line. The plot can be adjusted forward or backward, the position can be reversed, or the entry or exit delayed in an attempt to begin the new trade at the time when the trend has decidedly taken a new direction. Even if prices have begun what will become a major downtrend, an entry into a short position too soon may be subjected to sharp reversals caused by conflicting fundamental and technical elements at these turning points. The simplest way to avoid these price variations is by using a band.

A *band* is an area surrounding a trendline above and below that acts as a zone of commitment for the trader and allows time, as measured by movement and risk, for prices to settle into their new direction. Bands can be created in many ways, the most popular being a percentage of the current price or the current trendline value. A band that is formed from the trendline will be

(upper band) $B_U = M_t + cM_t$

(lower band) $B_L = M_t - cM_t$

where c is a percentage, $0 \leq c \leq 1$. Since the moving average is a smoothing, the band will be uniform as well. If the current price is used instead of the moving average then

$$B_U = M_t + cP_t$$

$$B_L = M_t - cP_t$$

The band will vary in width at a much faster rate using price. During an uptrend, the band based on prices will get very wide. Another popular type of band is based on *absolute point value*, for example, silver 5¢, corn 5¢, or cattle 25 points; each represents a dollar risk to the trader. The use of this type of band is usually found coordinated with a money-management program that limits losses on trades to a specific number or to a maximum percentage of the portfolio being managed.

The *independent smoothing* of the high and low daily prices forms a *volatility band*. Although it may be practical to use the same technique or the same relative smoothing (e.g., 10-day or 10% smoothing constant) for the high, low, and closing prices, it is not a requirement. If the same smoothing criterion is used, the band will be uniform with respect to the moving average of the closing price; if not, all three trendlines may weave around one another. A *volatility function* can also be used to create a band. Rather than the simple percentage calculation shown first, the band may be increased at rates equal to the price-volatility relationship discussed earlier in this book. All of the methods of forming bands are subject to *scaling*. Scaling will increase or reduce the sensitivity of any technique used for calculating the band. If S is a scaling factor we have

$B = M_t \pm S \times c \times M_t$	(percentage smoothing)
$B = M_t \pm S \times c \times P_t$	(percentage smoothing using price)
$B = M_t \pm S \times R$	(fixed risk using absolute point value)
$\left.\begin{array}{l} B_U = S \times f(H_t) \\ B_L = S \times f(L_t) \end{array}\right\}$	(independent smoothing of highs or lows)
$B = M_t \pm S \times (H_t - L_t)$	(volatility of high-low)
$B = M_t \pm S \times V(P_t)$	(volatility function at price level)
$B = M_t \pm S \times V(M_t)$	(volatility at moving average level)

When $S = 1$, the scaling effect is nullified; for $S > 1$, it magnifies the band; and for $S < 1$, it reduces the band.

Different bands are not mutually exclusive. A variable band may be used to time the entries and exits subject to a maximum risk established by another band. It may also be convenient to have separate exit and entry bands, the first more sensitive, such that a reversal of position is not always necessary. An exit band may be based on the intraday high or low prices—while entries are determined by closing prices.

Rules for Using Bands

Regardless of the type of band that is constructed, rules for using bands to generate trading signals are limited. The first decision to be made is whether a current position will be liquidated or reversed, causing the entry into a new position in the opposite direction. Assuming a reversal from long to short and from short to long, the following rules apply:

Buy (close-out shorts and go long) when the price penetrates the upper band.
Sell (close-out longs and go short) when the price penetrates the lower band.

This technique is always in the market with a maximum risk (without execution costs) equal to the width of the band on entry (see Figure 5-1). If a neutral position is preferred following the exit from each trade, there are the alternative rules:

Buy (go long) when prices penetrate the upper band. Close-out longs when prices reverse and go below the moving average value.
Sell (go short) when prices break below the lower band. Cover your shorts when prices penetrate back through the moving average value.

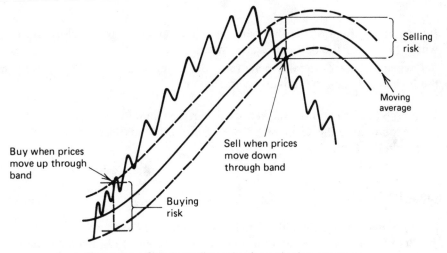

Figure 5-1 Simple trading rules for a moving average.

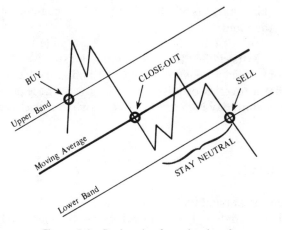

Figure 5-2   Basic rules for using bands.

The band is then used to enter into new long or short trades, and the moving average within the band is used only for liquidation. If prices are not strong enough to penetrate the opposite band on the close of the same day, the trade is closed-out but not reversed. The next day, penetration of either the upper or lower band will signal a new long or short trade, respectively.

This technique allows a trade to be reentered in the same direction in the event of a "false breakout." If a pullback occurs after a close-out while no position is being held (as shown in Figure 5-2), an entry at a later date might be at a better price. A disadvantage occurs when the price changes direction and moves so fast that both the close-out and the new signal occur on the same day. Reversing the position immediately would be better in a fast market.

The high and low of the day may also be used as penetration criteria. Again using the outer bands for entry and the moving average for exit, apply the following rules:

Buy when the high of the day penetrates the upper band and close-out longs when the low of the day penetrates the moving average.

Sell when the low of the day penetrates the lower band and cover shorts when the high penetrates the moving average.

With both the first and second set of rules, risk is limited to half of the full band. In the second case, the chances of exiting one trade and remaining neutral are greater than the first.

Timing the Order

The type of order placed when following a system will have a long-term effect on its results. The use of a band with a single moving average identifies change of trends when a breakout occurs. Buying during an upside break or selling during a downside break often causes poor entry prices, and has been known to place the trader in a new trend at the point where prices are ready for a "technical adjust-ment." The most frequent complaints of trend followers is that their new positions usually show losses and that it takes a long time before the technical adjustment ends and the new trend returns to its entry price level. This reasoning has caused many variations from the original rules:

Buy (or *sell*) on the close after an entry signal has been indicated.

Buy (or *sell*) on the next market open following a signal.

Buy (or *sell*) with a delay of 1, 2, or 3 days after the signal.

Buy (or *sell*) after a price retracement of 50% (or some other value) following a signal.

Buy (or *sell*) when prices move to within a specified risk relative to a stop-loss point.

These modifications are for the purpose of entering a new position with an imme-diate profit or preventing excessive risk. Some can be categorized as "timing" and others as "risk management." If intraday prices are used to signal new entries and exits, a rule may be added that states:

Only one order can be executed in one day; either the liquidation of a current position or an entry into a new position.

The improvement of exit and entry points is worth the time and effort. With limited capital, the conservation of the investment is important when the greater number of trades are expected to lose money. Better entry points will reduce the risk on a larger part of the trades and allow longer strings of poor performance.

Waiting for the "right time" to enter a trade may have more disadvantages than is apparent. In tests on a trend-following system conducted over 1 year with a few hundred commodity trades, it was shown that positions entered at the market opening on the day following the system signal improved fill prices about 75% of the time but resulted in smaller overall profits for the year. Why? Many breakouts never adjusted back to allow the trader to enter at a better price. The three out of four better fills were more than offset by the one bad one.

APPLICATIONS OF SINGLE MOVING AVERAGES

The selection of the moving average speed is as important as any of the system's rules. The speed determines the activity of trading and the nature of the trend to be isolated. To help this decision, some of the preceding sections have shown comparisons of the different speeds as well as approaches, based on minimizing the magnitude of the forecast errors. Without a computer, extensive examination of alternatives is impossible. Chapter 15 concentrates on the use of the computer for selection of trend speed and risk parameters for single- and multiple-average systems, as well as breakout systems. It also includes an analysis of results.

Prior to "optimization," the moving average span was based on multiples of calendar periods, expressed as trading days. In doing this, there is an opportunity to be in phase with behavioral patterns of traders and brokerage houses, who may work within weekly or monthly spans. The most popular intervals for selection have been: 3 days, the expected duration of a short price move; 5 days, a trading week; 20 to 21 days, a trading month, and so on. Included in the next sections are well-known systems using single moving averages, followed by examples of multiple-average systems.

MPTDI (A Step-Weighted Moving Average)

In 1972, Robert Joel Taylor published a system called the Major Price Trend Directional Indicator (MPTDI), which was reprinted in summary form in the September 1973 *Commodities Magazine*. The system was promoted and implemented through Enterex Commodities in Dallas and was historically tested by Dunn and Hargitt Financial Services in West Lafayette, Indiana, in 1972. It was one of the few well-defined published systems and served as the basis for much experimentation for current technicians and aspiring analysts.

MPTDI is based on a step-weighted moving average of varying lengths, with a band of changing widths relative to volatility. It is unique in its complete dependence on incremental values for all aspects of the system: the moving average, entry, and stop-loss points. For example, Table 5-1 shows what conditions it might be assigned to gold.

If gold were trading in an average range of 250 to 350 points each day, the weighting factor for the moving average would be TYPE C, indicating medium volatility (TYPE A is lowest). Using TYPE C with a 15-day moving average, the most recent 5 days are given the weight 3, the next 5 days 2, and the last 5 days are weighted by 1. The buy and sell signals use the corresponding entry-signal penetration of 250 points above the moving average as a buy signal and below as a sell entry. The highs or lows of intraday trading are used to activate the entry based on values calculated after the close of trading on the prior day. A stop-loss point is fixed at the time of entry equal to the value on the same line as the proper volatility. The penetration of the stop-loss will cause the liquidation of the current trade. A new signal in the reverse direction will serve as both a stop-loss and reentry point.

There is a lot to say in favor of the principles of MPTDI. It is individualized with respect to commodities and self-adjusting with changing volatility. The stop-

Table 5-1 MPTDI Variables

Average Trading Range	Number of Days in Calculation	Weighting-Factors Progression	Entry-Signal Penetration	Approximate Stop-Loss Point
50–150	25 days	TYPE A	100 pts	150 pts
150–250	20 days	TYPE B	200 pts	300 pts
250–350	15 days	TYPE C	250 pts	350 pts
350–450	10 days	TYPE D	350 pts	450 pts
450+	5 days	TYPE E	450 pts	550 pts

loss serves to limit the initial risk of the trade and allow the coordination of a money-management approach. The fixed risk differs from moving averages using standard bands because a moving average and its band can back away from system-entry points on a gradual reversal of the price trend. But there are some rough edges to the system. The incremental ranges for volatility, entry points, and stops seem a crude measure. Even if they are accurate in the center of the range, they must get doubtful at the extremes at the point of change from one range to another.

The Volatility System

Another method that includes volatility and is computationally simple is the Volatility System.[1] Signals are generated when a price change is accompanied by an unusually large move relative to average volatility. If the average volatility measured over N days is

$$V_t(N) = \frac{1}{N} \sum_{i=1}^{N} D_{t-i+1}$$

where D is the maximum of

(a) $|H_i - C_{i-1}|$

(b) $|H_i - L_i|$

(c) $|L_i - C_{i-1}|$

and H_i is the high on day i
 C_i is the close on day i
 L_i is the low on day i

Trading rules are given as

Sell if the close drops by more than $K \times V(N)$ from the previous close.
Buy if the close rises by more than $K \times V(N)$ from the previous close.

K is generally about 3.0.

Note that the average volatility should not include the current day t. A comparison of today's volatility using an average containing that value might cause inconsistent signals.

The 10-Day Moving Average Rule

The most basic application of a moving-average system was proposed by Keltner in his 1960 publication, *How to Make Money in Commodities* (The Keltner Statistical Service). Of three mechanical systems presented by Keltner, his choice of a moving average was based on performance and experience. The system itself is quite simple: a 10-day moving average based on the average of the daily high, low, and closing prices, with a band on each side formed from the 10-day moving

[1] Richard Bookstaber, *The Complete Investment Book*, Scott, Foresman, Glenview, IL, 1984, p. 231.

average of the high-low range. A buy signal occurs on penetration of the upper band and a sell signal when the lower band is broken; positions are always reversed.

The 10-day moving-average rule is basic, but it does account for the fundamental volatility principle and serves as an example of the actual use of moving averages. Keltner expresses his preference for this particular technique because of its identification of minor rather than medium- or long-term trends, and there are some performance figures that substantiate his conclusion. As an experienced trader, he prefers the speed of the 10-day moving average, which follows the market prices with more reasonable risk than slower methods. A side benefit to the selection is that the usual division required by a moving-average calculation can be substituted by a simple shift of the decimal place; who knows how much impact that convenience had on Keltner's choice?

Triple Exponential Smoothing

A triple exponential smoothing technique was described by Hutson as another approach to trend-following.[2] Substituting the log of the price, he applied an exponential smoothing three times using the same smoothing constant. A buy signal was generated when the triple smoothed series rose for 2 consecutive days; a sell signal followed a 2-day decline.

The smoothing constant selected would normally be faster (less than a 20-day equivalent, when $2/(n + 1)$ is used to convert the n days to a smoothing constant) for a triple smoothing than for a single smoothed line. It is interesting to see what actually happens when a series is smoothed three times. For example, a triple smoothing of a straight 3-day moving average gives the following:

$$P = (P_1, P_2, \ldots, P_n)$$

The single moving average at day n is

$$M_n = \frac{(P_{n-2} + P_{n-1} + P_n)}{3}$$

Smoothing the new series M gives

$$M'_n = \frac{(M_{n-2} + M_{n-1} + M_n)}{3}$$

$$= \frac{(P_{n-4} + 2P_{n-3} + 3P_{n-2} + 2P_{n-1} + P_n)}{9}$$

and the third smoothing gives

$$M''_n = \frac{(M'_{n-2} + M'_{n-1} + M'_n)}{3}$$

$$= \frac{(P_{n-6} + 3P_{n-5} + 6P_{n-4} + 7P_{n-3} + 6P_{n-2} + 3P_{n-1} + P_n)}{27}$$

[2] Jack K. Hutson, "Good TRIX," *Technical Analysis of Stocks & Commodities*, July 1983.

The weighting puts increased importance on the middle values, reducing the significance of both ends. With exponential smoothing as well, the increased emphasis will be placed on the $n - 2$ value, the price which is repeated most often.

The Parabolic Time/Price System

One of the primary complaints about trend-following systems is that the intrinsic lag destroys the trade. In the Parabolic Time/Price System,[3] Wilder has reduced the lag by increasing the speed of the trend (shortening the days) whenever prices achieve new profitable levels. The philosophy of the Parabolic System is that time is an enemy. Once a position is entered, it must continue to be profitable or it will be liquidated.

The Parabolic Time/Price System is always in the market; whenever a position is closed-out, it is also reversed. The point at which this occurs is called the Stop and Reverse (SAR). When plotted, it is similar to a trendline although it has a decreasing lag (the distance between the current price and the trendline, or SAR point), as shown in Figure 5-3.

To calculate the SAR value, first assume a long or short position. If the market has recently moved lower and is now above the lows of that move, assume a *long*. Call the lowest point of the previous trade the SAR initial point (SIP) because it will be the starting point for the SAR calculation ($SAR_1 = SIP$).

Calculate each following SAR as

$$SAR(tomorrow) = SAR(prior) + AF \times [High(today) - SAR(prior)]$$

This is an exponential smoothing using the prior high price. It is unique because the smoothing constant AF, called the acceleration factor, changes. The AF is set

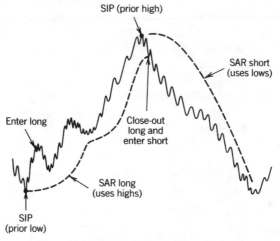

Figure 5-3   Parabolic Time/Price System.

[3] J. Welles Wilder, Jr., *New Concepts in Technical Trading Systems*, Trend Research, Greensboro, NC, 1978.

to .02 at the beginning of the trade. Each day that a new extreme occurs (a new high when long, or a new low when short) the AF is increased by .02. In moving average days, the AF begins at 99 days and increases speed to a maximum of a 9-day moving average, but not in a linear fashion.

In the SAR calculation, the High(today) is used when a long position is held, and Low(today) is used when a short is held. An additional rule also prevents premature reversal by not allowing the SAR to enter the price range of the most recent 2 days:

> If *long*, the SAR may never be greater than the low of today or the prior day. If it is greater than this low, set the SAR to that low value. A reversal will occur on a new intraday low which penetrates the SAR.
>
> If *long*, the SAR is calculated in the same way based on the highs.

Wilder's Parabolic Time/Price System has a new and interesting idea—varying the exponential smoothing constant. This could also be accomplished by varying the moving average days, but not as effectively. The constant increment of .02 and the limitations of the range, .02 to .20, are likely to be shortcomings. Traders might want to relate the changing speed to more basic price phenomena. For those readers interested in the further development of this method, the Parabolic Time/ Price System is combined with Directional Movement (described in Chapter 18) to form the Directional Parabolic System discussed in Chapter 6.

The Master Trading Formula

Another method of variable speed is Mart's Master Trading Formula.[4] It is based on an exponential smoothing formula where the smoothing constant and band are calculated daily, based on market volatility. Mart averages the extended daily range (using the maximum of yesterday's close and today's high and low) and the net price movement over the same interval to define a *correlated volatility factor*. This value is then used to look up a smoothing constant in a modified log-scale table, where an 8% smoothing (24-day equivalent) is used for the lowest volatility and a 33% smoothing (2-day equivalent) for the greatest volatility, with the median value at 14% (13-day equivalent).

A band is also placed around the trendline, based on an inverse relationship to the correlated volatility factor. The band is widest when there is low volatility and the smoothing constant produces a slow trend; it is narrowest in fast, highly volatile markets.

Rules for trading Mart's Master Formula are centered around the basic band trading rules. The system is always in the market, taking long positions when the upper band is broken and short positions when the lower band is crossed.

TECHNIQUES USING TWO MOVING AVERAGES

This section is restricted to applications of moving averages; however, do not assume that these constitute the only timing methods. Any secondary system that

---

[4] Donald S. Mart, *The Master Trading Formula*, Winsor Books, Brightwaters, NY, 1981.

analyzes a shorter time period than the primary system can be considered as a timing device. For example, a 3-day moving average could act as a timing technique for a 10-day average. The delays of 1, 2, 3, or more days, discussed earlier, are for timing; but a 5-day delay would not be used with a 3-day moving average since the two would not make sense together. Plotting of lag and lead moving-average values is another possible timing method. In this section, the use of more than one moving average will be examined (any type of moving average would apply) to create a system; a standard moving average will be used here.

In using two averages, the slower one, requiring more calculation days, will determine the long-term trend. The faster average will be used for timing. A long-term moving average generates a signal with respect to the long-term trend, regardless of recent patterns. A trader would be more comfortable knowing that there is a recent short-term surge of prices in the direction of the new position at the moment of entry. To resolve this problem, select two moving averages, one noticeably faster than the other, and apply either of the two following rules:

1. *Buy* when the faster moving average crosses the slower moving average going up. *Sell* when the faster moving average crosses the slower moving average going down.
2. *Buy* when the current price crosses above both moving averages and close-out long positions when prices cross below either moving average. *Sell* when the current price crosses below both moving averages and close-out short positions when prices cross above either moving average (Figure 5-4).

The first set of rules results in constant trading, going from long to short and back as the long-term trend is violated by the faster trend. The second set of rules allows for a neutral position when the current position is closed-out and the long-term trend is not penetrated. One problem with this second approach is that the faster moving average may cause whipsaws by being too close to the current price. This can be solved in the same way as the single moving average by placing a band around one or both of the trendlines. There are other variations of these rules that can be listed, but they are not materially different from these two.

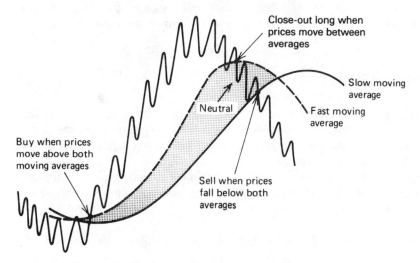

Figure 5-4   Trading system using two moving averages.

Donchian's 5- and 20-Day Moving Average System

The combined use of two moving averages has been popular among professional advisors. Of these, the most well-known is Donchian's 5- and 20-Day Moving Average,[5] a method claiming one of the longest recorded operational results, beginning January 1, 1961. There is no explanation for the selection of these two values, but in 1961 when moving averages were more the state-of-the-art than now, they were a reasonable choice. The selections can be justified because of their close relationship to the trading days in a week and a month; even now, calendar periods might add some desirable features to a system.

Donchian's idea is to use a volatility-penetration criterion relative to the 20-day moving average, but with some added complication. The current penetration must not only cross the 20-day moving average but also exceed any previous 1-day penetration of a closing price by at least one volatility measure.

The 5-day moving average serves as a liquidation criterion (along with others) and is also modified by prior penetration and volatility. These features tend to make Donchian's volatility measurement "self-adjusting." Even if selected poorly, the new penetration must exceed prior breakouts; without thorough testing, it may be difficult to determine which rule has more significance. To maintain a human element, Donchian requires execution of certain orders to be delayed a day if the signals occurred on specific weekdays or before a holiday. The combination of different factors is generally the result of refinement over years of actual operation, but neither complexity nor sophistication guarantees success; only the results will tell.

MULTIPLE MOVING AVERAGES

If two moving averages improve trading, it should follow that three or more are even better—but it doesn't. With the use of two moving averages, there is a main trend identifier and a timing device; the addition of one or more averages or indicators must fulfill a distinct purpose. When more moving averages must agree on the same signal, there is less chance and less time to trade. The results of moving average systems using two and three moving averages are covered in Chapter 15.

COMPREHENSIVE STUDIES

Considering the availability of the computer and computer programs that allow testing of alternative systems, there have been very few comprehensive studies published within the past 10 years. These studies have been included in Chapter 15. Among them are systems similar to the single- and double-moving average methods just discussed as well as the selection of a third trend for entry timing. An important objective of the optimization discussion is the longevity of the parameters selected through the testing process.

[5] Richard D. Donchian, "Donchian's 5- and 20-Day Moving Averages," *Commodities Magazine*, Dec. 1974.

SELECTING THE RIGHT MOVING AVERAGE[6]

Up to now, the selection of the *right* (or desired) moving average has only been discussed in general terms. The best moving average speed for a hedger may not be the same as for a speculator. For example, a hedger may be marketing cattle each month and may need to choose a time at which to preprice his or her product. A 3-day moving average might generate five sell signals in 1 month, each one indicating a 2-day trend—an ineffective tool for the hedger. The hedger needs an average of one sell signal per month to be a useful timing tool; the speculator has no such concerns.

For the speculator, the *right* moving average speed is the one that produces the best performance profile. This profile could be simply maximum profits, or it could be a more complex combination of profits, equity variation, and use of margin. In Chapter 15, the computer is used to find the combination of speed, stop-loss, and other rules that best satisfy a preset criterion; a computer, however, is not always necessary.

Computer testing of a moving average system or other trading strategies sometimes leads to solutions that are highly fitted. The computer may find that a 3-day moving average was more profitable with lower risk than a 20-day trend, which was only slightly worse in performance. Our logic tells us that the results of the 3-day system will be more difficult to attain in real trading because execution costs in fast markets with many trades may be higher than expected. A slower selection is more conservative and more likely to return the expected results. However, the trader must be the judge of whether the selection is reasonable.

Selecting the Trend Speed

Observation of a price chart will show the trends of the market. The trends that two traders see will often be different. Some traders "see" long-term price trends, others see much shorter movements. To find your own best moving average speed without the use of a computer, look at a price chart and mark the beginning and end of each price move that you would like to capture. These trends may occur every few days, or only three or four times each year. In this exercise, the major trends were selected from the chart for August 1985 pork bellies (Figure 5-5).

Use the fact that a moving average of n-day speed will be neutral over a period of n days where the price returns to the same level. If the daily price changes are nearly equal, one leg of this move (the trends identified in Figure 5-5) will occur in $n/2$ days. To be cautious, select moving average intervals slightly longer than two times the worst retracement within the trend in order to prevent being "stopped-out" of the trend.

When calculating profits generated by a moving average, part of the trend movement is lost at the beginning and end of the trade. This part is equivalent to the price change over $\frac{1}{2}$ of the moving average speed, since it requires that much time for the moving average to "break even," or become neutral with respect to the price move.

[6] Perry J. Kaufman, "Moving Averages" in Todd Lofton (Ed.), *Trading Tactics: A Livestock Anthology*, Chicago Mercantile Exchange, Chicago, 1986.

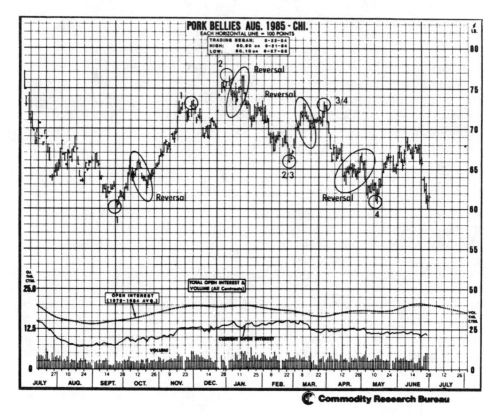

Figure 5-5 Selected trends and reversals.

Keeping these two points in mind, the best trend speed can be selected from presenting the moves and largest reversals, as shown in Table 5-2.

The longest period to offset the largest reversal is 3.1 weeks (each week is 5 days), and it takes a 16-day moving average to neutralize the largest move. A 16-day moving average usually requires 8 days to break even. Allowing 2 weeks (10 days) of price movement to reach the break-even point, the following profitability remains:

Trade	Move/Week	Profitable Weeks	Total Profit
1	1.30	8	10.4
2	1.25	6	7.5
3	1.40	3	4.2
4	1.70	5	8.5
Total			30.6

Naturally, there will be periods of uncertain direction and small losing trades with this or any price series; however, capturing these four price trends will go a long way towards profitability.

Table 5-2   Selecting Trends and Reversals

Trade		Range (cents)	Total Move (cents)	Duration (weeks)	Move per Week	Needed[a] to Offset (weeks)
1. Sustained move	up	60–73	13	10	1.3	3.1
Largest reversal	down	66–62	4	1	4.0	
2. Sustained move	down	76–66	10	8	1.25	2.4
Largest reversal	up	73–76	3	1	3.0	
3. Sustained move	up	66–73	7	5	1.4	2.9
Largest reversal	down	73–69	4	1	4.0	
4. Sustained move	down	73–61	12	7	1.7	1.2
Largest reversal	up	63–67	4	2	2.0	

[a] The number of weeks of profitable movement needed to recover the loss due to the largest reversal.

LIVING WITH MOVING AVERAGES

The advantages and disadvantages of moving averages are those of most disciplined systems. The first question that a trader should ask is: ''What can I expect from a moving average?'' The speed of a moving average will change the profitability, size of individual profits and losses, and reliability. This is covered thoroughly in Chapter 17. Fast moving averages enter trades on the first strong reversal day; slower averages take more time to identify a trend change. No matter what its speed or how well-timed, a moving average can never be precise; consequently, watching commodity prices vary with respect to the moving average will be frustrating. The moving average system will rarely enter or close out a position at just the right place. It is intended to extract profits from the middle of a trend and hold losses to a minimum. The risks and magnitude of reward are intrinsic to the speed of the moving average although the risk/reward ratio may be similar for many moving averages. The success of such a system can only be judged by its actual performance; thus, the weekly or monthly accumulated results should be studied rather than simply observing the relationship of the trendline to prices.

The slower the moving average, the further behind it will lag. Professional traders lean towards the faster trends and portfolio managers towards the slower. When trading only one commodity, individual trade risks can be kept small using faster moving averages. The portfolio trader can offset the long-term adverse move in one commodity with an equally long favorable trend in another. The advantage of diversification and long-term trends is that each commodity will move in the direction of the trend a majority of days, even though that may mean only 6 out of 10. A portfolio of 10 commodities, each with a 60% probability of a move in the trend direction, should result in six moving in a profitable direction. It is more likely that all of them will be profitable on the same day than it is that all will be losers.

Slower moving averages are more likely to endure than faster ones. These slower trends often profit from fundamental market changes, such as seasonality, production cycles, and inflation. They stick to a trend while it develops. The faster moving averages are attempting to catch shifts in market psychology, short-term cycles caused by trading patterns and current events, and wide swings in high-priced, uncertain markets. The patterns that make fast trading profitable also change quickly. A 3-day moving average may be highly profitable for one month, then produce consistently losing trades.

"Take Your Profits and Let Your Losses Run"

Many traders are guilty of profit-taking with moving average systems. Cutting losses short is an intrinsic quality of a moving average system as is its lag. It is inevitable that a trader will want to close out a trade that has a $1,000 profit and a stop-loss at a level that captures only $300. However, this places an arbitrary limit on potential profits while letting losses remain at their natural size. A trend-following system compensates for many small losses when prices sustain a trending move. Don't cut it short.

6

Momentum and Oscillators

The study of momentum and oscillators is an analysis of changes in price rather than price levels. Among technicians, momentum establishes the pace of the commodity and the rate of ascent or descent. In geometry, momentum is analogous to slope, the angle of inclination as measured from a horizontal line representing time. Momentum is also thought of as force or impact. As in Newton's Law, once started it tends to remain in motion in a straight line.

Rate of change indicators, such as momentum and oscillators, are used as leading indicators of price change. They can identify when the current trend is no longer maintaining its same level of strength. This gives the trader an opportunity to begin liquidating the open trend trades before prices actually reverse. A more aggressive strategy will develop rules for an early reversal of the market positions based on an overbought or oversold signal from a rate-of-change indicator.

MOMENTUM

Momentum is usually calculated by taking the difference between prices at a fixed interval. For example, today's 5-day momentum value $M(5)$ would be the difference between today's price P_t and the price 5 days ago:

$$M(5)_t = P_t - P_{t-5}$$

The momentum value $M(5)_t$ will increase as the change in price increases over the 5-day period. Figure 6-1 shows that a price increase will cause both angle a to become larger and the hypotenuse of the triangle, marked "momentum," to increase. If the 5-day momentum is 100, the slope of the momentum line can be expressed as $\frac{100}{5} = 20$. If prices had increased by 150 points, the slope would be $\frac{150}{2} = 30$, and the momentum would be 150.

$M(5)_t$ can range in value from the maximum upward move to the maximum downward move that the commodity can make in 5 days; the momentum is zero if prices are unchanged after 5 days. Figure 6-2 shows the possible moves in the momentum calculation. Consider a commodity with a 20 point daily limit. Starting at point A, the 5-day price change *increased at a faster rate* for 8 days (up 2, up 4, etc.) until at point B, prices were moving at their fastest 5-day rate. At point B, the

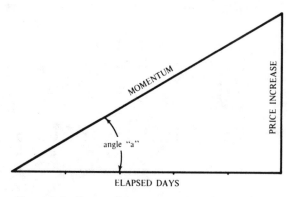

Figure 6-1   Geometric representation of momentum.

5-day price change was ⅔ of the maximum 100 point change, or 60 points. From point *B* to point *C*, prices still increased but at a slower rate; until the 5-day difference at point *C* was zero. Prices then declined at an increasing rate until at point *D* the maximum 5-day decline of 40 points was reached; at point *E*, the 5-day difference was again zero. Note that at point *B* prices did not start down but only increased at a slower rate; only at *C* did prices first begin their 5-day decline.

Alternate Momentum Calculations

It is common for the term momentum to refer to the difference between today's price and a corresponding moving average value. The properties of the resulting value remain the same. As the momentum becomes larger, prices are moving away from the moving average at a faster rate. When it gets smaller, the prices are converging with the moving average. Unlike the first definition of momentum, a value that is positive but converging towards the moving average may actually be

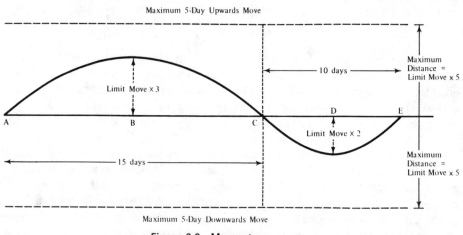

Figure 6-2   Momentum range.

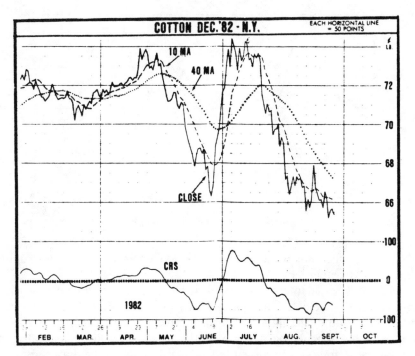

Figure 6-3 Momentum as "relative strength," the difference between prices and a moving average, or between two moving averages. (*Source:* Commodity Resource Bureau.)

declining rather than advancing at a slower rate. The major similarity is that the maximum profit is near the extreme points of the momentum chart. Figure 6-3 shows a typical use of this technique by the Commodity Research Bureau; it is often referred to as a *relative strength* indicator.

Momentum may also be defined as the difference between two moving averages. This method further smooths the results. Because both moving averages are lagged, the peaks identified by the difference between the two will also be lagged. This is contrary to the usual purpose of the momentum indicator, which is to identify the moment when an extreme has been reached. Looking at Figure 6-3 again, it can be seen that the peak formed by the widest difference between the two moving averages would have occurred about 1 week after the highest point shown, on about July 9.

Momentum as a Trend Indicator

The momentum value is a smoothing of price movement and is very similar to a standard moving average. By looking at the net increase in prices over the number of days designated by the momentum indicator, intermediate fluctuations are ignored, and the price trend can be seen. The longer the span between the observed points, the smoother the results. This is equivalent to faster and slower moving averages. In the case of momentum and oscillators, however, the focus is

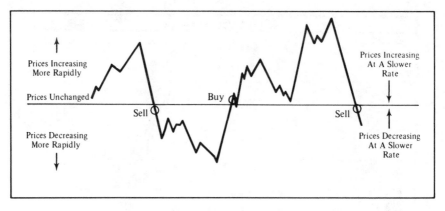

Figure 6-4 Price momentum signals.

usually the identification of abnormal price movements. This is best done by avoiding the extremely long time frame.

The use of the momentum value as a trend indicator is straightforward. The momentum span is selected and plotted as in Figure 6-4. A buy signal occurs whenever the value of the momentum turns from negative to positive and a sell signal is when the opposite occurs. If a band is used to establish a neutral position or a commitment zone, as discussed in Chapter 5, it should be drawn around the horizontal line representing the momentum value of zero.

In order to find the best choice of a momentum span, a sampling of different values could be tested for optimum performance, or a chart could be examined for some natural price cycle. Identify the significant tops and bottoms of any bar chart and average the number of days between these cycles, or find the number of days that would closely approximate the occurrences of these peaks and valleys. These natural cycles will often be the best choice of momentum span (Figure 6-5a).

Identifying Extremes

An equally popular and more interesting interpretation of the momentum chart is based on an analysis of tops and bottoms. All momentum values are bounded in both directions by the maximum move possible during the time interval represented by the span of the momentum. The conditions at the points of high positive and negative momentum are called *overbought* and *oversold,* respectively. A market is overbought when it can no longer sustain the strength of the current trend and a downward price reaction is imminent; an oversold market is ready for an upward move. Faster momentum calculations will reach these maximum values more often and stay there for extended periods of high upward or downward momentum. The use of a slow momentum period, however, will produce values which rarely test its limits. If the momentum system uses the horizontal zero line to enter and exit trades, it is of no consequence how often the bounds are touched; once a position is entered, the high momentum condition serves as positive reinforcement for the trade. However, the maximum positive and negative momentum values can be measured and used to anticipate the end of a trend. For this

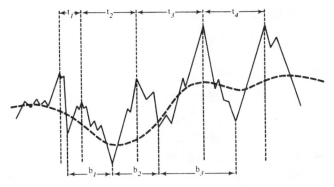

Tops and Bottoms Determine Momentum Value

(a)

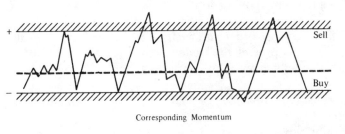

Corresponding Momentum

(b)

Figure 6-5   Relationship of momentum to prices. (a) Tops and bottoms determine momentum value. (b) Corresponding momentum.

purpose, momentum values that are too fast will obscure the trading signals—the momentum *index* must be allowed to reach its full value.

A system that takes advantage of the momentum extremes may be created by drawing two horizontal lines on the momentum graph (Figure 6-5b) above and below the zero line in such a way that the tops and bottoms of the major moves are isolated. These lines may be selected visually so that once the line is penetrated, prices reverse shortly afterwards. Another selection might simply be based on a percentage of the maximum possible momentum value. A third statistical approach would be to use a multiple of the standard deviation, or some other probability distribution function so that the band is formed by the zero line, plus or minus two standard deviations. That is, about 95% of all values within the area are bounded by the two horizontal lines.

When positioning these bands, there is always a trade-off between finding more trading opportunities and entering the market too soon. This can be a complicated choice and is discussed in "System Trade-Offs," Chapter 17. Once these lines have been drawn, the basic trading rules will be one of the following:

1. Enter a new long position when the momentum value penetrates the lower bound and a new short position when the value penetrates the upper bound.
2. Enter a new short position on the first day the momentum value turns down after penetrating the upper bound (the opposite for longs).

3. Enter a new short position when the momentum value penetrates the upper bound coming down (the opposite for longs).
4. Enter a new short position after the momentum value has remained above the upper bound for t days (the opposite for longs).

To close-out a profitable position there are the following alternatives:

1. Close-out long positions or cover shorts when the momentum value satisfies the entry condition for a reverse position.
2. Cover a short position when the momentum penetrates the zero line, minus one standard deviation (or some target point, e.g., halfway between the zero line and the lower bound).
3. Cover a short position if the momentum recrosses the zero line moving up after penetrating that line moving down.

A protective stop-loss order may be used to prevent giving up all profits (as in the last point) or to protect the trader from a sustained move that causes the momentum value to remain on the outside of the overbought/oversold lines.

1. Place a protective stop above or below the most extreme high or low momentum value.
2. Follow a profitable move with a nonretreating stop based on fixed points or a percentage.
3. Establish zones that act as levels of attainment (using horizontal lines of equal spacing) and do not permit reverse penetrations once entered.

These precautions are due to both normal price variability and volatility. As prices reach higher levels, increased volatility will cause momentum tops and bottoms to widen; at lower levels, they may not be active enough to penetrate the bounds. A penetration level established when coffee prices were 50¢ per pound and the maximum daily range was 2¢ would not work with coffee at $2.50 per pound and limits of 4¢. A reasonable modification to the momentum plot would be the use of a band or stop-loss which is a percentage of price, or a percentage of the permissible limit move (a volatility function). The tops and bottoms would remain more in line although the risk would increase appreciably. This, however, is the intention of the *oscillator*.

When selecting trading rules for a countertrend technique, risk must be the primary concern. Using entry option 1, a short signal will occur upon penetration of the upper level; this may happen when the market is very strong. If an immediate reversal does not occur, large open losses may accrue. One solution might be to place a fixed stop-loss at the time of each entry. To determine the proper stop-loss amount, a computer test was performed using an immediate entry based on penetration of an extreme boundary, with a close stop-loss for risk protection. The first results were thought to have outstanding profits and consistency until it was discovered that the computer had done exactly the opposite of what was intended: It *bought* when the momentum crossed the upper bound and placed a close stop-loss *below* the entry. It did prove, for a good sampling of commodities, that high momentum periods continued for enough time to capture small but consistent profits. It also showed that entry rule 1, anticipating an early reversal, would be a losing strategy.

OSCILLATORS

Because the representation of the momentum index is that of a line fluctuating above and below a zero value, this technique has often been termed an *oscillator*. Even though it does oscillate, the terminology is confusing. In this presentation, the term oscillator will be restricted to a specific form of momentum, or rate-of-change indicator, which is normalized and expressed in terms of values ranging between $+1$ and -1, $+1$ and 0, or 100 and 0, as in percent.

To transform a standard momentum calculation into the normalized form (maximum value of $+1$, minimum value of -1), divide the momentum calculation by the maximum attainable value of the momentum index. A 5-day index for silver with a 20¢ limit move could be divided by \$1.00 to find the normalized value. If silver were to move its limit up for 5 days, the oscillator would have the value of $+1$ rather than the momentum value of 100. If the limits were to expand, the divisor would change as well, giving the technique a means of adjusting for varying volatility. Using the normalized momentum, or oscillator, the top and bottom zone becomes volatility-adjusted at any level.

Erratic movements in the simple momentum and oscillator make it a very difficult tool to apply without additional work. Some of these problems can be eliminated by making the buying and selling zones more extreme or by smoothing the indicator values. In the following sections, a few of the applications of this technique are shown.

RELATIVE STRENGTH INDEX

One of the most popular indicators for denoting overbought and oversold conditions is the *Relative Strength Index* (RSI) developed by Wilder.[1] It is a simple measurement that expresses the relative strength of the current price movement as increasing from 0 to 100. It is calculated as

$$\text{RSI} = 100 - \left(\frac{100}{1 + \text{RS}}\right) = 100 \times \left(\frac{\text{RS}}{1 + \text{RS}}\right)$$

where $\text{RS} = \dfrac{AU}{AD}$

AU = the total of those days closing higher during the past 14 days
AD = the total of those days closing lower during the past 14 days

---

[1] J. Welles Wilder, Jr., *New Concepts in Technical Trading Systems,* Trend Research, Greensboro, NC, 1978.

Once the first calculation has been made, both the AU and AD values can be calculated daily using an "average off" method:

$$AU_{today} = AU_{prior} - \frac{AU_{prior}}{14} + \text{today's up close or zero}$$

$$AD_{today} = AD_{prior} - \frac{AD_{prior}}{14} + \text{today's down close or zero}$$

This method essentially drops an average value and adds the new value, if any. The daily calculation of the RSI becomes simple.

Wilder has favored the use of the 14-day measurement because it represents one-half of a natural cycle. He has set the significant levels for the RSI at 30 and 70. The lower level is indicative of an imminent upturn and the upper level of a pending downturn. A plot of the RSI can be interpreted in the same manner as a bar chart, with the "head and shoulders" formation as the primary confirmation of a change in direction (Figure 6-6).

In fact, Wilder relies heavily on "top" and "bottom" formations for RSI signals. More often than head and shoulders, the "failure swing" or divergence denotes an unsuccessful test of a recent high or low RSI value.

Modifying the RSI

An obvious objection to the RSI might be the selection of a 14-day half-cycle. Maximum divergence is achieved by the use of a moving average that is exactly one-half the length of the dominant cycle, but 14 days may not be that half-cycle. In addition, the need to use chart interpretation might mean that the RSI value remains outside the 70–30 zones for extended periods rather than signaling an immediate turn.

In practical terms, the use of a 14-day criteria means that a sustained move in one direction which exceeds 14-days will retain a very high RSI value and may result in losses. If the trading of the RSI seems to have high risk, increase the overbought and oversold levels by moving them from 70–30 to 80–20, or higher. This will cause a signal at a more extreme level.

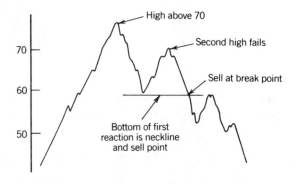

Figure 6-6   RSI top formation.

The generalized calculation for an N-day RSI on day t is given as

$$RSI_t(N) = 100 - \left(\frac{100}{1 + \left(\dfrac{Up_t(N)}{Down_t(N)} \right)} \right)$$

where

$$Up_t(N) = \frac{1}{N} \sum_{i=1}^{N} D_t \qquad \text{for } D_t > 0$$

$$Down_t(N) = \frac{1}{N} \sum_{i=1}^{N} D_t \qquad \text{for } D_t < 0$$

and $D_t = (P_{t-i+1} - P_{t-i})$ is the daily price change.[2]

A study by Aan[3] on the behavior of the RSI, with respect to the occurrence of divergence, showed that the average value of an RSI top and bottom was consistently grouped near 72 and 32, respectively. Therefore, 50% of all RSI values lie between 72 and 32, which is evenly distributed and similar in proportion to a standard deviation. This would suggest that the 70–30 levels proposed by Wilder are too close together to act as selective overbought/oversold values, but should be moved farther apart.

The frequency at which the market will reach these extreme levels can be adjusted by changing the 14-day criteria. If the interval is lowered, there will be more frequent trades and higher risk. If the time period is increased, there will be safer but fewer trades (discussed in more detail in Chapter 17). It is always safer to err on the side of less risk. If there are too many trades being generated by the RSI, a combination of a longer interval and higher confidence bands will be an improvement.[4]

STOCHASTICS

A *stochastic* is an oscillator that measures the relative position of the closing price within the daily range. It is based on the commonly accepted observation that closing prices tend to cluster near the day's high prices as an upwards move gains strength and near the lows during a decline. When the market is about to turn from up to down, for instance, it is often the case that the highs are higher, but the closing price settles nearer the lows. This makes the stochastic oscillator different from most oscillators which are normalized representations of the *relative strength*, the difference between the closing price and a selected trend speed.

The three indicators that result from the stochastic measurement are called %K, %D, and %R. The latter one, %R, was improved by Larry Williams and is

[2] Richard Bookstaber, *The Complete Investment Book*, Scott, Foresman, Glenview, IL, 1985, pp. 239–241.

[3] Peter W. Aan, "How RSI Behaves," *Futures*, Jan. 1985.

[4] For a more sophisticated approach to RSI optimization, see John F. Ehlers, "Optimizing RSI With Cycles," *Technical Analysis of Stocks & Commodities*, Feb. 1986.

discussed in a following section. The first two calculations form the normal concept of the stochastic oscillator and are calculated for today t as

$$\text{Initial } \%K_t = 100 \times \frac{C_t - L_t(5)}{R_t(5)}$$

$$\%D = \text{``}\%K\text{-slow''} = \frac{\%K_t + \%K_{t-1} + \%K_{t-2}}{3} = \frac{\left(\sum\limits_{i=t-2}^{t} \%K_i\right)}{3}$$

$$\%D_t\text{-slow} = \frac{\left(\sum\limits_{i=t-2}^{t} \%D_i\right)}{3}$$

where C_t is today's closing price

$L_t(5)$ is the low price of the last 5 days

$R_t(5)$ is the range of the last 5 days (highest high minus lowest low) as of today[5]

Notice that $\%D$ is a 3-day moving average of $\%K$, and $\%D$-slow is a 3-day moving average of $\%D$. The 5-day high, low, and range selections tend to make the smoothed stochastics, $\%D$ and $\%D$-slow, front-loaded calculations. Figure 6-7 shows the price of July 1984 cotton plotted with the corresponding $\%D$-slow and $\%D$ ($\%K$-slow) stochastic. Notice that the extremes do not correspond to what would be expected using a 5-day simple momentum. Points A and B appear much weaker in the stochastic than on the line chart while points C and D are more pronounced. The low at point E is confusing, perhaps due to the gap in data; otherwise, the stochastic would seem a unique and useful tool. The smoothed value $\%D$-slow does not lag as much as the 3-day average would imply, supporting the premise that there is significant weighting given to the more recent prices. The first calculation, $\%K$, is not used due to its instability.[6]

Interpreting the Stochastic

The initial trading signal occurs when the $\%D$-slow crosses the extreme bands, suggested in the range of 75 to 85% on the upside, and 15 to 25% on the downside. The order, however, is not placed until the $\%K$ line (from here on referring to $\%K$-slow) crosses the $\%D$-slow line. Even though the extreme zone helps assure an adverse reaction of minimum size, the crossing of the two lines acts in a way similar to a dual moving average system. By waiting for the crossover, the trader cannot be trapped into shorting an extremely bullish move or buying a bearish one.

[5] Harry Schirding, "Stochastic Oscillator," *Technical Analysis of Stocks & Commodities*, May/Jun. 1984. For a pocket computer version of these calculations, see C. F. Johnson. "Stochastic Oscillator Program for the HP-41C(V)," *Technical Analysis of Stocks & Commodities*, Sept./Oct. 1984.

[6] It is common practice to use the notation $\%K$ and $\%D$ to mean *%K-slow* and *%D-slow*, respectively. All writings on the stochastic use the smoothed values, rather than the initial $\%K$ calculation, regardless of the omission of "*-slow*." Any use of $\%K$ in this text will also refer to *%K-slow* unless specifically stated.

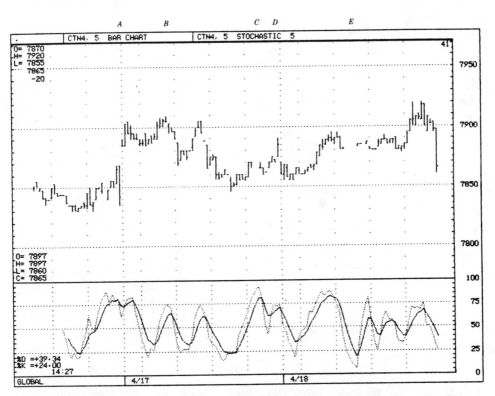

Figure 6-7   The stochastic. A 5-minute bar chart of July 1984 cotton futures (New York Cotton Exchange) as recorded by a Commodity Quite-Graphics TQ-20/20 satellite system. Cotton's 5-period stochastic is plotted below the bar chart through the close of April 18, 1984.

The emphasis in interpretation of the stochastic is its divergence from the apparent direction of prices. Referring again to Figure 6-7, points *A* and *B* are declining while new high prices at *A* are tested at *B*. This divergence is an important confirmation of the sell indication.

Patterns noted by Lane[7] are more extensive than other writings. They include:

Left and Right Crossovers. Typically, the faster %*K* will change direction sooner than the %*D*-slow, crossing the %*D*-slow line while it is still moving in the prior trend direction. The opposite case, when the %*D*-slow turns first, indicates a slow, stable change of direction and is a more favorable pattern (Figure 6-8*a*).

Hinge. A reduction in the speed of either the %*K* or %*D*-slow lines, shown as a flattening out, indicates a reversal on the next day (Figure 6-8*b*).

Warning. An extreme turn in the faster %*K* (2 to 12%) indicates at most 2 days remaining in the old trend.

---

[7] George C. Lane, "Lane's Stochastics," *Technical Analysis of Stocks & Commodities,* May/June 1984.

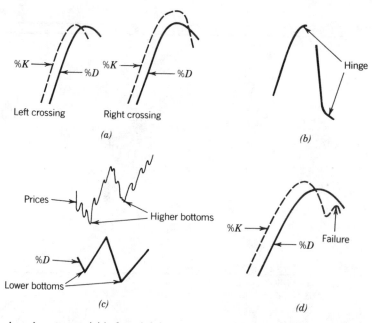

Figure 6-8   Lane's patterns. (a) Left and right crossings. (b) Hinge. (c) Bear market set-up. (d) %
K failure.

Extremes. Reaching the extreme %K values of 0 and 100 requires 7 consecutive
days of closes at the highs (lows). The test of this extreme, following a pullback, is
an excellent entry point.

Set-Up. Although the line chart shows higher highs and lows, if the %D-slow line
has lower lows, a *bear market set-up* has occurred. Look for a selling opportunity
on the next rally (Figure 6-8c).

Failure. An excellent confirmation of a change in direction occurs when %K
crosses %D-slow (after penetrating the extreme level) then pulls back to the %D-
slow line, but fails to cross it again (Figure 6-8d).

LARRY WILLIAMS' OSCILLATORS

Larry Williams has been known for his development of trading methods based on
oscillators since his publication of the *A/D oscillator* in 1972. Although they have
changed over the 14 years spanning these systems, some similarities are apparent
in Williams' three techniques which follow.

A/D Oscillator

In 1972, Jim Waters and Larry Williams published a description of their *A/D
Oscillator* in *Commodities* magazine. For their system, "A/D" means accumula-

tion/distribution rather than the usual notation of advance/decline, a well-known interpretive index for stocks. They used a unique form of relative strength, defining *buying power* BP and *selling power* SP as

$$BP = high - open \qquad SP = close - low$$

where the values used were today's open, high, low, and closing prices. The two values BP and SP show the additional buying strength (relative to the open) and selling strength (compared to the close) in an effort to measure the implied direction of the day's trading. The combined measurement, called the *Daily Raw Figure* (DRF) is calculated as

$$DRF = \frac{BP + SP}{2 \times (high - low)}$$

The maximum value of 1 is reached when a commodity opens trading at the low and closes at the high: $BP - SP = high - low$. When the opposite occurs and the market opens at the high and closes on the lows, the DRF will be 0. Each commodity will develop its own patterns, which can be smoothed or traded in many ways similar to a momentum index. The Waters/Williams A/D Oscillator solves problems of volatility and physical limits. DRF completely adjusts to higher or lower trading ranges because the divisor itself is a multiple of the day's range; and because each day is treated independently, the cumulative values of the momentum index are not part of the results. This day-to-day evaluation causes DRF to vary radically and requires some smoothing technique or cycle interpretation to make it useable. As an example, look at the January 1977 Soybean contract for the two months before delivery, November and December 1976. Table 6-1 shows the calculations for the daily raw figure and for the smoothed DRF using an exponential moving average with a smoothing constant of 30% (selected arbitrarily). DRF is plotted as the solid line on a scale of .00 to 1.00 in Figure 6-9 and is extremely erratic in its movements. The dotted line is the smoothed DRF. Once plotted, two horizontal lines can be drawn to isolate the peaks and bottoms of DRF; the top part becomes a zone representing an overbought condition and the bottom zone represents oversold. Bear in mind that these lines were drawn after the DRF was plotted and cannot be construed as predictive; however, in the article by Waters and Williams, their example of soybean oil had lines drawn in a similar place. Corresponding broken lines were drawn to indicate the overbought and oversold state for the smoothed DRF.

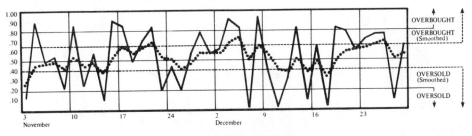

Figure 6-9   A/D Oscillator.

Table 6-1 A/D Oscillator—January 77 Soybeans

						DRF		30% DRF Smoothing		
1976 Date	Open	High	Low	Close	DRF	DRF[a] Signal	Price	30% Smoothed DRF	30% Smoothed Signal[a]	Price
11-01	682	686	674¾	678½	.34			.34		
11-03	679	683	655	658½	.13			.28		
11-04	658	676	658	671½	.87	Sell		.45		
11-05	674	678	665	673½	.48		674	.46		
11-08	673	685	671	674¼	.54			.48		
11-09	673	673	660	666	.23			.41		
11-10	667	676½	665	675	.85	Sell		.54		
11-11	660	662½	645	651	.24		660	.45		
11-12	652	658	650½	653	.57			.49		
11-15	652	652	627	632½	.11	Buy		.37	Buy	
11-16	639½	655	636½	654¼	.90	Sell	639½	.53		639½
11-17	653	671	649	668½	.85		653	.63		
11-18	667	674½	658	666½	.48			.58		
11-19	670	691	669½	678¾	.70			.62		
11-22	680	691	675½	690½	.84	Sell		.68	Sell	
11-23	689	696½	674½	675¾	.20	Buy	689	.54		689
11-24	681	686	678½	680	.43		681	.51		
11-26	678	681½	670½	671¾	.21	Buy		.42		
11-29	670	675	661½	672	.57		670	.46		
11-30	668	677½	666	674½	.78			.56		
12-01	676	681½	673	677	.56			.56		
12-02	678	681½	675	679½	.61			.57		
12-03	679	687	679	685¾	.92	Sell		.68	Sell	
12-06	690	698½	689	696½	.84		690	.73		690
12-07	700	700	690	690½	.02	Buy		.51		
12-08	691	708	691	706	.94	Sell	691	.64		
12-09	705	712	702	703	.40		705	.57		
12-10	704	704	696	696½	.03	Buy		.41		
12-13	693	695	690½	691½	.33		693	.38	Buy	
12-14	696	701½	694	701	.83	Sell		.52		696
12-15	701	702	684	687	.11	Buy	701	.39	Buy	
12-16	688½	692	685	690½	.64		688½	.47		688½
12-17	690	690	676	677½	.05	Buy		.34	Buy	
12-20	680	684½	679½	683¼	.82	Sell	680	.49		680
12-21	682	688	679	687½	.80		682	.58		
12-22	688	693	686½	689¼	.60			.59		
12-23	689	693	684½	692½	.71			.62		
12-27	695	705	694	700¾	.76			.66		
12-28	701	706½	697½	705¾	.76			.69	Sell	
12-29	708	710	699	699½	.11	Buy		.52		708
12-30	703½	708	698	706½	.65		703½	.56		

Basic DRF Performance[b]		30% Smoothed DRF Performance[b]	
16 signals		7 signals	
4 compounded signals		3 compounded signals	
12 profits		5 profits	
Average profit	13.08¢	Average profit	22.10¢
4 losses		2 losses	
Average loss	14.25¢	Average loss	6.50¢
Net profit/loss	99.96¢	net profit/loss	97.50¢

[a] Signals taken the following day on open.

[b] No commissions have been deducted.

The rules for using the A/D Oscillator were not defined in the *Commodities* magazine presentation, but some simple rules could be:

Sell when the DRF (or smoothed DRF) penetrates into the overbought zone. Close-out all accumulated long positions if any and go short on the open of the next trading day.
Buy when the opposite condition occurs.

If the DRF (or smoothed DRF) enters an overbought or oversold zone more than once without the opposite zone being entered, one additional position is added at each reentry. Following these rules, the A/D Oscillator showed excellent success for both the raw and smoothed values. Accepting the after-the-fact designation of zones, the results still show that the method is viable and that a smoothing technique can be applied to DRF to vary the speed of trading.

Waters and Williams used a simple 10-day momentum for their example of the A/D Oscillator. The choice of interval can be determined by examining the tops and bottoms of a chart for the natural cycle of the prices.

In reviewing the A/D Oscillator, there are modifications to be considered. Conceptually, the value of the oscillator should be +1 when prices are rising rapidly. The most extreme example is a locked-limit no-trading day, representative of the strongest (or weakest) market. But for that case, the open, high, low and closing prices are all the same and DRF cannot be determined (since the divisor is zero). A more basic problem concerns gap openings. A much higher opening with a stronger close would also upset the resulting DRF. For example, the following trading occurs:

	Open	High	Low	Close	DRF	ΔDRF	$\Sigma\Delta$DRF
Monday	43.00	44.00	40.00	41.00	.25		
Tuesday	42.00	42.00	39.00	40.00	.17	−.17	−.17
Wednesday	38.50	38.50	38.00	38.00	.00	+.17	.00
Thursday	42.00	42.00	39.00	40.00	.17	−.33	−.33
Friday	40.00	43.00	40.00	42.00	.83	+.50	+.17

Note that on Wednesday, the ΔDRF indicates that the momentum has reversed, but in fact the price is falling rapidly and give no indication of recovering; it may actually be gaining momentum. On Thursday the price soars up and closes in the midrange, but the ΔDRF shows a new downward momentum. The problem seems to be related to lack of association with the prior closing price. The daily movement can take on different appearances if the entire range was above or below the closing price. To form this link, replace the current high or low with the prior closing price if that price was outside the current trading range. The following example shows the results smoothed out and leaves the trend intact.

	Open	High	Low	Close	DRF	ΔDRF	ΣΔDRF
Monday	43.00	44.00	40.00	41.00	.25		
Tuesday	42.00	42.00	39.00	40.00	.17	−.17	−.17
Wednesday	38.50	(40.00)	38.00	38.00	.37	+.04	−.13
Thursday	42.00	42.00	(38.00)	40.00	.25	−.12	−.25
Friday	40.00	43.00	40.00	42.00	.83	+.58	+.33

Another construction of an oscillator can be made using the highs and lows relative to the prior close:

$$O_t = \frac{H_t - C_{t-1}}{H_t - L_t}$$

The two days are linked together and the ratio of the high price relative to the prior close is measured against the total range for the day. For the normal case, $H_t \geq C_{t-1} \geq L_t$; but if $C_{t-1} > H_t$ or $L_t > C_{t-1}$, C_{t-1} replaces either H_t or L_t to extend the range. The value of O_t will be either 1 or 0 for these extreme cases. As with the A/D Oscillator, the values derived from this method may also be smoothed.

Oscillators are not the only tools for measuring momentum or for determining overbought or oversold conditions. Because it is very different from either a charting technique or a moving average, it is valuable either on its own or as a confirmation of another method.

A word of caution: Trading against the trend can be exciting and profitable, but at considerably greater risk than a trend-following system. The problem with selling an overbought condition is that there is no way to hold losses to a minimum. Once a short position is entered, the momentum or the oscillator value could sustain its strength and move against the position.

%R Method

After the publication of Williams, *How I Made A Million Dollars Last Year . . Trading Commodities* (Conceptual Management), the %R oscillator became well-known. It is a simple way of calculating where today's closing price fits into the recent trading range. Using the last 10 days, define

$$\%R = \frac{\text{buying power}}{\text{range}} = \frac{\text{high}_{10} - \text{close}_{\text{today}}}{\text{high}_{10} - \text{low}_{10}}$$

Williams' %R is actually what is now called a *10-day stochastic,* using the high price rather than the low price in the numerator. The 10-day interval smooths out some of the irregularities of the initial %K (see the preceding section) without the front-loading. With a chart that has 0 at the top and 100 at the bottom, a value below 95% will give a buy signal, and one over 10% a sell. Williams viewed this as a timing device to add positions within a major technical or fundamental trend. Trades were not to be entered if they contradicted the major market direction.

The %R method is not precise and can only be used in combination with a more complete system. It has no risk control and, considering the short 10-day period,

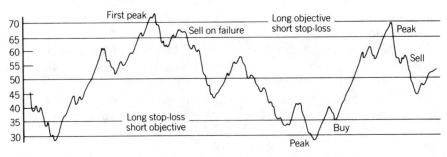

Figure 6-10   Williams' "Ultimate Oscillator."

can encounter frequent bull and bear markets which would lock the value at either 0 or 100%.

The "Ultimate Oscillator"

In the *Ultimate Oscillator*, Williams seems to combine his original idea of the A/D Oscillator with a great deal of Wilder's RSI.[8] He adds the unique feature of three concurrent time periods in order to offset the negative qualities of the short time period of the %R, without slowing the system too much. The Ultimate Oscillator works as follows:

1. Calculate today's *buying pressure* B_t by subtracting the "true low" from the closing price. The "true low" is today's low or yesterday's close, whichever is lower.
2. Calculate today's "true range" R_t, by taking either the greater of today's high and low, today's high and yesterday's close, or yesterday's close and today's low.
3. Total the "buying pressure" B_t separately over the three intervals 7, 14, and 28 days, designated as SB_7, SB_{14}, and SB_{28}.
4. Total the "true range" R_t over the same three periods, SR_7, SR_{14}, and SR_{28}.
5. Divide the sum of the buying pressures by the corresponding true range, that is, SB_7/SR_7 and scale by multiplying the 7-day value by 4 and the 14-day value by 2. All three calculations are now in the same scale.

Notice that the nearest seven values for the buying pressure and the true range are each used seven times, that is, they are multiplied by both the scaling factors of 4 and 2, and used once more in the 28-day calculation. Williams has created a step-weighted momentum, assigning values of 7, 3, and 1 to the first 7 days, second 7 days, and last 14 days, respectively. The last 14 days accounts for only 10% of the total.

The rules for using this oscillator (see Figure 6-10) are:

1. A sell signal occurs when the oscillator moves above the 50% line (an upward divergence), and the oscillator peaks and then fails to break the peak on the

[8] Larry Williams, "The Ultimate Oscillator," *Technical Analysis of Stocks & Commodities*, Aug. 1985.

next rally. Then, a sell order can be placed when the oscillator fails (on the right shoulder).

2. If holding a short position, close-out the short when a long signal occurs, or when the 30% level is reached, or if the oscillator rises above 65% (the stop-loss point) after being below 50%.

3. A buy signal occurs using the opposite techniques as the short signal (rule 1).

4. If a long position is held, close-out longs when a short signal occurs, or when the 70% level is reached, or if the oscillator falls below 30% (after being above 50%).

Williams' Ultimate Oscillator has combined many important features, including weighting time periods, setting objectives, stop-loss points, and chart interpretation. There are two obvious weaknesses in this approach.

1. The chart rules add a great deal of subjectiveness to the method. Waiting for a failure of a second peak is another way of looking for a broadening top—a slower rise, followed by a rounding pattern. Waiting for a pattern may add reliability if interpreted properly, but it defeats the effect of the oscillator being a "leading indicator."

2. The stop-loss rules apply only after the oscillator has crossed 50%. If it moves the wrong way immediately, there is no risk control.

VELOCITY AND ACCELERATION

A method conceptually similar to momentum is derived from the concepts in physics of velocity and acceleration; elements of the science of motion. *Velocity*, as defined in mechanics, is the rate of change of position with respect to time (also called *speed*). There are two types of velocity, *average* and *instantaneous*. The average velocity is simply calculated as the mean velocity over a fixed distance and for a fixed time interval. In working with commodity prices, the time interval used will be days and the distance is measured in points; so that if silver moved 40 points in 6 days, its average velocity is

$$\bar{v} = \tfrac{40}{6} = 6\tfrac{2}{3} \text{ points per day}$$

In general, the average velocity is expressed

$$\bar{v} = \frac{D}{T}$$

where D is the total elapsed distance over the time interval T. For a geometric interpretation of momentum, D, the change in price, can be related to T, the length of the momentum span, to get exactly the same results for average velocity as for slope (see Figure 6-11).

The instantaneous velocity v, which is the velocity calculated at a specific point in time, will be different. In order to determine the instantaneous velocity, a mathematical technique called *differentiation* is used. It effectively looks at smaller and smaller time intervals and consequently smaller distances on the price

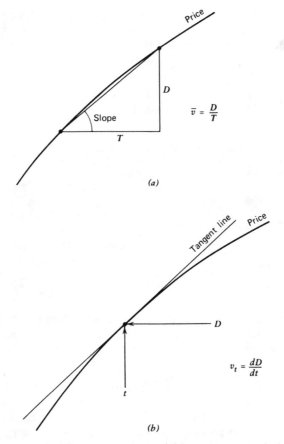

Figure 6-11   (a) Average velocity. (b) Instantaneous velocity.

curve until the slope calculation is reduced to a single point. The results of the process of differentiation is called the *derivative* and is expressed

$$v_t = \lim_{\Delta t \to 0} \frac{\Delta D}{\Delta t} = \frac{dD}{dt}$$

This shows that the velocity taken at any point is the result of the time interval (Δt) becoming progressively smaller without reaching zero. The rules for differentiation can be found in any advanced mathematics book. Only the results will be presented. The velocity v_t represents the speed or momentum of the price at the point in time t. If v gets larger for $t_0, t_1, t_2, \ldots$, then the velocity is increasing; if v gets smaller, the velocity is decreasing. Because the velocity also denotes direction, it can be both positive and negative in value and appear similar to a momentum indicator. Systems applied to momentum may equally be applied to velocity. Of course, some of the basic equations have constant velocity and cannot be used for a velocity trading plan since the values never change. The straight line, simple and weighted moving averages, and exponential smoothing all have constant velocities. Only those equations with ''second-order smoothing'' will work.

When the processes of differentiation is reapplied to the equation for velocity, it results in the rate of change of the speed with respect to time, or *acceleration*. This type of acceleration tells whether the velocity is increasing or decreasing at any point in time. The acceleration, also called the *second derivative*, adds another dimension to momentum and may improve the timing of trades.

Let's assume that the velocity and acceleration have been calculated (Table 6-2). The following are the possible combinations that can occur:

Vel	Acc	Price movement
+	+	Price is moving up at an increasing rate
+	0	Price is moving up at a constant rate
+	−	Price is moving up at a decreasing rate
0	0	Price is static
−	+	Price is moving down at a decreasing rate
−	0	Price is moving down at a constant rate
−	−	Price is moving down at an increasing rate

Using the acceleration feature, a change of velocity (or momentum) can be detected or the strength of a current price move can be confirmed.

Quick Calculation of Velocity and Acceleration

A less precise but very convenient way of determining velocity and acceleration is the calculation of first and second differences. The purpose of these values is to find more sensitive indicators of price change, and most traders will find this quick calculation satisfactory. The results can be used in exactly the same way as the formal mathematical results. Consider the following examples:

1. A price series 10, 20, 30, 40, . . . is moving higher by a constant value each day. The first differences are 10, 10, 10, . . . , showing a consistent velocity of 10. The second differences, formed by subtracting sequential values in the first differenced series, are 0, 0, 0, . . . showing that there is no change in speed, therefore the acceleration is zero.
2. Another price series is shown with its first and second differences as

t	1	2	3	4	5	6	7	8	9	10	11	12
S	10	15	20	30	45	50	45	35	25	20	25	40
V		+5	+5	+10	+15	+5	−5	−10	−10	−5	+5	+15
A			0	+5	+5	−10	−10	−5	0	+5	+10	+10

where S is the price series
V is the velocity (first differences)
A is the acceleration (second differences)

Table 6-2 Equations for Velocity and Acceleration

	Basic Equation	Velocity at x_t[a]	Acceleration at x_t
Straight line	$y_t = a + bx_t$	$v_t = b$	$a_t = 0$
Curvilinear	$y_t = a + bx_t + cx_t^2$	$v_t = b + 2cx_t$	$a_t = 2c$
Logarithmic (base a)	$y_t = \log_a x_t$	$\left\{\begin{array}{l} v_t = (\log_a e)/x_t \quad \text{or} \\ v_t = 1/(x_t \ln a) \end{array}\right\}$	$a_t = -1/(x_t^2 \ln a)$
Logarithmic (natural log)	$y_t = \ln x_t$	$v_t = 1/x_t$	$a_t = -1/x_t^2$
Exponential	$y_t = e^{ax_t}$	$v_t = ae^{ax_t}$	$a_t = a^2 e^{ax_t}$
Moving average	$y_t = \dfrac{x_t + x_{t-1} + \cdots + x_{t-n+1}}{n}$	$v_t = 1$	$a_t = 0$
Weighted moving average	$y_t = \dfrac{a_1 x_t + a_2 x_{t-1} + \cdots + a_n x_{t-n+1}}{n}$	$v_t = \dfrac{a_1 + a_2 + \cdots + a_n}{n}$	$a_t = 0$
Exponential smoothing	$y_t = y_{t-1} + c(x_t - y_{t-1})$	$v_t = c$	$a_t = 0$

[a] Since velocity and acceleration are time derivatives, all equations implicitly include the factor $\dfrac{d(x_t)}{d_t}$ as part of the right member.

The original series S has two turns in trend clearly shown by the velocity and acceleration. The velocity V continues to be positive through the sixth value as the underlying price moves from 10 to 50. Whenever prices change direction, the velocity changes sign. The basic upward trend can be associated with a positive velocity and a downward trend with a negative one.

The acceleration, or second difference, show the change in speed. At the sixth item, the acceleration becomes negative, even though the velocity was positive, because prices moved higher at a slower rate. They had been gaining by 5, 10, and 15 points each day, but on day 6, the gain was only 5 points. This reversal in acceleration was a leading indicator of a trend change. A similar situation occurred on day 8, when the acceleration slowed and reversed on day 10, one day ahead of the actual price reversal.

The relationship between velocity and acceleration using first and second differences can be interpreted using the same logic as previously discussed. Velocity and acceleration are increasingly more sensitive directional indicators; the slightest variation in price movement will cause the acceleration to reverse. It is an indicator of great value when it is used selectively.

OTHER RATE-OF-CHANGE INDICATORS

On-Balance Volume

A momentum technique recently popularized by Joseph Granville accumulates the daily volume by assigning it to either upward or downward pressure. Although it is treated as an oscillator, it is covered in detail at the end of Chapter 8, along with a modification called the *Volume Accumulator*.

Projected Crossovers

If moving averages can successfully be used to identify the trend direction, it follows that a projection of the moving average will be valuable in anticipating when the trends will change. If a moving average trading strategy used a single trend, the price at which the standard N-day moving average line would cross the price CP1 is

$$CP1 = \frac{\text{sum of last } N - 1 \text{ prices}}{N - 1} = \frac{\left(\sum_{t-N+2}^{t} P_i \right)}{(N - 1)}$$

To calculate the price at which two moving averages would cross requires the following

$$CP2 = \frac{N \times (\text{sum of last } N - 1 \text{ prices}) - M \times (\text{sum of last } M - 1 \text{ prices})}{(M - N)}$$

where N and M are the lengths of the two moving averages.[9]

[9] Donald R. Lambert, "The Market Directional Indicator," *Technical Analysis of Stocks & Commodities,* Nov./Dec. 1983. This article also contains a BASIC computer program to calculate the MDI.

The projected crossover price is most useful when it is likely that a trend change will occur within a few days, that is, when the two moving average begin converging and become close in value. Acting on the expected price would give the trader a great advantage in order execution. A plot of this, however, may not be much different than a simple *relative strength* measurement. The difference between the price and the moving average line constitutes the relative strength.

The change in the projected crossover is considered a more valuable tool by Lambert. He creates a *Market Direction Indicator* (MDI) with the following formula:

$$MDI = \frac{100 \times (\text{crossover price yesterday} - \text{crossover price today})}{\text{average of past 2 day's prices}}$$

The point at which the MDI crosses the zero line moving higher is a buy signal, and the point where it crosses moving lower is a sell signal.

Demand Index

Based on dividing volume by price changes, the Demand Index was developed by James Sibbett.[10] Using volume in addition to buying and selling pressure familiar to stochastics and Williams' A/D Oscillator, it relies on the premise that "price change is inversely proportional to the net result of sell pressure."

Combining a Trend and Oscillator

Directional Parabolic System. The *Directional Parabolic System*[11] is a combination of two of Wilder's well-known techniques, Directional Movement and the Parabolic Time/Price System. Directional Movement is covered fully in Chapter 17. It gained popularity as a method of selecting the commodities that were most likely candidates for trend-following systems. The Parabolic Time/Price System is covered in Chapter 5. Although a full reading of both techniques are necessary, the essence of the combined systems can be understood with the following definitions:

+DI14	The 14-day upward Directional Index
−DI14	The 14-day downward Directional Index
ADX	The average Directional Movement Index
DPS	The Directional Parabolic stop

Although shown as −DI14, the downward Directional Index is a positive number based on the sum of those days that closed lower. The ADX is a ratio of those days that closed higher with those that closed lower over the past 14 days. The

---

[10] Sibbett Publications, Pasadena, CA.
[11] J. Welles Wilder, Jr., *Chart Trading Workshop 1980,* Trend Research, Greensboro, NC, 1980.

ADX is an oscillator based on the scaled ratio of $+DI/-DI$. The two systems combine according to the following rules:

1. If the ADX is up (the $+DM14$ is greater than the $-DM14$), take only long Parabolic System trades; if the ADX is down, take only short trades.
2. If the two systems conflict, no trade is entered. A trade may be entered at the time they agree.
3. If a position is held, the Parabolic stop is used. (The stop is now called the DPS instead of the SAR because it no longer requires a reversal of position.)
4. If no position is held, the Directional Movement *equilibrium point* is used (the high or low of the day on which the $+DM14$ crosses the $-DM14$).

Directional Parabolic Revision. In 1980, the entry rules were revised to include an added use of the ADX when it is greater than the $+DI14$ or the $-DI14$. Because the ADX serves as an oscillator and indicates turning points in the trend, when the ADX exceeds the magnitude of the current $+DI14$ or $-DI14$ and reverses, the current position should be closed-out. If the ADX remains above both the $+DI14$ and $-DI14$, the market is extremely strong and liquidation should stop. The ADX is intended to be a leading indicator for liquidation only. Reversal of the current position only occurs when the Parabolic stop has been penetrated, and the new trade agrees with the direction of the Parabolic System.

The addition of an oscillator to a trend-following system allows trades to be closed-out at more favorable positions than the usual trend exits. If the new direction carries through and the position is reversed, the added feature has worked perfectly; however, if prices turn back in the original direction, a reentry may not be possible. The revised rules are unclear concerning reentry into a position if prices fail to penetrate the DPS and signal a reversal. A reentry might occur if the ADX falls below both the $+DI14$ and $-DI14$, indicating that prices are no longer extreme, then turns back in the trend direction. Once reestablished, the DPS can be used and additional exits using the revised rules would apply.

Cambridge Hook

A combined indicator that has received some promotion is the "Cambridge Hook," used by one commodity trading advisor.[12] It is intended to identify an early reversal of the current trend by combining the following indicators (applied to an existing uptrend):

1. An outside reversal day (a higher high followed by a lower close)
2. Wilder's RSI must exceed 60% (moderately overbought)
3. Volume and open interest must be increasing

The result is a high likelihood of a downward trend reversal (the opposite applies to upward trend reversals). Protective stops are placed above the high of the hook on the day that signaled a downward reversal.

[12] Elias Crim, "Are You Watching the 'Right' Signals?" *Futures*, June 1985.

A WORD OF CAUTION

Momentum and oscillators are not the only tools for determining overbought and oversold conditions. Because they are very different from either a charting technique or moving averages, they have taken their place as timing indicators within other more structured systems. When the time interval for calculation is small, these indicators can be highly unstable, jumping from frequent overbought signals to just as frequent oversold ones. Both faster and slower speeds have the problem of risk control. The method implies that a position be entered contrary to the direction of price movement. Although chart interpretations attempt to remedy this, unusually large losses may result.

7

Seasonal and Cyclic Analysis

Chapter 3 introduced the components of a time series: The trend, the seasonal pattern, the cycle and chance movement, and included various ways of finding the trend using statistical analysis and forecasting techniques. In Chapter 4, this was extended to autoregressive methods of moving averages. It is now time to turn our attention to two other principal components, the seasonal and cyclic movements.

Seasonality appears in almost all commodities, whether crops or nonperishables. The essential habits of the consumer can cause a seasonal pattern in metals as weather does for agricultural products. The seasonal component is a special case of a cycle. It has all the characteristics of a cycle, varying with a constant period of 12 months and fluctuating, when adjusted, equally above and below the average price. Seasonality, a product of a well-defined calendar year, is always present, even when it is not a dominant force in price movement.

Commodity cycles are not as regular as seasonal patterns. The storage and carry-over of large supplies of grain has a dampening effect on farm prices; the shutting of mines will have a slow upward influence on metals. The frequency of cycles can be irregular if they are based on such business decisions as exploring for oil or opening a new mine. Once such decisions are made, they are not likely to be reversed.

Despite what would appear to be unpredictable timing in the making of these decisions, regular cycles have appeared in most commodities. For example, the supply of corn appears to peak every 4 years whereas coffee reserves reach minimum levels normally in 3-year cycles. Of course, these cycles may change due to basic changes in each industry. The magnitude, or amplitude, of the price increase during the high demand periods is not consistent although the base price during the high-surplus times of the cycle may be determined to some degree by government support programs and production costs.

It is important to be able to identify both seasonal and cyclic patterns. The proper moving average speed selected for trend-following will always be out-of-phase with the major cycle. For example, a 40-day cycle can be traded with a trend system using a moving average equal to or less than the half-span of the cycle—in this case, 20 days. Mathematical approaches for finding seasonal patterns are simple; the identification of cycles can use sophisticated trigonometric formulas or moving averages adapted to finding a specific pattern. These methods will be discussed in this chapter followed by some practical applications.

THE SEASONAL PATTERN

Seasonal patterns are easier to find than the longer-term cycles or economic trends, because they must repeat each calendar year. Although any 12-month period can be used to find the seasonal pattern, academic studies usually begin with the new-crop year, just following harvest, when prices tend to be lowest. This approach will make the carrying charges, which increase steadily throughout the crop year, more apparent. For uniformity, this analysis will consider carrying charges as an integral part of price and will always use a calendar year, which assumes no knowledge of where the "season" starts.

United States production is used here as the standard for "seasonal," even though a wheat crop is harvested continuously throughout the year in different parts of the world. Prices are expected to be lower during the U.S. harvest and highest during the middle of the growing season. The influence of world stocks and anticipated harvest from other major producers will serve as an overall dampening or inflating effect on prices, rather than to change the seasonal pattern. Costs of transporting grain to the United States would restrict its direct competition, but the world market will select a supplier at the best price. This has a first-order impact on the U.S. market, which must alter its local price based on export demand.

Other commodities have seasonal price variation based on demand. Silver, although used as an electrical conductor, for jewelry, and as a general hedge against inflation, rises and falls primarily according to photographic demand and is more heavily consumed during the summer months. Almost half of all copper is used in electrical and heat conductivity, with much of it in the form of an alloy with nickel and silver. Its seasonality is heavily related to the housing industry, where it is required for both electrical and water systems. New sources of ore are introduced infrequently, and the possibility of discovery or expansion rarely enters price movement as short-term anticipation. Primary supply problems are related to labor as well as social and political changes in producing countries.

Corn will be used as an example in the following sections due to the clear seasonality of U.S. crops. The economic factors of inflation and recession will be isolated and removed as independent trends in the seasonal studies.

Yearly Averages

The most basic way of measuring or describing seasonality is by the monthly variation from the yearly or crop average, usually calculated as a ratio or percentage. The results of this technique using the 1975 corn prices can be seen in Table 7-1.

It is apparent that the highest prices occur in January and August and the lowest at harvest, confirming expectations of the corn season. The extent of variation throughout the year ranges 13.7% above and below the average. By applying

Table 7-1   Percent of Monthly Corn Prices to Average

	Avg	Jan	Feb	Mar	Apr	May	Jun
Price[a]	2.70	3.07	2.86	2.67	2.68	2.66	2.68
Percent	100.0	113.7	105.9	98.9	99.2	98.5	99.2

	Jul	Aug	Sep	Oct	Nov	Dec
Price	2.72	2.95	2.76	2.62	2.33	2.37
Percent	100.7	109.2	102.2	97.0	86.3	87.8

[a] Mid-month U.S. farm price, 1975.

this method to the 20 years of data for corn shown in Table 7-2, the percentage variation can be shown in the corresponding Table 7-3.

The long-term seasonality, called the *seasonal adjustment factor*, is the monthly average of these percentages, shown at the bottom of Table 7-3 and in Figure 7-1. In both cases, the analysis has been separated into the two periods, 1956–1970 and 1971–1975, to indicate the changing volatility and slight change in pattern. The shaded area represents the range in the percentage variation for the 1956–1970 period, and the broken lines show the corresponding 1971–1975 results. Figure 7-1 shows that the highest and lowest points remained the same, but the sharper fluctuations were reduced to intervals of shorter duration. It is obvious that a seasonal pattern exists but that there is a considerable wide range of

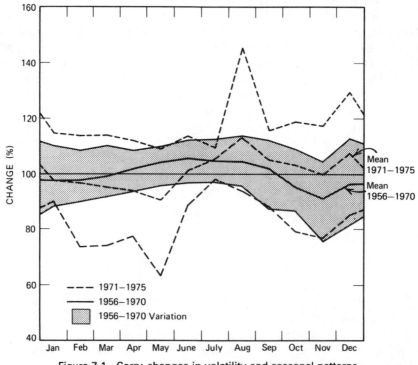

Figure 7-1   Corn: changes in volatility and seasonal patterns.

Table 7-2 Corn Cash Prices

Year	Avg	Jan	Feb	Mar	Apr	May	Jun	Jul	Aug	Sep	Oct	Nov	Dec
1956[a]	1.30	1.14	1.16	1.19	1.32	1.41	1.44	1.45	1.46	1.45	1.12	1.22	1.23
1957	1.25	1.22	1.16	1.18	1.18	1.20	1.20	1.21	1.22	1.13	1.04	.98	1.01
1958	1.10	.97	.98	1.04	1.18	1.20	1.23	1.23	1.24	1.15	1.02	.94	1.04
1959	1.09	1.05	1.06	1.08	1.17	1.18	1.19	1.17	1.17	1.09	.96	1.00	.99
1960	1.03	1.03	1.04	1.04	1.09	1.11	1.11	1.11	1.09	1.07	.97	.82	.92
1961	1.01	.99	1.03	1.04	.98	1.04	1.04	1.06	1.04	1.02	1.00	.91	.94
1962	.98	.94	.95	.96	.98	1.03	1.03	1.02	1.01	1.00	.94	.91	1.00
1963	1.11	1.03	1.05	1.06	1.09	1.12	1.19	1.21	1.21	1.23	1.04	1.02	1.20
1964	1.13	1.12	1.09	1.13	1.15	1.18	1.17	1.14	1.14	1.17	1.05	1.04	1.14
1965	1.18	1.16	1.17	1.19	1.22	1.25	1.26	1.24	1.20	1.18	1.10	1.04	1.13
1966[b]	1.25	1.19	1.20	1.17	1.19	1.21	1.20	1.27	1.34	1.35	1.29	1.26	1.29
1967	1.17	1.28	1.26	1.28	1.26	1.25	1.26	1.21	1.11	1.12	1.04	.97	1.03
1968	1.04	1.04	1.06	1.06	1.06	1.09	1.07	1.04	.99	1.01	.96	1.04	1.05
1969	1.12	1.08	1.09	1.09	1.12	1.19	1.18	1.08	1.18	1.15	1.12	1.07	1.09
1970	1.24	1.12	1.14	1.13	1.15	1.18	1.21	1.24	1.27	1.38	1.34	1.29	1.39
1971	1.27	1.42	1.43	1.43	1.41	1.38	1.43	1.36	1.19	1.11	1.00	.97	1.08
1972	1.17	1.09	1.09	1.10	1.13	1.15	1.13	1.14	1.15	1.22	1.19	1.20	1.42
1973	1.86	1.39	1.35	1.37	1.42	1.16	1.99	2.03	2.68	2.15	2.17	2.18	2.39
1974	2.92	2.59	2.76	2.68	2.41	2.45	2.57	2.91	3.37	3.30	3.45	3.32	3.27
1975	2.70	3.07	2.86	2.67	2.68	2.66	2.68	2.72	2.95	2.76	2.62	2.33	2.37
Average		1.30	1.30	1.29	1.31	1.32	1.38	1.39	1.45	1.40	1.32	1.28	1.34
1976		2.44	2.48	2.50									

[a] 1956–1965 Mid-month Illinois Farm Prices (U of I).
[b] 1966–1975 Mid-month U.S. Farm Prices (CRB Yearbook).

119

Table 7-3 Corn Price as Percentage Average (Annual)

Year	Avg	Jan	Feb	Mar	Apr	May	Jun	Jul	Aug	Sep	Oct	Nov	Dec
1956	1.30	87.6	89.2	91.5	101.5	108.5	110.8	111.5	112.3	111.5	86.1	93.8	94.6
1957	1.25	97.6	92.8	94.4	94.4	96.0	96.0	96.8	97.6	86.9	86.9	75.4	80.8
1958	1.10	88.2	89.1	94.5	107.3	109.1	111.8	111.8	112.7	88.5	92.7	85.4	94.5
1959	1.09	96.3	97.2	99.1	107.3	108.2	109.2	107.3	107.3	100.0	88.1	91.7	90.1
1960	1.03	100.0	101.0	101.0	105.8	107.8	107.8	107.8	105.8	103.9	94.2	79.6	89.3
1961	1.01	98.0	102.0	103.0	97.0	103.0	103.0	104.9	103.0	101.0	99.0	90.1	93.1
1962	.98	95.9	96.9	97.9	100.0	105.1	105.1	104.1	103.1	102.0	95.9	92.8	102.0
1963	1.11	92.8	94.6	95.5	98.2	101.0	107.2	109.0	109.0	110.8	93.7	91.9	99.1
1964	1.13	99.1	96.5	100.0	101.8	104.4	103.5	100.9	100.9	103.5	92.9	92.0	100.9
1965	1.18	98.3	99.1	100.8	103.4	105.9	106.8	105.1	101.7	100.0	93.2	88.1	95.8
1966	1.25	95.2	96.0	93.6	95.2	96.8	96.0	101.6	107.2	108.0	103.2	100.8	103.2
1967	1.17	109.4	107.7	109.4	107.7	106.8	107.7	103.4	94.9	95.7	88.9	82.9	88.0
1968	1.04	100.0	101.9	101.9	101.9	104.8	102.9	100.0	95.2	97.1	92.3	100.0	101.0
1969	1.12	96.4	97.3	97.3	100.0	106.2	105.3	96.4	105.3	102.7	100.0	95.5	97.3
1970	1.24	90.3	91.9	91.1	92.7	95.2	97.6	100.0	102.4	111.3	108.1	104.0	112.1
1956–1970 Avg		96.3	96.9	98.1	100.9	103.9	104.7	104.0	103.9	101.5	94.3	90.9	96.1
1971	1.27	111.8	112.6	112.6	111.0	108.7	112.6	107.1	93.7	87.4	78.7	76.4	85.0
1972	1.17	93.2	93.2	94.0	96.6	98.3	96.6	97.4	98.3	104.3	101.7	102.6	121.4
1973	1.86	74.7	72.6	73.6	76.3	62.4	107.0	109.1	144.1	115.6	116.7	117.2	128.5
1974	2.92	88.7	94.5	91.8	82.5	83.9	88.0	99.6	115.4	113.0	118.1	113.7	112.0
1975	2.70	113.7	105.9	98.9	99.2	98.5	99.2	100.7	109.2	102.2	97.0	86.3	87.8
1971–1975 Avg		96.4	95.8	94.2	93.1	90.1	100.7	102.8	112.1	104.5	102.4	99.2	106.9

possibilities during any one month. All methods of determining seasonality will suffer from those years in which overwhelming factors caused prices to move counter to normal seasonal patterns. A later section will discuss the advantages of distinguishing seasonal and nonseasonal years by "filtering."

A general formula for the monthly average is:[1]

$$APP_i = 100 \left\{ \frac{1}{N} \left[12 \sum_{n=1}^{N} \left(P_{in} \bigg/ \sum_{j=1}^{12} P_{jn} \right) \right] \right\}, \; i = 1, 12$$

where APP_i is the Average Percentage Price in month i
  i is the calendar month from 1 to 12
  N is the number of years in the analysis
  P_{jn} is the average price for month j of year n

This formula may be applied to weekly or quarterly average prices by changing the 12 to 52 or 4, respectively.

The use of an annual average price can obscure a clear seasonal pattern because of its inability to account for a long-term trend in the price of the commodity. If the rate of inflation in the United States is 6%, there will be a tendency for each month to be $\frac{1}{2}$% higher, resulting in a bias toward higher prices at the end of the year. The steady rise in grain prices from 1972–1975, followed by a longer decline in the 1980s, will obscure or even distort the seasonality.

Removing the Trend

Jake Bernstein, most well-known for his seasonal studies,[2] uses the method of first differences to remove the trend from prices before calculating the seasonal adjustment factor. He offers the following steps for determining the cash price seasonal tendencies:

1. Arrange the data used in a table with each row as one year. Columns can be daily, weekly, or monthly although most analyses will use monthly. Average prices are preferred for each period.
2. Compute a second table of month-to-month differences by subtracting month 1 from month 2, month 2 from month 3, and so on. This new table contains *detrended* values.
3. Calculate the sum of the price differences in each column (month) in the new table. Find the average for that column by dividing the number of years of data (columns may have different numbers of entries). This is the average price change for that month.
4. From the table, count the times during each month (column) that prices were up, down, or unchanged. This will give the frequency (expressed as a percent) of movement in each direction.

Bernstein adds the average monthly changes together, expresses the frequency of upwards price changes, and presents the results of corn in Figure 7-2.

[1] David Handmaker, "Low-Frequency Filters for Seasonal Analysis," in Perry J. Kaufman, *Handbook of Futures Markets,* Wiley, New York, 1984.
[2] Jacob Bernstein, *Seasonal Concepts in Futures Trading,* Wiley, New York, 1986.

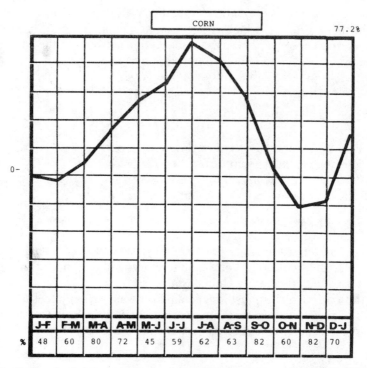

Figure 7-2   Seasonal price tendency in monthly cash average corn prices (1936–1983). (*Source:* Bernstein, J. *Seasonal Concepts in Futures Trading,* Wiley, New York, 1986, p. 31.)

The Method of Link Relatives

Another interesting and important way of identifying the seasonal price variations and separating them from other price components involves the use of *link relatives*. Each month is expressed as a percentage by taking the ratio of that average monthly price to the average price of the preceding month in a manner similar to an index. The results of using 1960 and 1961 corn prices from Table 7-2 are shown in the first two lines of Table 7-4.

After the initial calculation of 1960 and 1961 link relatives, it is necessary to find the average or median (which is preferred if an adequate sample is used) of the monthly ratios expressed in rows (1) and (2). The average in row (3) represents monthly variation as a percentage of change; each calculation is a function of the preceding month. Thus far, this is the same as Bernstein's average monthly price changes, expressed as a percent of the prior price.

In order to establish a fixed base, *chain relatives* are constructed using January as 100; each monthly chain relative is calculated by multiplying its average link relative by the average link relative of the preceding month. The March chain relative is then $1.005 \times 1.025 = 1.030$, and February remains the same since it uses January as a base.

A constant trend throughout the test period can be found by multiplying the December chain relative (4) by the January average link relative. If prices showed

Table 7-4 Corn Prices Expressed as Link Relatives

	Jan	Feb	Mar	Apr	May	Jun	Jul	Aug	Sep	Oct	Nov	Dec
(1) 1960	1.040	1.010	1.000	1.048	1.018	1.000	1.000	.982	.982	.907	.845	1.122
(2) 1961	1.053	1.040	1.010	.942	1.061	1.000	1.019	.981	.981	.980	.910	1.031
(3) Average	1.047	1.025	1.005	.995	1.040	1.000	1.010	.982	.982	.944	.878	1.077
(4) Chain relatives	1.000	1.025	1.030	1.000	1.035	1.040	1.010	.992	.964	.927	.829	.946
(5) Corrected chain relatives	1.000	1.024	1.028	.997	1.032	1.036	1.005	.986	.958	.920	.822	.937
(6) Indices of seasonal variations	1.022	1.046	1.050	1.019	1.054	1058	1.027	1.007	.979	.940	.840	.957

no tendency for either upward or downward movement, the result would be 1.00; but, inflation should cause an upward bias and therefore the results are expected to be higher. From line (4), the December entry times the January entry on line (3) gives .946 × 1.047 = .990, leaving a negative factor of .1% unaccounted. This means that the 1960–1961 years showed a .1% deflation or that the standard inflationary rate was offset by some other economic factor, such as the accumulation of grain stocks by the U.S. government.

The chain relatives must be corrected by adding the negative bias back into the values, using the same technique as in computing compound interest. For example, from 1967–1977, the Consumer Price Index increased from 100 to 175, a total of 75% in 10 years. To calculate the annual compounded growth rate for that period, apply the formula:

$$\text{Compound rate of growth} = \sqrt[N]{\frac{\text{ending value}}{\text{starting value}}} - 1$$

where N is the number of years or the number of periods over which the growth is compounded.

$$R = \sqrt[10]{\frac{175}{100}} - 1$$

$$= 1.05755 - 1$$

$$= .05755$$

This indicates a compounded rate of inflation equal to 5.75% per year. If the rate had been greater than 1.00 instead of .990, the growth rate would be subtracted from each month to offset the upward bias. In this case, the results are added back into the chain relative to compensate for the negative influence. A .1% decline, compounded over 12 consecutive entries gives:

$$R = \sqrt[12]{\frac{.99}{1.00}} - 1$$

$$= .99916 - 1$$

$$= -.00084$$

This is a compounded deflation of about $\frac{8}{100}$ of 1%. The corrected chain relative was found by multiplying the February entry by $(1 + R) = .99916$, March by $(1 + R)^2 = .99832$, and December by $(1 + R)^{11} = .99076$.

The chain relatives have been calculated on a base of January, which was important in order to correct the compounded bias throughout the test period. The final step is to switch the corrected chain relatives to a base of the average value. The average (.97875) of line (5) is used to create line (6), taking the ratio of the corrected chain relative entries to their average. The final result is the *Index of Seasonal Variation*. The accuracy of this result can be proved by averaging the entries of line (6), which will be 1.00. A complete study of seasonals using this method can be found in Smith, *Seasonal Charts For Futures Traders* (Wiley).

The Moving-Average Method

The moving average is a popular means for determining seasonal patterns. Looking again at Table 7-4, take the average quarterly prices for the years 1960–1965 rounded to the nearest cent. More practical results may be obtained by repeating this procedure for monthly prices.

Because every four entries completes a season, the 4-quarter moving average is calculated and recorded in such a way that each value lags $2\frac{1}{2}$ quarters, corresponding to the center of the 4 points used in the calculation. Column (2) of Table 7-5 shows the 4-quarter moving average positioned properly; Figure 7-3 is a plot of both the quarterly corn prices and the lagged moving average. By using the exact number of entries in the season, the moving average line is not affected by any seasonal patterns.

Because there was an even number of points in the moving average, each calculation falls between two original data points. Column (3) of Table 7-5 is constructed by averaging every two adjacent entries in column (2) and placing the results in a position corresponding to the original data points. This avoids smoothing the initial prices. The difference of column (1) minus column (3) is the *seasonal adjustment factor* (4) in cents per bushel; the *seasonal index* (5) is taken as the

Table 7-5 Seasonal Adjustment by the Moving-Average Method

Year	Quarter	Average Quarterly Price	4-Point Moving Average	Corresponding 4-Point Values	Seasonal Adjustment Factor	Seasonal Index
1960	Jan–Mar	104				
	Apr–Jun	110				
	Jul–Sep	109	$103\frac{1}{4}$	103	+6	1.06
	Oct–Dec	90	$102\frac{3}{4}$	$101\frac{3}{4}$	$-11\frac{3}{4}$	.88
1961	Jan–Mar	102	$100\frac{3}{4}$	$100\frac{1}{8}$	$+1\frac{7}{8}$	1.02
	Apr–Jun	102	$99\frac{1}{2}$	$100\frac{1}{8}$	$+1\frac{7}{8}$	1.02
	Jul–Sep	104	$100\frac{3}{4}$	$99\frac{7}{8}$	$+4\frac{1}{8}$	1.04
	Oct–Dec	95	99	$98\frac{7}{8}$	$-3\frac{7}{8}$	.96
1962	Jan–Mar	95	$98\frac{3}{4}$	$98\frac{3}{8}$	$-3\frac{3}{8}$	.96
	Apr–Jun	101	98	98	+3	1.03
	Jul–Sep	101	98	$99\frac{1}{4}$	$+1\frac{3}{4}$	1.02
	Oct–Dec	95	$100\frac{1}{2}$	102	-7	.93
1963	Jan–Mar	105	$103\frac{1}{2}$	$106\frac{1}{8}$	$-1\frac{1}{8}$	.99
	Apr–Jun	113	$108\frac{3}{4}$	$110\frac{3}{4}$	$+2\frac{1}{4}$	1.12
	Jul–Sep	122	$112\frac{1}{4}$	$113\frac{1}{4}$	$+8\frac{3}{4}$	1.08
	Oct–Dec	109	$113\frac{3}{4}$	$114\frac{1}{4}$	$-5\frac{1}{4}$	.95
1964	Jan–Mar	111	$114\frac{3}{4}$	$113\frac{7}{8}$	$-2\frac{7}{8}$	.97
	Apr–Jun	117	113	$113\frac{7}{8}$	$+4\frac{1}{8}$	1.04
	Jul–Sep	115	$112\frac{3}{4}$	$112\frac{7}{8}$	$+1\frac{1}{8}$	1.01
	Oct–Dec	108	$114\frac{1}{4}$	$113\frac{1}{8}$	$-7\frac{1}{8}$	.94
1965	Jan–Mar	117	116	$116\frac{3}{4}$	$-\frac{1}{4}$	1.00
	Apr–Jun	124	$117\frac{1}{2}$	$117\frac{7}{8}$	$+6\frac{3}{8}$	1.05
	Jul–Sep	121	$117\frac{3}{4}$			
	Oct–Dec	109				

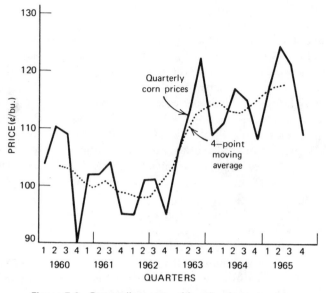

Figure 7-3 Detrending corn with a moving average.

ratio of column (1) divided by column (3). The periodic fluctuation of prices becomes obvious once these values have been recorded. A generalized seasonal adjustment factor and seasonal index is calculated by taking the average of the quarterly entries for the 5 complete years (Table 7-6).

X-11

The seasonal adjustment method X-11 (Census Method II-X-11) is most widely used for creating a seasonally adjusted series of such information as car and housing sales, as well as other consumer products. It is very extensive, involving both an initial estimation and reestimation. Because of the interest expressed, an outline of its steps follows.[3]

1. Calculate a centered 12-month moving average (MA). Subtract this MA from the original series to get an initial detrended seasonal series.
2. Apply a weighted 5-term MA to *each month separately* to get an estimate of the seasonal factors.
3. Compute a centered 12-month MA of the seasonal factors (step 2) for the entire series. Fill in the six missing values at either end by repeating the first and last available MA values. Adjust the seasonal factors from step 2 by subtracting the centered 12-term MA. The *adjusted seasonal factors* will total approximately zero over any 12-month period.
4. Subtract the seasonal factor estimates (step 3) from the initial detrended sea-

---

[3] A more detailed account of X-11 and *Henderson's weighted moving average* (step 9) can be found in Abraham, Bovas, and Johannes Ledolter, *Statistical Methods for Forcasting,* Wiley, New York, pp. 178–191. Their book also includes a computer program for "seasonal exponential smoothing."

Table 7-6 Average Seasonal
Variation Using the
Moving-Average Method

Average of All Years	Seasonal Adjustment Factor	Seasonal Index
Jan–Mar	−1.15	.988
Apr–Jun	+3.53	1.052
Jul–Sep	+4.43	1.042
Oct–Dec	−7.00	.932

sonal series (step 1). This is the *irregular component series* used for outlier adjustment.

5. Adjust the outliers in step 4 by the following procedure:

   a. Compute a 5-year moving standard deviation s of the irregular component series (step 4).

   b. Assign weights to the series components c_i as follows:

   $$0 \text{ if } c_i > 2.5s$$

   linearly scaled from 0 to 1 for $2.5s \geq c_i \geq 1.5s$

   $$1 \text{ if } c_i < 1.5s$$

   Use this weighting function to adjust the detrended series in step 1.

6. Apply a weighted 7-term MA to the adjusted series (step 5) to get the *preliminary seasonal factor*.

7. Repeat step 3 to standardize the seasonal factors.

8. Subtract the series resulting in step 7 from the original series to find the *preliminary seasonally adjusted series*.

9. To get the trend estimate, apply a 9-, 13-, or 23-term *Henderson's weighted moving average*[4] to the seasonally adjusted series (step 8). Subtract this series from the original data to find a second estimate of the detrended series.

10. Apply a weighted seven-term MA to each month separately to get a second estimate of the seasonal component.

11. Repeat step 3 to standardize the *seasonal factors*.

12. Subtract the final seasonal factors from the original series to get the final *seasonally adjusted series*.

Winter's Method

Another technique for forecasting prices with a seasonal component is *Winter's method*, a self-generating, heuristic approach.[5] It assumes that the only relevant

---

[4] A specialized symmetric assignment of weighting values. A specific example can be found in Abraham, Bovas, and Johannes Ledolter, *Statistical Methods for Forcasting*, Wiley, New York, p. 178.
[5] *Winter's method,* as well as other advanced models, can be found in Douglas C. Montgomery and Lynwood A. Johnson, *Forecasting and Time Series*, McGraw Hill, New York, 1976, and Abraham and Ledolter (1983).

characteristics of price movement are the trend and seasonal components, which are represented by the formula

$$X_t = (a + bt)S_t + e_t$$

where X_t is the estimated value at time t
   $(a + bt)$ is a line that represents the trend
   S_t is the seasonal weighting factor
   e_t is the error at each point

If each season is represented by N data points, S_t repeats every N entries and

$$\sum_{t=1}^{N} S_t = N$$

The unique feature of Winter's model is that each new observation is used to correct the previous components a, b, and S_t. Without that feature, it would have no applicability to commodity price forecasting. Starting with 2 or 3 years of price data, the yearly (seasonal) price average can be used to calculate both a and b of the linear trend. Each subsequent year can be used to correct the equation $a + bt$ using any regression analysis. Winter's method actually uses a technique similar to exponential smoothing to estimate the next components a and b individually. The seasonal adjustment factors are assigned by calculating the average variance from the linear component, expressed as a ratio, at each point desired. As more observations are made, each component can be refined. Consequently, it will take on the form of the general long-term seasonal pattern.

Seasonal Filters

Seasonal studies often yield results that are not as clear as desirable; the results may be rejected because of the obvious lack of consistency. David Handmaker shows that separating the data into "analogous" years can give strikingly better results.[6]

For example, crop production is primarily determined by weather. Poor weather will cause sharp rallies during the growing season whereas good weather results in a dull, sideways market. Bad weather develops slowly. A draught is not caused by the first hot day but prolonged days of sunshine and no rain. Delayed planting due to wet fields or a late winter will set the stage for an underdeveloped crop. A trader can see the characteristics of a "weather market" in time to act on it.

In Figure 7-4a, the seasonal corn pattern has been separated into those years with good weather and those with bad weather. In a later study by ContiCommodity,[7] soybean seasonality was separated into "bull" and "bear" years (Figure 7-4b). "Bull" years include all bad weather years but also years with such inci-

---

[6] David Handmaker, "Low Frequency Filters in Seasonal Analysis," *Journal of Futures Markets*, Vol. 1, No. 3, Wiley, New York, 1981.

[7] ContiCommodity, *Seasonalty in Agricultural Futures Markets*, ContiCommodity Services, Chicago, 1983.

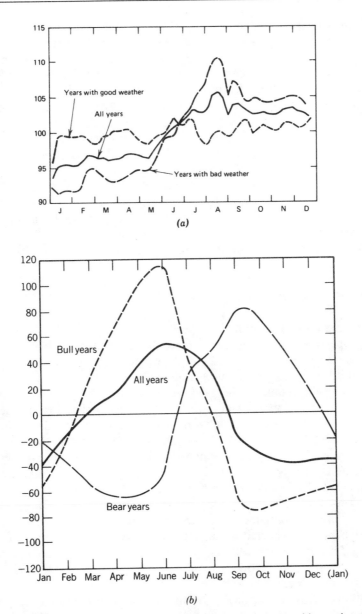

Figure 7-4 (*a*) Corn price seasonality separated into all years, years with good weather, and years with bad weather. (*b*) Soybeans (10 years) shown with separate bull years (5 years) and bear years (5 years).

dents as the 1973 Soviet grain sale. Because other events are not confined to the growing months, they may distort rather than clarify the patterns. "Bear" would represent mostly good weather patterns; however, markets that decline steadily all year following a bull market would also be included.

During the bad weather years, the corn chart shows a prolonged rise during the primary growing months, May through August. The study of bull years for soybeans shows a longer sustained rise from the beginning of the new crop in October into the following June. In the case of good weather and bear markets, corn shows a rise from May to June, some sideways hesitation from June to July (possibly the last anticipation of bad weather), then a return to previous price levels. Soybeans show steady declines through April and then a short rally through the summer.

The corn analysis shows a critical point around July 1, when the market decides that the weather is not a factor. The soybean analysis is completely different showing nearly the opposite patterns for bull and bear markets. Because the resulting pattern of combining both bull and bear markets looks very similar to the bull pattern, the magnitude of the bull moves must overwhelm the overall picture. In fact, the magnitude of the bull moves are often three to four times greater than the bear markets.

Separate studies of similar years can show clear patterns for many products. This approach need not be limited to seasonality but may be applied to identify a pattern that is likely to repeat for a specific set of events.

Seasonals for Trading

Whatever method is used to find the seasonal pattern, it is equally important to apply it properly when trading. Select a commodity that has a dominant seasonal pattern. The crops always qualify, with the exception of potatoes which are fully stored and do not react to the harvest depression. Livestock tends to be more complex than other commodities because of the joint dependency on both feed grain prices as well as their own production and consumption factors. Both crops and livestock have primarily supply-oriented seasonal trends, depressed at harvest and highest during the growing months—or depressed in the fall when the supply becomes greatest due to liquidation before winter. Metals patterns are caused by demand since they have no dependence on weather and production is usually constant. The summer months still see the highest prices due to increased consumption—copper in housing and silver in photography.

Select a delivery month most likely to reflect the pattern to be traded. If a sharp rise in soybeans is expected in July, trade the August contract. Prices of the November delivery, which will also be active, will not move as much because it is both deferred and a new crop. In more extreme cases, February pork bellies do not reflect events occurring in the previous July or August contracts.

Exceptions occur in seasonal patterns, as they do in any model. There are events that may overwhelm normal seasonality such as runaway interest rates or inflation, rapid change in the U.S. dollar, or Soviet grain embargoes. Even though the seasonal variation still exists, the size of the price change resulting from these other factors is much greater and tends to obscure the seasonals. It is usually easy to recognize a nonseasonal pattern—prices simply go steadily up when they normally go down, or down when they are expected to go up. From 1972–1974, corn prices increased steadily with only small adjustments in September and October. Once this variation occurs, it is necessary to wait until another season has reestablished the normal pattern.

The systems and methods that follow are based entirely on seasonal patterns and may be used alone or to filter other methods.

Seasonal Studies and Key Dates

Most agricultural commodities exhibit traditional, reliable price moves at one or more periods throughout the year. The grains grown in the Northern Hemisphere have a high likelihood of a rally during the late spring and early summer, when the chance of draught will have the greatest effect on yield. When prices show the normal harvest lows, followed by a modest rise and sideways pattern throughout the winter, the potential is good for a rally during the early growing season. Because prices start at relatively low levels, the risk is small. Once prices have moved higher, there is rarely a season where a short sale of corn, soybeans, cotton, or sugar will not net a good profit within the 2 months before harvest begins.

Seasonal studies are intended to provide information on when the largest move will occur. The following studies, (1) Grushcow and Smith (1980), (2) ContiCommodity (1983), and (3) Bernstein (1986) will be used to compare the seasonals in some of the more interesting commodities. A summary of the results is shown in Table 7-7. Each study offers a different perspective on seasonality. Grushcow and Smith analyze both cash and individual futures markets over a fairly long period and present complete statistics; ContiCommodity used mostly the past 10 years, but included a unique volatility analysis; Bernstein, the most recently published study, gave the most complete background on calculations, including separate studies of bullish and bearish years and an exceptionally long time period for cash market analysis.

The number of years in the seasonal analysis counts heavily in determining the normal patterns. As Table 7-7 shows, the ContiCommodity results, based on a maximum of 10 years, is often quite different from the other two studies. For trading safety, it would be best to select those patterns that have proved reliable over many years; however, because inconsistency in the past 10 years cannot be ignored, a trader must be able to identify a nonseasonal, bullish, or bearish pattern.

The periods that seem consistent throughout all studies are:

Corn and soybeans. September and October major harvest pressure.

Cattle. End of the year liquidation and mid-winter rally.

Coffee and juice. No common moves.

Some commodities are clearly more seasonally consistent than others. Both the coffee and orange juice markets were expected to show patterns that reflect a rise as the possibilities of a freeze increase. It must be that the "normal" seasonality of these products is distorted by the inconsistent and highly volatile periods which follow a freeze. These markets would be candidates for an "analogous years" study.

The three studies shown here, as well as most others, include recommended trades based on key dates, which reflect the patterns in Table 7-7. By selecting those trades common to all of them, you have found those that are most reliable. In a summary by Bernstein, which catalogues commodities by those months with the highest reliability, the agricultural products are clearly the most seasonal. The only nonagricultural commodity that shows any consistent seasonality is copper.

Table 7-7 Results of Seasonal Studies

	J-F	F-M	M-A	A-M	M-J	J-J	J-A	A-S	S-O	O-N	N-D	D-J
					Corn							
24 years[a]	.5	−1.1	1.6	3.6	3.4	.5	1.5	−5.3	−8.5	−1.3	.5	2.1
10 years[b]	2.2	−1.3	−2.3	−1.2	2.3	7.7	4.5	1.4	−7.5	−1.3	−6.4	1.8
46 years[c]	−.6	2.0	3.0	2.9	2.3	3.8	−1.5	−3.2	−6.7	−3.7	5.4	1.5
%[a]	58	58	67	92	50	46	50	54	88	63	83	71
%[c]	52	60	80	72	45	59	62	63	82	60	82	70
					Soybeans							
24 years[a]	7.4	7.5	8.4	9.5	6.4	−.7	−1.3	−25.8	−7.5	4.2	5.8	.3
10 years[b]	−2.3	21.1	23.7	12.6	20.0	14.7	−11.7	−14.9	−46.7	−9.8	−8.9	2.1
42 years[cd]	3	11	8	8	3	−1	−5	−20	−8	10	3	2
%[a]	67	50	67	50	42	38	58	83	63	75	67	79
%[c]	62	53	57	51	42	37	64	74	64	76	72	70
					Cattle							
25 years[a]	−.4	.1	.6	.1	−.1	.4	.4	−.3	−.4	−.5	−.1	.4
10 years[b]	1.4	.2	.8	1.8	.4	−1.2	−.4	−.7	−1.3	−.5	−.3	−.2
50 years[cd]	1	12	13	4	−1	7	3	4	−9	−9	−2	2
%[a]	64	60	48	44	56	60	56	44	76	64	52	72
%[c]	52	70	59	52	52	59	55	42	60	71	51	62

Orange juice

10 years[a]	-1.6	-.1	-.3	-.9	-.9	-.3	.1	-.2	1.2	-2.3	-.3	1.7
10 years[b]	-1.9	2.4	-1.1	-.7	.0	1.6	1.8	2.3	.2	.0	.0	-4.7
34 years[c]	27	14	4	-3	-8	-1	1	3	-2	-2	-13	-4
%[a]	78	45	67	56	45	45	56	67	45	45	56	56
%[c]	61	64	50	58	50	65	66	81	61	40	67	62

Coffee

22 years[a]	-.2	.9	-.5	-.4	.1	.1	-.7	-.3	.1	.3	-.5	.1
8 years[b]	-6.5	1.8	7.6	5.0	-.3	3.3	-11.5	-2.0	4.3	-8.6	4.7	2.2
53 years[cd]	0	-10	2	-4	1	4	18	2	19	-10	-4	-2
%[a]	41	64	50	50	59	46	46	55	41	64	50	77
%[c]	56	58	43	53	50	48	56	56	51	59	54	49

[a] Grushcow and Smith (change in price).
[b] ContiCommodity (% change in seasonal factor).
[c] Bernstein (% change in seasonal factor).
[d] Approximate values.
% refers to the reliability of monthly seasonality.

Table 7-8 Seasonal Calendar

	Mar Corn	May Corn	Jul Corn	Sep Corn	Dec Corn	Mar Wheat	May Wheat	Jul Wheat	Sep Wheat	Dec Wheat	Mar Oats	May Oats	Jul Oats	Sep Oats	Dec Oats	Jan Soybeans	Mar Soybeans	May Soybeans
1 Jan				76			29				66	66					29	
2											66			66				
3	66							22	23	37							66	
4							27			33	37						37	
5 Feb						31		35	37	31								66
6		27				64				75	66							
7	35											31	37	33				
8	35	29				22	27				27						70	
9 Mar	66						35		31	25		23	37	37			35	
10								27	37	31								
11			72			35		35	23	29								
12																		37
13 Apr			66	66			72		79			76	64	81				78
14		77										66	64					70
15						37			33									35
16						33								25	37			26
17		27						22				22						
18 May						37			29	18		83						76
19	35											82	76					
20	70			66			33											
21						37	33										66	
22 Jun				37					31	29				37		64	35	
23	33		33	35		76			35	28			37	37				
24	76			76		33			64	82							70	
25	33			27	36				37	29						76		64
26 Jul	66		70	66	63								64					
27			66						64					29	26			
28		35						64						35		13		23
29	22	22			21									31		25	17	29
30		27		23	36		27											
31 Aug					35	33												
32												70		66				
33												66		66				
34						83		64					64	66	66	37		
35 Sep				35		72		70	64			66		37				
36								64										66
37			31									70				29		29
38	29				31									35			33	
39																		
40 Oct												64		64	76			64
41						66		72		64					25			35
42				63								66						
43						27	33				70							
44 Nov			27	66	37	33		26				72			31	33		
45									35					79	64			
46															29	33	35	
47			64					64										
48 Dec						29		35						66	64			
49	18		35						33					66				
50											35			29	66	25		
51											64			35	35	27	37	
52						66												

Table 7-8   Seasonal Calendar (cont.)

Jul Soybeans	Aug Soybeans	Sep Soybeans	Nov Soybeans	Jan Soybean Meal	Mar Soybean Meal	May Soybean Meal	Jul Soybean Meal	Sep Soybean Meal	Dec Soybean Meal	Mar Soybean Oil	May Soybean Oil	Jul Soybean Oil	Sep Soybean Oil	Dec Soybean Oil	Feb Live Cattle	Apr Live Cattle	Jun Live Cattle	Aug Live Cattle	Oct Live Cattle
37							33			35									
64	64										66					64			
								29			77	66					64		
	37					33			66	66					66			66	
	64	70			28			37	37	70	64	62			64		76		
					37										66			75	
64	64												66		76			64	
							35			33								37	
	35					66	35	23	23	35						77	76	66	
					66	64		70		70	66						66	66	66
						37	35									66	70		
37										33							37		
	64					70	70			72					72	76	71		
64			63					70	66						64	66	76		
	25								37								64	75	66
23					29	17				33		66							
		36						29	29	70					64			66	
75										27							64		33
70	64	66				64			70						70				66
								64	75	27		33					70	75	66
23	33	37		66		66	31		31		27	33	22		64		64		
64									76			33	66	66					
37				64	81	66		66	66	70	33		66	66					33
	70			72						72								66	
75		66				64		66	70		72		72	66	77		73		
	64			66		76		64						37				77	
		63		66	29			64					33						
	33	25	15	33	20	35		29	25		29								
			28				35	35				64							
							35	35										66	
					37			37											
							70	75		33									
	37				37		29	35	27	64		29	10						37
64	35					64				64			64	66	35			70	
29		66				29		76	66	27				37					
									37					66					
														37					
64		36	72											35	33				
35		73		66		36		76	64					72					
		35						23							27	35	31		
								64						33	35				
64		77	66		70									70	72	13	64		
	76		75		64									64	70	75			
			66						16					66	70	76			
	37			35			37	29	66			27				66			
			66	66	72			66	33			33							
								70											
33	29			35	31			66	29			66	66						
37	35	31						11	27	22		64			66				

135

Table 7-8 Seasonal Calendar (cont.)

	Dec Live Cattle	Mar Feeder Cattle	Apr Feeder Cattle	Sep Feeder Cattle	Oct Feeder Cattle	Nov Feeder Cattle	Feb Live Hogs	Apr Live Hogs	Jun Live Hogs	Jul Live Hogs	Aug Live Hogs	Oct Live Hogs	Dec Live Hogs	Feb Pork Bellies	Mar Pork Bellies	May Pork Bellies	Jul Pork Bellies	Aug Pork Bellies	Mar Cocoa	May Cocoa	Jul Cocoa	Dec Cocoa
1 Jan									66					64			37					
2							70	77		76				70	66							33
3			66						66	80	76				66	64	64		35			
4									73	64						66				62		
5 Feb		70								64	66			64	81							
6	66						64								37					64		
7																	35			35	33	
8		20		36			35	66										66		66		
9 Mar	80	80	70	63				66									70			75	66	
10				63	70																	
11			35					33										64	35	27	27	
12		37		63									73				66				68	
13 Apr									66			70	64					79				
14	72		90	80	63	90		77	78	87			71		33			31			38	
15			80	81	72	66							33		66			78		66		
16				81											23			23			22	38
17												64	64									
18 May				30	33	30			66	73												
19				27					80									27	37	29	27	
20			70									29	31				35			64	66	
21			63	81	80												17	35				33
22 Jun					77					35	26	27	35				35	23				
23	33		36		30				31						37				37			33
24	70				36				70					70			70				66	
25				72	63						64	66					70		76	77		
26 Jul	66			72	66						35				66		75					72
27				36	80							64							64	77	66	72
28				36	27							35						66			77	64
29												35	37									
30				27																		
31 Aug				36							66						64			64	66	
32				72	63							76	66	72						64		36
33				36								70		76	66			64		33		
34				63	30								37	38						64	83	
35 Sep	70			63	80								73	66	70	66	81			70		77
36				63	72	70								66							33	66
37						70									37							
38						30																
39	27																			33		
40 Oct	33				70								31	29			33	29	23			
41														27	31					29	33	
42	35				36													37	70			
43	22													66	33		75				72	64
44 Nov							82	83	71					72	64	66	72	66	70	29		
45	70													77	70			80	25	33	33	
46		70					84							77								27
47																						
48 Dec							64							35			35		64	66		72
49	33		66										66									
50														76		37	66	64				
51									64					73			77	76				
52																						

Table 7-8 Seasonal Calendar (cont.)

Jan Orange Juice	May Orange Juice	Sep Orange Juice	Nov Orange Juice	Mar Sugar	May Sugar	Jul Sugar	Oct Sugar	Mar Coffee	May Coffee	Jul Coffee	Sep Coffee	Dec Coffee	Mar Cotton	May Cotton	Jul Cotton	Oct Cotton	Dec Cotton	Jan Lumber	Mar Lumber	May Lumber	Jul Lumber	Sep Lumber	Nov Lumber
31	35	29								63				75	87	86			66				
	35					77	70	63		66						75	66					28	
37								27	18	27						64		30		69			
	35			35					66	75					35	33				69	64		
					35			63		63	72	81							71	69	69	66	
					70				66	91	75	63							15	64	63		
		35								72	33	70	35	37	18	37							76
	35	29	33	62	72	35		36	25		66		64	64	70	68			21	7	28	72	28
						70	66					72							30		35	16	
25	31		64	29	37	36	36	33		33					37	35	31					33	
26	29	12	16		27	37	36	80	75		83	72			35				35	69			30
			22							66	33				70	75					15	25	35
31	64					70				75	36	36										36	7
31		37	37				36		66	66	66	72			66							33	
75				33	37						63	63									70		
75	64	76	76						63	66	75	27		29	26								
																	30						
						77	33	36		72	72	80		75		68		27		30	7	25	23
							35				72	66	63		76		70			35	33		35
68		35								36	75	72	72		70	66	23					25	
68										66		36	35		37	31	35	69			28	83	14
33		64					64					29				29					78	33	83
35			33	33				36	36		33				70		37		66				35
		35				33	36						27	70			75	69				75	64
66	35	27			29			36			33		36		64								
					35							36	64										
73		66										36				68		37	30				35
	64				29								70		35		72		15	35			28
		64						36	63			66			76				?			66	71
									36				64										
	70							63		66	80												28
37											72	66	63	37		37							71
73			66							27		36	64	64		37						66	
73		82	66			76		36	75			36				66							
		70	66							72		66	36		35	35			30				69
							36				63	33	63	35	35	37		25	7			25	28
75						27	37	36	63	66		63	23	37	29	12			35	23			28
												63					23						
81	82		64	11		35		36	33			81						33					28
		64															81	66	75				
	76				72	66	70	68	36			63	27	70	68	68		76					
75	64				66	72	64	75		66	75	83				37					69		28
80						72		90	66	75	83	63	64	64					66	66	71	76	71
									63	63													71
				70		72	70	63		63	66		35	35	35	37	35	84	69	69			64
						66	64								63	64	66						64
					64					72	75	75	66		35	37							
					64	70					72	66	63						33			30	
			66	33				72	83	83	75	63	64		35				69		76	85	83
26	18			33		35				63											76	66	

137

Although there may be interesting arguments for the forces of demand on silver, currencies, and financial markets, their inconsistency is apparent and they are not candidates for seasonal trading.

Seasonal Calendar. Because Bernstein's work covers the cash markets over an extremely long period, it must be considered the most reliable source of basic seasonal patterns. Table 7-8 is part of the weekly seasonal calendar, which appears in *Seasonal Concepts in Futures Trading*. The numbers that appear show those weeks with consistent historic moves. Weeks of 64% and higher represent upwards moves; weeks of 36% and lower display downward trends. This calendar can be extremely useful when combined with some simple trading logic which asks, "Is the market acting in a seasonal manner?" before the position is entered.

CYCLES

The cycle as a trading tool has raised many questions among traders. There is no doubt that cycles exist as an integral part of all price movement. It is one of the three primary components of fundamental analysis along with the trend and seasonal components, but the ability to profit from their use has been subject to many studies. Cycles come in many forms—seasonality, production startup and shutdown, inventory or stocks, behavioral, and astronomical. Seasonality is a special case of a calendar cycle. Some of the cycles are clearly *periodic*, having regular intervals between peaks and valleys; others are more uniform in their *amplitude* or height but irregular in period. The most definitive cycle remains the seasonal, which is determined by periodic physical phenomena.

The second part of this chapter will discuss the major commodity cycles that result from business decisions, government programs, and long-term commodity characteristics. Short-term cycles are usually attributed to behavior and will be covered in a later chapter on pattern recognition. There are a few important ways to find the cycle, the most common being *trigonometric curve fitting* and *Fourier (spectral) analysis*. Both will require a computer and will be explained in the following sections. Examples of solutions will be included in the explanation of the methods and applications will follow. Computer programs that solve the trigonometric problems can be found in Appendix 4 along with additional examples.

Observing the Cycle

Before selecting a commodity for cycle analysis, it is necessary to observe that a dominant cycle exists. This is best done for commodities in which you have reason to believe that there are fundamental and/or industrial reasons for cycles. The basis for a cycle could be the change in stocks, breeding patterns, seasonality, or other economic factors. Figure 7-5 shows a clear 9 to 11 month cycle in live cattle futures prices[8] over the past 6 years. The peaks and valleys vary by plus or minus 1 month, making the pattern reliable for use as part of a trading strategy.

[8] Jacob Bernstein, "Cyclic and Seasonal Price Tendencies in Meat and Livestock Markets," in Todd Lofton (Ed.), *Trading Tactics*, Chicago Mercantile Exchange, Chicago, 1986.

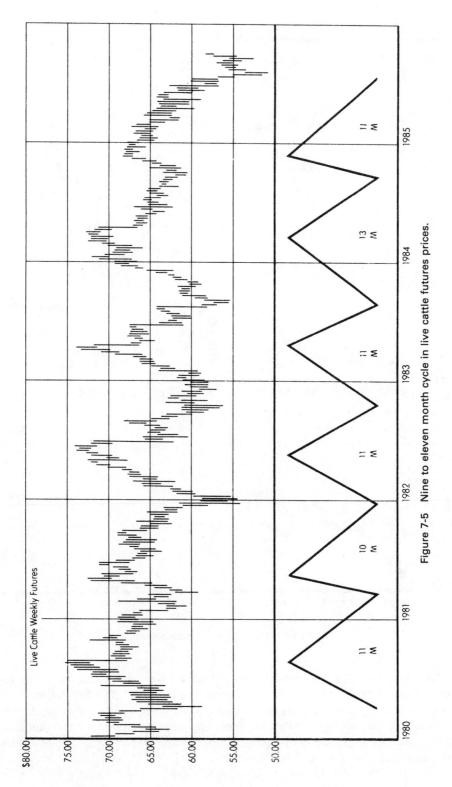

Figure 7-5   Nine to eleven month cycle in live cattle futures prices.

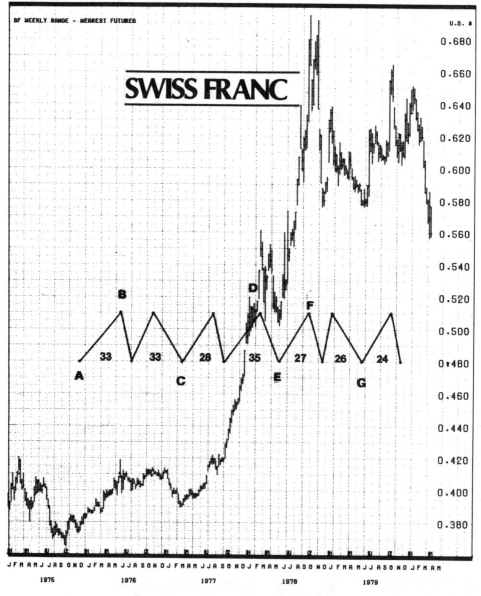

Figure 7-6 Cycles in Swiss franc futures.

The Swiss franc cycle demonstrated in Figure 7-6 is quite different.[9] It ranges from 24 to 35 weeks with a 40% variance compared to 20% for cattle. Most important, the cycle in the Swiss franc cannot be related to any specific fundamental reason. Given enough variance, a repeating pattern can be found in any data. Confidence in trading a cycle pattern is based on the reason for its existence and the confidence that it should continue.

[9] Jacob Bernstein, *The Handbook of Commodity Cycles*, Wiley, New York, 1982.

The most newsworthy cycles have probably been the least practical or accurate, such as the Kondratieff wave, which shows a 54-year economic cycle. Unfortunately, a 10% shift in any one peak could cause a trading signal to buy or sell 5 years too soon. Determining cycles for any commodity has the same problem—the actual market will never correspond exactly to the predicted peaks and valleys.

The dominant half-cycle can be found by locating the obvious price peaks and valleys, then averaging the distance between them. A convenient tool for estimating the cycle length is the Ehrlich Cycle Finder.[10] It is an expanding device with evenly spaced points, allowing you to align the peaks and valleys to observe the consistency in the cycle. For finding a single pattern, it is just as good as some of the high-powered mathematics that follows.

Cycles can be obscured by other price patterns. A strong trend, such as the one in Swiss francs (Figure 7-6) or the seasonality of crops, may overwhelm a less pronounced cycle. Proper cycle identification will remove these factors by detrending and by deseasonalizing. The resulting data will then be analyzed and the trend and seasonal factors added back once the cycle has been found. To find a subcycle, the primary cycle may be removed and a second cycle analysis performed on the data. The methods that follow (trigonometric regression and spectral analysis) locate the dominant cycles using integrated processes.[11]

Trigonometric Price Analysis

Most cycles can be found using the trigonometric functions *sine* and *cosine*. These functions are also called *periodic waves* because they repeat every 360° or 2 radians (where $\pi = 3.141592$). Because radians can be converted to degrees using the relationship

$$1 \text{ degree} = \frac{2\pi}{360}$$

all work that follows will be in degrees. Some other necessary terms are:

Amplitude (a): The height of the wave from the center (x = axis).

Frequency (ω): The number of wavelengths that repeat every 360°, calculated as $\omega = 1/T$.

Period (T): The number of time units necessary to complete one wavelength (cycle).

A simple sine wave fluctuates back and forth from +1 to −1 (0, +1, 0, −1, 0) for each cycle (one wavelength) as the degrees increase from 0° to 360° (see Figure 7-7). To relate the wavelength to a specific distance in boxes (on graph paper), simply divide 360° by the number of boxes in a full wavelength, resulting in the box size (in degrees). For example, a 100-box cycle would give a value of 3.6° to

[10] Ehrlich Cycle Finder Company, 2220 Noyes Street, Evanston, IL 60201.
[11] A more specific presentation of trigonometric curve fitting can be found in Claude Cleeton, *The Art of Independent Investing*, Prentice-Hall, Englewood Cliffs, NJ, 1976, Chapter 8. The material covered in this section is carried further in that work.

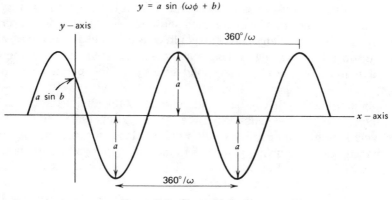

Figure 7-7   Sinusoidal wave.

each box. The *wavelength* can be changed to other than 360° by using the frequency as a multiplier of the angle of the sine wave

$$\sin \omega\phi$$

If $\omega > 1$, the frequency increases and the wavelength shortens to less than 360°; if $\omega < 1$, the frequency decreases and the wavelength increases. Because ω is the frequency, it gives the number of wavelengths in each 360° cycle. To change the *phase* of the wave (the starting point), the value b is added to the angle

$$\sin (\omega\phi + b)$$

If b is 180°, the sine wave will start in the second half of the cycle; b serves to shift the wave to the left. The *amplitude* can be changed by multiplying the resulting value by a constant a. Because the sine ranges from $+1$ to -1, the new range will be $+a$ to $-a$ (Figure 7-8). This is written $a\sin(\omega\phi + b)$.

There are few examples of commodity-price movement that can be represented

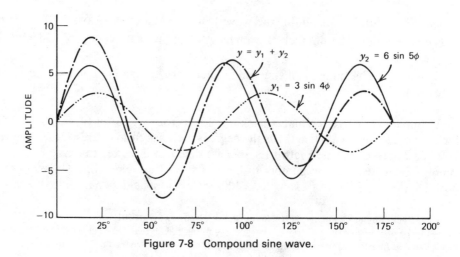

Figure 7-8   Compound sine wave.

by a single wave; thus, two sine waves must be added together to form a *compound wave*:

$$y = a_1 \sin(\omega_1\phi + b_2) + a_2 \sin(\omega_2\phi + b_2)$$

Each set of characteristic variables, a_1, ω_1, b_1, and a_2, ω_2, b_2, can be different, but both waves are measured at the same point ϕ at the same time. Consider an example that lets the phase constants b_1 and b_2 be zero:

$$y_1 = 3 \sin 4\phi$$

$$y_2 = 5 \sin 6\phi$$

$$y = y_1 + y_2$$

Figure 7-8 shows the individual regular waves y_1 and y_2, and the compound wave y over the interval 0° to 180°. Note that both y_1 and y_2 began the normal upward cycle at 0°; but by 180°, they are perfectly out-of-phase. During the next 180°, the two waves come back into phase.

When combining periodic waves, it is useful to know the maximum and minimum amplitude of the resulting wave. Because the peaks of the two elementary waves do not necessarily fall at the same point, the maximum amplitude of either wave may not be reached. A mathematical technique, called *differentiation*, is used to find the maximum and minimum amplitudes. The first derivative, with respect to angle ϕ, is written $dy/d\phi$ or y', where y is the formula to be differentiated. The rules are:

$$\frac{d}{d\phi}(\sin \phi) = \cos \phi; \qquad \frac{d}{d\phi}(\cos \phi) = -\sin \phi$$

$$\frac{d}{d\phi}(\sin \omega\phi) = \omega \cos \omega\phi$$

$$\frac{d}{d\phi}(\sin(\omega\phi + b)) = \omega \cos(\omega\phi + b)$$

$$\frac{d}{d\phi}(a_1\sin(\omega_1\phi + b_1) + a_2\sin(\omega_2\phi + b_2))$$

$$= a_1\omega_1\cos(\omega_1\phi + b_1) + a_2\omega_2\cos(\omega_2\phi + b_2)$$

Applying this method to the previous example,

$$y = 3 \sin 4\phi + 6 \sin 5\phi$$

$$\frac{dy}{d\phi} = y' = 12 \cos 4\phi + 30 \cos 5\phi$$

The points of maximum and/or minimum value occur when $y' = 0$. For $y_1' = 12 \cos 4\phi$, the maxima and minima occur when $4\phi = 90°$ and 270 ($\phi = 22\frac{1}{2}°$ and $67\frac{1}{2}°$) (Figure 7-8). For $y_2' = 30 \cos 5\phi$, the maximum and minimum values occur at $5\phi = 90°$ and $270°$ ($\phi = 18°$ and $54°$). It must be pointed out that the first derivative identifies the location of the extreme highs and lows, but does not tell which one is the maximum and which is the minimum. The second derivative, y'', calculated by taking the derivative of y', is used for this purpose as follows:

If $y'(x) = 0$ and $y''(x) > 0$, then $y(x)$ is a minimum.

If $y'(x) = 0$ and $y''(x) < 0$, then $y(x)$ is a maximum.

Then, $y_1 = 22\frac{1}{2}°$ and $y_2 = 18°$ are maxima and $y_1 = 67\frac{1}{2}°$ and $y_2 = 54°$ are minima.

Anyone interested in pursuing the analysis of extrema will find more complete discussions in a text on calculus. Rather than concentrating on these theoretical aspects of curves[11] consider a practical example of finding a cycle in the price of scrap copper, shown in Table 7-9 and charted in Figure 7-9. The price peaks seem evenly spaced, occurring at mid-1966, January 1970, and January 1974, about 4 years apart. The solutions to these problems are tedious; therefore, calculations will be performed using the computer programs in Appendix 4.

The results obtained by using actual copper prices will not be as clear as using fictitious data. It is important to be able to understand the significance of practical results and apply them effectively.

Because trigonometric curves fluctuate above and below a horizontal line of value zero, the first step is to detrend the data using the least-squares method. This results in the equation for a straight line representing the upward bias of the data. The value of the detrending line is then subtracted from the original data to produce copper prices that vary equally above and below the line from positive to negative values.

Table 7-9 Dealer's Buying Price, No. 2
Heavy Copper Scrap at New York[a]

Year	Average Quarterly Price (¢/lb)			
	1st	2nd	3rd	4th
1963	22.12	22.46	22.17	22.00
1964	23.18	24.56	25.57	30.59
1965	28.23	33.77	35.90	40.05
1966	46.22	51.48	40.76	40.16
1967	36.51	29.30	30.36	36.42
1968	39.75	30.07	29.08	32.13
1969	38.94	42.95	43.38	46.23
1970	47.70	46.98	35.78	27.35
1971	25.40	29.45	27.15	28.48
1972	32.74	33.53	30.01	29.25
1973	36.82	45.07	55.13	65.51
1974	66.56	70.06	47.30	35.62
1975	32.06	31.46	35.75	36.46
1976	38.22	43.24	45.46	38.96
1977	37.08	38.72	34.01	33.00
1978	35.07	40.23	41.63	44.95
1979	51.12	63.71	59.56	63.38

[a] Based on prices from the American Metal Market.

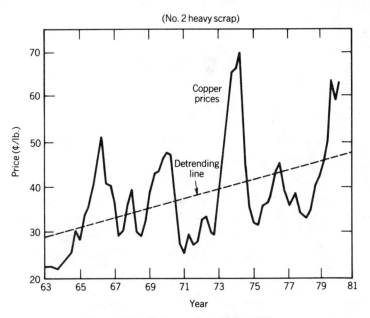

(No. 2 heavy scrap)

Figure 7-9   Copper prices 1963–1979.

The straight line $y = a + bx$, which best represents the trend, can be found by solving the least-squares equations:

$$b = \frac{N\Sigma xy - \Sigma x\Sigma y}{N\Sigma x^2 - (\Sigma x)^2}$$

$$a = \frac{1}{N}(\Sigma y - b\Sigma x)$$

To do this, let x be the date and y be the price on that date. For convenience, instead of letting $x = 1967, 1967\frac{1}{4}, 1967\frac{1}{2}, \ldots$, let $x = 1, 2, 3, \ldots$. The solution, using a computer program in Appendix 2 (also an integral part of the programs in Appendix 4) or the hand-calculation method, is

$$y = 28.89 + .267x$$

Figure 7-9 displays the original copper prices and the regression line. The original prices can now be "detrended" using the equation above, subtracting the line values from the corresponding prices. Complete step-by-step results for this example can be found in Appendix 4. The detrended data is now used in the general trigonometric single-frequency wave:

$$y_t = a \cos \omega t + b \sin \omega t$$

The variable t replaces ϕ in order to consider the angle in integer units rather than in degrees. This will be more convenient to visualize and to chart.

To find the frequency ω, it will be necessary to first solve the equation:

$$\cos \omega - \tfrac{1}{2}\alpha = 0$$

using the system of equations,

$$\alpha y_2 = y_1 + y_3$$

$$\alpha y_3 = y_2 + y_4$$

$$\vdots$$

$$\alpha y_{n-1} = y_{n-2} + y_n$$

This is expressed as a summation (similar to least-squares) in which the values for c and d must be found:

$$\alpha \Sigma c^2 = \Sigma cd$$

where $c = y_n$ and $d = y_{n-1} + y_{n+1}$. Summing the detrended values c^2 and cd gives $\Sigma c^2 = 6338.4$ and $\Sigma cd = 9282.2$, resulting in $\alpha = 1.464$. The value for α is substituted into the intermediate equation and solved for the frequency ω:

$$\cos \omega - \tfrac{1}{2}(1.464) = 0$$

$$\cos \omega = .732$$

$$\omega = 42.9$$

The period T is $360/42.9 = 8.4$ calendar quarters. The last step in solving the equation for a single frequency is to write the normal equations:

$$a\Sigma \cos^2 \omega t + b\Sigma \cos \omega t \sin \omega t = \Sigma y_t \cos \omega t$$

$$a\Sigma \sin \omega t \cos \omega t + b\Sigma \sin^2 \omega t = \Sigma y_t \sin \omega t$$

and solve for a and b, where $t = 1, \ldots, 40$, and $\omega = 42.9$. As in the other solutions, a computer program is best for finding the sums (using detrended data) necessary to solve the equations. The sums are

$$\Sigma \cos^2 \omega t \qquad \Sigma \sin \omega t \cos \omega t \qquad \Sigma y_t \cos \omega t$$

$$\Sigma \sin^2 \omega t \qquad \Sigma y_t \sin \omega t$$

Then, a and b can be found by substituting in the following equations:

$$b = \frac{\Sigma y_t \sin \omega t \Sigma \cos^2 \omega t - \Sigma y_t \cos \omega t}{\Sigma \sin^2 \omega t \Sigma \cos^2 \omega t - \Sigma \cos \omega t \sin \omega t}$$

$$a = \frac{\Sigma y_t \cos \omega t - b\Sigma \cos \omega t \sin \omega t}{\Sigma \cos^2 \omega t}$$

The results $a = -.603$ and $b = 1.831$ give the single-frequency curve as:

$$y_t = -.603 \cos 42.9t + 1.831 \sin 42.1t$$

Taking $t = 1$ to be 1967 and $t = 68$ to be $1979\tfrac{3}{4}$ and adding back the trend, the resulting periodic curve is shown in Figure 7-10.

The single-frequency curve shown in Figure 7-10 matches seven out of the eight peaks in copper; however, it is not much more than could have been done using the Ehrlich Cycle Finder mentioned in the previous section. A single-frequency curve can be created simply by identifying the most dominant peaks, averaging the distance (period), and applying the single-frequency formula.

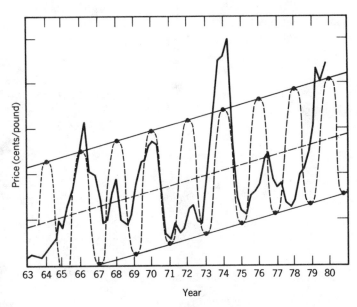

Copper prices 1963–1979

Figure 7-10   Copper prices 1963–1979: single-frequency copper cycle scaled to approximate amplitude.

Two-Frequency Trigonometric Regression

The combination of more than one set of sine and cosine waves of varying amplitudes and frequencies will be a better fit than a single-frequency solution. This is analogous to the use of a second-order (curvilinear) solution instead of the first-order linear. The equation for the two-frequency cycle is

$$y_t = a_1 \cos \omega_1 t + b_1 \sin \omega_1 t + a_2 \cos \omega_2 t + b_2 \sin \omega_2 t$$

To find the results of this complex wave, apply the same techniques used in the single-frequency approach to the detrended copper data. The algebra for solving this problem is an expanded form of the previous solution, and the use of a programmable calculator or computer is a requirement. The programs necessary to solve this one appear in Appendix 4. The frequencies ω_1 and ω_2 are found by solving the quadratic equation:

$$2x^2 - \alpha_1 x - (1 + \alpha_2/2) = 0$$

where $x = \cos \omega$, using the standard formula:

$$x = \frac{\alpha_1 \pm \sqrt{\alpha_1^2 + 8(1 + \alpha_2/2)}}{4}$$

The same least-squares method as before can be used, derived from the general form:

$$\alpha_1(y_n + y_{n+2}) + \alpha_2 y_{n+1} = y_{n-1} + y_{n+3}$$

The least-square equations for finding α_1 and α_2 are:

$$\alpha_1 \Sigma c^2 + \alpha_2 \Sigma cd = \Sigma cp$$

$$\alpha_1 \Sigma cd + \alpha_2 \Sigma d^2 = \Sigma dp$$

where $c = y_n + y_{n+2}$, $d = y_{n+1}$, and $p = y_{n-1} + y_{n+3}$. These equations can be solved for α_1 and α_2 using:

$$\alpha_2 = \frac{\Sigma dp \Sigma c^2 - \Sigma cp \Sigma cd}{\Sigma d^2 \Sigma c^2 - (\Sigma cd)^2}$$

$$\alpha_1 = \frac{\Sigma cp - \alpha_2 \Sigma cd}{\Sigma c^2}$$

Then, ω_1 and ω_2 are calculated from the two solutions x_1 and x_2 of the quadratic equation. The next step is to solve the normal equations to find the amplitudes a_1, b_1, a_2, and b_2:

$$a_1 \Sigma \cos^2 \omega_1 t + b_1 \Sigma \cos \omega_1 t \sin \omega_1 t + a_2 \Sigma \cos \omega_1 t \cos \omega_2 t$$
$$+ b_2 \Sigma \cos \omega_1 t \sin \omega_2 t = \Sigma y_t \cos \omega_1 t$$

$$a_1 \Sigma \sin \omega_1 t \cos \omega_1 t + b_1 \Sigma \sin^2 \omega_1 t + a_2 \Sigma \sin \omega_1 t \cos \omega_2 t$$
$$+ b_2 \Sigma \sin \omega_1 t \sin \omega_2 t = \Sigma y_t \sin \omega_1 t$$

$$a_1 \Sigma \cos \omega_2 t \cos \omega_1 t + b_1 \Sigma \cos \omega_2 t \sin \omega_1 t + a_2 \Sigma \cos^2 \omega_2 t$$
$$+ b_2 \Sigma \cos \omega_2 t \sin \omega_2 t = \Sigma y_t \cos \omega_2 t$$

$$a_1 \Sigma \sin \omega_2 t \cos \omega_1 t + b_1 \Sigma \sin \omega_2 t \sin \omega_1 t + a_2 \Sigma \sin \omega_2 t \cos \omega_2 t$$
$$+ b_2 \Sigma \sin^2 \omega_2 t = \Sigma y_t \sin \omega_2 t$$

Once the sums are obtained, the final step is to create a 4×5 matrix to solve the four normal equations for the coefficients a_1, b_1, a_2, and b_2. When plotting the answer it will be best to plot the original two-frequency equation in its component forms as well as in combination:

$$y_t' = a_1 \cos \omega_1 t + b_1 \sin \omega_1 t$$

$$y_t'' = a_2 \cos \omega_2 t + b_2 \sin \omega_2 t$$

$$y_t = y_t' + y_t''$$

where $a_1 = 3.635$, $b_1 = -.317$, $a_2 = -.930$, and $b_2 = .762$. The solution to the two-frequency problem gives the following values:

$$\alpha_1 = .535, \qquad x_1 = .830$$

and

$$\alpha_2 = .133, \qquad x_2 = -.764$$

and finally the frequencies:

$$\omega_1 = 33.9 \qquad \text{and} \qquad \omega_2 = 139.8$$

correspond to 10.6 and 2.6 calendar quarters (Figure 7-11).

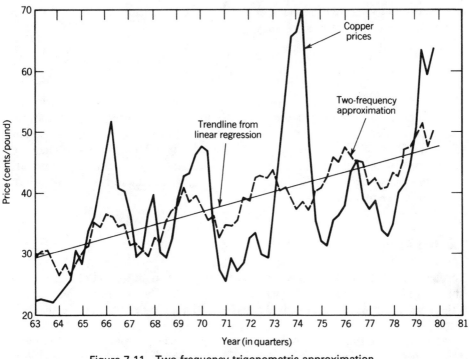

Figure 7-11   Two-frequency trigonometric approximation.

Fourier Analysis: Complex Trigonometric Regression

Developed by the French mathematician John Baptiste Joseph Fourier, *Fourier analysis* is a method of complex trigonometric regression, which expresses any data set as a series of sine and cosine waves of the same type as discussed in the previous section.

Assuming that there is a cycle and that there are N data points in each repetition of this cycle, the Fourier method of analysis shows that the N points lie on the regression curve:

$$y_i = 1 + \sum_{k=1}^{(N/2)} \left(u_k \cos \frac{2\pi ki}{(N/2)} + v_k \sin \frac{2\pi ki}{(N/2)} \right)$$

where the regression coefficients u_k and v_k are given by:

$$u_k = \frac{1}{(N/2)} \sum_{i=1}^{N} y_i \cos \frac{2\pi ki}{(N/2)} \qquad k = 1, 2, \ldots, \frac{N}{2}$$

$$v_k = \frac{1}{(N/2)} \sum_{i=1}^{N} y_i \sin \frac{2\pi ki}{(N/2)} \qquad k = 1, 2, \ldots, \frac{N}{2}$$

$$v_{N/2} = 0$$

It is important to see that the mean of all the points on one cycle is equal to 1. The N values of y_i will have the property

$$\sum_{i=1}^{N} y_i = N$$

Applying the Fourier series to the seasonal component will help clarify this method. Seasonal data form the most obvious cycle; using average monthly prices, detrended to avoid any skew, let $N = 12$. It is also known that seasonally adjusted prices will vary about the mean; hence the weighting factors will have the same property as the above equation. With this information, the trigonometric curve which approximates the seasonals can be generated and compared with the results of other methods.[12]

Spectral Analysis

Derived from the word *spectrum*, spectral analysis is a statistical procedure that isolates and measures the cycles within a data series. The specific technique used is the Fourier series as previously discussed, although other series have also been used.

When studying the cycles that comprise a data series, it is important to refer to their *phase* with respect to each other. Phase is the relationship of the starting points of different cycles. For example, if one cycle has the same period as another but its peaks and valleys are exactly opposite, it is *180° out-of-phase*. If the two cycles are identical in phase, they are *coincident*. Cycles with the same period may lead or lag the other by being out of phase to various degrees.

A tool used in spectral analysis to visualize the relative significance of a series' cyclic components is the *periodogram*. Weighting the cyclic components in the periodogram will give the more popular *spectral density* diagram, which will be used to illustrate the results of the spectral analysis. "Density" refers to the frequency of occurance. Figures 7-12*a* and 7-12*b* show the spectral density of a series composed of three simple waves (*D* is the Fourier series made up of waves *A*, *B*, and *C*).[13] The cycle length, shown at the bottom of the spectral density chart, corresponds exactly to the cycle length of the component waves *A*, *B*, and *C*. The spectral density, measured along the left side of Figure 7-12*b*, varies with the amplitude squared of the cycle and the magnitude of the "noise," or random price movements, which obscures the cycle. In Figure 7-12*b*, the result is based on a series composed of only three pure waves. Had there been noise of the same magnitude as the underlying cycle amplitude, those cycles identified by the spectral analysis would have been completely obscured. Readers who have studied ARIMA will recognize the similarity between the spectral density and the correlogram.

[12] A continuation of this development can be found in Warren Gilchrist, *Statistical Forecasting*, Wiley, London, 1976, pp. 139–148; a more theoretical approach is to be found in C. Chatfield, *The Analysis of a Time-Series: Theory and Practice*, Chapman and Hall, London, 1975, Chapter 7.
[13] William T. Taylor, "Fourier Spectral Analysis," *Technical Analysis of Stocks & Commodities*, July/Aug. 1984.

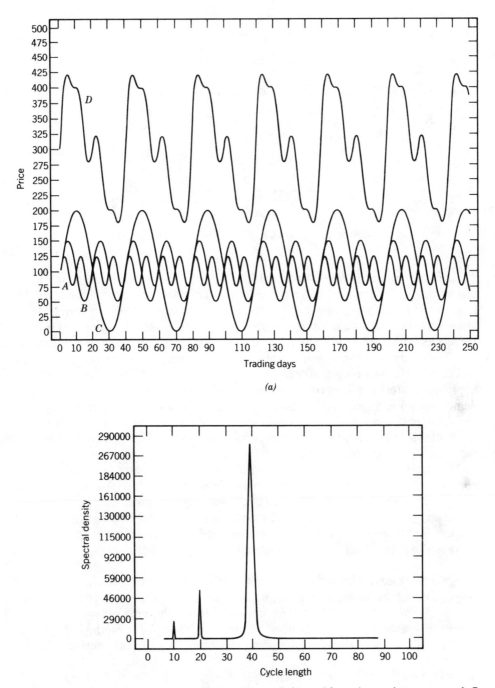

Figure 7-12 Spectral density. (a) A compound wave D, formed from three primary waves, A, B, and C. (b) Spectral density of compound wave D.

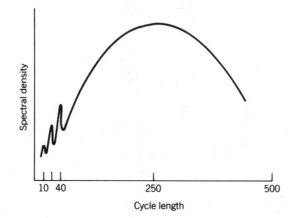

Figure 7-13   10-, 20-, and 40-day cycles, within a 250-day seasonal.

As in trigonometric regression analysis, the other basic price components can distort the results. A noticeable trend in the data must be removed or it will be interpreted as the dominant cycle. The familiar methods of first differencing or linear regression can be used to accomplish this. The seasonal component is itself a cycle and does not need to be removed from the series. Because spectral analysis will identify both the seasonal and cyclic component, the success of the results will depend on the strength of these waves compared to the noise that remains. In applying this technique to real data, it would not be surprising to see the results demonstrated in Figure 7-13. Three subcycles of length 10, 20, and 40 days are shown as part of a 250-day (seasonal) cycle. Notice that, as the cycle lengthens, the width of the spectral density representation widens. This does not mean that the wider peaks are more important.

The trader is most interested in those cycles with greater spectral density, corresponding to a larger price move. The minimum amount of data necessary to find these cycles must include the full cycle that might be identified. For example, to see any seasonal pattern, a full 12 months is needed. More data is better when using spectral analysis to confirm the consistency of the cycle. A single year is not adequate to support any seasonal findings.

Weighting Factors. The most important part of spectral analysis is finding the proper estimators, or weighting factors, for the single-frequency series of cosine waves. When looking for long-term cycles, it is worth being reminded that the trend and seasonal components must be removed because the method of spectral analysis will consider these the dominant characteristics and other cycles may be obscured.

As in the other trigonometric formulas, the basic time-series notation is used, where y_t, $t = 1, 2, \ldots, N$ are the data points and $\hat{y}_t$ will be the resulting estimated points on the spectral analysis. Then

$$\hat{y}_t(\omega) = \frac{1}{\pi} \left(c_0 + 2 \sum_{k=1}^{N-1} c_k \cos \omega k \right)$$

where

$$c_k = \sum_{t=1}^{N-k} \frac{(y_t - \bar{y})(y_{t+k} - \bar{y})}{N}$$

Methods of performing spectral analysis vary due to the choice of weighting functions that compensate for the fact that the accuracy of c_k decreases as k increases. The two most popular techniques for adjusting for this problem introduce an estimator λ_k called a *lag window* and a truncation point $M < N$ so that the values of c_k for $M < k < N$ are no longer used and the values of c_k for $k \le M$ are weighted by λ_k.

The spectral analysis approximation is then written:

$$\hat{y}_t(\omega) = \frac{1}{\pi} \left(\lambda_0 c_0 + 2 \sum_{k=1}^{M} \lambda_k c_k \cos \omega k \right)$$

where λ_k can be either of the following:

(a) *Tukey window*

$$\lambda_k = \frac{1}{2} \left(1 + \cos \frac{\pi k}{M} \right) \qquad k = 0, 1, \ldots, M$$

(b) *Parzen window*

$$\lambda_k = \begin{cases} 1 - 6 \left(\dfrac{k}{M} \right)^2 + 6 \left(\dfrac{k}{M} \right)^3 & 0 \le k \le \dfrac{M}{2} \\ 2 \left(1 - \dfrac{k}{M} \right)^3 & \dfrac{M}{2} \le k \le M \end{cases}$$

Using a Fast Fourier Transform Program. There are computer programs that apply a *Fast Fourier Transform* to perform a spectral analysis. Anthony Warren's approach[14] can be found in Appendix 5. He has published the BASIC program code and preparation necessary to apply the COMPU-TRAC Fast Fourier Transform. The program detrends the data and reduces endpoint discontinuity, which can produce large unwanted cycles. This is accomplished by multiplying the data by a bell-shaped "window" and extending the endpoints to give a more definitive structure to the detrended data, without effecting the results (as discussed in the previous section).

A second filter is applied using selected moving averages. The moving average will reduce or eliminate the importance of those cycles, which are equal to or shorter than two times the length of the moving average, letting the more dominant cycles appear. For example, the use of a 10-day moving average will eliminate cycles of length less than 20 days (frequencies greater than 12.5 per year). Figure 7-14 shows the output of the computer program.

[14] Anthony Warren, "A Mini Guide to Fourier Spectrum Analysis," *Technical Analysis of Stocks & Commodities,* Jan. 1983. A very useful series of articles on spectral analysis has been published in *Technical Analysis* beginning in January 1983, authored by both Anthony W. Warren and Jack K. Hutson. Much of the information in this section was drawn from that material.

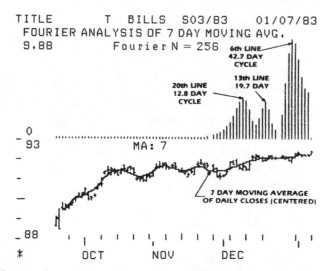

Figure 7-14 Output of spectral analysis program. (*Source:* Hutson, Jack K. "Using Fourier," *Technical Analysis of Stocks & Commodities,* Jan. 1983 p. 10.)

Subsequent works by Warren and Hutson[15] present a computer program to calculate moving average weighted filters using linear, triangular, and Hanning weights.

Sample Results. A fast method for observing the possible results is to use weekly rather than daily data. This will be a close approximation for low frequency waves but will be less representative for the high frequencies. Averaging the data points can yield results very similar to the daily analysis.

Maximum Entropy. Warren, who has written extensively on spectral analysis, has also developed a *Maximum Entropy* method as an alternative to using a Fourier series.[16] It is the basis for Maximum Entropy Spectral Analysis (MESA), a system of current interest. This approach is intended to use less data and identify more current cycles. Warren explains that most commodity price series are "nonstationary," that is, their patterns are constantly shifting. The ability to find cycles within recent data would therefore be more meaningful.

However, if the price series are not stationary, there is no reason to believe that those current cycles are reliable. They could also be in the process of changing. The most dependable cycles are those having a fundamental basis; they tend to be long term and require years of data to identify. Their period is too long to be the sole basis for trading but may successfully be incorporated into a shorter-term strategy. Conclusions based on the recent appearance of a cycle may prove to be risky.

[15] Anthony Warren and Jack K. Hutson, "Finite Impulse Response Filter," *Technical Analysis of Stocks & Commodities,* May 1983.
[16] Anthony Warren, "An Introduction to Maximum Entropy Method (MEM)," *Technical Analysis of Stocks & Commodities,* Feb. 1984. See the bibliography for other articles on this topic.

Cycle Channel Index

A trend-following system that operates for a commodity with a well-defined cyclic pattern should have specific qualities not necessary in a generalized smoothing model. In order to confirm the cyclic turning points, which do not often occur precisely where they are expected, a standard moving average should be used, rather than an exponentially smoothed one. Although exponentials always include some residual effect of older data, the determination of a cyclic turning point must be limited to data that is nearer to one-fourth of the period, combined with a measure of the relative noise in the series which may obscure the turn.

These features have been combined by Lambert[17] into a *Commodity Cycle Index* (CCI), which is calculated as follows:

$$\text{CCI}_t = \frac{x_t - \bar{x}_t}{.015\text{MD}}$$

where $x_t = (H_t + L_t + C_t)/3$ is the average of the daily high, low and close

$$\bar{x}_t = \sum_{i=t-N+1}^{t} x_i \text{ is the moving average over the past } N \text{ days}$$

$$\text{MD} = \sum_{i=t-N+1}^{t} |x_i - x| \text{ is the mean deviation over the past } N \text{ days}$$

N is the number of days selected (less than $\frac{1}{4}$ cycle)

Since all terms are divided by N, that value has been omitted. In the CCI calculations, the use of .015MD as a divisor scales the result so that 70% to 80% of the values fall within a +100 to −100 channel. The rules for using the CCI state that a value greater than +100 indicates a cyclic turn upward; a value lower than −100 defines a turn downward. Improvements in timing rest in the selection of N as short as possible but with a mean-deviation calculation that is a consistent representation of the noise. The CCI concept of identifying cyclic turns is good because of the substantial latitude in the variance of peaks and valleys, even with regular cycles.

Phasing

One of the most interesting applications of the cyclic element of a time-series is presented by J. M. Hurst in *The Profit Magic of Stock Transaction Timing* (Prentice-Hall); it is the "phasing" or synchronization of a moving average to represent cycles. This section will highlight some of the concepts and present a simplified example of the method. It is already known that to isolate the cycle from the other elements, the trending and seasonal factors should be subtracted, reducing the resulting series to its cyclic and chance parts. In many cases, the seasonal and

[17] Donald R. Lambert, "Cycle Channel Index," *Commodities*, 1980, reprinted in *Technical Analysis of Stocks & Commodities*.

cyclic components are similar but the trend is unique. Hurst treats the cyclic component as the dominant component of price movement and uses a moving average in a unique way to identify the combined trend-cycle.

The system can be visualized as measuring the oscillation about a straight-line approximation of the trend (centered line), anticipating equal moves above and below. Prices have many long- and short-term trends, depending on the interval of analysis. Because this technique was originally applied to stocks, most of the examples used by Hurst are long-term trends expressed in weeks. For commodities the same technique could be used by applying the nearest futures contract on a continuous basis.

As a simple example of the concept, choose a moving average of medium length for the trending component. The "full-span" moving average may be selected by averaging the distance between the tops on a price chart. The "half-span" moving average is then equal to half the days used in the full-span average.

The problem with using moving averages is that they aways lag. A 40-day moving average is always 20 days behind the price movement. The current average is plotted under the most recent price, although it actually represents the price pattern if the plot were lagged by half the value of the average. This method applies a process called *phasing*, which aligns the tops and bottoms of the moving average with the corresponding tops and bottoms of the price movement. To phase the full- and half-span moving averages, lag each plot by half the days in the average; this causes the curve to overlay the prices (Figure 7-15). Then project the phased full- and half-span moving averages until they cross. A line or curve connecting two or more of the most recent intersections will be the major trendline. The more points used, the more complicated the regression formula for calculating the trend; Chapter 3 discusses a variety of linear and nonlinear techniques for finding the "best fit" for these intersections. Once the trendline is calculated, it is projected as the center of the next price cycle.

With the trend identified and projected, the next step is to reflect the cycle about the trend. When the phased half-span average turns down at point A (Figure 7-16), measure the greatest distance D of the actual prices above the projected trendline. The system then anticipates the actual price crossing the trendline at point X and declining an equal distance D below the projected trendine. Once the projected crossing becomes an actual crossing, the distance D can be measured exactly and the price objective firmed. Rules for using this technique can be listed as follows:

1. Calculate the full-span moving average for the selected number of days; lag the plot by half the days. If the full-span moving average uses F days, the value of the average is calculated at $t - F/2$, where t is the current day. Call this phased point PH_t.
2. The half-span moving average is calculated for H days and plotted at $t - H/2 + PH_t$.
3. Record the points where the two phased averages PH_i and PF_i cross and call these points $X_n, X_{n-1}, \ldots$.
4. Find the trend by performing a linear regression on the crossing points $X_n, X_{n-1}, \ldots$. If a straight line, then $Y_T = a + bX_T$.
5. Record the highest (or lowest) values of the price since the last crossing, X_n.

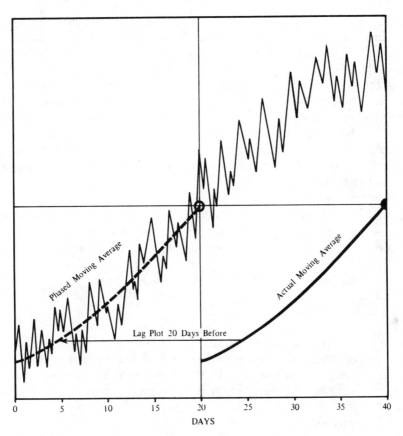

Figure 7-15   Phasing.

6. Calculate the projection of the half-span by creating a straight line from the highest (or lowest) half-span value since the last crossing (A) to the last calculated half-span value. This equation will be $Y_C = c + dX_C$.
7. Find the point at which the projected trendline crosses the projected cyclic line by setting the equations equal to one another and solving for X and Y. At the point of crossing $(X_T, Y_T) = (X_C, Y_C)$, giving two equations in two unknowns, which is easily solvable (X is time in days; Y is price).

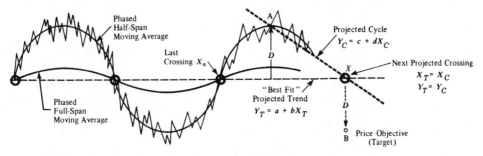

Figure 7-16   Finding the target price.

8. If the half-span is moving down, the maximum price reached by the commodity since the last crossing is subtracted from the Y coordinate of the projected crossing. This distance D is subtracted again from the Y coordinate to determine the price objective. If the half-span is moving up, the price objective uses the minimum price and reflects the distance above the projected crossing. It should be noted that this calculation of distance is simplified because the trend is established by a straight line; for nonlinear fits, the measurement of D will be more complicated.

9. Recalculate the moving averages, the half-span projection (6), the projected crossing (7), and price objective (8) each day until the actual crossing occurs. At that time D is fixed.

10. Follow the trading rules:

    a. Enter a new long position when the half-span moving average turns up; cover any existing short positions regardless of the price objective.

    b. Enter a new short position when the half-span moving average turns down; close-out any long positions.

    c. Close-out both long and short positions if the price objective is reached. An allowable error factor is considered as 10% of the height of the full cycle (lowest to highest point).

This approach to cycles should be studied carefully as an example of a complex problem solved using elementary mathematics. There are many techniques for determining trends and a number of seasonally oriented systems, but a cyclic approach is rare. Whereas Hurst's explanation is more complete and more sophisticated, the interpretation presented in this section should be considered only a reasonable approximation.

8
Charting

Nowhere can a picture be more valuable than in price forecasting. Elaborate theories and complex formulas may ultimately be successful, but the loss of perspective is rarely corrected without a simple chart or illustration. For example, an investor, anxious after a long technical presentation by a research analyst, could only blurt out, "But is it going up or down?" Even the most sophisticated market strategies must capture the obvious trends or countertrends. Before any trading method is accepted, the buy and sell signals should be plotted on a chart. The signals should appear at logical points, otherwise the basis of the strategy or the testing method should be questioned.

Through the years, chart interpretation has held its place in technical analysis. Most traders begin as chartists, and many return to it or use it along with their other methods. William L. Jiler, a great trader and founder of Commodity Research Bureau, wrote:

One of the most significant and intriguing concepts derived from intensive chart studies by this writer is that of characterization, or habit. Generally speaking, charts of the same commodity tend to have similar pattern sequences which may be different from those of another commodity. In other words, charts of one particular commodity may appear to have an identity or a character peculiar to that commodity. For example, cotton charts display many round tops and bottoms, and even a series of these constructions, which are seldom observed in soybeans and wheat. The examination of soybean charts over the years reveals that triangles are especially favored. Head and shoulders formations abound throughout the wheat charts. All commodities seem to favor certain behavior patterns.[1]

In addition to Jiler's observation, the cattle market is recognized as also having the unusual occurrence of "V" bottoms. Both the silver and pork belly markets have tendencies to look very similar, with long periods of sideways movement and short-lived, but violent "price shocks," where prices leap rather than trend to a new level.

Charting is a most popular and practical form for evaluating commodity price movement, and numerous works have already been written on the various inter-

---

[1] William L. Jiler, *How Charts Are Used in Commodity Price Forecasting*, Commodity Research Publications, New York, 1977.

pretations. This chapter will summarize some of the accepted approaches to charting, and then consider the topic in terms of advanced concepts of both standard charting methods and systems directly related to its behavioral implications. Some conclusions will be drawn as to what is most likely to work and why.

A price chart is often considered as a representation of human behavior. The goal of any chart analyst is to find consistent, reliable, and logical patterns to predict price movement. In the classic approaches to charting, there are consolidation forms, trend channels, top-and-bottom formations, and a multitude of other patterns that can only be created by the repeated action of large groups of people in similar circumstances. At this time, there has not been a quantitative study relating the psychology of behavior to the reliability of chart formations. The philosophy of trading that is treated in most of the well-read stocks and commodities literature may be the cause of the repeated patterns. Novice speculators approach the problem with great enthusiasm and often some rigidity in an effort to stick to the rules. They will sell double and triple tops, buy breakouts, and generally do everything to propagate the standard formations. In that sense, it is wise to know what are the most popular and well-read techniques and act accordingly.

There are many habits of speculators taken as a whole that can be used to interpret charts and help trading. The typical reader not on the exchange floor will place an order at an even number, 5 to 10¢ increments in the grains, 10 to 50 points in other products. Who would think of buying corn at 278¾? The public is also known to enter into the bull markets always at the wrong time. Once the major media, such as television news, syndicated newspapers, and radio, carry stories of outrageous prices in cattle, sugar, or coffee, the public enters in what W. D. Gann calls the "grand rush," causing the final runaway move before the collapse; this behavior is easily identifiable on a chart. Gann also talks of "lost motion," the effect of momentum that carries prices slightly past its goal. A common notion of the professional trader who is close to the market is that a move may carry 10% over its objective. A downward swing of soybeans from 8.00 to a support level of 7.50 could violate the bottom by 5¢, without being considered significant.

The behavioral aspects of prices appear rational. In the great bull markets, the repeated price patterns and variations from chance movement are indications of the effects of mass psychology. The greatest single source of information on this topic is Mackay's *Extraordinary Popular Delusions and the Madness of Crowds* originally published in 1841. In the preface to the edition of 1852 the author says:

We find that whole communities suddenly fix their minds on one object, and go mad in its pursuit; that millions of people become simultaneously impressed with one delusion. . . .

In 1975, sugar was being rationed in supermarkets at the highest price ever known. The public was so concerned that there would not be enough at any price that they would buy (and horde) as much as possible. This extreme case of public demand coincided with the peak prices, and shortly afterwards the public found itself with an abundant supply of high-priced sugar in a rapidly declining market.

Charting is a broad topic; the chart paper itself and its scaling are sources of controversy. A standard bar chart (or line chart) representing highs and lows can be plotted for daily, weekly, or monthly intervals in order to smooth out the price movement over time. In the other direction, large increments representing price levels will reduce the volatile appearance of price fluctuations. Bar charts have been drawn on logarithmic and exponential scales[2], where the significance of greater volatility at higher price levels is put into proportion with the quieter movement in the low ranges. Each variation gives the chartist a unique representation of price action. The shape of the box and its value of height/width will alter subsequent interpretations based on angles. Standard techniques applied to bar graphs, point-and-figure charts, and other representations use support and resistance trendlines, frequently measured at 45° angles (and in more complex theories at various other angles). Selection of the charting paper may have a major effect on the results. This chapter will use daily price charts and square boxes unless otherwise noted.

It may be a concern to today's chartist that the principles and rules that govern chart interpretations were based on the early stock market, using averages instead of individual contracts. This will be discussed in the next section. For now, refer to Edwards and Magee, who said that the similarity of an organized exchange trading "anything whose market value is determined solely by the free interplay of supply and demand" will form the same graphic representation. They continue to say that the aims and psychology of speculators in either a stock or commodity environment would be essentially the same; the effect of postwar government regulations have caused a "more orderly" market in which these same charting techniques can be used.[3]

INTERPRETING THE BAR CHART

The *bar chart,* also called the *line chart,* became known through the theories of Charles H. Dow, who expressed them in the editorials of the *Wall Street Journal.* Dow first formulated his ideas in 1897 when he created the stock averages for the purpose of evaluating the movements of stock groups. After Dow's death in 1902, William P. Hamilton succeeded him and continued the development of his work into the theory that is known today. Those who have used charts extensively and understand their weak and strong points might be interested in just how far our acceptance has come. In the 1920s, a New York newspaper was reported to have written:

One leading banker deplores the growing use of charts by professional stock traders and customers' men, who, he says, are causing unwarranted market declines by purely mechanical interpretation of a meaningless set of lines. It is impossible, he contends, to figure values by plotting prices actually based on supply and demand; but, he adds, if too many persons play with the same set of charts, they tend to create the very unbalanced supply and demand which upsets market trends. In his opinion, all charts should be confiscated, piled at the intersection of Broad and Wall and burned with much shouting and rejoicing.[4]

Since then, charting has become part of the financial industry, whether the analyst is interested in the fundamentals of supply and demand or pure price

---

[2] R. W. Schabacker, *Stock Market Theory and Practice,* Forbes, New York, 1930, pp. 595–600.
[3] Robert D. Edwards and John Magee, *Technical Analysis of Stock Trends,* John Magee, Springfield, MA, 1948, Chapter 16.
[4] Richard D. Wyckoff, *Stock Market Technique, Number One,* Wyckoff, New York, 1933, p. 105.

movement. The earliest authoritative works on chart analysis are long out of print, and most of the essential material has been recounted in newer publications. If, however, a copy should cross your path, read the original *Dow Theory* by Robert Rhea;[5] most of all, read Richard W. Schabacker's outstanding work *Stock Market Theory and Practice,* which is probably the basis for most subsequent texts on the use of the stock market as an investment or speculative medium. The most available book that is both comprehensive and well written is *Technical Analysis of Stock Trends* by Robert D. Edwards and John Magee. It is confined entirely to chart analysis with related management implications and a small section on commodities. For the reader who prefers concise information with few examples, the monograph by W. L. Jiler, *Forecasting Commodity Prices with Vertical Line Charts,* and a complementary piece, *Volume and Open Interest, A Key to Commodity Price Forecasting,* are available.[6]

The Dow Theory

In its basic form, the Dow theory is still the foundation of chart interpretation and applies equally to commodities as to stocks. Its major premise is that averages discount all extraneous motion; Dow's averages were groups of stocks. The difficulty with interpreting stock movement is in the thinness of a specific issue; its fixed number of shares and light volume made the movement of one stock an unreliable indicator of an economic turn. Taken in total, it would be improbable to move the average by the manipulation of a single issue; hence, the averages become the subject of analysis. Commodities, especially the financial and index markets, differ from stocks in their enormous volume; trading can be distributed in one or more contracts with little distortion because of "local spreading." The possibility of cornering a commodity market is remote to the point of no concern; a single product can substitute for a stock-related group average.

The Dow theory defines price motion, as represented by the average, in three distinct primary, secondary, and minor trends. These elements have often been compared to the tide, the wave, and the ripple. The primary trend denotes the main move and will exceed a magnitude of 20% of the original price; the secondary trend is an adjustment or correction, and the minor movements are day-to-day fluctuations. The theory emphasized the main move. As Angas said: "Be simple. Take the grand view." It is easier to identify the dominant trend than to worry about every change in direction.

Accumulation and distribution are the beginning phases of a bull or bear market. Accumulation is the period where the insiders begin to acquire a long position in anticipation of a bull move. In charting, this is traditionally a wide formation at a low price with increasing open interest and erratic peaks in volume representing large purchases. The distribution phase serves the same function for anticipated bear moves.

A unique part of the Dow theory that distinguishes it from application in com-

[5] Robert Rhea, *Dow Theory,* Vail-Ballou, Binghamton, NY, 1932.

[6] Two newer works worth studying are Appel, Gerald, *Winning Market Systems: 83 Ways to Beat the Market,* Signalert, Great Neck, NY, 1974, and Appel, Gerald, and Martin E. Zweig, *New Directions in Technical Analysis,* Signalert, Great Neck, NY, 1976.

modities is the principle of confirmation, requiring that a signal be produced by more than one average. There has been some criticism with regard to the relationship of an industrial group being confirmed by a rail, but the principle is not unreasonable. If the purpose of the Dow theory is to identify major trends in the economy, it is unlikely that the average of one stock group would be going up and the other group down in a well-defined inflationary or deflationary period. In the same way, one would not expect the price of corn to increase and the price of wheat to decrease in absolute terms. A period of inflation should uniformly affect stocks and commodities; any items varying from the total pattern should be justified on an individual basis.

The relationship of sales to motion is characterized by saying that "volume expands with the trend." Whether a bull or bear market, activity increases as the trend becomes clear. In commodities, the open interest has been treated in the same manner, with increased positions, especially during the accumulation and distribution phases, a sign of a new move forming.

The Dow theory has other points that have been incorporated into most other chart interpretations. The exclusive use of closing prices is important for two reasons: They are most closely followed by the typical speculator, and they discount the effects of any positions taken by floor traders for 1-day profits. Support and resistance lines were introduced as a substitute for the secondary move, which may have been difficult to define. Lastly, the theory expressed some trading philosophy by stating that a trend should be assumed to be intact until a reversal occurred.

CHART FORMATIONS

Chart analysis uses both trendlines and geometric formations extensively. Rather than discuss the placement and identification of these elements in detail, they will be summarized and described in trading situations.

Trendlines

The *trendline* remains the most popular and readily recognized tool of chart analysis. It is used as:

A *support line,* drawn to connect the bottom points of a price move

A *resistance line,* drawn across the price peaks

A *channel,* the area between the support and resistance lines that contains a sustained price move. When the support and resistance lines are relatively horizontal, or sideways, the channel is called a *trading range.*

Geometric Formations for Accumulation (Distribution)

The most effort in charting goes into the identification of tops and bottoms. Because many of these formations "unfold" over fairly long periods of development, they have been called *accumulation* at the bottom, where investors slowly buy into their position, and *distribution* at the top, where the ownership is dispersed. The most popular of these formations are:

Head-and-shoulders bottom (top)

Common rounded upwards (downwards) turn

Triangular bottom (top) of an ascending, descending, or symmetric shape, such as a *triangle, flag,* or *pennant*

Ascending bottom (top)

"V"-bottom (a "V"-top is usually referred to as a *spike*)

Double bottom (top)

Complex bottom (top), including a triple bottom (top) or a combination of other formations

Broadening bottom (top)

Most of these patterns are self-explanatory and are covered in detail in many books devoted entirely to the topic. In addition to the volume by Edwards and Magee and the monograph by Jiler, the reader can find considerable value in Arthur Sklarew's *Techniques of a Professional Commodity Chart Analyst* and John Murphey's "Bar Charting" in Kaufman, *Handbook Of Futures Markets.*[7]

Individual Patterns

A number of patterns defining specific situations have been noted by the chartist. They are:

Gaps

Spikes

Reversal days

Thrust days

These will be covered in the following sections.

Major and Minor Formations

Throughout the study of charting, it is important to remember that the same patterns will appear in short- as well as long-term charts. An upward trendline can be drawn across the bottom of a price move that only began last week, or it can represent a sustained 6-month move in coffee or a 3-year trend in the financial markets. In general, the longer the time interval, the more significant the formation. Contract highs and lows, sustained trading ranges, trendlines using weekly

[7] Arthur Sklarew, *Techniques of a Professional Commodity Chart Analyst,* Commodity Research Bureau, New York, 1980, and Murphy, John. "Bar Charting" in Perry J. Kaufman (Ed.), *The Handbook of Futures Markets,* Wiley, New York, 1984.

charts, and head-and-shoulder formations are carefully watched by traders. The obscure patterns and new formations are not supported by most chartists, and without the support of the traders, conclusions drawn from those formations have no substance. The basic charting course also includes interpretation of volume and open interest, and a variety of rules for using the formations.

TRADING RULES

The simplest formations to recognize are the most commonly used: horizontal support and resistance lines, bullish and bearish support and resistance lines, and channels. Proper use of these basic lines is essential for successful trading. More complex formations are likely to enhance good performance but cannot compensate for poor trend identification.

Once the support and resistance lines have been drawn, a penetration of those lines creates the basic trend signal (Figure 8-1a). The bullish support line defines

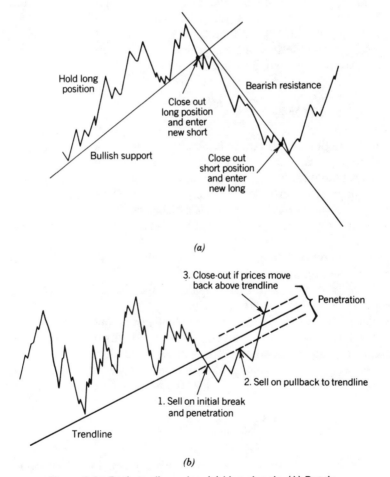

(a)

(b)

Figure 8-1   Basic trading rules. (a) Line signals. (b) Bands.

the upward trend, and the bearish resistance line denotes the downward one. For long-term charts and major trends this is often sufficient, but small penetrations of both long- and short-term trendlines can be included in the rules by placing a band around both lines (Figure 8-1*b*). A short signal occurs when both the trendline and the band have been penetrated. Because of the basic charting rule—"Once broken, a resistance level becomes a support level and a support level becomes a resistance level"—the original trendline (or trendline plus/minus band) can be used as a stop-loss. If prices penetrate the stop-loss point, then return to the original formation, there has been a "false breakout" and the original trendlines are still valid.

Experienced traders often wait for the first pullback after the breakout before entering their position. This technique results in a higher percentage of profitable trades. The position is placed when the new direction is confirmed following a test of the old support or resistance levels (and the theoretic stop-loss). If the test fails, which frequently occurs, the trade is not entered and a loss is prevented (Figure 8-1*b*). Unfortunately, most of the biggest profits result from breakouts that never pull back. Catching only one of these breakouts will compensate for all the small losses due to false signals. Many professional traders may be steady winners, but they do not often find the big move. The same basic rules can be applied to intraday trading but with less latitude for error. It is common practice to buy or sell a breakout from the opening range as though it were bounded on top and bottom by resistance and support lines.

TOPS AND BOTTOMS

Most of the formations important to bar charting can be traded using a penetration of one of the support or resistance lines as a signal. The most interesting and potentially profitable trades occur on breakouts from major top or bottom formations. The simplest of all bottom formations, as well as one that offers great opportunities, is the *extended rectangle* at contract lows. Fortunes have been made by applying patience, some available capital, and the following plan:

1. Find the commodity with a long consolidating base and reduced volatility (with increasing open interest).
2. Buy whenever there is a test of its major support level, placing a stop-loss to liquidate all positions on a new, low price.
3. After the initial breakout, buy again when prices pull back to the original resistance line (now a support level). Close-out all positions if prices penetrate back into the consolidation area and start again at step 2.
4. Buy whenever there is a major price adjustment in the bull move. These adjustment, or pullbacks, will become shorter and less frequent as the move develops.
5. Liquidate all positions at a prior major resistance point, a top formation, or the breaking of a major bullish support line.

Building positions in this way can be done with a relatively small amount of capital and risk. The closer the price comes to major support, the shorter the distance from the stop-loss; however, fewer positions can be placed. In his book, *The Professional Commodity Trader* (Harper & Row), Stanley Kroll discussed "The Copper Caper—How We're Going To Make a Million," using a similar technique for building positions. It can be done, but it requires patience, planning, and capital. The opportunities are there.

This example of patiently building a large position does not usually apply to bear markets. Although there is a great deal of money to be made on the short side of the market, prices move faster and may not permit the accumulation of a large position. There is also the possibility of exceptionally high risk and false signals caused by greater volatility. Within consolidation areas at low levels, there is an underlying demand for a product, the cost of production, government price support (for agricultural products), and low volatility. There is also a well-defined trendline that may have been tested many times. A careful trader will not enter a large position at an anticipated top, but there will be growing volume and open interest at a well-defined major support level.

Head and Shoulders

The classic top and bottom formation is the *head and shoulders,* accepted as a major reversal indicator. This pattern, well-known to chartists, appears as a left shoulder, a head, and a right shoulder (Figure 8-2).

The head-and-shoulders top is developed in the following manner:

1. A strong upward breakout reaching new highs on increased volume. The move appears to be the continuation of a long-term bull move.
2. A consolidation area formed with diminishing volume. This can look much like a descending flag predicting an upward breakout, or a descending triangle indicating a downward breakout.
3. An upward breakout on continued reduced volume forms the head. This is the key point of the formation. The new high is not confirmed by increased volume and prices fall off quickly.

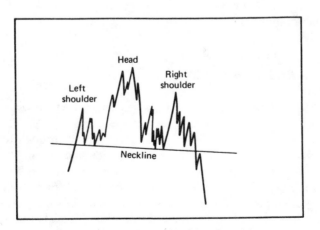

Figure 8-2   Head-and-shoulders formation.

4. Another descending flag or triangle on further reduced volume followed by a minor breakout without increased volume. This last move forms the right shoulder and is the third attempt at new highs for the move.
5. The lowest points of the two flags, pennants, or triangles become the "neckline" of the formation. A sale is indicated when this neckline is broken.

Trading Rules for Head and Shoulders

There are three approaches to trading a head-and-shoulders top formation involving increasing degrees of anticipation:

1a. Sell when the final dip of the right shoulder penetrates the neckline. This represents the completion of the head-and-shoulders formation. Place a stop-loss just above the entry if the trade is to be held only if there is a sharp break, or place the stop-loss above the right shoulder or above the head in order to liquidate on new strength.
   b. Sell on the first rally after the neckline is broken. (Although more conservative, the lost opportunities usually outweigh the improved entry prices.) Use the same stops as in Step 1a.
2a. Sell when the right shoulder is being formed. A key place would be when prices have retraced their way half of the distance to the head. A stop-loss can be placed above the top of the head.
   b. Wait until the top of the right shoulder is formed and sell with a stop either above the high of the right shoulder or above the high of the head.

Both steps 2a, and 2b, allow positions to be taken well in advance of the neckline penetration with logical stop-loss points. If the high of the head is used for a protective stop, added confidence is gained from the old rule: "Always sell a triple top."

3. Sell when the right part of the head is forming, with a stop-loss at about the high of the move. Although this represents a small risk, it has less chance of success. It is for traders who like to find tops and are willing to suffer frequent small losses to do it. Even if the current prices become the head of the formation, there may be numerous small corrections that will look like "absolute tops" to an anxious seller.

Other Top and Bottom Formations

The experienced trader is most successful when prices are testing a major support or resistance level, usually a contract or seasonal high or low. The more often those levels are tested, the less likely prices will break through to a new level without a change in the fundamental supply and demand factors.

Repeated tests of tops are visually clearer, but not as exact as bottoms because of the added volatility of higher prices. The *double top* is a more speculative trade than successive multiple tops; it is more frequent than the other formations and is the first opportunity for picking the top of a bull move. It is also easy to position a stop-loss above the previous highs. As with other chart patterns, declining volume

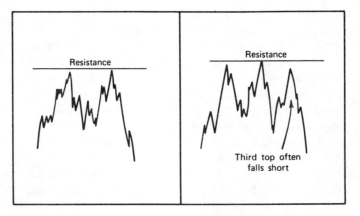

Figure 8-3 Double and triple tops.

would be a welcome confirmation after the formation of the first top and accompanying each additional test of the top (Figure 8-3).

Triple tops are reliable opportunities for selling. Because they are easily seen, there is frequently anticipation that causes the third top to look more like a right shoulder, lower than the previous highs. Traders waiting for a near-test of the highs to achieve less risk could find themselves without any position at all. Among professionals, the fourth top is considered the final test; whichever direction prices turn at that time will determine the new major trend.

Double and triple bottoms also occur but are generally of lesser magnitude than tops. Because low prices can be sustained at cost-of-production levels, it is not necessary for the new upward trend to begin in the near future. In most markets, the profitability associated with these bottom formations is much lower and can be related to the lower risk. With the exception of the financial markets, for which bottoms are really tops (peak interest rates), double and triple bottom formations are most often found in the currency and cattle markets.

Now You See It, Now You Don't!

The "V-top" (actually an inverted V), or *spike,* is probably the most difficult top formation to anticipate and trade. Its frequency in the 1974 and 1980 markets tended to deceive new speculators. V-tops are caused by critical shortage and demand and emphasized by public awareness. In 1974, it was a combination of domestic crop shortage, severe pressure on the U.S. dollar abroad, and foreign purchases of U.S. grain. The news was so well-publicized that novice commodity traders withdrew their funds from their declining stock portfolios and bought any commodity available as a hedge against inflation.

It could not continue for long. When the top came in soybeans, silver, and most other commodities, there was no trading for days in locked-limit markets; paper profits dwindled faster than they were made, and the late entrants found their investments unrecoverable. The public often seems to enter at the wrong time. The case of cattle is an example.

Live cattle prices are based on a combination of consumer demand, substitute foods, and the price of various feed grains. During 1973 as the price of feed increased, cattle prices rose steadily from under 40¢ per pound to almost 54¢ in August. Prior to that, live beef prices had never been over 37¢ (in 1952). The price of soybean meal, used as a high-protein feed, continued to move prices higher. How high could it go? Between August and October, live-cattle prices formed a V-top and declined back to under 40¢, giving up the 8-month gain in 2 months. How could the supply-and-demand factors change so quickly? They can't. Fast rises are always followed by fast, usually extensive declines.

The psychology of the "runaway" market is interesting. In the case of beef, the consumers do not tend to consider pork, fowl, or fish as an actual substitute and will bear increased costs longer than expected. As prices neared the top, the following changes occurred:

The cost became a major factor in the standard household budget

Rising prices received more publicity

Movements for public beef boycotts began

Grain prices declined due to the new harvest

This is the *Elastic Theory*. It can be applied to the 1973 soybean and 1980 silver markets as well. The Elastic Theory is based on the principle that when prices get high enough, a number of phenomena occur:

1. Previously higher-priced substitutes become practical (synthetic for cotton)
2. Competition becomes more feasible (corn sweetener as a sugar substitute)
3. Inactive operations start up (southwest gold mines and marginal production of oil)
4. Consumers would rather avoid the produce (beef and silver)

Consequently, the demand suddenly disappears.

Announcements of additional production, more acreage, new products, boycotts, and a cancellation of orders all coming at once cause highly inflated prices to reverse sharply. These factors form a V-top that is impossible to anticipate with reasonable risk. Further impetus is given to the reversal because of the scramble to liquidate after the first reversal day. This is followed by those latecomers or pyramiders who entered their most recent positions near the top and cannot afford a continued adverse move. The rush to close-out long positions, put on new shorts, and liquidate deficit accounts only prolongs the sharpness of the V-top, causing a liquidity void at many points during the decline.

GAPS

A *gap* is a formation caused by a jump in price from one point to the next; it is noted for its relationship to support and resistance lines. It is an open area on a chart created by prices trading entirely above or below the prior trading range. Gaps will usually occur at the point where prices breakout of a clearly identified formation, such as a long-term trendline, a consolidation area, or during a prolonged major price move. Gaps are the result of either extreme demand (upside gap) or oversupply (downside gap); it is the consequence of a lack of speculators willing to take the opposing position causing a thinly traded or illiquid market. In the most interesting situations, the *breakaway gap* is the result of many stop-loss orders placed at new highs or lows, at major trendlines as protection against unfavorable breakouts with respect to existing positions, or as an entry to a new position. The breakaway gap usually signifies a change from the previous, well-established pattern.

The *common gap* is the least glamorous. It occurs within a well-defined trading range or pattern, and is not indicative of a change of direction nor does it have other special attributes. Hence it is called "common." Both *runaway gaps* and *mid-way gaps* refer to those price jumps occurring within a strong trend. They are associated with periods of illiquidity within a move; this could be the result of additional news to encourage the bulls or bears, or it could be a critical chart formation or anticipated reversal point that fails. Runaway gaps indicate stronger moves.

The *exhaustion gap* or *island reversal* is the culmination of a major move; unfortunately, it is a formation only identifiable after the fact. If the price move has been exceptionally extended, it is likely that the first gap reversal will be the beginning of the trend change; however, there is a great risk associated with it.

Gaps are a hindrence rather than an asset to trading. A breakaway gap usually causes stop-loss orders to be executed far away from the stated price. If a long position is entered in anticipation of a breakout, that breakout never occurs and a high price is guaranteed. If the breakaway gap occurs on light volume, a position might be entered on a pullback. In the final analysis, if the breakout represents a major change, a trade should be entered immediately at the market price. The poor executions will be offset by a single time when prices move quickly and no pullback occurs. A breakaway gap on high volume should be more indicative of such a major change.

Many traders believe that prices will retrace and "fill the gap" that occurred sometime earlier. There are analysts who never give up, but waiting to fill a gap that is more than 2 years old may be carrying this technique too far. There is no doubt that the gap represents an important point at which prices move out of their previous pattern and begin a new phase. The breakaway gap will often be a position just above the previous "normal" price level. Once the short-term demand situation has passed, prices should return to near-normal (perhaps slightly above the old prices), but also slightly below the gap.

KEY REVERSAL DAYS

A formation that has been endowed with great forecasting power is the *key reversal day,* sometimes called an "outside reversal day." It is a weaker form of an island reversal. It first forms a new high in an upward trend, then reverses and closes outside the prior day's range and opposite to the trend. It is considered more reliable when the prior trend is well-established.

Recent studies have shown mixed results using the key reversal as a sole trading indicator. The most complete analysis[8] concluded that the performance

---

[8] Eric Evans, "Why You Can't Rely on 'Key Reversal Days,'" *Futures,* Mar. 1985.

was "strikingly unimpressive." Based on this, it must be concluded that other factors unconsciously enter into the normal perception of a "key reversal." A trader's senses should not be underestimated; the extent and speed of the prior trend, a change in liquidity, a quieter "tone," or some external news may be essential in confirming the important reversals.

EPISODIC PATTERNS

There is little argument that commodity prices change quickly in response to unexpected news. The transition from one major level to another is termed an *episodic pattern;* when these transitions are violent, they are called *shocks*. The coffee and oil markets have received the greatest number of shocks; however, all markets are continually adjusting to new price levels and all experience an occasional shock.

The pattern that results from episodic movement is exactly what one might expect. Following the sharp price movement is a period of declining high volatility, narrowing until a normal volatility level is found and remaining at that level (Figure 8-4).

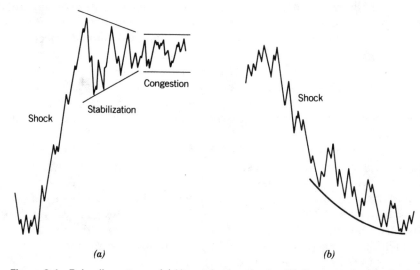

Figure 8-4   Episodic patterns. (*a*) Upward price shocks. (*b*) Downward price shocks.

Patterns that result from rising prices are not the same as falling prices. Although higher price moves usually overshoot the price level at which they normally settle, sharp declines do not reach their final levels during the first shock.

PRICE OBJECTIVES FOR BAR-CHARTING

There is some satisfaction in having a price objective for a trade that has just been entered. If this objective can be determined to a reliable degree, those trades would be selected that have the best profit potential as compared to the risk. It is also comforting to know that profits will be banked at a specific point. Unfortunately, prices sometimes don't recognize the objective that has been set and react in a way contrary to plans.

The simplest and most logical price objective is a major support or resistance level established by previous trading. When entering a long position, look at the most well-defined resistance levels above the entry point. The testing of those levels by the current price move will probably result in one of the top formations just reviewed; when those prior levels are tested, there is generally a technical adjustment or a reversal. In the case of a strong upward market, the volatility often causes a short penetration before the setback occurs. Placing the price objective at a reasonable distance below the prior major resistance level will always be safe; the intermediate resistance levels can be used for adding positions on technical reversals. The downside objective can be handled in a similar manner: Find the major support level and place a stop just above it.

When using both support and resistance price objectives, watch carefully for a violation of the current trend; don't be rigid about the position. Take advantage of each reaction to add to the position, but if the major trendline is broken before the objective is reached, get out. On the other hand, if the goal is reached and prices react as predicted but then reverse and break through the previous highs or lows, the trade may be reentered on the breakout and a new price objective calculated.

There are other, more analytic ways to determine the objective of a trade. Bear in mind that these methods are considered guidelines and are not precise. If the price objective falls very near to a support or resistance level that level should be substituted for a calculated level.

The head-and-shoulders top has a downside objective which is associated with its volatility. This objective is measured from the point where the right shoulder penetrates the neckline and is equal to the distance from the top of the head to the neckline (Figure 8-5). For a major top, this goal seems modest, but it will be a

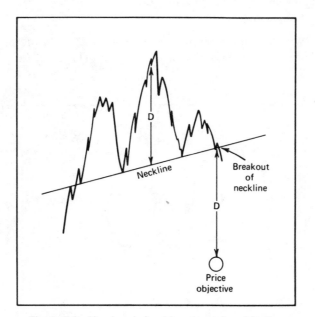

Figure 8-5   Head-and-shoulders top price objective.

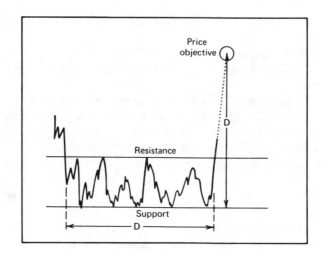

Figure 8-6   Consolidation price objective.

good measure of the initial reaction and will generally be safe, even if a new high price is reached later.

A *consolidation area,* both top and bottom, has a counting method based on the width of the rectangle or consolidation pattern. For a basing formation, the objective is the vertical distance above the support line equal to the width of the consolidation area (Figure 8-6). For downside objectives, measure vertically downward from the resistance line forming the upper bound of the congestion area. This technique says, "The longer the consolidation area, the bigger the move." The same method can be seen later in point-and-figure charting.

Trendlines can also be used to measure the expected price move. The following are some accepted ways:

1. The channel width which bounds a trend will be equal to the price objective measured from the point of the channel breakout (Figure 8-7).

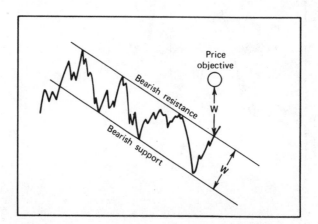

Figure 8-7   The channel width as a price objective.

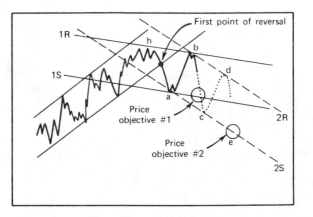

Figure 8-8   Forming new channels to determine objectives.

2. Once a breakout of an upwards channel has occurred, construct a new descending channel. This is done by connecting the high of the uptrend with the high of the first reversal following the break, then drawing a parallel support line across the low of the first breakout. The new channel will be shallow but will serve as a guideline for the price change. A second channel, drawn after the next reversal, should indicate the final direction of the new move.

In Figure 8-8, the original channel around the uptrend was broken at the point marked by the dot, followed by prices moving down to point a and reacting back up to point b. When a new high is not made at point b, a resistance line (1R) can be drawn from the prior high h to the top of the latest move b. A line parallel to 1R can be constructed at point a, forming the initial downward channel. Price objective 1 is on the support line of the new channel (1S) and is used once the top at point b is determined. Price objective 1 cannot be expected to be too precise due to the early development of the channel. If prices continue to point c and then rally to d, a more reasonable channel can now be defined using trendlines 2R and 2S. The support line will again become the point where the new price objective is placed. The upper and lower trendlines can be further refined as the new high and low reactions occur. The primary trendline is always drawn first, then the new price objective becomes a point on the parallel trendline.

Triangles and *flags* have objectives based on volatility in a manner consistent with other patterns. The triangle objective is equivalent in size to the initial reaction which formed the largest end of the triangle (Figure 8-9a). The flag is assumed to occur midway in a price move; therefore, the objective of a new breakout must be equal to the size of the move preceding the flag (Figure 8-9b).

The Rule of Seven

Another measurement of price objectives, the *Rule of Seven,* is credited to Arthur Sklarew.[9] It is based on the volatility of the prior consolidation formation and

[9] Sklarew, *Chart Analyst,* 1980. (See ref. 7 on p. 164.)

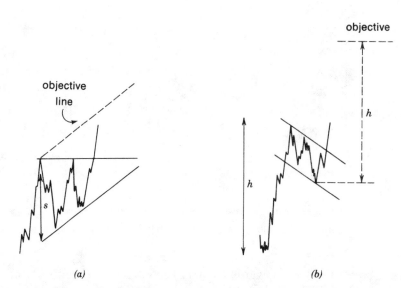

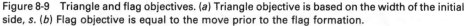

Figure 8-9   Triangle and flag objectives. (*a*) Triangle objective is based on the width of the initial side, *s*. (*b*) Flag objective is equal to the move prior to the flag formation.

computes three successive price objectives in proportion to one another. The Rule of Seven is not symmetric for both uptrends and downtrends. Sklarew believes that, after the initial leg of a move, the downtrend reactions are closer together than the reactions in a bull market. Because the downside of a major bear market is limited, it is usually characterized by consolidation. Major bull markets tend to run away as they develop.

To calculate the objectives using the Rule of Seven, first measure the length L of the initial leg of a price move (from the previous high or low, the most extreme point before the first pullback). The objectives are:

1. In an *uptrend:*

$$\text{OBJ } 1 = \text{prior low} + (L \times 7/4)$$
$$\text{OBJ } 2 = \text{prior low} + (L \times 7/3)$$
$$\text{OBJ } 3 = \text{prior low} + (L \times 7/2)$$

2. In a *downtrend:*

$$\text{OBJ } 1 = \text{prior high} - (L \times 7/5)$$
$$\text{OBJ } 2 = \text{prior high} - (L \times 7/4)$$
$$\text{OBJ } 3 = \text{prior high} - (L \times 7/3)$$

The three objectives apply most clearly to major moves. During minor price changes it is likely that the first two objectives will be bypassed. Sklarew's experience says that, regardless of whether any one objective is missed, the others still remain intact.

VOLUME AND OPEN INTEREST

Patterns in volume and open interest have always been tied closely to chart analysis in both the stock and commodities markets. There has been little research published that relates these factors to futures markets; its popular use has assumed the same conclusions as in stock market analysis. Open interest, however, is a tool not available in securities markets: It is the netting out of positions that has only been approximated by stock methods such as On-Balance Volume.

Standard Interpretation

The traditional interpretation of changes in volume and open interest can be summarized as follows:

Volume	Open interest	Interpretation
Rising	Rising	Confirmation of trend
Rising	Falling	Position liquidation (at extremes)
Falling	Rising	Slow accumulation
Falling	Falling	Congestion phase

Some of the generally accepted notions for the use of volume and open interest are:

1. Open interest increases during a trending period.
2. Volume may decline but open interest builds during an accumulation phase. Volume occasionally spikes.
3. Rising prices and declining volume/open interest indicate a pending change of direction.

Volume exceptions exist in the stock market. There are days or periods when volume is expected to change. For example, volume is lighter:

On the first day of the week
On the day before a holiday
During the summer

In the futures markets, there are similar patterns. Lighter volume will exist during holiday periods and summer months, but may be heavier on Fridays and Mondays during a trending market or a "weather market." Liquidation often occurs before the weekend and positions are reentered on the first day of the week.

On-Balance Volume

Made famous by Joseph Granville, *On-Balance Volume* (OBV) is now a byword in stock analysts circles. On days when prices close higher, it is assumed that all volume is representative of the buyers; on lower days, the volume is controlled by the sellers.[10] The result is a volume-weighted series, similar to a relative strength

[10] Curtis Arnold, *The Personal Computer Can Make You Rich*. Weiss Research, West Palm Beach, FL, 1984.

calculation (e.g., Wilder's RSI). Determining the OBV is a simple accumulation process as follows:

Table 8-1   Calculating On-Balance Volume

Closing Price	Daily Volume (in 1000s)	On-Balance Volume
310	25	25
315	30	55
318	27	82
316	15	67
314	12	55
320	28	83

In Table 8-1, there was greater volume on days in which prices rose and lower volume on declining days. This is expected in a market with a clear uptrend. The advantage of recording the OBV is in observing when the trend of the prices diverges from the OBV values. The general interpretation of OBV is given in Table 8-2.

Table 8-2   Interpreting On-Balance Volume

Price Direction	OBV Direction	Interpretation
Up	Up	Clear uptrend
	Sideways	Moderate uptrend
	Down	Weak uptrend near reversal
Sideways	Up	Accumulation period (bottom)
	Sideways	No determination
	Down	Distribution period (top)
Down	Up	Weak downtrend near reversal
	Sideways	Moderate downtrend
	Down	Clear downtrend

Volume Accumulator

A modification to Granville's OBV system is Mark Chaiken's *Volume Accumulator*. Instead of assigning all the volume to either the buyers or the sellers, the Volume Accumulator uses a proportional amount of volume corresponding to the relationship of the closing price to the intraday mean price. If prices close at the high or low of the day, all volume is given to the buyers or sellers as in the OBV calculation.[11]

[11] Both OBV and the Volume Accumulator are characterized as "momentum" systems. See Chapter 6 for more information on similar techniques.

Volume Momentum

A straightforward way of using volume and open interest was proposed by Waxenberg.[12] Based on the traditional interpretation, a 10-day moving average of the volume is calculated as "normal." A change in trend must be confirmed by a 20% increase in volume above the normal value. Extremes in a trending move can be found at points which exceed approximately a 40% volume increase. Applied to the stock market, Waxenberg used the extreme volumes to indicate the end of a sell-off.

Alternately, using 13 days of volume, subtract the total down volume from the total up volume. A plot of the results will serve as a momentum indicator from which overbought and oversold levels can be identified. If these values are unstable due to lack of liquidity, they may be smoothed using a short-term moving average.

USING THE BAR CHART

Charting is not precise and the construction of the trendlines, other geometric formations, and their interpretation can be performed with some latitude. When using the simplest trendline analysis, it often happens that there will be a small penetration of the channel or trendline followed by a movement back into the channel. Some think that this lack of adherence to the rule makes charting useless; however, many experienced analysts interpret this action as confirmation of the trend. The trendline is *not* redrawn so that the penetration becomes the new low of the trend, but it is left in its original position.

Multiple Signals

Some of the impreciseness of charting can be offset with confirming signals. A simultaneous short- and long-term trend break is a much stronger signal than either one considered separately. The break of a head-and-shoulders neckline that corresponds to a channel support line is likely to receive much attention. Whenever there are multiple signals at a single point, whether based on moving averages, Gann, cycles, or phases of the moon, that point gains significance. In chart analysis, the occurrence of multiple signals at one point can compensate for the quality of the interpretation.

Pattern Failures

The failure to adhere to a pattern is equally as important as the continuation of that pattern. Although a trader might anticipate a reversal as prices near a major support line, a break of that trendline is significant in continuing the downward

---

[12] Howard K. Waxenberg, "Technical Analysis of Volume," *Technical Analysis of Stocks & Commodities,* Mar. 1986.

move. A failure to stop at the support line should result in setting short positions and abandoning plans for higher prices.

A head-and-shoulders formation that breaks the neckline, declines for a day or two, then reverses and moves above the neckline is another pattern failure. "Post-pattern" activity must confirm the pattern. Failure to do so means that the market refused to follow through and therefore should be traded in the opposite direction. This is not a case of identifying the wrong pattern; instead, price action actively opposed the completion of the pattern. Wyckoff calls this "Effort and Results," referring to the effort expended by the market to produce a pattern that explains the price direction. If this pattern is not followed by results that confirm the effort, the opposite position should be set.

Consider a trading day where prices open, move higher, then close lower. The expectation is for prices to open lower the next day. If an inside day or a higher open follows, there is a strong sign of higher prices to come. As Thompson concludes, "A strongly suggestive pattern that is aborted is just as valuable as a completed pattern."[13]

Change of Character. Thompson also discusses the completion of a pattern or price trend by identifying a "change of character" in the movement. As a trend develops, the reactions, or pullbacks, tend to become smaller. Traders looking to enter the trend wait for reactions to place their orders; as the move becomes more obvious, these reactions will get smaller and the increments of trend movement will become larger. When the reaction suddenly is larger, the move is ending; the change in the character of the move signals a prudent exit, even if prices continue erratically in the direction of the trend.

Testing Your Skill

Recognizing a pattern is both an art and science. Not everyone has an eye for patterns; others will see formations where no one else would. How much of the chart do you use? By choosing a short interval, a trendline may be drawn where none was possible over a longer period; a longer sequence of points may form a pennant whereas the most recent part forms a triangle; a short-term trendline may have been broken but not a long-term one. Additional variables in both the construction and reading of the charts are the time element and scale. Are the formations different if the scale is expanded or reduced?

The timeliness of the identification is another major problem. Can the formation be interpreted in time to act on a breakout, or is the pattern always seen afterwards? At different stages of development, the lines may appear to form different patterns. Before using your charting skills to trade, practice simulating the day-to-day development of prices as follows:

1. Hold a piece of the paper over the right side of the chart, covering the most recent months, or better still, have someone else give you the partial chart.

[13] Jesse H. Thompson, "What Textbooks Never Tell You," *Technical Analysis of Stocks & Commodities,* Nov./Dec. 1983.

2. Look at the chart and analyze the formations.
3. Determine what action will be based on your interpretation. Be specific.
4. Move the paper one day to the right, or have someone else give you the next day's price.
5. Record any orders that would have been filled based on the prior day's analysis. Don't cheat.
6. Determine whether the new day's price would have altered your formations and plans.
7. Return to step 3 until finished.

This simple exercise might save a lot of money—and may be discouraging. With practice you will become better at finding and using formations and will learn to select the ones that work best. Very few traders base their trading decisions entirely on bar charts. Many consult the charts for confirmation of separate technical or fundamental analysis; others will only use the most obvious major trendlines, looking for points at which multiple indicators converge. The general acceptance of bar charting analysis makes it a lasting tool.

9

Point-and-Figure Charting

Point-and-figure charting is credited to Charles Dow, who is said to have used it just prior to the turn of the twentieth century. This method differs from ordinary charting in three important ways:

1. It eliminates price reversals that are below a minimum (box) value.
2. It has simple, well-defined trading rules.
3. It has no time factor. As long as prices fail to change direction by the *reversal value,* the trend is intact.

When point-and-figure charting first appeared, it did not contain the familiar boxes of Xs and Os. The earliest published book containing the subject is reported to be *The Game in Wall Street and How to Play it Successfully,* published by Hoyle (not Edmond Hoyle, the English writer) in 1898. The first definitive work on the subject was by Victor de Villiers, who in 1933 published *The Point and Figure Method of Anticipating Stock Price Movement.* De Villiers worked with Owen Taylor to publish and promote a weekly point-and-figure service, maintaining their own charts; he was impressed by the simple scientific methodology. As with many of the original technical systems, the application was intended for the stock market, and the rules required the use of every change in price appearing on the ticker. The rationalization for a purely technical system has been told many times by now, but an original source is often refreshing. De Villiers said:

"The Method takes for granted:

1. That the price of a stock at any given time is its correct valuation up to the instant of purchase and sales (a) by the concensus of opinion of *all* buyers and sellers in the world and (b) by the verdict of *all* the forces governing the laws of supply and demand.
2. That the last price of a stock reflects or crystalizes *everything* known about or bearing on it from its first sale on the Exchange (or prior), up to that time.
3. That those who know more about it than the observer *cannot* conceal their future intentions regarding it. Their plans will be revealed in time by the stock's subsequent action." [1]

---

[1] Victor De Villiers, *The Point and Figure Method of Anticipating Stock Price Movements,* Trader Press, NY, 1966 (Reprint of 1933 edition), p. 8.

The unique aspect of the point-and-figure method is that it ignores the passage of time. Unlike bar charts, you do not make a single vertical mark and then move to the right a uniform distance. Each column of a point-and-figure chart can represent any length of time. The measurement of a significant change in price direction alone determines the pattern of the chart.

The original "figure charts" were plotted with only dots or with the exact price in each box or with a combination of X's and occasional digits (usually 0s and 5s every five boxes) to help keep the chart aligned. A geometric representation was also created by connecting the points in each column with a vertical line and closing the gap between columns with a crossbar on top for a reversal down and a bar at the bottom if the next column goes up. Charts using one, three, and five points were popular, where each point represented a minimum price move. In the 5-point method, no entry was recorded unless the price change spanned 5 points.

PLOTTING PRICES USING THE POINT-AND-FIGURE METHOD

To plot prices on a point-and-figure chart, start with a piece of graph paper and mark the left scale using a conveniently small price increment. For example, each box may be set at $1 for gold and platinum, 1¢ for soybeans and silver, and so forth (see Figure 9-1). The choice of a box size will make the chart more or less sensitive to changes in price direction as will be seen in later examples. The smaller the price increment, the more changes in direction will be seen. This also corresponds to longer or shorter trends or major and minor trends. Therefore, a point-and-figure chartist looking for a long-term price movement will use a larger box size. Box sizes are often related to the current volatility of the markets.

Once the graph paper has been scaled and the prices entered on the left side, the chartist can begin. The first box to be entered is that of the current closing price of the commodity. If the price of silver is 852.50 and a 1¢ box is being used, a mark is placed in the box beside the value 852. An X or an O is used to indicate that the current price trend is up or down, respectively. Either an X or O may be used to begin—after that, it will be determined by the method.

Silver

854.0	X								
853.0	X	O	X						
852.0	X	O	X	O					
851.0		O	X	O	X				
850.0		O		O	X	O			
849.0				O	X	O			
848.0				O	X	O			
847.0				O					
846.0									

Figure 9-1   Point-and-figure chart.

The rules for plotting point-and-figure charts are easily shown as a flowchart (Figure 9-2). In general, preference is given to price movements that continue in the direction of the current trend. Therefore, if the trend is up (represented by a column of Xs), the new high price is tested first; if the trend is down, the low price is of greatest importance. The opposite price is checked only if the new price fails to increase the length of the column of the current trend.

The traditional point-and-figure method calls for the use of a "three-box reversal," that is, the price must reverse direction by an amount equal to three boxes from the most extreme box of the last column (it actually must fill the forth box since the extreme box is left blank) before a new column can begin. The importance of keeping the three-box reversal has always been questioned by experienced point-and-figure traders. It should be noted that the net reversal amount (the box size times the number of boxes in the reversal) is the critical value. For example, a $4 box for gold, with a three-box reversal means that gold must reverse

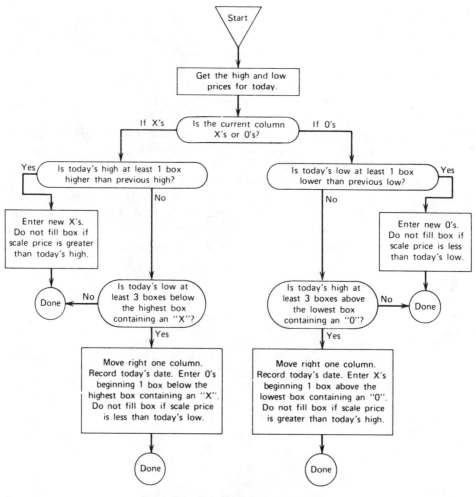

Figure 9-2 Point-and-figure daily rules.

by $12 to indicate a trend change. The opposite combination, a $3 box and a four-box reversal, would actually signal a reversal of trend at the same time. The proper selection is based on the subsequent sensitivity of the box size following the reversal. Therefore, a smaller box size may interpret the smallest price movements as a continuation of the trend and ultimately capture more of the price move; it is considered the preferable alternative. The choice of box size and reversal boxes will be considered later in more detail.

CHART FORMATIONS

It would be impossible for the average speculator to follow the original method of recording every change in price. When applied to stocks, those charts became so lengthy that interpretations similar to the line chart were necessary to select the best patterns. In 1965, Robert E. Davis published *Profit and Profitability,* a point-and-figure study that detailed eight unique buy and sell signals. The study covered two stocks for the years 1914–1964, and 1100 stocks for 1954–1964. The intention was to find specific bull and bear patterns that were more reliable than others. The best buy signal was an ascending triple top and the best sell signal was the breakout of a triple bottom (Figures 9-3 and 9-4).

Plotted daily, commodity prices do not offer the variety of formations available in the stock market. Limited sets of commodities and the high correlation of movement between many of the delivery months makes signal selection impractical. It is necessary to limit the trading rules to the simple buy signal, an X in the current column one box above the highest X in the last column of Xs, and the simple sell signal which is an O plotted below the lowest O of the last descending column. The variability in the system lies in the size of the box; the smaller the size, the more sensitive the chart will be to price moves. In 1933, Wyckoff noted that it was advisable to use a chart with a different box size when the price of the stock varied substantially.[2]

Trendlines

The bullish and bearish trendlines important to bar charting also exist for point-and-figure charts. The top or bottom box that remains blank when a reversal

```
    Ascending Triple Top        Breakout of a Triple Bottom
            X ← BUY                  X   X
           X X                     0 X 0 X 0
    X    X 0 X                     0 X 0 X 0
    X 0 X 0 X                      0   0   0
    X 0 X 0                                0 ← SELL
       0
```

Figure 9-3 Best formations from Davis' study.

[2] Richard D. Wyckoff, *Stock Market Technique, Number One,* Wyckoff, New York, 1933, p. 89.

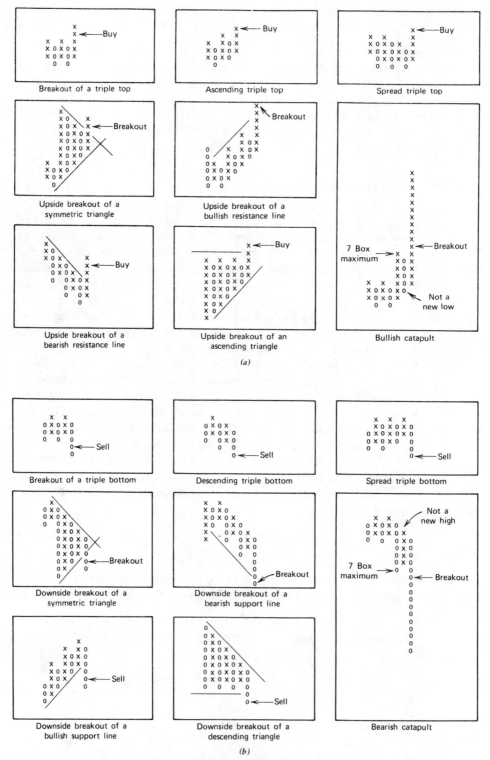

Figure 9-4 (a) Compound point-and-figure buy signals. (b) Compound point-and-figure sell signals.

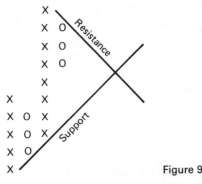

Figure 9-5   Point-and-figure trendlines.

occurs often forms the beginning of a descending or ascending pattern at a 45°
angle (providing the graph paper has square boxes). These 45° lines represent the
major anticipated trends of the commodity. Once a top or bottom has been identified, a 45° line can be drawn down from the upper corner of the top boxes of Xs
toward the right, or up from the bottom of the lowest box of Os toward the right
(Figure 9-5). These trendlines are used to *confirm* the direction of price movement
and often "filter" the basic point-and-figure trading signals so that only those
signals are taken that agree with the 45° trendlines.

Point-and-Figure Studies

In 1970, Charles C. Thiel, Jr., with Robert E. Davis, completed the first purely
commodity point-and-figure study[3] that calculated profitability of good samples of
commodities by varying both the value of a box and the reversal criteria (the
number of boxes necessary to start a new column). With the standard 3-box
reversal and only simple buy and sell formations, the tests showed 799 signals of
which 53% were profitable; the average net profit on all trades was $311 realized in
approximately 50 days. The period studied was 1960 through 1969. More recently,
Zieg and Kaufman[4] performed a computerized study using the same rules but
limiting the test period to 6 months ending May 1974, an extremely active market
period. For the 22 commodities tested, 375 signals showed 40% of the trades were
profitable; the net profit over all the trades was $306 and the average duration was
12.4 days. It is interesting to note that the most significant difference in the results
of the two studies is in the average length of a trade, from 50 to 12.4 days,
indicating a change potentially induced by more volatile markets. Although the
two tests varied in many of the details, the results are a strong argument for the
consistency of the point-and-figure method as a trading tool.

In its current role, point-and-figure differs from other forms of charting because
it provides a rigid set of rules for entering long and short positions. Many of the

---

[3] Charles Thiel and R. E. Davis, *Point and Figure Commodity Trading: A Computer Evaluation*, Dunn
& Hargitt, West Lafayette, IN, 1970.
[4] Kermit C. Zieg, Jr. and Perry J. Kaufman, *Point and Figure Commodity Trading Techniques*,
Investors Intelligence, Larchmont, NY, 1975. This book contains complete tabularized results of both
point-and-figure tests.

formations are still subjected to interpretation and are frequently used in the original sense by floor traders; but as a tool for the speculator without access to intraday prices and the experience to understand the subtleties of chart analysis, point-and-figure fills an important gap. It will tell the trader exactly what penetration of a resistance or support level is necessary to generate a buy or sell signal and exactly where the stop-loss order should be placed to limit risk. It is this well-defined nature of point-and-figure charting that allows computer testing and evaluation.

Table 9-1a Point-and-Figure Box Sizes[a]

Commodity	Year	Prior to 1975[b] Box Size	1975[c] Box Size	1977[c] Box Size	1977[d] Box Size	1986[c] Box Size
Grains						
Corn	1971	½¢	2¢	2¢	2¢	1¢
Oats	1965	½¢	1¢	1¢		1¢
Soybeans	1971	1¢	10¢	10¢	5¢	5¢
Soybean meal	1964	50 pts	500 pts	500 pts		100 pts
Soybean oil	1965	10 pts	20 pts	20 pts		10 pts
Wheat	1964	1¢	2¢	2¢	2¢	1¢
Livestock and Meats						
Cattle	1967	20 pts	20 pts	20 pts		20 pts
Hogs	1968	20 pts	20 pts	20 pts		20 pts
Pork bellies	1965	20 pts	20 pts	20 pts		20 pts
Other Agricultural Products						
Cocoa[e]	1964	20 pts	100 pts	100 pts	50 pts	10 pts
Coffee		(20) pts	100 pts	100 pts	50 pts	100 pts
Cotton		(20) pts	100 pts	100 pts		50 pts
Lumber		(100) pts	100 pts	100 pts		100 pts
Orange juice	1968	20 pts	20 pts	100 pts		100 pts
Sugar	1965	5 pts	20 pts	20 pts	20 pts	10 pts
Metals						
Aluminum						50 pts
Copper	1964	20 pts	100 pts	100 pts	50 pts	50 pts
Gold			50 pts	100 pts		400 pts
Palladium						100 pts
Platinum	1968	200 pts	100 pts	200 pts	200 pts	400 pts
Silver	1971	100 pts	200 pts	200 pts	400 pts	1000 pts

[a] All box sizes use a 3-box reversal and are in *points* (decimal fractions treated as whole numbers) unless otherwise indicated.
[b] Cohen (1972); parentheses indicate approximate values.
[c] Courtesy of Chartcraft Commodity Service, Chartcraft, Inc., Larchmont, NY.
[d] Chart Analysis Limited, Bishopgate, London. Values are for long-term continuation charts.
[e] Cocoa contract changed from cents/pound to dollars/ton.

Table 9-1b   Point-and-Figure Box Sizes

Commodity	1986 Box Size	Commodity	1986 Box Size
Oils		*Currencies*	
Crude	10 pts	British pound	50 pts
Gasoline	50 pts	Canadian dollar	10 pts
Heating oil	50 pts	Japanese yen	10 pts
		Swiss franc	10 pts
		Deutschemark	10 pts
Financials		*Index*	
Eurodollars	10 pts	S&P 500	50 pts
GNMAs	$^{16}\!/_{32}$ pts	Major market	50 pts
Treasury bonds	$^{16}\!/_{32}$ pts	NYSE	50 pts
Treasure bills	10 pts	Value line	50 pts
Certificates of deposit	10 pts		

The basic study of the point-and-figure method involves rules of charting, buy and sell signals, trendlines, geometric formations, and price objectives. Since these points have been covered effectively in at least two books currently available,[5] they will not be repeated here. More advanced point-and-figure topics will be discussed, including its relationship to bar charting, alternate plotting rules, risk-limited trading, and varying box size.

POINT-AND-FIGURE BOX SIZE

The box size used in a point-and-figure chart determines the sensitivity, or frequency of signals, and allows the identification of trends and trading ranges of various duration. *Chartcraft* is the only major service that produces a full set of point-and-figure charts (see Table 9-1).

Over the past 10 years, all markets have had one or more major price moves reaching levels often greater than twice their normal price. Sugar and silver each topped at 10 times their starting value. These moves necessitate changes in box size in order to control the impact of the increased, and later decreased, volatility.

In the past few years, most commodities have been in a devaluing period with the exception of currencies (which are constantly shifting), oil, and coffee. Table 9-1 shows part of the history of changing box sizes using a 3-box reversal. By noting the historic price moves, the change in volatility can be related to the change in box size. Whereas most commodities show a pattern of small to large to small box sizes, coffee and orange juice have remained volatile. Silver and gold maintain large box sizes as a result of their long steady declines; however, current levels would favor a reduction. Rules for varying box sizes and risks associated with these changes will be discussed in the next sections.

[5] A. W. Cohen, *How To Use the Three-Point Reversal Method of Point and Figure Stock Market Trading,* Chartcraft, Larchmont, NY, 1972, and Zieg and Kaufman, *Point and Figure Commodity Trading Techniques,* 1975.

THE PROBLEM OF RISK

I go long or short as close as I can to the danger point, and if the danger becomes real I close out and take a small loss.

Jesse Livermore to Richard Wyckoff[6]

If the point-and-figure method is accepted as successful, why is it necessary to modify the basic signal and use trendlines and geometric formations to interpret new signals? The answer involves the risk of an individual trade. The difference in treatment of the same price move can be seen by looking at both a bar chart and a corresponding point-and-figure chart for the same period (Figure 9-6). The bar chart uses support and resistance trendlines to define a rectangular trading range; when the resistance line is penetrated, a long position is taken. A stop-loss is also placed below the resistance line in order to close out the position in the event of a false breakout. An alternate place for the stop-loss could have been below the support line allowing the new bull move some latitude to develop. The interpreted bar chart makes the selection of the entry point and the placement of stops seem obvious; however, when trading, the placement of the support and resistance lines is not as clear. The time to enter a trade after a breakout is never certain, and the position for the stop depends on the volatility of prices and the risk that can be assumed.

In contrast to the ambiguity of the bar chart, the point-and-figure method defines the support and resistance levels exactly, establishes a place to buy in advance, and designates the position for the stop-loss below the rectangular congestion area. The rigidity of the method allows only one place for the stop-loss and fixes the risk as the difference between the support and resistance lines, a total of five boxes in this example. In the bar chart, the risk might have been held to the equivalent of two boxes using the first strategy; however, it may not be possible to stay with the trend with such low risk.

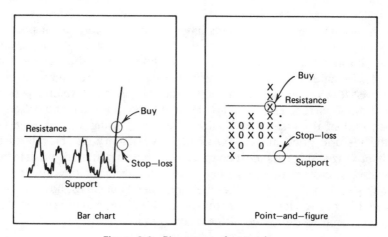

Figure 9-6   Placement of a stop-loss.

[6] Wyckoff, *Market Techniques*, 1933, p. 2.

TRADING TECHNIQUES

There are alternate methods for selecting point-and-figure entry and exit points that have become popular. Buying or selling on a pullback after an initial point-and-figure signal is one of the more common modifications to the system because it can limit risk to any level and still maintain a logical stop-loss point. Of course, the smaller the risk, the fewer the opportunities. There are two approaches that are recommended for entering on limited risk:

1. **Wait for a reversal back to within an acceptable risk, then buy or sell immediately with the normal point-and-figure stop.** Figure 9-7 shows various levels of risk using corn (5000 bushels or $50 for each 1¢ move). The initial buy signal is at 258, with the simple sell signal for liquidation at 249, giving a risk of 9¢, or $450 per contract. Wait for a reversal following the breakout, and buy when the low for the day penetrates the box corresponding to the predetermined risk. Buying into a declining market assumes that the support level will hold preventing the stop-loss point from being reached. Because of this, the base of the formation should be as broad as possible. The testing of a triple bottom or a spread triple bottom after a buy signal is a more reasonable place to go long than a simple buy after a small reversal in the middle of a move.

   It is not advisable to reduce risk by entering on the simple buy signal and placing a stop-loss at the point of the first reversal (three boxes below the highs). The advantage of waiting for the pullback is that it uses the logical support level as a stop. A stop-loss placed nearby following a breakout has no logical basis and will usually result in a short, losing trade.

2. **Enter the market on the second reversal back in the direction of the original signal.** As shown in Figure 9-8, the first reversal following a signal may not be within the desirable risk, but by placing a trailing entry order using the point-and-figure reversal value, while prices are moving counter to the direction of the signal, an entry will occur on a confirmation of the original direction with a stop-loss at the minimum 4-box distance.

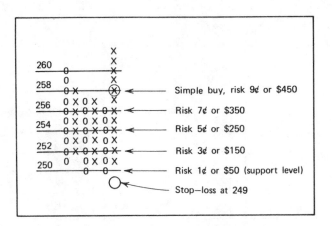

Figure 9-7   Entering on a pullback.

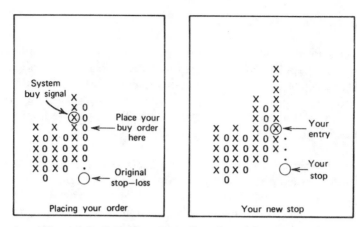

Figure 9-8   Entering on a confirmation of the new trend.

This technique is frequently used by traders who firmly believe that a reversal follows immediately after a breakout and prevents both high risk and false signals. If the pullback that follows the breakout continues in an adverse direction, penetrates the other support or resistance level, and triggers the original system stop-loss, no entry occurs, thus saving a substantial whipsaw loss.

The reversal principle in step 2 can also be effective for building positions. In bar charting, a pullback to a bullish support line or a bearish resistance line was a point for adding to a position with a risk limited to penetration of the major trendline. The equivalent procedure using point-and-figure is to add on each reversal back in the direction of the trend using the newly formed stop-loss point to exit the entire position as shown in Figure 9-9.

Take It and Run!

There comes a time in most substantial moves when there is ample profit and apprehension about how much of the paper profit will be returned before the

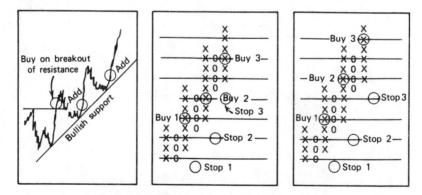

Figure 9-9   Three ways to compound positions.

system close-out signal is reached. Some traders prefer to take the profits. If the profit currently held in open positions is enough to sustain a life of leisure, a home in the mountains or South Seas, a country club and a small investment in a hotel or restaurant to occupy your time, then take it and run!

If you cannot sleep nights because you need money to meet personal commitments, you have just the right amount in unrealized profits, and one or two adverse days would ruin the opportunity, take the profits and begin again with a small investment. If you want a logical place to cash in on current open profits but you have some time and latitude, as long as you do not lose more than 10 to 25% of the existing profits, use the point-and-figure reversal value. The *reversal value*, the box size times the number of boxes in a reversal (usually three), is meant to indicate a significant contrary move and can be used as an objective indication of a change of direction. One approach to taking profits is shown in Figure 9-10.

In Figure 9-10*a*, a trailing 3-box reversal value is used for the stop-loss once there is a sustained move of at least 10 boxes. To reenter the move in the same direction, the same technique is used, (Figure 9-10*b*), adding another four boxes of profits while keeping the new risk small. In Figure 9-10*c*, this method lost four boxes of the potential profits when the reversal was short lived.

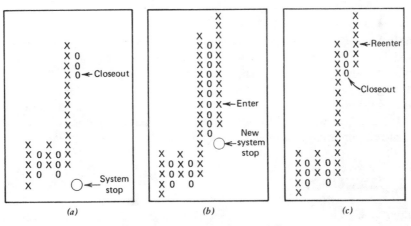

Figure 9-10 Cashing in on profits.

In general, taking profits in this way does not improve performance. It most often results in missing the biggest moves. A new rule should be carefully tested to know its effect on different market conditions. If successful, it should always be used. Selective use will limit potential profits but will not reduce losses.

Alternate Treatment of Reversals

Traditional point-and-figure charting favors the continuing trend. On highly volatile days, it is possible for both a trend continuation and a reversal to occur. Point-and-figure rules require that the trend continuation be recorded and the reversal ignored. Figure 9-11 shows a comparison of the two choices. In the example, prices are in an uptrend when a new 1-box high and a 3-box reversal both occur on

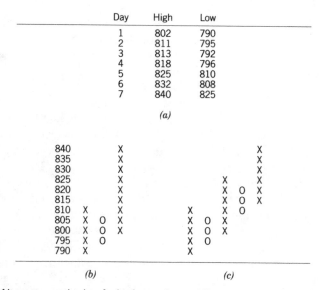

Figure 9-11 Alternate methods of plotting point-and-figure reversals. (a) Sample prices for plotting. (b) Traditional method. (c) Alternate rule taken on day 6.

day 6. In Figure 9-11b, the traditional approach is taken, resulting in a continuous upward trend with a stop-loss at 790. Taking the reversal first as an alternate rule, Figure 9-11c shows the same trend with a stop-loss at 805.

Plotting the reversal first will usually work to the benefit of the trader; both the stop-loss and change of trend will occur sooner. Subsequent computer testing proved this to be true. The alternate rule will not help when the reversal value is small and the optional reversals occur daily.

PRICE OBJECTIVES

Point-and-figure charting has two unique methods for calculating price objectives: *horizontal* and *vertical counts*. These techniques do not eliminate the use of the standard bar charting objectives, such as support and resistance levels, which apply here as well.

The Horizontal Count

The time that a commodity spends in a consolidation area is considered important in determining its potential move. One technique for calculating price objectives was to measure the width of the consolidation and project the same measurement up or down as the potential limits of the move. The point-and-figure horizontal-count method is a more exact approach to the same idea.

The upside price objective is calculated as

$$H_U = P_L + (W \times RV)$$

where H_U is the upside horizontal-count price objective,

$\quad$ P_L is the price of the lowest box of the base

$\quad$ RV is the reversal value of the commodity (number of boxes times the value of one box).

In order to complete this formula, the *base* needs to be identified. Count the number of columns (W) not including the breakout column and multiply that width by the value of a minimum reversal (RV); then add that result to the bottom point of the base to get the upper price objective. The base can always be identified after the break has occurred. For example, Figure 9-12 shows the March 74 contract of London Cocoa (£4 box) forming a very long but clear base. The reversal value is £12, and the width of the base is 19 columns (not counting the last column, which resulted in a breakout). Added to the lowest point of the base (£570) this gives an objective of £798, reached on the left shoulder of the topping formation. Another alternative is the wider base, marked as $W_2 = 25$. Using this selection results in a price objective of £870, by adding $25 \times £12 = 300$ to £570, the lowest point of the base.

The downwide objective is calculated in the same manner as the upside objective:

$$H_D = P_H - (W \times RV)$$

where H_D is the downside horizontal-count price objective

$\quad$ P_H is the price of the highest box of the top formation

$\quad$ W is the width of the top

$\quad$ RV is the reversal value

Some examples are given for downside objectives in the same Cocoa diagram (Figure 9-12). A small correction top could be isolated at the £720 level and two possible top widths, W_3 and W_5, could be chosen. W_3, the broader top, has a width of nine and a downside objective of £632. W_5 has a smaller width of five and a downside objective of £680. Although the lesser objective, calculated from W_5, is easy to reach, the farther one is reasonable because it coincides with a strong intermediate support level at about £640.

The very top formation was small and only produced a nearby price objective similar to the first downside example; there would be no indication that prices were ready for a major reversal. The top also forms a clear head-and-shoulders, which could be used in the same manner as in bar charting to find an objective. The height of the top of the head to the point on the neckline directly below is 20 boxes; the downside price objective is 20 boxes below the point where the neckline was penetrated by the breakout of the right shoulder, at £776, giving £696 as an objective.

The Vertical Count

The vertical count is a simpler and more definitive calculation than the horizontal count. As with the horizontal count, there is adequate time to identify the formations and establish a price objective before it is reached. The vertical count is a measure of volatility, the amount of rebound from a top or bottom, and can be

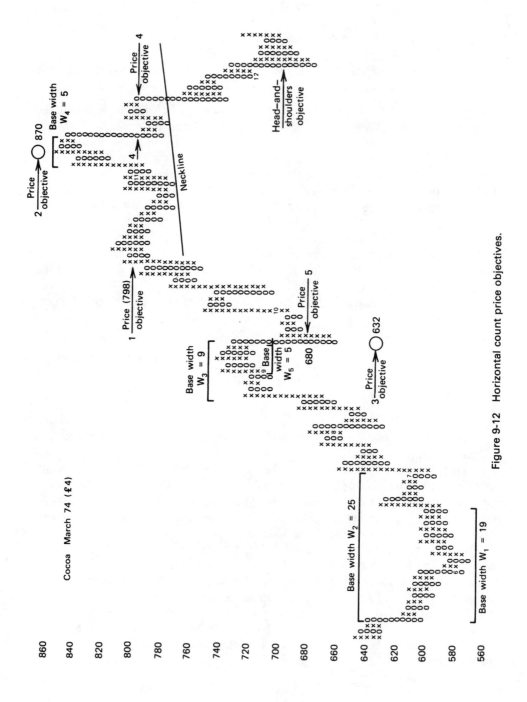

Figure 9-12 Horizontal count price objectives.

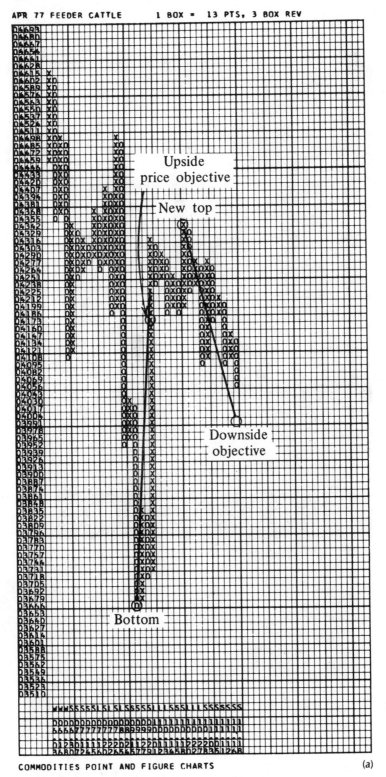

APR 77 FEEDER CATTLE   1 BOX = 13 PTS, 3 BOX REV

Upside price objective

New top

Downside objective

Bottom

COMMODITIES POINT AND FIGURE CHARTS   (a)

Figure 9-13 (*a*) April 77 feeder cattle point-and-figure chart. (*b*) May 77 corn point-and-figure chart.

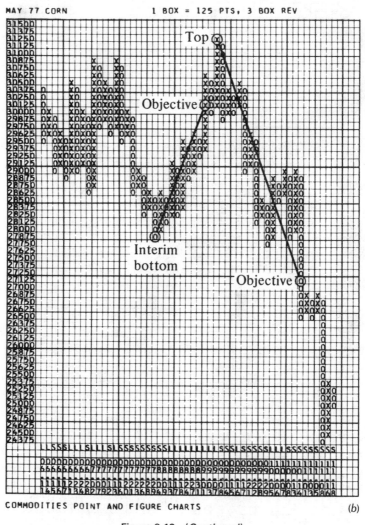

COMMODITIES POINT AND FIGURE CHARTS   (b)

Figure 9-13   (*Continued*)

used to determine the size of a retracement after a major price move. To calculate the upside vertical count price objective, locate the first reversal column after a bottom. To do this, a bottom must be established with one or more tests or a major resistance line must be broken. The vertical count price objective is then calculated:

$$V_{up} = \text{lowest box} + (\text{number of boxes in first reversal} \times \text{minimum number of boxes in a chart reversal})$$

The downside vertical count price objective is just the opposite:

$$V_{down} = \text{highest box} - (\text{number of boxes in the first reversal} \times \text{minimum number of boxes in a chart reversal})$$

Examples illustrating the vertical count are easy to find. Consider the following cases:

1. The April 77 feeder cattle chart (Figure 9-13*a*) has an obvious bottom at 36.66 and a 13-box reversal immediately following. Using the vertical count, a retracement of three times the primary reversal (13 boxes) is added to the low of the bottom. The price objective is then 41.73, 39 boxes above the low.
2. Following that upward move in April 77 feeder cattle, there is a top of 43.42 followed by a downward column of 9 boxes. The price objective becomes 27 boxes below the high, or 39.91, a likely goal on the chart because it is also the center of the only technical adjustment during the downtrend.
3. May 77 corn (Figure 9-13*b*) topped at 312½ and had an 11-box reversal in the next column; the price objective is 33 boxes lower at 271¼. Although that goal fell short of the lows by quite a distance, it netted about a 27¢ profit from the system sell signal. Earlier in the contract, there was an intermediate bottom at 278¾ with a 6-box reversal. The price objective of 301¼ was in the center of the prior major resistance level and resulted in another good trade.

As a simple measurement tool from contract highs or lows, this technique seems to have some reliability once the bottom or top becomes clear. It is, however, far from perfect.

A STUDY IN POINT-AND-FIGURE OPTIMIZATION

Throughout the point-and-figure discussion, there has been constant reference to "reversal value" or "3-box reversal" although there was no explicit suggestion of any alternative. In looking back at Table 9-1, it can be seen that the box sizes used prior to 1971 were generally smaller than the 1975 box sizes. In addition, larger boxes are used for long-term continuation charts and smaller ones for individual contracts of maximum term 1 to 1½ years. These differences are due to changing price levels and volatility as Wyckoff had suggested.

Prior to 1971, prices had been steadily increasing but at a much slower rate than 1974–1976. In a single year, the price fluctuation of any one commodity was easy to anticipate. Since 1969, prices have moved to unprecedented levels and back, with high volatility.

In 1969, sugar prices were plotted on a 5-point scale while prices ranged from 2.86¢ to 3.95¢ per pound; the possible span of point-and-figure boxes that could be filled was 22. In 1973, sugar prices went to almost 60¢ per pound, approximately 20 times their 1969 price. The daily limits were expanded from ½¢ to 2¢—more than the price had moved in 1 year. The use of a 5¢ point-and-figure box would result in a new reversal column on any day the market failed to continue its prior direction, and it no longer served the function of smoothing the price movement. It took 1200 boxes (10 feet of graph paper) to record the moves all the way up to 60¢.

One reason why the sugar scale changed from 5¢ to 20¢ boxes or soybeans from 1¢ to 10¢, was the practical need to fit the point-and-figure chart on a single page. Oddly enough, rescaling to fit a piece of paper of constant size has considerable merit. Look at soybeans in 1970. The range of the January 71 futures contract was

251⅝ to 315 and required a page of graph paper with only 64 boxes and an assigned value of 1¢ per box. Table 9-2 demonstrates what happens if the same number of boxes is used each year and if the scale is changed to accommodate the full price range. The reversal value is forced to increase so that the size of the point-and-figure chart and formations will look the same regardless of the price level. This is called *keeping the sensitivity constant*. The point-and-figure method, with its increased reversal value due to larger box size, will generate about the same number of reversals and buy and sell signals at any price level. Had prices increased without the box size increasing, the system would have had more frequent reversals, as in the sugar example, and it would be considered *more sensitive* to price changes.

The relationship of reversal value to the average price for the contracts 1971–1977 gives a price-volatility relationship, shown in the last column of Table 9-2. It is important to know to what degree prices will fluctuate as they advance and decline. This can become a valuable risk management tool.

Before continuing, certain questions must be asked of this method:

Why were soybeans started with a 1¢ box . . . why not ½¢ or 5¢?

Does this price-volatility relationship represent the best approach to rescaling?

How can it be used?

It can only be assumed that the original selection of a 1¢ box was a combination of both a smoothing attempt (chosen as a multiple of the minimum move) and convenience. The convenience part is easy to see; all the box sizes in Table 9-1 were even numbers. The first point-and-figure charts were drawn using the smallest allowable move and later refined to larger increments to identify long-term trends, and major support and resistance levels. However, it is necessary to find a more logical selection of starting parameters.

To answer the second question, the impact of rescaling on trading must be considered. As prices rise, boxes become larger and the minimum risk becomes proportionately greater. The risk of trading one contract increases at the same rate as the volatility expressed as a percentage of average price. If the box sizes are not

Table 9-2   Soybeans (January Futures Contract) Keeping the Size of the Chart the Same

Jan	High	Low	Average	Box Size	Reversal	Total Number of Boxes	Reversal Value	Reversal as Percentage of Average (%)
1971	315	251⅝	283¼	1¢	3	64	3¢	1.06
1972	346	282⅛	314	1¢	3	64	3¢	.95
1973	444	300	372	2¼¢	3	64	6¾¢	1.81
1974	915	349	632	9¢	3	63	27¢	5.27
1975	961	509	735	7¢	3	65	21¢	2.86
1976	705	439½	572¼	4¢	3	66	12¢	2.10
1977	782	490	636	4½¢	3	65	13½¢	2.12

increased when prices rise, risk can be kept small, but frequent losses will occur and trading will be based on extremely short-term trends.

There are few alternatives to rescaling, the two most reasonable being:

Method 1. Rechart at new prices levels using larger box values in order to keep the size of the chart constant and the sensitivity fixed as shown in Table 9-2.

Method 2. Increase the box value at a rate based on a fixed percentage of the current price so that a chart with a box value of 3 points at a price of 300 (1% value) would have a 6-point box at a price of 600.

Both approaches effectively increase the box value and risk while reducing the sensitivity of the chart as prices increase.

Solving the Scaling Problem

Before the price-volatility method can be used, it is necessary to perform a regression analysis on the average price and box size to find a formula for the relationship. A linear approximation was performed using the values in Table 9-2, based on a 3-box reversal, with the following results:

$$100 \times \text{volatility} = -28.8 + .485 \times \text{average price}$$

$$\text{box size} = -3.347 + .0147 \times \text{price}$$

The exact figures for the box size corresponding to specific price levels are shown in Table 9-3. Understanding that box sizes must be in practical increments, a variable-box point-and-figure chart can be constructed that changes box size as the price increases according to the table. These box sizes are shown with their corresponding price levels in Table 9-4.

Scaling by Constant Rate

The second choice of scaling requires answering the first question: "Why were soybeans started with a 1¢ box?" The long-term charts show that prior to 1970, prices were relatively stable and fluctuated in "normal" ranges. Finding the proper box size for the initial interval forms the basis for continuing into more volatile years. In 1970, Thiel and Davis published a study entitled *Point and*

Table 9-3   Point-and-Figure Price-Volatility Relationship (Method 1)

Average price	250	300	350	400	450	500	550	600
Percentage volatility	92	117	140	165	189	214	240	262
Box size	.328	1.06	1.80	2.54	3.20	4.01	4.75	5.49
Average price	650	700	750	800	850	900	950	1000
Percentage volatility	286	311	335	359	383	408	432	456
Box size	6.22	6.96	7.70	8.43	9.17	9.91	10.65	11.38

Table 9-4   Point-and-Figure Variable-Box Size for Specific
Price Levels (Method 1)

Box	Price	Box	Price	Box	Price	Box	Price	Box	Price
$\frac{1}{4}$	245	$2\frac{1}{4}$	380	$4\frac{1}{4}$	516	$6\frac{1}{4}$	652	$8\frac{1}{4}$	787
$\frac{1}{2}$	262	$2\frac{1}{2}$	397	$4\frac{1}{2}$	533	$6\frac{1}{2}$	669	$8\frac{1}{2}$	804
$\frac{3}{4}$	279	$2\frac{3}{4}$	414	$4\frac{3}{4}$	550	$6\frac{3}{4}$	686	$8\frac{3}{4}$	821
1	295	3	431	5	567	7	703	9	838
$1\frac{1}{4}$	312	$3\frac{1}{4}$	448	$5\frac{1}{4}$	584	$7\frac{1}{4}$	720	$9\frac{1}{4}$	855
$1\frac{1}{2}$	329	$3\frac{1}{2}$	465	$5\frac{1}{2}$	601	$7\frac{1}{2}$	736	$9\frac{1}{2}$	872
$1\frac{3}{4}$	346	$3\frac{3}{4}$	482	$5\frac{3}{4}$	618	$7\frac{3}{4}$	753	$9\frac{3}{4}$	889
2	363	4	499	6	634	8	770	10	906

Figure Commodity Trading: A Computer Evaluation (Dunn & Hargitt). In this analysis, they approach the problem of variable box size and reversal value strictly scientifically. They proceeded to test a good sampling of commodities, varying both the box size and reversal value, and recorded the resulting profits or losses and the reliability of the combination (percentage of profitable trades). For example, the January 66 soybean contract test results are presented in Table 9-5.

The study included the years 1960–1969, with data supplied by Dunn and Hargitt.[7] This coincides exactly with the time interval needed to determine the basic box size and reversal. In their study, Thiel and Davis draw conclusions and present alternatives for their selections, but the interests of this analysis are slightly different. Table 9-6 shows the final choice. The most important part of Table 9-6 is the reversal value, expressed as a percentage of the 10-year fluctuation. This figure represents the best choice of value for rescaling as a fixed percentage of the commodity's average price. The proper reversal criteria for each price level can now be selected using the rate of increase shown in the first and second formulas and the base price from Table 9-6.

For convenience, all box sizes will be chosen to correspond to the standard 3-box reversal. In general, a reversal value of 6¢ for soybeans would be profitable if plotted on a scale of 2×3, 3×2, 6×1, or 1×6, where the first number is the box size and the second is the number of boxes for a reversal. By having the percentage reversal value, the box and reversal criteria can be varied in a logical manner as the prices rise or fall. Using the January soybean contract, boxes can be assigned in such a way that the reversal value is close to 2.38% of the annual range (taken from Table 9-6). The results are the parameters shown in Table 9-7.

Variable-Scale Comparative Results

A simple way of determining the best selection of scaling is to plot the results. The choice of equal-percentage increases presented no problem. A standard point-

Table 9-5 Thiel and Davis' Results, January 66 Soybeans

Box Size	Reversal Boxes	Results		
		Profitability	Profit	Per Trade
0.500	4	2 of 12	−14.874	−1.239
0.500	5	2 of 12	−14.874	−1.239
0.500	6	2 of 10	−15.124	−1.512
⋮	⋮	⋮	⋮	⋮
1.000	4	1 of 2	3.00	1.500
⋮	⋮	⋮	⋮	⋮
4.000	1	1 of 1	7.25	7.25
⋮	⋮	⋮	⋮	⋮

Table 9-6 Optimum Box and Reversal Criteria for 10 Years—1960–1969 (Davis and Thiel)

	Approximate Price Range 1960–1969	Average	Box Size	Reversal	Reversal Value	10-Year Fluctuation (%)
Wheat	113–225	169.0	1½¢	3 boxes	4½¢ = $225	2.66
Corn	88–154	121.0	1½¢	4 boxes	6¢ = $300	4.95
Soybeans	196–309	252.0	2¢	3 boxes	6¢ = $300	2.38
Soybean meal	48–102	75.0	75 pts	2 boxes	150 = $150	2.00
Soybean oil	7.3–12.3	9.8	25 pts	1 box	25 = $150	2.55
Cattle	19–34	26.5	20 pts	2 boxes	40 = $160	1.50
Pork bellies	18–55	36.5	25 pts	6 boxes	150 = $540	4.10
Potatoes	1.9–8.4	5.15	5 pts	3 boxes	15 = $75	2.91
Copper	29–52	40.5	50 pts	4 boxes	200 = $500	4.93
Sugar	2–12	7.0	10 pts	5 boxes	54 = $560	7.14
Cocoa	12–51	31.5	25 pts	7 boxes	175 = $525	5.55
Silver	85–245	165.0	100 pts	2 boxes	200 = $200	1.21

Table 9-7 Holding the Chart to a 2.38% Reversal Value[a]

Soybean Contract	Highest Price	Lowest Price	Annual Range	Reversal Value	Box Size
Jan 71	315	251⅝	63⅜	1½	½
Jan 72	346	284⅞	61⅛	1½	½
Jan 73	444	300	144	3½	1⅛
Jan 74	915	354¼	560¾	13⅜	4½
Jan 75	961	509	452	10¾	3½
Jan 76	705	439½	265½	6⅜	2⅛
Jan 77	782½	490	292½	7	2⅜

[a] All values in cents.

and-figure chart was drawn with incremental price ranges assigned the necessary box size as follows:

Price range (¢/bu)	Box size (¢/bu)
240–286	2¢
286–351	2½¢
351–417	3¢
417–480	3½¢
480–544	4¢
544–598	4½¢
598–648	5¢
648–725	5½¢
725–917	6¢

Once the master chart is constructed, it will never have to be changed. If prices rise above the top of the scale, additional boxes can be numbered with larger increments. Using the standard three-box method of charting, each January soybean futures contract was plotted in Figure 9-14 and the results shown in Table 9-8. The profits were consistently good except for 1976. It should be noted that the number of trades increased as the average price increased throughout the test period. This can be expected since the box size does not increase as quickly at higher prices as does the price-volatility relationship. Because of this steady lag, the sensitivity of the system will increase noticeably at peak levels.

The chart based on the price-volatility approximation taken from Tables 9-3 and 9-4 is much smaller than the one used for equal percentage increases. Because the box sizes increase so rapidly, the formations appear more uniform at all price levels and the number of trades occurring during each contract was reasonably

Table 9-8 Results Using Equal Percentage Increases (Method 2)

	Trades		Net P/L[a]
	Total	Profitable	(¢/bu)
January 1966	2	1	+22
January 1971	4	3	+21
January 1972	3	2	+8½
January 1973	2	1	+93⅜
January 1974	20	9	+23⅜
January 1975	12	7	+554⅜
January 1976	16	7	−175¼
		Total	+548⅛

[a] 1¢ commissions deducted.

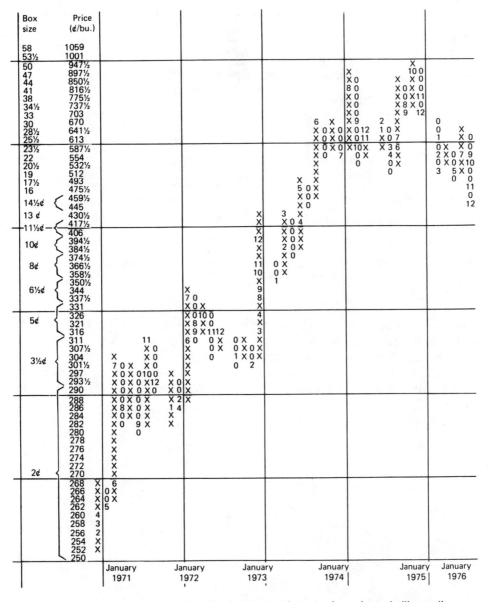

Figure 9-14   Point-and-figure chart for January soybeans using price-volatility scaling.

constant. The results of this method show that its application to a long-term chart would be practical. Any one contract contained only a small number of reversals and was able to generate from one to three trades (Table 9-9).

The plotted results appear to be much better than the tabulated results. This can be attributed to the increased risk at higher price levels. Although the number of boxes in a losing reversal remained small, the value of the loss increased by a factor of 25 from the bottom to the top of the chart. The few profits and losses that

Table 9-9   Results Using Price-Volatility Scaling

Individual Contracts	Trades		Net P/L[a] (¢/bu)
	Total	Profitable	
January 1971	3	1	-28
January 1972	2	1	$+\frac{1}{4}$
January 1973	1	1	$+109$
January 1974	2	1	$+32$
January 1975	1	0	-24
January 1976	3	1	-234
			Total $-144\frac{3}{4}$
Continuous trading 1971–1976	10	5	-70

[a] 1¢ commission deducted.

occur at higher price levels will be so significant in the final results that the earlier trading performance is unimportant.

Both variable-box approaches offer unique possibilities for identifying trends but increase the problems of risk management. Some of these effects can be offset by reducing the invested margin as prices rise. Other techniques are discussed in Chapter 18.

10
Charting Systems

The rapid growth of computerization has had a marked impact on technical trading. Most of the methods affected are of the moving average type including systematic testing. Recently, econometric analysis, cycles, and pattern recognition have been the subject of new computerized research. With the exception of point-and-figure, charting systems have not yet been bombarded with automated analyses.

The following systems are all based on charting. They do not all require the presence of a chart to be followed, but they are clearly interpretations of natural price patterns. The time that it takes for a price to move from one level to the next is not significant in many of these charting systems; it is only the level itself that is important.

SWING TRADING

The foundation for the largest number of chart-based systems is the "swing chart." Similar to point-and-figure, a swing is an upward or downward movement of a minimum size, regardless of the time it takes to achieve that move. Unlike point-and-figure, there are no "boxes," and the notation does not use Xs and Os. The basis of a swing chart is the *swing filter*. Once prices have reversed from a high or low point by the distance specified by the swing filter, a new vertical line is drawn in a column to the right of the current one. An example of a swing chart is given in Figure 10-1.

Rules for using the swing chart generally follow those of point-and-figure. New buy and sell signals occur at points where the new swing penetrates the level of the prior swing in the same direction. Secondary signals are given if the new signal is in the same direction as the trend. Stop-loss orders can be placed at trend reversal levels or at a point of fixed dollar loss.

The following systems are all unique, but at the same time they are clearly simple variations of the swing method of charting.

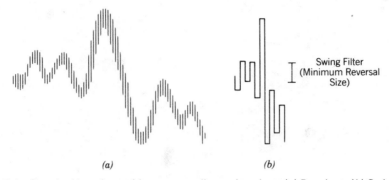

Figure 10-1   Standard bar chart with corresponding swing chart. (*a*) Bar chart. (*b*) Swing chart.

The Livermore System

Known as the greatest trader on Wall Street, Jesse Livermore was associated with every major move in both stocks and commodities during the 30-year period from 1910 to 1940. Livermore began his career as a "board boy," marking prices on the high slate boards that surrounded the New York Stock Exchange floor. During this time, he began to notice the distinct patterns or "habits" in the price movement that appeared in the columns of numbers.[1]

As Livermore developed his trading skills and eventually took his position as a professional trader, he maintained the habit of writing prices in columns headed Secondary Rally, Natural Rally, Up Trend, Down Trend, Natural Reaction, and Secondary Reaction. This may have been the basis for what is now considered a *swing chart*.

Livermore's approach to swing trading required two filters, a larger *swing filter* and a *penetration filter* of one-half the size of the swing filter. Penetrations were significant at price levels he called "pivot points." A pivot point is defined in retrospect as the top and bottom of each new swing and are marked with letters in Figure 10-2.[2]

As mentioned earlier, the swing chart differs primarily from the point-and-figure chart by having no box size. By measuring the change in trend as a reversal of the swing filter size from the last high or low swing, the pivot points are always posted at the exact price at which they occurred. In point-and-figure charting, using a 10-point box, a price rally that fails 5 points above the previous box will not be posted; a point-and-figure reversal is measured from the last posted box; therefore, the size of the price reversal needed to indicate a directional change may vary up to the size of one box.

Livermore's trading technique is a unique interpretation of the swing chart. Positions are taken only in the direction of the major trend. This trend is defined by confirming higher highs and higher lows (uptrend), or lower lows and lower

[1] Edwin Lefevre, *Reminiscences of a Stock Operator*, Books of Wall Street, Burlington, VT 1980. (First published by George H. Doran, 1923).
[2] Jesse Thompson, "The Livermore System," *Technical Analysis of Stocks & Commodities*, May 1983.

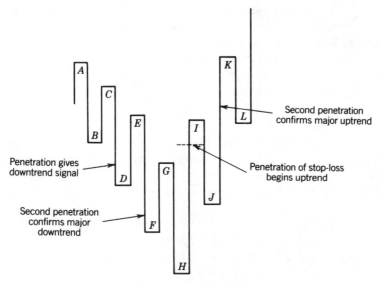

Figure 10-2   Trend change.

highs (downtrend), where the "penetration" filter is not broken in the reverse direction. That is, an uptrend is still intact as long as prices do not decline below the previous pivot point by as much as the penetration filter size (seen in Figure 10-2). Once the trend is identified, positions are added each time a new penetration occurs, confirming the trend direction. A stop-loss is placed at the point of penetration beyond the prior pivot point.

Failed Reversal. In the Livermore system, the first penetration of the stop-loss calls for liquidation of the current position. A second penetration is necessary to confirm the new trend. If the second penetration fails (at point K in Figure 10-3), it

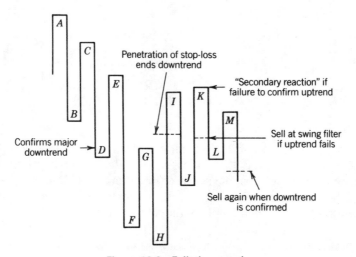

Figure 10-3   Failed reversal.

is considered a "secondary reaction" within the old trend. The downtrend may be reentered at a distance of the swing filter below K, guaranteeing that point K is defined, and again on the next swing, following pivot point M, when prices reach the penetration level below pivot point L. It is easier to reenter an old trend than to establish a position in a new one.

Wilder's Swing Index

An automated way of determining swings is presented with trading rules in Wilder's *Swing Index System*.[3] Wilder has determined that the five most important positive patterns in an uptrend are:

1. Today's close is higher than the prior close
2. Today's close is higher than today's open
3. Today's high is greater than the prior close
4. Today's low is greater than the prior close
5. The prior close was above the prior open

In a downtrend, these patterns are reversed.

The *Swing Index* (SI) combines these five factors, then scales the resulting value to fall between -100 and $+100$ as follows:

$$\text{SI} = 50 \left(\frac{(C_t - C_{t-1}) + .5(C_t - O_t) + .25(C_{t-1} - O_{t-1})}{R} \right) \frac{K}{M}$$

where K is the largest of $\begin{cases} H_t - C_{t-1} \\ L_t - C_{t-1} \end{cases}$

M is the value of a limit move
R is calculated from the following two steps:

1. Determine which is the largest of
   a. $H_t - C_{t-1}$
   b. $L_t - C_{t-1}$
   c. $H_t - L_t$
2. Calculate R according to the corresponding formula:
   a. $R = (H_t - C_{t-1}) - .5(L_t - C_{t-1}) + .25(C_{t-1} - O_{t-1})$
   b. $R = (L_t - C_{t-1}) - .5(H_t - C_{t-1}) + .25(C_{t-1} - O_{t-1})$
   c. $R = (H_t - L_t) + .25(C_{t-1} - O_{t-1})$

Although the usefulness of the SI cannot be determined without proper testing, the formulas combine factors that have a great deal of interest. The SI calculation uses three price relationships, the net price direction (close-to-close), the strength of today's trading (open-to-close), and the "memory" of yesterday's strength (prior open-to-close). It then employs the additional factor of volatility as a per-

[3] J. Welles Wilder, Jr., *New Concepts in Technical Trading Systems*, Trend Research, Greensboro, NC, 1978.

centage of the maximum possible move (K/M). The rest of the formula simply scales the results to within the required -100 to $+100$ range. In the first step of the calculation of R, the concept of the *true range* reappears.

The daily Swing Index values are added together to form an *Accumulated Swing Index* (ASI), which substitutes for the price chart, allowing ready identification of the significant highs and lows as well as clear application of Wilder's trading rules.

Terms used in the trading rules are as follows:

HSP The *high swing point*. Any day on which the ASI is higher than both the previous and the following day.

LSP The *low swing point*. Any day on which the ASI is lower than both the previous and the following day.

SAR *Stop and reverse* points of three types: *Index SAR* points are generated by the ASI calculation, *SAR* points apply to a specific price, and *Trailing Index SAR*, which lags 60 ASI points behind the best ASI value during a trade.

The Swing Index System rules are:

1. Initial entry:
   a. Enter a new long position when the ASI crosses above the previous HSP.
   b. Enter a new short position when the ASI crosses below the previous LSP.
2. Setting the SAR point:
   a. On entering a new long trade, the SAR is the most recent LSP; the SAR is reset to the first LSP following each new HSP. A *trailing SAR* is determined as the lowest daily low occurring between the highest HSP and the close of the day on which the ASI dropped 60 points or more.
   b. On entering a new short trade, the SAR is the most recent HSP; the SAR is reset to the first HSP following each new LSP. The *trailing SAR* is determined as the highest daily high occurring between the lowest LSP and the close of the day on which the ASI rose by 60 points or more.

Keltner's Minor-Trend Rule

One of the classic trading systems is the Minor-Trend Rule published by Keltner in his book *How to Make Money in Commodities* (The Keltner Statistical Service). It is still followed closely by a great part of the agricultural community and should be understood for its potential impact on markets.

Keltner defines an upward trend by the failure to make new lows (comparing today's low with the prior day) and a downtrend by the absence of new highs. This notion is consistent with chart interpretation of trendlines by measuring upward moves along the bottom and downward moves along the tops. The Minor-Trend Rule is a plan for using the daily trend as a trading guide. The rule states that the *minor trend* turns up when the *daily trend* sells above its most recent high; the *minor trend* stays up until the *daily trend* sells below its most recent low, when it is considered to have turned down. In order to trade using the Minor-Trend Rule, buy when the minor trend turns up and sell when the minor trend turns down; always reverse the position.

The Minor-Trend Rule is a simple short-term trading tool, buying on new highs and selling on new lows. It is a breakout method in the style of "swing" trading and can be used as a "leading indicator" of the major trend. It requires frequent trading in most markets, with risk varying according to the volatility of the commodity. Keltner's Minor-Trend Rule is the basis for a number of current technical systems that vary the time period over which prior highs and lows are established and consequently increase the interval between trades and the risk of each trade. An advantage of the Keltner approach is that it imposes no arbitrary restrictions on the analysis of prices (e.g., breakouts of 100 points).

Donchian's Four-Week Rule

Playboy's *Investment Guide* reviewed Donchian's Four-Week Rule as "childishly simple . . . was recently discovered to rank premiere among a dozen widely followed mechanical techniques." And the rules are simple:

1. Go long (and cover shorts) when the current price exceeds the highs of the previous 4 full calendar weeks.
2. Go short (and liquidate longs) when the current price falls below the lows of the previous 4 full calendar weeks.
3. Roll forward if necessary into the next contract on the last day of the month preceding expiration.

In 1970, *The Traders Note Book* (Dunn and Hargitt Financial Services), rated the Four-Week Rule as the best of the popular systems of the day. Based on 16 years of history, the best performers were December wheat, June cattle, May copper, August bellies, January soybean oil, and May potatoes.

The system satisfies the basic concepts of trading with the trend, limiting losses and following well-defined rules. It bears a great resemblance to the principle of Keltner's Minor-Trend Rule, modified to avoid trading too often. The system is so simple that the only comments about it must also be simple: can a Four-Week Rule work for all commodities? If the volatility of a commodity increases dramatically, the high and low for a 4-week period could become astronomical while at the same time lower prices could cause narrow ranges in another commodity. The solution may be a price-level-modified rule that reduces the number of weeks (or days) in the high-low measured period as prices and volatility increase. A change of this sort would keep risk on a more even level but still relate to the basic volatility principle of the original system. The concept can easily be tested by any trader without the need of a computer.

Modified for the Final 3 Months. An actual system based on the Four-Week Rule uses only the last 3 months of each contract. Beginning 3 months before the delivery month, plot the highs and lows according to the Four-Week Rule. For example, trading December silver, start on September 1 and plot for 4 weeks. The first time the market price crosses the high or low of that 4-week period, take the appropriate long or short position and place a stop-loss of $2\frac{1}{2}\%$ of the entry price. If not stopped out, liquidate the position on the last day of the month prior to delivery. If stopped out reenter a new position using the high and low established during the original 4 weeks.

The theory behind the modification is that breakouts are more valid and larger in the period just prior to delivery. An advantage of the system is that it trades very little and has a low commission burden. The disadvantage is that when tested over a diversified market, it showed only 6 profits out of 23 trades and a net loss of $6900.

The N-Day Rule

Computers have allowed us to take many simple ideas and examine them in great detail. One of the first projects was to change the Four-Week Rule into the *N-Day Rule*. The rationale seems logical. If the Four-Week Rule works but the equity drawdown is too large, shortening the time period should improve results.

The N-Day Rule states that a buy signal occurs when the current price exceeds the highest price of the past N days; a sell signal occurs when the current price falls below the lowest price of the past N days. The determination of N is critical to the success of this system. The most obvious approach to finding N is by testing a broad range of values (as will be shown in the next section). It has also been suggested that N could be variable based on the relationship of "normal" volatility to "current" volatility.[4]

$$N_t = N_I \times \frac{V_n}{V_c}$$

where N_t is the number of days used for today's calculation

N_I is the initial days used for "normal" markets

V_n is the normal volatility measured over historical data

V_c is the current volatility measured over a fixed period shorter than the "normal" volatility

As the current volatility increases, the number of days used in today's calculation decreases.

Testing the N-Day Rule. Hochheimer tested weekly breakouts, a limited case of the N-Day Rule; his report called it the *Weekly Price Channel*. Weekly breakouts produce a slow trading system that depends on major moves for profits. About 75% of those commodities tested in this 1982 study[5] showed higher risk (some very high), than the crossover systems tested earlier (see Chapter 15).

The original purpose for the *Weekly Rule* was to look at prices only on Friday. The close on Friday is considered in the same sense as the daily close—the

[4] Andrew D. Seidel and Philip M. Ginsberg, *Commodities Trading,* Prentice-Hall, Englewood Cliffs, NJ, 1983.
[5] Frank L. Hochheimer, *Computerized Trading Techniques 1982,* Merrill Lynch Commodities, New York, 1982.

evening up at the end of the day. Traders are attributed with the feeling that holding a position over a weekend is the only thing worse than holding it overnight. This "evening-up" will prevent false signals that may never occur mid-day or mid-week.

Typical trading rules for a Weekly Price Channel system would be

1. *Buy* (and close-out shorts) if the closing price on Friday exceeds the highest closing price of the past *N* weeks.
2. *Sell* (and close-out longs) if the close on Friday is below the lowest closing price of the past *N* weeks.

Because this model is always in the market, it is possible for the risk to become very high. The commitment to a new long position is the difference between the highest and lowest closing prices of the past *N* weeks. In addition, even if penetrated, the position is not liquidated until the close of Friday. This could be a very risky proposition.

Alternate rules were tested by Hochheimer in his study. Buy and sell signals were taken at the time that the intraday new high or new low occurred. No comparison was available to determine whether the risk was greater or less than the conventional approach. Hochheimer also tested the Weekly Rule with the week ending on days other than Friday. It was not apparent that any one day was better.

WILLIAM DUNNIGAN AND "THE THRUST METHOD"

Dunnigan's work in the early 1950s is based on chart formations and is purely technical. Although an admirer of others' ability to perform fundamental analysis, his practical approach is represented by these statements:

"If the economists are interested in the price of beans, they should, first of all, learn all they can about the *price of beans*." Then, by supporting their observations with the fundamental elements of supply and demand they will be "certain that the bean *prices will reflect these things*."[6]

Dunnigan did extensive research before his major publications in 1954. A follower of the Dow theory, he originally created a "breakaway system" of trading stocks and commodities, but was forced to drop this approach because of long strings of losses even though the net results of his system were profitable. He was also disappointed when his "2⅜ swing method" failed after its publication in *A Study in Wheat Trading*. But good often comes from failure and Dunnigan had realized by now that different measurements applied to each commodity at different price levels. His next system, the *Percentage Wheat Method,* used a combination of a 2½% penetration and a 3-day swing, introducing the time element into his work and perhaps the first notion of *thrust,* a substantial move within a predefined time interval. With the 2½%, 3-day swing, a buy signal was generated if the price of

[6] William Dunnigan, *Selected Studies in Speculation*, Dunnigan, San Francisco, 1954, p. 7.

wheat came within 2% of the lows, then reversed and moved up at least an additional $2\frac{1}{2}\%$ over a period of at least 3 days.

For Dunnigan, the swing method of charting[7] represented a breakthrough; it allowed each commodity to develop its natural pattern of moves, more or less volatile than any other commodity. He had a difficult time trying to find a criterion for his charts that satisfied all commodities, or even all grains, but established a $2 swing for stocks where Rhea's *Dow Theory* used only $1 moves. His studies of percentage swings were of no help.

The Thrust Method

Dunnigan's final development of the *Thrust Method* combined both the use of percentage measurements with the interpretation of chart patterns, later modified with some mathematical price objectives. He defines a *downswing* as a decline in which the current day's high and low are both lower than the corresponding high and low of the highest day of the prior *upswing*. If currently in an upswing, a higher high or higher low will continue the same move. The reverse effect of having both a higher high and low would result in a change from a downswing to an upswing. The "top" and "bottom" of a swing are the highest high of an upswing and the lowest low of a downswing, respectively. It should be noted that a broadening or consolidation day, in which the highs and lows are both greater or both contained within any previous day of the same swing, has no effect on the direction.

In addition to the swings, Dunnigan defines the five key buy patterns:

1. *Test of the bottom,* where prices come within a predetermined percentage of a prior low.
2. *Closing-price reversal,* a new low for the swing followed by a higher close than the prior day.
3. *Narrow range,* where the current day's range is less than half of the largest range for the swing.
4. *Inside range,* where both the high and low fall within the prior range.
5. *Penetration of the top* by any amount, conforming to the standard Dow theory buy signal.

All of these conditions can be reversed for the sell patterns. An entry buy signal was generated by combining the patterns indicating a preliminary buy, with a thrust the next day confirming the move. The *thrust* was defined as a variable price gain based on the level of the commodity (in 1954 wheat, this was $\frac{1}{2}$ to $1\frac{1}{2}$¢). Dunnigan's system attempted to enter the market long near a bottom and short near a top, an improvement on the Dow theory. Because of the risks, the market was asked to give evidence of a change of direction by satisfying two of the first four patterns followed by a thrust on the next day. Any variance would not satisfy the conditions and an entry near the top or bottom would be passed.

[7] W. D. Gann, *How To Make Profits in Commodities,* Lambert-Gann, Pomeroy, WA, 1976. This book devotes a large section to swing charts and includes many examples of markets prior to Dunnigan's work.

The same buy and sell signals applied for changes in direction that did not occur at prior tops and bottoms but somewhere within the previous trading range. In the event all the conditions were not satisfied and prices penetrated either the top or bottom, moving into a new price area, the fifth pattern satisfied the preliminary signal and a thrust could occur on any day. This was not restricted to the day following the penetration. So that if nothing else happened, Dunnigan followed the rules of the Dow Theory to insure not missing a major move.

It has been said by followers of Dunnigan's method that his *repeat* signals are the strongest part of his system; even Dunnigan states that they are more reliable although they restrict the size of the profit by not taking full advantage of the trend from its start. Repeat signals use relaxed rules not requiring a new thrust because the trend has already qualified. Two key situations for repeat buy signals are:

1. A test of the bottom followed by an inside range (market indecision).
2. A closing price reversal followed by an inside range.

A *double thrust* occurs when the first thrust is followed immediately by a second thrust; or, after the first thrust, a congestion area develops, followed by a second thrust in the same direction as the first. Although Dunnigan used a fixed number of points to define his "thrust," today's traders may find the standard deviation of the daily price changes a more practical basis for identifying significant price moves.

"One-Way Formula"

Dunnigan worked on what he hoped would be a generalized version of his successful *Thrust Method* and called it the *One-Way Formula*. Based on his conclusions that the Thrust Method was too sensitive, causing more false signals than he was prepared to accept, he modified the confirmation aspect of the signal and made the thrust into the preliminary signal. He also emphasized longer price trends.

With the upswing and downswing remaining the same, Dunnigan modified the thrust to have its entire range outside the range of the prior day. For a preliminary buy, the low of the day must be above the high of the prior day. This is a stronger move than his original thrust but only constitutes a preliminary buy. The confirmation occurs only if an additional upthrust occurs after the formation of, or test of, a previous bottom. There must be a double bottom or ascending bottom followed by a thrust to get a buy signal near the lows. If the confirmation does not occur after the first bottom of an adjustment, it may still be valid on subsequent tests of the bottom.

For the *One-Way Formula,* repeat signals are identical to original confirming signals. Each one occurs on a pullback and test of a previous bottom, or ascending bottom, followed by an upthrust. Both the initial and repeat signals allow the trader to enter after a reaction to the main trend. The Dow approach to penetration is still allowable in the event all else fails. The refinement of the original thrust method satisfied Dunnigan's problem of getting in too soon.

The Square-Root Theory

The two previous methods show a conspicuous preponderance of entry techniques and an absence of ways to exit. Although it is valid to reverse positions when an opposite entry condition appears, Dunnigan spends a great effort in portfolio management[8] and risk-reward conditions that were linked to exits. By his own definition, his technique would be considered "trap forecasting," taking a quick or calculated profit rather than letting the trend run its course (the latter was called "continuous forecasting").

A fascinating calculation of risk evaluation and profit objectives is the *Square-Root Theory*. He strongly supported this method, thinking of it as the "golden"[9] key, and claiming recognition by numerous esoteric sources such as *The Journal of the American Statistical Association, The Analysts Journal,* and *Econometrica*. The theory claims that prices move in a square root relationship. For example, a commodity trading at 81 (or 9^2) would move to 64 (8^2) or 100 (10^2); either would be one point up or down based on the square root. The rule also states that a price may move to a level that is a multiple of its square root. A similar concept can be found greatly expanded in the works of Gann (Chapter 12).

NOFRI'S CONGESTION-PHASE SYSTEM

Commodity markets spend the greater part of their time in nontrending motions, moving up and down within a range determined by near-stable equilibrium of supply and demand. Most trend-followers complain about the poor performance that results from markets that fail to move continuously in one direction. However, their systems are designed to conserve capital by taking repeated small losses during these periods in order to capture the "big move." Eugene Nofri's system, presented by Jeanette Nofri Steinberg, is used during the long period of congestion, returning steady but small profits. Nofri's system does not concern itself with the long move, therefore the user of the Congestion-Phase System can wait to be certain of a well-defined congestion area before beginning a trading sequence.

The basis of the system is a third-day reversal. If prices are within a congestion range and have closed in the same direction for 2 consecutive days, take the opposite position on the close of day 2, anticipating a reversal. If this is correct, take the profits on the close of trading the next (third) day. Nofri claims a 75% probability of success using this technique, and the Theory of Runs supports that figure. If there is a 50% chance of a move either up or down on day 1, there is a 25% chance of the same move on the next day, and $12\frac{1}{2}$% chance on day 3. Considering both commissions and variation in the distribution, an assumption of 75% is reasonable.

Because the basis of the Congestion-Phase System is an unlikely run within a sideways price period, the substitution of a 4-day run instead of the current 3-day

---

[8] Each of his writings on systems contained examples of multiple-fund management of varied risk.
[9] Refers to the Greek description of Fibonacci ratios.

run should increase the profitability and reliability of the individual trades while reducing the number of opportunities.

The Congestion-Phase System is only applied to markets within a trading range specifically defined by Nofri. Users are cautioned not to be too anxious to trade in a newly formed range until adequate time has elapsed or a test of the support and resistance has failed. The top of the congestion area is defined as a high, which is immediately followed by 2 consecutive days of lower closing prices; the bottom of the congestion area is a low price followed by 2 higher days. A new high or low price cancels the congestion area. Any 2 consecutive days with prices closing almost unchanged ($\frac{1}{2}$¢ for grains) are considered as 1 day for the purposes of the system. These ranges occur frequently and can be found by charting prices from only the last 10 days. In cases where the top or bottom has been formed following a major breakout or price run, a waiting period of 10 additional days is suggested to ensure the continuance of the congestion area and limit the risk during more volatile periods. Remember, systems that trade only within ranges offer many opportunities which should be exercised with patience.

A congestion area is not formed until both a top and bottom can be identified. Penetration of a previous top and formation of a new top redefines the range without altering the bottom point; the opposite case can occur for new bottoms. If a false breakout occurs lasting 2 or 3 days, safety suggests a waiting period of 7 days. Logical stops are also possible, the most obvious places being the top and bottom of the current congestion area, but closer stops could be formulated by measuring price volatility.

The Congestion-Phase System can stand alone as a short-term trading method or can be used to complement any longer technique. When trying to improve entry or exit fills, the system qualifies as a timing device but only within the congestion areas defined by the rules. It is not intended to be used in all situations. The converse of the system says that an entry signal given outside of a congestion area should be taken immediately because longer periods of prolonged movement in one direction are most likely. But in a trading range, the Congestion-Phase System may turn a moving average technique from a loser to a winner.

OUTSIDE DAYS WITH AN OUTSIDE CLOSE

There are numerous chart patterns that can be profitable if they are properly identified and traded consistently. Unfortunately, any one pattern may not appear very often and traders may become impatient of waiting for the opportunities. For others who may feel that overall trading success is a combination of small victories, the *outside day with an outside close* is one such successful pattern.

An outside day has the high and low outside the range of the previous day; that is, the high is higher and the low is lower. An outside close is one where the closing price is higher or lower than the prior day's high or low, respectively. This is considered an attempt to move in one direction followed by a strong push in the other direction. If the close was in the direction opposite to a recent price move, this is called a *key reversal day;*[10] however, because the previous price direction is

---

[10] See the discussion of key reversals in Chapter 8.

not distinguished it is not necessarily a reversal but may be a renewal of the trend direction.

A brief study by Arnold[11] showed that this pattern proved profitable for a small sample of currencies, metals, and financials using the following rules:

1. *Buy* on the close of an outside day if the close is above the prior high; *sell* if the close is below the prior low.
2. If buying, place a stop-loss just below the low of the outside day; if selling, place the stop just above the high.
3. Close-out the position on the close 3 days after entry.

After studying exits on days 1 through 5 following the trade entry, Arnold concluded that this formation predicts reasonably consistent price movements for the next 3 days.

ACTION AND REACTION

The human element in the market is not responsible for the ultimate rise and fall of prices, but for the way in which prices find their proper level. Each move is a series of overreactions and adjustments. Many stock and commodity analysts have studied this phenomenon and base entire systems and trading rules on their observations. Elliott's *Wave Principle* is the clearest of the theories founded entirely on this notion. Tubbs' *Stock Market Correspondence Course* is the first to define the magnitude of these reactions in the *Law of Proportion*; more recently, the Trident System has been based on both the patterns and the size of the action and reaction.

Retracement of a major bull campaign is the most familiar of the market reactions and the one to which almost every theory applies. It is virtually unanimous that a 100% retracement, back to the beginning of the move, encounters the most important support level. The 100% figure itself has been discussed in terms of unity, referring to its behavioral significance. The next most accepted retracement level is 50%, strongly supported by Gann and commonly discussed by experienced speculators. The other significant levels vary according to different theories:

Schabacker accepts an adjustment of $\frac{1}{3}$ or $\frac{1}{2}$, considering anything larger to be a trend reversal.
Angas anticipates 25% reactions for intermediate trends.
Dunnigan and Tubbs look at the larger $\frac{1}{2}$, $\frac{2}{3}$, or $\frac{3}{4}$ adjustment.
Gann takes inverse powers of 2 as behaviorally significant: $\frac{1}{2}$, $\frac{1}{4}$, $\frac{1}{8}$, . . .
Elliott based his projections on the Fibonacci ratio and its complement (.618 and .382).

Predicting advances into new ground is also based on prior moves. Gann believed in multiples of the lowest historic price as well as even numbers; prices

---

[11] Curtis Arnold, "Your Computer Can Take You Beyond Charting," *Futures*, May 1984.

would find natural resistance at \$2, \$3, . . . , at intermediate levels of \$2.50, \$3.50, . . . , or at two to three times the base price level. Elliott looked at moves of 1.618% based on a Fibonacci ratio.

These rules cannot be proved scientifically but they are accepted by most traders. In general terms, the retracement theories, or "revelation methods," can be categorized as either *proportional retracements* or *time-distance goals*. Proportional retracement states that prices will return to a level which is clearly related, by proportion or ratio, to the length of the prior price move. The larger the move, the clearer the retracement. The percentages and ratios expected to be successful are those that are most obvious: 100%, 50%, 33%, and so on in addition to the Fibonacci ratio 1.618 and its inverse 0.618. The time-distance rule is popularized in the works of Gann (see Chapter 12). Gann's retracement objectives can best be thought of as forming an arc of a circle, with the center at the price peak. The goal is satisfied when prices touch any point on the circle.

Tubbs' Law of Proportion

The technical point of Tubbs' course in stock market trading is heavy chart interpretation. The *Law of Proportion* presented in Lesson 9 is a well-defined action-and-reaction law. In cases where the nearby highs or lows of a swing were not broken, Tubbs claims four out of five successful predictions with his principle. The law states:

Aggregates and individual stocks tend to run on half, two-thirds, three-fourths of previous moves. First in relation to the next preceding move which was made. Then in relation to the move preceding that.

Graphically, an initial move from \$4 to \$6 in silver, would react $\frac{1}{2}$ to \$5, $\frac{2}{3}$ to \$4.67, or $\frac{3}{4}$ to \$4.50. Tubbs does allow for support as a major obstacle to the measured price move, and so unity may be added to the three proportions. Figure 10-4 shows subsequent reactions to the silver move just described; the second reversal could be any of three magnitudes (or back to major support at \$4.00), ending at \$4.50, a $\frac{3}{4}$ reversal. Reversals 3, 4, and 5 are shown with their possible objectives. The last reversal, 5, becomes so small that the major support levels are considered as having primary significance (horizontal broken lines), along with proportions of moves 1 and 2. Major support at \$4.00 coincides with $\frac{1}{2}$ of move 1 and $\frac{2}{3}$ of move 2. This would normally be sufficient to nominate that point as the most likely to succeed. Tubbs indicates that these points rarely occur with exactness, but proportions serve as a valuable guideline. The principle is one of reaction in relationship to an obvious preceding action.

Trident

The Trident Commodity-Trading System received its fair share of publicity when it was introduced at the beginning of 1975. An article in the 1977 *Dow Jones Commodities Handbook* has an excellent review of the background of the system

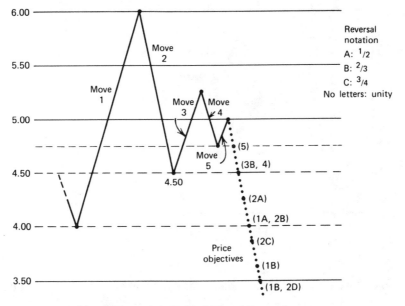

Figure 10-4 Tubbs' Law of Proportion.

and some of the conflicts surrounding its presentation and subsequent successes and failures. The system itself is not unique in concept but in its implementation. It is based upon the principle of price action and reaction with formations similar to the "waves" of R. N. Elliott. For each price move, there is a point of under-value and overvalue with subsequent reaction, or adjustments, in price as it moves irregularly in the direction determined by the ultimate balance of supply and demand.

The object of the system is to trade in the direction of the main trend but take advantage of the reaction (or waves) to get favorable entry and exit points. The concept of trading with the trend and entering on reactions is discussed in commodity technical analysis as early as 1942 by W. D. Gann and in the preceding section on action and reaction. The goal is to predict where the reactions will occur and what profit objective to set for each trade.[12] Trident's approach is easy to understand: Each wave in the direction of the main trend will be equal in length to the previous wave in the same direction. The target is calculated by adding this distance to the highest or lowest point of the completed reaction. As with Elliot's principle, the determination of the tops and bottoms of the waves is dependent on the time element used; the complex form of primary and intermediate waves would hold true with Trident (Figure 10-5).

Because there are inaccuracies in the measurement of behavioral phenomena, Trident emphasizes the practical side of its theory by offering latitude in its choice of entry and exit points. By entering after 25% of the anticipated move has occurred and exiting 25% before the target, there is ample time to determine that the downward reaction has ended before your long position is taken and enough

---

[12] Gann's work also discusses this topic specifically.

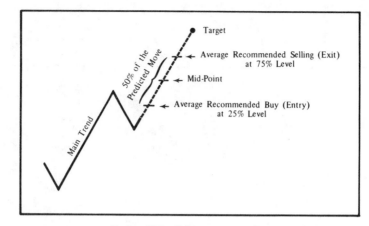

Figure 10-5   Trident entry-exit.

caution to exit well before the next reaction. A critical point in each main trend is midway between the start of the move and the target. If the midpoint is not reached, there is a change in direction of the main trend causing a reevaluation of the main trend and the reactions. A change of direction is considered conclusive if a reversal equal in size to 25% of the last reaction occurs during what was expected to be an extension of the main trend. That 25% value becomes the trailing stop-loss on any trade in the event the objective is not reached.

This discussion is not intended to be a complete representation of the Trident System, but a brief description of its essential ideas. The actual system has substantial refinements and subleties in target selection for major and minor trends and corrective moves; it includes points to reverse positions based on the trailing stop.

In a later bulletin to Trident users, it was suggested that a modification to the system be implemented with respect to money management. Using a technique similar to the Martingale System, each loss is followed by an increase in the number of positions traded. The trader only has to continue to extend his positions and stay with the system until he wins. A comprehensive version of this classic gambling approach can be found in the section *Theory of Runs,* in Chapter 17. The Trident concepts are all reasonable and generally accepted by experienced traders. The concepts are advance and retracement, trade the trend, and don't pick tops and bottoms, but take the center out of each move and use a trailing stop. It is more carefully defined than most charting systems and it should be interesting to follow.

CHANNEL RULES

A *channel* is a term used to describe a chart formation consisting of a trendline and an additional parallel line drawn to envelop price movement. A mathematical way of representing a channel might use the average of the high, low, and close to designate the center and a band based on the highs and lows. The midpoint M and range R can be calculated

$$M_t = \frac{1}{3N} \sum^{N} (H_t + L_t + C_t)$$

$$R_t = \frac{1}{N} \sum^{N} (H_t - L_t)$$

Then, the upper and lower channel bands forecasted for the next day are

$$U'_{t+1} = M_t + (M_t - M_{t-1}) + wR_t$$

$$L'_{t+1} = M_t + (M_t - M_{t-1}) - wR_t$$

The bands are created by extrapolating the average midpoint and adding or sub-tracting the average daily range R multiplied by a scaling factor w. A long position is taken when the new price $P_{t+1} > U'_{t+1}$; a short is taken when $P_{t+1} < L'_{t+1}$. If a "channel" profit objective is used, it can be calculated at a point equal in distance to the channel width from the channel breakout as follows

Long objective: $UO_{t+1} = U'_{t+1} + 2wR_t$

Short objective: $LO_{t+1} = L'_{t+1} - 2wR_t$

Because the value wR_t represents one-half the band width, $2wR_t$ would place the objective an equal band width above or below the breakout point on any day. The objective may remain fixed at the price level determined on the day of the breakout, or preferably, will change each day to remain one band width from the new channel value (Figure 10-6).

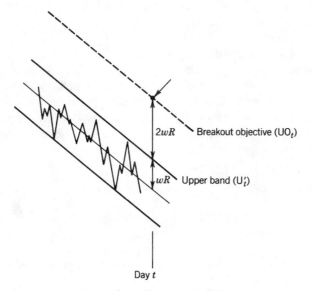

Figure 10-6 Channel calculation.

An alternate way of defining a channel would be to use a regression analysis (*linear* for a straight channel, *log* for a curved one) and use the standard deviation of the errors to define the band. The other rules would remain the same.[13]

COMBINING TECHNIQUES

Richard D. Wyckoff relied solely on charts to determine the motives behind price behavior. He combined the three most popular methods, bar charting, point charts (the predecessor of point-and-figure charts), and waves to identify the direction, the extent, and the timing of price behavior, respectively.[14]

To Wyckoff, the bar chart combined price and volume to show the direction of the price movement. In general terms, it shows the trading ranges in which supply and demand are balanced. The volume complemented this by giving the intensity of trading, which relates to the *quality* of the long or short position. Wyckoff used *group charts,* or indices, to select the stocks with the most potential, rather than looking at individual stock price movement.

Point-and-figure charts condense price action. If prices move from lower to higher levels due to events, the time it takes to reach the new level is unimportant. Point-and-figure charts record events, not time. As long as prices rise without a significant reversal, the chart uses only one column; when prices change direction, a new column is posted (see Chapter 9 as well as the swing trading section of this chapter). Price objectives can be determined from formations in a point-and-figure chart usually related to the length of the sideways periods or "horizontal formations." These objectives are very different and normally closer than objectives found using similar bar chart formations.

The *wave chart,* similar to Elliott's theories, represents the behavior of investors; the natural rhythm of the market. Wyckoff uses these waves to determine the points of buying and selling within the limitations defined by both the bar chart and point-and-figure charts. He considered it essential to use the wave charts as a leading indicator of price movement.

Wyckoff used many technical tools but not rigidly. He did not believe in unconfirmed fundamentals but insisted that the market action was all you needed to know—the market's primary forces of supply and demand could be found in charts. He did not use triangles, flags, and other formations, which he considered to be a type of Rorschach test, but limited his analysis to the most basic patterns, the horizontal or congestion areas. He used time-based and event-based charts to find the direction and forecast, then relied on human behavior for timing. His trading was successful and his principles have survived.

---

[13] For a further discussion of channels, see Donald Lambert, "Commodity Channel Index," *Technical Analysis of Stocks & Commodities,* Oct. 1980, and John F. Ehlers, "Trading Channels," *Technical Analysis of Stocks & Commodities,* Apr. 1986.
[14] Jack K. Hutson, "Elements of Charting," *Technical Analysis of Stocks & Commodities,* Mar. 1986.

11
Spreads

Positions taken in opposing directions in related items are a *spread,* or "straddle." The most common use of the term relates to two delivery months for the same commodity. For example, a trader may take a long position in March Treasury bonds and a short position in the June contract (for the same year). The expectation is that prices will rise and that near-term delivery will rise faster than the deferred, netting a larger profit on the long position and a smaller loss on the short.

A spread is most often a way to reduce both the risk and, consequently, the potential profit that exists in a single, long or short commodity position. A spread is commonly placed in two delivery months of the same commodity, or in a combination of futures and physicals in the same market. The reduction in risk depends on the relationship between successive delivery months, which varies considerably with the commodity traded. These can be summarized as follows:

Financial markets nearest to delivery react faster and with greater magnitude to changing supply and demand situations. The deferred contracts will respond slower because the lasting effect on the commodity is not as clear.

Precious metals markets are noted for "pure carry." Successive delivery months always trade at a higher price based primarily on interest rates. If the price of the metal rises or interest rates rise (financial prices decline), the cost of carry increases and the spread between months widens. If metal prices or interest rates decline, the spread narrows. If metal prices and interest rates move in opposite ways, the effect on the spread is dampened to varying degrees.

Industrial metals, such as copper, will show normal carrying charges under most circumstances but are affected by demand to the extent that prices have been known to "invert" for significant periods of time.

Foreign exchange rates are dependent on the prevailing economic outlook for the specific country. A stable economy will show nearly unchanged forward rates; a weakening economy will cause the deferred contracts to be discounted. Because exchange rates must be quoted vis-à-vis other currencies, everything must be viewed as relative to another economy.

225

Agricultural products (*crops*) contain a well-defined carrying charge within each crop year. Expected variations in both supply and demand have made delivery month patterns differ from one another; however, prices rarely achieve "full carry." (Note that potatoes are an exception to the normal patterns shown by agricultural products.)

Livestock markets are noted for products that cannot be stored and redelivered; therefore, the prices for any one contract month are based on anticipated supply and demand at the time of delivery. Feedlots and farmers have been known to deliver early when prices were high or when production costs were

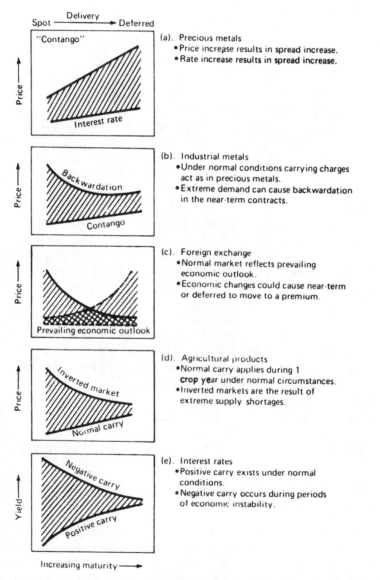

(a). Precious metals
- Price increase results in spread increase.
- Rate increase results in spread increase.

(b). Industrial metals
- Under normal conditions carrying charges act as in precious metals.
- Extreme demand can cause backwardation in the near-term contracts.

(c). Foreign exchange
- Normal market reflects prevailing economic outlook.
- Economic changes could cause near-term or deferred to move to a premium.

(d). Agricultural products
- Normal carry applies during 1 crop year under normal circumstances.
- Inverted markets are the result of extreme supply shortages.

(e). Interest rates
- Positive carry exists under normal conditions.
- Negative carry occurs during periods of economic instability.

Figure 11-1   Interdelivery price relationship and terminology. (*a*) Precious metals. (*b*) Industrial metals. (*c*) Foreign exchange. (*d*) Agricultural products. (*e*) Interest rates.

rising; however, this will cause an unreplaceable shortage in the nearest deferred months (Figure 11-1).[1]

Spreads are often unique to a specific commodity situation and cannot be generalized for all products. The trader must first understand the basis of the spread relationship before the most common technical analysis can be applied. This chapter will present many approaches to spreading that are clearly limited in scope to the examples specifically associated with the techniques. Further generalization should be approached with caution.

SPREAD RELATIONSHIPS

The nature of the spread will determine the type of trading strategy that may be applied. The types of spreads that are most often watched are:

1. *Substitute products,* such as wheat and corn or cattle and hogs. Product substitution ranges from those commodities that are nearly identical (e.g., 3-month T-bills and 3-month Eurodollars), to cotton and soybeans, which share the same land and growing season.
2. *Location spreads,* including gold in New York, Chicago, and London, cocoa in New York and London, and interbank currency rates.
3. *Carrying charge spreads* and *cash-and-carry,* where one delivery month is out-of-line with others.
4. *Product relationships,* such as crude oil versus heating oil and gasoline, and soybeans versus soybean meal and oil.
5. *Usage spreads,* including the hog–corn ratio, feeder cattle–corn–fat cattle, cocoa–sugar, broilers–corn, and lumber–plywood.

Arbitrage

When the two legs of a spread are highly correlated and therefore the opportunity for profit from price divergence is of short duration (less than 1 or 2 days), the trade is called an *arbitrage*. True arbitrage has essentially no trading risk; however, it is offset by small profits and limited opportunity. For example, a "spacial" arbitrageur using the interbank market might call one bank in Tokyo and another in Frankfurt to find their rates on the Mexican peso. If they differ, the trader would buy the peso from one bank and sell the peso at another provided:

1. The price difference was greater than the bid-asked spread, representing the cost of converting the currencies.
2. The arbitrageur has proper credit established with both banks.
3. The transaction can be performed *simultaneously* (by telephone). This requires one telephone in each ear or two traders working side-by-side.

[1] Perry J. Kaufman, "Technical Analysis," in Nancy H. Rothstein (Ed), *The Handbook of Financial Futures,* McGraw-Hill, New York, 1984.

Large-scale arbitrage has become the domain of major financial institutions who employ many traders, each provided with computer displays and telephones. These traders specialize in specific interest-rate markets, foreign exchange, or less often, precious metals. They constantly scan world quotes for price differences, then act quickly using cash, forward and futures markets. They trade large quantities to profit from small variations. For the interest rate markets, there are computer programs that compare the various types of coupons and maturities in order to identify an opportunity quickly. Such operations have become an integral part of the banking industry; they keep rates in-line with other banks and generate steady profits.

One well-known, second-order arbitrage combines foreign exchange forward rates with interest rate parity. Consider the following: A U.S. corporation would like to invest \$1 million for the next 6 months. The current U.S. T-bill return for the next 6 months is lower than the rate in West Germany and the inflation rate is about the same. The corporation is faced with the decision of whether to convert U.S. dollars to Deutschemarks and invest in West German time deposits or accept the lower U.S. rates. The decision is made easier if the corporation purchases goods from West Germany, since it must eventually convert U.S. dollars to Deutschemarks to satisfy payments; the conversion cost will then exist with either choice.

What if the value of the Deutschemark loses 1% against the U.S. dollar during the 6-month investment period? A corporation whose payment is stated in Deutschemarks suffers a 1% loss in the total interest received. If the 6-month return was 4%, interest received is now valued at \$400 less than the \$40,000 total; a small amount for the corporation making payment in Deutschemarks. A speculator would face a different problem because the entire return of \$1,040,000 would be reduced by 1% to \$1,029,600 netting a return of only 2.96%, less the additional cost of conversion. For the speculator, shifts in exchange rates often overwhelm the relative improvement in interest rate return.

The *interest rate parity theorem* will normally explain the differences between the foreign exchange rates and the relative interest rates of countries. It states that *the forward rate of a currency is equal to its present value plus the interest earned in that country for the period of the forward rate.*[2] Using the futures or interbank market for the forward rate ($DM_{1\,yr}$ is 1 year forward) and the spot rate for the current value (DM_{spot}), the annual interest rate in West Germany (I_{Ger}) is applied to obtain the relationship

$$DM_{1\,yr} = DM_{spot}(1 + I_{Ger})$$

Because the forward value of the U.S. dollar can be expressed similarly as

$$U.S._{1\,yr} = U.S._{spot}(1 + I_{U.S.})$$

Compute the *implied interest-rate/forward-rate parity* by dividing the second equation by the first:

$$U.S./DM_{1\,yr} = U.S./DM_{spot} \frac{1 + I_{U.S.}}{1 + I_{Ger}}$$

[2] James E. Higgens and Allen M. Loosigian, "Foreign Exchange Futures," in Perry J. Kaufman, (Ed.) *Handbook of Futures Markets*, Wiley, New York, 1984.

For example, if U.S. interest rates are 8%, West German rates are 6%, and the U.S./DM$_{spot}$ is 0.5000, the 1-year forward rate would be

$$U.S./DM_{1\ yr} = 0.5000\ \frac{1.08}{1.06}$$

$$U.S./DM_{1\ yr} = 0.5094$$

Class B Arbitrage. A recent development is *Class B arbitrage,* which takes advantage of the difference between the futures and the interbank forward markets. "Class B" actually refers to the category of membership on the International Monetary Market of the Chicago Mercantile Exchange, which provides exclusively for this type of arbitrage.

Intermarket Spreads. The propogation of financial and stock index futures markets have expanded the variety of intermarket spreads (location spreads) that are possible. Prior to these markets, only silver in New York, London, and Chicago, and gold in New York and Chicago received much attention. Now there is a selection of 3-month interest rate vehicles and a number of stock index markets, all competing for their share of hedgers and speculators. Figure 11-2 shows the spread between the Value Line Index, the first stock index market in Kansas City, and the S&P 500 in Chicago, the most active. Once the delivery months becomes liquid, they provide classic spread opportunities.

Traders must be cautious when attempting intermarket spreads. Because they are on different exchanges, no reduction in margin occurs. In addition, the simultaneous execution of both legs cannot be assured by either exchange. Legs must be entered "at the market" with orders placed at "almost" the same time. Further care must be taken so the contracts are as closely related as presumed; the three wheat contracts in Kansas City, Minneapolis, and Chicago trade wheat of different types for different purposes. Intermarket wheat spreads can often go the wrong way. Even the S&P 500 will shift relative to the Value Line when market participants concentrate on "blue chips."

Product Spreads

Product spreads are closely watched. The "soybean crush," the most popular among futures traders, has been used for many years. Product spreads usually involve three commodities, which may be of different delivery months, depending on the processing time. Possible product spreads are:

Raw product(s)	Resulting primary product(s)
Soybeans	Meal and oil
Crude oil	Gasoline and #2 heating oil
Feeder cattle and grain	Fat cattle
Feeder pigs and corn	Live hogs
Live hogs	Pork bellies

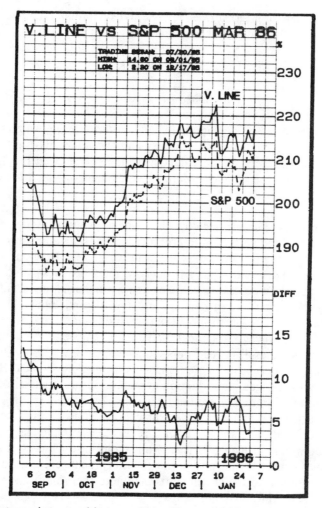

Figure 11-2 Intermarket spread between Value Line and S&P 500. (*Source:* Commodity Research Bureau Weekly Chart Service.)

Exchanges often allow reduced margins when these spreads are entered in the proper proportion at the same time.

Product spreads do not always correct for distortions within the time needed to be profitable for the trader. When the combined return on soybean meal and oil is below the cost of crushing the soybeans, processors may execute a *reverse soybean crush* spread, in which they sell the soybeans and buy the products. Even though this appears to be a clever way of keeping prices in-line, it is not done until the crushing margin is very negative. Processors cannot readily reduce their level of operation and lay-off employees; a reverse crush means that they are buying products as well as producing them—a position of significantly increased risk.

CHANGING SPREAD RELATIONSHIPS

Although some spread relationships will always exist, others may change due to:

1. Price level, such as during the silver bull market of 1980.
2. Consumer tastes, such as a shift away from red meat.
3. Health reasons, such as those often concerning nitrates in bacon.
4. New competition, such as increased supply of edible oils from the Far East impacting the soybean product relationship, or the effect of high-fructose corn sweeteners on the sugar industry.

Even though there may be anticipation of change, unexpected events relating to health or interruption of supply can produce a price shock which will affect many spreads.

Gold/Silver Ratio

A relationship that has always been followed with keen interest is the gold/silver ratio, traditionally considered normal at 33 : 1. It serves as a good example of the variability of many perceived spreads. When gold was $35 per ounce and silver about $1 per ounce, the relationship was never very stable. Between 1930 and 1945, silver prices dropped to about $.50 per ounce; from 1951 to 1962, they remained just under $1 per ounce and afterwards began its accelerating move to $38 per ounce in January 1980. Between 1944, when the International Monetary Fund (IMF) was formed, and 1971, the price of gold was fixed at $35 per ounce although in a few years before the cancellation of the agreement, the price varied above the designated value. From the late 1960s until the silver crisis of 1980, the gold/silver ratio ranged from about 20 : 1 to 45 : 1 in a slow cycle. During the crisis (September 1979–September 1980), the ratio fluctuated around 33 : 1 in a highly volatile pattern moving only slightly above and below its historic pattern. Following the silver crisis, the value of silver declined faster than gold reaching a ratio of 56 : 1 in June 1982, with gold at $314 and silver at $5.57. A year later, the ratio touched 33 : 1 and rapidly widened to 66 : 1 in June 1986.

Is the gold/silver ratio tradable? Was it ever a good spread trade? Probably not. The relationship is mainly dependent on public perception of both items as an enduring store of value. The same is true for the platinum/gold ratio (Figure 11-3), or the value of gems. Prices remain strong as long as the public confidence is unshaken. There is no fundamental reason for these prices remaining in the same ratio as there is for feedgrain prices to adjust relative to their protein content.

The public was hurt during the silver crisis. Many people made their purchases during the latter part of 1979, then lost heavily in 1980. At the same time that the U.S. dollar was gaining incredible strength and interest rates were still high, gold and silver prices were dropping rapidly.

Naturally, the value of gold did not decline as much as other "investments." Many countries still hold gold as a store of value. But times change and there has been a noticeable shift to the U.S. dollar as an international standard. Investors

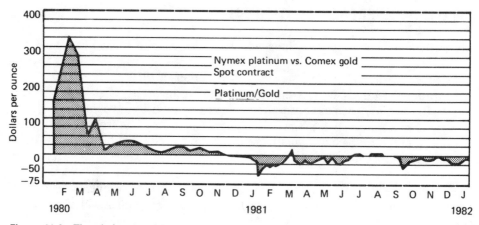

Figure 11-3   The platinum/gold spread, similar to gold/silver, shows periods where it might be successfully traded; however, markets such as 1980 always remain a possibility. (*Source:* New York Mercantile Exchange.)

feel safe with their money in U.S. banks and in U.S. dollars; they are willing to suffer short-term currency swings in exchange for security and diversification. For example, the price for oil, the largest traded commodity in the world, is quoted in U.S. dollars rather than gold.

There is no doubt the U.S. dollar will lose glamour if U.S. leadership or its economy weakens; if world peace becomes a reality, the security of the dollar will also be less important. There may be a return to gold and diamonds as an implied standard. However, these relationships are too uncertain to be tradeable, except at great risk.

CARRYING CHARGES

The *carrying charge* structure of a commodity determines the underlying differences in the relative price of each contract. For metals and most storable commodities, these charges consist of interest, storage costs, and insurance. All else being equal, a market with "normal carry" can be expected to show steadily higher prices for deferred contracts based entirely on the cost of carry. Prices that move out-of-line may be corrected by taking delivery of the nearby and redelivering against the next contract.

It is always possible for changes in supply and demand to alter the relationship of futures contracts so that the carrying charge pattern no longer appears "normal." Although this is not likely to occur in the metals, it often happens that an immediate demand for food can cause short-term increases in prices without substantial effect on more deferred months. This situation is called an *inverted market,* or "negative carry," even though the carrying charges are implicit in the price regardless of the pattern.

In the financial markets, a similar situation occurs when the demand for money increases dramatically in the short term. If the market expects that the demand will be short-lived, the rates on short-term maturities are significantly affected whereas the longer-term vehicles may show only a minor change.

In the metals markets, a normal carry is called "contango" (a term coined by the London Metals Exchange when referring to copper) and a negative carry is "backwardation." Changes in supply and demand that lead to backwardation are most likely to occur in the industrial metals where the commodity is consumed at a greater rate. Gold, silver, and platinum, the *precious-metals* markets, have a uniform price relationship in the deferred delivery months. Any deferred delivery price can be calculated by adding the current rate of interest (plus storage and insurance) to the value in the cash market. If interests rates rise and the price of gold remains the same, the carrying charges and the spread will increase. If the price of gold rises but interest rates remain constant, the carrying charges and spread will also increase because the increased value of the contract results in higher interest costs. Similarly, lower carrying charges and a narrowing spread will occur if either or both the rate of interest or the price of gold declines.

The terms used in referring to carrying charges in the financial markets are the same as those just mentioned, but the concepts are different. "Carry" is a term describing the yield-curve relationship. The concept of positive or normal carry is a curve that increases in yield with the time of maturity. The longer an investor is willing to commit money, the greater the yield. Negative carry can also exist for short periods of time. When economic conditions become unstable, the interest on short-term investments may increase sharply although longer-term rates will increase only slightly. Investors anticipate a correction in these short-term distortions, and do not often move money committed for longer periods for fear that rates will return to positive carry. The various relationships and terminology that exist in each commodity group can be found in Figure 11-1.

Implied Interest Rates

A "pure carry" market is one in which the forward price is entirely comprised of the costs of holding the physical product until a predetermined delivery date. As previously mentioned, these costs are those of storage, insurance, and the loan rate. As an example, consider gold, which is a classic "pure carry" market.

Assume that spot gold is selling for $300 per ounce and the 6-month forward contract for $313.50, an increase of 4.5%. With interest rates at 7%, there is a possibility of increasing the return on investment by purchasing gold at the current spot price of $300 per ounce and selling a futures contract 6-months deferred for $313.50. The gross profit is the difference between the futures price and the value of a comparable cash investment. Compare this with an initial investment of $30,000, which corresponds to the size of a 100 oz. futures contract of gold. That is,

6-month return on $30,000 cash at 7%	=	$ 1,050
6-month futures price	=	313.50
Less the spot price		−300.00
Gives the profit per oz.	=	13.50
Times the contract size of 100 oz.	=	$ 1,350

The gross improvement over the cash investment is $300, or 1% over the 6-month investment period.

However, there are costs involved in this "cash-and-carry" that do not exist in a straight time deposit. In addition to the storage and insurance of the physical gold, there are transaction costs involved in the trading of futures. Because these costs are relatively fixed, they are known in advance and the potential profit level of the cash-and-carry can be calculated.

The "Limited-Risk" Spread

If the nearby month of a storable commodity is at a discount to a deferred month by more than the cost of carry, a *limited-risk* spread may be entered by buying the nearby and selling the deferred. The trader then takes delivery of the nearby and redelivers it against the later contract. When trading commodities, which are significantly influenced by supply and demand, the outcome of this trade is never certain.

For example, the crude oil and copper markets are not affected by weather or planting conditions, and their supply is readily available. Demand has caused both markets to become inverted for long periods of time. Anticipation of lower prices, reduced demand, or a poor economy may result in a hand-to-mouth purchasing policy. This causes a concentrated short-term demand in the spot market and little activity in the deferred months, resulting in higher prices in the nearby months than further out. Carrying charges are still an integral part of the deferred price; if they were absent, the inversion would be more extreme. Even when they appear to have "normal carry," these markets are not candidates for an implied interest rate or cash-and-carry spreads.

The "limited-risk" spread may be better terms a "limited-profit" spread. Whereas the carrying charges provide a theoretical limit to the premium that a deferred month may have over a nearby, there is no limit to the discount that a month may take on. An increase in the expected supply might change a normal carry market to an inverted one, resulting in large losses.

The Carrying Charge Spread

The *carrying charge spread* is a popular trade based on anticipation of interest rate change and is therefore a lower risk than a net long or short position in any commodity. Consider gold again as an example.

In 1978, the price of gold was low (under $200 per ounce) as were interest rates (about 6%). An investor who had the foresight to expect both gold and interest rates to rise but who wanted to limit the risk of a speculative position, could have entered a *bull spread* by buying a deferred contract and selling a nearby contract of gold. The number of months between the contracts would determine the potential for both profit and risk; the further apart, the larger the carrying charges and the greater the expected spread movement.

Intracommodity and Intercommodity Financial Spreads

Spread relationships in financial markets represent anticipation of economic policy. The spread values themselves are well-defined by the interrelationship of all interest rate vehicles, but they will vary on the interpretation of the impact of government policy on money supply in reaction to the balance of trade, unemployment, expanding economy, and the time period in which the action will occur.

An *intracommodity spread,* or *delivery month spread* in a single financial instrument, such as T-bills, is a conservative speculation in changing policies as discussed in the previous section. A *bull spread,* long the nearby and short the deferred, shows a belief in temporarily declining interest rates. An *intercommodity* financial spread, involving different maturities, is a speculation in the changing yield curve. A ''long bonds/short bills'' position favors a negative carry, whereas ''long bills/short bonds'' expects a return to normal carry (with respect to futures prices).

Intercrop Spreads

A special case involving carrying charges is the *intercrop spread* which can be highly volatile, even though there is an old crop ''carry-over'' that ties the two seasons together. Soybeans, for example, are harvested mainly in September and October. The August delivery is clearly the old crop, and November is the first new crop month; the September contract often reflects the shift from old to new.

Normally, the old crop trades at a premium to the new crop. Carrying charges, accumulating since the previous winter, are part of the August price; export demand may cause shortages in the old crop, which move prices further above the cost of carry. Figure 11-4a shows the anticipated price pattern resulting from carrying charges during a normal year. The minimum storage commitment for the 3 months immediately following harvest is shown as a faster rise. Normal carry adds equal amounts to the price until the following September, where old and new crop mix. Finally, any carry-over must assume the price of the new crop which is in greater supply.

The theory behind an intercrop spread is that prices must come together when the old crop merges with the new crop. But can it be a profitable trade? Examine the two possible events which affect this trade:

1. Problems involving development of the new crop making supply uncertain. Prices in the new crop rise faster than the old crop (Figure 11-4b).
2. Export demand in the old crop results in old crop prices rising faster than new crop prices (Figure 11-4c).

In case 1, the spread between crops narrows and can only be traded *short the old crop, long the new crop.* This spread has limited potential since the November delivery cannot exceed the old crop by more than the normal carrying charge. At that point, processors will buy, store, and redeliver the old crop against the new crop. When prices in the new crop are nearing the old crop value, it makes sense

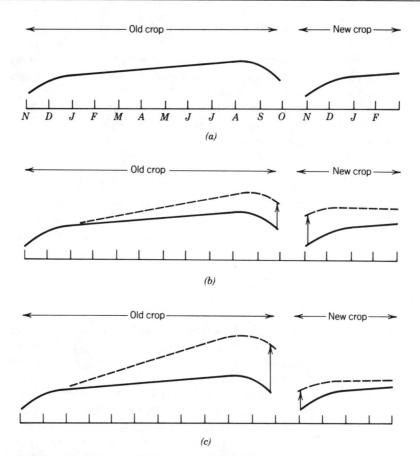

Figure 11-4 Intercrop spreads. (a) Normal carrying charge relationship. (b) New crop supply problems result in narrowing spreads. (c) Export effects the old crop more than the new, resulting in a widening spread.

to liquidate or even to reverse the spread. Once reversed, there is little risk that the spread can move adversely. A revised crop estimate that showed better yield than originally expected would cause the new crop to decline sharply and the spread to widen.

In case 2, export demand in the old crop causes the intercrop spread to widen at first. A spread trader will typically wait until export commitments are complete, then sell the old crop and buy the new. When old crop prices rise to a large premium over the new crop, many processors will reduce purchasing based on:

1. Low or negative profit margins at the current price levels.
2. Use of reserves or inventory to carry processing through until the lower new crop prices are available.

It is remarkable how demand is inversely related to price even when it is considered "inelastic." When a delay in purchasing or processing will result in greater profits for the commercial, it is somehow achieved.

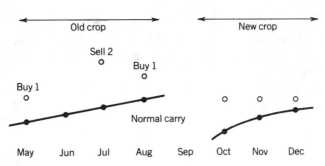

Figure 11-5   Delivery month distortions in the old crop making a *butterfly spread* possible.

Butterfly Spreads

A *butterfly spread*, normally referred to as just a "butterfly," is a low risk technique for capturing short-term interdelivery distortions. It is most appropriate in highly volatile markets, where the concentration of trading in one or two delivery months causes those contract prices to move away from the normal delivery month relationship.

For example, in April a combination of poor planting, declines in the U.S. dollar, and new export agreements changes the soybean prices as shown in Figure 11-5. Increased demand results in sharply higher July futures prices with a tapering-off of the effect in the more deferred contracts. The normal carrying charge relationship is shown as a straight line in the old crop, beginning again in the new crop. A butterfly entered in the old crop would mean selling two contracts of July soybeans and buying one contract each of May and August. This is the same as executing two spreads: long May, short July and short July, long August.

Each spread in the butterfly has a good chance of being profitable; the combination of the two is exceptionally good. The July contract cannot remain out-of-line with the deliveries on both sides because a trader could take delivery of the May contract and redeliver it in July at a profit exceeding the cost of carry. Under normal circumstances, commercial users of soybeans will defer their purchases to later months, depleting their reserves, to avoid paying a short-term premium and causing July prices to drop.

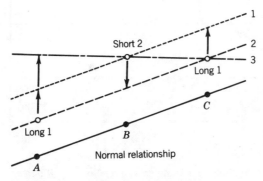

Figure 11-6   Corrections to interdelivery patterns.

The butterfly spread guarantees that any adjustment in the three contacts back to a normal relationship will prove profitable. If the price of both May and August rise to be in-line with July or if May rises to form an inverted relationship, the spread will be profitable (Figure 11-6).

The problem with such an ideal spread is the short life and difficult execution. Because profits are nearly riskless, opportunity is small. The beneficiaries of these trades are usually the floor traders who can act quickly. Once the position is entered, liquidation can be easily accomplished.

TECHNICAL ANALYSIS OF SPREADS

Once the spread components have been selected and there is full confidence in the underlying fundamental relationship (even if temporary), the extreme levels and trends may be found to determine which spread trades may be entered.

Most technical analysis of intracommodity spreads (e.g., March–December T-bonds) is represented as variations or distortions from the "normal" price relationship. In this method of trading, the distortions are also called "overbought" and "oversold" conditions and the approach is "countertrend." By subtracting the deferred price from the nearby (e.g., December from March of the same year) over the life of the contract for many years, the investor can measure the historic patterns (see Figure 11-7). These spread relationships will vary in a manner that allows the trader to set objectives. When March is trading $1\frac{1}{2}$ points over December, the spread can be sold; when March trades under December by $1\frac{1}{4}$ points, the spread can be bought.

Historical Comparisons

Those spreads with a sound fundamental basis will show clear patterns in their price history. Analysis of longer historic periods will result in a better understanding of the consistency and risk involved in trading the spread. A long-term study will reveal seasonal and cyclic moves as well as periods of lower and higher volatility.

Figure 11-7   Intracommodity interest rate spread relationship. (*Source: Handbook of Financial Futures,* p. 359.)

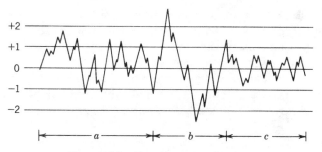

Figure 11-8   Changing spread ranges.

Many spread opportunities result from understanding changing spread patterns. For example, Figure 11-8 is a long-term spread that has three distinct ranges, shown along the bottom as a, b, and c. Spread traders during period a would have identified +1 and −1 as the extreme levels and entered positions at those points; the risk varied but remained within an acceptable range. The higher volatility during period b would have caused large losses for those traders used to the prior market patterns. Unprecedented shifts in the spread relationship would prompt traders to liquidate spreads. As period c begins, traders change their objectives to wait for a spread opportunity at ±2. Although they could not profit from the original extreme because spreads were entered too early, they are prepared for the next time. But instead of repeating itself, the spread narrows until it settles in a range of ±½. If it is now traded in this range, an increase to the prior "normal" levels of period a will produce a large loss.

This dilemma is common to spreading; spread prices shift from one range to another. When the range decreases, few spreads are taken, and when it increases, a large loss occurs. The following outlines possible solutions to this problem:

1. *Underlying price-volatility relationship*. Higher prices allow the spread to widen whereas lower prices force the spread price to narrow. The spread between heating oil and gasoline must be greater when those products are trading at $1.00 per gallon than when they are at one-half that price. Figure 11-8 could easily be related to changing price levels, where a is a long-term bull market, peaking in period b, and followed by a decline to lower levels in period c.
2. *Normal seasonal patterns*. Seasonality causes spreads to narrow and widen in predictable ways. During harvest, the *basis spread* (the difference between the spot and cash markets) widens, reflecting the available supply. After harvest, the basis will continue to narrow as a function of demand.
3. *Specific events*
   a. A freeze in coffee or orange juice results in a prolonged shift in prices, which will then make the next years' crop even more sensitive to a potential freeze.
   b. Events that cause seasonal price changes, such as exceptional crop demand, will nullify the seasonal patterns for the remainder of the crop year and often the next season.

c. Combination of similar circumstances, such as low inventory, stocks, or carry-over; prior year higher export demand; and dry, hot weather midway in the growing season will result in a "nervous" market, causing prices to rally in anticipation of problems becoming real. By observing past similar situations, the extent of the rally can be observed as large enough to use a medium to fast trend-following method, with profit-taking either at the time the trend turns or 1 month before harvest begins, whichever comes first.

Relative Spread Opportunities

A long-term analysis of a spread relationship will show the extent of variability and include most patterns. When the spread range is wide due to shifts cause by inventory cycles, changing public opinion, and other factors, a *relative* measure will be of interest. Figure 11-9*a* shows a simple example of a more complicated spread pattern.

The safest spread trades are those taken at historic highs and lows (H_1, L_3, H_6), anticipating a return to normal levels; these trades do not occur often. Instead, there are many opportunities to sell a *relatively overbought* (H_2, H_3, H_4, . . .) level or buy a *relatively oversold* level (L_1, L_2, L_4, . . .). There is less risk if the relative level is closer to the historic extreme.

The relative spread levels can be found by taking the difference between the spread price and a moving average. The number and magnitude of the relative tops and bottoms will vary with the speed of the trend; the faster the moving average (3 to 5 days), the more relative highs and lows will appear and the smaller the magnitude of those moves. Figure 11-9*b* shows a detrended spread chart based

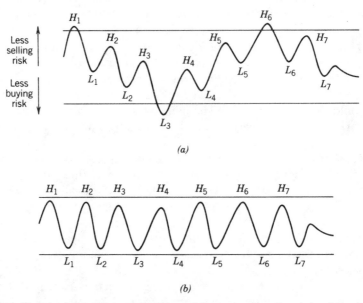

(a)

(b)

Figure 11-9 "Relative" spread opportunities. (a) Spread prices showing relative swings. (b) Prices adjusted to identify relative spread opportunities.

on the patterns in Figure 11-9a. The highs and lows are clear; however, it is not possible to distinguish those that have less risk from those with greater risk. When actually trading, selling H_3 is more likely to result in a loss than a profit. It will be necessary to use both charts to select the proper trades: one to locate the relative highs and lows, the other to determine risk.

Trend Analysis of Spreads

Moving averages, point-and-figure, and other trend-following methods are usually inappropriate for intracommodity spreads. The time necessary to develop a buy or sell signal using a trending approach often takes most of the potential profit from the trade. The magnitude of the profits and losses resulting from these spread trades is usually small compared to an outright long- or short-market position.

Trend-following methods apply to spreads when the movement of the spread is large enough to justify sacrificing both the beginning and end of the move in order to determine the direction of the trend. Using T-bonds and GNMAs as an example, the trader selects the delivery month to be analyzed (usually the same one) and subtracts the GNMA price from the bond price. The resulting price is treated as a single new commodity; a moving average, point-and-figure method, or another trend-following technique can be applied to these new numbers. When a buy signal occurs, the spread is bought (bonds are increasing in price with respect to GNMAs), and when a sell signal is generated, the spread is sold (bonds are decreasing in price with respect to GNMAs). These techniques can work as well as any analysis of the individual commodities.

Spreads that typically allow trend analysis are those with very wide swings extending for long time intervals. Some examples of these spreads (Figure 11-10) are:

Short- versus long-term interest rates

Hogs versus cattle

Gold versus silver

One currency versus another (e.g., British pound versus Deutschemark)

Bull and Bear Spreads. A spread can be a low risk substitute for an outright long- or short-trend position. In grains and foods, a bull market will result in prices of the nearby delivery months rising faster than deferred months. A *bull spread* can be placed by entering a long position in the nearby and a short position in a deferred month. Both risk and reward are reduced; the greater the time between months, the more volatile the spread (Figure 11-11). Once the price peaks in the uptrend, the spread must be reversed, as in an outright position, because the nearby delivery will decline faster than the deferred. By selling the nearby and buying the deferred contract, a *bear spread* is established.

The analysis that identifies the time to enter a bull or bear spread can be a standard trend-following approach based on the nearby contract only. Many traders believe that the spread must also confirm the trend before a position is taken; therefore, a moderate-speed moving average may be applied to the spread series.

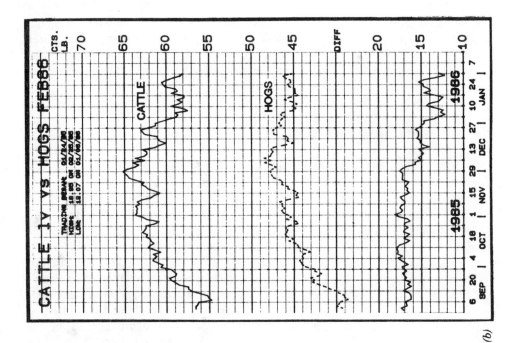

(b)

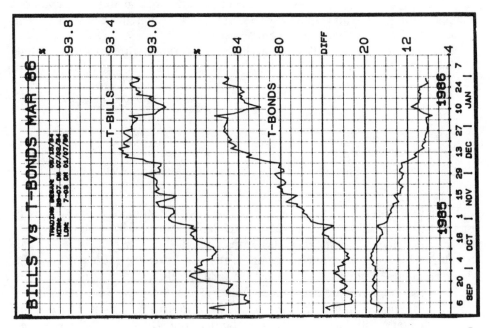

(a)

242

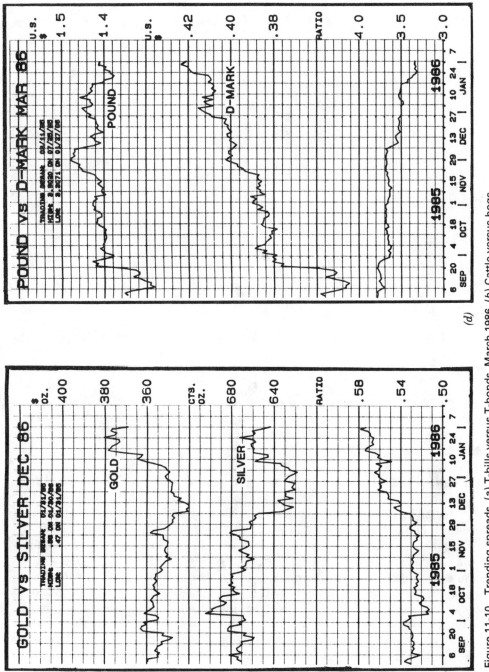

(d)

(c)

Figure 11-10   Trending spreads. (*a*) T-bills versus T-bonds, March 1986. (*b*) Cattle versus hogs,
February 1986. (*c*) Gold versus silver, December 1986. (*d*) Pound versus Deutschemark, March
1986. (*Source:* Commodity Research Bureau Weekly Chart Service.)

243

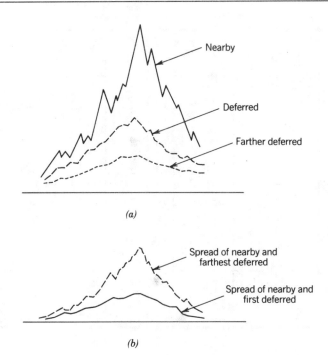

(a)

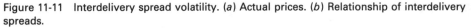

(b)

Figure 11-11   Interdelivery spread volatility. (a) Actual prices. (b) Relationship of interdelivery spreads.

This would provide a signal based on the relative change in spread direction. A simple 1-day change might be enough for the fast trader. An upward trend signal in the nearby delivery and a bear spread movement is a conflict that should be passed.

Legging-In and -Out of a Spread.   When both contract, or "legs," of a spread are not entered or closed-out at the same moment, trading risk is increased. An unprotected leg of a spread is simply an outright long or short position and must be managed carefully. Consider a bull spread in a fast-moving market. Although both legs can be entered simultaneously using a spread order, the long position (in the trend direction) might be entered first, followed by the short leg within a few minutes or a few days. If the market is trending steadily, profits in the long position can be protected when the short leg is entered. It is a rewarding philosophy when it works. If it doesn't work, there is a large loss on the outright position, which will be difficult to offset with the lower profits from the spread. If the purpose of trading a spread is to reduce risk, legging-in or legging-out is not going to accomplish that goal.

Protecting an existing trend position in the nearby month by spreading against the next deferred is not as good as simply liquidating the initial position. If the market has been going up and indicates a temporary downturn, some traders will "hedge" by selling the first deferred contract. A bull spread is held instead of an outright long. If correct about the turn, the trade risk is reduced but there is still a loss. If wrong about the change of direction, profits are reduced. Why hedge to reduce losses when closing-out the position eliminates them? In addition, the greater liquidity in the nearby contract favors the simple close-out over the spread.

When the trend turns from up to down, it is necessary to switch the spread from bull to bear. If large profits have been made in the bull move and both the trend and spread signal a downward turn, it could be tempting to lift the long leg, and hold the outright short using accrued profits to offset the increased risk. A more conservative trader might enter a bear spread in the first and second deferred months rather than the spot and first deferred, thereby reducing risk even further and allowing smaller profits—conserving prior success.

Reverse Response to Trending Markets. Some commodity spreads respond in just the opposite way to trends. For precious metals and potatoes, an upward trend results in the deferred contracts rising faster than the nearby. For example, consider the rising price of gold which results in a larger total contract value and consequently a higher interest charge based on that value.

Traders familiar with the potato market will know that higher prices, which reflects greater demand and product disappearance, will result in critical tightness in the last winter trading month. The perishable potato crop must last to early June when the first spring potatoes reach the market. Early demand on the stored crop will be magnified by the end of spring. For both metals and potatoes, a bull spread can be entered by selling the nearby and buying the deferred contracts.

Markets That Do Not Apply. During a trending period, most commodities exhibit a clear relationship between delivery months. Cattle, hogs, broilers, and eggs are nonstorable, however, and show little relationship in the response of deferred contracts to the same bullish or bearish news.

During periods of exceptional demand, livestock has been marketed early resulting in similar price moves in most nearby contracts. Even in the most extreme cases, this cannot be carried far into the future.

VOLATILITY AND SPREAD RATIOS

Higher price levels result in increased volatility in both individual commodities and their related spreads. Fast price movements and large swings associated with high price levels will create spread opportunities that are more profitable than normal with added execution latitude; markets with small movement are not candidates for spreads. The combination of two low-volatility markets produce spreads with such small potential that execution costs often exceed the expected profits.

The two sides of a spread rarely have the same volatility. When badly mismatched, a spread will act the same as an outright position in the more volatile side of the spread. For example, Figure 11-12a shows what appears to be an excellent spread relationship; however, Figure 11-12b reveals that the pattern is the result of two sideways markets, one highly volatile (A) and the other with low volatility (B). Market B offers little protection if market A were to move sharply higher instead of sideways.

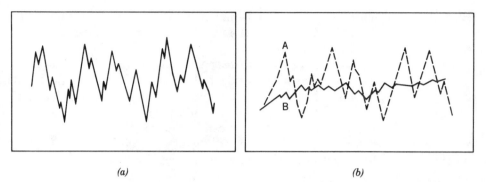

(a)   *(b)*

Figure 11-12   Poor spread selection. (*a*) Spread price. (*b*) Spread components.

The same illustration would be appropriate if a gold–silver spread were created by subtracting the price of silver from that of gold rather than taking a ratio. Equal moves of 10% in gold from $300 to $330 and silver from $6.00 to $6.60 would result in a spread price change from $294.00 to $323.40, effectively mirroring the gold change rather than maintaining an unchanged spread.

Spread Ratio

The individual markets which offer sound spread opportunities will vary in their absolute price range or volatility. For example, during 1984, the price of spot live hog futures varied from 43.80¢ to 58.00¢ per pound, whereas pork bellies ranged from 54.70¢ to 74.10¢ per pound. Both appear to be consistent in volatility as seen from the ratios, yet more than a 50% difference occurred in the size of the price change.

Had the ratio been seen to drop to 1.15, a long bellies, short hogs spread would have been entered. If the ratio had moved to 1.35, a spread would have been entered to buy hogs and sell bellies. Assume that this distortion occurred at prices near the lows and that prices then adjusted to 1.27 at the highs shown in Table 11-1. There are two possible trades that might have occurred:

	Spread Price	High	P/L		Contract Size	Net P/L
Case 1: Long bellies	50.00	74.10	$24.10	×	38,000	$9,158
Short hogs	43.48	58.00	(14.52)	×	30,000	(4,356)
Ratio	1.15	1.27				$4,802
Case 2: Short bellies	54.70	74.10	(19.40)	×	38,000	($7,372)
Long hogs	40.52	58.00	17.48	×	30,000	5,244
Ratio	1.35	1.27				($2,128)

In Case 1, the trade produces a profit while the relationship adjusts to normal; in Case 2, it results in a loss even though the same adjustment occurs. Two factors cause this: the different contract sizes and the absolute price range. If the contract

Table 11-1   Price Movement of Pork Bellies and
Live Hogs in 1984

	Low	High	Average	Range	Mean Volatility
Pork bellies	54.70	74.10	64.40	19.40	30%
Live hogs	43.80	58.00	50.90	14.20	28%
Ratio	1.25	1.27	1.27		
Spread	10.90	16.10	13.50		

sizes were adjusted to equal units, which can be done by trading four bellies and five hog contracts, the results would be:

		P/L per Contract	Number of Contracts	Total P/L
Case 1:	Long bellies	$9,158	4	$36,632
	Short hogs	(4,356)	5	21,780
	Spread results			$14,852
Case 2:	Short bellies	($7,372)	4	($29,488)
	Long hogs	5,244	5	26,220
	Spread results			($ 3,268)

This is slightly closer to the correct results but not yet right. Adjusting the number of contracts for volatility means attempting to equalize percentage moves per unit size. The range of 14.20 in hogs and 19.40 in bellies combined with their contract size gives:

	Range	Contract Size	Total	Ratio
Bellies	19.40	38,000	$737,200	
Hogs	14.20	30,000	$426,000	.5779 : 1

For convenience, the ratio will be taken as 1:2, which means trading two hog contracts for every one pork bellies contract. Then:

		P/L per Contract	Number of Contracts	Net P/L
Case 1:	Long bellies	$9,158	1	$9,158
	Short hogs	(4,356)	2	(8,712)
	Spread results			$ 446
Case 2:	Short bellies	($7,372)	1	($7,372)
	Long hogs	5,244	2	10,488
	Spread results			$3,116

Using the relative volatility and contract size to produce a *spread ratio* gives the correct results.

Table 11-2   Metals Volatility and Spread Ratios

	Cash Prices			Contract			Ratio to Gold
	1978	1980	1985	Size	Range	Total	
Gold ($/oz)	150	850	300	100 oz	700	70,000	—
Platinum ($/oz)	170	420	300	50 oz	250	12,500	.18
Silver ($/oz)	5.00	38.00	6.50	5,000 oz	33.00	165,000	2.36
Copper ($/lb)	.60	1.35	.65	25,000 lb	.75	18.750	.27

Metal Relationships

Most metals markets showed extreme volatility in early 1980 as a result of the silver crisis. Table 11-2 gives the comparable price moves of the four major futures metals markets and shows the spread ratios that should have been used.

Gold is seen to be much more volatile than either platinum or copper but less than silver. During this volatile period, a spread of five platinum to one gold, four copper to one gold, and two silver to five gold would have been necessary. Unfortunately, this spread ratio represents an exceptionally volatile period. From the beginning of 1985 through June 1986, the monthly average spot gold price varied from $302 to $345 per ounce—silver prices ranged from $5.11 to $6.45 per ounce. This produces the following relationship:

	Range	Contract Size	Total	Ratio to Gold	Contracts in Spread
Gold	$43/oz	100 oz	$4,300		3
Silver	$1.34/oz	5,000 oz	$6,700	1.56	2

The ratio of three gold to two silver is normally most practical but is not safe enough when prices move above these levels.

Volatile Spreads

Trading a high-priced spread is always riskier than one where both legs are at "normal" levels for the following reasons:

1. If only one leg is at a high level, the profitability of the spread depends entirely on the profitable trading of the most volatile leg.
2. If both legs are volatile, specific events may cause them to move independently creating unprecedented spread levels.
3. Highly volatile spreads are usually in nearby months and may not adjust to "normal" before the expiration of the contract. At expiration, extreme demand in the cash market may cause further unusual spread differences.

4. A highly volatile spread may have greater risk than a single outright position in one leg. This is not usually the purpose of a spread trade.

LEVERAGE IN SPREADS

Because a spread is the difference between two or more fundamentally related commodities or delivery months, the risk is usually less than that of an outright long or short position. Interdelivery spreads within the same crop year, or in nonagricultural products, are recognized by the exchange as having lower risk. The result is that spread margins can be less than 20% of the margin required for a nonspread position.

The profit potential is also less for a spread than for a net long or short position. It may be more or less than 20% of the profit possible in a nonspread trade. In agricultural products, the bull and bear spreads can be highly volatile; for metals, the potential will be equal only to the change in interest caused by higher and lower contract values. Traders manage to compensate for the lower profits and risks by taking advantage of the smaller margins and entering more positions. With five contracts, the trader has managed to convert a conservative spread trade into the same magnitude risk/reward as a nonspread trade—perhaps even higher risk—without added capital. The small trader, however, does not have to leverage the spread to the utmost degree.

Some trades that derive the benefit of spread margins are not always of proportionately less risk. For example, when the IMM began, any two currencies could be spread with reduced margin. A short position in the Deutschemark against a long position in the Mexican peso would hardly have been considered reduced risk when the first devaluation of the peso occurred. The trader must keep in mind that the decrease in margin, which accompanies spreads entered on the same exchange, will cause a substantial increase in leverage and may counteract the intrinsic risk reduction in a spread that was related to the smaller price movement. Spreads are not necessarily less speculative or safer than trading a single net long or short position.

12

Behavioral Techniques

There are some approaches to commodity trading that are more directly dependent on human behavior than the purely mathematical techniques. When used in the short term, most systems will be more representative of behavior than economic factors, but the concepts presented in this chapter deal specifically with human reactions. *Measuring the News* covers an area that has been greatly overlooked by technicians and offers the greatest single opportunity for research. *Contrary Opinion* takes the form of a poll or consensus of opinions of traders and commodity publications. It may help answer the question, "What is everyone else doing?", or at least, "What are they thinking of doing?"

The principal works of Elliott and Gann are covered in the envelope of *Mathematics and the Mystic*. It is not intended that these two approaches be taken lightly, but some of the assumptions upon which these systems are based are abstract and not capable of being substantiated other than by the success of the systems themselves. Both are fascinating and open areas of creativity essential to commodity traders. They are grouped together with discussions of natural phenomena and astrological forecasting, all of which should leave you thinking.

MEASURING THE NEWS

If you can keep your head when all about you are losing theirs, maybe you haven't heard the news.

Rudyard Kipling[1]

The news is one of the greatest single elements affecting all free markets. As a medium, it carries both fundamental and technical information about all commodities, directly or indirectly, and is indispensable. If not objective, the news services could materially alter any opinion by the inclusion or omission of relevant information. The impact of news is so great that a speculator holding a market position according to a purely technical system would do best not reading, listening to, watching, or in any sense being exposed to news that might be cause for deviating

[1] Adam Smith, *The Money Game,* Random House, New York, 1967, p. 48.

250

from the system. In a study commissioned by the *Wall Street Journal,* it was shown that 99% of the financial analysts polled read the paper regularly, and 92% considered it the "most valuable" publication they read.[2]

As an element of a program or as an indicator of its own, the news is invaluable. If we could measure the impact of unexpected news, the importance of the *Wall Street Journal* or the wire service articles, the USDA crop reports and the CFTC positions reports,[3] and the anticipation of news, we might know the direction of the markets. But first we must be aware of the complications of analyzing the news. There is the problem of objectively selecting which items are relevant and which sources are most important. The most difficult problem is quantifying the news—how do you rank each item for measurement, and on what scale do you determine cumulative importance? Some news items are known to have more of an affect on the market—weather disasters, major trade agreements, key crop reports—but these must be ranked against themselves and other issues to produce a numerical system of analysis. On a single day, an address by the President about foreign trade may be ranked as a "+6," a continued lack of rain in the west as a "+2," large grain stocks as "−4," and a key article in the *Wall Street Journal* on the improved Russian harvest as "−5," giving a net score of "−1" to the news—interpreted as neutral. Such a ranking scheme would be considered analytic in nature since it tries to weigh relevance on a predetermined scale without knowledge of individual effects.

Klein and Prestbo attempted such a study by assigning values of 3, 2, and 1 to articles in the *Wall Street Journal* of decreasing importance. Their interest was the stock market, but their work was straightforward and some of the conclusions general in nature. They showed a direct correlation between the relevant positive and negative news articles and the direction of the stock market. As it was scored over 6-week intervals before and after major turning points in the Dow Jones Industrial Averages, the news would stay about 70% favoring the current market direction. Having eliminated the possibility of the market influencing the news, they could conclude that, in retrospect, the market reflected the nature of the news.

The sources that influence commodity prices are different from those that move the stock market because of the fewer, more specific, items, and the purpose of those trading commodities. Specific news releases and economic reports are an implicit part of commodity prices; newspaper releases become important in the last phase of a long move. The most important news items in commodities are:

U.S. economic news

News relating to the availability of funds

Government reports on production and stocks

Unexpected news of any type from any medium

Trade information—balance of trade, legislation

Weather

[2] Frederick C. Klein and John A. Presbo, *News and the Market,* Henry Regnery, Chicago, 1974, p. 3.
[3] A thorough analysis of the CFTC *Commitment of Traders* report can be found in Chapter 16. It should be noted that other government reports released on the same day may complicate the interpretation.

In-depth studies by the *Wall Street Journal*

Front-page news articles (or television, etc.) on high prices, strikes, etc.

Market letters, research reports and comments from accepted authorities and known organizations

Ranking and Measuring

The problem of ranking and assigning values to news items requires a knowledge of how others see the news. Klein and Prestbo also studied this problem for the stock market and concluded that about 90% of the *Wall Street Journal* readers perceived news in the same way (bullish, bearish, or neutral). The same relationship can be assumed for commodities. A reason for the uniform interpretation of the news articles in any field is the publicized analysis. Shortly after the release of a USDA stocks report, the wire services begin to quote independent and poll opinions of the meaning of the report, then transmit those interpretations over their news media to be relayed to most traders. The "professional analysis" is taken as correct and later discussions based on that interpretation serve to solidify the opinion.

News can also be measured empirically, by studying the immediate impact of an expected or surprise news item. It is necessary to make the assumption for this type of measurement that the effects of a news release are most important in the short term, and that their influence on the market is diluted daily. A place to start in assigning a quantitative value to this reduced influence would be with a modification of the standard physics formula

$$I = \frac{1}{D^2}$$

where I is the net influence and D is the elapsed days since the release of the news. In science, this phenomenon of a sharp decline in effect as distance increases is applicable to many areas.

Measured empirically, the USDA and CFTC reports are worth studying. The CFTC releases its *Commitments of Traders* report each month on the 10th, accurate as of the last day of the previous month. It tells the distribution of holdings among large and small speculators and hedgers as a percent of total open interest. This report is watched because it is assumed that the small speculators are always wrong and the large hedgers right (see Chapter 16).

It is important to understand the difference between the analytic and empirical approach to news. In the analytic method, the value of specific events are determined in advance, and then when they occur their preassigned value is compared with the effects. Using the empirical method, the historic effects of each event are analyzed for a fair sample and then applied to subsequent news items.

The analytic approach has the advantage of working in an environment where multiple events are occurring simultaneously; the sum of all news items can be calculated for a new measurement. When testing the empirical approach, the event of interest may not be clearly distinguished from other news of importance occurring at the same time. Getting a pure measurement may be impossible. The primary disadvantage of the analytic approach is that it does not account for the discounting or anticipation of the news. An event of modest importance may become neutral or very significant relative to other concurrent or anticipated events; the empirical method would not be subject to that problem since it measures reaction and not expectation.

Trading on the News

Even without a sophisticated method of measurement, there are many professional speculators who trade on the news. When a bullish news item or report is introduced and the market fails to respond upward, the experienced trader looks for a place to sell. It shows that there is too much apprehension about higher prices and possibly a large numbers of sellers above the market. Similarly, *opening calls,* available for most commodities, are transmitted via wire services within half an hour of the opening bell. Regardless of the means for determining the opening direction, an experienced trader may take advantage of a higher opening call to place a sell order. There are frequent cases of so many traders wanting to sell a higher opening that the influx of orders after a call, before the opening, has changed the direction from higher to sharply lower on the open.

Weather markets are purely news reactions. Traders with long positions wait for the 5-day forecast hoping for no rain; they anticipate a loss of a specific number of bushels per acre for every dry day once the rainfall is below a given level. Weather markets are nervous and are characterized by evening-up on weekends; they rely heavily on anticipation and emotion. It is said that a farmer loses his crop three times each year, once for drought, once for disease, and once for frost. In 1976, the news carried numerous articles on the desperate wheat crop in the western states, showing films of virtually barren fields, and yet the United States harvested one of their largest wheat crops on record emphasizing the danger in using weather for long-term predictions.

The *discounting of news* is well-known by "insiders," but the public remains unaware. An old saying in the market, "Buy the rumor, sell the fact," implies that anticipation drives the price past the point where it would realistically adjust to news. When the actual figures are released, there is invariably an adjustment back to their proper level.

Market Selectivity

The market seems to focus on a single news item. Although the same factors are always there to affect prices, they must reach a point of newsworthiness before they become the primary driving factor. For heating oil, the combination of unexpected, sustained cold weather compared to available inventory will activate a weather market. Interest rates, the U.S. dollar, and tension in the Middle East will either be magnified out of proportion or completely ignored, while the anticipation of demand rises sharply. A market analysis of shortages not supported by news may as well be discarded—it is combined opinions that move the market, not one person.

CONTRARY OPINION[4]

The contrarian lies somewhere between the fundamentalist and the technician, basing actions on the behavior of crowds, in this case the commodity speculators. The contrarian sees the end of a bull market occurring when everyone is bullish. Once all long positions have been set, there is diminishing influence by the bulls; moreover, opportunities always lie in the reverse direction from crowd thinking.

Contrary opinion alone is not meant to signal a new entry into a position; it identifies situations that qualify. It is more of a filter than a trading system, a means of finding an opportunity. Consider the patterns that appear in every prolonged bull or bear move. First, there is a point where the direction is generally accepted as the major trend. After that, traders wait for a reversal to reenter in the direction of the trend at a more favorable price. These price "corrections" become smaller or disappear when everyone wants to "buy a lower open" or "sell a higher open" until you have the ultimate "blow-off" and a reversal of a major bull or bear market. The dynamic end is generally credited to the entrance of the public; when the masses are unanimously convinced that prices are going higher, who is left to buy?

The other important ingredient to a contrarian is that all the facts cannot be known. The widely accepted belief that "prices will go higher" must be based on presumptions; if the final figures were out, the market would adjust to the proper level. This idea is older than *The Art of Contrary Thinking*. In 1930, Schabacker discussed cashing out a long position if the market rallied on news that was general rather than specific.

The practical application of the theory of contrary opinion is the *Bullish Consensus*[5] and the *Market Sentiment Index,* created from a poll of market letters prepared by the commodity departments of brokerage firms and professional advisors. In the Bullish Consensus (see Figure 12-1), these opinions are weighted according to the estimated exposure of these letters until a final index value is determined. This value will range from 0 to 100%, indicating an increasingly bullish attitude. Because of the psychology of the novice commodity trader, the neutral consensus point is 55%. The normal range is considered from 30 to 80%, although each commodity must be individually evaluated.

The principle of contrary opinion does not require the user to look always for a trade in the opposite direction of the current price movement. Within the normal range, the contrarian will take a position in the direction of the trend. Frequently, the Bullish Consensus will begin increasing prior to the price turning higher, indicating that the attitude of the trader is becoming bullish. It is considered significant when the index changes 10% in a 2-week period. Once the Bullish Consensus reaches 90% during an upward move or 20% during a bear move, the commodity is considered overbought or oversold, and the contrarian looks for a convenient point to exit from the current trade. Positions are not reversed until prices show that they are not continuing in the original direction. This could be

[4] For the most definitive works, see Humphrey Neill, *The Art of Contrary Thinking,* Caxton Printers, Caldwell, OH, 1960, who is credited with having first formulated the concept, and Earl R. Hadady, *Contrary Opinion,* Hadady, Pasadena CA, 1983.
[5] The *Bullish Consensus* is a product of Sibbett-Hadady, Pasadena, CA; a Market Sentiment Index is published in *Consensus,* Kansas City, MO.

**Bullish
Consensus
Percentage**

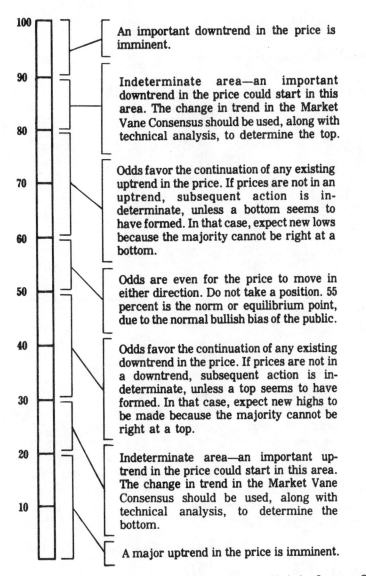

100	An important downtrend in the price is imminent.
90	Indeterminate area—an important downtrend in the price could start in this area. The change in trend in the Market Vane Consensus should be used, along with technical analysis, to determine the top.
80	
70	Odds favor the continuation of any existing uptrend in the price. If prices are not in an uptrend, subsequent action is indeterminate, unless a bottom seems to have formed. In that case, expect new lows because the majority cannot be right at a bottom.
60	
50	Odds are even for the price to move in either direction. Do not take a position. 55 percent is the norm or equilibrium point, due to the normal bullish bias of the public.
40	Odds favor the continuation of any existing downtrend in the price. If prices are not in a downtrend, subsequent action is indeterminate, unless a top seems to have formed. In that case, expect new highs to be made because the majority cannot be right at a top.
30	
20	Indeterminate area—an important uptrend in the price could start in this area. The change in trend in the Market Vane Consensus should be used, along with technical analysis, to determine the bottom.
10	
	A major uptrend in the price is imminent.

Figure 12-1   Interpretation of the Bullish Concensus. (*Source:* Hadady, *Contrary Opinion*)

identified using a moving average. Remembering Schabacker's advice, the occasion of a general news release that moves the market further in the direction of the general opinion would be an opportune moment to enter a contrary trade; specific news that fails to move prices would be a good indication of an exhausted trend when the consensus is overbought or oversold. A typical contrarian situation given by Hadady is given in Figure 12-2.

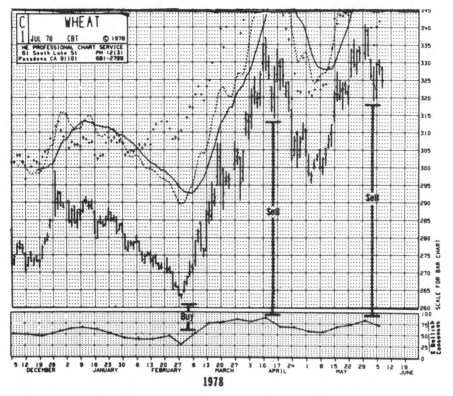

Figure 12-2 Typical contrarian situation—wheat, 1978.

R. Earl Hadady said about the system that he sponsors: "The principle of contrary opinion, by definition, works 100% of the time. The problem is getting an accurate consensus."[6] Timeliness is another problem with an index; if 60 to 70 market letters are reviewed, read, and weighted to form an index, the results may be dated before they can be used. The theory of contrary opinion also emphasized its use as a timing device for entering trades at an opportune moment and for filtering out the ambiguous trades; the theory is not readily applicable to exiting a position unless the reverse consensus occurs. It is not always prudent to wait for a confirmation before exiting a trade.

MATHEMATICS AND THE MYSTIC

Even though we may not understand the cause underlying a particular phenomenon, we can, by observation, predict the phenomenon's recurrence.

R. N. Elliott[7]

History is a great record of achievement in the face of disbelief: the explorations of Columbus, Magellan, Marco Polo; the science of da Vinci, Galileo, Copernicus;

[6] George Angell, "Thinking Contrarily," *Commodities,* Nov. 1976.
[7] R. N. Elliott, *Nature's Law: The Secret of the Universe,* Elliott, New York, 1946 p. 4.

and the philosophy of Socrates and other men now known to be great. We are more observant today and less apt to condemn those who delve into areas still unknown. Of these, astrology is the most obvious, but its acceptance may be partly because of its harmless nature; in its common form, it attempts to classify personality and behavioral traits. If the predictive aspect of astrology were emphasized, there would be fewer that would accept its premises. And still, the positions of our moon and planets, the energy given off, and the gravitational phenomenon are directly responsible for physical occurrences of tides and weather—should they not have a measureable affect on behavior? This will be considered in the following sections.

Let us look first at the fascinating subject of symmetry in nature. Science is familiar with the symmetric shapes of crystalline substances, snowflakes, spherical planets, and the human body. The periodicity of the universe—sun spots, eclipses, and other cyclic phenomena—is also understood, but its bearing on human behavior is not yet known. Work in biorhythms is only at the point of being a curiosity; the relationship of behavior to nonbiological functions, such as planetary positions, is too abstract.

In 1904, Arthur H. Church wrote about phyllotaxis, the leaf arrangement of plants,[8] showing its relationship to a mathematical series based on the works of Leonardo Pisano (Fibonacci).[9] This mathematical series of numbers has been attributed the quality of representing human behavior. Examples have been given which appear to be more than "interesting coincidences."

Fibonacci and Human Behavior

It is not certain how Fibonacci conceived his summation series. His greatest work, *Liber Abaci,* written in the early part of the 13th century was not published until 1857.[10] It contained a description of a situation involving the reproduction of rabbits in which the following two conditions hold: Every month each pair produces a new pair, which, from the second month on become productive; deaths do not occur. This becomes the famous *Fibonacci summation series*

$$1, 2, 3, 5, 8, 13, 21, 34, 55, 89, 144, \ldots$$

(more currently written 1, 1, 2, 3, . . .). It can be easily seen that each element of the series is the sum of the two previous entries.

Those who have studied the life of Fibonacci often attribute the series to his observations of the Great Pyramid of Gizeh. This pyramid, dating from a preliterary, prehieroglyphic era, contains many features said to have been observed by Fibonacci. In the geometry of a pyramid there are 5 surfaces and 8 edges, for a total of 13 surfaces and edges; there are 3 edges visible from any one side. More specifically, the Great Pyramid of Gizeh is 5813 inches high (5-8-13, and the inch is the standard Egyptian unit of measure); and the ratio of the elevation to the base is

---

[8] A. H. Church, *On the Relation of Phyllotaxis to Mechanical Laws,* Williams and Newgate, London, 1904.

[9] In the appendices to Jay Hambridge, *Dynamic Symmetry: The Greek Vase,* Yale University Press, New Haven, CN, 1931, pp. 141–161, there is a full discussion of the evolution of this number series within science and mathematics, together with further references.

[10] *Il Liber Abaci di Leonardo Pisano,* Baldassare Boncompagni, Rome, Italy, 1857.

.618.[11] The coincidence of this ratio is that it is the same as the ratio that is approached by any two consecutive Fibonacci numbers; for example,

$$\tfrac{2}{3} = .667, \qquad \tfrac{3}{5} = .600, \qquad \tfrac{5}{8} = .625, \qquad \ldots, \qquad \tfrac{89}{144} = .618$$

It is also true that the ratio of a side to a diagonal of a regular pentagon is .618.

Another phenomenon of the pyramid is that the total of the 4 edges of the base, measured in inches, is 36524.22, which is exactly 100 times the length of the solar year. This permits interpretations of the Fibonacci summation series to be applied to time.

The Greeks showed a great fascination for the ratios of the Fibonacci series, noting that while $F_n/F_{n+1} = .618$, the reverse $F_{n+1}/F_n = 1.618$ was even more amazing. They expressed these relationships as "golden sections" and used them either consciously or not in the proportions of such works as the Parthenon, the sculpture of Phidias, and classic vases. Leonardo da Vinci consciously employed the ratio in his art. It has always been a curiosity that the great mathematician, Pythagoras, left behind a symbol of a triangle with the words "The Secret of the Universe" inscribed below.

Church, in his work in phyllotaxis, studied the sunflower, noting that one of normal size (5 to 6 inches) has a total of 89 curves, 55 in one direction and 34 in another. In observing sunflowers of other sizes, he found that the total curves are Fibonacci numbers (up to 144) with the two previous numbers in the series describing the distribution of curves. The chambered nautilus is considered a natural representation of a "golden spiral," based on the proportions of the Fibonacci ratio.

Up to now, aspects of the Fibonacci series have been intriguing, but here it goes a step beyond. The numbers in the series represent frequent or coincidental occurrences:

The human body has five major projections; both arms and legs have three sections; there are five fingers and toes, each with three sections (except the thumb and great toe). There are also five senses.

In music an octave means eight, with 8 white keys and 5 black, totaling 13.

There are three primary colors.

The United States had 13 original states and 13 is an unlucky number.

The legal age is 21 and the highest salute in the army is a 21-gun salute.

The human emotional cycle has been determined at 33 to 36 days by Dr. R. B. Hersey.[12]

The wholesale price index of all commodities is shown to have peaks of 50–55 years according to the Kondratieff wave: 1815 after the war of 1812, 1865 after the Civil War, 1920 after the World War I, and about 1975 after . . .[13]

---

[11] Jay Hambridge, *Dynamic Symmetry*, pp. 27–38.

[12] R. N. Elliott, *Natures Law*, p. 55. Elliott quotes other human emotional relationships.

[13] *Cycles*, Jan. 1976, p. 21; see also *The Kondratieff Wave: The Future of America Until 1981 and Beyond*, Dell, New York, 1974, which is based on the theory developed by the Russian economist early in this century.

These examples are not meant to prove anything in the strict sense, but to open an area that may not have previously been considered. Human behavior is not yet a pure science and probes of this sort may lead the way to further understanding. The following sections deal with ideas such as these—sometimes reasonable and other times seeming to stretch the imagination.

ELLIOTT'S "WAVE PRINCIPLE"

R. N. Elliott was responsible for one of the more highly regarded and complex forms of market technical analysis. The *Elliott Wave Theory* is a sophisticated method of price motion analysis and has received careful study by A. H. Bolton (1960), and later by Charles Collins. His works are fully covered in two more recent publications by Robert Prechter; brief summaries of the analysis appear in some of the comprehensive books on commodities.[14] This presentation of Elliott's technique will include both the original principles and extensions with examples.

The Wave Theory is an analysis of behavioral patterns based on mathematics and implemented using price charts; its original application was stocks and it is credited with predictive ability with respect to the Dow Jones Industrial Averages that is second only to the occurrence of Haley's comet. It is understood that Elliott never intended to apply his principle to individual stocks, perhaps because the thinness of trading might distort those patterns that would have appeared as the result of mass behavior. If so, caution must be exercised when applying this method to individual commodities markets.

The successes of the Elliott Wave Theory are fascinating and reinforce the use of the technique; most summaries of Elliott's work recount them and the reader is encouraged to read these. The "waves" referred to in the theory are price peaks and valleys, not the formal oscillations of sound waves or harmonics described in the science of physics. The waves of price motion are overreactions to both supply and demand factors within major bull moves developed in five waves and corrected in three. His broad concept was related to "tidal wave bull markets" that have such large upward thrusts that each wave could be divided into five subwaves satisfying the same principle. After each primary wave of the major bull trend there was a major corrective move of three waves, which could be further divided into subwaves of three (see Figure 12-3).

The types of waves could be classified into the broad categories of triangles and ABCs representing a main trend and a correction, respectively. The term *triangle* was taken from the consolidating or broadening shape that the waves form within trendlines, although in later works Elliott eliminated the expanding form of the triangle (see Figure 12-4).

An interesting aspect of the theory is its compound-complex nature, by which each sequence of triangles can occur in subwaves within waves (Figure 12-5). More recent work suggests that in commodities, a 3-wave development is more

---

[14] Robert R. Prechter, Jr., *The Major Works of R. N. Elliott*, New Classics Library, Chappaqua, NY (circa. 1980) and A. J. Frost and Robert R. Prechter, Jr., *Elliott Wave Principle*, New Classics Library, Chappaqua, NY, 1978; Merrill (1960) Appendices 5 and 6 contain one of the more thorough summaries and analyses of the basic Wave Theory, including performance.

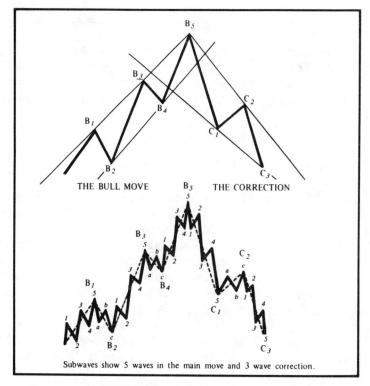

THE BULL MOVE   THE CORRECTION

Subwaves show 5 waves in the main move and 3 wave correction.

Figure 12-3   Basic Elliott wave.

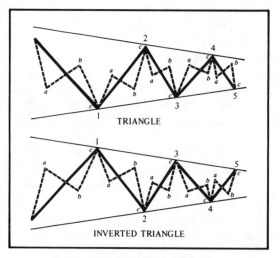

TRIANGLE

INVERTED TRIANGLE

Figure 12-4   Triangles and ABCs.

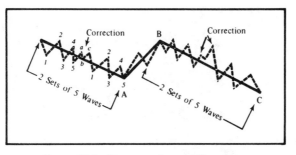

Figure 12-5   Compound correction waves.

common than 5 waves. Prechter, a well-known interpreter of Elliott's principles, has shown many major stock index moves which conform to the ratio of 1.618. The stock index, which has great participation, is most likely to represent the generalized patterns of human behavior.[15]

Elliott's Sideways Markets

Occasionally, the market pauses during a major move; or, it may move sideways in a volatile pattern after completing the fifth leg of a wave. This has been described as "stock prices seen to be waiting for economic fundamentals to catch up with the market expectations."[16] These periods can be represented by a single "three," a simple zigzag or flat formation, or by the more extended "double" or "triple three" (Figure 12-6).

A small variation of the single three has been noted to occur following the third wave, when the zigzag forms a minor swing reversal with *b* lower than its preceding top, and *c* lower than *a*. Elliott has also recognized this as a *descending zigzag* in an upward trend.[17]

Fitting the Market to the Patterns

One point to remember when applying an intricate set of rules is that an exact fit will not occur often. The best trading opportunities that will arise will be for those price patterns that fit best as the move is progressing; each successful step will serve as positive reinforcement for continuing. The critical period in the identification process is the fifth wave. The failure of the fifth wave to form indicates that the last correction of three waves will be retraced. In a bull market, an extension of the fifth wave is often followed by a corrective 3-wave function. In addition, the

[15] Robert R. Prechter, Jr., David Weiss, and David Allman, "Forecasting Prices with the Elliott Wave Principle," in Todd Lofton (Ed.), *Trading Tactics: A Livestock Futures Anthology,* Chicago Mercantile Exchange, 1986.

[16] See Robert R. Prechter, *Forecasting Prices,* 1986.

[17] Robert R. Prechter, Jr., "Computerizing Elliott," *Technical Analysis of Stocks & Commodities,* July 1983, gives some general observations on how he would go about adapting Elliott's interpretations to a computer program.

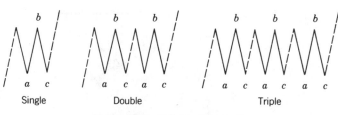

Figure 12-6 Elliott's "threes."

recognition of a 5-wave sequence should be followed by further analysis to determine whether that cycle was part of a more complex series. One of the difficulties in the method is the orientation of the current position to the wave formation; the multitude of primary and secondary waves makes some of the situations subjective until further developments clarify the position. Anyone interested in the further complexities of wave formation should refer directly to Bolton's work.

Elliott's Use of the Fibonacci Series

The application of the Elliott wave theory is unique in its use of the Fibonacci series. Besides the natural phenomena mentioned earlier, the summation series has the mathematical properties that

The ratio of any number to its successor (F_i/F_{i+1}) approaches .618.

The ratio of any number to its previous element (F_{i+1}/F_i) approaches 1.618

The ratio of F_{i+2}/F_i is 2.618

The two ratios (F_i/F_{i+1}) $\times$ (F_{i+1}/F_i) = .618 $\times$ 1.618 =1

Elliott was also able to link certain measurements of the Great Pyramid to the Fibonacci series and connect the number of days in the year as well as the geometric figure of a circle to his theory. Both time and the circle will play a role in Elliott wave analysis.

While Elliott used the lower end of the Fibonacci series to describe the patterns in the stock market, it should be noted that there are increasingly larger gaps between successive entries as the series increases. To be consistent with the original principle, each gap could be subdivided into another Fibonacci series in the same manner that the waves take on a complex formation. Harahus offers an alternate approach to filling these spaces by use of Lucas numbers, formed in the same way as the Fibonacci summation beginning with (1, 3) and resulting in (1, 3, 4, 7, 11, 18, 29, 47, 76, 123, 199, . . .). The two sets are combined, eliminating common numbers, to form (*1, 2, 3,* 4, 5, 7, *8, 13,* 18, *21,* 29, *34,* 47, 55, 76, *89,* 123, *144,* 199, *233,* . . .). The Fibonacci numbers have been italicized since they will receive the most emphasis, whereas the Lucas numbers will serve as intermediate levels of less significance. The numbers themselves are applied to predict the length in days of a price move. A bull move that lasts for more than 34 days should meet major resistance or reverse on the 55th day or on the 89th day (considering Fibonacci numbers only). It is suggested that a penetration of the 89th day should permit the series to start again with the beginning of the series added to 89 (e.g., . . . , *94,* 96, *97, 102,* 107, *110,* 118, *123,* 136, . . .), including the more important Lucas and Fibonacci numbers from the original series. This effect is similar to the complex wave-within-a-wave motion.

The same numbers are used to express key levels in a trend reversal. For example, a bull move that carries prices up for about 47 days before a reversal should meet resistance at the price level on the 34th day. If that price does not stop the reversal, either the behavioral implications of the number series do not hold for this situation or prices are in a different part of the cycle.

With the introduction of Lucas numbers (L) there are some additional key ratios. In the combined Fibonacci–Lucas series (FL), denote an element with j if it is the first element of the other series following entry i; L_j is the first Lucas number entry following F_i that is a Fibonacci number. This results in the ratios $F_i/L_j = .72$, $L_i/F_j = .854$, and $F_i/F_{i+2} = L_i/L_{i+2} = .382$.

The important ratio of a Fibonacci number to its following entry can be represented by the ratio of successive numbers ($\frac{1}{2}$, $\frac{2}{3}$, $\frac{3}{5}$, $\frac{5}{8}$, $\frac{8}{13}$, $\frac{13}{21}$, $\frac{21}{144}$, . . .). When expressed in decimal, these ratios approach the number .618 in a convergent oscillating series (1.000, .500, .667, .625, .615, .619, . . .). These ratios, the key Fibonacci–Lucas ratios and the alternate-entry ratios, represent the potential resistance levels (in terms of percentage) for price adjustments within a well-defined move. For example, a price advance of $1.00 in silver to $5.00 might correct 100, 50, or 62%, to $4.00, $4.50, or $4.38, respectively, according to the most important ratios.

Trading Elliott

Elliott also knew that there was great variability in this adherence to waves and ratios. The appearance of the waves is not regular in either length or duration and should not be expected to continually increase as they develop, although the fifth wave is generally the longest. The waves must be identified by peaks only. Elliott introduced a channel into his theory in order to determine the direction of the wave being analyzed as well as to establish intermediate price objectives. Looking back at the diagram of the basic wave, note the channel drawn touching the peaks and bottoms of the bull move. For every two peaks, a channel can be drawn that will serve as a trendline for price objectives. This same technique is covered in detail in a later section of Chapter 10. The lower trendline in the bull move will serve to tell when a correction has begun.

The Elliott Wave Theory is very intricate and should not be attempted without careful study of the original material, but some rules are presented here in order to help understand the nature of the method:

1. Identify a main trend.
2. Determine the current status of the main trend by locating the major peaks and bottoms that will form the five key waves.
3. Look for three wave corrections and five wave subtrends or extensions.
4. Draw trendlines to determine the direction.
5. Measure the length of the waves in days to determine its adherence to the Fibonacci–Lucas sequence; measure the size of reactions as compared to FL ratios.
6. Watch for reactions at points predicted by the FL sequence and corresponding

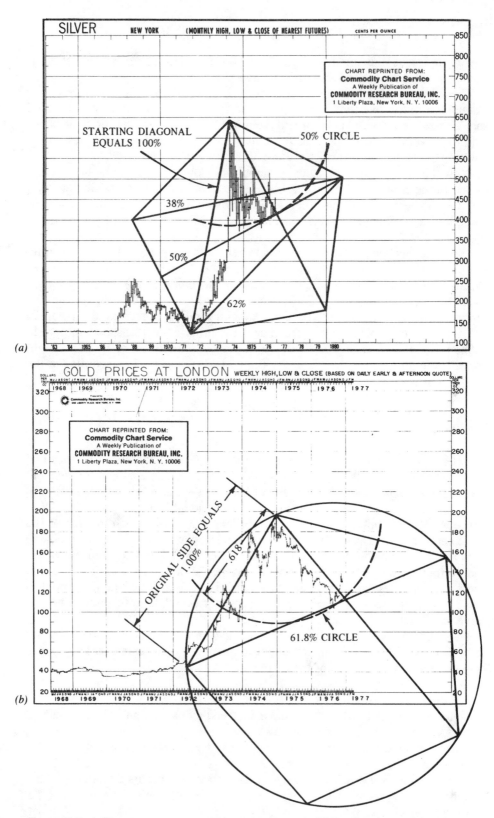

(a)

(b)

Figure 12-7 (a)Pentagon constructed from one diagonal. (b) Pentagon constructed from one side.

to the patterns described by the five-wave main trend and three-wave correction.

7. Use the ratios, day counts, and trendlines as predictive devices to select price objectives.

8. Use the trendlines to determine changes of direction.

Constructions Using the Fibonacci Ratio

Harahus shows interesting constructions using Fibonacci ratios; these are referred to as the "golden rectangle," "golden triangle," and "golden spiral." Although there is no doubt of their importance, the application to markets is not trivial. As a behavioral model, any technique is subject to gross inaccuracy at times. In using a method as sophisticated as the Elliott Wave Theory, it is necessary to select situations that are representative examples of the phenomenon described by the *FL* sequence. Confirmation of such action can only be found by careful monitoring and development of an awareness of the nature of the price motion important to the system.

Harahus further introduced the regular pentagon as a tool for measuring correction. This geometric figure has the property that any diagonal is 1.618 times the length of a side; exactly a Fibonacci ratio.

By constructing a regular pentagon so that the major trend falls along one diagonal (or one side), the other line connecting the corners of the pentagon will serve as support or resistance to price moves. In addition, the circumscribed and inscribed circle will serve as a measurement of support and/or resistance (Figure 12-7).

Harahus further extends the charting techniques of the Elliott Wave Theory using circles and arcs. A circle drawn from the top or bottom of a wave, representing the 38, 50, or 62% levels serves as a convenient measurement of either elapsed time or a price adjustment, either of which could occur within the bounds of the rules. Prices are expected to meet resistance at any attempt to penetrate the key circles formed about either *A* or *B* in Figure 12-8.

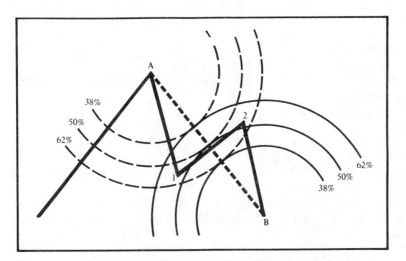

Figure 12-8   Using circles to find support and resistance.

The Elliott Wave Theory is highly regarded, although it is an odd combination of mathematics and chart interpretation bordering slightly on the mystic. Because it is primarily based on chart patterns it has been criticized as being too interpretive. The development of the fifth wave receives the most comment—sometimes it never develops; at other times, it must be extended into another subset of waves. In an analysis by Merrill, it is shown that the median stock market bull move has seven legs and the bear move has five legs; this may account for the need for the compound form of the Elliott wave. Those analysts who find this study of interest should also read the works of W. D. Gann and Edson Gould, both of whom concentrated on mathematical approaches to charting.

FISCHER'S GOLDEN SECTION COMPASS SYSTEM

Although there are many systems that use the Fibonacci ratios, Fischer's *Golden Section Compass* (GSC) *System* is the only one based primarily on that concept.[18] The system is founded on the premise that human behavior reflects the Fibonacci ratios; the human decision-making process unconsciously selects points to act that "appear" to be the right time or the right price level. The behavior-based rules are combined with practical entry and stop-loss rules to eliminate those situations that do not properly develop.

Fischer is not alone in his observation of these patterns. Elliott, discussed in the previous sections, defined market cycles in 5 wave patterns with 3 wave corrections (Figure 12-9). In *Nature's Law,* Elliott shows the "complete" market cycle[19] as:

Number of	Bull Market	Bear Market	Total	
Major waves	5	3	8	complete cycles
Intermediate waves	21	13	34	complete cycles
Minor waves	89	55	144	complete cycles

Time-Goal Days

The GSC System states that a new price direction will begin on, or shortly after, the day calculated as:

$$T_k = 1.618 \times (L_i - L_{i-1}) + L_i$$

or

$$T_{k+1} = 1.618 \times (H_i - H_{i-1}) + H_i$$

where L_i and H_i are the days on which lows and highs occurred, and L_i occurred before H_i.

For simplicity, an extreme may be used only twice—once as the first point and once as the second. Figure 12-10 shows the order in which the calculations occur.

[18] Robert Fischer, Fibonacci Trading, Ltd., Hamilton 5, Bermuda.
[19] Robert Fischer, *The Golden Section Compass Seminar,* Fibonacci Trading, 1984.

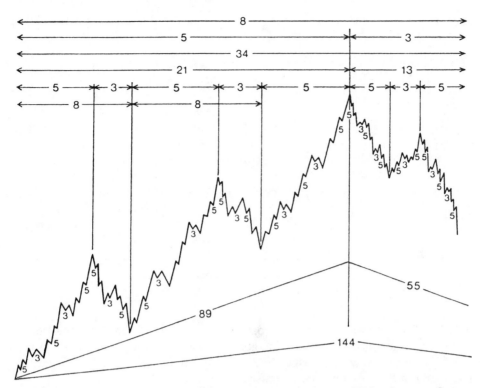

Figure 12-9 Elliott's complete wave cycle. (*Source:* Fischer, Golden Section Compass System Seminar, 1984 p. 28.)

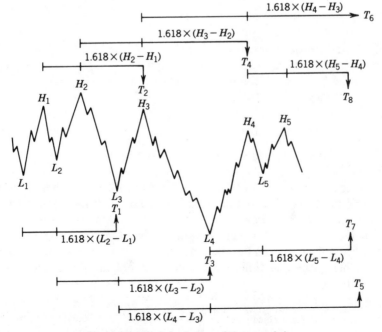

Figure 12-10 Calculation of time-goal days.

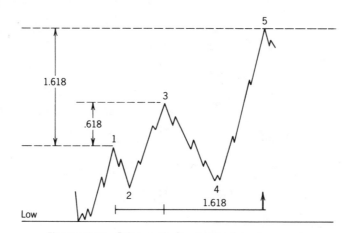

Figure 12-11   Price goals for standard s-wave move.

Time-goal day T_5 was calculated from lows L_3 and L_4 before time-goal day T_7 occurred. When more than one time-goal day occurs at the same point, or when the highs or lows which formed the time-goal days are more significant, the likelihood of a major reversal increases.

Specific entry signals occur on a 5-day price reversal. A long signal is given following a time-goal day when the closing price is higher than the high of the past 5 days. This is sufficient to identify a trend change and allows the stop-loss to be the recent low or a fixed point below the entry point.

Price Goals

Price objectives are determined using the same highs and lows. Elliott's Wave Theory is refined by Fischer, as shown in Figure 12-11. Once the low has been found, followed by wave 1, the price objectives for waves 3 and 5 can be calculated as a function of wave 1:

Wave 3 objective = .618 × (wave 1 − low) + low

Wave 5 objective = 1.618 × (wave 1 − low) + low

The pullbacks to points 2 and 4 are not determined in this calculation, and the probability of the 5-wave formation occurring is not confirmed unless the wave 3 objective is satisfied. Price goals are used for profit-taking rather than new entry points. The GSC System, however, does not require that markets move in 5-wave patterns. Price objectives can be calculated from long-term lows as *1.618 × initial move up*. When price and time goals occur at the same point, there is greater reliance on the signal.[20]

---

[20] Examples of time and price objectives can be found in Tucker J. Emmett, "Fibonacci Cycles," *Technical Analysis of Stocks & Commodities*, May 1983 and Mar./Apr. 1984.

In general, retracements from sustained moves can be expected to approximate or exceed 38.2% (1 − .618) of the initial move. Once a high level objective has been reached and a reversal occurs, consistent profits may be taken using this goal. If prices fail to make new highs following the first retracement, objectives for the next lower levels down can be set according to the inverted Elliott wave patterns, or simply, *1.618 × initial downward move*.

Filtering Highs and Lows

The GSC System can be made to identify more significant highs and lows by increasing the *selection filter*. For example, a sensitive system would select highs and lows in gold that are separated by a minimum swing of $10 per ounce. More significant points may be identified by swings of $20 per ounce. It can be demonstrated that a small filter will generate highs and lows that are produced by noise rather than significant behavioral actions. The system cannot be forced to producing more signals than the natural patterns allow.

The *selection filter* should be adjusted for market volatility. At higher price levels, the noise also increases and will obscure the more important high and low points. Although Fischer only briefly touches on this, traders who apply this method should be prepared to adjust the selection filter from time to time.

W. D. GANN, "TIME AND SPACE"

The works of W. D. Gann cannot be explained with any thoroughness in a few words, but some of his main ideas have been selected and presented in this section. Gann was a pure technician using charts for all his analyses. His methods varied substantially from conventional charting techniques, but his philosophy was one of a professional trader: Conserve your capital and wait for the right time. Gann traded primarily grains for many years, and in his writings he attempted to summarize his most important observations; some of them are reminiscent of other well-known market lore.

Price moves are never exact. Gann was a believer in support and resistance lines, but expected some violation of the objectives because of "lost motion," his way of accounting for the momentum that carries prices higher or lower than their likely goals. Nearly a cross between Elliott's "waves" and Angas' "cycles," Gann classifies bull and bear moves into four "stages," each one compared to a trending move and a subsequent reversal culminating in a major top or bottom. He observed that bull markets last longer than bear markets. He concluded that reversal patterns must reduce in magnitude as the move develops and persists. A similar argument is expressed in the "theory of contrary thinking." Much of Gann's work is related in 1940 cents and requires an economic inflator close at hand.

Gann's techniques combine mathematics and geometry with time and space; he finds duration as important as the size of the price change. One of his principles reflects the idea of a longer consolidation period resulting in a longer price move after a breakout. One approach to price objectives in bar charting is exactly this idea.

"Time and Price"

Gann proposed certain natural divisions, expressed as percents. Zero and 100% are the most important of these. Based on behavioral awareness, he considered a potential resistance level at 100% of the original point of the move or 100% of the highest or lowest (the best guide) price of that commodity. In a reversal, 100% was a full retracement of the original move. The rationale for this theory is behavioral, as is his conclusion that most traders like even numbers; for this reason orders in grains are most often placed at 5 and 10¢ levels.

After the 100% level, decreased importance goes to increments of 50%, 25%, 12½%, and so on. For a grain, this would mean that major resistance could be expected at the even dollar levels with the next resistance at 50¢ intervals, then every 25¢, and so on; after a bull move of $1, the major support would be $1 lower, then 50¢, 25¢ and 75¢, and so on. The use of successive halving of intervals was also extended to time. A year is a full cycle of 360°, which makes half of a year equal to 26 weeks, a quarter of a year 13 weeks, an eighth of a year 45 days, and a sixteenth of a year 22½ days. In cases of conflict, time always took precedence over price. The combination of a key price level (percentage move) occurring at a periodic time interval is the basis for much of Gann's work.

Geometric Angles

Gann often used geometric angles for relating price and time. By using square graph paper, it was not necessary to know the exact angle because the construction was based on boxes up versus boxes to the right. A 1×1 angle (45°) was drawn diagonally from the bottom of the lowest point of a price move through the intersection 1 box up and 1 box to the right. This is the primary bullish support line. A bearish resistance line is drawn down from left to right from the highest price using the 1×1 angle. The next most important angles in order of significance are 2×1, 4×1, and 8×1; for lower support areas there is also 1×2, 1×4, and 1×8. Places where the support and resistance lines cross are of special significance, indicating a major congestion area.

Figure 12-12 is taken from Gann's private papers and shows the use of geometric angles in an actual trading situation. Lines were first drawn where Gann expected a bottom, then redrawn. The initial upward move followed the primary 45° line; the second important support line, 1×2, met the primary downward line at the point of wide congestion at the center of the chart. The highest point on this congestion phase became the pivot point for the next 45° downward angle defining the next breakout. Traders have found the primary 1×1, or 45° line, an important tool for staying with the major trend. It is used to filter out small reversals in both standard charting techniques and point-and-figure.

Gann combined this method with a more remarkable technique, the *squaring of price and time*. It was fortunate to find a chart that complemented Figure 12-12, based on the lowest recorded cash price of soybeans, 44¢ per bushel. Figure 12-13 shows how Gann constructed this square, beginning with the lowest price at the center and moving one square to the right, circling counterclockwise and continuing the process. The basic geometric lines (horizontal, vertical, and diagonal)

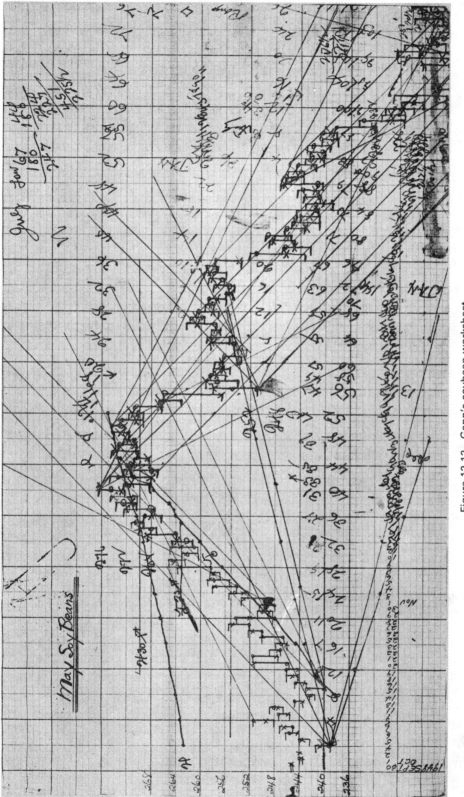

Figure 12-12   Gann's soybean worksheet.

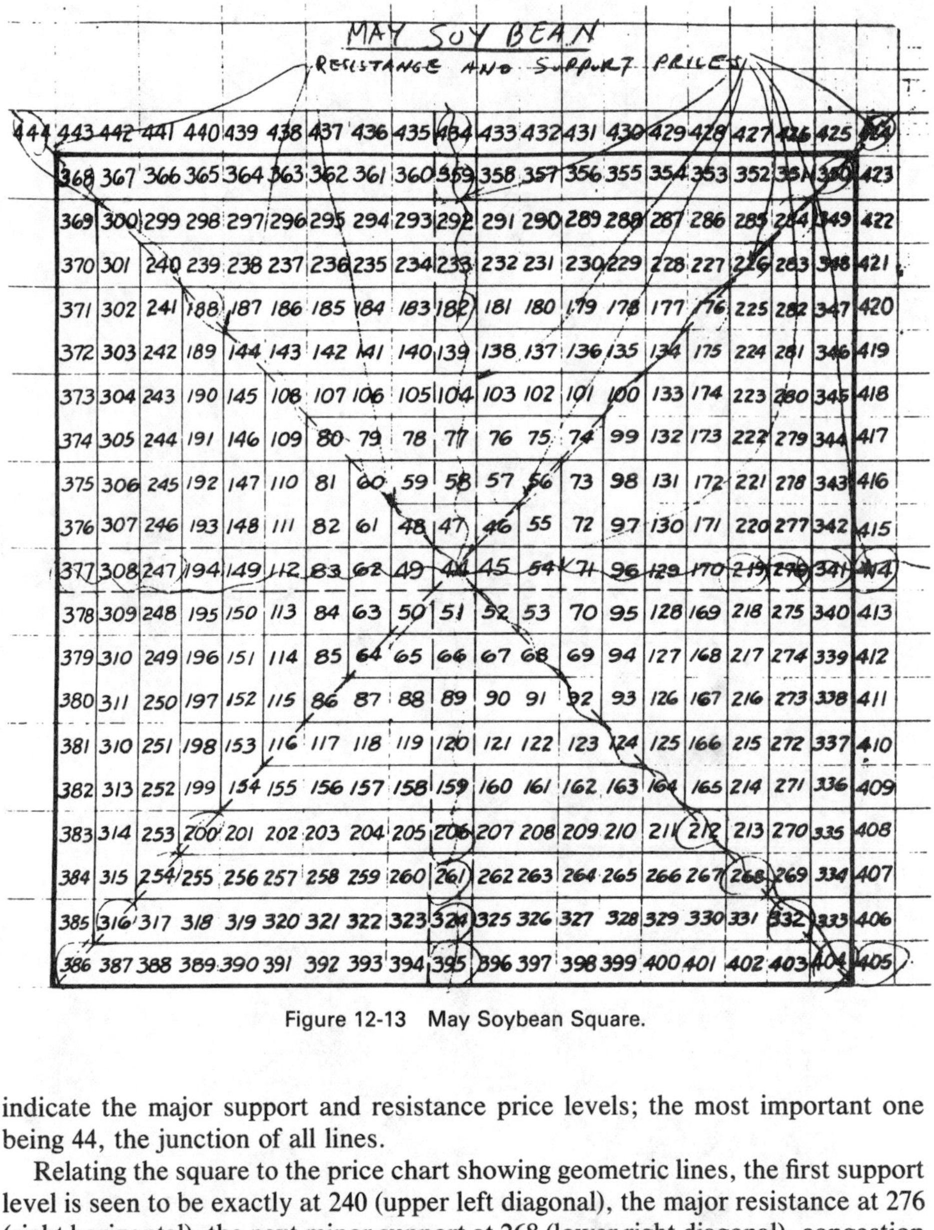

Figure 12-13   May Soybean Square.

indicate the major support and resistance price levels; the most important one being 44, the junction of all lines.

Relating the square to the price chart showing geometric lines, the first support level is seen to be exactly at 240 (upper left diagonal), the major resistance at 276 (right horizontal), the next minor support at 268 (lower right diagonal), congestion area support at 254 and 262 (1 box off), and back down to support at 240. Notice that the distance between the lines on the square become wider as prices increase, conforming to the notion of volatility. It is also expected that soybeans at $10 will have some "lost motion" near these key support and resistance levels.

The Hexagon Chart

Gann generalized his "squaring method" to include both geometric angles and the main cyclic divisions of 360°. By combining these different behavioral concepts, the strongest levels of support and resistance are found where all three coincide. The generalized construction for this purpose is the *Master Calculator,* based on aligning the chart at a point representing a multiple of the lowest historic price for that commodity; crisscrossing angles will then designate support and resistance for the specific commodity. Other time charts of importance are the *Square of Twelve* (one corner of the Master Calculator), the *Hexagon Chart,* and the *Master Chart of 360°.* The Hexagon Chart can be used as an example of the combined effect.

As shown in Figure 12-14, the inner ring begins with six divisions, giving Gann the basis for the chart name. Each circle gains six additional numbers as it proceeds outward, which relates to the overall continuity of the construction. In using the hexagon, the degrees represent time and the numbers in the circle are price; a major support or resistance point exists when both time and price occur simultaneously.

For example, consider the 360° of the hexagon relating to the calendar year, or perhaps the crop year for grains. In his own work on grain, Gann equated 0° to March 20, near to the first day of spring when the sun crosses the equator going

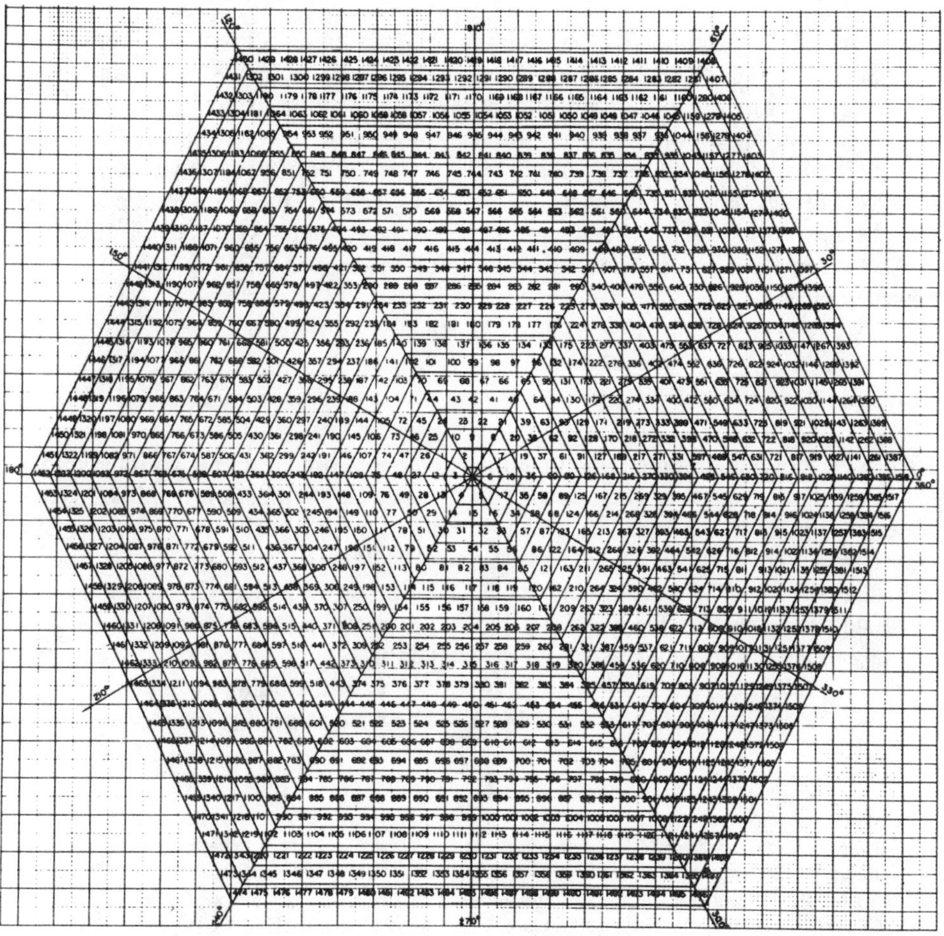

Figure 12-14 The Hexagon Chart.

north. Then, the 45° line is on May 6, 90° on June 21 (the first day of summer), 180° on September 23 (fall), and 270° on December 21 (winter). These primary divisions also represent the most significant places for price support and resistance. The other lines represent secondary levels.

When looking at price and time together on the Hexagon Chart, the distance between the major degree lines become greater as prices increase showing the importance of volatility. Using the price of November 77 soybeans, the chart shows that between 90° and 180°, or June 21 to September 23, 1977, the price of soybeans should have support at 567 and then move its major support level to 507 and its major resistance to 588 with next higher and lower support and resistance at 432 and 675, respectively. As it turned out, this was a very accurate prediction.

Gann's work is more difficult to grasp than most methods; his tools are less conventional than others. If Gann were asked for a word of advice, there is no doubt that he would caution to patience, stating: *When price meets time, a change is imminent.*[21]

THE MOON: "BUY FULL, SELL NEW"

It is known that the moon's effect on our planet is great—it is vitally connected with the movement of all fluids. The moon is also believed to affect human behavior in strange ways, especially during a new or full moon.

In an experiment conducted on an arbitrary set of commodities for the year 1972,[22] it was shown that short-term movements of prices react with some uniformity with respect to the phases of the moon. In fact, the commodities chosen for observation—silver, wheat, cattle, cocoa, and sugar—showed an uncanny ability to form a rising market following a full moon and a falling market after a new moon.

"Corn Is Rising"

Astrology seeks a common bond in human behavior, similar to the work in biological rhythms and cycles. The impact of astrology on civilization has been great; observations of the periodicity of the moon is traced back 32,000 years. Star charts were known to have been in Egypt about 4200 B.C., and the earliest written ephemerides were in the 7th century B.C.[23] The pyramids at Ghiza are said to have sloping corridors leading from the faces to the interior that were used as sighting tubes for Egyptian astrologers for making accurate forecasts. The acceptance of astrology throughout history is widespread, including virtually all civilizations. Can these beliefs relating to behavior be used to predict the movements of prices?

[21] Computer software is available for calculating and plotting much of Gann's works. See "Ganntrader I," *Technical Analysis of Stocks & Commodities,* Jan./Feb. 1984, or contact Gannsoft Publishing Co., 311 Benton St., Leavenworth, WA 98826 or Lambert-Gann, P.O. Box O, Pomeroy, WA 99347.
[22] Todd Lofton, "Moonlight Sonata," *Commodities,* July 1974.
[23] Derek Parker and Julia Paricor, *The Compleat Astrologer,* McGraw-Hill, New York, 1971, p. 12.

Jack Perrine in an article entitled "Taurus the Bullish" presented an adaptation that may be a start of a new predictive approach to trading. The method considers each planet as representative of one or more commodities as well as traits; for example, Mars is cattle, heavy industry and railroads; Uranus is corn, revolution, change, and larger corporations; and the moon is gold and silver. The positions of the planets are also significant. The "aspect," a measurement of the angular separation between two planets as seen from the Earth, are termed "hard" and "soft" for scarce and plentiful. Aspects reach peak effectiveness at specific positions: very hard at 90° and very soft at 120°; they seem to oscillate in their interpretation as they continue in one direction.

The "signs" are associated with angular sectors in the geocentric system of astrology. Beginning with Aries in the spring, the 12 familiar signs relate to varying degrees of bullish and bearish influence. The months alternating with Aries (April) are bearish, with the exception of December, which is bullish instead of bearish. The relationship of the "signs" to the market is not apparent to the casual observer.

Perrine uses his rules to predict the turns in the markets for a near and a long-term forecast. Some of the aspects are interpreted as:

Jupiter in conjunct to Pluto—very bearish for the financial world

Jupiter square to Neptune—sky-high interest rates[24]

In subsequent analyses by Perrine, he says: ". . . Mars will be square to the Sun, a friendly sign for precious metals." However, a strong bearish influence approaching may cause many commodities that are otherwise strong to "get swept down in their powerful bearish currents." Are you going to be the one to say that this won't work?

---

[24] Jack Perrine, "Taurus the Bullish," *Commodities*, Sept. 1974, p. 36.

13

Pattern Recognition

Pattern recognition forms the basis for most trading systems. Charting is entirely the identification of common formations; even moving averages attempt to isolate, using mathematical methods, what has been visually determined to be a trend. Traders have always looked for patterns in market price movement. Because they were not equipped with computers, their conclusions are considered market lore rather than fact. The conclusions are handed down from generation to generation as proverbs, such as "Up on Monday, down on Tuesday," "Locals even-up on Fridays," and "Watch for key reversals." Because these three sayings have endured, they are candidates for analysis later in this chapter.[1]

The earliest technical systems using patterns were of the form: "If after a sharp rise the market fails to advance for 3 days, sell." In recent years, the extreme mathematical approach has also been taken. By observing the closing prices starting at an arbitrary day, it is possible to record *all* patterns of higher and lower closes and their tendency to repeat periodically. A computer is well-equipped to perform this task. First, the 2- and 3-day patterns are eliminated; the recurrence of up-down or down-up and the equivalent 3-day patterns would be too frequent to be meaningful. Then, the closing prices are scanned for occurrences of predefined patterns. For example, if an up-up-down-up-down-up is to be matched, every six consecutive prices must be tested. From a table of occurrences, it can be determined whether these patterns can be predicted in advance or whether they are leading indicators of other price moves. The combination of events used to forecast profitable situations is discussed later in this chapter.

Pattern recognition may appear more like a game than a business, but it is a source of many valuable ideas. Figure 13-1, a graph of the New York Stock Exchange (1854–1959), shows the simplification of patterns to the point where it is difficult not to count the recurrences of the more obvious patterns and look for the formations that precede them in order to see whether they could be predictive. For example, in 1922, 1924, and 1927, there were sharp advances in the market; the years preceding those showed an identical *U* pattern. It would be interesting to see whether another occurrence of a symmetric *U* was followed by a similar rise.

---

[1] The only other known work that concerns similar patterns, although for the stock market, is by Arthur A. Merrill, *Behavior of Prices on Wall Street*, Analysis Press, Chappaqua, NY, 1966.

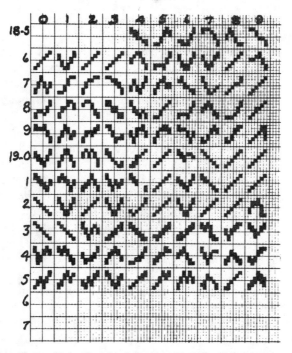

Figure 13-1 Graph of the New York Stock market.

Another pattern that stands out is that of two consecutive years of sharp rise, 1862–1863, 1908–1909, 1918–1919, and 1927–1928; in no case was there a third consecutive year but neither the preceding nor following years seem consistent.

Patterns frequently provide the foundation for a trading method or the justification for beginning work in the development of a method. They have been applied in many ways to commodity analysis, from the time of day to place an order, to the compound relationship of price, volume, and open interest. Daily trading opportunities may be a function of patterns based on the strength or weakness of the daily opening price. These are discussed in the next section. Weekly and weekend traits are studied, as well as types of reversals and their effects. These techniques can be considered complementary when used sequentially or can confirm the results of another test when used together. The end of this chapter discusses more general issues in pattern recognition.

TIME OF DAY

Market participants, especially floor traders, are the cause of periodic movement during the day. Angas called these the "tides of the daily prices." Over the years, the great increase in participants have added liquidity to each pit but have not altered the intraday time patterns.

There are a number of reasons for the regular movement of prices. Because most of the daily volume is the result of day-trades, those positions entered in the morning will be closed-out by the afternoon thus no margin is required. Orders that originate off the floor are the result of overnight analysis and are executed at the open. Scalpers and floor traders who hold trades for only a few minutes frequently have a mid-morning coffee break together; this natural phenomenon causes liquidity to decline and may result in a temporary price reversal. All traders develop habits of trading at particular times. Some prefer the opening, others 10 minutes after the open. More recently, large funds and managed accounts have been using close-only orders.

A day trader must watch certain key times. The opening moments of trading are normally used to assess the situation. A floor trader will sell a strong open and buy a weak one; this means the trade must be "evened-up" later and thus reinforces the opening direction. On a strong open without a downward reaction, all local selling is absorbed by the market and later attempts of the locals to liquidate will hold prices up. In any event, floor trades can be expected to take the opposite position to the opening direction usually causing a reversal early in the session.

Tubbs' Stock Market Correspondence Lessons, Chapter 13, explains the dominant patterns in the stock market (given a 10:00 A.M. to 3:00 P.M. session).

1. If a rally after the open has returned to the opening price by 1:00 o'clock, the day is expected to close weaker.
2. If the market is strong from 11:00 to 12:00, it will continue from 12:00 to 1:00.
3. If a reversal from 1:00 to 1:30 finds support at 1:30, it will close strong.
4. If the market has been bullish until 2:00 o'clock it will probably continue until the close and into the next day.
5. A rally that continues for 2 or 3 days as in (4) will most likely end on an 11:00 o'clock reversal.
6. In general, a late afternoon reaction down after a strong day shows a pending reversal.

Putting these together, the following patterns (among others) can be expected:

1. A strong open with a reversal at 11:00 not reaching the opening price, then strength from 11:00 to 1:00, a short reversal until 1:30, and then a strong close; according to (5), another strong open the following day.
2. A strong open that reverses by 11:00, continuing lower until 1:00, reverses again until 1:30, and then closes weak.

Merrill's work shows the hourly pattern of the stock market in Table 13-1. The grid clearly indicates a bullish bias with 1963 the most obvious. The pattern is

Table 13-1   Merrill's Hourly Stock Market Patterns

	Time During Trading Session					
	10:00	11:00	12:00	1:00	2:00	3:00
1962	−	+	−	−	+	−
1963	+	+	+	+	+	−
1964	+	+	−	−	+	−
1965	+	+	−	−	−	−

uniform and similar to what would be expected: early trending, an adjustment, then a wave of down-up-down. Contrary to commodities, these 4 years show extremely consistent strength on the opening with a sell-off on the close. Commodity prices may have regular patterns, but these patterns will occur with downward moves as well as upward ones. It is just as likely to see an opening sell-off with a rally on the close.

In commodities, the patterns are similar but may be compacted, as in the case of agricultural products, due to shorter, earlier hours (9:30 to 1:15 for most Chicago grains and livestock), or shifted as with currencies that open earlier. Knowing the daily time patterns would not only help a day trader but would also aid any speculator to enter an order at a better place. Figure 13-2 shows the time pattern for the Chicago Mercantile Exchange live cattle contract (open from 9:05 to 12:45). Seventy-six consecutive trading days were tabulated for the June 75 contract from February 1 through May 31, 1975, an active period for cattle. The left scale of the chart shows the frequency of occurrences and the bottom shows the time of day. A line appearing in the top half of the chart indicates price movement in the direction of the opening price (from the prior close); the lower half shows a reversal trend. Measurements were first taken every 5 minutes and later every 15 minutes, due to a more variable price direction near the open.

Figure 13-2 shows that trading in the direction of the opening price slows down immediately and by 9:30, 25 minutes after the open, the price direction has usually reversed. There is a subsequent steady change in direction back and forth throughout the day. This pattern is remarkably similar to Merrill's stock market observations.

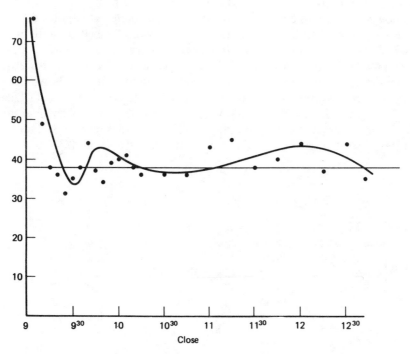

Figure 13-2   Intraday time patterns, June 75 cattle.

Table 13-2   Accumulating Time-of-Day Data

Time		Price	Direction From Last	Direction From Open
Monday				
9:05	(1)	45.15	+	O
9:30	(2)	45.25	+	O
10:00	(3)	45.10	−	X
10:30	(4)	45.05	−	X
11:00	(5)	45.20	+	O
11:30	(6)	45.30	+	O
12:00	(7)	45.40	+	O
12:30	(8)	45.30	−	X
Tuesday				
9:05	(9)	45.25	−	O
9:30	(10)	45.35	+	X
10:00	(11)	45.45	+	X
10:30	(12)	45.40	−	O
11:00	(13)	45.50	+	X
11:30	(14)	45.40	−	O
12:00	(15)	45.20	−	O
12:30	(16)	45.05	−	O

By showing 2 consecutive days of cattle price movement, Table 13-2 demonstrates how the data was accumulated. Although the table actually used 5-minute intervals from 9:00 to 10:15 and then 15-minute intervals from 10:15 until the close at 12:45, Table 13-2 is summarized in half-hour increments. If Friday's closing price was 45.00, Monday's open of 45.15 was indicated by a "+" for absolute direction and an *O* for opening direction. Any half-hour interval showing a price rise was marked with the relational symbol *O* and a reversal with an *X*. Tuesday opened lower, but the opening direction is still given as an *O*. Every interval that followed with lower prices is in the opening direction and is marked *O*. Adding the 76 test days together resulted in the scores shown in Table 13-3.

Table 13-3   Time Reversal Patterns[a]

9:05	76	9:35	38	10:05	35	11:15	31
9:10	27	9:40	32	10:10	38	11:30	38
9:15	38	9:45	39	10:15	40	11:45	36
9:20	40	9:50	42	10:30	40	12:00	32
9:25	45	9:55	37	10:45	40	12:15	39
9:30	41	10:00	36	10:00	33	12:30	32
						Close	41

[a] A more recent look at June 1976 Cattle showed very similar results.

Knowing the direction of the price movement does not mean that trading these intervals will be profitable. In order to evaluate the potential, it is necessary to know the approximate size of the price move; the interval can then be selected with the greatest potential for movement in the direction of the time-of-day pattern. By observing Figure 13-2, the intervals to study can be picked from the tops and bottoms of the cycles:

Selected Time Intervals

   a. Opening to 9:20
   b. 9:20 to 10:00
   c. 10:00 to 11:00
   d. 9:20 to 11:00
   e. 9:20 to 12:00
   f. 12:00 to closing

For each interval, the average range from high to low (volatility) and the net result of this span (additive bias) were measured without considering the "relative direction" that was used to create the curve of time patterns. The results, shown in Table 13-4, indicate that the narrowest ranges, (b) and (c), were early in the day moving only a total of 14 points. The combined period (d) was 21.7 points, 50% greater than the individual periods (b) and (c). Figure 13-3 describes the likely combination of the intervals.

The results show a midmorning drift that nets a total of 4.6 points in the direction of the opening price, and a maximum potential profit of 21 points by entering a position between 9:20 and 10:00 and then liquidating between 10:00 and 11:00. During the test period, the magnitude of the cattle move did not appear worth the risk, but the same pattern might be profitably traded in a market with higher value per point.

When trying to find other market patterns, it might be best to observe only stronger or weaker openings. For example, a gap open of 5 to 20 points in cattle would indicate a potentially more volatile day allowing greater price reactions. More uniform results can be expected as seen in both the *reversal patterns* and *gap analysis,* which appear later in this chapter. Restricting trading to days of higher volatility will reduce the trading opportunities but improve results.

Table 13-4   Summarized Time Data

Time	Average Volatility	Additive Bias	Points Moved in Direction of Open
a. Open–9:20	17.3	+4.9	+4.4
b. 9:20–10:00	14.3	+1.5	+.6
c. 10:00–11:00	14.2	+3.7	+3.9
d. 9:20–11:00	21.7	+5.3	+4.6
e. 9:20–12:00	25.8	+7.2	+3.3
f. 12:00–Close	19.6	+3.2	−1.2

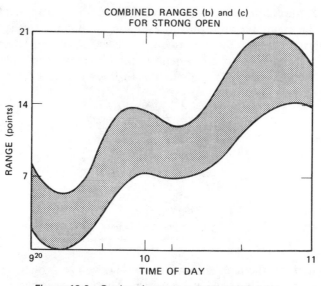

Figure 13-3   Cattle price ranges 9:20–11:00 A.M.

Trading the Early Patterns

The best opportunity for trading against the trend would be 5 minutes after the open. The opening momentum that carries prices further in the opening direction can be used to advantage without waiting. After 20 or 30 minutes, the opening reversal should have occurred and a trade may be entered in the same direction as the opening but at a more favorable price.

Relating the Opening Trade to the Prior Day

Another analysis performed on the time-pattern chart was a correlation to determine whether the period from market open to 9:20 (15 minutes), related to the prior day's direction, could help predict the direction of the "tides" during the current day. The 15-minute interval was chosen as sufficient time to react to results and place an order. The two situations distinguished were the relationship of the first trade to the prior day's direction and the direction of the early trading, using the first 15 minutes. Because the same 76 days of cattle trading were used, it should be noted that the conclusions are based on a small sample. Even though they are believed to be valid, there should be some variation between these results and those based on a large sample.

   Four cases were observed using the time intervals shown in Table 13-5. The percentages are calculated as the likelihood of movement in a specific direction relative to the conditions of the opening price and opening interval:

1. The opening price continued in the same direction as the prior day's open-to-close direction.

2. The opening 15-minute interval was consistent with the direction of the opening price as in (1).
3. The opening price and opening interval both continued the direction of the prior day.
4. The opening price and opening interval both continued opposite to the direction of the prior day.

Note that most of the intervals observed moved opposite to the opening price direction. This will support the more extensive work in the tables of reversal patterns and gap analysis. The two most extreme entries are the 39% in (1) and the 35% in (3). The first shows that by 9:20 there have been reversals 61% of the time further supporting the previous conclusions. The second case, in (3), shows that an opening price and opening interval that continues in the direction of the prior close has reversed 65% of the time in the 10:00 to 11:00 A.M. interval.

Table 13-5 Likelihood of Movement in the Same Direction as the Open

	Cases			
	(1)	(2)	(3)	(4)
Open– 9:20	39%	—	—	—
9:20–10:00	52%	57%	58%	50%
10:00–11:00	43%	40%	35%	48%
9:00–11:00	45%	47%	43%	48%
9:20–12:00	43%	49%	43%	44%
12:00–Close	46%	53%	48%	42%

Highs and Lows of the Day

In selecting a place to enter the market for a single day trade, it would be a great advantage to know the time of day at which the highest or lowest price is likely to occur. To understand this, Figure 13-4 presents a combined tabulation of both the daily highs and lows positioned at the time they occurred. The pattern clearly indicates that the opening and closing ranges are most likely to be the highest or lowest price, with 11:00 o'clock as the only midday alternative. No attempt was made to determine whether a high at the open had a low at 11:00 o'clock or at the close, nor was any relative positioning of the high-low observed. Separate charts of only highs and only lows proved that there was no distinction in the patterns— highs were just as likely to occur at the three peaks as were lows.

There are simple ways in which this small piece of information could be of advantage. After the opening range has been formed, watch for the breakout of the range and assume the other direction is a high or low. In the example, the breakout will occur to the upside, and the bottom of the range will be considered the daily low. *Buy* the opening breakout with a stop below the opening range. Look for the high of the day at 11:00 o'clock. If there is a test of the highs at 11:00,

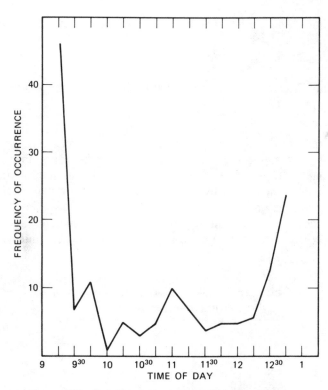

Figure 13-4   Combined occurrence of highs and lows.

liquidate the position assuming that the resistance will hold. If there is another upside breakout, buy again in anticipation of the highs of the day at the close. If no test of the highs occur at 11:00, hold the position until the close; if support is broken, close-out or reverse and expect the lows of the day at the close.

OPENING GAPS AND INTRADAY PATTERNS

The daily price fluctuations and intraday patterns of a commodity may be related to the strength or weakness of the daily opening. A *gap opening* of considerable size allows a correspondingly greater reaction, and may show more consistency in the subsequent intraday patterns than a market that opens nearly unchanged. A gap analysis was performed to study this situation. A strong open followed by a stronger close would allow a trader to buy on a reaction, whereas a consistently weak close after a strong open would require a short position to be taken. The specific entry timing can be improved by using the patterns discussed in the previous section.

The gap analysis for the Deutschemark (Table 13-6) is divided into two parts:

1. The position of the closing price following a gap opening.
   a. The close continued in the direction of the gap.

    b. The close was between the gap opening and the prior close.

    c. The close reversed the direction of the opening gap, that is, if the open was higher, the close was lower.

2. The type of trading range pattern that occurred.

    a. Prices crossed the prior closing price (but did not necessarily close there).

    b. Prices reversed from the open but did not cross the prior close.

    c. Prices continued in the direction of the open and never reversed.

In addition, a record is shown of the percentage of times that price *continued on the following open* in the same direction as the current gap.

The Deutschemark can be used to interpret the gap analysis table. For opening gaps less than +/−40, the market does not show any special tendency. As the gap increases, there is a greater chance the opening move will continue on the close. The chance of a closing-price reversal is less likely as the opening gap is greater. In almost all cases, there is a pullback following a gap greater than +/−20 points. A trader, looking to buy after a strong opening, would be advised to wait for a pullback. The Deutschemark does not show a tendency to continue in the direction of the gap on the next day's open except at the extremes.

Pork bellies (Table 13-7) display a slightly different pattern. They show a decreasing tendency to continue in the gap direction as the gaps increase, and a high likelihood of a closing price reversal in the range of +/−50 point opening gaps. As the gaps increase, a follow-through on the next open is more likely.

Table 13-6   Gap Analysis for the Deutschemark from January 3, 1977 for 1788 Trading Days[a]

	Close			Trading Range			Cont. Next Day	No. of Cases
Gap	Cont. Dir.	Below Open	Rvrsd. Dir.	Cross Pr.Cls.	Adj. Open	Cont. Only		
1.20	.0	100.0	.0	.0	33.3	66.7	66.7	3
1.00	80.0	20.0	.0	.0	100.0	.0	40.0	5
.80	55.6	44.4	.0	11.1	88.9	.0	33.3	9
.60	64.8	33.3	1.9	3.7	96.3	.0	40.7	54
.40	50.0	39.1	10.9	17.3	82.1	.6	44.9	156
.20	44.0	26.1	29.9	55.4	40.7	3.9	51.1	612
.00	.0	.0	.0	.0	.0	.0	.0	50
−.20	45.9	25.0	29.1	56.9	38.6	4.5	53.5	645
−.40	46.1	45.1	8.8	16.1	82.9	1.0	50.8	193
−.60	54.8	40.5	4.8	9.5	88.1	2.4	52.4	42
−.80	63.6	36.4	.0	.0	100.0	.0	54.5	11
−1.00	20.0	80.0	.0	.0	80.0	20.0	80.0	5
−1.60	.0	100.0	.0	.0	.0	100.0	100.0	1
−2.00	.0	100.0	.0	.0	100.0	.0	100.0	1

[a] Values are shown as the percent of cases in each line category.

Table 13-7   Gap Analysis for Pork Bellies from January 3, 1977 for 1788 Trading Days[a]

Gap	Close			Trading Range			Cont. Next Day	No. of Cases
	Cont. Dir.	Below Open	Rvrsd. Dir.	Cross Pr.Cls.	Adj. Open	Cont. Only		
6.50	100.0	.0	.0	.0	100.0	.0	100.0	1
4.25	.0	100.0	.0	.0	100.0	.0	.0	1
3.50	.0	100.0	.0	.0	100.0	.0	.0	1
2.50	.0	100.0	.0	.0	50.0	50.0	50.0	2
2.25	8.7	87.0	4.3	13.0	30.4	56.5	78.3	23
2.00	26.7	66.7	6.7	6.7	66.7	26.7	60.0	15
1.75	42.9	52.4	4.8	23.8	76.2	.0	57.1	21
1.50	40.9	50.0	9.1	31.8	68.2	.0	68.2	22
1.25	57.5	22.5	20.0	35.0	62.5	2.5	70.0	40
1.00	59.2	14.1	26.8	42.3	57.7	.0	47.9	71
.75	51.5	16.7	31.8	62.1	37.9	.0	64.4	132
.50	52.8	11.2	36.1	73.4	26.2	.4	49.8	233
.25	49.5	4.4	46.0	90.2	8.3	1.6	51.1	315
.00	.0	.0	.0	.0	.0	.0	.0	21
−.25	48.0	5.3	46.7	89.5	9.9	.6	52.9	323
−.50	48.3	13.8	37.9	71.3	27.1	1.7	57.9	240
−.75	55.4	13.1	31.5	54.6	44.6	.8	53.8	130
−1.00	60.9	15.9	23.2	46.4	50.7	2.9	52.2	69
−1.25	56.4	17.9	25.6	41.0	59.0	.0	56.4	39
−1.50	61.9	14.3	23.8	33.3	66.7	.0	47.6	21
−1.75	57.9	31.6	10.5	10.5	89.5	.0	68.4	19
−2.00	24.1	62.1	13.8	27.6	51.7	20.7	51.7	29
−2.25	5.9	94.1	.0	5.9	17.6	76.5	76.5	17
−5.25	.0	100.0	.0	.0	100.0	.0	100.0	1
−9.50	.0	100.0	.0	.0	100.0	.0	.0	1

[a] Values are shown as the percent of cases in each line category.

THREE STUDIES IN MARKET MOVEMENT—WEEKLY, WEEKEND, AND REVERSAL PATTERNS

The next three sections are concerned with longer periods of time. The first, *weekly patterns,* looks only at the closing prices during a 5-day week from Monday through Friday in order to find recurring close-only patterns. A week is often considered to have integrity as a single unit of time. The study attempts to isolate predictive patterns; for example, if Monday through Thursday were all higher, what is the possibility of Friday being higher? If the weekly trend can be clearly identified, should a correction on Friday be expected due to "evening up"? Because patterns represent human behavior, the results could prove interesting.

Weekend patterns are considered independently in the second study. The opening direction on Monday could restore the trend of the prior week, if those traders who liquidate on Friday intend to resume their positions. The weekend is also an extended period for unexpected news or a build-up of public interest. The study will attempt to relate the direction of the Monday opening price to some pattern or trend of the preceding week.

Reversal patterns are not based on a day of the week but may be a leading indicator. They may also be used as a filtering or timing device.

Weekly Patterns

During their constant exposure to the market, professional traders often observe patterns in weekly price movement; their acceptance of these patterns are as old as the market itself. In *Reminiscences of a Stock Operator,* the fictional character Larry Livingston (assumed to be Jesse Livermore) begins his career recording prices on a chalk board above the floor of the New York Stock Exchange eventually becoming aware of patterns within these prices. The most accepted occurrence of a pattern is the Tuesday reversal, which is taken as commonplace by close observers of the market. When questioned why a strong soybean market on the first of the week is followed by a weak day, a member of the Board of Trade would shrug his shoulders and quote: "Up on Monday, down on Tuesday." If this is true, there is a trading opportunity.

If a commonly accepted idea is not enough to be convincing, consider the additional rationalization about human behavior: The weekend allows a build-up of sentiment, which should result in greater activity on Monday. Coupled with adding back positions that were liquidated prior to the weekend this may cause a disproportionate move on Monday, especially early in the session. This pattern may be further exaggerated when a clear trend exists. With this overbought or oversold condition, it is likely that Tuesday would show an adjustment. So much for hypothesizing.

The first aspect of the test was to define the weekly pattern. This was done in terms of the Friday-to-Monday move (close-to-close). Monday always received the value X, regardless of whether its direction from Friday was up or down. For each day that closed in the same direction as the Friday-to-Monday move, another X is used; when the close reversed direction, an O is recorded. Therefore, XOXXO means that Tuesday and Friday, represented by O, closed in the opposite direction from the prior Friday-to-Monday move whereas Wednesday and Thursday were in the same direction. This could have meant either of the situations:

		(1)	(2)
Monday	X	Up	Down
Tuesday	O	Down	Up
Wednesday	X	Up	Down
Thursday	X	Up	Down
Friday	O	Down	Up

It might be that there is a distinction between the weeks that begin with an upward move on Monday rather than a lower price, but all cases were combined. This assumes that the pattern, rather than the direction is most important.

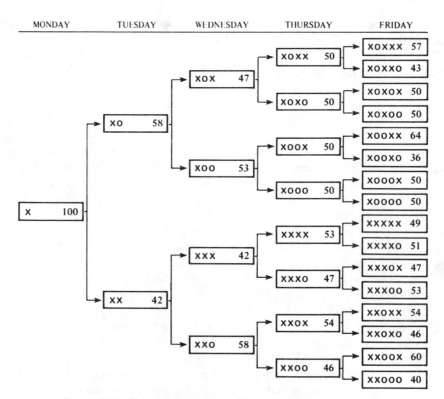

Figure 13-5   Twenty-three commodities 1976 (873 weeks tested).

Figure 13-5 shows the aggregate results of the weekday patterns for a sampling of 23 commodities tested for 1976. The numbers next to the corresponding patterns indicate the percentage of occurrences of each new day's pattern. For example, if the Monday-Tuesday pattern was XX, an O followed 58% of the time and X followed 42%.

In the first edition of this book, combinations of patterns that occurred most often were shown as trading opportunities. Figure 13-6a shows the cattle patterns (1970–1975) and the *high probability trades* that were found. Weekly patterns were recalculated for the period January 1977–January 1984, with the results shown in Figure 13-6b. Some of the prior frequent patterns are the same while some are not. In a complete evaluation of a wide sampling of 1970–1975 markets versus 1977-1984, there were consistent patterns but they were not necessarily the same. Appendix 6 contains a sampling of the original charts and a selection of the more interesting results from the recent study.

Daily Sequences

The additional study that points out the inconsistencies in weekday patterns means that other information must be used if these patterns are to be traded. The sequential relationship of the daily reversals or continuations satisfies that need. Consider Figure 13-5 in terms of how each day relates to the prior day. For example, on Tuesday the XO pattern was prevalent; this means a reversal was most likely. On Wednesday, both cases of higher occurrences were in the reverse trend direction (O). On Thursday, all situations greater than 50% were in the direction of the Friday–Monday move (trend), and on Friday $\frac{3}{4}$ of the cases above 50% favored the trend. Rather than count on specific patterns, the general weekday moves could be said to relate to the Monday move as:

	Direction
Tuesday	Opposite
Wednesday	Opposite
Thursday	Same
Friday	Same

HIGH PROBABILITY TRADES:

IF **XOX** THEN EXPECT **X** ON THURSDAY   IF **X** OCCURS HOLD UNTIL FRIDAY'S CLOSE,
                                               OR ELSE REVERSE OF THURSDAY AND C/O FRIDAY

IF **XOOX** THEN EXPECT **X** ON FRIDAY

IF **XOOO** THEN EXPECT **X** ON FRIDAY

IF **XXXX** THEN EXPECT **X** ON FRIDAY

IF **XXOX** THEN EXPECT **X** ON FRIDAY

IF **XXOO** THEN EXPECT **X** ON FRIDAY

DO NOT TRADE IF **XXXO** PATTERN OCCURS

(a)

Figure 13-6 (a) Cattle 1970–1975. (b) Weekday patterns for cattle, January 3, 1977–February 3, 1984 (1787 days).

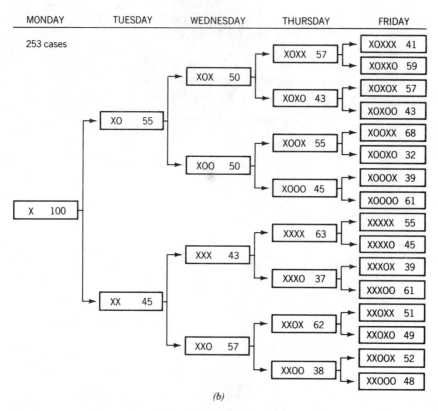

(b)

Figure 13-6 (*Continued*)

In the notation used for this study, this is XOOXX which shows as 58-53-50-64 sequential daily frequencies.

Two other sequences are important: the frequency of *switching* or *continuing* the direction of the day before. Whether a day was an X or O, it may be that the next day shows all high-frequency situations in the same direction (*C* for continuation) or opposite (*S* for switched direction). Looking again at Figure 13-5, four of the six cases over 50% on Friday were a continuation of the prior day's direction. Then, the best Friday trade is in the direction of the Thursday move but even better if Thursday is an X.

Table 13-8 summarizes the daily sequences for the 1970–1975 tests and Table 13-9 shows the results of the 1977–1984 tests. Asterisks designate those columns where 100% of the patterns favored the direction shown. Sugar was neither X nor O on Friday but always favored the same move as Thursday. Soybeans (+) had seven out of eight cases favor the same as Thursday but also leaned toward an O on Friday. Although cotton consistently switched from Thursday to Friday and favored an X on Friday, it was inconsistent from the earlier study. At that time, it showed Friday as a *CR* rather than the current *S*T*, a situation to treat cautiously.

Table 13-9 shows those markets that trend from those that do not. The Deutschemark and the Swiss franc both show

R   S   CT   CT*

Table 13-8 Weekday Sequential Patterns (1970–1976)[a]

Commodity	Tuesday	Wednesday	Thursday	Friday
23 combined (1976)	*R*	*R*	*T*∗	*C T*
Grains (1976)	*R*	*R*	*S R*	*T*
Metals (1976)	*R*	*R*		*T*
Cotton (1970–1975)		*R*	*C*∗	*C R*
Cocoa (1970–1975)	*R*	*S*∗		*T+*
Cattle (1970–1975)		*S*∗	*C*∗	*C T*
Copper (1970–1975)		*R*	*S T*	*C T*

[a] *T* is a *trend move*, in the direction of the prior Friday-Monday
  R is a *reversal*, opposite to the Friday-Monday move
  S is a *switch*, a reversal of the prior day's direction
  C is a *continuation*, the same direction as the prior day
  ∗ indicates all cases were the same
  + indicates that seven out of eight possible cases were the same

Table 13-9 Weekday Sequential Patterns (1977–1984)[a]

Commodity	Tuesday	Wednesday	Thursday	Friday
Corn	*R*	*T*	*S*	*C T*
Wheat	*R*	*R*		*C T*
Soybeans	*R*	*S*∗		*C+R*
Cotton		*R*	*S*∗	*S*∗*T*
Sugar	*R*	*T*	*C T*	*C*∗
Cocoa			*S T*	*S T*
Coffee		*T*	*C*∗	*C R*
Cattle	*R*	*S*∗*R*	*T*∗	*C T*
Pork bellies		*S*∗	*T*∗	*C T*
Gold	*R*	*S*∗	*S*∗	*S T*
Silver	*R*	*T*	*C T*	*C T*
Copper		*R*	*S*∗	*R*
Swiss franc	*R*	*S*∗	*C T*	*C T*
Deutschemark		*S*∗	*C T*	*C T*
Treasury bills	*T*	*T*	*C*∗	*S T*
Treasury bonds (20-year)	*R*	*S*∗		*T*
S&P 500	*R*	*S*∗	*S*∗	*S*

[a] *T* is a *trend move*, in the direction of the prior Friday-Monday
  R is a *reversal*, opposite to the Friday-Monday move
  S is a *switch*, a reversal of the prior day's direction
  C is a *continuation*, the same direction as the prior day
  ∗ indicates all cases were the same
  + indicates that seven out of eight possible cases were the same

This means a reversal on Tuesday, then renewing the trend Thursday and Friday (XOXX) or reversing on Wednesday, most likely followed by a trend continuation (XXOXX) but possibly XXOOO.

Gold and the S&P 500 both have the greatest inconsistencies with the pattern

$$R \quad S* \quad S* \quad S$$

Each day tended to reverse the direction of the day before. Wednesdays and Thursdays were exceptionally consistent.

Trading Weekday Patterns

The weekday patterns can be traded by using market-on-close orders. For example, to take advantage of the sugar trends ($R \quad T \quad CT \quad C*$), an order should be placed on Tuesday's close to buy if Monday was up or sell if Monday was down. A continuation of the trend is expected through Friday, when the position is liquidated on-the-close or on a favorable move Friday. If prices move opposite to the trend on Thursday (O), the trade is reversed and carried into Friday. The $C*$ indicates a strong likelihood of a continuing Thursday–Friday move.

Weekend Patterns

Of all patterns studied, this test was expected to be the most promising. Two factors lead to the anticipation of strong weekend patterns:

1. "Friday liquidation," the aversion of traders to hold a market position over the weekend.
2. Setting of new positions and resetting of old ones on Monday, especially during a trending market.

If the patterns can be identified, the 2-day weekend delay should result in large price jumps and good profits for those willing to take the weekend risk. As in the case of the weekday patterns, a 1976 study was available for comparison (commodities tested for 5 years ending June to December 1975 depending on contracts selected).

Not knowing what to expect but anticipating combining the results with the study of weekly patterns, a number of different trend indicators and patterns were tested. These were limited to closing price relationships.

Trend indicators:
Prior Friday-to-Monday direction
Friday-to-Friday direction
Most frequent direction last week
Direction of Thursday-to-Friday

Patterns
Unique Wednesday-Thursday-Friday patterns

Table 13-10 Weekend Patterns for Sugar from January 3, 1977 to February 6, 1984 for 1777 Days

Trend Direction	No. Cases	Trend/Pattern Continued Monday on . . .					
		Open	%	Close	%	Extreme	%
Case 1: Friday to Monday	289	139	48%	145	50%	233	80%
Case 2: Friday to Friday	289	146	50	132	45	228	78
Case 3: Most frequent direction	266	141	53	125	46	214	80
Case 4: Thursday to Friday	289	174	60	132	45	239	82
Case 5: (a) X-XXX	44	23	52	15	34	35	79
(b) X-XXO	25	17	68	9	36	24	96
(c) X-XOX	36	24	66	15	41	31	86
(d) X-OXX	65	34	52	33	50	52	80
(e) X-XOO	44	29	65	25	56	37	84
(f) X-OOX	30	20	66	19	63	27	90
(g) X-OOO	45	27	60	16	35	33	73

Following each of the trends or patterns, the prices on Monday were tabulated to determine the frequency and consistency of the opening price, closing price, and high or low prices with respect to the trend or patterns. For example, Table 13-10 lists the results for sugar. Of the trend cases 1–4, only the *Thursday-to-Friday* shows some follow-through on the open of the next Monday. None of the cases show that prices continued in the "trend" direction on Monday's close. In general, the open was more likely to be in the direction of the trend than the close.

The *extreme* in Table 13-10 includes the actual price direction. It shows the frequency of Monday's high greater than Friday's close when the trend is up, or Monday's low less than Friday's close when the trend was down. For all cases, this is greater than 75%. It is not surprising that there is an opportunity for profit sometime during the next day as most trading days span the prior close.

The Wednesday-Thursday-Friday patterns are much clearer. For sugar, patterns ending with XX were followed by reversals on Monday. The best trend continuation followed X-XXO. This is the ideal case where a strongly trending week succombs to Friday liquidation, renews the trend on Monday's open (68%), is followed by an intraday trend continuation (98%), but fails badly by the close Monday (36%).

In general, the two patterns that have the most frequent follow-through are X-XXO and X-OOX, which can be seen in Tables 13-11 and 13-12. The pattern X-XXX has a very low frequency of continuing in the same direction. Further tests can be found in Appendix 6.

Combining Weekday and Weekend

It is natural to consider combining the weekday and weekend patterns. If the two result in holding a trade for another day or two, profits can be increased considerably. In Table 13-9, the currencies are seen to be highly trending, but the weekend

Table 13-11   Cattle Weekend Patterns, from January 3, 1977 to
February 3, 1984 for 1786 Days

		Trend/Pattern Continued Monday on . . .					
Trend Direction	No. Cases	Open	%	Close	%	Extreme	%
Case 1: Friday to Monday	290	143	49%	138	47%	237	81%
Case 2: Friday to Friday	290	124	42	138	47	231	79
Case 3: Most frequent direction	275	122	44	116	42	215	78
Case 4: Thursday to Friday	290	148	51	111	38	231	79
Case 5: (a) X-XXX	32	10	31	6	18	19	59
(b) X-XXO	45	26	57	19	42	40	88
(c) X-XOX	26	14	53	14	53	22	84
(d) X-OXX	89	47	52	29	32	72	80
(e) X-XOO	28	13	46	7	25	19	67
(f) X-OOX	30	22	73	18	60	27	90
(g) X-OOO	40	16	40	18	45	32	80

patterns (Appendix 6) show them to be exceptionally poor risks for continuing. On the other hand, sugar shows a high probability of continuing the prior trend, except for the patterns X-XXX and X-OOO (Table 13-10). If a trend position is held on Friday (which is favored), it should be continued over the weekend and closed-out on Monday.

A Comment on Testing and Holidays

The weekday and weekend tests did not distinguish holidays as a special case. Weekends were defined as any period where the market did not trade for 2 or

Table 13-12   Weekend Patterns for Pork Bellies, January 3, 1977 to
February 6, 1984 for 1787 Days

		Trend/Pattern Continued Monday on . . .					
Trend Direction	No. Cases	Open	%	Close	%	Extreme	%
Case 1: Friday to Monday	291	146	50%	149	51%	245	84%
Case 2: Friday to Friday	291	148	50	141	48	246	84
Case 3: Most frequent direction	274	141	51	143	52	233	85
Case 4: Thursday to Friday	291	160	54	140	48	249	85
Case 5: (a) X-XXX	41	18	43	21	51	34	82
(b) X-XXO	34	20	58	16	47	30	88
(c) X-XOX	29	22	75	19	65	25	86
(d) X-OXX	86	47	54	38	44	73	84
(e) X-XOO	30	13	43	14	46	24	80
(f) X-OOX	34	20	58	16	47	31	91
(g) X-OOO	37	20	54	16	43	32	86

Table 13-13   Merrill's Holiday Results

Period Tested	Holiday or Holiday Period	% Upward Moves
1897–1964	Day prior to all holidays	67.9%
1897–1964	Day after all holidays	50.8
1897–1964	Thanksgiving to New Year	74
1897–1964	July 4th to Labor Day	69
1931–1965	Before Christmas	74
1931–1965	Before New Year	75

more days. Weeks used in the weekly tests required 5 consecutive trading days; those patterns that made sense with a 4-day week were included. Note that it may have been that a "Friday" was really a "Thursday" in a 4-day week.

It is commonly accepted that the action prior to holidays is the same as those before weekends. The only available work in this area is by Merrill, whose results are based on the stock market, and demonstrates a strong bullish tendency before a holiday with a weak day immediately after. Remembering the bullish bias of the stock market (about 54% of all days were higher from 1897–January 1964), Merrill's results are shown in Table 13-13. In relation to commodity trading, this would indicate the possibility of a sharp trending move prior to or throughout a holiday season.

Reversal Patterns

The last of the three studies is on the nature of reversals. The intention is to find a pattern in the open, high, low, and closing price of the day that will help predict the next day's pattern or direction. One reversal of special interest is the *key reversal*, which is usually associated with the extreme of a clearly trending move. The reversals and patterns analyzed in this study are defined as follows:

Intraday Trend Continued. The current opening price was above (below) the prior closing price, and the current close was above (below) the current open. The market has continued to rise (or fall) steadily.

Key Reversal. The current high (low) was above (below) the prior high (low), and the current close was below (above) the prior close.

Both trend and reversal were filtered using the following trend indicators:

1-Day. The reversal must be counter to yesterday's price direction.

1-Week. The reversal must be counter to the prior 5-day net price direction.

Table 13-14 shows the results of an individual test for 20-year T-bonds. The reversals, shown first, indicate that the 1-day direction was a very good forecast of the key reversal for both the subsequent opening and closing prices. The 5-day trend was much less reliable.

Table 13-14　Reversal Analysis for 20-Year Treasury Bonds, August 22, 1977 through February 6, 1984 for 1622 Days

	Key Reversals Down			Key Reversals Up		
	No Dir.	1-Day	5-Day	No Dir.	1-Day	5-Day
Total	199			211		

Continued in Reversal Direction Next OPEN

	No Dir.	1-Day	5-Day	No Dir.	1-Day	5-Day
Number	126	98	65	105	79	66
% total	63%	49%	32%	49%	37%	31%
% cont.		77%	51%		75%	62%

Continued in Reversal Direction Next CLOSE

	No Dir.	1-Day	5-Day	No Dir.	1-Day	5-Day
Number	92	75	45	79	60	50
% total	46%	37%	22%	37%	28%	23%
% cont.		81%	48%		75%	63%

	Trend Moves Down			Trend Moves Up		
	No Dir.	1-Day	5-Day	No Dir.	1-Day	5-Day
Number	824	370	446	748	317	340
% cont.	50%	44%	54%	46%	42%	45%

Table 13-15　Key Reversal Patterns[a]

		Reversals Down		Reversals Up	
	Total	— % Continued on the Next . . . —			
Commodity	Reversals	Open	Close	Open	Close
Corn	197	81	79	84	81
Soybeans	265	78	77	83	84
Sugar	242	83	81	76	76
Coffee	211	79	80	87	86
Cocoa	214	82	78	78	78
Cattle	266	86	82	75	80
Pork bellies	274	87	86	86	82
Gold	229	79	77	72	68
Silver	223	73	75	69	61
Swiss franc	162	68	73	64	73
Deutschemark	166	73	71	62	59
Treasury bills	188	73	77	80	77
Treasury bonds	199	77	81	75	75
S&P 500	79	88	83	90	88

[a] Approximately 1780 trading days were used for each product. There was an average of 15% reversal days tabulated. The S&P 500 had only 480 days tested.

The *trend continuation* proved to be inconsistent for all tests on all markets, regardless of the 1- or 5-day filter. This implies that price moves are determined by overnight jumps; the close may be higher or lower than the open without any trend consequences. Table 13-15 summarizes key reversals based on the 1-day filter. The results are very consistent.

Trading a 1-Day Reversal

A 1-day reversal does not stand alone as a trading method, but the consistency of the results deserves attention. The occurrence of a reliable indicator on 15% of the trading days can help improve any trading method. Traded by itself, a short position can be entered on the close of a downward key reversal day, then closed-out on the open or sometime during the following day. Combined with weekday or weekend patterns, this could be parlayed into a longer trade.

COMPUTER-BASED PATTERN RECOGNITION

The methods previously discussed were based on patterns familiar to traders. The weekly and weekend studies, as well as the intraday time patterns shown in the previous sections, were originally verified by hand and later recalculated using a computer. There is a type of pattern recognition, however, that would hardly be considered without the availability of a computer.

Rather than the conventional price patterns where recurring sequences of higher and lower days are found within certain qualified intervals, *computer-based pattern recognition* refers to *sets of descriptors* and *classes of interest*. For example, Aronson[2] describes the sets and values which must be satisfied by a professional jockey as:

Descriptor	Value-Range
Height	Under 5'5"
Weight	Under 120 lbs.
Age	16 to 35
Years riding horses	Over 10

The *set* of people who satisfy all four conditions are said to *contain* all professional jockeys. The converse, that all people satisfying these conditions *are* professional jockeys, is not true. It will be necessary to qualify this set further to create a set that contains *only* professional jockeys; however, these four conditions go a long way toward reducing the field.

[2] David R. Aronson, *Artificial Intelligence Methods,* (privately published). Also see David R. Aronson, "Artificial Intelligence/Pattern Recognition Applied to Forecasting Financial Market Trends," *Market Technicians Association Journal,* May 1985, pp. 91–131.

How can this tool be applied toward the development of a trading strategy? If the system is defined in terms of the *trade profile,* it becomes obvious. Consider the following characteristics of a trade:

1. The price moves higher or lower by at least 3% of the starting price.
2. The price move occurs within 20 days.
3. There is no loss exceeding .5%.

Either a computer or an analyst can locate all price moves that satisfy these conditions within a price series. Each of the 5 days preceding an upward move, which satisfies these conditions, can be marked as *buy* days, and the 5 days preceding a downward movement can be designated *sell* days (see Figure 13-7).

The computer now contains the set of all buy and sell days; those days on which it would be good to get a buy or sell signal. Next, some likely indicators must be specified to be used for identifying that these trades are about to begin. The following might be used:

1. The moving average direction.
2. An overbought/oversold indicator such as a *relative strength indicator* (RSI) or *contrary opinion.*
3. The direction of changes in trading volume.
4. A 10-day momentum.

By entering a broad selection of indicators and trying to avoid duplication, the computer can find unique values for combinations of indicators that primarily occur during the days selected as buy and sell periods. Ideally, all buy signals should occur when one indicator, or the value of combining indicators, exceeds a specific value. For example, all buy signals occur when the average value of the

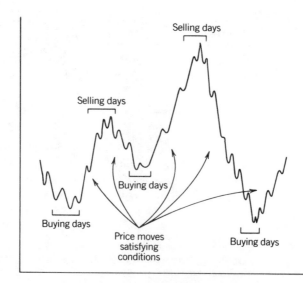

Figure 13-7 Specific buying and selling days.

RSI and the market sentiment (contrary opinion) is below the 10% level. However, having all buy signals occur here is not enough. Poor signals may appear at this level, which cause large losses. The perfect system will have *no losing signals* occur in this zone.

Unfortunately, in the real world there are no perfect solutions. The trades that are signaled by the combinations of indicators will have to be studied for net return, risk, and other performance criteria. However, the technique of setting up classes of indicators, buy and sell days, is a new and valid approach to system development. It is analogous to the multiple regression method used by econometricians to find the relationship between statistics and prices. Although the econometricians use inflation, supply, interest rates, and so forth, pattern recognition can employ technical indicators and discrete patterns to forecast a buy or sell day.

ARTIFICIAL INTELLIGENCE METHODS

Artificial Intelligence refers to a computer process that performs an operation corresponding to or approaching, human thinking. The state-of-the-art in artificial intelligence is the separation of two ideas. The collection of information that is stored in the brain has been termed the *knowledge base*. This is distinguished from reason, rules, and logic, called the *inference engine*. These ideas are not very different from the data base and trading strategies that are discussed here.

The closest practical approach to artificial intelligence is *heuristic* programming. This refers to computer learning in very much the same way as finding the way out of a maze. The computer starts with rules relative to the problem, then records the successful and unsuccessful experiences. Eventually, it has a complete table of what to do for each situation or at least a table of probable solutions. This is a realistic, intelligent approach when the same events can be expected to recur in the same way. It does not help in new situations without the added complication of extrapolation, basic relationships (e.g., price level to volatility), and other forms of "expectation."

The danger of the heuristic approach to pattern recognition is that it may continue to define longer combinations of patterns that have already produced inconsistent or poor results. Allowing the computer to identify a limitless collection of patterns is just another case of overfitting, but this time at a highly sophisticated level.

Heuristic programs have improved current technology in searching, optimization, and game-playing strategies; however, they are not readily available. There is no doubt that this technique will be quickly absorbed into trading strategies as it develops.[3]

---

[3] Two books of interest that represent the state-of-the-art in heuristics and game playing are Judea Pearl, *Heuristics,* Addison-Wesley, Reading, MA, 1984 and M. A. Bramer, *Computer Game-Playing: Theory and Practice,* Halsted Press, New York, 1983.

14

Day Trading

A *day trade* is a position entered and liquidated during a single trading day. The techniques of *time of day* and *daily patterns,* discussed in such rigid form in Chapter 13, are put to use by the day trader. Day trading requires extreme discipline, excellent planning, and psychic anticipation. The need for a fast response to changing situations tends to exaggerate any bad trading habits; as in other fields, the shorter the response time, the greater the chance for error.

In order to keep mistakes to a minimum, daily strategy must be planned in advance. It should focus on the most likely situations that might occur, based on the nature of the current price movement. It should also have alternatives for the extreme unexpected moves in either direction. Making spot decisions during market hours will cause more frequent errors.

Computers have increased the number of day traders who rely on systems. The availability of graphic display at brokerage offices and the use of home computers to receive intraday prices have made it possible for the trader with less of a technical background to use an orderly approach to day trading. Although these methods reduce risk, they are still greatly limited in selection. Commercial software rarely provides more than displays of moving averages, relative strength, and their variations. As discussed here, these methods might not be enough.

For the arbitrageur, computers have changed the entire nature of trading. Instant display of movements in cash and futures markets combined with computerized screening of opportunities have allowed professionals in interest rate and foreign exchange arbitrage to flourish. For the independent trader, few of these opportunities are available. With an increase in risk, however, spread trading can be improved using similar displays. The intraday picture of spread relationships makes it possible to see distortions in intermarket, interproduct, and intercrop spreads, which would have been missed previously. This faster response must improve profits and reduce risk in any day trading method.

IMPACT OF TRANSACTION COSTS

Transaction costs are the greatest deterrent to day-trading profits. The failure to execute near the intended price and commission costs can be a disproportionate part of potential profitability. An aspiring day trader has two ways of improving performance: by paying lower commissions and by careful selection of opportunities. Table 14-1 presents a brief evaluation of the significance of low retail commissions for various commodities. In major brokerage firms, these rates may be double; as an exchange member, rates are negligible. When selecting a market to trade, the *typical daily range,* the *price level,* and the *volume* should be carefully weighed.

Liquidity

The importance of liquidity is magnified in day trading. A $100 execution skid (away from the intended price for "market" orders) will have little impact on a month-long trade netting $2000; however, it will be critical for a day trade with a profit objective of $300. The selection of day trading candidates begins with those markets of greater volume. Whether 1 contract or 1000, a thinly traded market will cut sharply into profits. In choosing between the S&P and Value Line, or T-bonds and T-bills, the choices are clear.

Occasionally, markets with light volume show larger price moves than similar markets traded on other exchanges. Traders will be tempted to profit from these moves but will consistently find that the execution of an order at the posted price is elusive. A market order is not advisable due to the thinness of the trading, a limit order does not get filled, and a spread is not quoted at anything resembling the apparent price relationships; there is no real way to take advantage of these perceived profits. If an execution succeeds, exiting the position must still be negotiated.

Price Ranges

The *active daily range* shows the price movement on a reasonably active day. Some commodities, such as copper and cotton, combine lack of liquidity with a narrow daily range and are easily disqualified from a day trade opportunity. On the other hand, grains, cattle, and silver have the volume but a smaller range than desirable for day trading. The S&P 500 stands out as having both qualities, followed by currencies and oil.

The price range over the past year is shown in both price and percentage. Whereas a high past volatility does not mean continued present activity, a low 1-year volatility, as seen in copper, Eurodollars, silver, and the grains, should eliminate those commodities.

Day traders may find daily trading limits a problem during high volatility periods. Day trading does best in markets that have wide swings not deterred by limits; a single locked-limit move can generate a loss which offsets many profitable day trades. High volatility and locked-limit moves present a conflict for day trading. Expanding limits have greatly helped reduce the frequency of locked-limit days. The livestock markets have not yet adopted this policy; consequently, pork bellies, one of the most volatile of all markets, has an exceptionally high percentage of days on which the limit is reached.

Table 14-1 Recent Volatility and Liquidity Factors[a]

	Active[b]					Percentage		Dir.[c]
	Spot Price	Daily Volume	Daily (pts.)	Range ($)	1-Year Range	Daily	1-Year	
Wheat	260	8,000	5	250	60	1.0	23	−
Corn	165	20,000	4	200	110	1.2	67	−
Soybeans	500	25,000	7	350	110	.7	22	−
Cattle	60.00	20,000	1.00	400	22.00	1.7	37	+
Hogs	62.00	7,000	1.00	300	22.00	1.6	35	+
Pork bellies	80.00	4,000	2.00	760	40.00	1.9	50	+
Coffee	170.00	4,000	4.00	1500	150.00	1.8	88	−
Sugar	7.00	15,000	.30	336	5.40	4.3	77	−
Cocoa	1900	3,000	75	750	700	3.9	37	m
Orange juice	100.00	400	1.50	225	45.00	1.5	45	m
Copper	58.00	7,000	.75	188	6.00	1.3	10	−
Silver	540.00	9,000	10.00	500	40.00	1.9	7	−
Gold	375.00	25,000	5.00	500	100.00	1.3	27	+
Platinum	520.00	3,000	10.00	500	50.00	1.9	10	+
T-Bills	94.00	7,000	.15	375	6.00	1.6	6	+
T-Bonds	99.00	225,000	1.16	1500	50.00	1.5	51	+
Eurodollars	93.00	40,000	.15	375	7.00	1.6	8	+
British pound	145.00	10,000	2.00	500	22.00	1.4	15	+
Deutschemark	48.00	15,000	.50	625	11.00	1.0	23	+
Japanese yen	65.00	20,000	.50	625	20.00	.8	31	+
Swiss franc	60.00	12,000	.75	938	13.00	.8	22	+
Cotton	31.00	3,000	.50	250	35.00	1.6	113	−
Heating oil	40.00	15,000	1.50	630	42.00	3.8	105	−
Crude oil	14.00	30,000	.60	600	17.00	4.3	121	−
S&P 500	230.00	80,000	3.00	1500	70.00	1.3	30	+
Value line	225.00	4,000	3.00	1500	51.00	1.3	23	+

[a] All values estimated as of mid-1986. A $30 commission was used for all commodities.
[b] Estimated daily trading range, high to low.
[c] Direction of the price move over the past year: up (+), down (−), currently mid-range (m).

Price Level

Traders can be assured of continuing volatility in markets that are abnormally high priced. Bull markets are followed by bear markets; the combination of the two means sustained activity. Prices that are volatile at low levels may be returning to older patterns and will not guarantee continued volatility. (Crude oil remains the exception to this rule, sustaining exceptional volatility due to control attempts). Foreign exchange markets have no "high" or low," and cannot be viewed in the same way. They are volatile when they are either higher or lower than their "normal" relationship to other currencies; although this may be a permanent shift caused by reevaluation, volatility will increase until prices settle or return to the prior norm.

Table 14-1 shows that gold, the S&P 500, pork bellies, and currencies combine all of the features necessary to be confident of a reasonable opportunity and relatively small impact from transaction costs. Bonds, while active at the moment, are lower vis-à-vis rates and should be considered declining as far as potential volatility.

APPLICABILITY OF TRADING TECHNIQUES

Most traditional methods of technical analysis are not used for trading intervals of less than 3 days; however, the price fluctuations during these shorter periods are nearly all "technical." An economic analysis of supply and demand cannot be relevant over such a short time span; that approach can only be used for establishing longer-term trading policy. Other than the immediate reactions to overnight cash market movement, anticipated daily price changes based on political events and weather have not been successfully measured.

Techniques appropriate for day trading also apply to short-term trading, that is, under 3 days. Both are concerned with timing to improve entry and exit points. The most common way to accomplish this is by a simple form of pattern recognition. Today's price movements are compared to the most recent significant levels such as the opening price, today's high and low, yesterday's closing price, yesterday's high and low, last week's high and low, significant older support and resistance points, and finally, life of contract high and low. When the same price satisfies more than one condition, there is greater confidence in the importance of that point.

Time and Day Patterns

Time of day and *short-term patterns* are combined in the most popular forms of day trading; the types of patterns have been discussed in Chapter 13. There are natural occurrences during the trading day that make certain times more important than others. The opening gap and the continuation of that direction usually takes the first 15 to 20 minutes of the trading day. After that, a price reversal occurs and a trading range is established which lasts until the middle of the session. The midmorning period, which may marginally expand the initial range, tends to have low volume as well because many of the orders originating off the floor are exhausted near the open.

Following midday, activity steadily increases and the existing daily range is tested. It is common for most day traders to buy the bottom of the range and sell the top. A break of either support or resistance after midday is considered a major directional change; traders quickly shift to the direction of the breakout with the expectation of holding that position for the balance of the day. A more thorough analysis of time is shown in Figure 14-1. This chart, created by Walt Bressert, uses the important recent highs and lows and is very specific about relationships between the developing range, the previous day's range, and the time of day. Readers may want to compare Bressert's relationship with those found in Chapter 13. Intraday highs and lows that correspond to key levels found on charts such as channel support and resistance, head-and-shoulders objectives, and so forth are also likely to have increased importance.

Overnight Positions

Holding a position overnight involves margin, larger commissions, and greater risk. It also increases the opportunity. In moderately active markets, the opening gap, the difference between the prior close and the next open, is one-half to two-thirds the size of the normal trading range. Whereas it is nearly impossible to capture the full trading range in a day trade, it is simple to executive orders "on the close" and "on the open"; therefore, the full overnight move can realistically be captured.

The limited potential for a systematic approach to trading during a single day causes many traders to hold overnight positions. With this concession, most of the standard technical systems can be adapted to short-term trading by running the intraday data from one day into the next.

Point-and-Figure for Short-Term Trading

Point-and-figure charting has been a primary tool of day traders for many years. Using the minimum price movement as the box size and a 3-box reversal, many traders will keep a continuous, although lengthy, chart of day-to-day price movement. Buy and sell signals can be taken in the standard manner, but day traders are most likely to use these charts for identifying countertrend support and resistance levels. Intraday point-and-figure, as well as moving averages, often require substantial changes of direction before a new buy or sell signal occurs, even when the minimum box size is used. Trend methods are best applied to short-term overnight positions where the size of the move is much larger.

Price reversals that occur during the day can be plotted using a slightly smaller point-and-figure box size than is common for daily charting. The more frequent reversals due to the combination of more data and smaller box size will define the trend sooner or bring the protective stop closer. Remember, stop-loss levels advance only when there are reversals. In this way, day traders' improvements are transparent to the point-and-figure users who work only with the daily high, low,

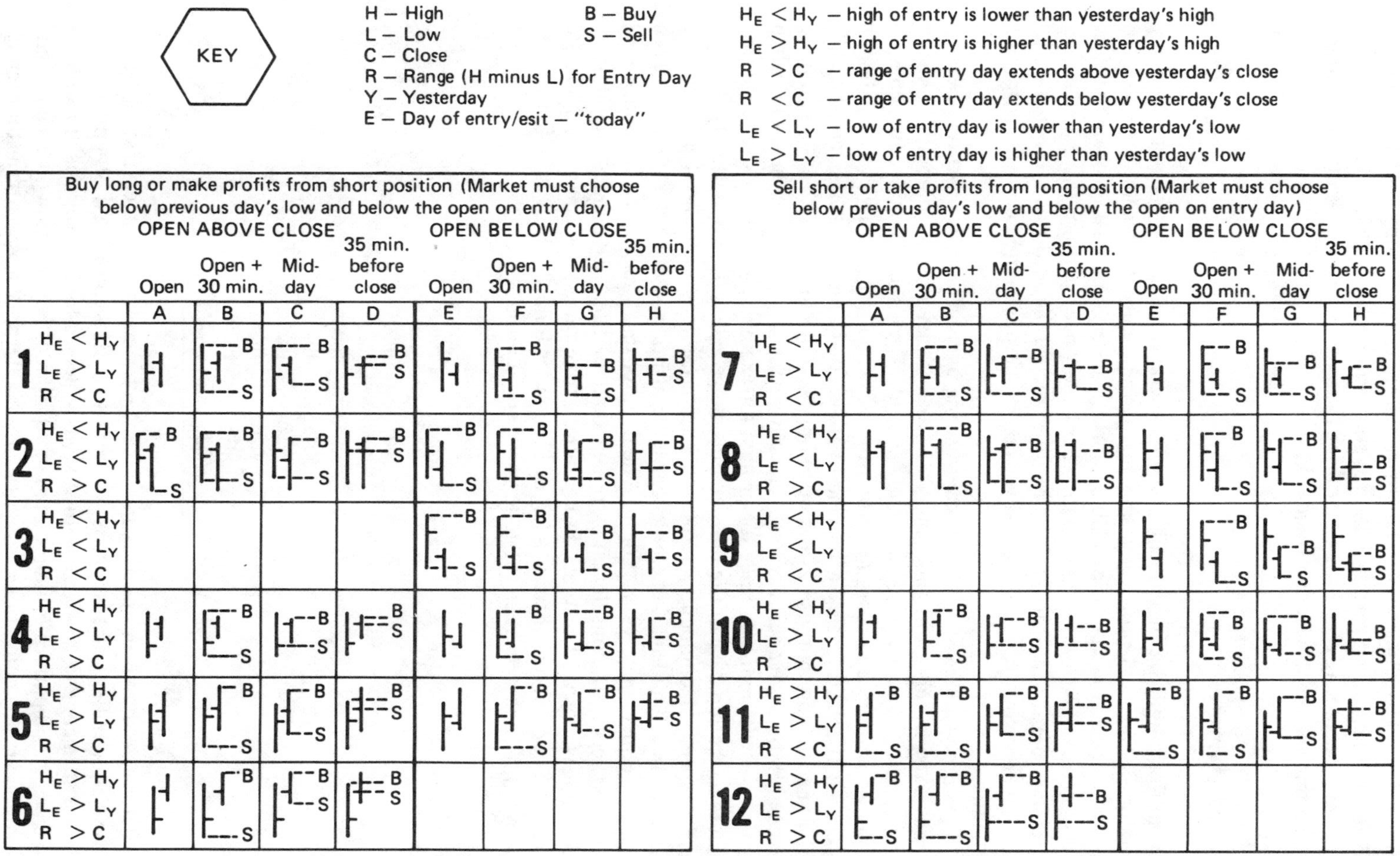

Figure 14-1 Intraday timing of market movement. (*Source:* Walt Bressert.)

and closing prices. In general, when there is a choice of plotting a point-and-figure trend continuation or reversal, the reversal should be plotted. This allows the chart to reflect the reversal sooner or bring the stop-loss closer—both possibilities are an improvement over the standard rules.

Moving Averages

The intrinsic time dependency of a moving average makes it less adaptable to day trading. To be used properly, a moving average must be recalculated at fixed intervals. If no computer is available, a practical decision must be made to select the interval based on the ability to record the price, perform the calculations, enter an order if necessary, and be ready to record the next price. It is not likely that anyone would do this manually when numerous computers will perform it instantly.

Two problems exist with intraday moving averages, both philosophical. Do trends exist in this short time interval? Does it make sense to apply a moving average to all intraday prices unevenly spaced? Trends are identified by eliminating noise and there appears to be more noise when prices are viewed in shorter intervals; therefore, using a moving average for intraday trading may be self-defeating. Its only purpose would be to impose a discipline on identifying a price reversal. Moving average reversals, even if sustained, could only be useful when they occur with ample latitude for profits; for example, an upwards reversal that occurs in the top 25% of the daily trading range offers little opportunity.

The speed of computers allows all intraday prices to be used in a moving average. In a liquid market, the occurrence of prices will be fairly regular even though volume may vary. For practical purposes, they might be considered evenly spaced. But consider an extreme example. The price of a less liquid product changes every 30 seconds during more active times, then quiets to 5-minute intervals; at one time, there is a lull of 15 minutes followed by a jump in price. Is there a difference between the following two patterns?

Time A	Price	Time B
1000	5005	1000
1001	5010	1005
1002	5005	1006
1003	5015	1016
1004	5025	1026
1005	5020	1028
1006	5015	1029
1007	5025	1044

Pattern A shows an upwards movement over equal time intervals; pattern B shows slow rallies and fast drops. Pattern B is often considered "toppy"; it is a market struggling to go higher with anxious sellers. Moving averages of pattern A taken as is and pattern B interpolated to equal intervals will show the same trend direction at each point; however, a trader will interpret these patterns differently.

MARKET PATTERNS

A trade that lasts from 1 to 3 days can be improved if short-term patterns or cycles can be found. For example, in a trending market there are outstanding weekly and weekend patterns. It is most common to find that the price movements from Thursday to Friday (close-to-close) are in the direction of the major trend and that the movement on Monday is a continuation of that trend. By Tuesday (or sometimes Wednesday), the strength of new buyers or sellers has faded, and the market reverses due to lack of activity and some profit taking. It often stays in this state through Wednesday or early Thursday when it again resumes the trend. In a sideways market, the Friday and Monday directions differ from the direction during the prior week and often differ from each other.

Support and Resistance

Support and resistance levels are important to the short-term trader. If prices start to move higher, slow down, and finally reverse, it is natural to consider the top price as a resistance point. Prices are thought to have been stretched to their extreme at that level. Any subsequent attempt to approach the previous high price will be met with professional selling in anticipation of prices stopping again at the same point. In addition, it is common for the same traders and others to place orders above the previous high prices in order to take new long positions or close-out shorts in the event of a breakout.

This method, very popular among floor traders and active speculators, tends to create and emphasize the support and resistance price levels until they define a clear *trading range*. Within a 1- to 3-day period, these ranges can be narrow and yet effectively contain price movement. During the life of the trading range, it will continue to narrow as the levels become clear to more traders and the anticipation of a reversal at those levels becomes imminent.

To take advantage of the smaller ranges caused in this manner, it is necessary to enter positions during the middle of a trading session, frequently holding that trade until the middle of the next session. An example using the Chicago Board of Trade December 75 Silver contract, during August 1975 will help to illustrate the problem. Prices on 4 consecutive days are seen in Table 14-2. The opening and closing prices for the first 3 days do not indicate any opportunity for trading. Prices were generally in the middle of the daily range. By using the high and low of the previous day, this situation can be traded either of two ways.

Table 14-2 December 75 CBT Silver

	Open	High	Low	Close
August 21	500.50	505.00	493.00	498.20
22	501.00	504.00	494.50	500.00
25	501.00	594.50	496.00	503.80
26	502.50	504.00	483.80	483.80

Thursday, August 21, forms a range of 505 to 493, closing near the center of the range. After the next open, buy just above 493 and sell just below 505 in order to be certain of entering and exiting the position. For protection, a stop can be entered at about 506 and 492 to reverse the position on a breakout.

Had this procedure been followed, entering 2¢ (200 points) before the bounds of the range, Table 14-3 shows how trades would have been executed:

Table 14-3   Trading December 75 Silver Using Support and Resistance

		Profit/Loss
August 22	Sold at 503.00	
	Closed-out short and bought at 495.00	+ 8.00
August 25	Closed-out long and sold at 502.00	+ 7.00
	Closed-out short and bought at 496.50	+ 5.50
August 26	Closed-out long and sold at 502.00	+ 5.50
	Closed-out short and bought at 498.00	+ 4.00
	Closed-out long and sold at 495.00	− 3.00
	Open position	+11.20

In each case, the entry was 200 points before the level where prices had reversed on the prior day. The stop-loss was placed to limit losses to a 100-point penetration. Although this is an ideal situation, professional traders frequently use this method. It can be seen that the support levels did actually rise from 493.00 to 494.50, and then to 496.00. When support was penetrated, prices rapidly broke to new lows of 483.80, down to the permissible limit. Similarly, the resistance level remained intact going from 505.00 to 504.00, 504.50, and, finally 504.00. It is generally accepted that the resistance level represents a more volatile area which must be watched closely for false breakouts.

Support and resistance levels gain importance the more time they remain intact. The high and low of the prior day are not as significant as the weekly or the monthly range. Each can be traded using the same technique. The major support and resistance levels are contract highs and lows, which rarely allow breakouts with less than one attempt. Longer-term price objectives can be identified using a continuation chart. This chart plots only the nearest (spot) futures contract of a specific commodity to allow the location of support and resistance levels when the current contracts are in a new high or low area.

Very few systems have been written on day trading because of the difficulties in finding a large enough audience and an experienced trader willing to set down his knowledge. The following method is a valuable part of the available literature.

The Taylor Trading Technique

In 1950, George Douglass Taylor published his *book method* of day trading which he had been using for many years in both the stock and grain markets. The method is one that requires the experience of discipline and timing, but is carefully set down and offered to the public in its full measure of sophistication and in a simplified state. The system is intrinsically cyclic, anticipating 3-day movements in the grains. These 3 days can vary in character when they are within an uptrend or downtrend. Taylor's explanation of his method is thorough and includes many valuable thoughts for traders interested in working with the market full time. The summary and analysis presented here cannot replace a reading of the original material.

Taylor developed his approach to trading through experience and a belief in a basic rhythm in the market. The dominant pattern is seen to be a 3-day repetition with occasional, although regular, intervals of 4- to 5-day patterns. Taylor's cycles are based on continuous trading days without regard to weekends and holidays. The 3-day cycle varies slightly if prices are in an uptrend or downtrend. The uptrend is defined as having higher tops and bottoms over some selected time period such as a week, month, or season. A downtrend is the reverse. During an uptrend the following sequence can be expected:

1. A *buying day objective,* where prices stop declining and a purchase can be made before a rally begins.
2. A *selling day objective,* at which the long position is closed-out.
3. A *short sale day objective,* where prices meet resistance and can be sold prior to a reversal.

Following the third day, after a short position is entered, the cycle begins again with a *buying day objective.* Because an uptrend is identified, Taylor has given extra latitude to the long position with part of the day between the liquidation of the long (2), and entering a new short (3) reserved to allow the upwards momentum to exhaust itself. Downtrends are the opposite, expecting some added time for the downward move to finish before the rally begins.

The actual *objectives* are extremely short-term support and resistance levels, usually only the prior day's high and low prices or occasionally the high and low of the 3-day cycle, which may be the same prices. On a buying day, the objective is a test or penetration of the prior day's low price, but only if it occurs first, before a test of the prior highs. Taylor's method is then a short-term countertrend technique, which looks for prices to reverse direction continuously. His belief was that speculation caused these erratic, sometimes large, cyclic variations about the long-term trend.

Taylor placed great emphasis on the order of occurrence of the high and low on each day. In order to buy, the low must occur first. If this is a buying day in an uptrend, a long position is entered after any lower opening whether or not the prior low is reached. Taylor reasoned that because an uptrend is generally stronger toward the close, the first opportunity must be taken on a buying day. However, if a high occurs first and prices then decline nearing the lows toward the end of the trading day, no long position is entered. This pattern indicates a lower open the following day which will provide a better opportunity to buy. During a downtrend, the violations of the lows, or penetrations towards the close, are more common. By waiting until the next day to purchase, the 3-day cycle is shifted to favor the short sale.

Consider the same problems with regard to closing out a long and entering a new short during an uptrend. If on the same day that the long was entered prices rallied sharply, touching or penetrating prior highs, a higher opening would be expected the next day at which time the long position would be closed-out. Because of the uptrend, a small setback and another test of the highs might be expected. It would then require another day to ensure that the strength was exhausted. If the highs of the *selling day* were tested on the open of the *short sale day,* a new short would be entered immediately. If the short sale day opened lower and finished higher, no position would be taken.

Shorter reactions to price moves are expected when a long position is entered on a buy day, or on the next open, when a downtrend exists. If prices rally sharply on the same day, the position is closed-out at a profit. This is important to remember because trading against the trend does not offer the latitude of waiting for the best moment; time is working against the position.

Taylor called this his "book method" because he recorded all the information necessary for trading in a small $3 \times 5''$ spiral notebook that he carried. The organization of the book is shown in Table 14-4, an example that uses the November 75 soybean contract. Of course in Taylor's book, there would be only one month per page due to its size. The first five columns contain the date and day, followed by the open, high, low, and closing prices. The first 10 days are used to determine where the cycle begins. Scanning the daily lows, circle the lowest of the first 10 days, in this case March 19. Then work backward and forward, circling every third low price. These are buying days. The sequences of 2 in-between days are circled in the high column and indicate the selling day and the short sale day, respectively. This example is especially simple because it assumes a consistent uptrend and shows no variation from the 3-day cycle.

In order to judge the opportunities for buying and selling, the next columns, marked *D* and *R*, indicate the number of points in the *decline* from the short sale to the buying day and the number of points in the *rally* from the buying day to the selling day. In both columns, the differences are taken using the highs and lows

Table 14-4   November 1975 Soybeans

1975		Open	High	Low	Close	D	R	BH	BU	Net
				March						
M	10	540	(x542)	535	540½					
T	11	435	560¼	(x535)	560¼	7		18¾	0	
W	12	560	(x572)	552	571½		37			
H	13	568	(x577)	559	560½					
F	14	553	559	(√549)	549½	28		0	10	+ 2¾
M	17	548	(√560)	548	558		11			
T	18	555	(x558)	538	538½					

Table 14-4 (*Continued*)

1975		Open	High	Low	Close	D	R	BH	BU	Net
W	19	530	546	(x529)	545¼	29		0	9	
H	20	543	(√555)	540	547½		26			
F	21	547½	(√567½)	547½	567½					−1½
M	24	573	581	(√561)	573	6½		13½	0	
T	25	573	(x575)	564	574		14			
W	26	577	(√594)	574	594					
H	27	587	590	(√579)	585	15		0	0	+31½
M	31	592	(√603½)	589	595½		24½			

April

T	1	599	(x599)	584	591½					
W	2	589	591½	(√575)	575¾	24		0	9	
H	3	570	(√573)	565	566¾		0			
F	4	570	(√578)	567	576¾					−12
M	7	577	577	(√562)	565¾	16		0	5	
T	8	566	(√579½)	563	568¼		17½			
W	9	565	(√574)	561½	573½					
H	10	571	575	(√556)	561¾	18		1	5½	
F	11	560	(x564½)	558	563½		8½			−9
M	14	561	(x568)	555½	561½					
T	15	565	569½	(√560½)	563½	7½		1½	0	
W	16	562	(x566)	553	559¼		5½			
H	17	560	(√565)	558	563½					
F	18	563	563	(√557)	559	8		0	1	−1

only. These values represent the maximum number of points that could have been made in those trades, provided the highs and lows occurred in the proper order. An "x" or a "√" in the circle next to the high or low means that the opportunity to buy or sell occurred first (if an x) or last (if a √). In the case of the first, the trade would have been entered that day and in the other case, Taylor would have waited.

The next two columns, BH and BU, show the adversity and opportunity of that day's prices to the buying objective. BH means a *buying day high* and is entered with the number of points that the day traded above the prior day's high (the *short sale day*), and BU shows the opportunity to *buy under*, by recording the number of points by which the day sold under the low of the prior day—the area to buy if the low occurred first. If neither situation occurred, zeros were entered.

A wide column on the right is used to indicate the net weekly change in direction by taking the difference between the prior Friday's closing price and the current Friday's price. This should be used to compare with the trading performance.

By observing columns *D* and *R* in Table 14-4, it can be seen that there was ample opportunity for profits on both the long positions and short sales, with only one case of a zero entry on April 3. The trades that would have been entered or liquidated can be approximated using the BH and BU columns and the x and √ notations. For consistency, it might be assumed that the √ indicates that a position was taken on the next open. In either case, the results would have been good.

Taylor's daily method requires care in monitoring the market, which only a full-time trader can provide. The order of the highs and lows must be observed as well as whether the new low is going to penetrate or fail to penetrate the prior lows. The trades must be timed carefully for maximum profit. In addition, it would be helpful to combine this method with a good trend identification technique as well as observe seasonal patterns to improve the choice of the overriding market direction.

For those who cannot watch the market constantly, Taylor offers a rigid *3-Day Trading Method,* which is a modification of his overall daily method. The cycles remain the same, but the buying and selling objectives are entered into the market in advance. This method is expected to work on balance, as are other well-defined systems. What is primarily lost by this approach is the order of occurrence of the highs and lows; otherwise, the concept of the system remains intact.

It is interesting that this technique profits from penetration of support and resistance levels. Most other methods consider a breakout of prior highs and lows as a major trend change indication, but Taylor views it as a better opportunity to do the opposite. It is one of the few examples of such an approach and could only succeed in the short term, where the behavioral aspects of trading are dominant.

15
Optimization

One of the most interesting techniques to develop from computerization is "optimization." It is the process of repeatedly testing data to find the best moving average speed, point-and-figure box size, stop-loss size, or other information. Optimization is an irresistible method when a computer is available, and, in an indiscriminate way, it has replaced logical selection. It is frequently the means of creating strategies referred to as "black box" methods, which invariably look better before they are traded.

Computers present a serious, often futile, dilemma for the analyst. If a trend-following system is desired and some form of smoothing technique is selected (simple moving average, exponentially or step-weighted moving average), how do you select the "right" speed?

Twenty years ago, the 5-, 10-, and 20-day moving averages were most popular because they represented a 1-week, 2-week, and 1-month time interval. They were also easy to calculate. In fact, the 10-day moving average was the most common because no division was necessary to arrive at the average. Unfortunately, that simple approach no longer exists.

Consider what is necessary to create a trading strategy. Once trend speed has been logically selected (e.g., 10-day) and the trading rules determined, you will want to know the performance of that choice over selected past markets. If it proves successful, you may trade using that method; however, if it does not meet expectations, what do you do? With a computer, the answer is easy: try another trend speed and see if the results are better. This follows a perfectly natural progression; after all, who would use a system today that has failed to be profitable in the past?

It is obvious that a trader with a talent for computers or one who has purchased a software package for testing will take an organized approach to experimenting with a broad selection of trend speeds, box sizes, stop-loss points, and trading rules to arrive at a system with an excellent trading profile. When no satisfactory combination can be found for a specific market, that market will not be traded. This method of "optimization" has become a dominant factor in the development of trading systems; it is dependent on the availability of a computer.

The following sections will discuss various aspects of optimization. Performed properly, extensive testing can teach a great deal; done incorrectly, it can be misleading and completely illogical. It is not always easy to know which case has been satisfied.

SETTING YOUR OBJECTIVE

There are a number of steps that must be carefully performed before testing can begin. These steps are more important than the actual testing and will determine the philosophy and structure of the test strategy and results. Correctly defined, the final system will have realistic goals and predictive qualities. Incorrectly done, it will look successful but fail in actual trading.

First, define the test objective. What results should the test present so that you can determine its success? Is it the highest profits possible from the test strategy, the frequency of profitable trades, or the average profit to average loss ratio? Most likely, it will be a combination of these and other values.

For example, maximum profits are used as the performance criteria, the resulting system may have 1 or 2 large profits (as silver in early 1980) and 40 small losses over the past 5 years. The same performance would also show a very impressive average profit to average loss ratio. The highest frequency of profitable trades can also be inadequate if there are very small profits and large losses.

A popular test profile is high profits with small variance. Variance is measured as "equity drop" (largest single decline in equity measured on a daily basis). The "test function" can be:

$$\text{Test function} = \text{net profits} \times (100 - \text{percentage equity drop})$$

This function will reduce the test profits according to the size of the equity drop. The larger the losses, the smaller the test function value.

IDENTIFYING THE PARAMETERS

Assuming the test strategy is known, the "parameters" to be tested must then be identified. A parameter is a value within the strategy that can be changed. For example, parameters include:

1. Moving average speed (in days)
2. Exponential smoothing constant (in percentages)
3. Stop-loss values (in points or percentages)
4. Size of a point-and-figure box (in points)

The simplest optimization would be a test of the number of days in a simple moving average system, where all other values are fixed. The test would then simulate the results of the trading strategy by stepping through the possible range of moving average days: one, two, three, and so forth until a satisfactory range has been covered. This is called a "one-dimensional" optimization.

Most systems have more than one important parameter. In the simple moving average system which is being used as an example, both the moving average speed and the stop-loss value are important. One test procedure selects the first moving average value, then tests all of the stop-loss values; the second moving average value is then set and all of the stop-loss values are retested. The process is repeated until all of the moving average values have been tested. This is a "two-dimensional" optimization.

When more than two parameters are tested, the optimization becomes much more complicated. It may be necessary to select fewer values to test for each parameter; otherwise, tests may become too long. For the moving average case, it is best to use all of the smaller values for the number of days and then fewer values as the numbers become larger. For example,

$$1, 2, 3, 4, 5, 6, 8, 10, 12, 15, 20, 25, 30, 40, 50$$

would be a good set of test values because there is a smaller, if any, difference in results when using a 30- or 31-day moving average, in contrast to the great difference in the results of a 2- or 3-day moving average.

SELECTING THE TEST DATA

Testing a trading strategy on a computer is different from verifying a charting technique or taking prices from the *Wall Street Journal* to check results manually. If a computer is to be used for testing, there must be a complete "data base," or price history available. Some computer systems, which are designed for commodity trading strategies, have created special "test series" specifically for optimization. This data can be of the form:

1. *Individual full contracts.* The entire futures contract, or more than one contract, are tested.
2. *Disjoint pieces of contracts.* Segments are selected as the last 30 to 90 days of a contract, or specific market pattern. They can be tested separately or they are combined together using "backward adjusting" or "indexing" as discussed in (3) and (4).
3. *Backward (or forward) adjusted data.* Data segments or entire contracts are combined by adjusting the data segments on a specific "roll" date by the difference between the prices of the new and old contract on that date. In a backward adjustment, all data prior to the adjustment date are changed by the differential on the roll date.
4. *Indexed data series.* A continuous series is constructed by adding the price change each day to the prior index value. When there is a change of contract, the price change is that of the new contract compared to its prior price.
5. *Constant forward series.* In the same manner as the London metals contracts are quoted (*n*-days out), an artificial price is calculated by interpolating the prices of the delivery months on both sides of the date needed for this price series. This type of data series has also been called a "perpetual" contract.

Which is best? Because analysts have gone to great lengths to prepare these different series, there will be some votes for each of them. But some of the forms clearly have more applicability and fewer problems than others. The individual contract in (1) seem to be the simplest approach; however, it is the least desirable for two reasons:

1. No one trades the entire contract. Most traders restrict their positions to the more liquid contracts nearest to delivery. Those contracts usually have greater price movement than the deferred contracts and may not result in the same parameter selection.

2. Full contracts often trade for more than 1 year and therefore overlap one another, causing some price movements to be duplicated. For example, a 1975 publication of trading systems displayed a well-organized approach to the testing of a single commodity. The length of each contract was 18 months, and 15 individual contracts ranging from July 1968–January 1972 were selected. Reasonable? Apparently so, but a closer look will show important problems.

The contracts selected for the test were:

Jul 1968	Dec 1967	Sep 1968	May 1970
Jul 1969	Dec 1968	Sep 1969	Jan 1971
Jul 1970	Dec 1969	Sep 1970	
Jul 1971	Dec 1970	Sep 1971	
	Dec 1971		

In a seasonal or cyclic commodity, there is good reason for selecting more than one delivery month during each year; new and old crop or production cycles can cause substantially unique price patterns during the same time period for different deferred deliveries. Even the proper overlapping of a traditionally nonseasonal product may pick up deviations due to anticipation or extreme short-term demand or surplus. But this commodity was not seasonal or cyclic, and the 18-month contract duration caused the overlapping time intervals shown in Figure 15-1a. Once the number of tests being performed at any one time is seen, it is easy to construct a distribution (Figure 15-1b) by counting the horizontal bars at specific points. This distribution will show the testing bias due to duplication. In the figure shown, there was only one delivery month tested in the last half of 1966, compared to six contracts tested during the middle period, tapering off to two contracts at the end of 1971.

In the last choice (5), a constant forward contract, the prices are not real. Because the prices did not actually occur, the trading strategy would be tested on prices that might not resemble the actual market.

The segmented data (2) have neither of the problems just discussed; they are exactly the data that would be traded. The short time periods, however, present many difficulties for a computer program. Most programs need "lead time" to wind up the statistics. If the trading strategy uses a 20-day moving average, the first 20 days of data cannot be used to generate trading signals due to the insufficient data to calculate the moving average. If a probability or frequency distribution is used, the amount of data will make the statistics unstable and unreliable.

The adjusted data series (3) and the index series (4) are almost identical. They both use real data, select only the portion of the contract that will be traded, and

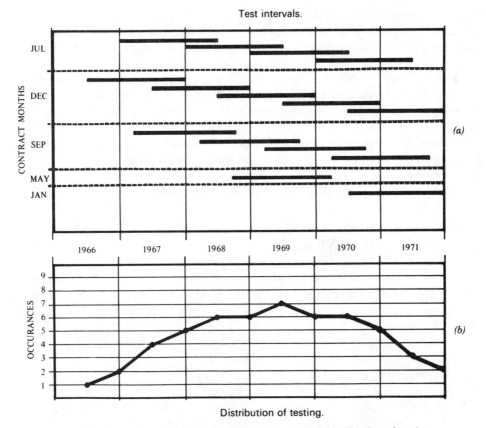

Figure 15-1   Selection of test data. (*a*) Test intervals. (*b*) Distribution of testing.

are long enough to provide a good test. The forward adjusted data series is actually identical to the index series. The only difference between the forward and backward adjustments is that, with the backward case, the data series prices match the actual current contract prices. The only criticism of these series is that they omit both the points at which the contracts switch and the transaction costs associated with either a closed-out position or a "roll-forward."

THE TEST VARIABLE ("PARAMETER")

The test variables can be of three forms: *continuous, discrete,* or *code* (alphabetic). In order to interpret and display test results properly, it is important to identify these forms in advance.

Continuous parameters refer to values (e.g., percentages) which can take on any value within a well-defined range. If a stop-loss point defined as a percentage is to be tested, this form might begin at .02% and increase in steps of .02 until 2% is reached.

Discrete parameters have distinct values. Discrete variables are usually integer values, such as the number of days in a moving average.

Code parameters represent a category of operations. For example, when the parameter value is *A*, a single moving average is used; when the value is *B*, a double moving average system is tested; and when the value is *C*, three moving averages are used.

It is important to distinguish between the first two parameter types, continuous and discrete, and the last one. The analyst can expect some pattern in the results when testing parameters which take on progressively larger or smaller values. The code parameter, however, usually causes rule changes. There is no reason why a change of rules, or systems, would result in any performance pattern—the first rule may be profitable, the second losing, and the third profitable. The display of results, discussed later, is only valid for continuous and discrete parameters tested in an incrementally ascending or descending manner.

OPTIMIZING TECHNIQUES

There are many complex techniques for optimizing; the two most basic will be discussed here. The first, and the only simple method, is to test all combinations of parameters. A single moving average system with a stop-loss might have the following tests:

1. All moving average days from 1 to 50
2. Stop-loss values from 1 to 100 points

The total number of tests would then be $50 \times 100 = 5000$. When three parameters are tested, the number of tests increase rapidly. Selecting the important values, as discussed earlier, is a simple way to reduce the test time without any loss in the range of results. When there are too many tests, even with selected values, a wider spacing of values can be used to locate the general pattern of performance. Once the approximate range of parameter values is known, more detailed retesting can be done.

Estimate the test time before beginning an optimization. It may be helpful if the computer prints something each time it begins another test or at fixed intervals. This allows a test to be stopped when it is too slow. One analyst waited 2 days before estimating the test time only to find out that the optimization that was being performed would be completed in $4\frac{1}{2}$ years.

Sequential Testing

If the number of tests and the number of parameters are too great, consider a different procedure:

1. Test one parameter
2. Find the "best" results and fix that value
3. Select the next parameter and test
4. Go back to (2)

Moving average days

	5	10	15	20	25
10	100	150	200	150	150
20	200	150	250	300	300
30	250	200	300	400	350
40	200	150	200	300	300
50	100	100	150	250	250

Stop-loss (points)

Figure 15-2   Results of a two-dimensional optimization.

This is a "sequential optimization." It has the advantage of reducing a three-parameter test case from $n1 \times n2 \times n3$ to $n1 + n2 + n3$. It has the disadvantage, however, of not always finding the best combination of parameter values. Figure 15-2 shows a two-dimensional map of test results. By testing all the combinations, the best choice was seen to be a 20-day moving average with a 30-point stop-loss. Using sequential testing, the best results cannot be found regardless of whether the test begins with the rows or columns. Even though the area of greatest profitability is clear, the best choices in the first row and column do not peak at values consistent with the overall best result.

There are two ways to avoid this problem. One method is to list the parameters in order of importance, that is, those that would have the greatest impact on profitability. If the selection of the days for calculating the moving average can result in a profit of $10,000 or a loss of $5000 and the selection of a stop-loss changes the results by a maximum of $2000, the number of days is obviously more important.

Another method is to choose logical starting values ("seeds") for the parameters. If tests begin in the right area of the test map in Figure 15-2, the results will be best. Run more than one test with different seed values. The total time for running three tests is still far less than testing all combinations of values. Begin testing with the slowest trends, largest stops, and so on. Conservative parameters are more stable and will tend to result in a more organized, continuous search.

DISPLAYING AND INTERPRETING THE RESULTS

Displaying the test results properly can eliminate most of the interpretation difficulties. For example, an optimization is run in which all parameters are fixed except for the number of days in a moving average. Three possible patterns of results are shown in Figure 15-3.

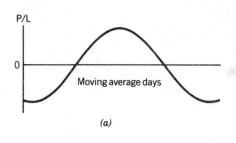

P/L

0

Moving average days

(a)

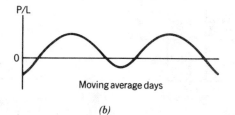

P/L

0

Moving average days

(b)

P/L

0

Moving average days

(c)

Figure 15-3 Possible resulting patterns from test, which vary only the moving average days.

In all three cases, the resulting profit or loss is shown on the left, and the number of moving average days is shown along the bottom. Figure 15-3*a* is a simple curve, indicating that both fast and slow parameters generate losses, although the midrange is profitable. It is easy to select the number of moving average days that produced the highest profit due to the good continuity around that point.

Figure 15-3*b* shows two possible areas of success. Because both are about equal in size, there is no reason for choosing one over the other. One possibility is to trade both moving averages. It is most likely that the longer-term results are more stable. Unless a very long data series was used, good performance in a fast trend-following system is usually just a temporary good fit.

The preceding case is exaggerated in Figure 15-3*c*. The fast system has much higher profits in a very narrow range whereas the long-term trend has a wide range of success. The spike in the area of the 3-day moving average is surrounded by losses, indicating that the high profits were probably caused by a pattern in the data that exactly conformed to that cycle.

The selection of a parameter that results in frequent trades should always be questioned. Trading a fast system can result in errors, poor execution prices, and large transaction costs. Unless these factors have been carefully incorporated into the trading strategy, a highly profitable simulation will result in large, real losses.

Two Parameter Tests

The most popular tests are those that have two parameters, either two moving averages or a moving average and a stop-loss value. Considering the moving average and stop-loss, it is evident that a *grid* (a two-dimensional table) can be formed, with the moving average days along the left (rows) and the stop-loss values at the bottom (columns). Figure 15-4 shows that the lowest number of days and the smallest stop-loss value will be given by the profit/loss value in the top left corner box.

By presenting the results as shown in Figure 15-4, there is a continuity of performance in all directions. The upper left corner represents the fastest system—the one with the most trades; the bottom right corner shows the results of the slowest strategy. The upper right and the lower left corners may show similar results if the days and stop-loss values were scaled properly. A faster trend speed with a large stop (top right) and a slow trend with a small stop (bottom left) are likely to have the same number of trades and similar profitability.

Depending on the data used for testing as well as the trading rules, three patterns are most likely to appear in the results of a two-dimensional display.

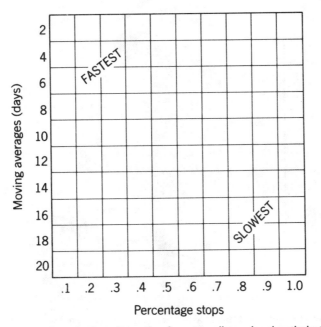

Figure 15-4 Standard configuration for a two-dimensional optimization.

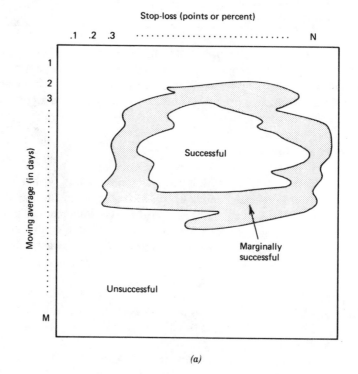

(a)

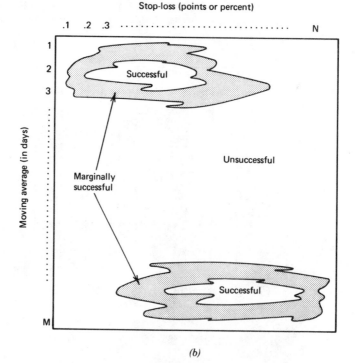

(b)

Figure 15-5   Patterns resulting from a two-dimensional optimization. (*a*) Single profitable area. (*b*) Two distinct profitable areas. (*c*) No obvious pattern.

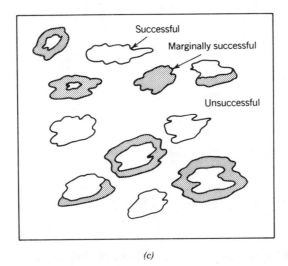

(c)

Figure 15-5 (*Continued*)

Figure 15-5*a* shows the simplest case of a single area of successful performance gradually tapering off. This is analogous to the single parameter test shown in Figure 15-3*a*. Selecting the parameters that gave the center of the best performance area is the most logical since moderate shifts in price patterns are still likely to be profitable.

Two areas of profitability are usually the results of a highly volatile market (Figure 15-5*b*). Prices that are moving quickly and sustain a major trend can be traded using a fast or slow model. The fast model is often more profitable because it captures more of the rising trend; it reacts faster and also profits from the decline. The slower trend-following approach gets less of the price move but keeps clear of the sharp reactions that stop out the middle-speed trends. The selection of parameters to use in real trading follows the same reasoning applied to Figures 15-3*b* and *c*.

The third case, shown in Figure 15-5*c*, is one of erratic profits and losses. The absence of a consistent pattern in the performance indicates that the trading strategy does not apply to the data. This is a sure sign that the system development is moving in the wrong direction.

Averaging the Results

Because the testing process is computer dependent, it is desirable to make the selection of the best parameters also automatic. This can usually be done effectively by averaging either the profits or other results displayed in the test map. In the case of a moving average system, first determine how broad the area of success must be so that it is not a "spike." For example, the results of a 3-, 4-, 5- and 6-day test show profits of 1000, 8000, 3000, and 4000, respectively. The 4-day case is clearly a spike and could be eliminated by replacing its value with the

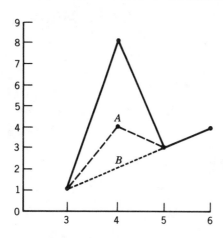

Figure 15-6   Replacing a spike with the average A, or an interpolation B.

average of the three values or by the interpolated value of the two adjacent points (Figure 15-6). In general the substitution process in which

$$PL_i' \text{ is replaced by } \frac{PL_{i-1} + PL_i + PL_{i+1}}{3}$$

will satisfy the problem. The best parameter set is the highest PL_i' once all values have been averaged.

It is more likely a spike or erratic results will appear in areas that test fewer days than in those that test slow trends. The difference between the results of a 2- and 3-day moving average are greater than those of a 30- or 31-day average or even a 30- or 40-day test. If the optimization was scaled properly, leaving more space between tests of higher value, the simple averaging technique will be a good substitute for testing every value.

Two-Parameter Averaging. The results of a two parameter test may also be averaged. Using the form discussed earlier (Figure 15-5), represent the results of each test by the notation PL_{ij}, the profit/loss associated with row i and column j of a two-dimensional display. The object is to replace each PL_{ij} with PL_{ij}', an average value of its surroundings. This is done, as seen in Figure 15-7a, by taking an average of the eight test results adjacent to the ijth value as well as the center value.

Exceptions must be made when the ijth result is not fully surrounded but on the perimeter of the test map. Figures 15-7b, 15-7c, and 15-7d show the averaging technique used when the ijth box is a top, side, or corner value. The 9-box average shown here is comparable to the 3-point average in the 1-parameter test. If the test is more detailed, that is, if there are smaller increments between tests and more test cases, an average of a larger area would be appropriate.

Test Continuity

Any system can be tested using a computer, but automatic selection of the best results only makes sense when they are continuous. For example, a simple mov-

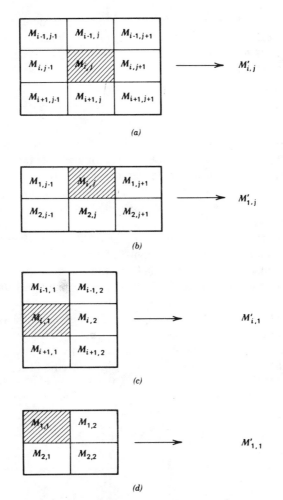

Figure 15-7 Averaging of map output results. (*a*) Center average (9 box). (*b*) Top edge average (6 box). (*b*) Left edge average (6 box). (*d*) Upper left corner average (4 box).

ing average system with stops is continuous in all directions. Adding a third dimension, an entry or exit delay (0, 1, or 2 days) will produce continuous results in the three directions. But not all tests satisfy this principle. Rule changes are the most likely cause of discontinuity. Consider a test where one variable is the speed of the trend and the other is a set of rules, L, S, and B, where L only takes long positions, S only takes short positions, and B takes both long and short positions. Although there may be interesting patterns and relationships, averaging these results does not make sense.

If each parameter tested has values that result in a continuous profit/loss curve, there are mathematical techniques available to locate the point of maximum profit with the minimum steps. One method, *optimization by steepest descent,*[1] uses

[1] F. R. Ruckdeschel, *BASIC Scientific Subroutines,* Vol. II, Byte/McGraw-Hill, Peterborough, NH, 1983.

both the profit and the rate of change of profitability to determine the size of the steps taken during the optimization process. This method can be suboptimal, however, if there is more than one profit peak.

CHANGING RULES

As testing progresses, it is inevitable that the analyst will want to modify a rule in the trading strategy. This is usually the result of inspecting the results of tests and noting that a specific pattern was not treated properly (or profitably). After some work, the analyst introduces a special rule, which turns a previously losing situation into a profit. Figure 15-8 shows two possible changes in the test performance pattern based on this change.

If the rule change improves one price pattern at the cost of others, the complete test results will appear as shown in Figure 15-8*a*. Higher profits at the previous peak and greater losses at the ends results in the same cumulative test profitability. The new rule caused the "fitting" of a specific pattern at the cost of added losses in other patterns. The rule is not an asset.

In Figure 15-8*b*, the new rule improves performance in all cases. This type of pattern is desirable in optimizations. It is possible, of course, that the improvement was caused by a rule that corrects one case only in a way that is so specific that it does not affect any other trade. That type of "rule fitting," on a sample of one pattern, is not likely to improve results in the long run.

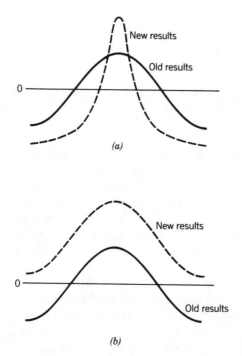

Figure 15-8 Patterns resulting from changing rules. (*a*) A rule change that improves one situation at the cost of others. (*b*) A rule change resulting in general improvement.

ARRIVING AT VALID TEST RESULTS

It is not unusual for the results of an optimization, especially one with many parameters, to appear perfect. All the trades could be profitable, the equity drops might be small, and the strategy might perform in changing markets, and yet, the final system might have no credibility at all. In order to create a system with predictive qualities rather than one which is historically fitted requires preparation in advance of testing.

The characteristics of a system with forecasting ability are:

1. **It must be logical.** Each rule and formula must be structured to identify a real fundamental or price phenomenon. *Discovering* a price pattern or cycle through optimization may seem to be a revelation, but it is more likely to cause losses. By testing enough patterns, it is statistically probable that one of them will seem to fit. Without a fundamental reason for the existence of that pattern, it is not safe to use it.
2. **It must adjust to changing market conditions.** A system that assumes constant price patterns will suffer large equity swings. Self-adjusting features might include an inflator or deflator, stop-loss values which adjust to volatility, and rule shifts based on seasonal or nonseasonal years.
3. **It must be tested properly.** The best procedure for proper testing is a sequence of optimizations over fixed length intervals, with performance measured using the *best* parameters on the "out-of-sample" period that immediately follows the test interval. Another test interval is then selected by dropping off old data and adding an equal amount of new data. The results of this second test are measured by the system performance during the time period immediately following the new test period. The method is continued until the out-of-sample results include all of the available test data. This method is also called *blind simulation* (further discussion will be found in the section "Reoptimization" later in this chapter).

Although all three points above are important, proper testing is critical. *Blind simulation* will show those rules that are unreliable because they will not work in the out-of-sample period. If prices remain within the same range as the test period and market patterns do not change, the self-adjusting rules will not be used in real trading.

Performance Criteria

Assuming that the proper principles have been followed, are the test results good enough? Although the strategy shows high steady profits with a low equity drop, could a naive system have done better? Did the famous skeptic on television throw darts at *buy* and *sell* signals on a board and show a 75% return while the system only netted 25%? Has he done it for 3 years in a row?

A number of performance criteria could be used to evaluate any trading strategy both during the test phase or under actual market conditions; a few are as follows:

1. **Average published performance.** Popular futures and financial magazines and newsletters publish the monthly performance of public funds and major pools. The minimum requirement for optimized results is that they are greater than the average real performance. Considering true-life execution difficulties and the ideal qualities used in simulation results, the optimized results should be nearer to the best published performance.

2. **Average test results.** Each optimization run should represent a broad sampling of tests over a wide range of parameter values. The total set should approach a random sampling if the analyst did not introduce an estimate of the "proper range" of values in the test specifications. Whether random or not, the performance of the trading model applied to the out-of-sample period should be no worse than the average test results over the same out-of-sample period. This can be determined from a subsequent optimization of the out-of-sample period.

3. **Stability over time.** In addition to one of the preceding measurement tests, the trading strategy should have consistently good performance over a broad sampling of market conditions. Be sure that the test data was long enough to have included changes in price level—a major bull and bear market as well as an extended sideway period at low volatility. The performance during these periods should be separated so that the trader understands what to expect.

4. **Elimination of "outlier" periods.** Realistically, a system should not base its profitability on a single major market move over the test interval. The parameters selected should be consistently profitable with this exceptional period removed. It might be practical to optimize over two sets of data, one full set and the other without the major market move. If the resulting parameter selection is the same, the system is stable; if not, the parameters must be selected according to the type of market most likely to occur.

Isolating and studying periods in which the system did not work is a way to find the faults in a system before they occur in real trading. Failure to account for shifting fundamentals and lack of proper risk control is often the cause of sustained losses.

Systems that Work in Only One Market

From time to time, all commodity traders receive mail offers for a highly specialized system called "The Cattle Trader," the "Silver Day-Trading System," or "Easy Profits Through Stock Index Trading." It is most likely that each of these systems have been finely tuned with rules unique to this one commodity. Once aware of the optimization process and its results, these offers must be viewed more critically; after all, by following the procedures in this chapter, a system could be produced with performance at least as good as the one being offered.

It should no longer be possible to accept a "black box" method of trading. Both rules and test procedure must be known. Even more, a comparison of the real trading profile compared to the expected performance based on testing should be available.

POINT-AND-FIGURE TESTING

The point-and-figure system is representative of the group of swing systems. Signals occur when prices move above or below previous highs and lows, respectively. The trend, in a point-and-figure method, is identified by a price reversal exceeding a specified number of points. Because it is a charting method, the reversal is shown in terms of boxes; the reversal criteria traditionally is expressed as a "3-box reversal" (for a complete explanation, see Chapter 9).

The size of the box and the number of boxes in a reversal are the two variables that make up the "reversal criteria." If silver were the object of the test, the box size might start as low as 10 points (the minimum move) and increase in increments of 10 points; the number of boxes in a reversal would be the integer values 1, 2, 3, ... Figure 15-9a shows that the expected pattern of results is symmetric, extending across the diagonal drawn from the top left to the bottom right corners. This example followed the convention of putting the fastest trend change in the upper left (smallest box size and a 1-box reversal) and the slowest in the lower right corners.

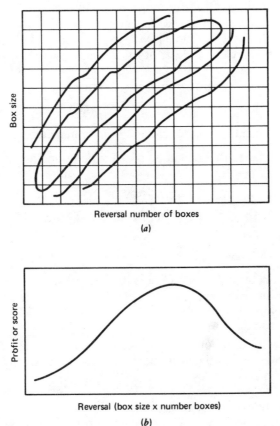

Figure 15-9   Point-and-figure mapping strategy. (a) Reversal number of boxes. (b) Reversal (box size × number boxes).

The symmetry is the result of very similar performance for equal reversal values, formed by the product of the box size and the number of boxes in a reversal. A trend change of 6¢ in silver could have occurred using combinations of 1¢ × 6, 2¢ × 3, 3¢ × 2, and 6¢ × 1. The difference in profitability occurs because the selection with the smallest box size will satisfy the penetration criteria sooner, giving slightly faster signals and more trades. The average profitability of all combinations of reversal size will appear as in Figure 15-9b. This representation can be used with the two-dimensional map to find the most consistent set of parameters.

The silver market has had an exceptionally wide price range over the past 10 years. The test just described would find the single parameter set that performed best over this period; however, there must be long periods of poor performance using any one set. For example, a reversal criteria of 20 points might represent a conservative trading method while prices were below $10 per ounce; but above $25 per ounce that value could have resulted in a reversal each day. Similarly, a 1¢ reversal (100 points) might have been best at the top of the market in 1980 but would generate no trades at the $7 per ounce level.

The problem of volatility was discussed in Chapter 9. It can be translated into optimization parameters by transforming the box size into a function of price. For example, instead of a 20-point box at $6 per ounce, a .033% box size is used. Then at $12 per ounce, the boxes would all be twice the size. If the rate increase is not enough, a *log* function can be used, or more simply, a *square root* function, as follows:

$$\text{Box size} = p \times \sqrt{\text{price}}$$

$$\text{Box size} = p \times \ln(\text{price})$$

where p is the percentage that is varied in the optimization.

This would be similar to the technique of using point-and-figure on a log-normal chart.

COMPARING THE RESULTS OF TWO SYSTEMS

Which system is better?

1. A simple moving average with a percentage stop-loss
2. A crossover using two exponentials
3. A point-and-figure system

A comparison of optimization results usually selects the one with the highest profits, but that may not be the best choice. Comparisons should account for the following minimum criteria:

1. A good sample of parameter combinations were tested. This will include those variables that cause frequent as well as slow trading. The distribution of fast and slow test results should be similar, which may involve scaling in different ways. One simple measure is the average number of trades per test on each system.

2. The average results of all tests and the variance of results should be compared. Significantly higher and more consistent overall results is a strong argument for a fundamentally sound approach.
3. Results should be scored in some way to include profitability and risk. Other measurements can be used, but stability is of great importance.
4. Results, or scores, should be averaged to avoid spikes or unusual distortions.
5. Execution costs, including liquidity factors must be included in the manner appropriate to each system. A trend-following system with entries and exits in the direction of the trend should have greater slippage than a countertrend entry method.
6. Make mistakes in the conservative direction. If two systems have comparable returns, select the one with the lower risk. If they have similar returns and risk, choose the one with fewer trades.

PROFITING FROM THE WORST RESULTS

The worst results of an optimization or test sequence can be of great interest. It can locate areas that can be used to improve entry and exit timing. Figures 15-10*a*

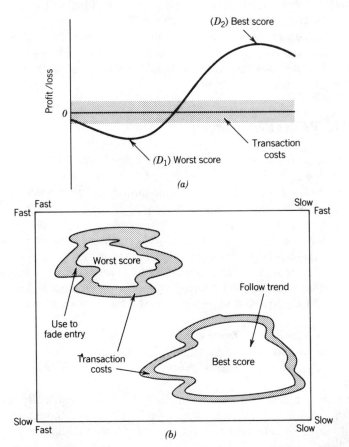

Figure 15-10 Dual use of test map. (*a*) Single-variable test. (*b*) Two-variable test.

and 15-10*b* show the continuous results of a one- and two-variable test. Both identify faster trading areas as having maximum loss and slower trends as having best performance.

The worst results are most useful if there is a net profit from taking the opposite position. This is the case only if the net loss is greater than the transaction costs. But even if the worst score has a near-zero return before transaction costs, it can be used profitably. Unprofitable results of a fast trend means that a long or short position taken at that point lasts only a few days and does not indicate a sustained trend. Use the following rules:

1. Trade a system of two moving averages, a long-term, designated by the "best score" D_2, and the short-term, selected as the worst score D_1.
2. When prices cross the long-term moving average, a long position becomes eligible. A long position is entered when the short-term moving average signals a short signal. Positions may be entered on a 1-day delay.
3. Short positions may be closed-out when prices cross above the long-term trendlines; they *must* be closed-out when a long position is entered.
4. Short positions and exits from long positions are the opposite of (2) and (3).

Because the short-term signals are not good indicators of trends, they can be used as a countertrend entry. That allows for better execution especially when trading larger positions. The choice of immediate exit or delayed exit is trader-preference. Once a position is being held, there is greater risk in waiting for a price move to reverse. Although profitability would be higher using the entry rule as an exit, it allows for unnecessary risk.

RETESTING PATTERNS

A single optimization is never the end of the testing process. Retesting is important to adjust the system to characteristics of new data. In some cases, the retest will include all of the original as well as the new data; other tests will optimize a fixed number of most recent data points. Most likely, the second case will result in a change in the parameter selection. Using the two-variable test as an example, a shift may be expected in the area of best performance as shown in Figure 15-11.

The size of the shift depends on the impact of the new data on the total set. The introduction of exceptionally unusual data (e.g., new high or low prices) would cause a large shift if the trading strategy cannot automatically adjust. This potential shift is less likely to result in trading losses if the following rules are observed:

1. Do not allow a large percentage of new days to be introduced without retesting. Ten percent should be used as an initial guideline.
2. An exceptional change in data characteristics should indicate an immediate retest.
3. Do not use data sets that are too small. The results are usually unstable.
4. Select the parameter values from an area that is broad enough to include any probable shifts in selection and still show profitable results.

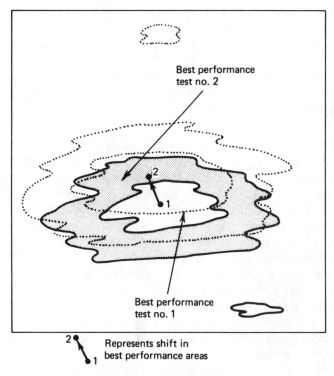

Figure 15-11 Consecutive tests.

COMPREHENSIVE STUDIES[2]

There are four known comprehensive studies of moving average systems: Maxwell, Davis and Thiel, Turner and Blinn, and the most recent, Hochheimer. In addition, "optimizations" of Wilder's *Directional Movement* and *RSI* will be found in the sections that discuss those techniques. They are all worth reading because they emphasize different features of trading that were important to the authors and would help someone whose interest is directed towards testing. But along with completeness in one area often comes a deficiency in another. Davis and Thiel analyze the greatest variety of commodities, covering virtually all of the U.S. crops as well as cattle, eggs, and the soybean complex. They include about 5 years of data and use relatively fast moving averages (up to 10 days); they introduce variations in lead-oriented plotting and in testing nonconsecutive days; the data used is close-only. The results are clearly presented in both detail and summary, and yield generally good returns.

The authors R. E. Davis and C. C. Thiel, Jr., present excellent credentials and experience in systems testing. Their study of moving averages use combinations of simple buy and sell signals, leading plots, and skips in the selection of sequen-

---

[2] Readers with an interest in performing optimizations such as these should read the basic material in Chapter 4 and the additional systems in Chapter 5.

tial prices used (e.g., a skip of two uses every other price). They test a total of 100 combinations of the three factors:

A *skip* from 1 day (none) to 5 days (1 week)
An *average* of 5, 6, 7, 8, or 10 days
A *leap* of 0 or 2 days.

Commodities tested were soybeans, bellies, cattle, cocoa, copper, corn, eggs, soybean meal, oats, soybean oil, potatoes, rye, sugar, and wheat.

Maxwell's study is extremely comprehensive but limited by its application to only one commodity, pork bellies. His idea was to apply combinations of features and test the results. The first feature was the choice of trend and included the possibilities of a simple mean, or a moving average of 3, 5, or 10 days, of either a conventional, average-modified, or weighted type. The second feature was the delay factor, used to improve timing of both entry or exit. Some of the possibilities were: (1) act without delay; (2) act if the signal condition persists for one additional day; (3) enter if the signal condition persists for two additional days, but liquidate without delay; and others. Combinations of two types of moving averages and a delay factor were tested, with and without fixed or moving stops. With ten types of averages, six delay factors, and different stops, Maxwell has a lot of combinations to examine.

The study is then expanded to 3-factor systems with a list of 18 combinations of rules to generate 324 systems of which the results of 285 are recorded, with 49% profitable and 51% losers. The largest loss was generated by a system with the rules:

Enter a new position when both the weighted 3-day and weighted 10-day moving averages cross the price-mean, as long as the signal condition persists for two additional days (buy if averages cross moving down, sell if up).

Liquidate positions when the 3-day average reverses its direction through the price-mean as long as it continues for one additional day.

No fixed stops are used.

The best profits in the 3-factor system required both a 5-day average-modified and a 10-day weighted average to move across the price-mean, provided the 5-day average lagged behind the 10-day. The current position was liquidated when the shorter-term average crossed the longer term. No fixed stops were used.

Maxwell's study represents a great amount of work and some simple and sound philosophy, but does not cover an adequate sampling of data to justify most of his conclusions. Conclusions were drawn based on a selected 50-day test period using May 72 pork bellies, leaving many questions regarding the success of this system or any other system when applied to this short test interval. Maxwell does test four other selected 50-day periods, but the reader cannot know how these periods were chosen. Considering the effort in outlining a testing program and establishing rules, the actual magnitude of the system testing is disappointing.

Turner and Blinn study silver, recording 13 computer-tested methods with professional competence. The systems they present are classified as:

A. Five profitable trading methods
   1. 40- and 5-day moving average
   2. 30- and 8-day moving average
   3. 30- and 5-day moving average
   4. 25- and 8-day moving average
   5. 25- and 5-day moving average

These double moving-average systems always have a position in the market, going from short to long when the faster moving average crosses above the slower one and from long to short when the opposite occurs.

B. Three terrible trading methods
   1. 10- and 1-day moving average
   2. 10- and 5-day moving average
   3. 15- and 2-day moving average

C. Two mediocre methods
   1. 40- and 2-day moving average
   2. 25- and 1-day moving average

A total of 15 combinations of "extreme price channel" breakouts and delays were then tested. The n-day channel was defined as bounded by the highest and lowest prices reached during the prior n days. A delay of m days means that the most recent m days are not included, but used to determine whether a signal has occurred. Using this technique the authors were noticeably successful with two choices, unsuccessful with two others, and mediocre with two, concluding that the waiting period seemed to be more significant than the length of the channel and that risks could be quite large. To improve the problems of the "extreme price channel" method, only the closing prices were used and the contracts retested in hopes of reducing the give-ups. This time shorter channels outperformed longer channels.

With the loss on exit still too large, Turner and Blinn moved to price objectives, using the theory that a price goal captures more profits and maintains the integrity of the system. Accordingly, various objectives ranging from 1000 to 2000 points were tested with some improvement and some reduction in profits. Additional testing included protective stops, which did not improve otherwise successful methods.

Trading Silver Profitably is clear and informative, and covers good samplings of moving-average systems. It is difficult to tell how thoroughly each system was tested because only a few results are presented. If testing were complete but profitable results were few and intermittent, these results would not be reassuring; if only a few tests were performed, there would not be an adequate sample. The important question becomes: Why were *those* results published?

Comparing Methods of Calculation

Hochheimer[3] performs two interesting studies: a comparison of three types of *moving average calculations* and a test of the use of *channels and crossovers*. In the first analysis, Hochheimer compares *simple, exponentially smoothed,* and *linearly weighted* moving averages, tested on a good sampling of markets (without financials and currencies, which did not exist during the 1970–1976 test period). The terms used are those that have already been covered in this book. The *simple* and *exponentially smoothed* calculations are reasonably standard, and the *linearly weighted* refers to *step-weighting,* where integer values are used and each successive day is incremented by one, the most recent day having the highest weighting factor.

The trading rules that apply regardless of which calculation was performed, were:

1. The trend calculation used the closing price only.
2. A *buy* signal occurred on an upwards penetration of the moving average by the closing price; a *sell* signal occurred under the opposite conditions.
3. The model is always in the market.
4. A trade cannot be executed when the day's high and low price are the same. It is assumed to be a "locked-limit" day.

The test covered 7 years of data from 1970–1976 and moving average days (or equivalent smoothing constant converted as $2/(days + 1)$), which appear to range from 2 to 70. The results shown in Table 15-1 are interesting and logical, considering the rules. The longer trends (using more days) were consistently better than shorter ones, regardless of which technique was used. This would imply that the longer trends are more reliable. With a few exceptions, the best selection of days ranged from 40 to 70.

A more careful look at the results will uncover some problems in the study. During the 7 years of test data, soybeans had 728 trades using a 55-day simple moving average. That is more than 100 trades each year, one every 2 or 3 days. Hogs had 1093 trades during the same period, and other commodities were similarly high. That seems contrary to thoughts about a slow moving average catching the big trend. In addition, the study never discusses the transaction costs or "slippage" due to execution liquidity, both significant items when trading quickly. It must be assumed that all of the trends were subject to numerous whipsaws because of the simple buy and sell rule. Although the longer trend is more conservative, this study shows that a moving average of any type and any speed requires a commitment to the trade rather than constantly reversing its position.

Channels and Crossovers

This study consisted of two tests. The first is a *crossover of two simple moving averages.* The short-term average (fast trend) ranged from 3 to 25 days and the

[3] Frank Hochheimer, "Moving Averages," and "Channels and Crossovers" in Perry J. Kaufman (Ed.), *Technical Analysis in Commodities,* Wiley, New York, 1980.

Table 15-1   Results of a Simple Moving Average Model

	Best Day	Best Range	Net P/L	Max. Run of Losses	Trades		
					Total	Profit	% of Prof. Tr.
Cocoa	54	53–59	$ 87,957	$−14,155	600	157	26%
Corn	43	43–46	24,646	− 6,537	565	126	22
Sugar	60	55–60	270,402	−15,563	492	99	20
Cotton	57	52–57	68,685	−11,330	641	121	19
Silver	19	—	42,920	−15,285	1,393	429	31
Copper	59	54–59	165,143	− 7,687	432	158	37
Soybeans	55	55–60	222,195	−10,800	728	151	21
Soy meal	68	65–70	22,506	−20,900	704	148	21
Wheat	41	40–45	65,806	−12,550	480	124	26
P Bellies	19	16–25	97,925	− 9,498	774	281	36
Soy oil	69	65–70	89,920	− 8,920	586	122	21
Plywood	68	65–70	1,622	− 3,929	372	98	26
Hogs	16	16–20	35,595	− 7,190	1,093	318	29

long-term from 5 to 50 days. The objective was to eliminate the whipsaws that were evident in the first study. The rules for this system were:

1. Each moving average used closing prices only; the long-term number of days was always greater than the short-term days.
2. A *buy* signal occurred when the short-term average moved above the long-term average; a *sell* signal occurred when the short-term average moved below the long term.
3. The model was always in the market.
4. If the high and low prices of the day were equal, a "locked-limit" day was assumed and no execution occurred.

In this test, the commitment to the new position is measured by the distance between the two moving averages and the price at the time an entry signal occurred. In a very quiet market, this distance would be small; in a fast market, it would be larger. As can be seen in Table 15-2, the number of trades were greatly reduced and the percentage of profitable trades was greatly increased—a most desirable quality.

Channels. The next two models attempted to break away from the moving averages used in the previous optimizations. They are based entirely on penetration of a band, defined as the high and low of the past *N* days. In the first model, the penetration, which causes a *buy* or *sell* signal, occurs if the intraday high or low price penetrates the band; in the second model, only the close is used to determine penetration. In the first model, it is possible for both a *buy* and *sell* signal to occur on the same day. In that case, only the first signal is taken.

Tables 15-3 and 15-4 show the results of the *intraday* and *interday* tests, respectively. Intuitively the closing price is expected to be a more reliable indicator than

Table 15-2   Results of Two Simple Moving Average Crossovers

	Best Days	Net P/L	Max. Run of Losses	Trades		
				Total	Profit	% of Prof. Tr.
Cocoa	7 25	$176,940	$− 4,436	468	199	43%
Corn	11 47	69,275	− 2,697	225	93	35
Sugar	5 50	335,843	−13,851	311	109	35
Cotton	16 25	304,485	− 4,755	485	233	48
Silver	3 26	100,790	− 8,610	661	262	40
Copper	17 33	212,939	− 3,057	354	177	50
Soybeans	16 50	286,440	−15,665	311	148	48
Soybean meal	18 50	117,155	− 8,155	272	118	43
Wheat	11 47	113,118	− 2,660	209	87	42
Pork bellies	25 46	13,124	−21,538	226	100	42
Soybean oil	14 50	121,749	− 6,585	327	128	39
Plywood	24 42	18,505	− 3,184	219	100	46
Hogs	3 14	97,448	− 7,805	793	321	40

the intraday high or low. This would seem confirmed by the pork bellies' results, which had 567 profitable and 847 losing trades in the intraday test, and only 51 profits and 43 losses in the interday model. Most of the other results are not as clear.

One thing is certain: The channel methods have much lower profits and proportionally greater risk than the crossovers; results tend to be more erratic as well.

Table 15-3   Results of Intraday Closing Price Channel

	Best Day	Net P/L	Max. Run of Losses	Trades		
				Total	Profit	% of Prof. Tr.
Cocoa	53	$135,689	$− 7,460	118	65	55%
Corn	38	40,834	− 5,798	159	66	42
Sugar	50	281,629	−16,687	119	54	45
Cotton	61	162,520	−12,685	110	48	44
Silver	15	87,470	−13,060	603	282	47
Copper	32	178,774	− 5,800	204	113	55
Soybeans	49	256,856	−10,525	157	76	48
Soybean meal	57	79,818	−12,602	311	66	21
Wheat	30	118,503	− 4,580	173	82	47
Pork bellies	5	196,521	−10,370	1,414	567	40
Soybean oil	47	135,804	− 9,086	162	76	47
Plywood	49	8,632	− 4,432	120	57	48
Hogs	10	87,061	− 8,425	743	299	40

Table 15-4   Results of Interday Closing Price Channel

	Best Day	Net P/L	Max. Run of Losses	Trades		
				Total	Profit	% of Prof. Tr.
Cocoa	53	$147,913	$− 6,248	110	60	55%
Corn	49	39,533	− 5,048	118	50	42
Sugar	40	296,027	−20,758	133	57	43
Cotton	62	206,575	− 6,870	89	48	54
Silver	14	27,690	−12,365	552	212	38
Copper	27	151,671	− 7,225	217	115	53
Soybeans	51	244,839	−11,325	120	68	57
Soybean meal	49	104,690	− 7,000	166	71	43
Wheat	23	111,087	− 6,900	205	80	39
Pork bellies	52	60,263	− 9,892	94	51	54
Soybean oil	51	8,646	− 3,622	109	48	44
Plywood	49	8,632	− 4,432	120	57	48
Hogs	9	83,702	− 9,854	606	253	42

Modified Three Crossover Model

The use of one or more slow moving averages may result in a buy or sell signal at a time when the prices are actually moving opposite to the position that is about to be entered. This may happen when:

1. Using rules that consider the crossover of the moving average, rather than a penetration of the price.
2. Using a simple moving average calculation when the change in the new price is less than the change in the oldest price that was dropped.

For example, if a long signal occurs and the oldest price showed a decline of 50 points while today's price declined 40 points, the new moving average value will rise by the difference, +10, divided by the number of days in the moving average. This may also occur using exponential smoothing under the special conditions

$$E_{t-1} - P_t > P_{t-1} - E_{t-1}$$

By using a third, faster moving average, the slope can be used as a confirmation of direction to avoid entry into a trade that is going the wrong way. This filter can be added to any moving average or multiple moving average system with the following rule:

Do not enter a new long (or short) position unless the slope of the confirming moving average (the change in the moving average value from the prior day to today) was up (or down).

The speed of this third, confirming moving average only makes sense if it is equal to or faster than the faster of the trends used in the Crossover System.

Test Results. Fortunately, the results of both the Crossover System as well as the Modified Three Crossover System were available for the same commodities and the same years. Because the crossovers used in the latter model are exactly those of the first system, the comparison will show whether the confirming feature improved overall results. From the 22 commodities tested, plywood was removed because its poor results on both systems tended to distort the comparison. The important statistics are shown in Table 15-5.

The difference in using the Modified Three Crossover System versus the simpler Crossover System are:

Average change in profits	(15.3)%
Average change in equity drop	(15.5)%
Average change in percentage of profitable trades	.9%
Average change in number of trades	(26.1)%

A decline in profits equal to a decline in equity drop (or risk) is the same as using the original Crossover System with a 15.4% smaller investment. The percentage of profitable trades increased negligibly, indicating that the confirmation filter did not eliminate more losing trades as was expected. The last point, however, shows a larger decline in the total number of trades, indicating that the profit per trade has increased. The new filter must catch the entries at a better point, and it eliminated a higher percentage of trades with smaller profits. This improvement means that there is more latitude for trading error. Although the overall profile of the Modified Three Crossover is not much better than the Crossover System, it would be the preferred choice.

4-9-18 Crossover Model Results

This model, using the same rules as the Modified Three Crossover System, was well-known before Hochheimer's studies. It can be assumed that the selection of 4, 9, and 18 days was a conscious effort to be slightly ahead of the 5, 10, and 20 days frequently used in moving average systems. It is likely that the system was not developed by extensive testing, since all commodities are traded with these same speeds.

As simple as it seems, there are a few very sound concepts in this approach:

1. Each moving average is twice the speed of the prior, enhancing their independence in recognizing different trends.
2. They are slightly faster than the conventional 5-, 10-, and 20-day moving averages.
3. They are the same for all products, implying that a logical selection should work.

Table 15-5 Comparison of Systems 1970–1979

	Crossovers				Modified Three Crossover				Change	
	P/L	No. Trades	% Drop	% Profitable Trades	P/L	No. Trades	% Drop	% Profitable Trades	% P/L	% Trades
Deutschemark	$ 96,510	259	7.6	54	$ 97,698	226	3.4	52	1.2	(12.7)
Japanese yen	94,575	131	3.1	51	92,287	111	2.9	58	(2.4)	(15.3)
Canadian dollar	71,940	158	7.0	52	69,690	116	5.2	60	(3.1)	(26.6)
British pound	80,262	113	8.2	46	69,808	81	8.3	53	(13.0)	(28.3)
Swiss franc	120,674	121	4.8	48	100,891	91	4.6	46	(16.4)	(24.8)
Cocoa	408,262	353	2.4	46	282,453	291	7.6	43	(30.8)	(17.6)
Coffee	83,586	332	3.9	39	56,338	231	5.8	35	(32.6)	(30.4)
Sugar	348,833	449	3.8	36	331,526	322	4.1	41	(5.0)	(28.3)
Cotton	378,440	697	2.8	47	282,460	483	3.3	41	(25.4)	(30.7)
Silver	96,995	1098	13.9	35	89,165	990	15.7	37	(8.1)	(9.8)
Copper	218,790	571	2.7	43	217,689	408	2.9	43	(.5)	(28.5)
Soybeans	386,137	483	4.8	47	308,233	317	5.7	48	(20.2)	(34.4)
Soybean meal	165,294	429	5.3	43	135,643	316	5.9	39	(17.9)	(26.3)
Wheat	151,871	305	2.7	43	90,093	207	6.9	44	(40.7)	(32.1)
Pork bellies	78,207	312	27.5	44	76,363	246	14.2	43	(2.4)	(21.2)
Soybean oil	125,848	488	5.2	39	89,834	346	9.3	40	(28.6)	(29.1)
Hogs	88,097	853	9.2	39	94,634	647	7.9	41	7.4	(24.2)
Cattle	162,280	1186	4.8	41	155,135	875	3.3	40	(4.4)	(26.2)
GNMAs	76,291	197	4.4	52	56,217	133	6.5	47	(26.3)	(32.5)
T-bills	28,210	388	27.0	38	20,436	284	3.4	37	(27.6)	(26.8)
Gold	131,325	275	1.6	53	98,030	158	2.2	57	(25.4)	(42.5)
Average:			7.3	45			6.1	45	(15.3)	(26.1)

It would not be possible for either the profits or the equity drops to be better in this model than an "optimized" strategy, such as the Modified Three Crossover Method. Out of 17 commodities simulated during the 1970–1976 period, only two lost money. There is a greater degree of confidence in this performance than in an optimized program.

Reoptimization (Retesting)

The testing performed to find the best set of parameters is never the last test. It is always important to monitor performance and compare the out-of-sample results with a new optimization to determine the success of the system rules and the testing process. A 1982 publication of Hochheimer,[4] provides a rare opportunity to see how the original tests fared and how parameter selection would have changed based on both additional data and changes in price patterns.

Crossovers Retested

In the 1982 update of the Crossover System optimization using data through 1979, it is interesting to note that 11 out of 17 commodities selected two moving average speeds either identical (in six cases) or nearly identical to the previous test. Five of the remaining six tests showed new selections which traded slower than the previous test. Only gold resulted in a faster selection, but the original test in 1976 could have had only one year of data.

Because the results of using the parameters selected in 1976 were not shown in the new study, it is difficult to assess their exact performance. Eleven cases, however, where the new parameters were either identical or had very small changes can be used as a conservative estimate. Their out-of-sample performance is shown in Table 15-6. If the parameters are not identical, the 1979 test must show results that are higher than the actual out-of-sample would have been.

The first reaction to the update of the 1976 crossover test should be very positive. Almost identical parameters for 11 out of 17 products originally tested were selected. This means that the traders who used this system were using the *optimum* parameters during the 3-year period from 1977–1979. How did they do?

Table 15-7 is a comparison of the "out-of-sample" period, 1977–1979. In the cases where the parameter selection was slightly different, it must be assumed that the total performance, 1970–1979, was better than the performance using the original parameters. Therefore, the out-of-sample period should be at least as good as the results actually achieved. Total profits were $201,649, trading one contract of each commodity.

Two additional factors should be considered. Although only 3 of the 11 showed losses, the fast nature of this system results in very low profits per trade in 4 of the remaining 8 commodities. This may not seem serious until the realities of trading are considered—the exact execution price is rarely achieved. A trend-following

[4] Frank L. Hochheimer, *Computerized Trading Techniques 1982*, Merrill Lynch Commodities, New York, 1982.

Table 15-6 Retesting of the Crossover System

	Through 1976					Through 1979		
	Best Days	Net P/L	Trades Profitable/ Total	%	Profits/ Trade	Best Days	Net P/L	Trades Profitable/ Total
Corn	11 47	$ 69,275	93/225	41	$ 308	12 48	$ 83,586	129/ 332
Sugar	5 50	335,843	109/311	35	1080	6 50	348,833	160/ 449
Cotton	16 25	304,485	223/485	46	628	16 25	378,440	329/ 697
Silver	3 26	100,790	262/661	40	152	3 26	96,995	385/1098
Copper	17 33	212,939	177/354	50	602	17 32	218,790	245/ 571
Wheat	11 47	133,118	87/209	42	637	12 48	151,871	130/ 305
Bellies	25 46	13,124	100/226	44	58	25 46	78,207	137/ 312
Soy oil	14 50	121,749	128/327	39	372	14 50	125,848	190/ 488
Plywood	24 42	18,505	100/219	46	84	20 46	2,667	132/ 351
Cattle	7 13	147,540	337/792	43	186	7 13	162,280	490/1186
T-Bills	6 18	39,710	69/148	47	268	6 18	28,210	148/ 388

system, with orders entered as intraday stops, must always allow for "slippage." Slippage is caused by lack of liquidity and is related directly to the size of the order being executed (see the discussion of liquidity in Chapter 18). In a fast market, this slippage can be large, often hundreds of dollars (in contract value) away from the intended price. Even "close-only" orders are subject to slippage. A buyer using a close-only order should expect to get the high of the closing range; a seller will get the low.

In Table 15-7, the furthest right column assumes a conservative slippage, one that should be included in any test program. In some cases such as copper and

Table 15-7 Out-Of-Sample Results for the Crossover System

	Net P/L	Trades Profitable/ Total	%	Profits/ Trade	1-Way Slippage (5% Daily Range)			
Corn	$ 14,311	36/107	34	$133[a]	½¢	=	25 × 250 =	$(5350)
Sugar	12,990	51/138	37	94[a]	10 pts	=	112	= (34,500)
Cotton	73,995	106/212	50	349	10 pts	=	50	= (21,200)
Silver	(3,795)	123/437	28	(9)	½¢	=	50	= (43,700)
Copper	5,851	68/217	31	27[a]	20 pts	=	50	= (21,700)
Wheat	18,753	43/ 96	45	195[a]	½¢	=	25	= (2,400)
Pork bellies	65,083	37/ 86	43	757	10¢	=	42	= (7,224)
Soy oil	4,099	62/161	39	25	5¢	=	30	= (9,660)
Plywood	(15,838)	32/132	24	(120)[a]	20 pts	=	15	= (3,960)
Cattle	14,740	153/394	39	37	10 pts	=	40	= (31,520)
T-Bills	(11,500)	79/240	33	(48)	2 pts	=	50	= (24,000)
Totals	$201,649							($205,214)

[a] Best case (could have been no better, possibly worse).

bellies, the slippage is small and does not seem to impact on profits; even the large profits of cotton survive well. But in the fastest trading commodities, even the smallest slippage will severely reduce large profits, frequently turning them into losses. The final total shows that those small costs when applied to every product were greater than the profits. Instead of making a killing in the market, these traders netted a loss.

Test Criteria

The method used in these tests is not bad, but real market factors must be included or the results are deceiving. Although the researchers may have been pleased with the out-of-sample profits, they were only paper profits. In real trading, the chances greatly favor losses.

Testing should closely approximate trading. If there is doubt about the costs, make them larger. A system that can profit under testing "penalties" should make money when actually traded. Even when using prepackaged computer optimization software, the slippage can be added by making the commission costs high; both are per trade costs. If a mistake is to be made, do it by being too conservative.

16
Advanced Techniques

MEASURING VOLATILITY

Volatility is an essential ingredient in many calculations, from Wilder's *RSI* to variable stop-loss points and point-and-figure box sizes. But volatility is more uniform than its short-term measurement would imply; it is a predictable component of a price series.

In general, the volatility of both a commodity price series and a spread of two series is directly proportional to the increase and decrease in the price level. This *price-volatility relationship* has been described as "lognormal" in the stock market and is similar for commodities, that is,

$$V(n) = c \times \ln(P_t - P_b)$$

where V is the n-day volatility

P_t is today's price

P_b is the base price of the commodity, somewhere below the cost of production

c is a scaling factor, near 1

This shows that, relative to its base price, the volatility of a commodity increases in an exponential relationship to the price.

Shifting the Volatility Base

It follows that prices are more volatile at higher levels and that most trading systems must cope with this change by adjusting its parameters. For example, a stop-loss in silver might be 20 points when the price is under $10 per ounce, 40 points at about $20 per ounce, and 200 points at $50 per ounce. A point-and-figure box size might vary in the same way as the stop-loss; as prices become higher, it requires a larger box size to maintain the same frequency of trend changes and signals.

Using the stop-loss as an example, most traders set a fixed value based on the risk that they are willing to take, regardless of whether this risk is too large or small for market conditions. A stop-loss that is related to margin offers some variability; however, the lag time in the change in margin by the exchange is too long to keep this relationship in-line. A percentage stop is a popular solution for analysts who realize that volatility increases with price, but it falls far behind during major bull and bear markets. A reasonable representation of long-term or underlying risk is the adjusted, lognormal *price-volatility relationship*. Although volatility may vary greatly at any price level, this relationship establishes a foundation for the "normal" level.

Base Price. The volatility relationship will be very inaccurate if it assumes zero volatility at zero price rather than at a higher level. All commodities have a *base price,* a level that is so low that trading is inactive and volatility becomes near zero. It is at this level that the volatility relationship begins.

Figure 16-1*a* shows that the base price can be found by detrending the data and formulating the volatility based on the detrended values. Although Figure 16-1*b* does not indicate a time period, volatility only makes sense when measured over some interval. The amount of price movement will increase over larger intervals. This relationship is shown in Figure 16-1*c*.

In Figure 16-1*c*, the volatility increases rapidly as the interval expands from its smallest value at one day. As it becomes larger, it will level off. Volatility, as a measure of net change, will flatten once the interval is longer than the largest sustained price move; it may still increase gradually when measured as the sum of the absolute price changes.

Alternate Measures

The three most used measures of volatility all satisfy the previous lognormal relationship. The one discussed so far has been *net price change over time*. This is equivalent to a momentum calculation $|P_t - P_{t-n}|$, where n is the time interval over which the volatility is calculated. This measure is most useful for establishing the probability of a price change at different levels.

Markets that do not have a significant price change may also be volatile. Many systems use the daily or weekly high-low range to define risk and volatility. This may also work although it does not always capture a full measure of activity. The *sum or the absolute price changes* is a more complete value. Using Figure 16-2, the three measures can be shown as:

1. Price change over time interval n:

$$V_t = P_{t+n} - P_t$$

2. The maximum fluctuation during the interval n:

$$V_t = \max(P_t, P_{t+n}) - \min(P_t, P_{t+n})$$

3. The sum of the absolute price changes over the interval n:

$$V_t = \sum_{i=1}^{n} |P_{t-i+1} - P_{t-i}|$$

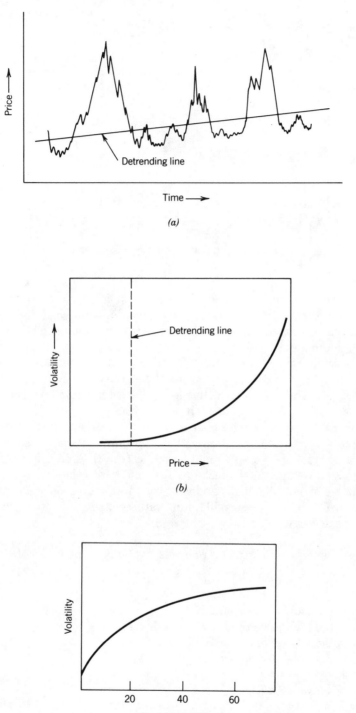

Figure 16-1 Measuring volatility from a relative base price. (a) Prices become less volatile relative to a long-term deflator (detrending line). (b) Volatility as a function of detrended price. (c) Change in volatility relative to the interval over which it is measured.

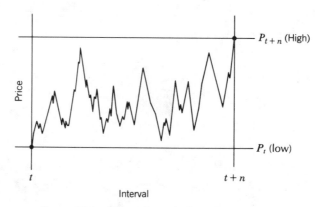

Figure 16-2   Alternative volatility measurements.

In (1), the volatility is entirely dependent on the relationship of the two points P_t and P_{t+n}, regardless of the interim activity. Over longer time periods, a predictable change can be expected, but in the short term this approach is not as good as either of the other two.

The maximum range (2) corrects for the dependence on only two points and will produce a more consistent measure of volatility, which may be used as an estimate of risk. This may be effective as the basis for a stop-loss as it defines the extent of the price fluctuation at each price level.

The sum of the absolute price changes (3) is the most accurate measurement of volatility although it is nondirectional. It clearly shows that prices are more or less active in cases that are not apparent to either (1) or (2). A price interval that tests the highs and lows alternately each day is much more volatile than one in which prices move slowly to the highs and then back to the lows once during the same time period. This measure is useful for indicating a change in market character, an increase, or decrease in activity.

Ratio Measurements. Bookstaber[1] presents a volatility measurement V, which is a ratio of successive closing prices, the high and low, or a combination of the two as follows,

where C_t is the closing price on day t
$\quad\quad H_t$ is the high price on day t
$\quad\quad L_t$ is the low on day t
$\quad\quad V_t$ is the volatility on day t

(a) *Close-to-close volatility*

$$R_t = \frac{C_t}{C_{t-1}}$$

and

$$A = \frac{1}{n} \sum_{i=1}^{n} \ln R_{t-i}$$

[1] Richard Bookstaber, *The Complete Investment Book,* Scott, Foresman, Glenview, IL, 1985, p. 349.

then

$$V_t^2 = \frac{1}{n-1} \sum_{i=1}^{n} (\ln R_{t-1} - A)^2$$

and

$$V_t = \sqrt{V_t^2}$$

(b) *High-low volatility*

$$V_t = \frac{.601}{n} \sum_{i=1}^{n} \ln \left(\frac{H_{t-i}}{L_{t-i}} \right)$$

(c) *High-low-close volatility*

$$S_t^2 = .5 \ln \left(\frac{H_t}{L_t} \right)^2 - .39 \ln \left(\frac{C_t}{C_{t-1}} \right)^2$$

$$V_t^2 = \frac{1}{n} \sum_{i=1}^{n} S_{t-i}^2$$

$$V_t = \sqrt{V_t^2}$$

Note that the current t may be a time interval rather than a single day. Then, C_t is the last price of the period, and H_t and L_t are the highest and lowest prices of the interval.

In the close-to-close estimation, the volatility V_t is the standard deviation of the closing price ratios. Bookstaber states that this measurement will follow a χ^2 distribution and that the actual volatility during the current period t can be set within the error bounds defined by the distribution.

Volatility System

The daily "volatility" can be used in a trading strategy, presented by Bookstaber,[2] as follows:

$$V_t(n) = \frac{1}{n} \sum_{i=1}^{n} D_{t-i+1}$$

where D_t is the maximum of:
    a. $|H_t - C_{t-1}|$
    b. $H_t - L_t$
    c. $|L_t - C_{t-1}|$

and H_t is the high on day t
    L_t is the low on day t
    C_t is the close on day t

[2] *Ibid*, pp. 224–236.

Note that D_t is the *extended range* concept that appears in many other works. V_t is the average extended range over the *n*-day interval. The trading strategy presented with this is

> *Buy* if the close C_{t+1} rises by more than $k*V_t(n)$ from the previous close C_t.
> *Sell* if the close C_{t+1} falls by more than $k*V_t(n)$ from the previous close C_t.

The volatility constant k is given as approximately 3 but can be varied higher or lower to make the trading signals less or more frequent, respectively.

PRICE-VOLUME DISTRIBUTION

Many systems that have excellent simulations fail when they are actually traded. These include models based on both intraday and daily data. One reason for this disappointing performance is the lack of understanding of market liquidity. Consider two systems:

> A *trend following method,* which signals a buy or sell order when prices rise or fall relative to a specific price during the day, and
> a *countertrend system,* which sells and buys at relative intraday highs or lows.

Although each system intends to profit with their opposing philosophies, both act when prices make a relatively unusual move. Figure 16-3 shows the normal distribution of intraday volume and the profitability associated with this distribution.[3]

The solid line *bb'* is the actual volume on an ideally normal day. Volume is greatest at the median *M* and declines sharply to the high and low endpoints *H* and *L*, where only one trade may have occurred. The dotted line *cc'* represents the apparent profit for a countertrend system that makes the assumption of a straight-line volume distribution. The endpoints are shown to contribute the largest part of the profits when, in reality, no executions may have been possible near those levels. Assuming the ability to execute at all points on the actual distribution *bb'*, the approximate profit contribution is shown as *dd'*.

For trend-following systems, no profits should be expected when buy or sell orders are placed at the extremes of the day. The actual price distribution *bb'* is the maximum that could be expected from such a system; in reality, the first day is usually a loss.

[3] Gary Ginter and Joseph J. Ritchie, "Data Errors and Profit Distortions," in Perry J. Kaufman (Ed.), *Technical Analysis in Commodities,* Wiley, New York, 1980.

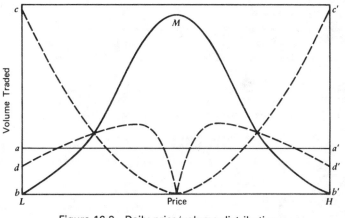

Figure 16-3   Daily price/volume distribution.

COMMITMENT OF TRADERS REPORT

Drawing from more than 20 years of experience in analyzing the CFTC's *Commitment of Traders Report,* William L. Jiler described a supplementary approach to identifying a major trend in his *1985 CRB Commodity Yearbook.*[4] With his usual thoroughness and clarity, Jiler presents material which had previously been unsuccessfully interpreted.

Released the eleventh day of each month, the *Commitment of Traders Report* summarizes the positions of "reporting" and "nonreporting" traders as of the last day of the previous month. Reported positions are those exceeding a minimum level determined for each futures market (e.g., 500,000 bushels in corn, wheat, or soybeans). The report subdivides the open interest into positions held by hedgers ("commercials") and speculators. By subtracting the reported positions from the total open interest, the total positions of small hedgers and speculators can be found. For grain reports (Figure 16-4), positions are further divided into "old crop" and "other" positions, which include new crop and intercrop spreading.

In order to analyze the shifts in position, Jiler has compiled tables of "normal" patterns, similar to a seasonal study (Figure 16-5). When the open interest of one group is significantly greater than their normal holdings, they express a definite opinion on the direction of the market. By tracking these changes for many years and observing the corresponding price changes, Jiler concludes that the large traders have the best forecasting record, with the large hedger better than the large speculator. The small traders were notably worse. Guidelines were stated as:

The most bullish configuration would show large hedgers heavily net long more than normal, large speculators clearly net long, small traders heavily net short more than seasonal. The shades of bullishness are varied all the way to the most bearish configuration which would have these groups in opposite positions—large hedgers heavily net short, etc.

[4] William L. Jiler, "Analysis of the CFTC Commitments of Traders Reports Can Help You Forecast Futures Prices," *1985 CRB Commodity Year Book,* Commodity Research Bureau, Jersey City, NJ, 1985.

SOYBEANS - CHICAGO BOARD OF TRADE
COMMITMENTS OF TRADERS IN ALL FUTURES COMBINED AND INDICATED FUTURES, FEBRUARY 28, 1985

FUTURES	TOTAL OPEN INTEREST	NON-COMMERCIAL LONG OR SHORT ONLY LONG	SHORT	LONG AND SHORT (SPREADING) LONG	SHORT	COMMERCIAL LONG	SHORT	TOTAL LONG	SHORT	NONREPORTABLE POSITIONS LONG	SHORT
					(THOUSAND BUSHELS)						
ALL	359,190	15,810	32,400	41,060	41,060	117,420	140,380	174,290	213,840	184,900	145,350
OLD	302,170	16,275	35,075	27,620	27,620	105,685	128,700	149,580	191,395	152,590	110,775
OTHER	57,020	9,280	7,070	3,695	3,695	11,735	11,680	24,710	22,445	32,310	34,575
			CHANGES IN COMMITMENTS FROM JANUARY 31, 1985								
ALL	-330	-9,240	15,575	18,280	18,280	16,560	-44,770	25,600	-10,915	-25,930	10,585
			PERCENT OF OPEN INTEREST REPRESENTED BY EACH CATEGORY OF TRADERS								
ALL	100.0%	4.4	9.0	11.4	11.4	32.7	39.1	48.5	59.5	51.5	40.5
OLD	100.0%	5.4	11.6	9.1	9.1	35.0	42.6	49.5	63.3	50.5	36.7
OTHER	100.0%	16.3	12.4	6.5	6.5	20.6	20.5	43.3	39.4	56.7	60.6
NUMBER OF TRADERS			NUMBER OF TRADERS IN EACH CATEGORY								
ALL	144	23	32	33	33	54	41	100	100		
OLD	134	23	32	23	23	51	39	88	90		
OTHER	32	8	8	5	5	9	6	21	17		

CONCENTRATION RATIOS
PERCENT OF OPEN INTEREST HELD BY THE INDICATED NUMBER OF LARGEST TRADERS

FUTURES	BY GROSS POSITION 4 OR LESS TRADERS LONG	SHORT	8 OR LESS TRADERS LONG	SHORT	BY NET POSITION 4 OR LESS TRADERS LONG	SHORT	8 OR LESS TRADERS LONG	SHORT
ALL	13.0	23.4	18.1	28.6	10.5	21.3	14.6	25.3
OLD	13.9	25.0	19.6	30.4	11.9	23.6	16.1	28.2
OTHER	18.6	20.6	27.4	28.7	18.6	20.2	27.3	26.8

Figure 16-4   Commitment of Traders Report.

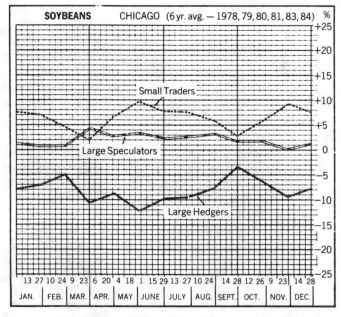

Figure 16-5   Jiler's "normal" trader positions.

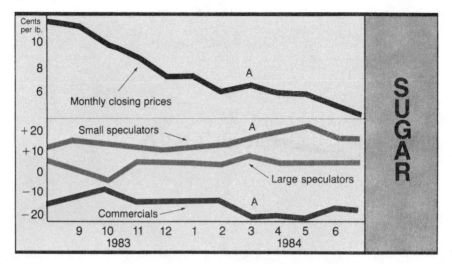

Figure 16-6   Arnold's trader position study.

There are two caution flags when analyzing deviations from normal. Be wary of positions that are more than 40% from their long-term average and disregard deviations of less than 5%.

This result is confirmed by Curtis Arnold,[5] who compared positions of large and small speculators with commercials for a 1-year period spanning 1983–1984. Arnold shows (Figure 16-6) that the position of commercials and small speculators tend to be opposite, with the commercials positioned to profit from the subsequent price move.

[5] Curtis Arnold, "Tracking 'Big Money' May Tip Off Trend Changes," *Futures*, Feb. 1985.

17

Practical Considerations

This chapter discusses areas of technical and mathematical analysis that cannot be regarded as systems yet are essential to the successful trader. The first part concerns the use of the computer. Recently, technical analysis and computers have become synonymous with each other; it would be rare to trade a new technical system without first running it through a computer to simulate its performance. Those who do not use a computer directly will be strongly influenced by the computer systems of others.

The second section, the Theory of Runs, is actually an application of gambling techniques, primarily Martingale, to commodities trading. What would seem more reasonable than assuming that the odds are against you in the commodities market and treating it as a gambling situation? The third section is about filtering, or selection, the tendency of all traders to seek ways to eliminate more losing trades. Instead, many end up by eliminating their capital. Filtering includes combining systems that focus on different market characteristics, and the understanding of the "trade-offs" inherent in each type of analytic method. Fourth is a short analysis of trading limits to show some of the problems and flaws of moving from a test to an operating environment. The last section reviews a recent study on the similarity of systems, to confront the issue of the impact of technical systems on futures markets.

USE AND ABUSE OF THE COMPUTER

Make sure your present report system is reasonably clean and effective before you automate. Otherwise your new computer will just speed up the mess.

Robert Townsend[1]

Computers are not a substitute for thinking. They excel in performing the same tedious task, over and over again, quickly and accurately—provided, of course, that correct information was entered. But even though technology has not yet reached the stage depicted in *Star Wars*, the computer is the only practical tool for

---

[1] Robert Townsend, *Up the Organization*, Knopf, New York, 1970, p. 36.

evaluating trading ideas. This section will consider both good and bad ways to approach a computer problem, none of which can be credited to or blamed on the machine. As a calculator, a computer can't be beat; many of the systems, advancements, and refinements presented in this book could not have been considered without it.

Computers come in many shapes and sizes, and can be purchased, rented, and borrowed. Their packaging has become second only to the car. The average life of a computer "generation" has been about 10 years; however, advances in technology are rapidly shortening the time between releases of significant new equipment. The past few years have seen a remarkable evolution in the computer industry. The acceptance of the personal computer (PC) has revolutionized data processing and brought the microcomputer into millions of homes. Because not everyone knows how to program a computer, software companies have developed "turn-key" packages, programs that are operated by menu selection. The combination of these two factors, cheap hardware and available software, has reached the commodities industry as well (Figure 17-1).

One of the first and foremost organizations to provide convenient computer research tools for the trader was the Technical Analysis Group (TAG), which began as a New Orleans-based user's group in 1975. It provides menu-driven capabilities for analysis of daily price data, using Apples or IBM-PCs for remote communication and local processing. More recently, new competition has arrived.[2] Traders may now select from among numerous companies providing daily and intraday services for:

1. *Price updates,* including contract history and daily data base maintenance.
2. *Trading strategy software,* such as standard trading techniques, optimization, and sometimes the ability to integrate user-written computer programs.

Data for system development is traditionally restricted to the daily open, high, low, close, volume, and open interest. Some companies are experimenting with historic intraday prices, but the volume and time necessary for transmission of past data makes this impractical for the PCs. Standard menu-driven programs are provided by service companies, allowing the user to:

1. List the contracts that are to be followed
2. Automatically dial and retrieve data via telephone communications
3. Correct data that was previously in error

The trading strategies that are part of the software package usually include:

1. All moving averages and multiple moving averages, whether standard, weighted, or exponential.
2. Specific public systems, such as stochastics, Relative Strength Index, On-Balance Volume, the Demand Index, and Convergence/Divergence (countertrend technique).

---

[2] Applied Decision Systems in St. Charles, IL has been noted as providing a commendable service.

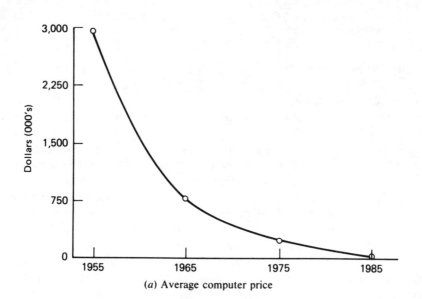

(a) Average computer price

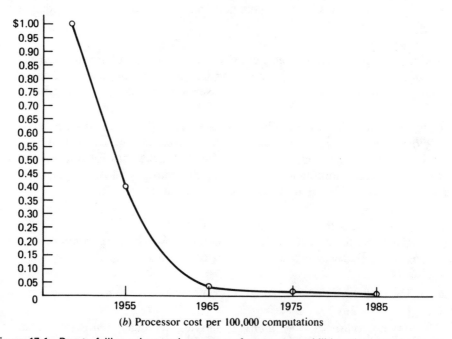

(b) Processor cost per 100,000 computations

Figure 17-1 Due to falling prices and greater performance capabilities, the cost of processor capacity has dropped dramatically. (a) Average computer price. (b) Processor cost per 100,000 computations. (c) Although the distinction between minicomputers and microcomputers grows increasingly hazy, the physical machinery size for a given level of processing power has gone down, so that as the trend continues, by 1985 there will be few applications requiring the behemoth computers. (Source: David Handmaker, "The Computer in a Commodity Futures Environment," in Perry J. Kaufman, Handbook of Futures Markets, Wiley, New York, 1984)

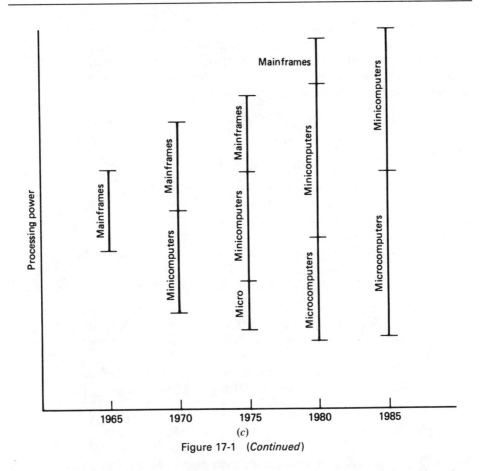

(c)

Figure 17-1   (Continued)

Companies are rapidly expanding their selection of systems and making them available for the study of intraday price movements.

Intraday

Using the computer to speed response to the market is a prime benefit of automation. By installing a communications port and attaching a standard telephone line, any trader can be "on-line" with all futures markets. The strategies that were once evaluated only at night can now give instantaneous response to both sudden price moves or subtle trend changes.

Special graphics are also part of both the intraday and daily computer programs. Screens can display bar charts, moving averages, volumes and open interest, relative strength, and other analyses on a single, full screen display or can be split into multiple displays.

Adding Your Own Decision Criteria

Some software packages allow you to enter your own formulas as part of the menu selection. To make this practical, series of values can be saved by the computer to be used in later calculations. David Handmaker, an expert in small systems, describes a way of comparing the various strategies by using three measures of performance: cumulative net gains, drawdown, and the total number of trades.[3] Single formulas may be entered using logic notation. For example, Handmaker shows that the following formula may be programmed into the system:

$$\text{IF}(((R_t > 0) \text{ AND } (R_t < B) \text{ AND } (DR_t > 0)) \text{ OR}$$

$$((R_t < 0) \text{ AND } (R_t > S) \text{ AND } (DR_t < 0))) \text{ THEN}$$

$$\text{SIGN}(R_t) * DP_t = \text{PROFIT}_t$$

where
    R_t is the relative strength, or oscillator, on day t
    B is the overbought level
    DR_t is the change in relative strength, R_t to R_{t-1}
    S is the oversold level
    $\text{SIGN}(R_t)$ is the positive or negative sign of R_t (direction of the change)
    DP_t is the price change $P_t - P_{t-1}$
    PROFIT_t is the profit from trading the system on day t

Menu-driven software for microcomputers won't always solve the problem. Sometimes it is necessary to invest time and money in programming a unique strategy. Often the testing of these strategies involves more "number crunching" than a PC is capable of. The optimization process, discussed in Chapter 15, has been known to take many hours on a mainframe; this could be equivalent to years of testing on a PC, even with special mathematical processing capabilities.

Developing the System

The specific computer that is needed for developing a trading strategy depends on many factors. The most important considerations reduce to a trade-off of time and money. Machines that run faster also cost more.

Picking a computer is not the best first step. Finding the machine for which data and supporting statistical and graphics programs are available will make the process much easier in the long run. Why make the solution more difficult than it already is? Find someone who has developed a trading system and ask them: Where did you get your data? Are you pleased? Were there other choices? Would you do it again if you were to start all over? After that, bombard them with the next set of questions: What machine did you choose? Why? Did you buy software or write it yourself? What did it cost? How long did it take to get? Did it work right away? Is the company dependable when things go wrong?

Without the help of another's experience this would be a long process. There are a number of commodity systems "user's groups," which are willing and able to give advice in these areas. Remember to keep everything in perspective. At 1986 prices, the cost of good equipment that will do everything necessary in the home will be about $5000. A few bad trades will cost more.

---

[3] David Handmaker, "Picking Software To Trade Technically," *Commodities* (now *Futures*), Aug. 1982 pp. 73–74.

Getting Data

The data needed for testing theories will always be available on the computers for which there is trading software already written. There are many services that advertise full commodity data bases on diskettes. Many are sold by the number of commodities and delivery months requested. By now, most of these should be free of errors. Simply select the most convenient one and purchase a modest sampling of different commodities, spanning 3 to 10 years. It is not necessary to obtain all years of all markets immediately; there is no chance of using all that data in the near future.

Data is also available in printed form from each exchange. The Chicago Board of Trade *Statistical Annual* or the Chicago Mercantile Exchange *Yearbook* contain all the prices, plus related statistics and charts. These books are valuable when data looks questionable; tests may also be selected by the type of price movement that can be seen on the chart. Do not even consider entering the data yourself. The time and inaccuracy involved in manual data entry is a poor alternative to purchasing the information.

Daily Updates. The *Wall Street Journal* is the standard choice for daily price updates. A few years ago, traders who entered prices manually began their day early over the commodities page of the *Wall Street Journal*. Now, there are other options:

Electronic quote machines. Every brokerage house and many homes are equipped with full-screen quote machines to display all futures prices as they change. In many cases, the same home computer that is used for research and analysis can be used as a real-time quote machine. Carried further, the data that is displayed can be captured on a hard disk and used later for analysis. Most traders will manually update their data base from prices copied off the displays of Reuter's, Quotron, Bunker-Ramo, Commodity Communications, Market View, and many others.

Dial-up services. For the trader interested in updating a wide variety of contracts to be processed daily by computer, dial-up data base updates are practical. Using a predefined format, the user activates a program which dials another computer. It then receives updates for a list of delivery months specified in advance. The communication program ends, and the user may then decode and distribute the new price data to the appropriate data files. Although the data base design is specified by the dial-up service, it takes little effort to convert the information into another format. The entire process may take less than one minute each day.

Time-Sharing

Before the small computer worked its way into the home, large machines dominated industry. The size and cost of this equipment made it desirable and feasible to share one machine among many users through *time-sharing*. Computer service bureaus thrived in the 1960s and 1970s, offering to sell usage on mainframes by the minute. The advantages of time-sharing are still the same:

1. The user pays only for the specific equipment and time used, such a computer memory, disk storage, printed lines.
2. Data is usually provided, ranging from only futures and stock prices to complete economic/statistical data.
3. Varied levels of software are available to specify trading strategies and graph results; many different programming languages can be used.
4. Communications equipment is small (portable) and inexpensive; only a terminal is needed rather than an entire computer.
5. Elapsed processing time ("throughput") is very fast, exceeding the home computer by a factor of 50 to 100.

Time-sharing companies found that the growing popularity of the PC severed a significant part of their customer base. But the large scale data base was something that could not be replaced; many companies shifted their emphasis to selling data. Now, an analyst sitting at home might use the PC for most testing and program checkout, download data from the mainframe when necessary, and occasionally use the large computer to run a test that would take too long on the microcomputer. The two worlds have learned to coexist.

Programming the System

Computer programming talent is not as rare as it was 20 years ago; however, explaining a commodity trading strategy to a programmer can be frustrating and very expensive. The safest approach to the problem is to purchase as much packaged software as possible, request the file layout (the internal specifications of the information storage), and build from there. Even though the actual program instructions ("source code") are not available by purchasing a system, the company selling the product should have no objections to added effort that uses the data generated by the program. Many User's Manuals that accompany the software will already contain the information.

Selecting a Programmer

If you are not going to program the computer yourself, try to find someone with the appropriate experience. Teaching a programmer all about trading strategies and calculation of profits and losses will take time. As a minimum, a scientific background is better than business programming experience.

Getting a programmer to say how much or how long it will take to solve a problem is going to be difficult—they just don't know. Programmers are incurable optimists, always thinking that the problem will be done at any moment. Even competent managers of programmers have difficulty in scheduling a project, based on the uncertainty of the debugging, or checking-out process. If it is necessary to contract the work or hire a programmer, do it on a fixed-price basis and avoid the problems that will occur later.

Define the Steps

Keep the work on schedule. Establish a programming plan in advance, starting with the end product, then the input, and finally the intermediate steps, in the following way:

1. Define the end product of this program—for example, a report showing results of various moving average systems, including profitability, number of total and profitable trades, and the largest drop in equity.
2. Simulate the form of the output report, *exactly* as it should appear.
3. Ask the question, "What is the minimum input necessary for this program to get the results shown on the output report?"
4. Write a technical description of how the results are calculated, using only the input data.
5. Draw a flowchart of the logic, or write a list in proper sequence, showing the handling of data, calculations, and so forth.
6. Write the program from the detailed flow.
7. Test the program with simple cases that can be verified by hand.
8. Run complete tests once you are sure that the program is operating properly.

Looking into the Past

The selection of how much data to use for testing is usually a practical problem. Generally, it is better to use as much data as possible. Some analysts will argue that older data is not representative of today's markets or that building a system that works in all prior periods will cause reduced performance in today's market. That's all true. A system that is general enough to be profitable over many years is not likely to capture all that is possible this year, or in any one year. But it is safer.

The practical problem faced by most traders who develop their own system is time. The home computer may take hours, or even days, to complete a single test of a commodity, searching for the best moving average. This time may be shortened by using selected markets if the system trades frequently. A system that trades less often can only be tested over long time periods in order to complete enough trades to be able to draw valid conclusions.

Finding the predictive qualities of a methodology (the combination of strategy and testing) is more complicated but can be calculated using a process of forward extrapolation. In other words, the following tests can be performed:

1. One-year test (single period).
   a. Test (optimize) the system for 1980, then use the best parameters to determine performance in 1981.

b. Repeat, testing 1981 data and use the new parameters for determining performance in 1982, and so on.

2. Two-year test (multiple period).

   a. Find the best system parameters for the combined 1981–1982 test period, then use the parameters for 1983 performance.
   b. Repeat, using 1982–1983 as a test period, then record the performance of the next forward period, 1984.

These simulated trading results will also help find the number of years of testing necessary to give the best predictive quality. It is similar to the way testing and trading actually happens, and it can be readily executed on a computer.

Holding Data Aside

Using all the available data for testing does not provide a chance to see how the final system might work on data that has not yet been seen. A system with many rules tested over a small data sample is likely to perform very well. The brute-force approach to testing all combinations of trends and rules will always result in a performance profile for the tested data, which looks too good to be true. It is too good to be true. *Overfitting* the data is a frequent problem in system development. Adding rules that correct specific price combinations leads to systems that can only work on past data.

To find out whether a newly created system is likely to be profitable, run it through data that has been held aside. Its performance should be similar to the tested profile—or only slightly worse. If the original tests showed no more than three consecutive losing trades, and the out-of-sample test shows six, take a closer look.

Out-of-sample data must be carefully chosen for most futures markets. Holding aside every other contract of gold will not work. The high correlation to other contracts trading on the same day is the same as testing all contracts. For these markets, hold aside the most recent year of data. When the system is shown to perform in the current market, retest the parameters to include that data. Live-stock markets, which are nonstorable, have little correlation between consecutive delivery months; random omission of data should work well.

Feedback. Care should be taken not to overuse out-of-sample data. If every test is followed by an examination of the out-of-sample data, *feedback* is introduced. The data that has been set aside is no longer out-of-sample.

Poor Use of Data

Data must be selected to represent different price movements and to avoid duplication. A classic example of poor selection was discussed in the section "Selecting the Test Data," which can be found in Chapter 15. The information in that section is equally appropriate here.

And the Results?

By the time a data base has been acquired, a programmer to implement the ideas, and computer time or equipment to "debug" and test the programs, there has been a substantial investment made. Hard work has resulted in proving one of four things:

1. The system is profitable.
2. The system is not profitable.
3. The system cannot be implemented effectively.
4. The whole process is too expensive.

If finances were exhausted without success, the trading philosophy is due to be reexamined. Trading strategies should be built slowly; each piece must be proved to be sound. It should be possible to stop at many points in the development of a system and begin trading, even though the trading profile is not ideal.

The third situation points out additional problems. It may indicate that the rules are too subjective—a valuable discovery. Many speculators believe that they are very clinical about their trading policies; they know exactly what will be done in every circumstance and therefore think that their approach can be well-defined in writing. But computerization requires no "maybes" and no "wait and see" and no exceptions at all.

The second result is that the system does not work using either the rules or the variables imposed by the program. If moving averages ranging from 20 through 50 were used, now try intervals of less than 20. If stop-loss points were too big or too small (judging by the size of frequency of the losses), try different sizes. Systems do not always work as expected and perhaps only a slight change to the rules is necessary. Negative results are important feedback. They help create a better strategy before it is too late. After all, if the answers were known in advance, this would all be unnecessary.

A common result is that the system works in some markets but not in others. This is usually the product of a constant rather than a changing rule. For example, a stop-loss of a small fixed value will work well in a quiet or low-volatility market but will cause many missed trades as activity increases. Try to locate the problem and make the rules more adaptable to changing conditions.

A Winner in Disguise

One important twist on performance should not be overlooked: A consistently bad performer can become a consistent winner by doing just the opposite. Finding a profitable trend system in the range of shorter time intervals may seem to be a hopeless effort. On the other hand, systematic losses means that the price movement fails to trend, and every buy signal and sell signal is actually an overbought and oversold condition, predictive of price change. This can happen in markets that are heavily traded using systems; trend changes are temporarily exaggerated due to massive buy and sell orders.

Consistent losses do not always mean that the reverse trade will work. The net losses may be less than the total transaction costs; therefore, the opposite action will show even larger losses. The successful reverse system is one where the net losses far exceed the transaction costs.

Simple or Complex?

It is not necessary to create or acquire a system that is exceptionally complex in order to be successful. Simple systems, such as a dual moving average crossover, will be profitable as well. The difference between the performance of a simple system and a well-developed complex method is the risk/reward ratio and the magnitude of the equity swings.

Simple systems will catch the trends and take as much profit from the big moves as the more sophisticated approaches. It is the different markets that make distinctions. Added features should reduce the losses and modify the trading patterns during nontrending periods. This may be accomplished by identifying a trading range, using positions of varying size, or by the inclusion of economic data. Sometimes, more complex systems are just more complex, without improving results. In that case, use the simple system but retain larger reserves than normal.

Just Because It Doesn't Work in Practice Doesn't Mean It Won't Work in Theory

You thought that you followed all the rules by:

1. Precisely defining the system
2. Using enough test data
3. Evaluating performance by forward extrapolation
4. Investing enough to survive the worst losing streak
5. Trading a diversified portfolio
6. Following every signal

And still you lost all your money. . . . What happened?

Most likely, one or more of the six guidelines were not followed properly. Careful reassessment will usually prove that some corners were cut during the development process. For example, new traders often only test their ideas "in general" by spot checking a few selected commodities during years that seem to have "interesting" or "typical" movement. They assume that these shortcuts do not affect the results of the system. The advantage of computerized testing is that *all* years can be tested easily—the procedure necessary to produce a system that works in most markets.

The creator of a system has the temptation to force a system to work if it failed because of one or two large losses. An analyst can impose a filter on the selected trades to eliminate those that would have caused the major losses. Some traders may just assume that circumstances would have caused them to "pass" the trade rather than buy or sell in an "obviously" adverse market. This type of tampering doesn't work.

Suppose all the rules were followed. Then, the most common problem is to misjudge the volatility of the market. If the average loss in testing is compared to the size of the real trading losses, it is likely that the actual losses are substantially higher than the theoretic ones. That's not surprising. Some prices are more volatile now than they have been in the past; consequently, losses are larger. Executions are worse in faster moving markets. The combination of changing volatility and transaction costs will cause a big impact on even the most carefully followed methods.

Start Slowly

Trading an exceptionally small portfolio, one that can be lost 10 times over, will not hurt at the beginning. There must be a chance to see if the system performs the way it appeared in testing. The size and frequency of the losses should be checked as well as the equity cycle. When everything passes inspection, the investment can be increased slowly. Patience is an important ingredient for success.

Once the system has been checked out, it is even safer to turn the day-to-day executions over to someone else. It may be the only certain way to follow the rules precisely. Then, take a trip and don't leave an address. Tell the broker to liquidate the account if losses exceed a specified level. At this stage, detachment and objectivity are necessary.

GAMBLING TECHNIQUE—THE THEORY OF RUNS

The application of Gambling Theory to commodity trading satisfies two important conditions. First, it presumes no statistical advantage in the occurrence of profits and losses but concerns itself with the probable patterns. Each day of commodity trading could be treated as an occurrence of red or black—up or down price moves or profits. Second, Gambling Theory stresses money management under adverse conditions. A successful professional gambler and a commodities trader must both be highly disciplined and conserve capital. This section will look at a gambler's approach to money management and risk, using the *Theory of Runs*.

If the assumption is made that each day of commodity trading is unrelated to the previous day or that each day prices have an equal chance of going up or down, the situation closely resembles roulette. In Monte Carlo, the roulette wheel has 37 compartments: 18 black, 18 red, and 1 white, assuring a loss of 2.7% in the same way that brokerage costs are a handicap to trading. Continuously betting on only red or black will break even, less 2.7%, over long betting periods. The only way to change the odds is by money management—varying the size of the bets.

The most well-known method for winning in a gambling situation is based on the probability of successive wins, the Theory of Runs. On each spin of the wheel, the likelihood of the same color (red or black) reoccurring is 50%, or $\frac{1}{2}$ (ignoring the white slot). In order to define a run of three reds, it is necessary to show a black on each side, that is,

$$Black\text{-}Red\text{-}Red\text{-}Red\text{-}Black$$

otherwise the run may not be complete. If each color had a 50% chance of occurring, the probability of a run of three is

$$\frac{1}{2} \times \frac{1}{2} \times \frac{1}{2} \times \frac{1}{2} \times \frac{1}{2} = \left(\frac{1}{2}\right)^5$$

One run of three can be expected for every 32 spins of the wheel (coups). Extending that to runs of n consecutive reds gives $(1/2)^{n+2}$. For 256 coups, which is both a power of two and the approximate number of trading days in a year, there are the following possibilities for runs of red:

Run of length	Probability of occurrence	Expected number of occurrences	Total appearances of red
1	$\frac{1}{8}$	32	32
2	$\frac{1}{16}$	16	32
3	$\frac{1}{32}$	8	24
4	$\frac{1}{64}$	4	16
5	$\frac{1}{128}$	2	10
6	$\frac{1}{256}$	1	6
		Total appearances:	120

A run of greater than six is not expected to occur. Notice, however, that the total appearances of red is only 120, short 8. These 8 appearances could increase any of the runs from 1 through 6, or become a run of 7 or 8. The likelihood of a run greater than 6 is calculated using a geometric progression to get the sum of all probabilities greater than 6, or $(1/2)^{n+2}$, where $256 \geq n \geq 7$:

$$P = (1/2)^9 + (1/2)^{10} + \cdots + (1/2)^{256}$$

$$= \frac{(1/2)^9}{1 - (1/2)} = \frac{1}{256}$$

There is a single chance that there will be a run greater than 6 in 256 tries. The average length of a run greater than 6 turns out to be 8, based on the decreasing probability of occurrences of longer runs. The average length of all runs greater than n will be $n + 2$. That makes the table of runs complete, with the number of occurrences of red equal to 128.

Martingale and Anti-Martingale

The classic application of the Theory of Runs is by Martingale. His approach was to double the bet each time a loss occurred and start again after each win. To demonstrate how this works, it is necessary to use a table of uniform random numbers (see Appendix 1) and let all those numbers beginning with digits 0 through 4 be assigned to red and 5 through 9 to black. Figure 17-2, read left to

COUPS GENERATED FROM RANDOM NUMBERS

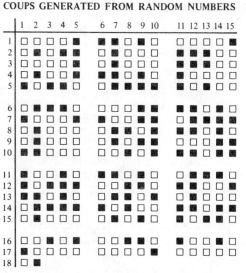

Figure 17-2   Coups generated from random numbers.

right, where open squares are red and solid squares are black, shows the first 257 assignments. Assuming that betting is on black, losses will depend on the longest run of red. The bet should be as large as possible and still withstand the longest run of red that is likely to occur. By using the results from the analysis of the length of runs, in 256 coups the likelihood is that only one run greater than six might occur, and that run would most probably be 8 in length. The probability of a run of 9 is $(1/2)^{11}$, or 1 in 1024. In 256 coups, the odds are about 3 to 1 against a run of 9 occurring.

Having decided that capitalization must withstand a run of 8, it can be figured that a bet of $1 doubled 8 times is $128. Divide the maximum amount of money to be risked by 128 and the result is the size of the initial bet. Each $1000 divided by 128 gives 7.8125, rounded down to $7; therefore, on the eighth consecutive occurrence of red, the bet will be $897. Counting the occurrences of runs on the simulated roulette table (Table 17-1), it is interesting to see that a run of eight but not seven appears.

Table 17-1   Random Occurrences of
Red and Black

Red	Black
35 runs of 1	35 runs of 1
12 runs of 2	14 runs of 2
7 runs of 3	11 runs of 3
7 runs of 4	3 runs of 4
2 runs of 5	2 runs of 5
2 runs of 6	
1 run of 8	
138 total occurrences	118 total occurrences

	1	2	3	4	5		6	7	8	9	10		11	12	13	14	15
1	1	2	4	8	[16]		[1]	[1]	1	[2]	1		2	4	8	16	[32]
2	1	[2]	1	[2]	[1]		1	[2]	1	2	4		[8]	[1]	[1]	1	2
3	4	8	16	32	[64]		1	[2]	1	2	4		[8]	[1]	[1]	1	2
4	4	[8]	1	2	[4]		[1]	[1]	1	[2]	1		[2]	1	2	4	8
5	[16]	1	[2]	[1]	1		2	[4]	[1]	[1]	[1]		[1]	1	[2]	1	2

Figure 17-3   Martingale betting pattern.

The results are within a reasonable approximation of expectations, and no runs greater than 8 occurred in either red or black. The betting would then proceed as shown in Figure 17-3, using an initial bet of $1. The numbers in the squares represent winning bets. Every occurrence of black is a winner. Although $64 is actually won on a single black coup, each sequence of runs nets only the initial bet due to the accumulated losses during that sequence. In the 256 coups represented in Table 17-1, there were a total of 65 distinct runs resulting in a profit of $65 ($455 based on a $7 initial bet), or about half of the initial capitalization ($128 or $1000, respectively). Without this strategy, betting on black to win equally, there would have been a loss of $20 on a $1 bet. The Martingale system therefore has a good chance of winning a reasonable amount.[4]

Anti-Martingale

The anti-Martingale approach offers a smaller chance of winning a large amount; it is exactly the opposite of the Martingale system. Instead of doubling each losing bet, the winners are doubled until a goal is reached. Because there is an excellent chance of 1 run of 6 in 256 coups and a similar chance of a longer run, this method counts on the long run occurring in the first half of the estimated coups (256 in this case).

A run of 6 would return $32 on a bet of $1, and a run of 8 would net $128. This would have lost if it had been applied to black in the test sequence; because there were 138 red coups with no runs greater than 5, there would have been a loss of $138. If the bet had been on red for a run of six, there would have been three wins, each for $94, and a loss of $118 for the total appearances of black. Waiting for a run of 8 would have won $128 and lost $117 on black by stopping right after the win. The success of the anti-Martingale method depends on how soon the long run appears. In 4096 coups, a run of 11 will occur once, returning $1024 on a bet of $1. In the same 4096 spins, there will be 2048 losses, showing that if the long run happens in the middle of play, the method breaks even; if sooner, it comes out ahead.

The Theory of Runs Applied to Commodities

Before applying either Martingale or anti-Martingale systems to commodity markets, it must be determined whether the movement of prices up or down is as

---

[4] The Martingale system is likely to work if the player could withstand adverse runs of 11, but casinos tend to limit bets to amounts significantly less than 2^{10} times the minimum bet.

uniform as in the case of roulette. A simple test was performed on a combined set of 21 diverse commodity contracts. The combined results of all up and down runs are shown in Table 17-2. The expected occurrences of both up and down were twice the probability of either a red or black coup occurring.

Certain differences between the expected and actual results should be noted in Table 17-2. Commodities consistently have fewer runs of one and more frequent runs of two, with a tendency also to fluctuate in a narrowing pattern about the expected length of a run (Figure 17-4). The probabilities might be used to decide the chances of the next trading day continuing in the direction of the prior days trend, noting that a 3- to 4-day run is as long as might be expected. The most interesting applications are in the betting strategies of the Martingale and anti-Martingale systems, applied to futures markets. The following sections show two possibilities.

Trading Daily Sequences. By combining the Theory of Runs with the direction of the trend, the chances of being on the correct side of the longest run are increased; the size of the price move in the direction of the trend may also tend to be larger. Assuming that the trend is up as determined from a chart or moving average, enter a long position on the close of a day in which the price moves lower.

If Martingale is being applied, double the position each day that prices move adversely. A single day in which prices move up should recoup all losses and net a reasonable profit. If the trend is sustained, there should be fewer days down and more days up, thereby yielding a better return to capitalization ratio. It may also be sound to hold the trade for 2 consecutive days in the profitable direction. If profits are taken while prices are moving higher and new long positions entered after 1 or even 2 days of lower prices, the ratio can all be much more favorable than a random occurrence of runs.

For the anti-Martingale approach, double the position after each profitable day. Take profits after runs of 3 and begin again after a reversal day. By trading with the trend, profit sequences may be increased to 4 days; it may also be expected that, on average, days in which prices move counter to the trend will be of lesser magnitude than those in the trend direction.

System Trading. A standard trend-following system has 30 to 40% successful trades (reliability) of varying profitability, which can be defined in terms of a profit/loss ratio. In considering the Martingale or anti-Martingale systems, it should be noted that the lower probability of occurrence of profitable trades would make the wait for a long run of profits less attractive. If there are 35% successful trades with a profit/loss ratio of 3 : 1, equal amounts of contracts traded have the following breakdown, assuming $750 each profit and $250 each loss:

Total trades	100 × $ 35 (comm.) =	$ −3,500
Profitable trades	35 × $750 =	$ 26,250
Losing trades	65 × $250 =	$−16,250
Net ($65 per trade)		$ 6,500

Taking these same figures and applying Martingale's system against a uniform sequence of two losses and one profit gives $285 as the first loss ($250 plus a $35

Table 17-2 Length of Commodity Runs

Length of Run	Expected Probability of Occurrence	21 Combined 1976 Occurrences		Cotton (6 years)		Copper (6 years)		Potatoes (6 years)	
		Expected	Actual	Expected	Actual	Expected	Actual	Expected	Actual
1	$\frac{1}{2}$	1225	1214	369	346	382	380	329	295
2	$\frac{1}{4}$	612	620	185	183	196	229	165	177
3	$\frac{1}{8}$	306	311	92	111	98	92	82	90
4	$\frac{1}{16}$	153	167	46	50	49	44	41	42
5	$\frac{1}{32}$	77	67	23	21	24	18	21	28
6	$\frac{1}{64}$	38	41	12	12	12	11	10	7
7	$\frac{1}{128}$	19	16	6	8	6	4	5	9
8	$\frac{1}{256}$	10	5	3	5	3	4	3	7
9	$\frac{1}{512}$	5	3	1	1	2	1	2	2
$\geqq 10$	$\frac{1}{1024}$	4	5	1	1	1	0	1	1
Total tested			2449		738		783		658

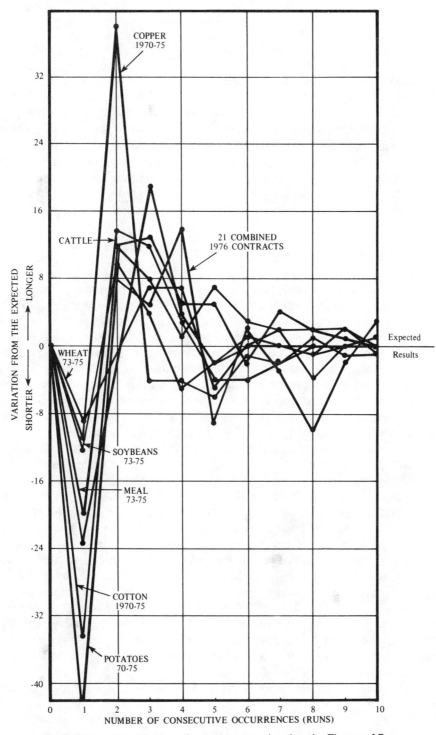

Figure 17-4 Actual commodity movement related to the Theory of Runs.

commission), \$570 for the second loss, then \$2145 for the profit, netting \$1290 for three trades, which would return \$145 per trade for equal contracts traded.

The disadvantage of the Martingale approach in commodities is that a long run of losing trades requires a large amount of capital. If it is necessary to keep a large reserve in the event of a series of losing trades, why not simply trade a larger number of contracts equally, without the Martingale system? Commodity trading differs from a pure gambling situation because a specific system will win in the long-term compared to losing at roulette. The results show that trading a larger number of contracts equally will return a higher profit than an application of the Martingale system requiring the same available capital; however, a less aggressive betting method that assumes favorable odds can improve return on investment.

SELECTIVE TRADING

Selective trading by manual intervention seems to be an unavoidable part of commodity trading. It is often based on the self-assurance that an individual analysis must be better than the combined perception of others. The beginning speculator has a special prejudicial filter, which works with great flexibility. It prevents the use of techniques that are counter to the "intuitive" senses; it allows the use of judgment to resist taking a small profit from the middle of a trend when there is much more possible in each move, and it helps interpret all news in favor of the position being held until it shows a profit. A trader who survives the first year has learned not to take a loss personally, to keep losses small, to establish and stay with a trading plan, and to filter out unsupported opinions.

Many technical systems are carried to extremes in an effort to automatically select only profitable trades. Two approaches to this are most common. The use of more than two moving averages is some way of isolating the "best" trend. In actually it may reduce the chances of identifying any trend. A system with many rules is another attempt at perfection. At its extreme, some of the rules apply to only one situation; it is not possible to know whether the rules are generally correct or simply a case of overfitting—most likely the latter.

Some degree of specialized selection is necessary in a trading system or plan. The rules must be clear and generalized. The use of other systems to enhance performance is not good because they often contain more complex interaction of rules that will be difficult to incorporate clearly within the main trading strategy. Not knowing everything about the other system, there may be inadvertent duplication of a faster trend, a 3-day cycle, or some other feature. Stay with pure elements. All ingredients of a plan can only be properly balanced if they are clearly identifiable.

Look for unique elements to combine, and use them only one. The selection of the speed of a moving average will be more important than how many moving averages to use. There may be an advantage to the double moving average approach, but a third, fourth, and so on, lose their significance. A momentum indicator bears a close resemblance to a moving average when its rules are to buy or sell on a move through the zero line. Both are heavily based on standard characteristics of a time-series and will not offer enough variation if both are applied to the same data. The methods should be fundamentally different. A technique that does not consider time would be a better complement to a moving average. A point-and-figure system or a support-and-resistance analysis of a charting nature would satisfy the requirements. The more complicated cycle and wave theories, contrary opinion, and other methods all view price movement in a completely different way than a moving average, even when applied to the same data. Two moving averages can be used without duplication when evaluating distinctly different data. A moving average of the closing price and one of the volume or open interest have no relationship other than the implications of the speed selection.

Filtering is a tool not restricted to price analysis, but applicable to money management, reliability, risk, portfolio selection, and other aspects of a trading program. The selection of which commodities to trade and how many contracts to enter is as important as the buy and sell signals. If the system itself corrects for high volatility markets by decreasing the distance of the stop-loss point (keeping the risk constant), it would be redundant to trade fewer positions of that commodity, thereby reducing the effects of any profits or losses relative to other commodities in a portfolio.

SYSTEM TRADE-OFFS

Most traders are continually searching for a well-defined system that has no losses; they are also realistic enough to know that most profit, loss, and risk decisions are all dependent on one another. Just as in Gambling Theory, a system can be structured to have frequent small losses and occasional large profits—or frequent small profits with large losses. One cannot create a system with such small losses that these losses are essentially zero without increasing the frequency of the losses to the point where profits rarely occur. In the commodities markets, the "cost of doing business" prevents such an approach from working.

The structure of a system requires the trader to choose between the frequency of profits to losses, the relative size of those profits and losses, and the number of opportunities that will be available to trade. These interrelationships will be interpreted differently for various types of systems.

Trend-Following Systems

The relative risks and rewards of a trend-following system are based on the selection of the trend speed. Using a simple moving average system (applied to closing prices) as an example, it can be seen in Figure 17-5 that a faster moving average (smaller number of days) will stay closer to the current price than a moving average that uses a larger number of days. The maximum risk is equal to the largest lag, as measured from the current price to the corresponding moving average value. This lag is limited by:

$$M = P - (L \times N)/2$$

where P is the current closing price, L is the limit move, and N is the number of days in the moving average.

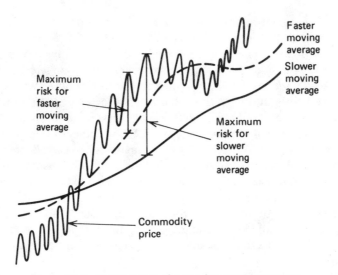

Figure 17-5   Relative risk of a moving average system.

The smaller losses of the faster trend system are kept in proportion to the profits because of the same system sensitivity. The price changes of smaller magnitude, which cause the moving average to change direction and hold losses to a minimum, also break the sustained trends into shorter movements. The net results are more frequent trades with relatively small losses and modest profits. Longer-term trends cause fewer trades by holding to the market direction for a longer time. This results in larger profits and correspondingly larger losses.

The risk of a single trade being small or large is not necessarily a complete measure of trading risk. Because there are more losses than profits in normal trend-following systems, it is important to consider the sequence of losses as part of the ultimate risk of trading. It is the combination of these losses that provides a reasonable comparison in determining whether a slow or fast moving average system has the best profit-to-loss ratio.

Countertrend Systems

The risk and reward structure of a countertrend method is different from that of a trend-following approach. Because a countertrend system, such as an oscillator, contrary opinion, or any "overbought/oversold" analysis, sets restrictions on prospective profits, it should not also limit losses. It is possible to distribute profits and losses in various ways with regard to their size and frequency. The combinations possible are:

1. A few large profits and frequent small losses
2. Many small profits and a few large losses
3. Larger profits less often
4. Smaller profits more often

5. More opportunities with greater risk
6. Fewer opportunities with less risk

The first two points are easily applied to trend-following; the others are most appropriate for countertrend trading. For example, consider a sideways market, or any price series that has been detrended as in Figure 17-6, so that it does not exhibit any overall trending bias. Assuming that there is a normal distribution of prices, there is a clustering near the center and less frequent peaks and valleys as prices move further away from the middle. Construct an overbought/oversold indicator, which can be categorized as *slightly* (S), *moderately* (M), or *extremely* (E) overbought or oversold, by drawing lines on Figure 17-6.

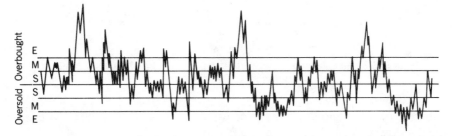

Figure 17-6   Countertrend alternatives using detrended price series.

It can be seen that there are more opportunities to buy a *slightly oversold* market and sell a *slightly overbought* market; all prices must pass through the area closest to the center before attaining a more overbought or oversold condition. Therefore, the *opportunities* must increase as profit goals decrease. But what about the risk? If profits are limited, risk must be restricted to a small part of the potential profits, or not limited by a dollar amount but by a patterned condition. For countertrend trading, an attempt to make losses small relative to a small profit is inconsistent. Considering the situation shown in Figure 17-6, the frequency of losses would increase so rapidly (as losses are kept smaller) that they would overwhelm the fixed profit potential. If losses are not restricted, they will be larger when there are more opportunities with smaller price objectives. The minimum risk occurs on a single trade taken at the absolute extreme points. Figure 17-7 shows the relationships that exist in a standard countertrend system.

All systems have trade-offs. In order to reduce the losses, either the profits or the frequency of opportunities must be reduced. A trend-follower looking for the big move must also take a big risk. In the development of a system or trading philosophy, each person must settle on the combination of risk, reward, and opportunity that best suits him or her.

The Commodex Method of Combining Elements

The *Commodex* system was first presented in 1959 and is still active, published daily by *Commodity Futures Forecast* in New York. Commodex combines the components most acceptable to the experienced trader in a unique weighting

Figure 17-7   Relationship of profits to risk per trade based on opportunities.

method. It includes moving averages, price momentum, and open interest to calculate a trend index.

The most interesting aspect of the Commodex system is its ranking process, intended to produce a relative strength value for each trend. Using a 10- and 20-day double moving average, the system scores the current market performance to establish the value of the trending component. Bullish and bearish values are calculated by looking at three situations independently: the simple moving-average signals derived from both the long- and short-term trends, and the double moving average signal generated by combining the two trends. The two techniques of single and double moving averages are exactly as treated in Chapter 5. The most important of the three factors is the long-term trend; second is the short-term trend, and last the relative position of the fast to the slow moving average. The strongest upward moving trend is generated when current prices are above both the faster and slower moving averages and the faster average is below the slower. The opposite positions would result in the strongest downward trending component. Trends are considered neutral if the most important element, the long-term moving average, conflicts with the other two factors.

The rate of change in open interest is considered a secondary reinforcement of the trend. Using a concept different from the usual charting techniques, Commodex considers it a bullish sign if there is an increasing "growth momentum" in open interest combined with rising prices. The growth momentum is the difference between the rate of increase of the open interest and the 20-day moving average of the open interest. The concept of continuing a bull move with rising prices and rising open interest is a classic concept of charting. The bear move is confirmed with rising open interest and falling prices. Commodex also considers a drop in open interest along with falling prices to be a bullish factor. The movement of volume is treated in the same manner as open interest and can confirm a bull or bear trend. An increasing volume momentum with rising prices is support of an upward move; other combinations indicate bear trends.

Added together the signals range from a strong "buy" to a strong "sell" with lesser degrees in between. The system must be given credit for the quantification and balancing of these elements, which are generally treated as highly interpretive charting techniques. The rules for applying the daily signals to trading combine both the individual strength of the signal with the movement of the Commodex trend index. The trend index itself acts as an overbought-oversold indicator, encouraging profits at specified levels and considering a position reversal in more extreme situations; stops are placed using the 20-day moving average with predetermined band penetrations. Additional objectives are based on the profits accrued from a trade, with a 50% return justifying a protective stop on part of the positions, and a 100% profit requiring the liquidation of half the position. These money-management concepts are an important aspect of any system and tend to round out Commodex.

The Commodex system has been used as an example of combining techniques that have been studied individually in previous sections. It is a good example because each element is simple to understand and avoids duplication; it has single and double moving averages (with and without bands), momentum indicators derived from volume and open interest, an overbought-oversold indicator formed from a combination of all elements, trading stops and liquidation based on money management and inverse pyramiding.

Combining Trends and Trading Ranges

Trends and trading ranges represent two distinct philosophies of technical analysis. A trend is concerned with the periodic tendency of prices to move in one direction without a limiting objective, and a trading range is a definition of price containment. The role of time is different for the two approaches. The trend must advance with regularity (time series) whereas prices within a trading range can move in any direction with varying speed, providing the upper and lower bounds are not violated.

Trading ranges and trends take turns dominating price movement. Long-term trends are most obvious, as seen in the buying power of the U.S. dollar and the Consumer Price Index. When there is no actual or anticipated change in fundamental factors, prices fluctuate in a narrow range, bounded by *support* and *resistance* levels. The top of a trading range is often wider than the bottom because of the inherently greater volatility at higher prices; but even with the broader formation, there is a clear point at which prices have gone higher and are no longer within the trading range.

It often happens that the two techniques of price trend and trading ranges are in conflict: The trend is up and a resistance level is encountered, or the downtrend is stopped by a support level. It makes sense to combine both features. The simplest way is to use the trading range while prices are within that area and follow the trend when prices break out either above or below (Figure 17-8).

The exact rules depend on the size of the trading range. If the range is narrow, a moving average buy or sell signal invariably occurs at the resistance or support level and is met with an initial reversal. For a larger range, a medium speed moving-average signal may occur closer to the center of the range and allow some

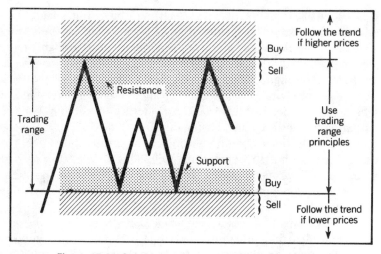

Figure 17-8   Combining the trend and trading range.

opportunity for trend profit before resistance is encountered. For very wide ranges, there may be ample latitude for a moving average to signal entry and close-out without the interference of support and resistance levels. One method of combining the two techniques is to use whichever signal is generated, regardless of the system. The following combinations of short position entry and exit are possible for medium to wide ranges:

1. Enter a new short position when the moving average turns down.
2. Enter a new short position when prices enter the sell zone around the resistance level.
3. Enter a new short position when prices fall below the support area, then close-out the short position when the moving average turns up.
4. Close-out a short position when prices enter the buy zone above the support level.
5. Close-out a short position when prices break through a resistance level moving up.

The same rules apply in reverse for long positions. The advantage of this filtering method is that new short trades are not entered at support levels, which causes immediate losses or prolonged trades of little result.

TRADING LIMITS—A DAMPENING EFFECT

The existence of trading limits in the U.S. markets has always been the concern of novice speculators who seem convinced that their first entry into the market will result in an adverse locked-limit move, stripping them of their future and happiness overnight. There is no doubt that many people have suffered from being "caught" on the wrong side of a move, but trading limits would tend to protect rather than harm them. The limits established by the exchanges were intended to allow free trading within the normal range of price fluctuation. If properly established, these limits should rarely be reached. As prices rise, the volatility of the market increases and so the limits must be expanded to correspond to the level. At this point, the risks become proportionately greater and margins are raised.

The purpose of limits is to prevent an immediate reaction to unexpected news from moving prices to unjustifiable levels. The first reaction to bad news is usually more extreme than is realistic and when proper assessment of the problem is completed, the results are rarely as bad as initially thought. Limits also serve to give the losing trader more time to capitalize the position, rather than be forced to liquidate.

Frequency of Limit Moves

Sugar prices, which had a spectacular rise in 1974, can serve as an extreme case of changing volatility. Beginning in 1969, Table 17-3 shows the remarkable price move seen in the frequency of limit moves. The contracts shown have no duplicate dates and do not include the actual delivery month.

The obvious conclusion to be drawn from the pattern of the sugar market is that limits did not expand quickly enough at higher price levels. In 1975, 22.6% of all trading days closed at the limit; at low price levels, the limits were of no consequence. The 1974 price of sugar increased by 15 times its 1969 price while the limits only expanded from 50 to 200 points, a factor of four. The use of a trading system tested in a market with few limit closes should not be expected to operate effectively in a limit-intense situation; speculators should be wary of these markets.

The only realistic way of comparing the effects of limit moves against a limitless market is to compare the U.S. and London exchanges. Using the May 77 Coffee contract for the month of February 1977, we can show three separate examples of limit moves in the U.S. contracts and the corresponding London action. Figure 17-9 illustrates the closing prices of markets on the same day. Two problems must be considered: the conversion of sterling to U.S. dollars, which was fixed at $1.70 for the entire comparison, and the overlapping hours of the New

Table 17-3 Frequency of Limit Moves

	Total Days Examined	Days Closing at Limit	Percentage of Limit Closes	Range of Closing Prices	Exchange Limits (¢/lb)
Sep 70	248	0	.0	2.91–4.01	.50
Sep 71	249	0	.0	2.74–5.08	.50
Sep 72	240	18	7.5	4.26–9.17	.50
Sep 73	239	9	3.8	5.44–10.50	.50
Sep 74	239	40	16.7	7.56–28.15	.50–2.00
Sep 75	239	54	22.6	11.51–50.82	1.00–2.00
Sep 76	238	3	1.3	12.07–18.65	1.00

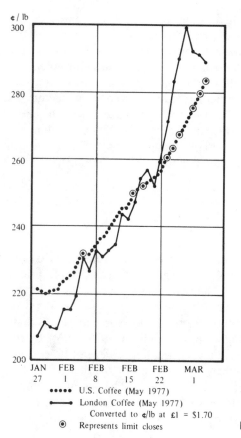

¢ / lb

U.S. Coffee (May 1977)
London Coffee (May 1977)
Converted to ¢/lb at £1 = $1.70
Represents limit closes

Figure 17-9   Limit moves, May 77 coffee.

York Coffee and Sugar Exchange and the London Sugar Exchange. The exchange hours may have some difference in the daily price but should not appreciably effect the comparison.

The first U.S. locked-limit day was on February 7, when the New York coffee prices for the May 77 contract moved to 230.82 (up 300 points). On the same day, London prices for the May 77 contract moved from 218.80 to 230.56 (actually 2883 to 3038 sterling). A trader who closed out his position on the open in the London market would have taken a fill of 2850 and a loss of 12.67 cents per pound relative to the U.S. market. The traders locked into their New York position could have gotten out on the open on February 8 at 233.50, a loss of 568 points. Had both the U.S. and London traders waited for the closing prices as shown in Figure 17-9, the corresponding losses would have been reduced to 1176 points in London and 318 points in New York.

The second case was on February 17 and 18 when the U.S. market stayed locked at the limit for two days. A trader entering the market in London on the prior day at 241.91 (3187.50 sterling) could have gotten out on the next day at 247.07 (3255.07) for a loss of 516 points. The corresponding New York trader would have entered at 246.00 and exited at 254.50 for a loss of 810 points.

Remarkably, the London coffee prices had moved to 252.04 by the time the New York market was trading again. London prices had gained 1013 points during the time that a locked-limit U.S. market gained only 850 points. In both cases, the volatility of the London market with no limits was much greater than the U.S. equivalent and the results do not show any disadvantage to trading limits.

The third case of locked-limit moves began on February 24. On the day prior to the first locked-limit day, the U.S. market traded actively even after the London Exchange moved up an equivalent of 698 points. There should have been ample time that day or even the prior day, when the U.S. market traded at the limit but closed lower for any trader to exit an undesirable position. Figure 17-9 shows the larger moves of the London market peaking and starting down to meet the plodding U.S. prices. The market with no limits has overreacted to the bullish news by at least 1000 points. Of course, for traders who didn't get out of New York coffee soon enough, the overreaction of the London market was not very gratifying.

Due to the frequency of locked-limit moves during the exceptional periods, most exchanges have changed the way daily trading limits are established. At one time, an exchange committee was convened to review limits; now, limits automatically expand to meet conditions. The normal policy is that, following a trading day in which prices closed "at the limit," limits expand to $1\frac{1}{2}$ their initial value. They may remain at this level for 1 or 2 days, provided prices continue to close at either limit (higher or lower). Limits will then expand to twice the initial range; if a locked-limit move persists, limits are removed for one day. After this, or after any day that prices do not close at the limit, the pattern begins again with the initial limit value. Occasionally, the initial value may be altered by the exchange.

GOING TO EXTREMES

In 1974, public awareness of inflation caused an overwhelming interest in all forms of hedging, with large numbers of naive investors purchasing silver and gold as currency protection. Many sophisticated investors turned to the futures markets, which offered leverage on their purchases; some learned how to use the markets themselves and others relied on advice.

One investment system that was sold at this time was more of a leveraged substitute for the purchase of bouillon than a trading strategy. At the time it was published, it had always worked—the sponsor of the system stood behind it with his reputation. The rules of the system were:

1. Trade silver futures because of their intrinsic value, historic performance, potential, and fundamental demand with short supply.
2. Use the futures contract between three and seven months from delivery to combine the advantages of liquidity and duration.
3. Always buy, never sell, because it is always successful.
4. Buy whenever you like. Although any sophisticated method can be used, it won't matter in the long run—any guess will do just as well. Follow the same method for adding to positions or reentering after closing out a trade.
5. Close-out the position when there is a profit, not before.
6. Meet all margin calls—don't let the market beat you.
7. Invest $5000 per contract (5000 troy ounces). This will allow a $1 per ounce adverse move (silver was at $4.50 per ounce).

8. Whenever you need reinforcement, reread the reasoning behind this system.
9. Do not let anyone or anything interfere with following this system.

How did the investors do? It depended on when they started. Entering in the first half of 1975, shortly after the system was released, showed individual contract returns ranging from profits of 51¢ to losses of 18¢ per ounce. A drop in silver prices then produced losses of up to $1.02 per ounce for the next 9 months, followed by a 2-month rally, and losses again. This system would have worked from 1979 to February 1980 and then lost for the next 6 years. An investor following these rules, entering at a chance place would have had more than a 10 : 1 likelihood of losing. Any profit made would have been given back if the investor persisted in following the method.

   In trying to understand how a system such as this can have a chance of reaching the public, remember the time in which it was introduced. With prices increasing drastically, food shortages, and publicity over the devaluing U.S. dollar, the rationale of the system seemed justifiable. There was serious talk about leveraged "inflation funds" using futures. These systems fill an immediate need, without regard to long-term consequences. There is no doubt that, if high inflation returns, systems just like this one will reappear.

SIMILARITY OF SYSTEMS

A primary concern of both the government regulatory agency (CFTC) and individual traders is the similarity of computer-based systems that are used to manage large positions. If the propagation of technical trading systems have similar foundation and testing methods, it is possible that many of them will produce signals on nearly the same day. That is, these systems may appear different in their rules and parameters, but they could be essentially quite similar.

   First, consider the extreme cases, where two systems with the same trend-following philosophy have the same profit over the same period of time. Will the signals occur on the same day? Are they on the same side of the market most of the time? Figure 17-10 shows one combination that has a low correlation given this situation.

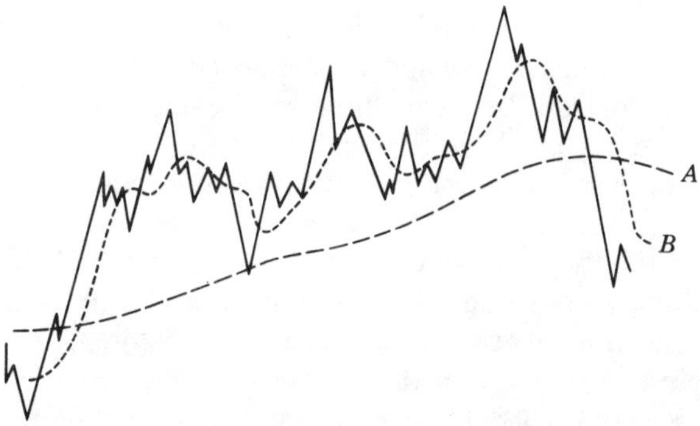

Figure 17-10   Two trend-following systems, with a low correlation in trading profile.

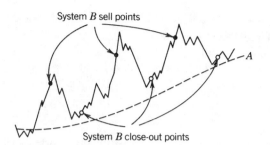

System B sell points

System B close-out points

Figure 17-11   Two systems that are negatively correlated: A is a long-term trend-following method, and B is a countertrend technique.

System A is a slow trend-following method, which avoids the choppy markets but nets only a small profit. System B jumps in and out, capturing profits quickly but with frequent losses. They both return the same profits. System B is on the same side of the market as A about 50% of the time because the overall trend was up; therefore, it cannot be negatively correlated but it could have a low positive correlation. If system B were not as fast as in this illustration, the positive correlation would be greater.

If system A remained a slow trend-following method and system B was a countertrend technique, there might be a negative correlation, as shown in Figure 17-11. When system A holds the same trend position, system B trades counter to that trend. Positions are always opposite; therefore, the correlation is negative. Both systems return the same profits.

From these examples, it is not clear that computer-based systems would result in highly correlated trades; however, the reality of the issue may be different from the theory. Lukac, Brorsen, and Irvin[5] performed such a study. They compared 12 popular trading techniques (mostly trend-following) over 12 varied commodities markets for the years 1978–1984. Each system was optimized, using three years of data, and the best parameters used to trade the next year. The systems selected were

1. *Channel systems*
    a. Closing price channel
    b. MII price channel
    c. L-S-O price channel
2. *Momentum/oscillators*
    a. Directional Indicator
    b. Directional Movement
    c. Range quotient
    d. Reference deviation
3. *Moving averages*
    a. Moving average with percent band
    b. Dual moving average

[5] Louis P. Lukac, B. Wade Brorsen, and Scott H. Irwin, *Similarity of Computer Guided Technical Trading Systems,* CSFM-124, Working Paper Series, Columbia Futures Center, Columbia University Business School, New York, Mar. 1986.

4. *Systems with trailing stops*
    a. Parabolic Time/Price System
    b. Alexander's Filter Rule
    c. Combined Directional Movement and Parabolic Time/Price System

The study used three measures to test system similarity:

1. The percentage of time systems are on the same side of the market (long or short).
2. The percentage of buy or sell signals that occurred on the same day, or within a few days of one another.
3. The correlation of aggregate monthly portfolio returns.

The results show a significant positive correlation in the system profitability (Table 17-4). However, there is no pattern that shows that one particular type of system is notably more correlated than others. The "Parabolic" and "Directional Parabolic" systems are most similar because one is based on the other.

Only four of the systems were significantly profitable: CHL, MII, DRP, and DMC. The correlations of those systems do not seem any more significant than others that were not profitable. In Table 17-5, the percentage of trades that occur on the same day is very low. Table 17-6, showing the percentage of trades that

Table 17-4   Correlations of Aggregate Monthly Returns from All Twelve Trading Systems[b,c]

System	CHL	PAR	DRM	RNQ	DRP	MII	LSO	REF	DMC	DRI	MAB
PAR	.57										
DRM	.72	.61									
RNQ	.70	.41	.70								
DRP	.65	.81	.79	.57							
MII	.75	.54	.67	.73	.67						
LSO	.59	.43	.53	.68	.54	.70					
REF	.55	.37	.57	.66	.52	.54	.60				
DMC	.72	.41	.68	.78	.55	.74	.58	.57			
DRI	.71	.42	.69	.77	.55	.70	.59	.66	.64		
MAB	.72	.55	.75	.74	.69	.69	.63	.60	.78	.72	
ALX	.58	.55	.62	.55	.57	.57	.58	.51	.52	.56	.57

[a] CHL = Channel   LSO = L-S-O Price Channel
    PAR = Parabolic   REF = Reference Deviation
    DRM = Directional Movement   DMC = Dual Moving Average Crossover
    RNQ = Range Quotient   DRI = Directional Indicator
    DRP = Directional Parabolic   MAB = Moving Average with % Price Band
    MII = MII Price Channel   ALX = Alexander's Filter Rule

[b] All coefficients significant at the .01% level, with the exception of REF and PAR coefficient which is significant at the .05% level.
[c] Shaded items indicate profitable systems.

Table 17-5 Percent of Trades That Occur on the Same Day[a,b,d]

System	Trading System[c]										
	CHL	PAR	DRM	RNQ	DRP	MII	LSO	REF	DMC	DRI	MAB
PAR	19*										
DRM	25**	21**									
RNQ	22**	9	15								
DRP	30**	93**	48**	10							
MII	20*	15	10	28**	17						
LSO	22**	13	17	27**	18	23**					
REF	12	7	7	11	9	12	14				
DMC	16	6	8	28**	6	12	18	19*			
DRI	18	9	14	38**	10	32**	22**	15	25**		
MAB	28**	18	23**	23**	27**	18	25**	11	19*	23**	
ALX	12	20*	12	19*	20*	9	17	10	10	16	17

[a] Percent of trades that occur on the same day by each pair of systems.
[b] Significance assuming a binomial distribution with * denoting 95% confidence limits and ** denoting 99% confidence limits.

[c] CHL = Channel   LSO = L-S-O Price Channel
   PAR = Parabolic   REF = Reference Deviation
   DRM = Directional Movement   DMC = Dual Moving Average Crossover
   RNQ = Range Quotient   DRI = Directional Indicator
   DRP = Directional Parabolic   MAB = Moving Average with % Price Band
   MII = MII Price Channel   ALX = Alexander's Filter Rule

[d] Shaded items indicate profitable systems.

Table 17-6 Percent of Trades That Occur Within a 5-Day Interval[a,b,d]

System	Trading System[c]										
	CHL	PAR	DRM	RNQ	DRP	MII	LSO	REF	DMC	DRI	MAB
PAR	47										
DRM	56*	52									
RNQ	48	32	42								
DRP	57*	97**	67**	43							
MII	49	44	48	71**	58**						
LSO	49	31	40	66**	43	46					
REF	32	22	33	43	30	28	37				
DMC	41	32	38	70**	48	35	53	57*			
DRI	51	35	44	68**	40	52	58**	43	52		
MAB	53	38	50	59**	54	43	53	38	58**	53	
ALX	33	42	39	51	54	30	45	32	31	50	62**

[a] Percent of trades that occur within a five day interval by each pair of systems.
[b] Significance assuming a binomial distribution with * denoting 95% confidence limits and ** denoting 99% confidence limits.

[c] CHL = Channel   LSO = L-S-O Price Channel
   PAR = Parabolic   REF = Reference Deviation
   DRM = Directional Movement   DMC = Dual Moving Average Crossover
   RNQ = Range Quotient   DRI = Directional Indicator
   DRP = Directional Parabolic   MAB = Moving Average with % Price Band
   MII = MII Price Channel   ALX = Alexander's Filter Rule

[d] Shaded items indicate profitable systems.

occurred within 5 days, is more difficult to assess since two fast systems may be out-of-phase but within 5 days of one another. Correlations are, in general, fairly high.

The study concludes that computer-based systems "trade on the same day significantly more often than would randomly be expected but the actual percentage of trades that occur on the same day is small." These systems have the potential to move market prices, but it is not expected to happen often.

18

System Management

A trading system alone will not assure success without an overall management program. Systems have losing streaks that will ruin any investor with inadequate resources and poor timing; a speculator must decide the initial capitalization, the commodities to trade, and when to increase or decrease the commitment. The first part of this chapter discusses capitalization and shows why many traders will be successful for months and then lose everything in only a few days. It will explain the choices in pyramiding and offer alternatives of less risk. The last section analyzes when a system is performing properly and when it is not living up to its expectations.

LIQUIDITY

The realities of trading are directly related to the liquidity of the market. Even though liquidity can have more than one meaning, lack of liquidity has only one trading result: poor execution. A *liquid* market does not necessarily mean good fills, but an *illiquid* market assures bad ones. Two types of illiquidity are most often encountered in the markets:

1. Fast moving markets, in which there are mostly buyers or sellers, and few traders willing to take the other side of the position
2. Inactive markets, usually in the deferred months where there is less interest in either hedging or speculating.

The fast market is the result of a supply/demand imbalance, or perceived imbalance, where the market is moving in a direction agreeable to all. The few hedgers and traders willing to take a position do little to offset the vast number of orders that flood the floor, pushing the price in the direction of the trend. In the inactive market, a premium must be paid to interest another trader in taking the opposite trade. This will only succeed in an inactive market when the bid or offered price clearly appears to give the other trader a "guaranteed" short-term profit.

The illiquidity of a market produces the most important execution cost, often greater than a sizable commission and sometimes unreasonably large. Ginter and Richie[1] have described this as a function of the order size, volume, and the speed of the market, in a single formula:

$$C = K \times \frac{Q \times V}{L_c \times L_o}$$

where C = cost of execution due to liquidity
Q = size of the order entered
V = volatility of the commodity
L_c = volume of the commodity (all deliveries)
L_o = volume of the specific option (delivery month)
K = constant factor

The volatility V might be the daily range (high minus low), or a factor of the standard deviation of the range. This would provide a measure of how much volume would move the market a specified number of points. The total volume (liquidity) L_c is important because it implies liquidity due to interdelivery spreading. Volume also serves as a measurement of the general interest in the product. More active trading in other contract months opens the possibility for trading in all months given the right circumstances.

The constant factor K will vary according to the nature of the order being placed and the current direction of the price with regard to that order. If prices are moving higher and a buy order is placed, K will be large; if prices are moving higher and a sell order is placed, K will be smaller. The investor can see that trading overhead, including both commissions and other execution costs, will have considerably greater impact on systems that trade more often, have smaller average profits, and trade in the direction of the trend. Given a choice between systems of equal gross profits, the investor should favor the method of fewest trades in the most liquid markets.

CAPITAL

Success does not depend on having enough capital, but in using it properly.

Dixon G. Watts

Every type of system has its own profit-and-loss cycle, depending on what price patterns or behavior it is measuring. A simple moving average will be profitable in a trending market and lose in a nontrending one; a system that operates within a trading range will profit from nontrending situations. It has been estimated that prices spend 70 to 80% of their total time in a nontrending movement; therefore, when using a trend-following system, it is likely that trading will begin in a nontrending period. Because the risk of the system during a sustained trendless market may be unknown, it is best to start small. Find the minimum amount that

[1] G. Ginter and J. Richie, "Data Errors and Price Distortions," in Perry J. Kaufman (Ed.), *Technical Analysis in Commodities*, Wiley, New York, 1980.

can be used to follow the system in a representative manner. During the start-up period, it is best to profit on 10 or 20% of capital than lose on 100%. Always begin slowly—actual trading performance is rarely as good as expected.

Establish the maximum margin based on the experiences of nontrending markets. If uncertain, keep the total margin well under 50% of available capital. The following sections review ways of increasing margin and compounding profits.

Diversification reduces both risk and reward; done properly, the risk is reduced more than the reward. Using a well-distributed portfolio for a system whose risks are known, a larger portion of the total capital can be allocated to margin. Advantages of statistics become apparent in the netting out of profits and losses daily; the majority of trades will move in a favorable direction a majority of the time. The volatility of a portfolio will be dampened by this netting effect; a trade with a slow upward trend and a distant stop-loss will be offset by a slow downward trending position in another commodity.

An undercapitalized account cannot be traded safely by selecting a system with a favorable risk-reward profile. Because there is very little "staying power," the trader must accept the fact that there is a small chance of success. There are two choices, based on the personality of the trader:

1. Try for the maximum profit possible on a single trade with the capital available. If it loses, trading is halted. If it profits, there may be enough capital for a diversified approach.
2. Take a low-risk approach, which allows the most losses for the given capital. This increases the time in the market, with comparably reduced profits. It is necessary to have an unusually long run of small profits to reach a point of success.

There are two important rules in managing an account. The first, *don't meet margin calls,* implies that a margin call represents an objective identification of a bad trade, or a system that is not meeting expectations. A margin call is a time to review trading performance. *Liquidate your worst position* when lightening up. The profitable trades have proved that they are trending or performing properly; the losing ones have proved they are not. Stay with the good positions and liquidate the worst.

The management of capital is especially important at the beginning stages of trading although it continually affects results. At some point, every trader wants to compound profits—a system that is profitable can be more profitable. This philosophy most often leads to disastrous results. The next sections present methods for measuring risk, followed by a traditional and a conservative approach to compounding and increasing leverage.

MEASURING RISK

An important part of both system development and money management is the recognition, measurement, and ultimately, the limiting of risk. Broadly speaking, money management is the art of limiting the risk of a portfolio while maximizing its return. To perform these tasks, it is first necessary to select, or develop, profitable trading strategies to be used for each commodity. It is the results of these strategies, both simulated and real, that will be used to structure a risk-controlled trading program (see the discussion of "System Trade-Offs" in Chapter 17).

Selecting a Trading Model

A trading model is a set of rules and formulas that, when applied to a price series, yields trading signals. These signals might be as simple as buy and sell "on the close" or complex contingent orders involving multiple delivery months and markets. To *simulate* results, the model must be well-defined, that is, all the rules must be logically stated and programmable. Interpretive methods, such as many charting techniques, cannot be simulated; they depend on patterns that cannot be defined in advance. The use of actual trading results for later analysis is always preferable and is not limited to computerized systems.

Suppose there is a choice of systems to trade, and the daily equity of each is available. If only one can be selected, which should it be? There are some characteristics of performance that are universal:[2]

1. Larger profits are better than smaller profits.
2. Small short-term fluctuations are better than large, short-term fluctuations.
3. Upwards equity surges (profits) are better than downward surges (losses).

Naive Performance Criteria. The use of a single piece of information is not sufficient to satisfy the basic criteria stated above. The system with the *maximum profit* is not necessarily a good choice. There might have been a run of losses greater than the investment before profitability was achieved. Similarly, the risk alone is not sensible. The system with the smallest risk is one that never trades. A valid performance measurement techniques must include a comparison of risk and reward.

The Sharpe Ratio. The classic measurement of performance is the *Sharpe Ratio* (SR), expressed as

$$SR = \frac{E - I}{\sigma}$$

where E is the expected return, I is the risk-free interest rate, and σ is the standard deviation, or fluctuation, of returns. For practical purposes, E should be an annualized rate of return in percent, and I can be omitted. The inclusion of I is important when a large part of the performance is a contribution of T-bill interest, or when the equity streams being compared are inconsistent in their use of interest income. The standard deviation of the equity is a way of measuring risk.

The SR satisfies the first criteria, that all else being equal, higher profits are

[2] Norm Strahm, "Preference Space Evaluation of Trading System Performance," in Perry J. Kaufman (Ed.), *Handbook of Futures Markets*, Wiley, New York, 1984.

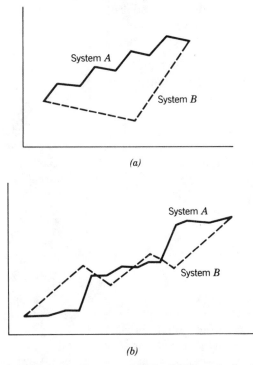

(a)

(b)

Figure 18-1   Two cases in which the Sharpe ratio fails. (a) The order in which profits and losses occur. (b) Surges in profits versus evenly distributed profits and losses.

better. It does not satisfy either of the other requirements because it cannot distinguish between:

1. Consecutive small losses (System B) and alternating small losses (System A).
2. Large surges of profits and large losses (Figure 18-1).

Clearly, System A is best in both cases.

Schwager[3] has presented a comprehensive study of evaluation techniques. Although each method may emphasize a particular equity trait, he seems to favor the *Average Maximum Retracement* (AMR). This method answers the question: "For each day, what would be the retracement if one had started trading the system on the worst possible trade entry date?" The AMR is the average of the daily maximum retracement values.

$$\text{AMR} = \frac{1}{N} \sum_{i=1}^{N} \text{POS}(MCE_i - TE_i)$$

where

$$\text{POS}(X) = \begin{bmatrix} x \text{ if } x > 0 \\ 0 \text{ if } x < 0 \end{bmatrix}$$

[3] Jack D. Schwager, *A Complete Guide to the Futures Markets*, Wiley, New York, 1984.

and *MCE* = closed-out equity (realized profits) on any trade entry date prior to *i*
    TE_i = total equity on day *i*
    N = total number of days of equity data

When $TE_i > MCE$, all traders will have a profit on day *i*, regardless of when they began. Schwager suggests that a much simpler computation would use only the low total equity day of each month; it would give a rough but good approximation.

Potential Risk. The measurement of risk may include other safety factors. Once a large loss has occurred, it is likely that a larger one may follow. It is unreasonable to think that all future losses will be smaller than the maximum already experienced. This *potential for loss* can be expressed as a probability by calculating the standard deviation of all equity drops, measured from lows to previous high equity points, and creating an *equity drop ratio* (EDR):

$$\text{EDR} = \frac{E}{\sigma(ED)}$$

where *E* is the annualized return (equity), and $\sigma(ED)$ is the standard deviation of the equity drops. Although this is not far from Schwager's approach, it satisfies all three of the original criteria: higher profits are favored, the order of profits and losses will result in larger and smaller net equity drops, and large gains are not penalized because only the drops are used to measure risk.

The conservative investors may want to include some additional simple considerations of potential risk. All else being equal, systems with greater risk will be:

1. Those tested with samples that are too small
2. Those that have not shown any (or few) equity drops
3. Those that concentrate on fewer product groups (not properly diversified)
4. Those that compound positions

Efficient Frontier. Using the risk measurement, it is always helpful to visualize how one system performs with respect to others. A plot of each system using its return and risk as coordinates will appear as in Figure 18-2.

Clearly, the best system would be the one that had the highest returns (*C*) if all of them had the same risk; or *A*, the one with the lowest risk, if it also had the

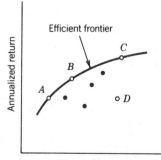

Risk measurement   Figure 18-2 Efficient frontier.

highest profit. The three systems, A, B, and C, are similar because they have the highest returns for their level of risk. However, each used a different degree of leverage, or reserves, and therefore had close to the same profit to risk ratio but in different magnitudes. The choice between systems A, B, and C is a personal preference and is discussed later.

RISK CONTROL

Risk can be reduced with the proper application of classic management techniques. These include capitalization, conservation of capital, varying leverage, and diversification.

Capitalization

The effects of larger and smaller investments has been discussed earlier in this chapter. For the purposes of risk control, it is necessary to invest an adequate amount to ensure survival during a reasonably unexpected losing period. A major reduction in risk is achieved by diversification, which requires adequate capital to trade a selection of commodities and/or systems.

Conservation of Capital

One of the objectives of a rational investor is the *conservation of capital*. It is the assurance that the investor has been given the most opportunities for success. This translates into keeping losses small using a stop-loss or comparable rules that respond quickly to negative price moves (''small'' is relative to capitalization or margin). A trend-following system is typically one of conservation of capital. Once a trend position is established, it is held as long as prices continue in the direction of the position; it is closed-out when the trend changes. The resulting performance profile is one of more frequent small losses and fewer large profits.

LEVERAGE

The consequences of leverage are readily seen in a risk/reward analysis, but it also plays a crucial role in the trading strategy itself. Commodities markets offer exceptionally high leverage opportunity, and most traders and analysts act as though they are obligated to take advantage of the maximum allowable. Without leverage, commodities prices show no more risk than stocks.

Consider the case of an investor with the substantial sum of $50,000 allocated to futures trading. If the price of soybeans is $6.00 per bushel and silver is $7.00 per ounce, a 5000-bushel contract of soybeans is worth $30,000 and a 5000-ounce contract of silver is valued at $35,000. With no leverage, the investor could only purchase one contract with the certainty of being able to hold that contract as long as necessary to achieve a profit. Let us assume that, because of fundamental

Table 18-1   Varying the Leverage of an Investment

Lever-age (%)	Soybeans			Silver			Total Return		
	Qty	Needed ($)	Profit ($)	Qty	Needed ($)	Profit ($)	Profit ($)	Needed ($)	% P/L
0%	0	30,000		1	35,000	20,000	20,000	35,000	40
10	0	27,000		1	31,500	20,000	31,500	31,500	40
20	0	24,000		1	28,000	20,000	28,000	28,000	40
30	1	21,000	10,000	1	24,500	20,000	30,000	45,500	60
40	1	18,000	10,000	1	21,000	20,000	30,000	39,000	60
50	1	15,000	10,000	2	17,500	40,000	50,000	50,000	100
60	1	12,000	10,000	2	14,000	40,000	50,000	40,000	100
70	2	9,000	20,000	3	10,500	60,000	80,000	49,500	160
80	3	6,000	30,000	4	7,000	80,000	110,000	46,000	220
90	7	3,000	70,000	8	3,500	160,000	230,000	49,000	460
95	15	1,500	150,000	15	1,750	300,000	450,000	48,750	900

reasons, the investor believes that soybean prices will move to $8 per bushel and silver to $11 per ounce within the next 6 months. The nonannualized gross return on investment will be 33% for soybeans and 57% for silver, equivalent to a 20 and 40% return on $50,000, respectively. With no leverage and not enough money to invest in both, the choice must be silver which has the highest return; in neither case could their be any "risk of ruin." In both cases there would be surplus capital.

But 100% capitalization is hardly necessary. Even the most conservative investor would agree that the price of either commodity would not drop to 30% of the current value; therefore, there is no significant risk in capitalizing 70%, rather than 100%, of the contract values. By reducing the individual capitalizations, the investor can then purchase both silver and soybeans, thus adding diversification and a much higher return on the available investment. Table 18-1 shows that 30% leverage would increase the return on investment from 40 to 60%, in addition to the way in which the investment could be allocated, given different levels of capitalization.

As the capitalization is lowered and leverage increased, both risk and return get rapidly larger. In Table 18-1, there are certain levels which are more significant than others:

30% leverage, the point where there is added diversification, an increase in return, and a negligible increase in risk.

90% leverage, equivalent to "exchange minimum" margin levels;[4] it allows well-capitalized traders to have margins averaging about 10% of the contract value.

95% leverage, equivalent to the margin level given to hedgers and spreaders, based on owning the physical product as offsetting risk.

---

[4] In futures trading, "initial margin" is the minimum amount required on deposit when the position is entered.

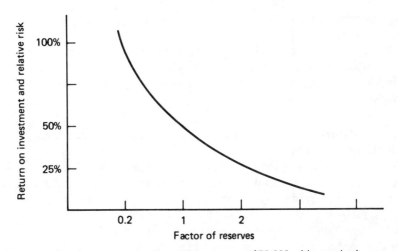

Figure 18-3   Varying reserves, assuming a 50% return on $50,000 with standard reserves (= 1).

At 90% leverage, the investor is required to use $49,000 for margin. The positions may be maintained without an additional investment as long as the account does not show a loss in excess of $12,250.[5] (With a total of 30 contracts, i.e., equivalent to a loss of $408 per contract, or 8¢ per ounce of silver and 8¢ per bushel of soybeans.) Because the daily trading range of both commodities exceeds that value, it is very possible to have a margin call on the first day the position is established. It is not possible for an investor to hold this position for long.

Reserves.   Most professional money managers use *reserves* to reduce the leverage and risk, thereby increasing their staying power. The size of the reserves usually average about 60% of the capital; however, ranges of 10 to 80% have been known. The use of a 50% reserve effectively halves the returns and the risk (Figure 18-3).

Looking again at Table 18-1, there is now only $25,000 of capital available for margin. If "exchange minimum" margin rates are used, there is 90% leverage available; this means each contract of soybeans requires a $3000 deposit and each contract of silver $3500. The 80% leverage line, with one-half the margin shown, would require a total margin commitment of $23,000, slightly under our limits. The net effect of 90% leverage on one-half the total investment is the same as 45% leverage. Returns are:

3 contracts of soybeans × $10,000 profit =	$30,000
4 contracts of silver × $20,000 profit =	60,000
Total profit	$90,000
Net return on investment	180%

[5] "Maintenance margin" is the level of capitalization that must be maintained in the account. Losses that reduce equity to below 75% (the current maintenance margin lever) of the initial margin level requires the investor to reestablish the capitalization to the full initial level.

Diversification

Diversification means spreading risk. This can be implemented using a broad selection of commodities within a single system, a selection of different trading models for one product, or multiple systems and products. The objectives of diversification are:

1. *Lower daily risk* due to the offsetting of losses in some markets and systems with profits in others.
2. *Ensure participation in major moves* by continuously trading those commodities in various groups that are likely to reflect fundamental changes. This avoids the need to identify which market will perform the best.
3. *To offset unexpected losses* caused by a system failing to perform in the current market, or a single trade that generates a large loss. It may be only bad luck that one system gave a short signal in coffee the day before the freeze that moved prices limit-up for 21 days, but another system might have given an offsetting buy signal.

Diversification is accomplished by applying as many of the following techniques as possible:

1. **Selecting commodities from different groups.** Trying to trade those products with as little relationship (low "covariance" or "correlation") to one another as possible. Traditionally, commodities have been categorized as grains, livestock, metals (industrial and precious), currencies, financials, foods, and miscellaneous. The last group accounts for fibers, woods, oil, and other products with little relationship to other markets. Recent expansion of stock index contracts may require an added group or a regrouping of existing markets.

    There is considerable interaction between the groups. Under normal circumstances each group will move according to its specific fundamentals; however, a radical change in the value of the U.S. dollar or interest rates would move all prices in the same direction. Less drastic moves in the currencies will affect the precious metals and export markets; changes in interest rates will directly impact the stock index. A crisis in the potato market, however, has little effect on other areas of the economy. When selecting those commodities to be used in a diversified portfolio it is necessary to check the historical similarity of equity patterns as well as consider the major forces that currently drive the market—both historic and predictive sides of the problem. When properly selected, diversification of commodities may reduce risk, as shown in Figure 18-4.
2. **Using more than one system** will reduce risk provided the systems are not similar. Techniques may appear different and yet be highly correlated. A moving average system, ARIMA model, and point-and-figure are very different methods, but all are trend-following. If the sensitivity of all three systems are similar (as determined by the number of trades per year), the equity patterns will also be similar. For system diversification, it is best to select strategies with different functional attributes, for example, the following list gives sys-

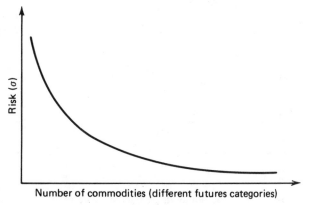

Figure 18-4   Effect of diversification on risk.

tems that are likely to be less correlated and techniques within each method that tend to be different.

a. Trend-following (moving averages or point-and-figure)
b. Countertrend (stochastic or contrary opinion)
c. Spreading (interdelivery, intercommodity, arbitrage, product)
d. Fundamental

All four techniques are very different. Fundamentals may be trending in nature but should have a longer time perspective. The four types of spreads all offer excellent diversification.

3. **Equalizing risk** is necessary if the selection of different commodities and systems is to offer proper diversification. Traditionally, price volatility or market value is used to equate risk; however, this method tends to concentrate trading in those products that are least active—and less likely to be profitable. For example in early 1986, corn was trading at $3 per bushel and the S&P 500 Index at 200, making their contract values $15,000 and $100,000, respectively. Equalizing contract values would mean trading seven corn to one S&P even though the likelihood profiting in corn is far less than that of the S&P.

Equalizing risk must account for the way the trading model performs in the selected markets; most systems do best in volatile periods. Because the most profitable strategies require some substantial price move, they concentrate on markets that have greater volatility. Therefore, it is both easier and better to diversify by distributing the investment among different systems and evaluating only the correlations in equity. A *dynamic capital allocation* will be necessary as one system becomes successful and its contribution to both profits and risk becomes disproportionately large. Withdrawing trading capital from the more successful systems at such times will maintain equal risk among systems and stabilize equity patterns.

These three justifications for diversification have their negative side as well. *Diversification can mean lower profits*. If there are equal returns from trading all commodities and all systems, the diversified returns reduce risk and leave profits at the same high level. However, this never happens. It is not likely that silver and

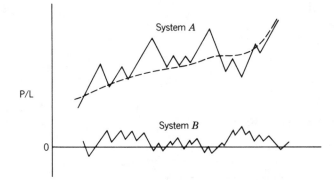

Figure 18-5 Stabilizing equity using negatively correlated systems.

soybeans will be profitable at the same rate, nor is it to be expected that two systems will parallel themselves in performance using two distinctly different techniques.

A classic example is the use of a system that actually loses money but has such a negatively correlated performance to one with a high return that the results of using them together are obviously better than either of them alone (Figure 18-5). Because system *B* returns only a small loss, it does little to affect the profitability of System *A*. It will, however, sharply reduce the equity drops by being profitable during periods when System *A* is losing.

COMMODITY SELECTION INDEX (CSI)

Among Wilder's trading tools is the *Commodity Selection Index* (CSI),[6] a calculation for determining which products are most likely to make the greatest move for each dollar invested. In this case, the movement measured is *directional* and therefore may apply more to trending models. The CSI combines directional movement, volatility, margin requirements, and commission costs into an index that allows for comparison and selection.

Directional Movement

The trending quality of the market, as defined by Wilder, begins with *directional movement,* the greater of either:

1. Plus DM (+DM), today's high minus yesterday's high, or
2. Minus DM (−DM), today's low minus yesterday's low.

The directional movement is *either* up or down, whichever is larger. It is the largest part of today's range which is *outside* yesterday's range. When an inside day occurs, the directional movement is zero (Figure 18-6).

[6] J. Welles Wilder, "Selection and Direction" in Perry J. Kaufman (Ed.), *Technical Analysis in Commodities,* Wiley, New York, 1980.

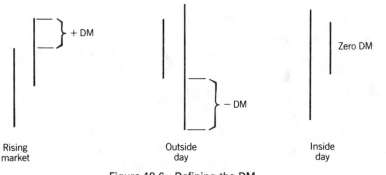

Figure 18-6 Defining the DM.

DM is expressed relative to the daily range (high minus low), defined as today's *true range* (TR1), the larger of the following:

1. Today's high minus today's low
2. Today's high minus yesterday's close
3. Yesterday's close minus today's low

The true range is always positive.

The relationship of the directional movement to the true range is called the *Directional Indicator*. Today's directional indicator is calculated using either the plus DM or the minus DM, whichever is greater.

$$+\text{DI}14 = \frac{+\text{DM}14}{\text{TR}14} \quad \text{or} \quad -\text{DI}14 = \frac{-\text{DM}14}{\text{TR}14}$$

Once the first DM14 is calculated, an "average off" technique is used to find each successive DM14 as follows:

$$\text{Today's } +\text{DM}14 = \text{prior } +\text{DM}14 - \frac{\text{prior } +\text{DM}14}{14} + \text{today's } +\text{DM}14$$

$$\text{Today's } -\text{DM}14 = \text{prior } -\text{DM}14 - \frac{\text{prior } -\text{DM}14}{14} + \text{today's } -\text{DM}14$$

The same procedure is followed for the true range:

$$\text{Today's TR}14 = \text{prior TR}14 - \frac{\text{prior TR}14}{14} + \text{today's TR}14$$

These results can also be produced using a smoothing constant of .93 as follows:

$$\text{Today's } +\text{DM}14 = .93 \times (\text{prior } +\text{DM}14) + \text{today's } +\text{DM}1$$

$$\text{Today's } -\text{DM}14 = .93 \times (\text{prior } -\text{DM}14) + \text{today's } -\text{DM}1$$

$$\text{Today's TR}14 = .93 \times (\text{prior TR}14) + \text{today's TR}1$$

At this point, the Directional Indicator can be used as a trading indicator, and is the subject of the next section; however, Wilder's interest was to use this in a more complete concept. Once the +DM14, −DM14, and the TR14 are calculated,

+DI14 and −DI14 follow, and the *true directional movement* is the difference between +DI14 and −DI14. When an upward trend is sustained, the +DI14 becomes larger, the −DI14 becomes smaller, and the true directional movement becomes greater. This is then "normalized" to allow it to be expressed as a value between 0 and 100.

$$DX = \frac{+DI14 \text{ minus } -DI14}{+DI14 \text{ plus } -DI14} \times 100 = \frac{DI \text{ difference}}{DI \text{ sum}} \times 100$$

where multiplying by 100 converts the percentage to a whole number. The DX is then smoothed out using a 14-day average (or 0.07 smoothing constant), and is called the *Average Directional Movement Index* (ADX).

$$ADX(today) = ADX(prior) + .07 \times [DX(today) - ADX(prior)]$$

One last adjustment is made to the extreme variance of the ADX by taking the 14-day difference of ADXs. This final rating is called the *Average Directional Movement Index Rating* (ADXR),

$$ADXR = \frac{ADX(today) + ADX(14 \text{ days ago})}{2}$$

The ADX and ADXR are shown plotted together in Figure 18-7. The ADX is seen to oscillate about the ADXR. Measuring the amplitude of the ADX from the zero line, a higher amplitude means higher directional movement and a stronger trend, whether up or down. The peaks are always the extremes in the same direction as the trend. If the major trend was down, the peaks would be extreme low points and the valleys would be relative high points. The greater the distance between the peaks and valleys, the greater are the reactions to the trend.

All this leads to the *Commodity Selection Index* (CSI), which is calculated as:

$$CSI = ADXR \times ATR14 \times \left[\frac{V}{M} \times \frac{1}{150 + C} \right] \times 100$$

where ADXR = average directional movement index rating
$\quad\quad$ ATR14 = 14-day average true range
$\quad\quad\quad\quad$ V = conversion factor; value of a 1¢ move (in dollars)
$\quad\quad\quad\quad$ M = margin (in dollars)
$\quad\quad\quad\quad$ C = commissions (in dollars)

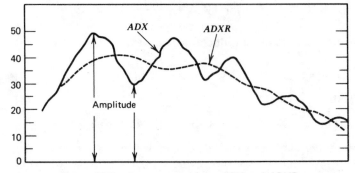

Figure 18-7 Appearance of the *ADX* and *ADXR*.

Note that for a particular commodity, the values in the bracket do not change. By calculating them once and calling that value K, the CSI can be expressed as:

$$CSI = ADXR \times ATR14 \times K$$

A portfolio allocation can be chosen by calculating the CSI daily (or weekly) for each commodity. Simply select those products to trade that have the highest CSI or allocate multiple contracts in proportion to their CSI value.

Optimizing Directional Movement[7]

The $+DI14$ and $-DI14$ are indicators that can be used in a simple trading strategy. Hochheimer, known for other studies of moving averages, crossovers, and channels, has defined the rules of a *Directional Movement System* in two ways.[8] The first set of rules are:

1. a. If the $+DI$ crosses above the $-DI$, enter a *buy stop* on the next day using today's high price. This order remains as long as it is not executed and $+DI$ remains higher than $-DI$.
   b. If the $-DI$ crosses below the $+DI$, enter a *sell stop* on the next day using today's low price. Maintain this order until it is executed and while $-DI$ remains below $+DI$.

Hochheimer calls the first case "Directional Movement with Delay." The second case is an immediate market entry following the crossing of the directional indicators:

2. a. If the $+DI$ crosses above the $-DI$, buy on the open of the next day.
   b. If the $-DI$ crosses below the $+DI$, sell on the open of the next day.

In both cases the system is always in the market.

Before seeing the actual results, it is possible to generalize the expected performance.

1. Case 2 must have more trades than case 1 as a result of always taking a position when a crossing occurs.
2. Because there is no commitment to the trade (i.e., no channel), there could be frequent whipsaws in case 2.
3. Because case 1 uses the high and low of the prior day, its entry prices will always be equal to or worse than case 2.
4. If the Directional Indicator gives a highly reliable signal, it would be better to enter immediately, as in case 2.

[7] For a general discussion of this topic, see Chapter 15.
[8] Frank L. Hochheimer, *Computerized Trading Techniques 1982*, Merrill Lynch Commodities, New York, 1982.

Parameters Defined. The purpose of the optimization was to see if changes in the time intervals caused improvements in results. Hochheimer chose the following parameters to test:

1. The +DM was calculated from 7 to 20 days,
2. The −DM varied from 5 above to 5 below the +DM value, and
3. Two *true ranges* (TR) were calculated, the first using the weight of the +DM, the other using the weight of the −DM.

The test data covered all information available from 1970–1981.

Results. Selected results are shown in Table 18-2. The pattern of the two cases are as expected. Case 2 has more trades, with a higher percentage of losses and higher risk. The profit/loss shown in case 1 is generally higher than case 2, indicating that, even under ideal conditions, the RSI generates many false signals using these rules.

It can also be seen that those commodities with a small amount of available data, T-bills, T-bonds, currencies, and gold, had the shorter intervals selected for calculation. By observing the tendency for the products with more data to use longer intervals, a "standard set" of days should have been chosen rather than allowing an apparent overfitting of the data.

The philosophy of these tests, however, should be questioned. Although the independent varying of the number of days in the +DM, −DM, and TR accounts for all combinations, it seems illogical. The Directional Movement Indicator is intended to be a measurement of relative strength over a fixed time period; it produces a percentage from 0 to 100. In this study, the TR (the denominator) may have a time interval smaller than one of the +DM or −DM, generating a value greater than 100.

The independent varying of the up and down segments of the indicator also allowed a long-term directional bias to appear. This can be seen in the optimum selection of those commodities with the shortest amount of data: the financials

Table 18-2   Comparative Performance of Directional Movement Systems

	Case 1				Case 2			
	Days	P/L	Equity Drop	No. of Trades	Days	P/L	Equity Drop	No. of Trades
Cocoa	22 17	$ 43,083	$(13,019)	723	23 18	$(4,117)	$(17,152)	1238
Corn	21 20	26,456	(7,072)	613	21 20	26,456	(7,072)	613
Cotton	18 21	37,495	(21,740)	1256	24 19	29,765	(18,340)	1462
Copper	18 20	219,639	(10,230)	633	12 14	88,561	(13,390)	1549
Deutschemark	8 13	140,538	(6,335)	277	14 14	101,476	(7,290)	423
Gold	15 10	827,980	(10,740)	504	16 12	664,390	(13,810)	1041
Cattle	22 19	(7,850)	(11,710)	474	20 20	(14,860)	(27,920)	808
Soybeans	16 20	254,495	(39,639)	895	19 20	177,584	(29,759)	1420
Silver	16 11	1034,825	(82,870)	788	22 17	351,360	(136,585)	1161
T-Bills	3 7	37,840	(12,005)	286	11 8	5,235	(17,545)	369
T-Bonds	8 7	185,371	(11,326)	436	9 8	118,256	(7,294)	739

markets and the currencies. In case 2, almost all of the products with 11 years of data produced interval selections that were nearly identical, in the area of either 14 or 20 days.

PROBABILITY OF SUCCESS AND RUIN

The relative size of trading profits and losses, the frequency of the losses, and the sequence in which they occur comprise the equity profile of traders and systems. This profile can be used to determine the capitalization necessary to maintain trading during the losing periods and allow the system to return to its full potential. In investment terminology and probability theory, the level at which you no longer have enough money to continue trading is called the *point of ruin,* and the chances of getting there is the *risk of ruin.* The probability of the *risk of ruin* is normally expressed as

$$R = \left(\frac{1 - A}{1 + A}\right)^c$$

where $0 \leq R \leq 1$, 0 indicates no risk, and 1 certain ruin

$A = P - (1 - P)$, P is the proportion of winning trades, also considered the "trader's advantage"

c = the beginning units of trading capital

A system of trading that has 60% profitable trades and trading capital in $10,000 units will have a risk of ruin calculated as follows:

$$A = 0.60 - (1 - .060) = 0.20$$

$$R = \left(\frac{1 - 0.20}{1 + 0.20}\right)^c = \left(\frac{0.80}{1.20}\right)^c = \left(\frac{1}{3}\right)^c$$

When $c = 1$ ($10,000), $R = 0.33$, and when $c = 2$ ($20,000), $R = 0.11$. Therefore, the greater the "trader's advantage" or the greater the capital, the smaller the risk of ruin (Figure 18-8).

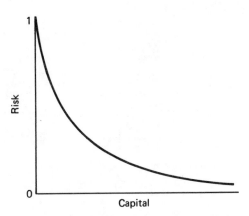

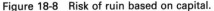

Figure 18-8   Risk of ruin based on capital.

When using profit goals, the chance of ruin should decrease as the goal becomes smaller. The relationship can be expressed as:

$$R = \frac{[(1 + A)/(1 - A)]^G - 1}{[(1 + A)/(1 - A)]^{c+G} - 1}, \quad 0 \le R \le 1$$

where all terms are the same as above, and G is the goal in units of trading capital.

Wins Not Equal to Losses

The basic equations just presented are generally applied to gambling situations, where the size of profits and losses are the same. This requires that the percentage of winning events exceed the losing events in order to avoid ruin. Commodity trading, however, often results in more losing trades than profitable ones and must therefore return much *larger* profits than losses. Such a structure is common to all conservation of capital, or trend-following, systems. This situation can be applied to the more complex form[9] where

C_T = the total capital available for trading (in units)
C_R = the cutoff point, where level of ruin is reached ($C_R < C_T$)
$C_A = C_T - C_R$, capital available to be risked
E = the expected mean return per trade, the probability-weighted sum of values that a trade might take

$$E = \sum_i^N [(PL_i)p_i]$$

where PL_i is the possible profit or loss value, and p_i is the probability of PL_i occurring ($0 < p_i < 1$).

E_2 is the expected squared mean return per trade, the probability-weighted sum of all the squared values of a trade,

$$E_2 = \sum_i^N [(PL_i^2)p_i]$$

where PL_i and p_i are defined above.

$$D = C_A/\sqrt{E_2}$$
$$P = 0.5 + E/(2\sqrt{E_2})$$

and the *risk of ruin* is

$$R = \left(\frac{1 - P}{P}\right)^D$$

Introducing an objective and a desired level of capital L, the *risk of ruin* R becomes

$$R = 1 - \frac{[(1 - P)/P)^D - 1]}{[(1 - P)/P)^G - 1]}$$

[9] F. Gehm, *Commodity Market Money Management,* Wiley, New York, 1983.

where

$$G = 1/\sqrt{E_2}$$

As in the first situation, using equal profits and losses, the risk increases as the objective L increases.

PYRAMIDING

At some point, all speculators find themselves pyramiding by choice or by accident. *Pyramiding* is the act of adding to, or compounding, one's position. Many traders view this as a means of "concentrating" on those commodities that have more potential. There are two lines of thinking among these traders. When a trade becomes more profitable, it is "confirming" its move and is thought to deserve more of a commitment than a trade that has not become profitable. On the other hand, by adding positions to a trade at preset intervals, the effect of a single poor entry point is reduced and a better average entry price is created. This later technique is called "scaled down buying" in the securities industry.

The following sections will assume that positions are added based on profitability as a means of increasing leverage. There are a number of techniques used by experienced traders, but the time to pyramid must be carefully selected. The situation chosen must have potential for a long move with limited risk; the sustained consolidation period of a commodity that is priced near its historic lows would be a candidate. No matter how well chosen, each method will result in the largest holdings at the highest (or lowest) price; when the market reverses, loses occur on a larger base and profits will disappear quickly. Pyramiding is very fragile, hard work and must be watched cautiously for a changing market; there are enough stories of speculators who pyramided small capital into a large fortune in less than a year's time and then lost it all in a week. As in all investments, the risk balances the opportunities.

The Scaled-Down Pyramid

The standard pyramid, or *upright pyramid,* has a larger base than its top. The largest portion of profits are developed early and an adverse price move is not as likely to be disastrous. The profit-compounding effect of this technique is comparably reduced. A favorite scaling method of this type adds one-half of the prior position at each opportunity (Figure 18-9a). The maximum number of contracts to be held must be planned in advance. The total position, if followed to completion, will be about twice the number of contracts that were initially entered; starting with 20 lots, 10, 5, 2, and 1 would be added respectively. An advantage of this or any other pyramiding method is that an initial loss will be based on a smaller number of contracts than the final commitment.

Adding Equal Positions

As larger commitments are added, an inverted pyramid is created (Figure 18-9b) in which the risk of an immediate loss due to a small reversal becomes greater.

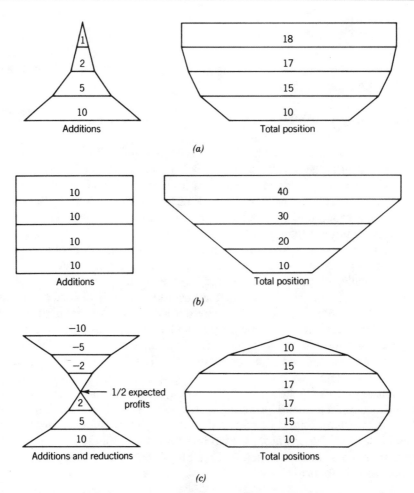

Figure 18-9   Pyramid structure. (a) Scaled-down (upright) pyramid offers a small amount of compounding. (b) Adding equal amounts (inverted pyramid) gives maximum leverage. (c) Reflecting pyramid combines leverage and profit-taking.

Adding equal numbers of contracts reduces the proportion of the original commitment in the event the trend does not materialize but increases later exposure (when, hopefully, there are large profits). The shift of risk can only be determined by the trader. With this approach as well as the other inverted-pyramid methods, the speculator should follow the rule that *no unsuccessful secondary purchase should offset the entire profits of the prior purchases*.

Adding Equal Amounts

To offset the effects of disproportionate risk, subsequent positions can be added based on the new value of the commodity being traded. Comparing this to the previous method of equal contracts, this would reduce the number of purchases in a rising market and increase them in a declining market. The effect of increased volatility at higher levels would substantiate this approach to adding as a means of maintaining the same relative effect of each new position to the prior ones.

Maximum-Leverage Pyramiding

The greatest risk and the most potential is in adding positions using all profits accumulated to date. To do this necessitates a close working arrangement with the

Table 18-3   Comparison of Pyramiding Methods[a]

							Scaled to 10		
Price	Add	Total	Equity	LiqVal	Risk	Equity/Risk	Equity	LiqVal	Risk
No Pyramiding									
0	10	10	0	(100)	100	0			
10	0	10	100	0	100	1.00			
20	0	10	200	100	100	2.00			
30	0	10	300	200	100	3.00			
40	0	10	400	300	100	4.00			
50	0	10	500	400	100	5.00			
60	0	10	600	500	100	6.00			
Scaled-Down (Upright) Pyramid									
0	32	32	0	(320)	320	0	0	(100)	100
10	16	48	320	(160)	480	.67	100	(50)	150
20	8	56	800	240	560	1.42	250	75	175
30	4	60	1360	760	600	2.27	425	237	187
40	2	62	1960	1340	620	3.17	612	418	193
50	1	63	2580	1950	630	4.11	806	609	196
60	0	63	3210	2580			1003	806	
Equal Positions									
0	10	10	0	(100)	100	0			
10	10	20	100	(100)	200	.50			
20	10	30	300	0	300	1.00			
30	10	40	600	200	400	1.50			
40	10	50	1000	500	500	2.00			
50	10	60	1500	900	600	2.50			
60	0	60	2100	1500					
Reflecting Pyramid									
0	10	10	0	(100)	100	0			
10	5	15	100	(50)	150	.67			
20	2	17	250	80	170	1.47			
30	0	17	420	250	170	2.47			
40	(2)	15	590	440	150	3.93			
50	(5)	10	740	640	100	7.40			
60	(10)	0	840	740					

[a] 1 point = $100.

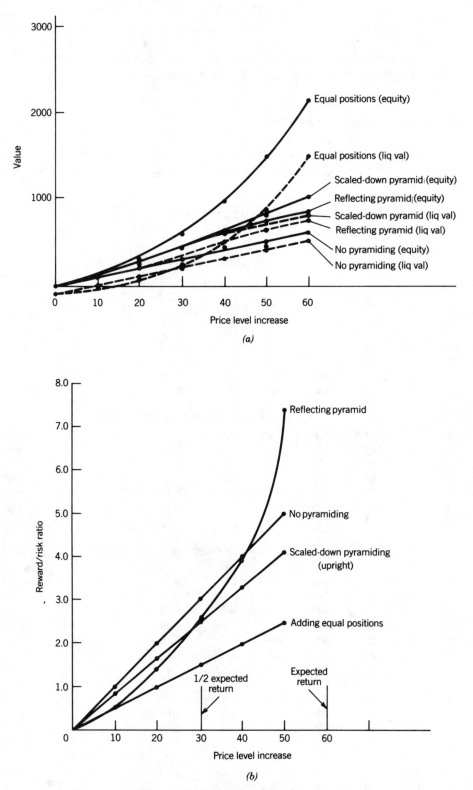

Figure 18-10   Returns and risks from pyramiding. (a) Equity and liquidated value (10-point reversal. (b) Reward to risk ratio.

margin department of a brokerage firm. They might even want to install a direct line. Whenever possible, new positions are added; profits are considered a confirmation of the trend. Being completely leveraged is a tenuous position, requiring constant monitoring of the market; there must be a well-defined stop-loss at all times in anticipation of a premature reversal.

Reflecting Pyramid

One way to reduce the extreme risks of pyramiding is to remove positions once a specific profit level has been reached. For example, if there is a reasonable expectation of an average profit of 60 points, a *reflecting pyramid* (Figure 18-9c) will add positions until the maximum commitment is reached at one-half the expected profit and then reduce positions until it is entirely closed-out at 60. This technique can be modified to apply to any of the methods of adding positions by requiring that the full commitment be achieved at a level below the expected profit; full liquidation may be targetted for a point above the average profit.

Comparison of Pyramiding Methods

Table 18-3 and Figures 18-10a and 18-10b show the risks and rewards of three methods of pyramiding compared to holding a single position from trade entry to exit. All methods of pyramiding increase both profits and risk. Holding an unchanged position shows consistently lower returns with a mostly higher reward/risk ratio, especially at early equity levels. Scaled-down additions show an improved return and less attractive ratio; equal additions show much higher returns with a much lower reward/risk profile. The reflecting pyramid has both higher returns than the single position and an improved ratio. At one-half the expected return, it is clearly a better choice than the other methods. As expected profits are neared, the investor must choose between the extremely high leverage and profits of adding equal positions and the excellent reward/risk ratio of the reflecting pyramid.

EQUITY CYCLES

Every system has profit-loss cycles that can be seen clearly by plotting its daily or weekly equity. Trending techniques show that once or twice each year, there are major increases in profits corresponding to a trending market; at other times, there is a steady decline and a stabilizing pattern to the total equity. For a system to operate as it is expected, the positions must be kept constant. Increasing positions as equity increases in a trending cycle results in always being fully invested at the top of the cycle, when losses begin. Losses will be on a larger base than profits, and equity will drop much faster than it increased.

The same effect can occur at the bottom of an equity cycle after a nontrending market period. A sustained losing streak may cause a speculator to reduce the investment in proportion to dwindling capital. If this happens, the result will be entering into a profitable period with a smaller investment than the prior losing period. The system must have disproportionately larger profits to recover the losses and achieve a net gain. An example of a typical system is shown, using a 100% gain for each profitable cycle, followed by a 50% loss cycle. Assume this cycle is repeated twice each year; in one year, the following equity pattern will occur:

	Change in equity	Total equity	
Original margin		$10,000	
Gain of 100%	+10,000	20,000	First 6 months
Loss of 50%	− 5000	15,000	
Gain of 100%	+10,000	25,000	Second 6 months
Loss of 50%	− 5000	20,000	

This leaves a net gain of 100% for the year. Each 100% profit was $10,000, and losses were $5,000—the rate of return is always based on the original margin. Had the cycle started with the losing phase, there would be a profit of 50% for the first year and 100% for each subsequent year.

Many traders would not net 100% each year from a system that performs as the one in the example. As their profits increased, positions would be added so that at the time the total equity was worth $20,000, the margin requirements would also be $20,000. The 50% loss is then applied to the total equity:

	Change in equity	Total equity	
Original margin		$10,000	
Gain of 100%	+10,000	20,000	First 6 months
Loss of 50%	−10,000	10,000	
Gain of 100%	+10,000	20,000	Second 6 months
Loss of 50%	−10,000	10,000	

Trading commodities would be a great deal of effort for no return.

Holding the investment constant as shown can also be viewed by studying the growth and decline of the account excess, called the *reserve*. The size of the reserve relative to total equity is the key to successful management. Starting with margin and reserves equal, reserves increase during profitable periods and decrease during losing ones. Proportionately more of the total equity is traded during losing phases. This pattern can be used to improve results safely, as follows:

	Change in equity	Margin	Reserve	Total equity	Reserve/ equity
Original investment		10,000	10,000	20,000	50%
Gain of 100%	+10,000	10,000	20,000	30,000	67%
Loss of 50%	− 5000	10,000	15,000	25,000	60%
Gain of 100%	+10,000	10,000	25,000	35,000	71%
Loss of 50%	− 5000	10,000	20,000	30,000	67%

Using the natural equity cycles, hold the number of positions the same and allow the reserve to increase during profitable periods; maintain the same position size through the beginning of the next losing period. When the equity drop has slowed or stabilized, the total equity can be redistributed into margin and reserve according to the original 50% formula. In the next example, the total equity of $25,000 is distributed 40% to margin and 60% to reserve at the end of the first cycle. It is redistributed so that the next profit phase will be entered with a larger base than the previous losing cycle. The result is a gradual increase in profits:

	Change in equity	Margin	Reserve	Total equity	Reserve/ equity
Original investment		10,000	10,000	20,000	50%
Gain of 100%	+10,000	10,000	20,000	30,000	67%
Loss of 50%	− 5000	10,000	15,000	25,000	60%
Redistribute		12,500	12,500	25,000	50%
Gain of 100%	+10,000	12,500	25,000	37,500	67%
Loss of 50%	− 5000	12,500	18,750	31,250	60%
Redistribute		15,625	15,625	31,250	50%

Trading on Equity Cycles

If a moving average technique is traded, the equity will fluctuate with the trending nature of the market. By applying a moving-average analysis to the equity itself, the trending and nontrending periods are identified by the "buy" and "sell" signals given by the equity series.

An equity "buy" means that the commodity market has begun trending; the length of this period depends on the speed of the moving average. A "sell" signal means that the market is no longer trending. These signals can be taken as "buy the system" or "short the system," that is, enter all positions that the system currently holds or liquidate the entire portfolio and hold cash. An equity "buy" could also be taken as the point to redistribute the equity into the original ratio of margin to reserve.

RISK PREFERENCE

Each investor has his or her unique objectives and attitudes toward risk. Some of the participants in futures markets would like to keep risks low and returns steady; others would like to risk all of their capital for a chance at the "big move." This trait is called the investor's *risk preference*. The risk preference or utility of an investor for a specific venture (in this case a trade) can be found by adding the expected value of the investor's utilities or preferences for the various outcomes of that event,

$$P = w_1p_1 + w_2p_2 + \cdots + w_np_n, \text{ where } \sum w_i = 1$$

where there are n possible outcomes. The weighting factors may be the results of personal bias or may be the calculated probabilities of each outcome. For example, a gold trade has a likely profit of $4000, with a risk of $1500. Adjust the reward values by dividing by 1000. If the probability of success is 60%, the total utility of the trade is:

$$P(\text{trade}) = 0.60 \times 4 + 0.40 \times (-1.5) = 1.8$$

If the probability of success were increased, the utility P would increase linearly. But investors do not feel the same about different rewards. Given a scale of 0 to 100 (negative to positive reaction), an investor may rank the 60% chance of a $4000 profit, with a 40% chance of a $1500 loss as a 65. If the reward is increased to $8000 while the risk remains at $1500, the investor might raise the preference of the trade to 80 although the utility would be 4.2, more than twice as large.

The various patterns of a curve drawn through the computed utilities represents the risk preference of the individual. Figure 18-11 shows the curve formations progressing from extreme risk aversion to extreme risk seeking. As the risk increases in (1), the trader is less likely to participate in the trade; in (3), there is equal chance of taking the trade at all risk levels; and in (5), the trader is more likely to enter a trade that has higher risk.

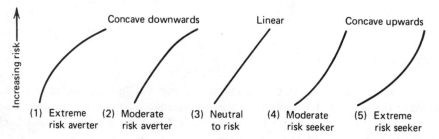

Figure 18-11   Investor utility curves. (*Source:* Teweles, R. J., C. V. Harlon, and H. L. Stone, *The Commodity Futures Games: Who Wins, Who Loses, Why?* McGraw-Hill, New York, 1974, p. 133.)

COMPARING EXPECTED AND ACTUAL RESULTS

In the development of an economic model or trading system, the final selection is usually the result of a performance comparison of the completed models. Often the results are given in terms of profit/loss ratios, annualized percentage profits, expected reliability (percentage of profitable trades to total trades), and potential risk. Although these statistics are common, their predictive qualities and sometimes their accuracy are not known. On occasion, these results are generated by a sample that is too small and usually they are not the results of a predictive but an historic test. This does not mean that the model will be unsuccessful, but that the pattern of success might vary far from the expected profit/loss ratio, reliability, and risk. In actual trading, every speculator experiences a series of losses far exceeding anything that was expected; at that point, it is best to know whether this situation could occur within the realm of the system's profile or whether the system has failed. For example, a moving-average system is expected to have $\frac{1}{3}$ profitable trades (reliability of 33%), with a profit/loss ratio of 4 : 1. But the first 10 trades of the system are losers. Should trading be stopped?

Binomial Probability

Consider the application of a random-number sequence to the trading model. What is the probability of l losses in n tries when the probability of a loss is p? Most of the work in this area of probability is credited to Bernoulli, whose study of a random walk is called a *Bernoulli process*. A clear representation of a random walk is shown by the Pascal triangle (Figure 18-12), where each box represents the probability of being in a particular position at a specific time in a forward random walk. The result of this process is called a *binomial distribution*.

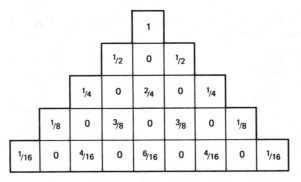

Figure 18-12 Pascal's triangle.

The forward random walk has an analogy to price movement, with the far edges of Pascal's triangle showing the probability of a continuous sequence of wins or losses using random numbers. The sequence $\frac{1}{2}, \frac{1}{4}, \frac{1}{8}, \ldots, (\frac{1}{2})^n$ is exactly the same as in the discussion of the Theory of Runs. The probability of successive losses can be calculated as the likelihood of a run of the same length, $(\frac{1}{2})^{n+2}$.

A binomial distribution is useful in considering the total number of losses that can occur in any order within a sequence of trades; it is the probability of getting to a specific point at the base of Pascal's triangle when there is a high probability of moving to the left (losses) rather than the right (profits). The formula for the binomial probability is:

$$B(l:p, n) = \frac{n!}{l!(n - l)!} p^l(1 - p)^{n-l}$$

where l is the number of losses

n is the total number of tries

p is the probability of a loss

and the symbol "!" is the factorial (e.g., $5! = 5 \times 4 \times 3 \times 2 \times 1$).

Consider the first five trades of a system with a probability of success of $\frac{1}{3}$. How many losses should be expected? To answer the question, find the binomial probability B for all possibilities and form a distribution function. Let $l = 4$. Then,

$$B(4:.667, 5) = \frac{5!}{4!1!} (.667)^4(.333)^l$$

$$= \frac{120}{24} \times (.19792)(.333)$$

$$= 5 \times .0659 = .32954$$

The binomial probability of having four losses out of the first five trades is about 33%. The following table shows the probability of losses for the first 5, 10, and 15 trades of a system, with a $\frac{1}{3}$ predicted reliability. Results show the highest probability of occurrence of loss is at the $\frac{2}{3}$ point (mean) for each sequence, but the standard deviation gives the range of variance about the mean, so that from 2.3 to 4.4, losses are expected in every 5 trades, 5.2 to 8.2 in 10 trades, and 8.2 to 11.8 losses in 15 trades (Table 18-4).

Table 18-4   The Probability of a Specific Number of Losses

5 Trades		10 Trades		15 Trades	
Losses	Probability (%)	Losses	Probability (%)	Losses	Probability (%)
0	1	0	0	0	0
1	4	1	0	1	0
2	16	2	0	2	0
3	33	3	2	3	0
4	33	4	5	4	0
5	13	5	14	5	1
		6	23	6	2
		7	26	7	6
		8	19	8	11
		9	9	9	18
		10	2	10	21
				11	20
				12	13
				13	6
				14	2
				15	0
$m^a = 3\frac{1}{3}$		$m = 6\frac{2}{3}$		$m = 10$	
$sd^b = 1.05$		$sd = 1.5$		$sd = 1.825$	

[a] Mean.

[b] Standard deviation.

Note that in the five-trade example, the chances of no losses is only 1% and there is a 13% chance of all losses. For the purpose of evaluation, it is easier to look at the maximum rather than the minimum number of losses. For 15 trades, there is an 8% chance of 13 or more losses; if the system has produced more than 12 losses in that period, there is something wrong with the predicted reliability.

In addition to the Pascal distribution, the reader may find the Poisson and various skewed distribution functions have application to system evaluation.

X^2—Chi-Square Test

Once a system has been traded and there is enough data to give a performance profile, a simple correlation between these actual results and the expected results can be found using the *chi-square test*. First, there must be enough data for a relevant answer. From the section on sampling, the formula for error is $1/\sqrt{N}$, where N is the number of items sampled. If there are 25 trades, the expected error in the calculation is $1/\sqrt{25}$, or 20%; 100 trades would give results accurate to 10%.

Assume that the real trading results show a reliability of 20% (1 out of 5) as compared to the expected reliability of 35%. What are the chances of getting these results? The chi-square test is

$$X^2 = \frac{(O - E)^2}{E}$$

where O is the observed, or actual result, and E is the expected or theoretical result. Then,

$$X^2 = \frac{(20 - 35)^2}{35} + \frac{(80 - 65)^2}{65}$$

$$= \frac{(-15)^2}{35} + \frac{(-15)^2}{65}$$

$$= \frac{225}{35} + \frac{225}{65} = 6.428 + 3.46$$

$$= 9.89$$

The percentage of actual winning trades is compared with the anticipated winning trades and the losing trades with the expected losing trades. The answer must be found in the first row of Table 18-5, which gives the distribution of X^2.

The probability is distributed unequally in the table because the results are only significant if the probability is small, showing less likelihood of the results occurring by chance. For this simple two-element test, the result P is classified as

Highly significant   if $P \geq 10.83$ (.1% or $\frac{1}{1000}$)
Significant   if $P \geq 6.64$ (1% or $\frac{1}{100}$)
Probably significant if $P \geq 3.84$ (5% or $\frac{1}{20}$)

Table 18-5   Distribution of X^2

Cases	Probability of Occurring by Chance								
Less 1	.70	.50	.30	.20	.10	.05	.02	.01	.001
1	.15	.46	1.07	1.64	2.71	3.84	5.41	6.64	10.83
2	.71	1.39	2.41	3.22	4.61	5.99	7.82	9.21	13.82
3	1.42	2.37	3.67	4.64	6.25	7.82	9.84	11.34	16.27
4	2.20	3.36	4.88	5.99	7.78	9.49	11.67	13.28	18.47
5	3.00	4.35	6.06	7.29	9.24	11.07	13.39	15.09	20.52
6	3.83	5.35	7.23	8.56	10.65	12.59	15.03	16.81	22.46
7	4.67	6.35	8.38	9.80	12.02	14.07	16.62	18.48	24.32
8	5.53	7.34	9.52	11.03	13.36	15.51	18.17	20.09	26.13
9	6.39	8.34	10.66	12.24	14.68	16.92	19.68	21.67	27.88
10	7.27	9.34	11.78	13.44	15.99	18.31	21.16	23.21	29.59

The answer $X^2 = 9.89$ is between .1% and 1% showing *significance*. For a large sample, the actual reliability should not have been 20% when 35% was expected.

The chi-square test can be used to compare actual price movement with random patterns to see whether there is appreciable variation. In the section on the Theory of Runs, Table 18-6 showed:

Table 18-6   Results from Analysis of Runs

Length of Run	Expected Results (E)	Actual Results (O)
1	1225	1214
2	612	620
3	306	311
4	153	167
5	77	67
6	38	41
7	19	16
8	10	5
9	5	3
≥10	4	5
≥ 8 [a]	19	13

[a] The last groups were combined in order not to distort the results based on a small sample.

Applying the actual data for runs of one through eight against a random distribution,

$$X^2 = \sum_{n=1}^{8} \frac{(O_n - E_n)^2}{E_n}$$

$$= \frac{(1214 - 1225)^2}{1225} + \frac{(620 - 612)^2}{612} + \frac{(311 - 306)^6}{306}$$

$$+ \frac{(167 - 153)^2}{153} + \frac{(67 - 77)^2}{77} + \frac{(41 - 38)^2}{38}$$

$$+ \frac{(16 - 19)^2}{19} + \frac{(13 - 19)^2}{19}$$

$$= \overset{(1)}{.09877} + \overset{(2)}{.10457} + \overset{(3)}{.08169} + \overset{(4)}{1.2810} + \overset{(5)}{1.2987}$$

$$\overset{(6)}{.23684} + \overset{(7)}{.47368} + \overset{(8)}{1.8947}$$

$$= 5.470$$

Table 18-5 gives the probability of about 55% for eight cases. The results are not significant; the Theory of Runs shows that all cases taken together give the same patterns as chance movement. Individual runs or sets of two or three adjacent runs can be inspected for distortion. In both cases, the results are further from normal but not mathematically significant. The two runs that differed the most were 4 to 5 days, which showed a 11% probability of occurring by chance.

Highly significant price runs can be found in the occurrence of extended runs, for example, 20 days, which is experienced occasionally in trending markets. By looking at the *asymmetry* of price movement, where a reverse run of 1 day is of negligible value, the significance of these runs will dramatically increase. Price movement is not a simple matter of random runs and equal payouts.

APPENDIX 1
Statistical Tables

PROBABILITY DISTRIBUTIONS TABLES

Normal Curve Areas

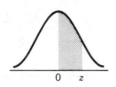

z	.00	.01	.02	.03	.04	.05	.06	.07	.08	.09
0.0	.0000	.0040	.0080	.0120	.0160	.0199	.0239	.0279	.0319	.0359
0.1	.0398	.0438	.0478	.0517	.0557	.0596	.0636	.0675	.0714	.0753
0.2	.0793	.0832	.0871	.0910	.0948	.0987	.1026	.1064	.1103	.1141
0.3	.1179	.1217	.1255	.1293	.1331	.1368	.1406	.1443	.1480	.1517
0.4	.1554	.1591	.1628	.1664	.1700	.1736	.1772	.1808	.1844	.1879
0.5	.1915	.1950	.1985	.2019	.2054	.2088	.2123	.2157	.2190	.2224
0.6	.2257	.2291	.2324	.2357	.2389	.2422	.2454	.2486	.2517	.2549
0.7	.2580	.2612	.2642	.2673	.2704	.2734	.2764	.2794	.2823	.2852
0.8	.2881	.2910	.2939	.2967	.2995	.3023	.3051	.3078	.3106	.3133
0.9	.3159	.3186	.3212	.3238	.3264	.3289	.3315	.3340	.3365	.3389
1.0	.3413	.3438	.3461	.3485	.3508	.3531	.3554	.3577	.3599	.3621
1.1	.3643	.3665	.3686	.3708	.3729	.3749	.3770	.3790	.3810	.3820
1.2	.3849	.3869	.3888	.3907	.3925	.3944	.3962	.3980	.3997	.4015
1.3	.4032	.4049	.4066	.4082	.4099	.4115	.4131	.4147	.4162	.4177
1.4	.4192	.4207	.4222	.4236	.4251	.4265	.4279	.4292	.4306	.4319
1.5	.4332	.4345	.4357	.4370	.4382	.4394	.4406	.4418	.4429	.4441
1.6	.4452	.4463	.4474	.4484	.4495	.4505	.4515	.4525	.4535	.4545
1.7	.4554	.4564	.4573	.4582	.4591	.4599	.4608	.4616	.4625	.4633
1.8	.4641	.4649	.4656	.4664	.4671	.4678	.4686	.4693	.4699	.4706
1.9	.4713	.4719	.4726	.4732	.4738	.4744	.4750	.4756	.4761	.4767
2.0	.4772	.4778	.4783	.4788	.4793	.4798	.4803	.4808	.4812	.4817
2.1	.4821	.4826	.4830	.4834	.4838	.4842	.4846	.4850	.4854	.4857
2.2	.4861	.4864	.4868	.4871	.4875	.4878	.4881	.4884	.4887	.4890
2.3	.4893	.4896	.4898	.4901	.4904	.4906	.4909	.4911	.4913	.4916
2.4	.4918	.4920	.4922	.4925	.4927	.4929	.4931	.4932	.4934	.4936
2.5	.4938	.4940	.4941	.4943	.4945	.4946	.4948	.4949	.4951	.4952
2.6	.4953	.4955	.4956	.4957	.4959	.4960	.4961	.4962	.4963	.4964
2.7	.4965	.4966	.4967	.4968	.4969	.4970	.4971	.4972	.4973	.4974
2.8	.4974	.4975	.4976	.4977	.4977	.4978	.4979	.4979	.4980	.4981
2.9	.4981	.4982	.4982	.4983	.4984	.4984	.4985	.4985	.4986	.4986
3.0	.4987	.4987	.4987	.4988	.4988	.4989	.4989	.4989	.4990	.4990

Figure A1-1   Normal curve areas.

T-Distribution

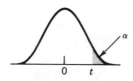

α d.f.	.10	.05	.025	.01	.005
1	3.078	6.314	12.706	31.821	63.657
2	1.886	2.920	4.303	6.965	9.925
3	1.638	2.353	3.182	4.541	5.841
4	1.533	2.132	2.776	3.747	4.604
5	1.476	2.015	2.571	3.365	4.032
6	1.440	1.943	2.447	3.143	3.707
7	1.415	1.895	2.365	2.998	3.499
8	1.397	1.860	2.306	2.896	3.355
9	1.383	1.833	2.262	2.821	3.250
10	1.372	1.812	2.228	2.764	3.169
11	1.363	1.796	2.201	2.718	3.106
12	1.356	1.782	2.179	2.681	3.055
13	1.350	1.771	2.160	2.650	3.012
14	1.345	1.761	2.145	2.624	2.977
15	1.341	1.753	2.131	2.602	2.947
16	1.337	1.746	2.120	2.583	2.921
17	1.333	1.740	2.110	2.567	2.898
18	1.330	1.734	2.101	2.552	2.878
19	1.328	1.729	2.093	2.539	2.861
20	1.325	1.725	2.086	2.528	2.845
21	1.323	1.721	2.080	2.518	2.831
22	1.321	1.717	2.074	2.508	2.819
23	1.319	1.714	2.069	2.500	2.807
24	1.318	1.711	2.064	2.492	2.797
25	1.316	1.708	2.060	2.485	2.787
26	1.315	1.706	2.056	2.479	2.779
27	1.314	1.703	2.052	2.473	2.771
28	1.313	1.701	2.048	2.467	2.763
29	1.311	1.699	2.045	2.462	2.756
30	1.310	1.697	2.042	2.457	2.750
40	1.303	1.684	2.021	2.423	2.704
60	1.296	1.671	2.000	2.390	2.660
120	1.289	1.658	1.980	2.358	2.617
∞	1.282	1.645	1.960	2.326	2.576

Source: Hoel, Elementary Statistics, 3d ed. (New York: John Wiley and Sons, Inc., 1971 c.).

Figure A1-2   T-distribution.

TABLE OF UNIFORM RANDOM NUMBERS

Table A1-3 Uniform Random Numbers

	1	2	3	4	5	6	7	8	9	10	11
1	10480	15011	01536	02011	81647	91646	69179	14194	62590	36207	20969
2	22368	46573	25595	85393	30995	89198	27982	53402	93965	34095	52666
3	24130	48360	22527	97265	76393	64809	15179	24830	49340	32081	30680
4	42167	93093	06243	61680	07856	16376	39440	53537	71341	57004	00849
5	37570	39975	81837	16656	06121	91782	60468	81305	49684	60672	14110
6	77921	06907	11008	42751	27756	53498	18602	70659	90655	15033	21916
7	99562	72905	56420	69994	98872	31016	71194	18738	44013	44840	63213
8	96301	91977	05463	07972	18876	20922	94595	56869	69014	60045	18425
9	89579	14342	63661	10281	17453	18103	57740	84378	25331	12566	58678
10	85475	36857	53342	53988	53060	59533	38867	62300	08158	17893	16439
11	28918	69578	88231	33276	70997	79936	56865	05859	90106	31595	91547
12	63553	40961	48235	03427	49626	69445	18663	72695	52180	20847	12234
13	09429	93969	52636	92737	88974	33488	36320	17617	30015	07272	84115
14	10365	61129	87529	85689	48237	52267	67689	93394	01511	26358	85104
15	07119	97336	71048	08178	77233	13916	47564	81056	97735	85977	29372
16	51085	12765	51821	51259	77452	16308	60756	92144	49442	53900	70960
17	02368	21382	52404	60268	89368	19885	55322	44819	01188	65255	64835
18	01011	54092	33362	94904	31273	04146	18594	29852	71585	85030	51132
19	52162	53916	46369	58586	23216	14513	83149	98736	23495	64350	94738
20	07056	97628	33787	09998	42698	06691	76988	13602	51851	46104	88916
21	48663	91245	85828	14346	09172	30168	90229	04734	59193	22178	30421
22	54164	58492	22421	74103	47070	25306	76468	26384	58151	06646	21524
23	32639	32363	05597	24200	13363	38005	94342	28728	35806	06912	17012
24	29334	27001	87637	87308	58731	00256	45834	15398	46557	41135	10367
25	02488	33062	28834	07351	19731	92420	60952	61280	50001	67658	32586
26	81525	72295	04839	96423	25878	82651	66566	14778	76797	14780	13300
27	29676	20591	68086	26432	46901	20849	80768	81536	86645	12659	92259
28	00742	57392	39064	66432	84673	40027	32832	61362	98947	96067	64760
29	05366	04213	25669	26422	44407	44048	37937	63904	45766	66134	75470
30	91921	26418	64117	94305	26766	25940	39972	22209	71500	64568	91402
31	00582	04711	87917	77341	42206	35126	74087	99547	81817	42607	43808
32	00725	69884	62797	56170	86324	88072	76222	36086	84637	93161	76038
33	69011	65795	95876	55293	18988	27354	26575	08625	40801	59920	29841
34	25976	57948	29888	88604	67917	48708	18912	82271	65424	69774	33611
35	09763	83473	73577	12908	30883	10317	28290	35797	05998	41688	34952
36	91567	42595	27958	30134	04024	86385	29880	99730	55536	84855	29080
37	17955	56349	90999	49127	20044	59931	06115	20542	18059	02008	73708
38	46503	18584	18845	49618	02304	51038	20655	58727	28168	15475	56942
39	92157	89634	94824	78171	84610	82834	09922	25417	44137	48413	25555
40	14577	62765	35605	81263	39667	47358	56873	56307	61607	49518	89565

Source: From Francis F. Martin, *Computer Modeling and Simulation*, p. 288. Copyright © 1968 by John Wiley & Sons, Inc. Reprinted by permission.

APPENDIX 2
Method of Least Squares

The following programs, written in Microsoft FORTRAN for the IBM PC,[1] solve the two-variable regression analysis using the *method of least squares*. The program allows for the regression of two series against one another, and the regression of one series against time.

OPERATING INSTRUCTIONS

In the following example, the user's entries are underlined:

LSTSQ

Enter data in sets of 2 (Y then X).
If second variable is omitted, sequential numbers will be used for x.
Extra ⟨return⟩ ends input.

Enter below:
YYYYYY XXXXXX
1.27   2.43
1.19   2.26
1.10   2.15
⟨RETURN⟩

Print data (Y/N)? Y

(Computer prints data and solutions)

Sample results (Y/N)?Y

Enter start, end and increments below
ssssss eeeee i i i i i i
1.00   7.00   .50

(Computer prints sample results)

---

[1] BASIC programs for both plotting and least-squares regression can be found in F. R. Ruckdeschel, *BASIC Scientific Subroutines, Volume I*, Byte/McGraw-Hill, Peterborough, NH, 1981.

Plot results (Y/N)?<u>Y</u>
Name for X-scale (9 chars)?
<u>SOYBEANS</u>
Name for Y-scale (9 chars)?
<u>CORN</u>

Which plot?
    1: Linear
    2: Logarithmic
    3: Exponential
    4: Curvilinear
Which number?<u>1</u>

(Computer plots)

Another plot (Y/N)?<u>Y</u>

Which plot?
    1: Linear

(and so forth)

COMPUTER PROGRAMS

```
 1  $TITLE: 'LSTSQ: LEAST SQUARES'
 2  $SUBTITLE: 'COPYRIGHT 1986 P J KAUFMAN'
 3  $STORAGE:2
 4          PROGRAM LSTSQ
 5  C---- Least Squares Regression Analysis for 2 variables
 6
 7          CHARACTER*1 ANS
 8          DIMENSION X(100),Y(100)
 9
10          DATA MAX/100/
11
12          OPEN(6,FILE='PRN')
13
14  C---- Read data in sets of 2 variables
15          I = 1
16          WRITE(*,7000)
17  7000  FORMAT(' Enter data in sets of 2 (Y then X).'/
18      +          ' If second variable is omitted, sequential numbers',
19      +          ' will be used for X.'/' Extra ⟨return⟩ ends input.'//
20      +          ' Enter below:'/
21      +          ' YYYYYY XXXXXX')
22  10    READ(*,5000)Y(I),X(I)
23  5000  FORMAT(BN,F6.2,F7.2)
24          IF(Y(I).EQ.0)GOTO 30
25          IF(X(I).EQ.0)X(I)=I
```

```
26              IF(I.EQ.MAX)THEN
27                  WRITE(*,7001)MAX
28      7001        FORMAT(' Data input reached max of',I5,'. Processing begins.')
29                  GOTO 30
30                  ENDIF
31              I = I+1
32              GOTO 10
33
34        30    N = I-1
35              WRITE(*,7002)
36      7002    FORMAT(' Print data (Y/N)?'\)
37              READ(*,5001)ANS
38      5001    FORMAT(A1)
39              IF(ANS.NE. 'Y')GOTO 50
40              WRITE(6,6000)
41      6000    FORMAT('1Least-Squares Regression Analysis',20X,'Data Input'//
42          +              '  Y (dep)   X (ind)'/)
43              DO 40 J = 1,N
44                  WRITE(6,6001)Y(J),X(J)
45      6001    FORMAT(2F8.2)
46        40    CONTINUE
47
48        50    CALL RA2V(Y,X,N)
49
50              CALL EXIT
51              END


 1 $TITLE: 'RA2V: Regression for 2 Variables'
 2 $SUBTITLE: 'Copyright 1986 PJ Kaufman'
 3 $STORAGE:2
 4              SUBROUTINE RA2V(Y,X,N)
 5
 6 C---- Regression Analysis for 2 Variables
 7 C----      With Linear, Power and Log Transformations
 8
 9 C---- Y = Dependent variable
10 C---- X = Independent variable
11 C---- N = Number of data entries
12
13              CHARACTER*1 ANS
14              CHARACTER*2 SIGN,SIGNC
15              CHARACTER*9 YNAME,XNAME
16
17              DIMENSION X(100),Y(100),ZA(4),ZB(4),ZR(4)
18
19              DATA MAX/100/
20
21 C---- Perform linear regression
```

```
22          ITYPE=1
23          CALL BSTFIT(Y,X,N,ZA(1),ZB(1),ZR(1),SD,ITYPE)
24          SIGN=' '
25          IF(ZB(1).GE.0)SIGN=' +'
26
27          WRITE(6,6000)ZA(1),SIGN,ZB(1),ZR(1),SD
28    6000  FORMAT(/54X, 'r2  St dev'//
29        +           ' LINEAR  Y=',F8.3,A2,F8.3,'*X',18X,F7.1,F9.3)
30
31          CALL LSTSQ2(Y,X,N,ZA(4),ZB(4),C,S4)
32
33          SIGN = ' '
34          IF(ZB(4).GE.0)SIGN = ' +'
35          SIGNC = ' '
36          IF(C.GE.0)SIGNC =' +'
37          ITYPE = 4
38
39          WRITE(6,6004)ZA(4),SIGN,ZB(4),SIGNC,C,S4
40    6004  FORMAT(/' CURVI  Y=',F8.3,A2,F8.3,'*X',A2,F8.3,'*X2',12X,F9.3)
41
42          ITYPE=2
43          CALL BSTFIT(Y,X,N,ZA(2),ZB(2),ZR(2),SD,ITYPE)
44          SIGN=' '
45          IF(ZB(2).GE.0)SIGN=' +'
46
47          WRITE(6,6001)ZA(2),SIGN,ZB(2),ZR(2),SD
48    6001  FORMAT(/' LOG     Ln(Y)=',F8.3,A2,F8.3,'*Ln(X)',10X,F7.1,F9.3)
49
50          ITYPE=3
51          CALL BSTFIT(Y,X,N,ZA(3),ZB(3),ZR(3),SD,ITYPE)
52          SIGN=' '
53          IF(ZB(3).GE.0)SIGN=' +'
54
55          WRITE(6,6002)ZA(3),SIGN,ZB(3),ZR(3),SD
56    6002  FORMAT(/' EXPON  Ln(Y)=',F10.3,A2,F10.3,'*X',10X,F7.1,F9.3)
57
58          WRITE(*,7000)
59    7000  FORMAT(' Sample results (Y/N)?'\)
60          READ(*,5000)ANS
61    5000  FORMAT(A1)
62          IF(ANS.NE. 'N')THEN
63              WRITE(*,7001)
64    7001      FORMAT(/' Enter start, end and increments below'/
65        +             ' ssssss eeeee iiiii')
66              READ(*,5001)P,END,STEPS
67    5001      FORMAT(BN,F6.2,2F7.2)
68
69              WRITE(6,6009)
```

```
70   6009    FORMAT(///12X, 'X LINEAR  CURVI  LOG  EXPON'/)
71
72 C----  Calculate all four fits at the same time
73   100     Y1 = ZA(1) + ZB(1)*P
74           Y2 = ZA(4) + ZB(4)*P + C*P*P
75           Y3 = ZA(2) + ZB(2)*ALOG(P)
76           Y3 = EXP(Y3)
77           Y4 = ZA(3) + ZB(3)*P
78           Y4 = EXP(Y4)
79
80           WRITE(6,6010)P,Y1,Y2,Y3,Y4
81   6010    FORMAT(5X,5F8.2)
82
83           IF(P.LT.END)THEN
84             P = P + STEPS
85             GOTO 100
86             ENDIF
87
88           ENDIF
89
90           WRITE(*,7002)
91   7002    FORMAT(/' Plot results (Y/N)?'\)
92           READ(*,5000)ANS
93           IF(ANS.NE. 'N')THEN
94             WRITE(*,7003)
95   7003    FORMAT(' Name for x-scale (9 chars)?')
96           READ(*,5002)XNAME
97   5002    FORMAT(A)
98           WRITE(*,7004)
99   7004    FORMAT(' Name for y-scale (9 chars)?')
100          READ(*,5003)YNAME
101  5003    FORMAT(A9)
102  120     WRITE(*,7005)
103  7005    FORMAT(/' Which plot?'/'  1: Linear'/'  2: Logarithmic'/
104     +              '      3: Exponential'/'  4: Curvilinear'/
105     +              ' Which number?'\)
106          READ(*,5004)I
107  5004    FORMAT(BN,I4)
108          TC = C
109          IF(I.NE.4)TC = 0
110          CALL PLOTRA(N,X,Y,ZA(I),ZB(I),TC,I,XNAME,YNAME)
111          WRITE(*,7006)
112  7006    FORMAT(/' Another plot (Y/N)?'\)
113          READ(*,5000)ANS
114          IF(ANS.NE. 'N')GOTO 120
115          ENDIF
116
117          RETURN
118          END
```

```
 1 $TITLE: 'LSTSQ2: 2nd Order Least Squares'
 2 $SUBTITLE: 'P. J. Kaufman'
 3 $STORAGE:2
 4           SUBROUTINE LSTSQ2(Y,X,N,A,B,C,S)
 5
 6 C---- Second Order (Curvilinear) Regression for 2 variables
 7
 8 C---- Y = Dependent variable
 9 C---- X = Independent variable
10 C---- N = Number of data entries
11 C---- A = Constant term
12 C---- B = Coefficient of X
13 C---- C = Coefficient of X**2
14 C---- S = Standard deviation of residuals
15
16           DIMENSION X(2),Y(2)
17
18           DOUBLE PRECISION SXX,SXY,SYY,SXX2,SX2X2,SYX2
19
20 C---- Find the mean of x and y
21           AX = 0
22           AY = 0
23           DO 10 I = 1,N
24               AX = AX + X(I)
25      10      AY = AY + Y(I)
26           AX = AX/N
27           AY = AY/N
28
29 C---- Initialize for summations
30           SXX = 0
31           SXY = 0
32           SYY = 0
33           SXX2 = 0
34           SX2X2 = 0
35           SYX2 = 0
36
37 C---- Sums
38           DO 20 I = 1,N
39               XI = X(I)
40               YI = Y(I)
41               XM = XI - AX
42               YM = YI - AY
43               XM2 = XI*XI - AX*AX
44               SXX = SXX + XM*XM
45               SXY = SXY + XM*YM
46               SYY = SYY + YM*YM
47               SXX2 = SXX2 + XM*XM2
48               SX2X2 = SX2X2 + XM2*XM2
49      20      SYX2 = SYX2 + YM*XM2
```

```
50
51          B = (SXY*SX2X2 − SYX2*SXX2) / (SXX*SX2X2 − SXX2*SXX2)
52          C = (SXX*SYX2 − SXX2*SXY) / (SXX*SX2X2 − SXX2*SXX2)
53          A = AY − B*AX − C*AX*AX
54
55 C----  Standard deviation of residuals
56          S = 0
57          DO 150 J = 1,N
58              TY = Y(J)
59              TX = X(J)
60              RV = A + B*TX + C*TX*TX
61              ERR = TY − RV
62              AVGY=AVGY+TY
63    150       S = S + ERR*ERR
64
65          S = SQRT(S/(N−1))
66
67          RETURN
68          END


 1 $TITLE: 'REGVAL: Get regression value'
 2 $SUBTITLE: 'Copyright 1986 PJ Kaufman'
 3 $STORAGE:2
 4          FUNCTION REGVAL(X,A,B,ITYPE)
 5
 6 C----  Transform data from log form to normal form based upon the
 7 C----       type of regression fit (transmitted via ITYPE)
 8
 9          GOTO (110,120,130),ITYPE
10
11 C----      Linear
12    110    TY=A+B*X
13          GOTO 140
14
15 C----      Log
16    120    TY=A+B*ALOG(X)
17          TY=EXP(TY)
18          GOTO 140
19
20 C----      Exponential
21    130    TY=A+B*X
22          TY = EXP(TY)
23
24    140 REGVAL=TY
25
26          RETURN
27          END
```

```
119
120          SUBROUTINE BSTFIT(Y,X,N,A,B,R,SD,ITYPE)
121
122 C---- Basic linear regression
123 C---- N      Number of input items
124 C---- X      Independent variable
125 C---- Y      Dependent variable
126 C---- A      Y-intercept
127 C---- B      Slope
128 C---- R      Correlation coefficient
129 C---- SD     Standard deviation of residuals
130 C----
131 C---- If ITYPE = 1 then linear (no prior x,y conversion)
132 C----           = 2 then log (x=log x, y=log y)
133 C----           = 3 then exponential (x=log x)
134
135          DIMENSION X(2), Y(2)
136
137          DOUBLE PRECISION SUMX2,SUMY2,XY
138
139          SUMX=0.
140          SUMX2=0.
141          SUMY=0.
142          SUMY2=0.
143          XY=0.
144
145          DO 100 I=1,N
146             TX=X(I)
147             IF(ITYPE.EQ.2)TX=ALOG(TX)
148             TY=Y(I)
149             IF(ITYPE.NE.1)TY=ALOG(TY)
150             SUMX=SUMX+TX
151             SUMX2=SUMX2+TX*TX
152             SUMY=SUMY+TY
153             SUMY2=SUMY2+TY*TY
154             XY=XY+TX*TY
155    100     CONTINUE
156
157          IF(N.LT.2)RETURN
158          B=(N*XY-SUMX*SUMY)/(N*SUMX2-SUMX*SUMX)
159          A=(SUMY-B*SUMX)/N
160
161 C---- Correlation coefficient
162          R1=N*XY-SUMX*SUMY
163          R2=(N*SUMX2-SUMX*SUMX)*(N*SUMY2-SUMY*SUMY)
164          R = ((R1**2)/R2)*100
165
166 C---- Standard deviation around fitted function
```

```
167          SD=0.
168          DO 150 J=1,N
169             TY=Y(J)
170             TX=X(J)
171             RV=REGVAL(TX,A,B,ITYPE)
172             T=TY−RV
173     150     SD=SD+T*T
174          SD=SQRT(SD/(N−1))
175
176          RETURN
177          END
```

LEAST-SQUARES SOLUTION FOR CORN SOYBEANS

Least-Squares Repression Analysis   Data Input

Y (dep)	X (ind)
1.27	2.43
1.19	2.26
1.10	2.15
1.10	2.07
1.05	2.03
1.00	2.45
.98	2.36
1.09	2.44
1.12	2.52
1.18	2.74
1.16	2.98
1.24	2.93
1.03	2.69
1.08	2.63
1.15	2.63
1.33	3.08
1.08	3.24
1.57	6.22
2.55	6.12
3.02	6.33
2.54	4.92
2.25	6.81
2.02	5.88
2.25	6.61
2.52	6.28
3.11	7.61
2.50	6.05

					r2	St dev
LINEAR	Y=	.274 +	.339*X		84.2	.278
CURVI	Y=	.310 +	.323*X +	.002*X2		.278
LOG	Ln(Y)=	−.616 +	.799*Ln(X)		86.3	.282
EXPON	Ln(Y)=	−.373 +	.195*X		87.3	.283

X	LINEAR	CURVI	LOG	EXPON
1.00	.61	.63	.54	.84
1.50	.78	.80	.75	.92
2.00	.95	.96	.94	1.02
2.50	1.12	1.13	1.12	1.12
3.00	1.29	1.29	1.30	1.24
3.50	1.46	1.46	1.47	1.36
4.00	1.63	1.63	1.64	1.50
4.50	1.80	1.80	1.80	1.66
5.00	1.97	1.97	1.95	1.83
5.50	2.14	2.14	2.11	2.01
6.00	2.31	2.31	2.26	2.22
6.50	2.48	2.48	2.41	2.45
7.00	2.65	2.66	2.56	2.70

Plot of Regression Analysis

```
CORN    +----+----+----+----+----+----+----B----+----+----+----+----+----+----+----+----+-
    3.07 :                                                                              X :
    3.03 :                                                                                :
    2.99 :                                                   X                            :
    2.95 :                                                                                :
    2.91 :                                                                                :
    2.87 :                                                                                :
    2.83 :                                                                                :
    2.79 :                                                                            **:
    2.76 :                                                                           *    :
    2.72 :                                                                        **      :
    2.68 :                                                                       *        :
    2.64 :                                                                    **          :
    2.60 :                                                                                :
    2.56 :                                                                  *             :
    2.52 :                                 X                 X X          **              :
    2.48 :                                                   X          *                 :
    2.44 :                                                          **                    :
    2.40 :                                                        *                       :
    2.36 :                                                     **                         :
    2.32 :                                                                                :
    2.28 :                                                 **                             :
    2.24 :                                              X X                               :
    2.20 :                                            **                                  :
    2.16 :                                           *                                    :
    2.12 :                                          *                                     :
    2.08 :                                       **                                       :
    2.05 :                                      *                                         :
    2.01 :                                    **            X                             :
    1.97 :                                                                                :
    1.93 :                                  **                                            :
    1.89 :                                 *                                              :
    1.85 :                               **                                               :
    1.81 :                                                                                :
    1.77 :                             **                                                 :
    1.73 :                                                                                :
    1.69 :                          **                                                    :
    1.65 :                         *                                                      :
    1.61 :                                                                                :
    1.57 :                       **                                                       :
    1.53 :                      *                          X                              :
    1.49 :                    **                                                          :
    1.45 :                   *                                                            :
    1.41 :                 **                                                             :
    1.37 :                *                                                               :
    1.34 :              **                                                                :
    1.30 :            X                                                                   :
    1.26 :      X    **                                                                   :
    1.22 :          **X                                                                   :
    1.18 : X      X*                                                                      :
    1.14 :        X    X                                                                  :
    1.10 :XX     X                                                                        :
    1.06 :   *X X      X                                                                  :
    1.02 :X  *     X                                                                      :
     .98 : **  XX                                                                         :
         +----+----+----+----+----+----+----+----+----+----+----+----+----+----+----+----+-
            2.75        3.54        4.34        5.14        5.94        6.73        7.5
                                         SOYBEANS

         LINEAR    A =       .274. B =        .339. C =       .000
```

432

Plot of Regression Analysis

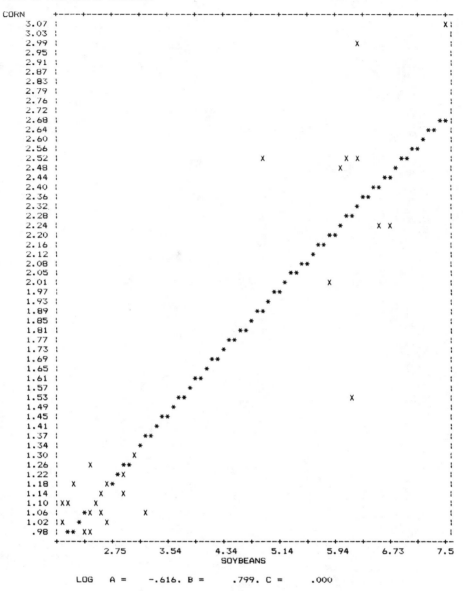

LOG   A =   -.616. B =   .799. C =   .000

Plot of Regression Analysis

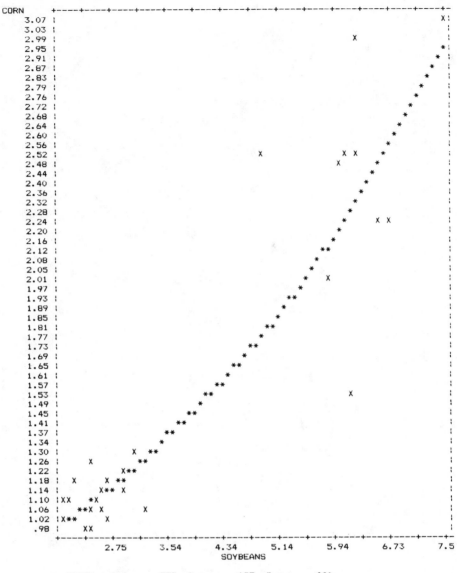

EXPON   A =   -.373. B =   .195. C =   .000

Plot of Regression Analysis

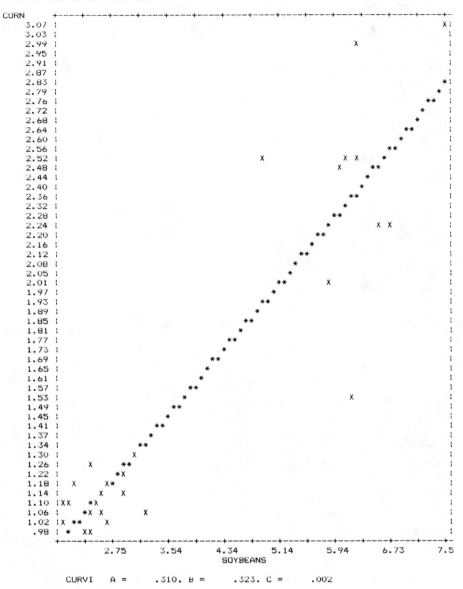

CORN

                                                                                            X
3.07 :   X :
3.03 :   :
2.99 :   X   :
2.95 :   :
2.91 :   :
2.87 :   :
2.83 :   * :
2.79 :   *   :
2.76 :   **   :
2.72 :   *   :
2.68 :   *   :
2.64 :   **   :
2.60 :   *   :
2.56 :   **   :
2.52 :   X   X X   *   :
2.48 :   X   **   :
2.44 :   *   :
2.40 :   :
2.36 :   **   :
2.32 :   *   :
2.28 :   **   :
2.24 :   X X   *   :
2.20 :   **   :
2.16 :   *   :
2.12 :   **   :
2.08 :   *   :
2.05 :   *   :
2.01 :   X   **   :
1.97 :   *   :
1.93 :   **   :
1.89 :   *   :
1.85 :   **   :
1.81 :   *   :
1.77 :   **   :
1.73 :   *   :
1.69 :   **   :
1.65 :   :
1.61 :   *   :
1.57 :   **   :
1.53 :   *   X   :
1.49 :   **   :
1.45 :   *   :
1.41 :   **   :
1.37 :   :
1.34 :   **   :
1.30 :   X   :
1.26 :   X   **   :
1.22 :   *X   :
1.18 : X   X*   :
1.14 :   X   X   :
1.10 :XX *X   :
1.06 : *X X   X   :
1.02 :X **   X   :
 .98 : * XX   :
        2.75   3.54   4.34   5.14   5.94   6.73   7.5
                              SOYBEANS

       CURVI   A =   .310. B =   .323. C =   .002

LEAST-SQUARES SOLUTION FOR SOYBEANS ONLY

Least Squares Regression Analysis   Data Input

Y (dep)	X (ind)
2.43	1.00
2.26	2.00
2.15	3.00
2.07	4.00
2.03	5.00
2.45	6.00
2.36	7.00
2.44	8.00
2.52	9.00
2.74	10.00
2.98	11.00
2.93	12.00
2.69	13.00
2.63	14.00
2.63	15.00
3.08	16.00
3.24	17.00
6.22	18.00
6.12	19.00
6.33	20.00
4.92	21.00
6.81	22.00
5.88	23.00
6.61	24.00
6.28	25.00
7.61	26.00
6.05	27.00

					r2	St dev
LINEAR	Y=	.987 +	.211*X		78.3	.881
CURVI	Y=	1.684 +	.112*X +	.004*X2		.830
LOG	Ln(Y)=	.271 +	.416*Ln(X)		58.0	1.212
EXPON	Ln(Y)=	.527 +	.053*X		83.1	.806

X	LINEAR	CURVI	LOG	EXPON
1.00	1.20	1.80	1.31	1.79
2.00	1.41	1.92	1.75	1.88
3.00	1.62	2.05	2.07	1.99
4.00	1.83	2.19	2.34	2.09
5.00	2.04	2.33	2.56	2.21
6.00	2.25	2.48	2.77	2.33
7.00	2.47	2.64	2.95	2.45
8.00	2.68	2.80	3.12	2.59
9.00	2.89	2.98	3.27	2.73
10.00	3.10	3.16	3.42	2.87
11.00	3.31	3.34	3.56	3.03
12.00	3.52	3.53	3.69	3.19
13.00	3.73	3.74	3.82	3.37
14.00	3.94	3.94	3.93	3.55
15.00	4.15	4.16	4.05	3.74
16.00	4.37	4.38	4.16	3.94
17.00	4.58	4.61	4.27	4.16
18.00	4.79	4.84	4.37	4.38
19.00	5.00	5.09	4.47	4.62
20.00	5.21	5.34	4.56	4.87
21.00	5.42	5.59	4.66	5.14
22.00	5.63	5.86	4.75	5.41
23.00	5.84	6.13	4.84	5.71
24.00	6.05	6.41	4.92	6.02
25.00	6.27	6.70	5.01	6.34
26.00	6.48	6.99	5.09	6.69
27.00	6.69	7.29	5.17	7.05
28.00	6.90	7.60	5.25	7.43
29.00	7.11	7.91	5.33	7.83
30.00	7.32	8.23	5.40	8.26
31.00	7.53	8.56	5.48	8.71
32.00	7.74	8.89	5.55	9.18
33.00	7.95	9.24	5.62	9.68
34.00	8.17	9.59	5.69	10.20
35.00	8.38	9.94	5.76	10.75
36.00	8.59	10.31	5.83	11.34
37.00	8.80	10.68	5.90	11.95
38.00	9.01	11.06	5.96	12.60
39.00	9.22	11.44	6.03	13.28
40.00	9.43	11.83	6.09	14.00

Plot of Regression Analysis

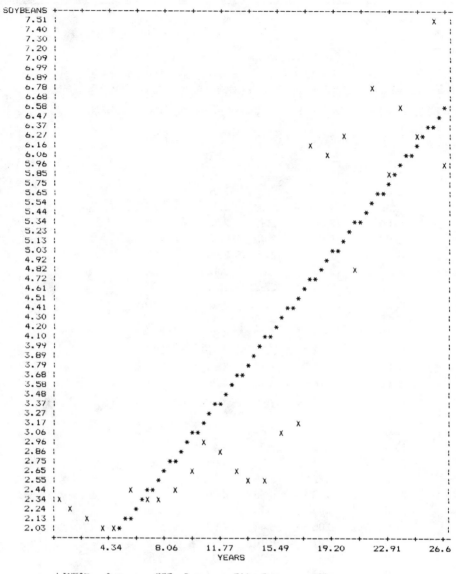

```
SOYBEANS +----+----+----+----+----+----+----+----+----+----+----+----+----+-
    7.51 :                                                              X  :
    7.40 :                                                                 :
    7.30 :                                                                 :
    7.20 :                                                                 :
    7.09 :                                                                 :
    6.99 :                                                                 :
    6.89 :                                                                 :
    6.78 :                                              X                  :
    6.68 :                                                                 :
    6.58 :                                                   X          *:
    6.47 :                                                              *  :
    6.37 :                                                             **  :
    6.27 :                                          X              X*      :
    6.16 :                                   X                         *   :
    6.06 :                                       X                  **     :
    5.96 :                                                         **    X:
    5.85 :                                                    X*           :
    5.75 :                                                    *            :
    5.65 :                                                  **             :
    5.54 :                                                 *               :
    5.44 :                                                *                :
    5.34 :                                              **                 :
    5.23 :                                             *                   :
    5.13 :                                                                 :
    5.03 :                                           **                    :
    4.92 :                                          *                      :
    4.82 :                                        X                        :
    4.72 :                                      **                         :
    4.61 :                                                                 :
    4.51 :                                     *                           :
    4.41 :                                    **                           :
    4.30 :                                                                 :
    4.20 :                                  *                              :
    4.10 :                                 **                              :
    3.99 :                                                                 :
    3.89 :                               *                                 :
    3.79 :                              *                                  :
    3.68 :                             **                                  :
    3.58 :                            *                                    :
    3.48 :                           *                                     :
    3.37 :                          **                                     :
    3.27 :                         *                                       :
    3.17 :                        *     X                                  :
    3.06 :                       **   X                                    :
    2.96 :                     *  X                                        :
    2.86 :                    *     X                                      :
    2.75 :                  **                                             :
    2.65 :                 *    X          X                               :
    2.55 :                *               X  X                             :
    2.44 :             X  **  X                                            :
    2.34 :X            **X X                                               :
    2.24 :  X                                                             :
    2.13 :     X     **                                                   :
    2.03 :    X X*                                                         :
         +----+----+----+----+----+----+----+----+----+----+----+----+----+-
            4.34      8.06      11.77     15.49     19.20     22.91     26.6
                                    YEARS
```

LINEAR   A =   .987. B =   .211. C =   .000

438

Plot of Regression Analysis

```
SOYBEANS +----+----+----+----+----+----+----+----+----+----+----+----+----+----+----+
   7.51 :                                                                      X  :
   7.40 :                                                                         :
   7.30 :                                                                         :
   7.20 :                                                                         :
   7.09 :                                                                         :
   6.99 :                                                                         :
   6.89 :                                                                         :
   6.78 :                                                   X                     :
   6.68 :                                                                         :
   6.58 :                                                      X                  :
   6.47 :                                                                         :
   6.37 :                                                                         :
   6.27 :                                               X              X          :
   6.16 :                                        X                                 :
   6.06 :                                          X                              :
   5.96 :                                                                      X :
   5.85 :                                                   X                     :
   5.75 :                                                                         :
   5.65 :                                                                         :
   5.54 :                                                                         :
   5.44 :                                                                         :
   5.34 :                                                                         :
   5.23 :                                                                         :
   5.13 :                                                                     * :
   5.03 :                                                                 ***     :
   4.92 :                                                               ****      :
   4.82 :                                          X          ***                 :
   4.72 :                                               ***                       :
   4.61 :                                             ***                         :
   4.51 :                                        ***                              :
   4.41 :                                      ***                                :
   4.30 :                                    **                                   :
   4.20 :                                 ***                                     :
   4.10 :                              ***                                        :
   3.99 :                            **                                           :
   3.89 :                           ***                                           :
   3.79 :                          **                                             :
   3.68 :                        **                                               :
   3.58 :                       **                                                :
   3.48 :                      **                                                 :
   3.37 :                    **                                                   :
   3.27 :                   **                                                    :
   3.17 :                 **                                                      :
   3.06 :                **             X                                         :
   2.96 :              *            X                                             :
   2.86 :             **        X                                                 :
   2.75 :            *                                                            :
   2.65 :          **      X       X                                              :
   2.55 :          *               X  X                                           :
   2.44 :        *   X      X                                                     :
   2.34 :X       *      X  X                                                      :
   2.24 :  X     *                                                                :
   2.13 :    X**                                                                  :
   2.03 :     *  X X                                                              :
        +----+----+----+----+----+----+----+----+----+----+----+----+----+----+----+
            4.34        8.06       11.77       15.49       19.20       22.91    26.6
                                         YEARS

             LOG   A =      .271. B =      .416. C =      .000
```

439

Plot of Regression Analysis

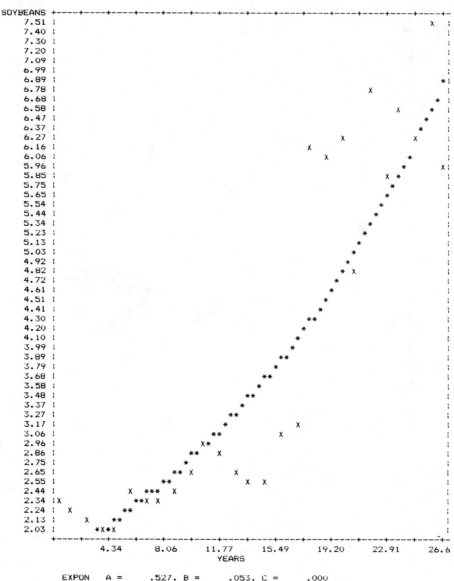

Plot of Regression Analysis

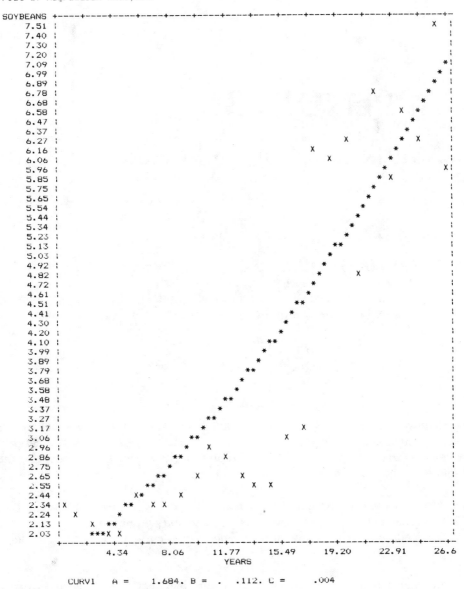

CURVI   A =   1.684. B = .   .112. C =   .004

APPENDIX 3

Matrix Solution to Linear Equations

GENERAL FORM

A matrix is a rectangular arrangement of elements into rows and columns. A matrix A is said to be $m \times n$ (m by n) if there are m rows and n columns in A.

$$a_{m \times n} = \begin{pmatrix} a_{11} & a_{12} & \cdots & a_{1n} \\ a_{21} & a_{22} & \cdots & a_{2n} \\ \vdots & \vdots & & \vdots \\ a_{m1} & a_{m2} & \cdots & a_{mn} \end{pmatrix}$$

Certain properties of a matrix make it a valuable tool for solving simultaneous linear equations. These elementary matrix operations, called transformations, allow you to alter the rows (which will represent equations) without changing the solution. There are three basic row operations:

1. Multiplication or division of all elements of the row by any number.
2. Interchanging of any two rows (and consequently of all rows).
3. The addition or subtraction of the elements of one row with the corresponding elements of another.

In order to relate the matrix to simultaneous linear equations, consider a three-equation example:

$$a_{11}x_1 + a_{12}x_2 + a_{13}x_3 = a_{14} \tag{1}$$

$$a_{21}x_1 + a_{22}x_2 + a_{23}x_3 = a_{24} \tag{2}$$

$$a_{31}x_1 + a_{32}x_2 + a_{33}x_3 = a_{34} \tag{3}$$

This is the same as the multivariate approximation in three variables once the sums are substituted and only the coefficients remain as unknowns.

The three elementary row operations can now be interpreted in terms of simple operations on an equation:

1. When both sides of an equation are multiplied or divided by the same value, the results are equal.

442

2. Any two equations in a system of equations can be interchanged with no effect.
3. When two equals are added or subtracted, the results are equal.

Putting these rules into use, write the coefficients of the three simultaneous linear equations as a 3×4 coefficient matrix,

$$\begin{pmatrix} a_{11} & a_{12} & a_{13} & a_{14} \\ a_{21} & a_{22} & a_{23} & a_{24} \\ a_{31} & a_{32} & a_{33} & a_{34} \end{pmatrix}$$

with the objective of reducing the matrix to the form

$$\begin{pmatrix} 1 & 0 & 0 & A_1 \\ 0 & 1 & 0 & A_2 \\ 0 & 0 & 1 & A_3 \end{pmatrix}$$

which would mean that $x_1 = A_1$, $x_2 = A_2$ and $x_3 = A_3$ since

$$1 \cdot x_1 + 0 \cdot x_2 + 0 \cdot x_3 = A_1$$
$$0 \cdot x_1 + 1 \cdot x_2 + 0 \cdot x_3 = A_2$$
$$0 \cdot x_1 + 0 \cdot x_2 + 1 \cdot x_3 = A_3$$

To achieve the results, perform the following steps. Divide the first equation by a_{11}, the first element, leaving

$$\left(1 \quad \frac{a_{12}}{a_{11}} \quad \frac{a_{13}}{a_{11}} \quad \frac{a_{14}}{a_{11}} \right) \tag{1-1}$$

and then multiply by a_{21} to get the first elements in rows one and two the same:

$$\left(a_{21} \quad \frac{a_{12}(a_{21})}{a_{11}} \quad \frac{a_{13}(a_{21})}{a_{11}} \quad \frac{a_{14}(a_{21})}{a_{11}} \right) \tag{1-2}$$

Now subtract (1-2) from (2) and get

$$\left(0 \quad a_{22} - \frac{a_{12}(a_{21})}{a_{11}} \quad a_{23} - \frac{a_{13}(a_{21})}{a_{11}} \quad a_{24} - \frac{a_{14}(a_{21})}{a_{11}} \right) \tag{2-1}$$

That successfully eliminates the first element a_{21} of the second equation. By going back and multiplying (1-1) by a_{31} and subtracting the resulting equation from (3), a_{31} can be eliminated from equation (3). Now column 1 looks like

$$\begin{pmatrix} 1 \\ 0 \\ 0 \end{pmatrix}$$

Column two or any column can be operated upon in the same manner as the first column:

1. Divide row n by the element in position $n(a_{nn})$, thereby setting $a_{nn} = 1$
2. Multiply row n by the corresponding element in row $i \neq n$, so that $a_{nn} \times a_{in} = a_{in}$

3. Subtract row n from row i, resulting in $a_{in} = 0$, and all other elements reduced by the corresponding element in row n

Continue this procedure for each row i until all elements

$$a_{1n}, a_{2n}, \ldots, a_{i-1n}, a_{i+1n}, \ldots, a_{mn} = 0 \quad \text{and} \quad a_{in} = 1.$$

For example, consider

$$\begin{pmatrix} 2 & 4 & 8 & 34 \\ 6 & 5 & 2 & 22 \\ 3 & 6 & 5 & 30 \end{pmatrix}$$

Divide row 1 by 2 (position a_{11}):

$$\begin{pmatrix} 1 & 2 & 4 & 17 \\ 6 & 5 & 2 & 22 \\ 3 & 6 & 5 & 30 \end{pmatrix}$$

Multiply row 1 by 6 to get (6   12   24   102) and subtract the new calculated row from row 2:

$$\begin{pmatrix} 1 & 2 & 4 & 17 \\ 0 & -7 & -22 & -80 \\ 3 & 6 & 5 & 30 \end{pmatrix}$$

Multiply row 1 by the number 3 to get (3   6   12   51), then subtract the calculated row from row 3:

$$\begin{pmatrix} 1 & 2 & 4 & 17 \\ 0 & -7 & -22 & -80 \\ 0 & 0 & -7 & -21 \end{pmatrix}$$

Column 1 is now completed. Divide Row 2 by -7 and get:

$$\begin{pmatrix} 1 & 2 & 4 & 17 \\ 0 & 1 & \dfrac{+22}{7} & \dfrac{+80}{7} \\ 0 & 0 & -7 & -21 \end{pmatrix}$$

Multiply row 2 by 2 and subtract the result (0   2   44/7   160/7) from row 1 in order to eliminate position 2 in the first row:

$$\begin{pmatrix} 1 & 0 & \dfrac{-16}{7} & \dfrac{-41}{7} \\ 0 & 1 & \dfrac{+22}{7} & \dfrac{+80}{7} \\ 0 & 0 & -7 & -21 \end{pmatrix}$$

Since the element in row 3 and column 2 is already 0, move to row 3. Divide row 3 by -7 and get

$$\begin{pmatrix} 1 & 0 & \dfrac{-16}{7} & \dfrac{-41}{7} \\ 0 & 1 & \dfrac{+22}{7} & \dfrac{+80}{7} \\ 0 & 0 & 1 & 3 \end{pmatrix}$$

Multiply row 3 by $-16/7$ and subtract the result $(0 \quad 0 \quad -16/7 \quad -48/7)$ from row 1:

$$\begin{pmatrix} 1 & 0 & 0 & 1 \\ 0 & 1 & \dfrac{+22}{7} & \dfrac{+80}{7} \\ 0 & 0 & 1 & 3 \end{pmatrix}$$

Multiply row 3 by $+22/7$ and subtract $(0 \quad 0 \quad +22/7 \quad +66/7)$ from row 2:

$$\begin{pmatrix} 1 & 0 & 0 & 1 \\ 0 & 1 & 0 & 2 \\ 0 & 0 & 1 & 3 \end{pmatrix}$$

The results show that $x_1 = 1$, $x_2 = 2$, $x_3 = 3$.

There are other ways to reduce the matrix to the final representation, but this technique is well-defined and lends itself to being programmed on a computer.

SOLUTION TO WEATHER PROBABILITIES EXPRESSED AS A MARKOV CHAIN

$$\text{Let } A = P(\text{clear})_{i+1} \quad = P(\text{clear})_i$$
$$B = P(\text{cloudy})_{i+1} = P(\text{cloudy})_i$$
$$C = P(\text{rainy})_{i+1} \quad = P(\text{rainy})_i$$

since when they converge all ith elements will equal $(i + 1)$th elements. The equations are

$$A = .7A + .2B + .2C \tag{1}$$
$$B = .25A + .6B + .4C \tag{2}$$
$$C = .05A + .2B + .4C \tag{3}$$

In addition

$$A + B + C = 1 \tag{4}$$

To solve this system of equations using matrices, convert and add equation (3) to (4),

$$-.3A + .2B + .2C = 0 \tag{1'}$$

$$.25A - .4B + .4C = 0 \tag{2'}$$

$$1.05A + 1.2B + .4C = 1 \tag{3'}$$

which becomes the matrix

$$\begin{pmatrix} -.3 & .2 & .2 & 0 \\ .25 & -.4 & .4 & 0 \\ 1.05 & 1.2 & .4 & 1 \end{pmatrix} \begin{matrix} (1') \\ (2') \\ (3') \end{matrix}$$

The following are key steps in the solution:

1. Reduce the first row,

$$\begin{pmatrix} 1 & -.6667 & -.6667 & 0 \\ .25 & -.4 & .4 & 0 \\ 1.05 & 1.2 & .4 & 1 \end{pmatrix}$$

and make the leading entries of rows 2 and 3 zero:

$$\begin{pmatrix} 1 & -.6667 & -.6667 & 0 \\ 0 & -.2333 & .5667 & 0 \\ 0 & 1.9000 & 1.1000 & 1 \end{pmatrix}$$

2. Reduce the second row,

$$\begin{pmatrix} 1 & -.6667 & -.6667 & 0 \\ 0 & 1 & -2.4291 & 0 \\ 0 & 1.9000 & 1.1000 & 1 \end{pmatrix}$$

and make the second entries of rows 1 and 3 zero

$$\begin{pmatrix} 1 & 0 & 2.2857 & 0 \\ 0 & 1 & -2.4291 & 0 \\ 0 & 0 & 5.7143 & 1 \end{pmatrix}$$

3. Reduce the third row,

$$\begin{pmatrix} 1 & 0 & 2.2862 & 0 \\ 0 & 1 & -2.4291 & 0 \\ 0 & 0 & 1 & .1750 \end{pmatrix}$$

and make the third entry of rows 1 and 2 zero:

$$\begin{pmatrix} 1 & 0 & 0 & .4000 \\ 0 & 1 & 0 & .4250 \\ 0 & 0 & 1 & .1750 \end{pmatrix}$$

Then $A = .4000$, $B = .4250$, and $C = .1750$.

COMPUTER PROGRAM SOLUTION

The following FORTRAN program accepts a system of ten equations in ten variables (unknowns) and applies the matrix method of solution. This is done using the method of Gaussian elimination discussed in the previous section.

```
$TITLE: 'MATRIX: MATRIX SOLUTION'
$SUBTITLE: 'COPYRIGHT 1986 PJ KAUFMAN'
$STORAGE:2
        PROGRAM MATRIX
C---- Matrix solution to simultaneous linear equations
C---- Copyright 1986 PJ Kaufman

        DIMENSION A(10,10), C(10)

        OPEN(6,FILE='PRN')

        WRITE(*,7000)
7000    FORMAT(' Enter matrix size (n)>'\)
        READ(*,5000)N
5000    FORMAT (BN,I4)
        IF(N.GT.10) STOP 'Matrix limited to 10 × 10'
        WRITE(*,7001) (I,I=1,N)
7001    FORMAT (' Enter matrix elements row by row under headings ...'/
      +          ' do not include constant to right of ='/
      +          7X,10(I2,'-xxxxx'))
        DO 20 I = 1,N
          WRITE(*,7003)I
7003      FORMAT(' Row',I2,':'\)
          READ(*,5003)(A(I,J),J=1,N)
5003      FORMAT(BN,10F8.0)
20        CONTINUE

        WRITE(*,7004)(J,J=1,N)
        WRITE(6,7004)(J,J=1,N)
7004    FORMAT(/' Input matrix is:'//9x,10(I2,'-col '))
        DO 30 I = 1,N
          WRITE(6,7005)I,(A(I,J),J=1,N)
```

```
    30      WRITE(*,7005)I,(A(I,J),J=1,N)
  7005      FORMAT(/' Row',I2,':',10F8.3)


          WRITE(*,7008)(I,I=1,N)
  7008   FORMAT(/' Enter constant vector under headings...'/
      +         1X,10(I1,'xxxxxx '))
          READ(*,5008)(C(I),I=1,N)
  5008   FORMAT(BN,10F8.0)
          WRITE(*,7009)(C(I),I=1,N)
          WRITE(6,7009)(C(I),I=1,N)
  7009   FORMAT(/' Constant vector is:'/10F8.3)


C----   Process row by row (Gaussian Elimination)
          DO 100 I = 1,N


          DIV = A(I,I)
          DO 40 J = 1,N
    40        A(I,J) = A(I,J)/DIV
          C(I) = C(I)/DIV


C----   Zero out column I for each row
          DO 60 J = 1,N
              IF(J.EQ.I)GOTO 60
              FACTOR = A(J,I)
              DO 50 K = I,N
    50            A(J,K) = A(J,K) - A(I,K)*FACTOR
              C(J) = C(J) - C(I)*FACTOR
    60        CONTINUE

   100      CONTINUE


          WRITE(*,7007)(C(I),I=1,N)
          WRITE(6,7007)(C(I),I=1,N)
  7007   FORMAT(/' Solution vector is:'/10F8.3)

          CALL EXIT
          END
```

MATRIX
Enter matrix size (N)>3
Enter matrix elements row by row under headings...
do not include constant to right of =

	1-xxxxx	2-xxxxx	3-xxxxx
Row 1:	2	4	8
Row 2:	6	5	2
Row 3:	3	6	5

Input matrix is:

	1-col	2-col	3-col
Row 1:	2.000	4.000	8.000
Row 2:	6.000	5.000	2.000
Row 3:	3.000	6.000	5.000

Enter constant vector under headings...

1xxxxxx	2xxxxxx	3xxxxxx
34	22	30

Constant vector is:
 34.000   22.000   30.000

Solution vector is:
 1.000   2.000   3.000

APPENDIX 4

Trigonometric Regression for Finding Cycles

The following computer programs and examples solve the cycle problems in Chapter 8.

SINGLE FREQUENCY TRIGONOMETRIC REGRESSION

The FORTRAN program TRIG1 and the subroutine LINREG are used to find the single-frequency representation of the copper cycle. The program output is clearly separated into the following information:

1. Input data, where each time period is the average cash price for a calendar quarter.
2. The solution to the linear regression, giving the detrending line. With $b = .267$, there is an inflationary bias of $+.267¢$ per quarter.
3. The detrended data resulting from subtracting the line values (2) from the original data (1).
4. Intermediate values for α, ω, and T.
5. The constant values a and b for the normal equations solving the single frequency problem.
6. The cycle resulting from the detrended data.
7. The final cycle with the trend added back.

The results show a copper cycle of approximately 8.4 quarters, or slightly more than $2\frac{1}{2}$ years.

An additional test was run on monthly cash corn prices from 1964 through 1983 to see if the seasonal cycle dominated the detrended pattern. The linear regression equation used for detrending was calculated as:

$$y = .939 + .01x$$

showing only a 1¢ per bushel per month rate of inflation, despite the bull markets in 1973 and 1980–1981. The cycle showed a period of 21.4 months, with the last highs in the cycle in August 1983 and the last lows in September 1982. Because this is clearly not a seasonal pattern it must be either:

1. Dominated by other supply/demand characteristics, such as stocks, or,
2. Distorted by the nonseasonal rallies of 1973 and 1980, which each took three years to return to the traditional seasonal pattern.

```
            PROGRAM TRIG1
C----   Single Frequency Trigonometric Regression
C----   Copyright 1986 PJ Kaufman

            DIMENSION X(250), Y(250), D(250), R(250)
            DOUBLE PRECISION SC2,SCD

            DATA MAX/250/

            OPEN(6,FILE='PRN')

C----   Read data, set X to incremental time
            I = 1
            WRITE(*,7000)
  7000    FORMAT(' SINGLE FREQUENCY TRIGONOMETRIC REGRESSION'/
      +           ' Enter data 1 per line'/' Extra ⟨return⟩ ends input'//
      +           ' Enter below:')

   10    WRITE(*,7001)I
  7001    FORMAT(I4,'>'\)
            READ(*,5000)Y(I)
  5000    FORMAT(BN,F8.2)
            X(I) = I
            IF(Y(I).NE.0)THEN
                IF(I.GT.MAX)STOP 'Maximum data exceeded'
                I = I+1
                GOTO 10
                ENDIF
            N = I−1
            WRITE(6,6000)
  6000    FORMAT('1Single Frequency Trigonometric Regression',20X,
      +           'Data Input'//' Time',16X,'Prices')
            DO 40 J = 1,N,4
   40        WRITE(6,6001)J,(Y(I),I=J,J+3)
  6001        FORMAT(I4,4F8.2)

C----   Linear regression analysis for detrending
            CALL LINREG(N,Y,A,B,SD)
            WRITE(6,6002)A,B
  6002    FORMAT(/' Linear regression results: A =',F8.3,', B =',F8.3)
```

```
C---- Detrend data into D and computer sums for equation (4)
      DO 60 I = 1,N
60       D(I) = Y(I) - (A+B*I)
C---- Print detrended data
      WRITE(6,6003)
6003  FORMAT(/' Detrended data'/)
      DO 65 I =  1,N,4
65       WRITE(6,6001)I,(D(J),J=I,I+3)
      SC2 = 0
      SCD = 0
C---- Solve equation (4) using detrended data
      DO 70 I = 2,N-1
         DI = D(I)
         SC2 = SC2 + DI*DI
70       SCD = SCD + DI*(D(I-1)+D(I+1))


      ALPHA = SCD/SC2
      WRITE(6,6004)SC2,SCD,ALPHA
6004  FORMAT(/'Sum C-squared =',F8.1,', Sum C x D =',F8.1,', Alpha =',
     +         F8.3)
C---- Solve for omega
      W = ACOS(ALPHA/2)
      T = 360/W
      WRITE(6,6014)W,T
6014  FORMAT(/' Omega (W) =',F5.1,' degrees, Period (T) =',F6.2,
     +            ' time units')


C---- Sums for normal equations
      COS2 = 0
      COSSIN = 0
      YCOS = 0
      SINCOS = 0
      SIN2 = 0
      YSIN = 0

      DO 80 I = 1,N
         C = COS(W*I)
         S = SIN(W*I)
         COS2 = COS2 + C*C
         COSSIN = COSSIN + C*S
         YCOS = YCOS + Y(I)*C
         SINCOS = SINCOS +S*C
         SIN2 = SIN2 + S*S
80       YSIN = YSIN + Y(I)*S


C---- Solve normal equations
      TB = (YSIN*COS2 - YCOS)/(SIN2*COS2 - COSSIN)
```

```
          TA = (YCOS − B*COSSIN) / COS2
          WRITE(6,6005)TA,TB
 6005     FORMAT(/' Solution to normal equations: A =',F8.3,', B =',F8.3)

C────  Values of fitted curve using detrended data
          DO 90 I = 1,N
   90        R(I) = TA*COS(W*I) + TB*SIN(W*I)
          WRITE(6,6006)
 6006     FORMAT(/' Trigonometric regression results using detrended data',
     +             /)
          DO 100 I = 1,N,4
  100        WRITE(6,6001)I,(R(J),J=I,I+3)

C────  Add trend back to result
          DO 110 I = 1,N
  110        R(I) = R(I) + A + B*I

          WRITE(6,6007)
 6007     FORMAT(/' Final regression results with trend added back '/)
          DO 120 I = 1,N,4
  120        WRITE(6,6001)I, (R(J),J=I,I+3)

          CALL EXIT
          END

          SUBROUTINE LINREG(N,DATA,A,B,SD)
C────  Generalized simple linear regression

          DIMENSION DATA(2)

C────  Initialize sums
          SX=0.
          SY=0.
          SXY=0.
          SX2=0.
          A=0.
          B=0.
          SD=0.
          IF(N.LE.2)RETURN

          DO 100 I=2,N
             X = I
             Y = DATA(I)
             SX=SX+X
             SY=SY+Y
             SXY=SXY+Y*X
             SX2=SX2+X*X
  100        CONTINUE
```

```
          M=N−1
          B=(M*SXY−SX*SY) / (M*SX2−SX*SX)
          A=(SY−B*SX) / M

C−−−−    Residuals
          SSR=0
          DO 200 I=2,N
             Y=DATA(I)
             R=Y−(A+B*I)
             SSR=SSR+R*R
   200       CONTINUE

          SD=SQRT(SSR/M)
          RETURN
          END
```

Single Frequency Trigonometric Regression

Time		Prices		
1	22.12	22.46	22.17	22.00
5	23.18	24.56	25.57	30.59
9	28.23	33.77	35.90	40.05
13	46.22	51.48	40.76	40.16
17	36.51	29.30	30.36	36.42
21	39.75	30.07	29.08	32.13
25	38.94	42.95	43.38	46.23
29	47.70	46.98	35.78	27.35
33	25.40	29.45	27.15	28.48
37	32.74	33.53	30.01	29.25
41	36.82	45.07	55.13	65.51
45	66.56	70.06	27.30	35.62
49	32.06	31.46	35.75	36.46
53	38.22	43.24	45.46	38.96
57	37.08	38.72	34.01	33.00
61	35.07	40.23	41.63	44.95
65	51.12	63.71	59.56	63.38

Linear regression results: A = 28.889, B = .267

Detrended data

1	−7.04	−6.96	−7.52	−7.96
5	−7.05	−5.93	−5.19	−.44
9	−3.06	2.21	4.07	7.95
13	13.86	18.85	7.86	7.00
17	3.08	−4.40	−3.61	2.19
21	5.25	−4.70	−5.96	−3.17
25	3.37	7.11	7.28	9.86

29	11.06	10.07	−1.39	−10.09
33	−12.31	−8.52	−11.09	−10.03
37	−6.04	−5.51	−9.30	−10.33
41	−3.02	4.96	14.75	24.86
45	25.65	28.88	−14.15	−6.10
49	−9.92	−10.79	−6.77	−6.32
53	−4.83	−.08	1.87	−4.89
57	−7.04	−5.67	−10.64	−11.92
61	−10.12	−5.23	−4.09	−1.04
65	4.86	17.19	12.77	16.32

Sum C-squared = 6338.4, Sum C × D = 9282.2, Alpha = 1.464

Omega (W) = .7 degrees, Period (T) =480.50 time units

Solution to normal equations: A = −.603, B = 1.831

Trigonometric regression results using detrended data

1	.81	1.78	1.80	.86
5	−.54	−1.66	−1.88	−1.10
9	.27	1.50	1.92	1.32
13	.01	−1.31	−1.92	−1.51
17	−.28	1.09	1.88	1.66
21	.56	−.85	−1.80	−1.79
25	−.82	.59	1.68	1.87
29	1.06	−.32	−1.53	−1.92
33	−1.28	.04	1.34	1.92
37	1.47	.23	−1.13	−1.89
41	−1.64	−.51	.89	1.82
45	1.77	.77	−.64	−1.71
49	−1.86	−1.02	.37	1.56
53	1.91	1.24	−.09	−1.38
57	−1.93	−1.44	−.19	1.17
61	1.90	1.61	.46	−.94
65	−1.83	−1.75	−.72	.69

Final regression results with trend added back

1	29.96	31.21	31.50	30.82
5	29.68	28.83	28.88	29.93
9	31.57	33.06	33.75	33.41
13	32.37	31.32	30.98	31.66
17	33.15	34.79	35.85	35.90
21	35.06	33.92	33.23	33.52
25	34.75	36.43	37.79	38.24
29	37.70	36.58	35.64	35.52
33	36.43	38.02	39.59	40.43

37	40.25	39.28	38.18	37.69
41	38.21	39.60	41.27	42.46
45	42.68	41.95	40.81	40.01
49	40.12	41.23	42.89	44.34
53	44.96	44.56	43.49	42.47
57	42.19	42.95	44.47	46.09
61	47.09	47.07	46.18	45.05
65	44.42	44.78	46.07	47.74

TWO-FREQUENCY TRIGONOMETRIC REGRESSION

The FORTRAN program TRIG2 and its subroutines LINREG (found in Appendix 4) and MTX are used to find the two-frequency representation of the copper cycle. The program output is clearly separated into the following steps.

1. Input data, where each time period is the average cash price for a calendar quarter.
2. The solution to the linear regression, giving the detrending line.
3. The detrended data resulting from subtracting the line values (2) from the original data (1).
4. Intermediate values for α_1, α_2, ω_1, and ω_2.
5. Resulting values a_1, b_1, a_2, and b_2, which are derived from the matrix solution using Gaussian elimination.
6. The cycle resulting from the detrended data.
7. The final cycle with the trend added back.

```
            PROGRAM TRIG2
C----   2-Frequency Trigonometric Regression
C----   Copyright 1986 PJ Kaufman

            DIMENSION X(250), Y(250), D(250), R(250), A(4,4), B(4)

            EQUIVALENCE (A(1,1),C2W1),(A(1,2),CW1SW1),(A(1,3),CW1CW2),
        +              (A(1,4),CW1SW2),(A(2,1),DUP1),(A(2,2),S2W1),
        +              (A(2,3),SW1CW2),(A(2,4),SW1SW2),(A(3,1),DUP2),
        +              (A(3,2),DUP3),(A(3,3),C2W2),(A(3,4),CW2SW2),
        +              (A(4,1),DUP4),(A(4,2),DUP5),(A(4,3),DUP6),
        +              (A(4,4),S2W2),(B(1),YCW1),(B(2),YSW1),(B(3),YCW2),
        +              (B(4),YSW2),(B(1),A1),(B(2),B1),(B(3),A2),(B(4),B2)
            DATA MAX/250/,NDIM/4/

            OPEN(6,FILE='PRN')

C----   Read data, set X to incremental time
            I = 1
            WRITE(*,7000)
    7000 FORMAT(' 2-FREQUENCY TRIGONOMETRIC REGRESSION'/
```

```
      +             ' Enter data 1 per line'/'Extra ⟨return⟩ end input'//
      +             ' Enter below:')

   10    WRITE(*,7001)I
 7001    FORMAT(I4,'>'\)
         READ(*,5000)Y(I)
 5000    FORMAT(BN,F8.2)
         X(I) = I
         IF(Y(I).NE.0)THEN
            IF(I.GT.MAX)STOP 'Maximum data exceeded'
            I = I+1
            GOTO 10
            ENDIF
         N = I−1
         WRITE(6,6000)
 6000    FORMAT('12-Frequency Trigonometric Regression'//
      +            'Time',16X,'Prices')
         DO 40 J = 1,N,4
   40       WRITE(6,6001)J,(Y(I),I=J,J+3)
 6001       FORMAT(I4,4F8.2)


C−−−−  Linear regression analysis for detrending
         CALL LINREG(N,Y,ALIN,BLIN,SD)
         WRITE(6,6002)ALIN,BLIN
 6002    FORMAT(/' Linear regression results: A =',F8.3,', B =',F8.3)


C−−−−  Detrend data into D and computer sums for equation (4)
         DO 60 I = 1,N
   60       D(I) = Y(I) − (ALIN+BLIN*I)
C−−−−  Print detrended data
         WRITE(6,6003)
 6003    FORMAT(/' Detrended data'/)
         DO 65 I = 1,N,4
   65       WRITE(6,6001)I,(D(J),J=I,I+3)
         SC2 = 0
         SCD = 0
         SCP = 0
         SD2 = 0
         SDP = 0
C−−−−  Solve for alpha1 and alpha2 using detrended data
         DO 70 I = 2,N−3
            C = D(I) + D(I+2)
            T = D(I+1)
            P = D(I−1) + D(I+3)
            SC2 = SC2 + C*C
            SCD = SCD + C*T
            SCP = SCP + C*P
            SD2 = SD2 + T*T
   70       SDP = SDP + T*P
```

```
        ALPHA2 = (SDP*SC2-SCP)/(SD2*SC2-SCD)
        ALPHA1 = (SCP-ALPHA2*SCD)/SC2
        T = SQRT(ALPHA1*ALPHA1+8*(1+ALPHA2/2))
        W1 = ACOS((ALPHA1+T)/4)
        W2 = ACOS((ALPHA1-T)/4)

        WRITE(6,6004)SC2,SCD,SCP,SD2,SDP,ALPHA1,ALPHA2,W1,W2
6004    FORMAT(/' Intermediate values:'//
     +          ' SUMS C2 =', F8.1,', C*D =',F8.1,', C*P =',F8.1/
     +          '        D2 =', F8.1,', D*P =',F8.1// ' Alpha1 =',F8.3,
     +          ',   Alpha2 =', F8.3,' Omega1 =',F5.2,', Omega2 =',F5.2)

C----   Sums for normal equations. . .to be used for matrix solution
        C2W1 = 0
        CW1SW1 = 0
        CW1CW2 = 0
        CW1SW2 = 0
        YCW1 = 0
        S2W1 = 0
        SW1CW2 = 0
        SW1SW2 = 0
        YSW1 = 0
        C2W2 = 0
        CW2SW2 = 0
        YCW2 = 0
        S2W2 = 0
        YSW2 = 0

        DO 100 I = 1,N
          DI = D(I)
          SW1 = SIN(W1*I)
          CW1 = COS(W1*I)
          SW2 = SIN(W2*I)
          CW2 = COS(W2*I)
          C2W1 = C2W1 + CW1*SW1
          CW1SW1 = CW1SW1 + CW1*SW1
          CW1CW2 = CW1CW2 + CW1*CW2
          CW1SW2 = CW1SW2 + CW1*SW2
          YCW1 = YCW1 + DI*CW1
          S2W1 = S2W1 + SW1*SW1
          SW1CW2 = SW1SW2 + SW1*CW2
          SW1SW2 = SW1SW2 + SW1*SW2
          YSW1 = YSW1 + DI
          C2W2 = C2W2 + CW2*CW2
          CW2SW2 = CW2SW2 + CW2*SW2
          YCW2 = YCW2 + DI*CW2
          S2W2 = S2W2 + SW2*SW2
100       YSW2 = YSW2 + DI*SW2
```

```
C----    Duplicate calculations for matrix
         DUP1 = CW1SW1
         DUP2 = CW1CW2
         DUP3 = SW1CW2
         DUP4 = CW1SW2
         DUP5 = SW1SW2
         DUP6 = CW2SW2

         WRITE(6,6009)
  6009   FORMAT(/' Coefficient matrix:'/)
         DO 110 I = 1,NDIM
   110       WRITE(6,6010)(A(I,J),J=1,4),B(I)
  6010       FORMAT(5F8.3)

C----    Solve using matrix Gaussian Elimination
         CALL MTX(A,B,NDIM)

C----    Solution vector
         WRITE(6,6011)(B(I),I=1,NDIM)
  6011   FORMAT(/' Solution vector:'/4F8.3)
C----    Values of fitted curve using detrended data
         DO 90 I = 1,N
    90       R(I) = A1*COS(W1*I) + B1*SIN(W1*I) + A2*COS(W2*I) +
        +             B2*SIN(W2*I)
         WRITE(6,6006)
  6006   FORMAT(/' Trigonometric regression results using detrended data',
        +              /)
         DO 105 I = 1,N,4
   105       WRITE(6,6001)I,(R(J),J=I,I+3)

C----    Add trend back to result
         DO 115 I = 1,N
   115       R(I) = R(I) + ALIN + BLIN*I

         WRITE(6,6007)
  6007   FORMAT(/' Final results with trend added back'/)
         DO 120 I = 1,N,4
   120       WRITE(6,6001)I,(R(J),J=I,I+3)

         CALL EXIT
         END

         SUBROUTINE MTX(A,C,N)
C----    Matrix solution to simultaneous linear equations
C----    Copyright 1986 PJ Kaufman

         DIMENSION A(4,4), C(4), A1(4,4), C1(4)

C----    Process row by row (Gaussian Elimination)
         DO 100 I = 1,N
```

```
            DIV = A(I,I)

            DO 40 J = 1,N
40              A(I,J) = A(I,J)/DIV
            C(I) = C(I)/DIV

C----  Zero out column I for each row
            DO 60 J = 1,N
                IF(J.EQ.I)GOTO 60
                FACTOR = A(J,I)
                DO 50 K = I,N
50                  A(J,K) = A(J,K) − A(I,K)*FACTOR
                C(J) = C(J) − C(I)*FACTOR
60              CONTINUE

100         CONTINUE

        RETURN
        END
```

2-Frequency Trigonometric Regression

Time		Prices		
1	22.12	22.46	22.17	22.00
5	23.18	24.56	25.57	30.59
9	28.23	33.77	35.90	40.05
13	46.22	51.48	40.76	40.16
17	36.51	29.30	30.36	36.42
21	39.75	30.07	29.08	32.13
25	38.94	42.95	43.38	46.23
29	47.70	46.98	35.78	27.35
33	25.40	29.45	27.15	28.48
37	32.74	33.53	30.01	29.25
41	36.82	45.07	55.13	65.51
45	66.56	70.06	27.30	35.62
49	32.06	31.46	35.75	36.46
53	38.22	43.24	45.46	38.96
57	37.08	38.72	34.01	33.00
61	35.07	40.23	41.63	44.95
65	51.12	63.71	59.56	63.38

Linear regression results: $A = 28.889$, $B = .267$

Detrended data

Time				
1	−7.04	−6.96	−7.52	−7.96
5	−7.05	−5.93	−5.19	−.44
9	−3.06	2.21	4.07	7.95
13	13.86	18.85	7.86	7.00
17	3.08	−4.40	−3.61	2.19

21	5.25	−4.70	−5.96	−3.17
25	3.37	7.11	7.28	9.86
29	11.06	10.07	−1.39	−10.09
33	−12.31	−8.52	−11.09	−10.03
37	−6.04	−5.51	−9.30	−10.33
41	−3.02	4.96	14.75	24.86
45	25.65	28.88	−14.15	−6.10
49	−9.92	−10.79	−6.77	−6.32
53	−4.83	−.08	1.87	−4.89
57	−7.04	−5.67	−10.64	−11.92
61	−10.12	−5.23	−4.09	−1.04
65	4.86	17.19	12.77	16.32

Intermediate values:

SUMS C2 = 17396.7, C*D = 8753.0, C*P = 10475.1
      D2 = 6126.9, D*P = 5499.2

Alpha1 = .151, Alpha2 = .898, Omega1 = .47, Omega2 = 2.52

Coefficient matrix:

34.206	.790	−.461	.426	124.829
.790	33.794	−.454	.479	−7.036
−.461	−.454	33.742	−.781	−33.500
.426	.479	−.781	34.258	28.219

Solution vector:
   3.635   −.317   −.930   .762

Trigonometric regression results using detrended data

1	4.29	.84	.69	−1.20
5	−3.72	−2.38	−4.57	−2.18
9	−1.06	−.43	3.23	2.12
13	4.21	3.45	1.39	1.82
17	−2.17	−1.93	−3.36	−4.39
21	−1.80	−2.78	.67	1.72
25	2.23	4.76	2.31	3.24
29	1.05	−1.35	−1.09	−4.45
33	−2.90	−3.25	−2.67	.70
37	.12	3.49	3.41	2.97
41	3.91	.27	.59	−2.04
45	−3.65	−2.57	−4.56	−1.50
49	−1.06	.38	3.44	2.19
53	4.54	2.79	1.38	1.20
57	−2.70	−1.91	−3.91	−3.91
61	−1.68	−2.44	1.44	1.69
65	2.86	4.60	2.08	3.19

Final results with trend added back

1	33.44	30.26	30.38	28.75
5	26.50	28.12	26.19	28.85
9	30.23	31.13	35.05	34.21
13	36.58	36.08	34.29	34.98
17	31.26	31.77	30.61	29.85
21	32.71	31.99	35.70	37.02
25	37.80	40.60	38.42	39.61
29	37.69	35.56	36.08	32.99
33	34.81	34.72	35.57	39.21
37	38.89	42.54	42.72	42.54
41	43.76	40.38	40.97	38.60
45	37.26	38.61	36.89	40.22
49	40.93	42.63	45.96	44.98
53	47.59	46.11	44.96	45.06
57	41.42	42.47	40.75	41.01
61	43.50	43.01	47.16	47.68
65	49.12	51.13	48.87	50.25

APPENDIX 5
Fourier Transformation

The original computer program that solves the Fourier transformation as described by Jack Hutson and Anthony Warren (*Technical Analysis of Stocks & Commodities*) is based on the Cooley-Tukey Fast Fourier Transform Algorithm (1965), developed at the IBM Thomas J. Watson Research Center. A full explanation of this program and its interpretation can be found in the two articles that appeared in the January 1983 edition of *Technical Analysis Of Stocks & Commodities*, then reprinted in the September 1986 issue.

The following program appeared in the September 1986 issue of *Technical Analysis of Stocks & Commodities*. It was written by John Ehlers and appended to the article "A Comparison of the Fourier and Maximum Entropy Methods."

FAST FOURIER TRANSFORM PROGRAM

```
 10  REM "FAST FOURIER TRANSFORM"
 20  REM FOR APPLE ][ WITH 2 DISKS USING
 30  REM DATA IN CSI OR COMPU-TRAC FORMAT
 40  REM BY JOHN F. EHLERS
 45  REM COPYRIGHT (C) 1986 BY TECHNICAL ANALYSIS, INC.
 50  HOME
 60  DIM DF$(20)
 70  HTAB 5: INVERSE : PRINT "* FAST FOURIER TRANSFORM *" :
     NORMAL
 71  HTAB 19: PRINT "BY"
 72  HTAB 14: PRINT "JOHN EHLERS"
 73  HTAB 16: PRINT "BOX 1801"
 74  HTAB 12: PRINT "GOLETA, CA 93116": PRINT
 80  LET D$ = CHR$(4)
 90  PRINT D$ + "OPEN MASTER,L40,D2"
100  FOR I = 1 TO 20
110      PRINT D$ + "READ MASTER,R";I
120      INPUT DF$(I)
130      IF LEFT$ (DF$(I),5) = "99999" GOTO 150
```

```
140      NEXT I
150 PRINT D$ + "CLOSE"
160 FOR J = 1 TO I−1
170      PRINT "⟨"; CHR$ (J + 64); "⟩"; MID$ (DF$(J),4,16)
180      NEXT J
190 PRINT "⟨V⟩ VIEW NEW DATA DISK"
200 PRINT "⟨X⟩ EXIT TO MENU": PRINT
210 PRINT "    SELECT ⟨ ⟩": CHR$(8); CHR$(8);
220 POKE − 16368,0: GET X$: PRINT X$; "⟩"; CHR$(8); CHR$(8);
230 IF X$ = "V" THEN
         HOME : VTAB 10:
         PRINT "INSERT NEW DATA DISK IN DRIVE 2":
         PRINT: PRINT "PRESS";: INVERSE: PRINT "RETURN";:
         NORMAL: PRINT "TO CONTINUE": VTAB 22:
         POKE − 16368,0: GET S$: GOTO 30
240 IF X$ = "X" THEN HOME
250 LET SF = ASC (X$) − 64
260 IF SF > 1 AND SF <= J − 1 THEN 290
270 HTAB 13: PRINT " ": CHR$(8);: GOTO 220
280 IF K < 120 OR K > LR THEN
         PRINT "OOPS − RUN AGAIN": END
290 HOME : VTAB 10: INVERSE: PRINT MID$ (DF$(SF),4,16):
    NORMAL: PRINT: PRINT
300 PRINT: PRINT D$ + "OPEN " + MID$ (DF$(SF),4,16) + ",L40":
    PRINT D$ + "READ " + MID$ (DF$(SF),4,16) +",R0":
    INPUT X$: LET LR = VAL (X$)
310 PRINT D$ + "CLOSE"
320 IF LR < 32 THEN 370
330 IF LR < 1024 THEN 410
340 PRINT "CONTAINS"; LR; " RECORDS"
350 PRINT "A MAXIMUM 1024 RECORDS ARE ALLOWED": PRINT
360 PRINT "PRESS ";: INVERSE: PRINT "RETURN";: NORMAL:
    PRINT " TO CONTINUE": VTAB 22
370 PRINT "CONTAINS ONLY "; LR; " RECORDS"
380 PRINT "AT LEAST 32 RECORDS ARE REQUIRED": PRINT
390 PRINT "PRESS ";: INVERSE: PRINT "RETURN";: NORMAL:
    PRINT " TO CONTINUE": VTAB 22
400 POKE − 16368,0: GET S$: HOME: CLEAR: GOTO 20
410 PRINT "CONTAINS "; LR; " RECORDS": PRINT
420 PRINT "ENTER ONLY 32, 64, 128, OR 256"
430 PRINT "FOR ANALYSIS.  THIS NUMBER MUST BE"
440 PRINT "LESS THAN THE FILE LENGTH.": PRINT
450 INPUT "RECORDS FOR ANALYSIS? "; N
460 IF (N = 32 OR N = 64 OR N = 128 OR N = 256 OR N = 512)
         AND N < LR THEN 480
470 PRINT: PRINT "OOPS −− RUN PROGRAM AGAIN": END

480 DIM DA$(1024), F(1024), A(257,8)
```

```
490 PRINT: PRINT D$ + "OPEN " + MID$ (DF$(SF),4,16) + ",L40"
500 FOR I = 1 TO N:
        PRINT D$ + "READ " + MID$ (DF$(SF),4,16) + ",R";
        (LR − N + I): INPUT DA$(I):
        NEXT I
510 PRINT D$ + "CLOSE"
520 REM *** DATA CONVERTER ***
530 IF MID$ (DA$(1),23,5) ⟨ ⟩ "99999" THEN 550
540 LET DA$(1) = DA$(2)
550 FOR I = 1 TO N
560     LET F(I) = VAL (MID$ (DA$(I),23,5))
570     IF MID$ (DA$(I),23,5) = "99999" THEN
            LET F(I) = F(I − 1)
580     NEXT I

590 REM *** SPECTRUM ANALYSIS ***
600 LET PI = 3.1415926
610 LET P0 = INT (N / 4): LET S0 = 8
620 FOR I = 1 TO R0 + 1:
        FOR J = 1 TO 8:  LET A(I,J) = 0:  NEXT J:
        NEXT I
630 FOR I = 1 TO R0
640     FOR J = 1 TO S0 STEP 2
650         LET K = 4 * (I − 1) + .5 * (J + 1)
660         LET A(I,J) = F(K)
670         LET A(I,J + 1) = 0
680         NEXT J
690     NEXT I
700 LET M  = LOG (N) / LOG (2): LET N2 = N / 2:
    LET N1 = N − 1:            LET J  = 1
710 FOR I = 1 TO N1
720     IF I > J THEN 850
730     LET R   = INT ((J − 1) / 4)
740     LET S  = 2 * J − 8 * R
750     LET R1 = INT ((I − 1) / 4)
760     LET S1 = 2 * I − 8 * R1
770     LET R1 = R1 + 1
780     LET R  = R + 1
790     LET T  = A(R,S)
800     LET A(R,S)   = A(R1,S1)
810     LET A(R1,S1) = T
820     LET T  = A(R,S − 1)
830     LET A(R,S − 1)   = A(R1,S1 − 1)
840     LET A(R1,S1 − 1) = T
850     LET K = N2
860     IF K > J THEN 910
870     LET J  = J − K
880     LET K  = K / 2
```

```
890      GOTO 860
900      NEXT I
910 LET J = J + K
920 NEXT I
930 LET L0 = 1
940 FOR L = 1 TO M
950      LET L1  = L0
960      LET L0  = 2 * L0
970      LET V   = 1
980      LET W   = 0
990      LET Z   = PI / L1
1000     LET W1 = COS (Z)
1010     LET W2 = SIN (Z)
1020     FOR J = 1 TO L1
1030         FOR I = J TO N STEP L0
1040             LET K  = I + L1
1050             LET R1 = INT ((K − 1) / 4)
1060             LET S1 = 2 * K − 8 * R1
1070             LET R1 = R1 + 1
1080             LET A1 = A(R1,S1 − 1)
1090             LET B1 = A(R1,S1)
1100             LET T  = A1 * V − B1 * W
1110             LET U  = A1 * W + B1 * V
1120             LET R  = INT ((I − 1)/ 4)
1130             LET S  = 2 * I − 8 * R
1140             LET R  = R + 1
1150             LET A(R1,S1 − 1) = A(R,S − 1) − T
1160             LET A(R1,S1)     = A(R,S) − U
1170             LET A(R,S − 1)   = A(R,S − 1) + T
1180             LET A(R,S)       = A(R,S) + U
1190             NEXT I
1200         LET U = V * W1 − W * W2
1210         LET W = V * W2 + W * W1
1220         LET V = U
1230         NEXT J
1240     NEXT L
1250 LET Z = − 1E6
1260 FOR I = 1 TO R0 / 2
1270     FOR J = 1 TO S0 STEP 2
1280         IF I = 1 AND J = 1 THEN 1310
1290         LET A(I,J) = SQR (A(I,J) * A(I,J) + A(I,J + 1) *
                 A(I,J + 1))
1300         IF A(I,J) > Z THEN LET Z = A(I,J)
1310         NEXT J
1320     NEXT I
1330 HOME: PRINT "SPECTRUM FOR " + MID$ (DF$(SF),4,16)
1340 PRINT
1350 PRINT "PERIOD    RELATIVE AMPLITUDE'
```

```
1360 PRINT "(DAYS)        (DB)": PRINT
1370 LET K = 0
1380 FOR I = 1 TO R0 / 2
1400     FOR J = 1 TO S0 STEP 2
1410         IF I = 1 AND J = 1 THEN 1460
1420         LET L = INT (N / K + .25)
1430         IF L + 1 > P THEN 1460
1440         LET P = L
1450         PRINT TAB( 2): L; TAB( 16);
                  INT (1000 * LOG (A(I,J) / Z) / LOG (10)) / 100
1460         LET K = K + 1
1470         NEXT J
1480     NEXT I
```

PROGRAM LENGTH: 152 LINES / 3304 BYTES

APPENDIX 6
Pattern Studies

WEEKDAY PATTERNS

The weekday patterns that follow are:

1. 1976 Study:
   Figure A6-1: 1976 Metals
   Figure A6-2: 1976 Grains and Soybean Complex
   Figure A6-3: Cotton, 1970–1975
   Figure A6-4: Copper, 1970–1975
   Figure A6-5: Cocoa, 1970–1975
2. 1985 Study:
   Figure A6-6: Soybeans, 1977–1984
   Figure A6-7: Sugar, 1977–1984
   Figure A6-8: Coffee, 1977–1984
   Figure A6-9: Pork bellies, 1977–1984
   Figure A6-10: Gold, 1977–1984
   Figure A6-11: Silver, 1977–1984
   Figure A6-12: Swiss franc, 1977–1984
   Figure A6-13: Treasury bills, 1977–1984
   Figure A6-14: S&P 500, 1982–1984

1976 Study

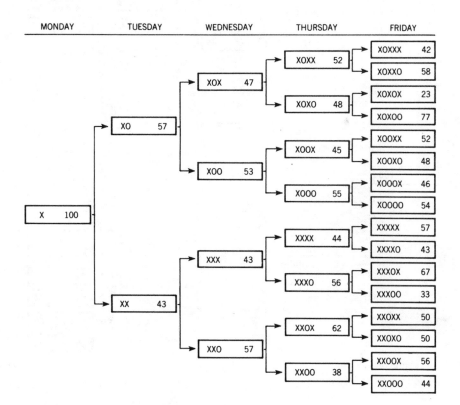

HIGH PROBABILITY TRADES:
IF XX THEN EXPECT O: IF XXO THEN REVERSE AND EXPECT XXOX
                 IF XXX THEN C/O
IF XXXO THEN EXPECT X
IF XOXO THEN EXPECT O

Figure A6-1   1976 metals (171 weeks tested).

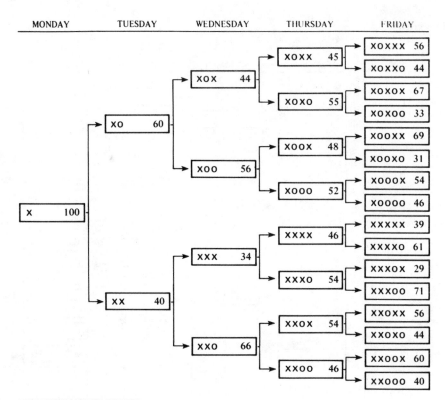

MONDAY	TUESDAY	WEDNESDAY	THURSDAY	FRIDAY

HIGH PROBABILITY TRADES:

IF **XOXO** THEN EXPECT **X** FRIDAY

IF **XOOX** THEN EXPECT **X** FRIDAY

IF **XXXX** THEN EXPECT **O** FRIDAY

IF **XXXO** THEN EXPECT **O** FRIDAY

IF **XXOO** THEN EXPECT **X** FRIDAY

IF **XX** THEN EXPECT **O** WEDNESDAY AND C/O

ALSO REVERSE MONDAY ON OPEN, C/O TUESDAY
IF ANOTHER REVERSAL, OR ELSE C/O WEDNESDAY
ON THE CLOSE.

Figure A6-2   1976 grains and soybeans complex.

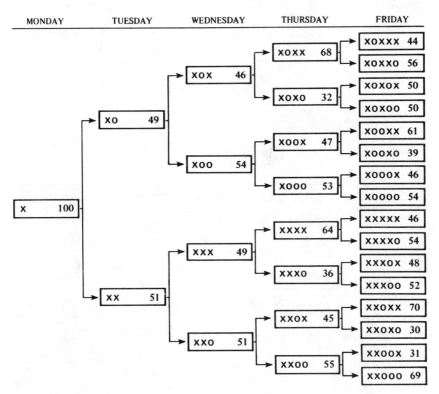

HIGH PROBABILITY TRADES:

IF **XOX** OCCURS, EXPECT **X** THURSDAY AND C/O

IF **XXX** OCCURS, EXPECT **X** THURSDAY AND C/O

IF **XOOX** OCCURS, EXPECT **X** FRIDAY

IF **XXOX** OCCURS, EXPECT **X** FRIDAY

IF **XXOO** OCCURS, EXPECT **O** FRIDAY

MAXIMUM OF I TRADE PER WEEK

Figure A6-3   Cotton 1970–1975.

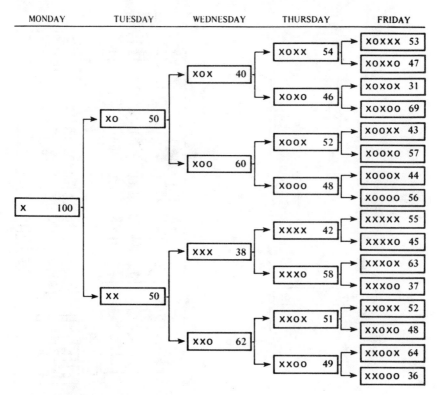

HIGH PROBABILITY TRADES:

IF **XX** OR **XO** THEN **O** ON WEDNESDAY, THEN C/O

IF **XOXO** THEN EXPECT **Q** ON FRIDAY

IF **XXXO** THEN EXPECT **X** ON FRIDAY

IF **XXOO** THEN EXPECT **O** ON FRIDAY

Figure A6-4   Copper 1970–1975.

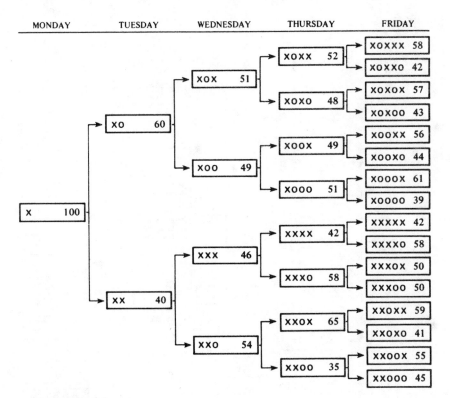

HIGH PROBABILITY TRADES:

IF **X** OCCURS THEN EXPECT **O** AND C/O

IF **XXO** OCCURS THEN EXPECT **X**; IF YES, THEN HOLD AND C/O FRIDAY

IF **XOOO** OCCURS THEN EXPECT **X**

Figure A6-5   Cocoa 1970–1975.

1985 Study

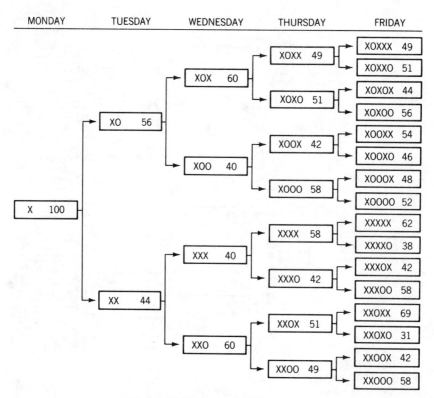

Figure A6-6   Soybeans 1977–1984.

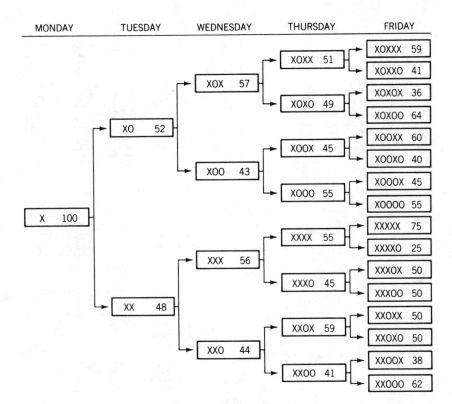

Figure A6-7   Sugar 1977–1984.

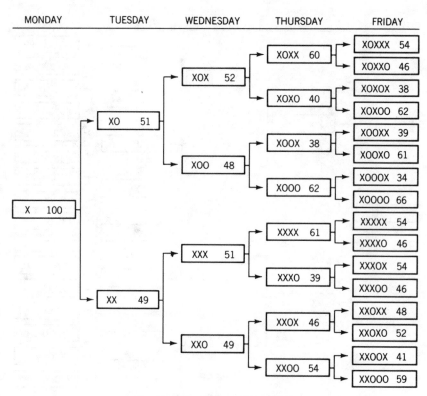

Figure A6-8   Coffee 1977–1984.

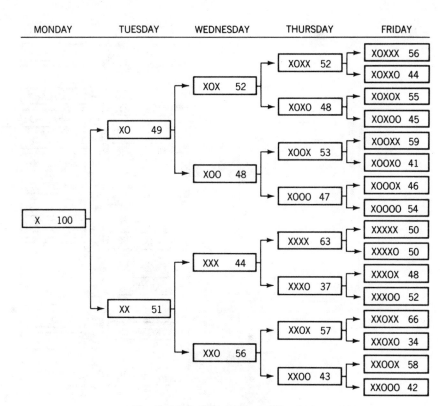
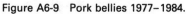

Figure A6-9   Pork bellies 1977–1984.

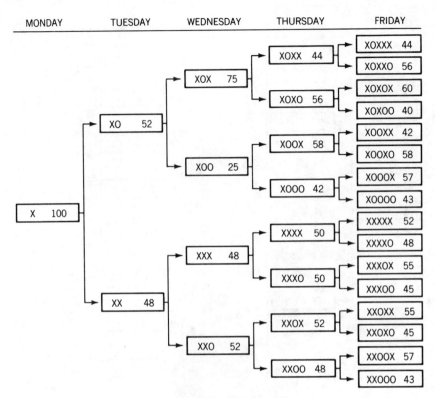

Figure A6-10 Gold 1977–1984.

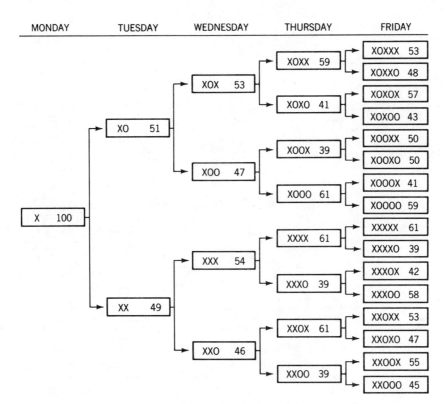

Figure A6-11   Silver 1977–1984.

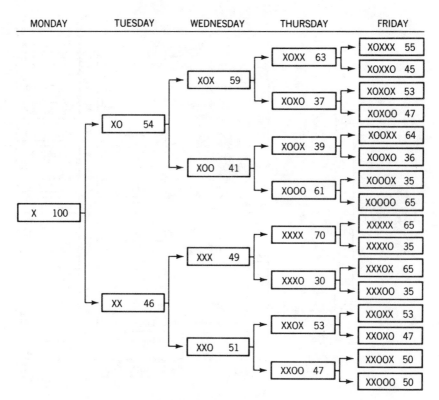

Figure A6-12   Swiss francs 1977–1984.

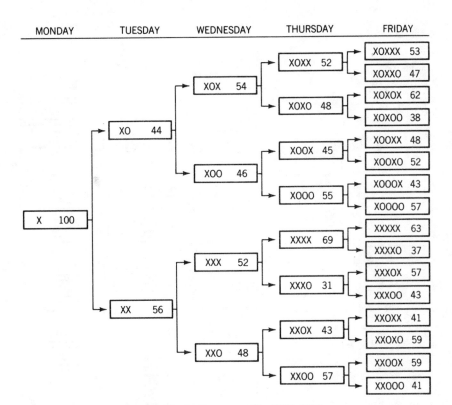

Figure A6-13   Treasury bills 1977–1984.

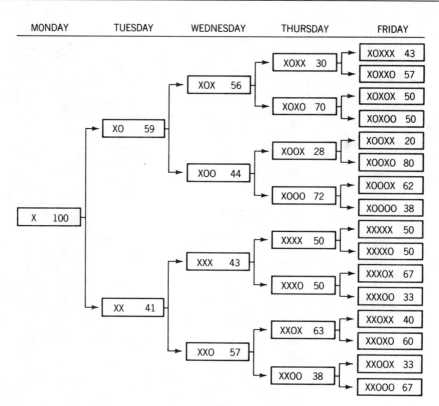

Figure A6-14   S&P 500 1982–1984.

WEEKEND PATTERNS

The weekend pattern tables that follow are:

1. 1976 Study:

   Table A6-1: 24 Commodities for 1976
   Table A6-2: Summary Results of Weekend Moves, 1970–1976

2. 1985 Study:

   Table A6-3: Soybeans, 1977–1984
   Table A6-4: Corn, 1977–1984
   Table A6-5: Coffee, 1977–1984
   Table A6-6: Gold, 1977–1984
   Table A6-7: Silver, 1977–1984
   Table A6-8: Deutschemark, 1977–1984
   Table A6-9: Treasury Bills, 1977–1984
   Table A6-10: Treasury Bonds, 1977–1984
   Table A6-11: S&P 500, 1982–1984

1976 Study

Table A6-1 24 Commodities for 1976

| | | Last Friday to Monday Direction | Friday–Friday Point Trend | Most Frequent Direction Last Week | Direction of Friday | Weekend Patterns[a] | | | | | Monday Move After Pattern | | | |
						WHF XXX	WHF XXO	WHF XOX	WHF OXX	WHF XOO	WHF OXO	WHF OOX	WHF OOO	Cases
May 76	Wheat	60	48	57	51	50	50	33	66	0	0	62	40	33
May 76	Corn	53	53	71	56	60	66	50	87	100	100	33	28	39
May 76	Soybeans	70	56	54	62	100	40	75	63	0	0	100	50	37
May 76	Oats	48	58	67	64	100	100	75	60	50	50	42	66	31
May 76	Soybean oil	65	56	68	59	100	40	100	71	100	100	40	28	32
May 76	Soybean meal	78	71	71	75	100	100	60	100	50	50	100	25	28
Apr 75	Cattle	57	50	67	53	50	0	66	100	75	75	25	40	28
Apr 76	Hogs	56	62	70	48	66	50	62	57	50	50	40	0	37
May 76	Pork bellies	38	66	56	51	0	100	40	60	40	40	50	100	39
Mar 76	Broilers	46	61	46	53	100	0	33	50	0	0	100	100	13
Mar 76	Eggs	53	38	61	61	50	0	100	50	50	50	66	66	13
Apr 76	Platinum	58	69	66	52	75	0	0	71	62	62	50	42	36
May 76	Copper	56	51	64	45	20	33	100	60	50	50	50	33	37
May 76	Silver NY	37	46	59	50	33	77	0	42	60	60	33	25	32
Mar 76	Gold–IMM	38	48	43	38	50	50	0	28	50	50	40	50	39
May 76	Lumber	40	59	53	53	50	50	50	25	66	66	50	100	32
May 76	Plywood	46	53	53	50	42	57	50	75	0	0	33	100	30
Mar 76	Orange juice	48	54	60	57	33	33	100	50	50	50	71	75	33
May 76	Cocoa (NY)	54	64	64	54	60	25	80	50	66	66	33	60	31
May 76	Coffee 'C'	36	70	70	60	100	100	66	25	100	100	12	75	30
May 76	Sugar (world)	42	44	68	50	28	75	25	80	75	75	44	42	38
May 76	Potatoes (Maine)	59	63	70	75	100	60	100	57	75	75	57	75	44
May 76	Cotton	58	74	66	63	80	33	66	77	37	37	14	100	39
Mar 76	Swiss franc	50	66	70	43	50	0	25	25	75	75	62	66	30
Totals		52	58	63	54	59	49	56	61	57	57	48	52	781

[a] Entries in the tables of this Appendix represent the percentage of situations where the following Monday closing price was a continuation of the same direction; for WHF indicates the "X" direction.

Table A6-2 Summary Results of Weekend Moves, 1970–1976

	Most Frequent Direction	Continuation Patterns[a]						
		WTF XXX	WTF XXO	WTF XOX	WTF OXX	WTF XOO	WTF OOX	WTF OOO
24 U.S. commodities (1976)	63	59	49	56	61	57	48	52
8 London commodities (1976)	61	70	45	40	50	59	60	57
Cattle (1970–1975)	60	59	52	61	60	44	60	73
Cocoa (1970–1975)	65	46	55	69	58	64	50	72
Copper (1970–1975)	58	48	42	62	61	28	52	46
Cotton (1970–1975)	61	64	53	60	58	50	51	58
Potatoes (1970–1975)	65	66	55	70	53	57	55	51
Silver (NY) (1970–1975)	63	77	53	54	56	56	51	47
Soybean meal (1970–1975)	68	70	66	88	66	27	55	22
Soybean oil (1970–1975)	66	70	54	77	66	37	58	46
Sugar (1970–1975)	55	53	50	51	51	46	67	39
Swiss franc (1970–1975)	69	65	16	80	42	61	38	64
(The following calculations exclude the 24 U.S. commodities)								
Mean	62.8	62.5	49.2	64.7	56.5	48.1	54.3	52.3
Standard deviation	4.3	9.9	12.6	13.9	7.2	12.9	7.4	14.9

[a] Figures represent percentage of situations of next Monday close in "X" direction.

Table A6-3   Weekend Patterns for Soybeans, 1977–1984

Trend Direction	No. of Cases	Trend/Pattern Continued Monday On . . .					
		Open	%	Close	%	Extreme	%
Case 1: Friday to Monday	292	144	49%	138	47%	246	84%
Case 2: Friday to Friday	292	112	38%	123	42%	237	81%
Case 3: Most Frequent Direction	280	113	40%	116	41%	227	81%
Case 4: Thursday to Friday	292	143	48%	129	44%	243	83%
Case 5: (a) X-XXX	39	19	48%	15	38%	28	71%
(b) X-XXO	35	22	62%	19	54%	29	82%
(c) X-XOX	35	17	48%	17	48%	32	91%
(d) X-OXX	65	33	50%	25	38%	51	78%
(e) X-XOO	36	16	44%	17	47%	32	88%
(f) X-OOX	39	23	58%	18	46%	34	87%
(g) X-OOO	43	13	30%	18	41%	37	86%

Table A6-4   Weekend Patterns for Corn, 1977–1984

Trend Direction	No. of Cases	Trend/Pattern Continued Monday On . . .					
		Open	%	Close	%	Extreme	%
Case 1: Friday to Monday	292	136	46%	138	47%	230	78%
Case 2: Friday to Friday	292	135	46%	131	44%	227	77%
Case 3: Most Frequent Direction	275	123	44%	127	46%	216	78%
Case 4: Thursday to Friday	292	149	51%	142	48%	234	80%
Case 5: (a) X-XXX	30	15	50%	11	36%	23	76%
(b) X-XXO	36	20	55%	17	47%	27	75%
(c) X-XOX	32	17	53%	17	53%	28	87%
(d) X-OXX	72	37	51%	35	48%	56	77%
(e) X-XOO	45	20	44%	23	51%	36	80%
(f) X-OOX	39	25	64%	24	61%	36	92%
(g) X-OOO	38	15	39%	15	39%	28	73%

Table A6-5 Weekend Patterns for Coffee, 1977–1984

Trend Direction	No. of Cases	Trend/Pattern Continued Monday On . . .					
		Open	%	Close	%	Extreme	%
Case 1: Friday to Monday	289	135	46%	150	51%	221	76%
Case 2: Friday to Friday	289	149	51%	135	46%	222	76%
Case 3: Most Frequent Direction	274	144	52%	133	48%	209	76%
Case 4: Thursday to Friday	289	181	62%	146	50%	239	82%
Case 5: (a) X-XXX	48	26	54%	24	50%	40	83%
(b) X-XXO	40	30	75%	20	50%	34	85%
(c) X-XOX	30	22	73%	19	63%	25	83%
(d) X-OXX	56	32	57%	23	41%	45	80%
(e) X-XOO	35	22	62%	19	54%	29	82%
(f) X-OOX	30	20	66%	19	63%	26	86%
(g) X-OOO	50	29	58%	22	44%	40	80%

Table A6-6 Weekend Patterns for Gold, 1977–1984

Trend Direction	No. of Cases	Trend/Pattern Continued Monday On . . .					
		Open	%	Close	%	Extreme	%
Case 1: Friday to Monday	293	139	47%	132	45%	224	76%
Case 2: Friday to Friday	293	125	42%	127	43%	213	72%
Case 3: Most Frequent Direction	276	120	43%	118	42%	204	73%
Case 4: Thursday to Friday	293	134	45%	100	34%	208	70%
Case 5: (a) X-XXX	36	14	38%	11	30%	20	55%
(b) X-XXO	43	24	55%	17	39%	32	74%
(c) X-XOX	51	26	50%	19	37%	40	78%
(d) X-OXX	63	28	44%	22	34%	45	71%
(e) X-XOO	39	14	35%	12	30%	25	64%
(f) X-OOX	31	17	54%	10	32%	28	90%
(g) X-OOO	30	11	36%	9	30%	18	60%

Table A6-7 Weekend Patterns for Silver, 1977–1984

Trend Direction	No. of Cases	Trend/Pattern Continued Monday On . . .					
		Open	%	Close	%	Extreme	%
Case 1: Friday to Monday	293	150	51%	147	50%	242	82%
Case 2: Friday to Friday	293	135	46%	135	46%	235	80%
Case 3: Most Frequent Direction	276	141	51%	131	47%	223	80%
Case 4: Thursday to Friday	293	154	52%	128	43%	234	79%
Case 5: (a) X-XXX	53	29	54%	24	45%	44	83%
(b) X-XXO	38	20	52%	19	50%	32	84%
(c) X-XOX	28	14	50%	17	60%	22	78%
(d) X-OXX	74	32	43%	27	36%	54	72%
(e) X-XOO	34	18	52%	15	44%	26	76%
(f) X-OOX	31	21	67%	11	35%	27	87%
(g) X-OOO	35	20	57%	15	42%	29	82%

Table A6-8 Weekend Patterns for Deutschemarks, 1977–1984

Trend Direction	No. of Cases	Trend/Pattern Continued Monday On . . .					
		Open	%	Close	%	Extreme	%
Case 1: Friday to Monday	291	142	48%	136	46%	214	73%
Case 2: Friday to Friday	291	135	46%	131	45%	210	72%
Case 3: Most Frequent Direction	267	129	48%	117	43%	196	73%
Case 4: Thursday to Friday	291	143	49%	116	39%	210	72%
Case 5: (a) X-XXX	39	23	58%	18	46%	29	74%
(b) X-XXO	36	16	44%	15	41%	27	75%
(c) X-XOX	28	12	42%	7	25%	18	64%
(d) X-OXX	69	28	40%	30	43%	45	65%
(e) X-XOO	31	18	58%	10	32%	24	77%
(f) X-OOX	28	17	60%	13	46%	24	85%
(g) X-OOO	60	29	48%	23	38%	43	71%

Table A6-9 Weekend Patterns for Treasury Bills, 1977–1984

Trend Direction	No. of Cases	Trend/Pattern Continued Monday On . . .					
		Open	%	Close	%	Extreme	%
Case 1: Friday to Monday	291	107	36%	122	41%	216	74%
Case 2: Friday to Friday	291	128	43%	128	43%	228	78%
Case 3: Most Frequent Direction	263	110	41%	107	40%	201	76%
Case 4: Thursday to Friday	291	140	48%	117	40%	225	77%
Case 5: (a) X-XXX	34	12	35%	12	35%	25	73%
(b) X-XXO	31	15	48%	14	45%	25	80%
(c) X-XOX	32	11	34%	12	37%	25	78%
(d) X-OXX	62	35	56%	27	43%	48	77%
(e) X-XOO	31	19	61%	13	41%	23	74%
(f) X-OOX	42	22	52%	18	42%	36	85%
(g) X-OOO	59	26	44%	21	35%	43	72%

Table A6-10 Weekend Patterns for Treasury Bonds, 1977–1984

Trend Direction	No. of Cases	Trend/Pattern Continued Monday On . . .					
		Open	%	Close	%	Extreme	%
Case 1: Friday to Monday	264	111	42%	108	40%	206	78%
Case 2: Friday to Friday	264	116	43%	116	43%	205	77%
Case 3: Most Frequent Direction	244	106	43%	99	40%	187	76%
Case 4: Thursday to Friday	264	121	45%	108	40%	210	79%
Case 5: (a) X-XXX	25	12	48%	9	36%	20	80%
(b) X-XXO	32	19	59%	20	62%	29	90%
(c) X-XOX	33	15	45%	15	45%	26	78%
(d) X-OXX	66	29	43%	22	33%	52	78%
(e) X-XOO	25	12	48%	11	44%	19	76%
(f) X-OOX	38	17	44%	13	34%	32	84%
(g) X-OOO	45	17	37%	18	40%	32	71%

Table A6-11   Weekend Patterns for S&P 500, 1982–1984

Trend Direction	No. of Cases	Trend/Pattern Continued Monday On . . .					
		Open	%	Close	%	Extreme	%
Case 1: Friday to Monday	78	32	41%	35	44%	70	89%
Case 2: Friday to Friday	78	29	37%	32	41%	68	87%
Case 3: Most Frequent Direction	73	23	31%	32	43%	65	89%
Case 4: Thursday to Friday	78	29	37%	26	33%	68	87%
Case 5: (a) X-XXX	6	2	33%	1	16%	6	100%
(b) X-XXO	7	4	57%	4	57%	5	71%
(c) X-XOX	12	3	25%	2	16%	9	75%
(d) X-OXX	17	8	47%	8	47%	15	88%
(e) X-XOO	11	3	27%	5	45%	10	90%
(f) X-OOX	13	5	38%	4	30%	13	100%
(g) X-OOO	12	4	33%	2	16%	10	83%

GAP ANALYSIS

The gap analysis tables that follow are:

Table A6-12: Corn, 2¢ Increments, 1977–1984
Table A6-13: Soybeans, 2¢ Increments, 1977–1984
Table A6-14: Soybeans, 5¢ Increments, 1977–1984
Table A6-15: Cattle, 50 Pt. Increments, 1977–1984
Table A6-16: Sugar, 10 Pt. Increments, 1977–1984
Table A6-17: Sugar, 25 Pt. Increments, 1977–1984
Table A6-18: Gold, $5 Increments, 1977–1984
Table A6-19: Silver, 5¢ Increments, 1977–1984
Table A6-20: Silver, 20¢ Increments, 1977–1984
Table A6-21: Treasury Bills, 10 Pt. Increments, 1977–1984
Table A6-22: S&P 500, 50 Pt. Increments, 1982–1984

Table A6-12 Gap Analysis for Corn, 2¢ Increments, 1977–1984

Gap	Close			Trading Range			Cont. Next Day	No. of Cases
	Cont. Dir.	Below Open	Rvrsd. Dir.	Cross Pr. Cls.	Adj. Open	Cont. Only		
12.00	.0	100.0	.0	.0	40.0	60.0	40.0	5
10.00	37.5	25.0	37.5	37.5	62.5	.0	37.5	8
8.00	44.4	33.3	22.2	22.2	77.8	.0	33.3	9
6.00	50.0	35.0	15.0	20.0	80.0	.0	45.0	20
4.00	56.9	33.3	9.7	20.8	79.2	.0	43.1	144
2.00	48.8	16.7	34.5	62.7	36.6	.7	60.5	754
.00	.0	.0	.0	.0	.0	.0	.0	86
−2.00	57.6	13.4	29.1	63.0	35.8	1.3	46.1	629
−4.00	62.2	22.4	15.3	27.6	71.4	1.0	53.1	98
−6.00	56.3	37.5	6.3	18.8	81.3	.0	31.3	16
−8.00	55.6	44.4	.0	.0	100.0	.0	22.2	9
−10.00	33.3	50.0	16.7	16.7	66.7	16.7	33.3	6
−12.00	.0	100.0	.0	.0	100.0	.0	.0	1

Table A6-13 Gap Analysis for Soybeans, 2¢ Increments, 1977–1984

Gap	Close			Trading Range			Cont. Next Day	No. of Cases
	Cont. Dir.	Below Open	Rvrsd. Dir.	Cross Pr. Cls.	Adj. Open	Cont. Only		
36.00	100.0	.0	.0	.0	100.0	.0	.0	1
32.00	.0	90.0	10.0	30.0	30.0	40.0	60.0	10
30.00	50.0	50.0	.0	25.0	75.0	.0	50.0	4
28.00	.0	100.0	.0	.0	100.0	.0	.0	1
26.00	.0	100.0	.0	.0	100.0	.0	.0	1
24.00	33.3	33.3	33.3	33.3	66.7	.0	33.3	3
22.00	60.0	10.0	30.0	30.0	70.0	.0	50.0	10
20.00	33.3	33.3	33.3	33.3	66.7	.0	33.3	6
18.00	50.0	50.0	.0	25.0	75.0	.0	50.0	4
16.00	75.0	12.5	12.5	25.0	75.0	.0	37.5	16
14.00	64.3	35.7	.0	7.1	92.9	.0	57.1	14
12.00	47.4	36.8	15.8	31.6	68.4	.0	52.6	19
10.00	55.6	29.6	14.8	29.6	70.4	.0	51.9	27
8.00	56.1	24.2	19.7	36.4	63.6	.0	40.9	66
6.00	56.5	22.4	21.2	46.3	53.7	.0	55.1	147
4.00	45.7	18.4	35.8	64.9	34.4	.7	52.8	282
2.00	47.3	6.7	46.0	88.8	11.2	.0	58.8	313
.00	.0	.0	.0	.0	.0	.0	.0	23
−2.00	47.7	8.7	43.5	86.5	12.3	1.3	47.7	310
−4.00	51.8	15.9	32.2	71.8	27.3	.8	49.0	245
−6.00	56.0	25.0	19.0	48.3	50.9	.9	55.2	116
−8.00	63.1	15.4	21.5	43.1	55.4	1.5	41.5	65
−10.00	73.0	13.5	13.5	27.0	70.3	2.7	54.1	37
−12.00	60.0	26.7	13.3	20.0	80.0	.0	60.0	15
−14.00	62.5	37.5	.0	25.0	75.0	.0	25.0	8
−16.00	80.0	20.0	.0	.0	100.0	.0	80.0	5
−18.00	80.0	20.0	.0	.0	100.0	.0	40.0	5
−20.00	66.7	16.7	16.7	33.3	66.7	.0	83.3	6
−22.00	14.3	42.9	42.9	57.1	42.9	.0	42.9	7
−24.00	57.1	42.9	.0	.0	100.0	.0	57.1	7
−26.00	100.0	.0	.0	.0	100.0	.0	.0	2
−28.00	33.3	66.7	.0	33.3	66.7	.0	33.3	3
−30.00	33.3	50.0	16.7	16.7	66.7	16.7	50.0	6
−32.00	.0	100.0	.0	.0	.0	100.0	100.0	1

Table A6-14 Gap Analysis for Soybeans, 5¢ Increments, 1977–1984

Gap	Close Cont. Dir.	Below Open	Rvrsd. Dir.	Trading Range Cross Pr. Cls.	Adj. Open	Cont. Only	Cont. Next Day	No. of Cases
40.00	100.0	.0	.0	.0	100.0	.0	.0	1
35.00	.0	90.0	10.0	30.0	30.0	40.0	60.0	10
30.00	40.0	60.0	.0	20.0	80.0	.0	40.0	5
25.00	50.0	21.4	28.6	28.6	71.4	.0	42.9	14
20.00	47.1	35.3	17.6	35.3	64.7	.0	35.3	17
15.00	61.9	28.6	9.5	19.0	81.0	.0	52.4	42
10.00	54.5	24.0	21.4	39.0	61.0	.0	48.1	154
5.00	48.2	13.7	38.2	73.6	26.1	.3	55.9	681
.00	.0	.0	.0	.0	.0	.0	.0	23
−5.00	50.2	13.4	36.3	76.6	22.3	1.1	49.1	619
−10.00	63.0	17.5	19.5	41.6	57.1	1.3	48.7	154
−15.00	61.5	30.8	7.7	19.2	80.8	.0	53.8	26
−20.00	76.9	15.4	7.7	15.4	84.6	.0	61.5	13
−25.00	35.7	42.9	21.4	28.6	71.4	.0	50.0	14
−30.00	45.5	45.5	9.1	18.2	72.7	9.1	36.4	11
−35.00	.0	100.0	.0	.0	.0	100.0	100.0	1

Table A6-15 Gap Analysis for Cattle, 50 Pt. Increments, 1977–1984

Gap	Close Cont. Dir.	Below Open	Rvrsd. Dir.	Trading Range Cross Pr. Cls.	Adj. Open	Cont. Only	Cont. Next Day	No. of Cases
2.00	.0	100.0	.0	.0	66.7	33.3	66.7	3
1.50	23.8	57.1	19.0	28.6	47.6	23.8	42.9	21
1.00	58.3	26.2	15.5	24.3	75.7	.0	48.5	103
.50	52.2	13.8	34.0	70.5	29.0	.5	53.5	749
.00	.0	.0	.0	.0	.0	.0	.0	23
−.50	46.3	14.5	39.2	73.8	25.6	.5	54.1	753
−1.00	43.3	33.0	23.7	39.2	60.8	.0	47.4	97
−1.50	55.2	41.4	3.4	10.3	82.8	6.9	55.2	29
−2.00	12.5	75.0	12.5	12.5	62.5	25.0	75.0	8

	Close			Trading Range				
Gap	Cont. Dir.	Below Open	Rvrsd. Dir.	Cross Pr. Cls.	Adj. Open	Cont. Only	Cont. Next Day	No. of Cases
2.60	.0	100.0	.0	.0	100.0	.0	.0	1
1.80	.0	100.0	.0	.0	100.0	.0	100.0	1
1.70	50.0	50.0	.0	.0	100.0	.0	50.0	2
1.60	.0	100.0	.0	.0	100.0	.0	.0	1
1.40	50.0	50.0	.0	.0	100.0	.0	.0	2
1.30	100.0	.0	.0	.0	100.0	.0	100.0	3
1.20	57.1	42.9	.0	.0	100.0	.0	85.7	7
1.10	30.8	69.2	.0	15.4	53.8	30.8	69.2	13
1.00	33.3	33.3	33.3	66.7	33.3	.0	66.7	3
.90	55.6	33.3	11.1	11.1	88.9	.0	66.7	9
.80	45.5	27.3	27.3	27.3	72.7	.0	54.5	11
.70	75.0	25.0	.0	16.7	83.3	.0	41.7	12
.60	37.5	37.5	25.0	58.3	37.5	4.2	50.0	24
.50	51.9	18.5	29.6	37.0	63.0	.0	55.6	27
.40	50.0	16.7	33.3	47.6	52.4	.0	73.8	42
.30	58.0	24.6	17.4	34.8	65.2	.0	65.2	69
.20	52.4	22.3	25.3	37.3	58.4	4.2	51.8	166
.10	46.9	13.2	39.9	65.2	27.7	7.0	51.2	469
.00	.0	.0	.0	.0	.0	.0	.0	55
−.10	47.1	17.0	35.9	63.9	34.6	1.5	55.6	482
−.20	47.7	27.0	25.3	39.7	59.8	.6	50.6	174
−.30	57.3	22.7	20.0	40.0	58.7	1.3	62.7	75
−.40	57.9	23.7	18.4	36.8	63.2	.0	47.4	38
−.50	55.6	27.8	16.7	22.2	77.8	.0	72.2	18
−.60	46.7	33.3	20.0	40.0	53.3	6.7	53.3	15
−.70	50.0	40.0	10.0	30.0	70.0	.0	60.0	10
−.80	80.0	.0	20.0	40.0	50.0	10.0	50.0	10
−.90	25.0	25.0	50.0	50.0	50.0	.0	75.0	4
−1.00	40.0	60.0	.0	10.0	50.0	40.0	50.0	10
−1.10	50.0	37.5	12.5	25.0	75.0	.0	37.5	8
−1.20	.0	100.0	.0	.0	100.0	.0	100.0	1
−1.30	60.0	20.0	20.0	20.0	80.0	.0	40.0	5
−1.40	50.0	50.0	.0	.0	100.0	.0	100.0	2
−1.50	66.7	33.3	.0	.0	66.7	33.3	.0	3
−1.60	50.0	.0	50.0	50.0	50.0	.0	.0	2
−1.70	.0	.0	100.0	100.0	.0	.0	100.0	1
−1.90	.0	100.0	.0	.0	100.0	.0	.0	1
−3.00	.0	100.0	.0	.0	100.0	.0	100.0	1

Table A6-17 Gap Analysis for Sugar, 25 Cent Increments, 1977–1984

| | Close | | | Trading Range | | | | |
| | Cont. Dir. | Below Open | Rvrsd. Dir. | Cross Pr. Cls. | Adj. Open | Cont. Only | Cont. Next Day | No. of Cases |
Gap								
2.75	.0	100.0	.0	.0	100.0	.0	.0	1
2.00	.0	100.0	.0	.0	100.0	.0	100.0	1
1.75	33.3	66.7	.0	.0	100.0	.0	33.3	3
1.50	66.7	33.3	.0	.0	100.0	.0	33.3	3
1.25	45.5	54.5	.0	9.1	72.7	18.2	77.3	22
1.00	47.1	29.4	23.5	29.4	70.6	.0	64.7	17
.75	50.0	33.3	16.7	40.5	57.1	2.4	47.6	42
.50	52.4	20.0	27.6	39.0	61.0	.0	65.7	105
.25	49.0	16.0	35.0	57.0	37.0	6.0	52.1	668
.00	.0	.0	.0	.0	.0	.0	.0	55
−.25	48.0	19.8	32.2	56.3	42.4	1.3	54.3	698
−.50	56.2	24.7	19.1	36.0	64.0	.0	61.8	89
−.75	53.1	28.1	18.8	40.6	53.1	6.3	56.3	32
−1.00	47.1	41.2	11.8	17.6	58.8	23.5	52.9	17
−1.25	36.4	45.5	18.2	27.3	72.7	.0	36.4	11
−1.50	75.0	25.0	.0	.0	87.5	12.5	50.0	8
−1.75	33.3	.0	66.7	66.7	33.3	.0	33.3	3
−2.00	.0	100.0	.0	.0	100.0	.0	.0	1
−3.00	.0	100.0	.0	.0	100.0	.0	100.0	1

Table A6-18 Gap Analysis for Gold, $5 Increments, 1977–1984

| | Close | | | Trading Range | | | | |
| | Cont. Dir. | Below Open | Rvrsd. Dir. | Cross Pr. Cls. | Adj. Open | Cont. Only | Cont. Next Day | No. of Cases |
Gap								
55.00	.0	100.0	.0	.0	50.0	50.0	.0	2
50.00	100.0	.0	.0	.0	100.0	.0	100.0	1
40.00	50.0	50.0	.0	.0	100.0	.0	50.0	2
35.00	.0	100.0	.0	.0	100.0	.0	.0	1
30.00	11.1	88.9	.0	.0	55.6	44.4	44.4	9
25.00	71.4	14.3	14.3	28.6	71.4	.0	57.1	7
20.00	41.7	50.0	8.3	8.3	91.7	.0	25.0	12
15.00	40.0	48.6	11.4	11.4	85.7	2.9	51.4	35
10.00	47.0	31.6	21.4	35.0	63.2	1.7	58.1	117
5.00	49.9	21.7	28.3	60.9	35.3	3.8	54.7	759
.00	.0	.0	.0	.0	.0	.0	.0	34
−5.00	46.6	21.1	32.3	61.2	35.0	3.8	44.9	626
−10.00	45.7	33.6	20.7	33.6	64.7	1.7	52.6	116
−15.00	43.6	43.6	12.8	23.1	76.9	.0	46.2	39
−20.00	63.6	36.4	.0	18.2	72.7	9.1	54.5	11
−25.00	33.3	55.6	11.1	11.1	77.8	11.1	66.7	9
−30.00	100.0	.0	.0	.0	100.0	.0	100.0	1
−35.00	100.0	.0	.0	.0	100.0	.0	.0	1
−45.00	100.0	.0	.0	.0	100.0	.0	100.0	1
−50.00	.0	100.0	.0	.0	50.0	50.0	100.0	2

Table A6-19 Gap Analysis for Silver, 5 Cent Increments, 1977–1984

| Gap | Close | | | Trading Range | | | | |
---	Cont. Dir.	Below Open	Rvrsd. Dir.	Cross Pr. Cls.	Adj. Open	Cont. Only	Cont. Next Day	No. of Cases
110.00	.0	100.0	.0	.0	100.0	.0	100.0	1
105.00	4.2	91.7	4.2	4.2	16.7	79.2	83.3	24
100.00	50.0	50.0	.0	25.0	75.0	.0	75.0	4
95.00	.0	33.3	66.7	66.7	33.3	.0	66.7	3
90.00	50.0	50.0	.0	.0	100.0	.0	50.0	2
85.00	.0	100.0	.0	.0	33.3	66.7	66.7	3
80.00	20.0	80.0	.0	.0	40.0	60.0	60.0	5
75.00	33.3	.0	66.7	66.7	33.3	.0	66.7	3
70.00	25.0	75.0	.0	25.0	75.0	.0	50.0	4
65.00	.0	50.0	50.0	50.0	.0	50.0	50.0	2
60.00	50.0	.0	50.0	50.0	50.0	.0	.0	2
55.00	33.3	66.7	.0	11.1	66.7	22.2	77.8	9
50.00	71.4	21.4	7.1	14.3	85.7	.0	78.6	14
45.00	36.8	57.9	5.3	42.1	42.1	15.8	36.8	19
40.00	62.5	25.0	12.5	12.5	87.5	.0	50.0	8
35.00	27.8	44.4	27.8	50.0	50.0	.0	66.7	18
30.00	53.6	32.1	14.3	28.6	71.4	.0	57.1	28
25.00	61.1	27.8	11.1	22.2	75.0	2.8	47.2	36
20.00	49.3	30.4	20.3	31.9	68.1	.0	40.6	69
15.00	49.5	23.1	27.5	49.5	49.5	1.1	57.1	91
10.00	44.1	23.2	32.8	61.0	38.4	.6	53.1	177
5.00	47.2	18.0	34.8	68.2	29.3	2.5	50.0	434
.00	.0	.0	.0	.0	.0	.0	.0	5
−5.00	43.8	12.7	43.5	76.3	22.0	1.7	38.1	354
−10.00	48.6	20.0	31.4	53.6	45.7	.7	47.1	140
−15.00	48.9	27.7	23.4	43.6	56.4	.0	47.9	94
−20.00	43.2	40.9	15.9	27.3	68.2	4.5	43.2	44
−25.00	48.5	21.2	30.3	42.4	57.6	.0	51.5	33
−30.00	58.8	20.6	20.6	26.5	70.6	2.9	44.1	34
−35.00	46.7	26.7	26.7	33.3	66.7	.0	53.3	15
−40.00	33.3	50.0	16.7	33.3	50.0	16.7	44.4	18
−45.00	75.0	16.7	8.3	8.3	83.3	8.3	50.0	12
−50.00	17.4	69.6	13.0	13.0	69.6	17.4	47.8	23
−55.00	40.0	20.0	40.0	80.0	20.0	.0	80.0	5
−60.00	33.3	66.7	.0	.0	100.0	.0	.0	3
−70.00	33.3	66.7	.0	33.3	66.7	.0	33.3	3
−75.00	.0	100.0	.0	.0	80.0	20.0	60.0	5
−80.00	100.0	.0	.0	.0	100.0	.0	100.0	1
−85.00	100.0	.0	.0	.0	100.0	.0	100.0	1
−90.00	100.0	.0	.0	.0	100.0	.0	100.0	1
−95.00	.0	100.0	.0	.0	.0	100.0	100.0	1
−100.00	5.4	89.2	5.4	5.4	21.6	73.0	78.4	37

Table A6-20 Gap Analysis for Silver, 20 Cent Increments, 1977–1984

Gap	Close			Trading Range				
	Cont. Dir.	Below Open	Rvrsd. Dir.	Cross Pr. Cls.	Adj. Open	Cont. Only	Cont. Next Day	No. of Cases
120.00	4.0	92.0	4.0	4.0	20.0	76.0	84.0	25
100.00	25.0	58.3	16.7	25.0	58.3	16.7	66.7	12
80.00	21.4	57.1	21.4	28.6	42.9	28.6	57.1	14
60.00	47.7	45.5	6.8	27.3	61.4	11.4	56.8	44
40.00	52.2	32.2	15.6	28.9	70.0	1.1	54.4	90
20.00	47.0	20.9	32.2	61.1	37.2	1.7	50.7	771
.00	.0	.0	.0	.0	.0	.0	.0	5
−20.00	45.6	18.5	35.9	63.0	35.6	1.4	41.9	632
−40.00	49.0	27.0	24.0	34.0	62.0	4.0	48.0	100
−60.00	37.2	48.8	14.0	18.6	69.8	11.6	48.8	43
−80.00	22.2	77.8	.0	11.1	77.8	11.1	55.6	9
−100.00	10.0	85.0	5.0	5.0	25.0	70.0	80.0	40

Table A6-21 Gap Analysis for Treasury Bills, 10 Pt. Increments, 1977–1984

Gap	Close			Trading Range				
	Cont. Dir.	Below Open	Rvrsd. Dir.	Cross Pr. Cls.	Adj. Open	Cont. Only	Cont. Next Day	No. of Cases
.70	.0	66.7	33.3	33.3	66.7	.0	33.3	3
.60	44.4	55.6	.0	.0	100.0	.0	66.7	9
.50	50.0	25.0	25.0	31.3	68.8	.0	25.0	16
.40	46.7	33.3	20.0	26.7	73.3	.0	33.3	15
.30	42.6	38.3	19.1	29.8	70.2	.0	55.3	47
.20	37.8	33.9	28.3	45.7	54.3	.0	48.8	127
.10	45.9	20.3	33.9	62.1	31.3	6.6	49.9	543
.00	.0	.0	.0	.0	.0	.0	.0	123
−.10	45.9	21.0	33.1	60.6	32.2	7.2	59.4	695
−.20	49.3	23.2	27.5	46.5	52.1	1.4	57.7	142
−.30	51.4	21.6	27.0	27.0	73.0	.0	45.9	37
−.40	43.8	31.3	25.0	31.3	68.8	.0	25.0	16
−.50	70.0	20.0	10.0	10.0	90.0	.0	60.0	10
−.60	25.0	75.0	.0	.0	50.0	50.0	50.0	4

Table A6-22   Gap Analysis for S&P 500, 50 Pt. Increments, 1982–1984

| | Close | | | Trading Range | | | | |
Gap	Cont. Dir.	Below Open	Rvrsd. Dir.	Cross Pr. Cls.	Adj. Open	Cont. Only	Cont. Next Day	No. of Cases
3.50	100.0	.0	.0	.0	100.0	.0	100.0	1
3.00	.0	.0	100.0	100.0	.0	.0	100.0	1
2.50	100.0	.0	.0	.0	100.0	.0	.0	2
2.00	50.0	.0	50.0	50.0	50.0	.0	50.0	4
1.50	47.4	21.1	31.6	47.4	52.6	.0	52.6	19
1.00	50.8	16.9	32.3	63.1	36.9	.0	55.4	65
.50	45.7	9.8	44.5	85.5	13.9	.6	60.7	173
.00	.0	.0	.0	.0	.0	.0	.0	5
−.50	44.8	6.3	49.0	85.3	14.0	.7	46.2	143
−1.00	52.1	12.5	35.4	64.6	35.4	.0	47.9	48
−1.50	42.9	21.4	35.7	57.1	35.7	7.1	50.0	14
−2.00	25.0	25.0	50.0	50.0	50.0	.0	75.0	4
−2.50	50.0	.0	50.0	50.0	50.0	.0	100.0	2
−3.00	75.0	25.0	.0	.0	100.0	.0	50.0	4

APPENDIX 7

Construction of a Pentagon

CONSTRUCTION OF A PENTAGON FROM ONE FIXED DIAGONAL

Establish the diagonal D by connecting the top and bottom of a major price move by a straight line. This diagonal will be toward the left and top of the pentagon to be constructed. (See Figure A7-1.)

1. Measure the length of the diagonal D. This diagonal connects two points of the pentagon.
2. With the point of a compass at one end of the diagonal and the tip on the other, draw a long arc to the right; placing the point on the other end of the diagonal, draw another arc to the right. These arcs should not cross to avoid confusion.
3. The length of a side of a regular pentagon is calculated from the diagonal by the formula

$$S = .618 \times D$$

Using a ruler, set the compass to the length of a side and place the point at one end of the diagonal. Draw an arc on both sides, crossing the arc on the right; do the same for the other end of the diagonal. The two new arcs will cross on the left. The three new crossings are the missing points of the pentagon.
4. The center of the pentagon can be found by bisecting any two sides. The point at which the two bisecting lines cross is the center. Use this point to circumscribe a circle around the pentagon.

CONSTRUCTION OF A PENTAGON FROM ONE SIDE

Establish the side S by connecting the top and bottom of a major price move with a straight line. As in the previous example this side will be toward the top and left of the pentagon, which will extend down and to the right. (See Figure A7-2.)

1. Calculate the length of the diagonal D by applying the formula $D = S/.618$. This will require a ruler to determine the length of S.

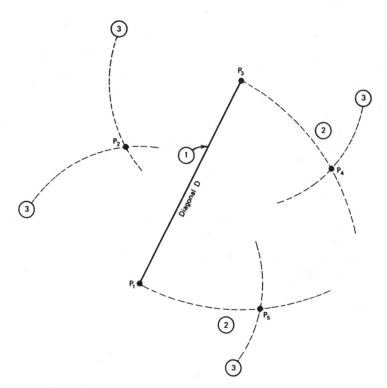

Figure A7-1 Construction of a pentagon from one diagonal.

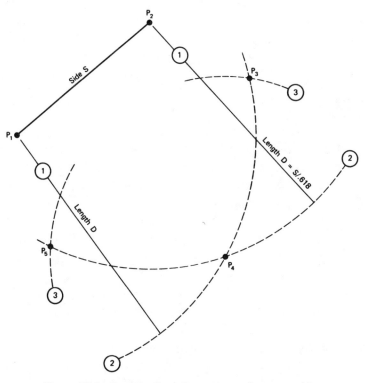

Figure A7-2 Construction of a pentagon from one side.

2. Using a ruler again, set your compass to the length of the diagonal calculated in the first step. Draw wide arcs of radius D from the endpoints of S crossing to the lower right of S. The place of crossing will be the third point of the pentagon P_4, opposite side S.
3. Set the compass back to length S and place the point at P_4. Cross the inner arcs drawn in step 2 with a small arc drawn on either side of P_4. The place of crossing will be the two remaining points of the pentagon.
4. The perpendicular bisectors of any two sides will cross at the center of the pentagon and allow you to circumscribe a circle around the pentagon.

The perpendicular bisector of any side is constructed by setting the compass to any length greater than half of the line being bisected, then placing the point at one end of the line. Draw an arc on both sides of the line in the area above the center of the line. Do the same by placing the point of the compass at the other end and crossing the arcs already drawn. A line through the two crosses will be the perpendicular bisector of the original line.

Bibliography

Aan, Peter W. "How RSI Behaves," *Futures,* Jan. 1985.

Abraham, Bovas, and Johannes Ledolter. *Statistical Methods for Forecasting,* Wiley, New York, 1983.

Ainsworth, Ralph M. *Profitable Grain Trading,* Traders Press, Greensville, SC, 1980 (originally 1933).

Andrews, W. S. *Magic Squares and Cubes,* Dover, New York, 1960.

Angas, L. L. B. *Investment For Appreciation,* Somerset, New York, 1936.

Angell, George. "Thinking Contrarily," *Commodities Magazine,* November 1976. (An interview with R. Earl Hadady.)

Angell, George. *Winning in the Commodities Markets,* Doubleday, New York, 1979.

Appel, Gerald, *Winning Market Systems: 83 Ways to Beat the Market,* Signalert, Great Neck, NY, 1974.

Appel, Gerald, and Martin E. Zweig. *New Directions in Technical Analysis,* Signalert, Great Neck, NY, 1976.

Arms, Richard W., Jr. "Equivolume—A New Method of Charting," *Commodities Magazine,* April 1973.

Arnold, Curtis M. *The Personal Computer Can Make You Rich in Stocks and Commodities,* Weiss Research, West Palm Beach, FL, 1980 (published in hardcover 1984).

———. "Tracking 'Big Money' May Tip Off Trend Changes." *Futures,* Feb. 1985.

———. "Your Computer Can Take You Beyond Charting," *Futures,* May 1984.

Aronson, David R. "An Introduction to Computer-Based Pattern Recognition." *Financial and Investment Software Review,* Jan./Feb. 1984.

———. "Artificial Intelligence/Pattern Recognition Applied to Forecasting Financial Market Trends." *Market Technicians Association Journal,* May 1985 pp. 91–131.

Barnett, Eugene H. *Programming Time—Shared Computers in BASIC,* Wiley–Interscience, New York, 1972.

Bernstein, Jacob. "Cyclic and Seasonal Price Tendencies in Meat and Livestock Markets," in Todd Lofton (Ed.), *Trading Tactics: A Livestock Futures Anthology,* Chicago Mercantile Exchange, 1986.

Beyer, William H. (Ed.), *Standard Mathematical Tables,* 24th ed. CRC Press, Cleveland, OH, 1976.

Bolton, A. Hamilton. *The Elliott Wave Principle, A Critical Appraisal,* Bolton, Tremblay & Co., Montreal, 1960.

Bookstaber, Richard. *The Complete Investment Book,* Scott, Foresman, Glenview, IL, 1985.

Box, G. E. P. and G. M. Jenkins. *Time Series Analysis: Forecasting and Control,* 2nd ed., Holden–Day, San Francisco, 1976.

Chatfield, C. *The Analysis of a Time Series: Theory and Practice,* Chapman and Hall, London, 1975.

Church, A. H. *On the Relation of Phyllotaxis to Mechanical Laws,* Williams and Newgate, London, 1904.

Cleeton, Claude. *The Art of Independent Investing,* Prentice–Hall, Englewood Cliffs, NJ, 1976.

Cohen, A. W. *How to Use the Three-Point Reversal Method of Point and Figure Stock Market Trading,* Chartcraft, Larchmont, NY, 1972.

Commodity Trading Manual. Chicago Board of Trade.

Commodity Traders Club. *Comparative Performances,* Messena, NY, 1969. (A reprint).

Commodity Yearbook 1975. Commodity Research Bureau, New York, 1975.

ContiCommodity. *Seasonality in Agricultural Futures Markets,* ContiCommodity Services, Chicago, 1983.

Control Data Corporation. *Control Data 6000 Series Computer Systems Statistical Subroutines Reference Manual,* St. Paul, 1966.

Cootner, Paul, ed. *The Random Character of Stock Market Prices,* MIT Press, Cambridge, MA., 1964.

———. "Speculation and Hedging," *Food Research Institute Studies, Vol. VII: 1967 Supplement,* Stanford University Press, Stanford, 1967.

Crim, Elias. "Are You Watching the 'Right' Signals?" *Futures,* June 1985.

Cycles, Foundation for the Study of Cycles, Pittsburgh, January 1976.

Davis, Robert Earl. *Profit and Profitability,* R. E. Davis, West LaFayette, IN, 1969.

Davis, R. E., and C. C. Thiel, Jr. *A Computer Analysis of the Moving Average Applied To Commodity Futures Trading,* Ouiatenon Management Co., West Lafayette, IN, 1970. (A research report)

DeVilliers, Victor. *The Point and Figure Method of Anticipating Stock Price Movements,* Trader Press, NY, 1966. (Reprint of 1933 edition)

Dewey, Edward R. and Og Mandino. *Cycles,* Hawthorn Books, New York, 1971.

Donchian, Richard D. "Donchian 5- and 20-Day Moving Averages," *Commodities Magazine,* December 1974.

Downie, N. M., and R. W. Heath. *Basic Statistical Method,* 3rd ed., Harper & Row, New York, 1970.

Dunn, Dennis. *Consistent Profits in June Live Beef Cattle,* Dunn & Hargitt, West Lafayette, IN, 1972.

Dunnigan, William. *One Way Formula,* Dunnigan, Palo Alto, CA, 1955.

——— *Select Studies in Speculation,* Dunnigan, San Francisco 1954. (Includes "Gain in Grains," and "The Thrust Method in Stocks")

——— *117 Barometers for Forecasting Stock Price,* Dunnigan, San Francisco, 1954.

Earp, Richard B. "Correlating Taylor and Polous," *Commodities Magazine,* September 1973.

Edwards, Robert D., and John Magee. *Technical Analysis of Stock Trends,* John Magee, Springfield, MA, 1948.

Ehlers, John F. "Optimizing RSI with Cycles," *Technical Analysis of Stocks & Commodities,* Feb. 1986.

——— "Trading Channels," *Technical Analysis of Stocks & Commodities,* Apr. 1986.

Elliott, R. N. *Nature's Law, The Secret of the Universe,* Elliott, New York. 1946.

——— *The Wave Principle,* Elliot, New York, 1938.

Emmett, Tucker J. "Fibonacci Cycles," *Technical Analysis of Stocks & Commodities,* May 1983 and Mar./Apr. 1984.

Ericsson, Christina. *Forecasting Success,* Kaufman, Westport, 1987.

Evans, Eric. "Why You Can't Rely on 'Key Reversal Days,'" *Futures,* Mar. 1985.

Fischer, Robert. *The Golden Section Compass Seminar,* Fibonacci Trading, P.O. Box HM 1653, Hamilton 5, Bermuda.

Floss, Carl William. *Market Rhythm,* Investors Publishing Co., New York, 1955.

Frost, A. J., and Robert R. Prechter, Jr. *Elliott Wave Principle,* New Classics Library, Chappaqua, NY, 1978.

Fuller, Wayne A. *Introduction to Statistical Time Series,* Wiley, New York, 1976.

Fults, John Lee. *Magic Squares*, Open Court, La Salle, IL, 1974.

Gann, William D. *The Basis of My Forecasting Method For Grain*, Lambert–Gann, Pomeroy, WA, 1976. (Originally 1935.)

―――― *Forecasting Grains By Time Cycles*, Lambert–Gann, Pomeroy, WA, 1976. (Originally 1946)

―――― *Forecasting Rules for Cotton*, Lambert–Gann, Pomeroy, WA, 1976.

―――― *Forecasting Rules for Grain–Geometric Angles*, Lambert–Gann, Pomeroy, WA, 1976.

―――― *How to Make Profits In Commodities*, Lambert–Gann, Pomeroy, WA, 1976. (Originally 1942)

―――― *Master Calculator for Weekly Time Periods to Determine the Trend of Stocks and Commodities*, Lambert–Gann, Pomeroy, WA, 1976.

―――― *Master Charts*, Lambert–Gann, Pomeroy, WA, 1976.

―――― *Mechanical Method and Trend Indicator for Trading in Wheat, Corn, Rye, or Oats*, Lambert–Gann, Pomeroy, WA, 1976. (Originally 1934)

―――― *Rules for Trading in Soybeans, Corn, Wheat, Oats and Rye*, Lambert–Gann, Pomeroy, WA, 1976.

―――― *Speculation: A Profitable Profession (A Course of Instruction In Grains)*, Lambert–Gann, Pomeroy, WA, 1976. (Originally 1955)

―――― *45 Years in Wall Street*, Lambert–Gann, Pomeroy, WA, 1949.

Gannsoft Publishing, "Ganntrader I," *Technical Analysis of Stocks & Commodities*, Jan./Feb. 1984.

Gehm, Fred. "Does Pyramiding Make Sense?" *Technical Analysis of Stocks & Commodities*, Feb. 1986.

―――― *Commodity Market Money Management*, Wiley, New York, 1983.

Gies, Joseph, and Frances Gies. *Leonard of Pisa and The New Mathematics of the Middle Ages*, Thomas M. Crowell, New York, 1969.

Gilchrist, Warren. *Statistical Forecasting*, Wiley, London, 1976.

Ginter G., and J. Richie. "Data Errors and Price Distortions," in Perry J. Kaufman (Ed.), *Technical Analysis in Commodities*, Wiley, New York, 1980.

Gotthelf, Edward B. *The Commodex System*, Commodity Futures Forecast, New York, 1970.

Gotthelf, Philip, and Carl Gropper. "Systems Do Work . . . But You Need a Plan" *Commodities Magazine*, April 1977.

Gould, Bruce G. *Dow Jones–Irwin Guide to Commodities Trading*, Dow Jones–Irwin, Homewood, IL, 1973.

Grushcow, J., and C. Smith. *Profits Through Seasonal Trading*, Wiley, New York, 1980.

Hadady, R. Earl. *Contrary Opinion*, Hadady, Pasadena CA, 1983.

Hallberg, M. C., and V. I. West. *Patterns of Seasonal Price Variations for Illinois Farm Products*, Circular 861, U. of Illinois College of Agriculture, Urbana, 1967.

Hambridge, Jay. *Dynamic Symmetry, The Greek Vase*, Yale University Press, New Haven, 1931.

―――― *Practical Applications of Dynamic Symmetry*, Yale University Press, New Haven, 1938.

Handmaker, David. "Picking Software To Trade Technically," *Commodities*, Aug. 1982.

Harahus, David. ". . . on Market Speculation . . . ," Harahus Analysis, Ferndale, MI, 1977.

Haze, Van Court, Jr. *Systems Analysis: A Diagnostic Approach*, Harcourt, Brace & World, New York, 1967.

Hieronymus, Thomas A. *Economics of Futures Trading*, Commodity Research Bureau, New York, 1971.

―――― *When to Sell Corn-Soybeans-Oats-Wheat*, University of Illinois College of Agriculture, Urbana, 1967.

Higgens, James E., and Allan M. Loosigian. "Foreign Exchange Futures," in Perry J. Kaufman (Ed.), *Handbook of Futures Markets*, Wiley, New York, 1984.

Hildebrand, F. B. *Introduction to Numerical Analysis*, McGraw–Hill, New York, 1956.

Hill, Holliston. "Using Congestion Area Analysis to Set Up for Big Moves," *Futures*, Apr. 1985.

Hochheimer, Frank L., and Richard J. Vaughn. *Computerized Trading Techniques 1982*, Merrill Lynch Commodities, New York, 1982.

Hurst, J. M. *The Profit Magic of Stock Transaction Timing*, Prentice–Hall, Englewood Cliffs, NJ, 1970.

Hutson, Jack K. "Elements of Charting," *Technical Analysis of Stocks & Commodities*, Mar. 1986.

—— "Good TRIX," *Technical Analysis of Stocks & Commodities*, Jul. 1983.

—— "Elements of Charting," *Technical Analysis of Stocks & Commodities*, Mar. 1986.

—— "Filter Price Data: Moving Averages Versus Exponential Moving Averages," *Technical Analysis of Stocks & Commodities*, May/June 1984.

—— "Using Fourier," *Technical Analysis of Stocks & Commodities*, Jan. 1983.

Hutson, Jack K., and Anthony Warren. "Forecasting with Maximum Entropy," *Technical Analysis of Stocks & Commodities*, Dec. 1984.

Jiler, William L. *Forecasting Commodity Prices With Vertical Line Charts*, Commodity Research Bureau, New York, 1966.

—— *Volume and Open Interest: A Key to Commodity Price Forecasting*, Commodity Research Bureau, New York, 1967.

Johnson, Charles F. "Stochastic Oscillator Program for the HP-41C(V)," *Technical Analysis of Stocks & Commodities*, Sep./Oct. 1984.

Kaufman, Perry J. *Handbook of Futures Markets*, Wiley, New York, 1984.

—— "High-Tech Trading," *Futures and Options World*, London, September 1985.

—— "Market Momentum Re-examined," Unpublished Article, November 1975.

—— "Moving Averages and Trends," in Todd Lofton (Ed.), *Trading Tactics: A Livestock Futures Anthology*, Chicago Mercantile Exchange, 1986.

—— "Safety-Adjusted Performance Evaluation," *Journal of Futures Markets*, Vol. 1, 1981.

—— "Technical Analysis," in Nancy H. Rothstein (Ed.), *The Handbook of Financial Futures*, McGraw–Hill, New York, 1984.

—— *Technical Analysis in Commodities*, Wiley, New York, 1980.

Kaufman, Perry J., and Kermit C. Zieg, Jr. "Measuring Market Movement," *Commodities Magazine*, May 1974.

Keltner, Chester W. *How to Make Money in Commodities*, The Keltner Statistical Service, Kansas City, 1960.

Kemeny, John G., and J. Laurie Snell. *Finite Markov Chains*, Springer–Verlag, New York, 1976.

Kemeny, John G., and Thomas E. Kurtz. *Basic Programming*, 2nd ed., John Wiley & Sons, New York, 1971.

Kepka, John F. "Trading with ARIMA Forecasts," *Technical Analysis of Stocks & Commodities*, May 1983.

Klein, Frederick C., and John A. Prestbo. *News and the Market*, Henry Regnery Co., Chicago, 1974.

Knuth, Donald E. *The Art of Computer Programming, Vol. 2: Seminumeric Algorithms*, Addison–Wesley, Reading, MA, 1971.

Kroll, Stanley. *The Professional Commodity Trader*, Harper & Row, New York, 1974.

Kroll, Stanley, and Irwin Shishko, *The Commodity Futures Market Guide*, Harper & Row, New York, 1973.

Kunz, Kaiser S. *Numerical Analysis*, McGraw–Hill, New York, 1957.

Labys, Walter C. *Dynamic Commodity Models: Specification, Estimation, and Simulation*, Lexington Books, Lexington, MA, 1973.

Lambert, Donald R. "Commodity Channel Index: Tool for Trading Cyclic Trends," *Commodities*, 1980. Reprinted in *Technical Analysis of Stocks & Commodities*, Jul. 1983.

—— "Exponentially Smoothed Moving Averages," *Technical Analysis of Stocks & Commodities*, Sep./Oct. 1984.

—— "The Market Directional Indicator," *Technical Analysis of Stocks & Commodities*, Nov./Dec. 1983.

Lane, George C. "Lane's Stochastics," *Technical Analysis of Stocks & Commodities,* May/Jun. 1984.

Lefevre, Edwin. *Reminiscences of a Stock Operator,* Books of Wall Street, Burlington, VT, 1980 (originally published in 1923 by George H. Doran Co., New York).

Lofton, Todd. "Chartists Corner," *Commodities Magazine,* December 1974. (Two series of articles.)

—— "Moonlight Sonata," *Commodities Magazine,* July 1974.

Lofton, Todd. *Trading Tactics: A Livestock Futures Anthology,* Chicago Mercantile Exchange, 1986.

Luce, R. Duncan, and Howard Raiffa. *Games and Decisions,* John Wiley & Sons, New York, 1957.

Lukac, Louis P., G. Wade Brorsen and Scott H. Irwin, *Similarity of Computer Guided Technical Trading Systems,* CSFM-124, Working Paper Series, Columbia Futures Center, Columbia University Business School, New York, Mar. 1986.

MacKay, Charles. *Extraordinary Popular Delusions and The Madness of Crowds,* Noonday Press (Farrar, Straus and Giroux), New York, 1932.

Macon, Nathaniel. *Numerical Analysis,* John Wiley & Sons, New York, 1963.

Mart, Donald S. *The Master Trading Formula,* Winsor Books, Brightwaters, NY, 1981.

Martin, Francis F. *Computer Modeling and Simulation,* John Wiley & Sons, New York, 1968.

Maxwell, Joseph R., Sr. *Commodity Futures Trading with Moving Averages,* Speer, Santa Clara, CA, 1974.

McKinsey, J. C. C. *Introduction to the Theory of Games,* McGraw–Hill, New York, 1952.

Mendenhall, William, and James E. Reinmuth. *Statistics for Management and Economics,* 2nd ed., Duxbury Press, North Scituate, MA, 1974.

Merrill, Arthur A. *Behavior of Prices on Wall Street,* The Analysis Press, Chappaqua, NY, 1966.

Mills, Frederick Cecil. *Statistical Methods,* Henry Holt & Co., New York, 1924.

Montgomery, Douglas C., and Lynwood A. Johnson. *Forecasting and Time Series,* McGraw–Hill, New York, 1976.

Morney, M. J., "On The Average and Scatter," in *The World of Mathematics,* Vol. 3 (James R. Newman, Ed.), Simon & Schuster, New York, 1956.

Neill, Humphrey. *The Art of Contrary Thinking,* The Caxton Printers, Caldwell, OH, 1960.

Oster, Merrill J. "How the Young Millionaires Trade Commodities," *Commodities Magazine,* March and April 1976.

Oster, Merrill, J., et al. *How to Multiply Your Money,* Investors Publications, Cedar Falls, IA, 1979.

Parker, Derek, and Julia Paricor. *The Compleat Astrologer,* McGraw–Hill, New York, 1971.

Perrine, Jack. "Taurus the Bullish," *Commodities Magazine,* September 1974.

Polous, E. Michael. "The Moving Average As A Trading Tool," *Commodities Magazine,* September 1973.

Powers, Mark J. *Getting Started in Commodity Futures Trading,* Investors Publications, Waterloo, Iowa, 1975.

Prechter, Robert R., Jr. "Computerizing Elliott," *Technical Analysis of Stocks & Commodities,* Jul. 1983.

—— *The Major Works of R. N. Elliott,* New Classics Library, Chappaqua, NY, c. 1980.

Prechter, Robert R., Jr., David Weiss, and David Allman. "Forecasting with the Elliott Wave Principle," in Todd Lofton (Ed.), *Trading Tactics: A Livestock Futures Anthology,* Chicago Mercantile Exchange, 1986.

Reiman, Ray. "Handicapping the Grains," *Commodities Magazine,* April 1975.

Rockwell, Charles S. "Normal Backwardation, Forecasting, and the Returns to Commodity Futures Traders," *Food Research Institute Studies, Vol. VII: 1967 Supplement,* Stanford University Press, Stanford, 1967.

Rothstein, Nancy H. *The Handbook of Financial Futures,* McGraw–Hill, New York, 1984.

Ruckdeschel, F. R. *BASIC Scientific Subroutines,* Vol. 1, Byte/McGraw–Hill, Peterborough, NH, 1981.

—— *BASIC Scientific Subroutines,* Vol. 2, Byte/McGraw–Hill, Petterborough, NH, 1983.

Schabacker, R. W. *Stock Market Theory and Practice,* B. C. Forbes, New York, 1930.

Schirding, Harry. "Stochastic Oscillator," *Technical Analysis of Stocks & Commodities*, May/Jun. 1984.

Schwager, Jack D. *A Complete Guide to the Futures Markets*, Wiley, New York, 1984.

——— *Risk and Money Management*, in Perry J. Kaufman, *Handbook of Futures Markets*, Wiley, New York, 1984.

Seidel, Andrew D., and Philip M. Ginsberg. *Commodities Trading*, Prentice–Hall, Englewood Cliffs, NJ, 1983.

Shaw, John E. B. *A Professional Guide to Commodity Speculation*, Parker Publ., West Nyack, NY, 1972.

Sklarew, Arther. *Techniques of a Professional Commodity Chart Analyst*, Commodity Research Bureau, New York, 1980.

Smith, Adam. *The Money Game*, Random House, New York, 1967.

Springer, Clifford H., Robert E. Herlihy, and Robert I. Beggs. *Advanced Methods and Models*, Richard D. Irwin, Homewood, IL, 1965.

——— *Probabilistic Models*, Richard D. Irwin, Homewood IL, 1968.

Statistical Annual, Chicago Board of Trade, Chicago, 1969–1975 eds.

Steinberg, Jeanette Nofri. "Timing Market Entry and Exit," *Commodities Magazine*, September 1975.

Strahm, Norman D. "Preference Space Evaluation of Trading System Performance," in Perry J. Kaufman, *Handbook of Futures Markets*, Wiley, New York, 1984.

Taylor, George Douglass. *The Taylor Trading Technique*, Lilly Pub. Co., Los Angeles, 1950.

Taylor, Robert Joel. "The Major Price Trend Directional Indicator," *Commodities Magazine*, April 1972.

Taylor, William T. "Fourier Spectral Analysis," *Technical Analysis of Stocks & Commodities*, Jul./ Aug. 1984.

Teweles, Richard J., Charles V. Harlow, and Herbert L. Stone. *The Commodity Futures Game, Who Wins? Who Uses? Why?*, McGraw–Hill, New York, 1974.

Thiel, Charles, and R. E. Davis. *Point and Figure Commodity Trading: A Computer Evaluation*, Dunn & Hargitt, West LaFayette, IN, 1970.

Thiriea, H., and S. Zionts, Eds. *Multiple Criteria Decision Making*, Springer–Verlag, Berlin, 1976.

Thompson, Jesse H. "The Livermore System," *Technical Analysis of Stocks & Commodities*, May 1983.

——— "What Textbooks Never Tell You," *Technical Analysis of Stocks & Commodities*, Nov./Dec. 1983.

Thorp, Edward O. *Beat the Dealer*. Vintage, New York, 1966.

Tippett, L. C. "Sampling and Standard Error," *The World of Mathematics*, Vol. 3 (James R. Newman, Ed.), Simon & Schuster, New York, 1956.

Townsend, Robert. *Up the Organization*, Knopf, New York, 1970.

Trading Strategies, Futures Symposium International, Tucson, AZ, 1984.

Tubbs. "Tubbs' Stock Market Correspondence Lessons." (Chap. 13, Tape Reading.)

Turner, Dennis, and Stephen H. Blinn. *Trading Silver—Profitably*, Arlington House, New Rochelle, NY, 1975.

Von Neumann, John, and Oskar Morgenstern. *Theory of Games and Economic Behavior*, Princeton University Press, Princeton, 1953. (First published 1943)

Warren, Anthony. "A Mini Guide to Fourier Spectrum Analysis," *Technical Analysis of Stocks & Commodities*, Jan. 1983.

——— "Fourier Analysis! In a Nutshell; Faster and Better," *Technical Analysis of Stocks & Commodities*, Dec. 1983.

——— "An Introduction to Maximum Entropy Method (MEM) Technical Analysis," *Technical Analysis of Stocks & Commodities*, Feb. 1984.

———— "Optimizing the Maximum Entropy Method," *Technical Analysis of Stocks & Commodities*, Mar./Apr. 1984.

Warren, Anthony, and Jack K. Hutson. "Finite Impulse Response Filter," *Technical Analysis of Stocks & Commodities*, May 1983.

Waters, James, J., and Larry Williams. "Measuring Market Momentum," *Commodities Magazine*, October 1972.

Watling, T. F., and J. Morley. *Successful Commodity Futures Trading*, Business Books Ltd., London, 1974.

Watson, Donald S., and Mary A. Holman. *Price Theory and Its Uses, 4th ed.*, Houghton Mifflin, Boston, 1977.

Waxenberg, Howard K. "Technical Analysis of Volume," *Technical Analysis of Stocks & Commodities*, Mar. 1986.

Weiss, Eric. "Applying ARIMA Forecasts," *Technical Analysis of Stocks & Commodities*, May 1983.

———— "ARIMA Forecasting," *Technical Analysis of Stocks & Commodities*, Jan. 1983.

Wilder, J. Welles, Jr. *Chart Trading Workshop 1980*, Trend Research, Greensboro, NC, 1980.

———— *New Concepts in Technical Trading*, Trend Research, Greensboro, NC, 1978.

Williams, Edward E., and M. Chapman Findlay III. *Investment Analysis*, Prentice–Hall, Englewood Cliffs, NJ, 1974.

Williams, J. D. *The Complete Strategyst*, McGraw–Hill, New York, 1966.

Williams, Larry R. *How I Made One Million Dollars . . . Last Year . . . Trading Commodities*, Conceptual Management, Carmel Valley, CA, 1973.

Williams, Larry. "The Ultimate Oscillator," *Technical Analysis of Stocks & Commodities*, Aug. 1985.

Williams, Larry, and Charles Lindsey. *The Trident System*, Lindsey, O'Brien & Co., Thousand Oaks, CA, 1975. (A report).

Williams, Larry, and Michelle Noseworthy. "How Seasonal Influences Can Help You Trade Commodities," *Commodities Magazine*, October 1976.

Winski, Joseph N. "A Sure Thing?" *The Dow Jones Commodities Handbook 1977*, Dow–Jones Books, Princeton, NJ, 1977.

Working, Holbrook. "Test of a Theory Concerning Floor Trading on Commodity Exchanges," *Food Research Institute Studies, Vol. VII: 1967 Supplement*, Stanford University Press, Stanford, 1967.

Wyckoff, Richard D. *The Richard D. Wyckoff Method of Trading and Investing in Stocks*, Wyckoff Associates, Inc., Park Ridge, IL, 1936. (Originally 1931)

———— *Stock Market Technique, Number One*, Wyckoff, New York, 1933.

———— *Wall Street Ventures and Adventures Through Forty Years*, Harper & Brothers, New York, 1930.

Zieg, Kermit C., Jr., and Perry J. Kaufman. *Point and Figure Commodity Trading Techniques*, Investors Intelligence, Larchmont, NY, 1975.

Index